The Letters of
Virginia Woolf

Volume VI: 1936-1941

Gisèle Freund

Virginia Woolf in 1939

The Letters of Virginia Woolf

Volume VI: 1936-1941

Edited by Nigel Nicolson
and Joanne Trautmann

Harcourt Brace Jovanovich
New York and London

Originally published in England as *Leave the Letters Till We're Dead*

Printed in the United States of America

First American edition

B C D E

Library of Congress Cataloging in Publication Data

Woolf, Virginia Stephen, 1882–1941.
The Letters of Virginia Woolf.

Vol. 1 first published under title: The flight of the mind.
Vol. 2 first published under title: The question of things happening.
Vol. 3 first published under title: A change of perspective.
Vol. 4 first published under title: A reflection of the other person.
Vol. 5 first published under title: The sickle side of the moon.
Vol. 6 first published under title: Leave the letters till we're dead.
Includes bibliographical references and indexes.
CONTENTS: v. 1. 1888–1912 (Virginia Stephen).—
v. 2. 1912–1922.—v. 3. 1923–1928.—v. 4. 1929–1931.—
v. 5. 1932–1935.—v. 6. 1936–1941.
1. Woolf, Virginia Stephen, 1882–1941—Correspondence.
2. Authors, English—20th century—Correspondence.
PR6045.072Z525   1975   823'.9'12   [B]   75-25538
ISBN 0-15-150929-8

"Lets leave the letters till we're both dead. Thats my plan. I dont keep or destroy but collect miscellaneous bundles of odds and ends, and let posterity, if there is one, burn or not. Lets forget all about death and all about Posterity."

Virginia Woolf to Ethel Smyth
17 *September* 1938

Contents

Editorial Note

AS we complete the sixth and last volume of Virginia Woolf's surviving letters, we renew our thanks to Quentin Bell and his sister Angelica Garnett, who own the copyright of the letters and invited us to undertake their publication; and to Olivier Bell who has helped us with her unequalled knowledge of the major and minor actors, scenes and incidents in the Bloomsbury story. Her edition of Virginia Woolf's Diary has set a standard of editorial skill which we have tried to emulate. The Diary has been a source of much detailed information, to which Mrs Bell has constantly added when reading the drafts of our successive volumes. She has lent us the typescripts of the Diary ahead of her own publication, and for this essential guide to Virginia Woolf's life, writings and correspondence we are also indebted to Lola L. Szladits, Curator of the Berg Collection, New York Public Library, which owns the original. Leonard Woolf's Diary has also recently become available in the Library of Sussex University, to which it was presented by Mrs Ian Parsons.

In Appendix B we publish letters which reached us too late for inclusion in their chronological order. For reasons of space, we have selected those which seemed most interesting, and omitted a higher proportion than in the main body of the volumes. This leaves us with about 230 relatively unimportant letters and postcards, many of them mere scraps, which we have omitted from all six volumes. A list of them (names of the addressees, dates when possible, and the present location of the originals) will be placed in the Berg Collection and in the library of Sussex University. After some years, we hope to publish in a scholarly journal any important letters which reach us after 1979.

Kate Stout has been our research-assistant for this volume, and we gratefully acknowledge her energy and resourcefulness in tracing to their origins the many obscure references to contemporary people, events, publications and jokes which inevitably speckle a private correspondence.

Several published books have been of special help to us. Vol. II of Quentin Bell's *Virginia Woolf*, 1972, with its detailed chronological Appendix; Leonard Woolf's two volumes of autobiography, *Downhill All the Way*, 1968, and *The Journey Not the Arrival Matters*, 1969; *A Bibliography of Virginia Woolf*, 1967, by B. J. Kirkpatrick; *A Checklist of the Hogarth Press*, 1976, by J. Howard Woolmer; and *Journey to the Frontier*, 1966, by Peter Stansky and William Abrahams, for its account of the life and death of Julian Bell.

ix

For allowing Professor Joanne Trautmann to spend part of her academic year working on this volume, we are grateful to the Department of Humanities and its Chairman E. A. Vastyan, the Pennsylvania State University College of Medicine, Hershey, Pennsylvania. We also acknowledge with thanks the grant of travel funds to Professor Trautmann by the Institute for the Arts and Humanistic Studies, Pennsylvania State University, directed by Professor Stanley Weintraub.

We wish to pay a final and congratulatory tribute to the printers of these volumes, T. & A. Constable Ltd of Edinburgh, for the care they have taken with a difficult task of type-setting and imposition; and to the Hogarth Press, specially Norah Smallwood, for the interest and understanding that they have shown throughout.

The names of the owners of the original letters are printed at the foot of each, and this information is also our method of thanking them for xeroxes or the loan of the originals, and for permission to publish them. In addition, we are indebted to the following for help on this volume: William Abrahams; Mark Arnold-Forster; Enid Bagnold; Dr Wendy Baron; Isabel Batten; the staff of the British Library (specially Miss J. M. Backhouse); John Burt (Sussex University Library); the Chicago Historical Society; Louise Collis; Angus Davidson; Pamela Diamand; Mrs T. S. Eliot; Professor Donald Gallup; Angelica Garnett; David Garnett; Victoria Glendinning; Amanda Golby (Fawcett Library); Geoffrey Grigson; Michael Halls (King's College Library); Philippa Hardman; Professor Katherine Hill; John House; Lord Hutchinson; Catherine Lacey (Tate Gallery); James Lees-Milne; John Lehmann; Jane Leigh-Breeze; Sir Henry Lintott; Lord Llewelyn-Davies; the staff of the London Library; Leila Luedeking (Washington State University); Jane Marcus; Professor Madeline Moore; Frank Muir; George D. Painter; Dr David Parker (Dickens House Museum); Mrs Ian Parsons; Dr Jane Petro; Dr Elaine Robson; George Rylands; May Sarton; A. M. Sayers; Anne Scott-James; Richard Shone; Professor Brenda R. Silver; Anthony Spalding; George A. Spater; Stephen Spender; Professor Peter Stansky; Su Hua-Ling (Mrs Chen); Angelica Thevos (George T. Harrell Library, Hershey Medical Center); Professor Stanley Weintraub; and Professor Jack Willis.

The typing of the letters has been shared between Valerie Henderson (assisted by Ann Erikson), Gretchen Hess Gage, Joan Bernardo and June Watson in the United States; and Pamela Kilbane and Jane Carr in England. In preparing the volume for press we have owed much to the secretarial help of Jane Carr.

NIGEL NICOLSON
JOANNE TRAUTMANN

Introduction

"WILL you destroy all my papers." These were the very last words which Virginia Woolf wrote, in the margin of her second suicide-note to Leonard. What did she mean? Was he to tear up the typescript of her last novel *Between the Acts*, the first chapter of her projected history of English literature (*Anon*), her scraps of autobiography, her diaries, notebooks, and all letters written to her? If so, Leonard disregarded her instructions. He published the novel, long extracts from the diary, and her letters to and from Lytton Strachey. He was careful to keep all her manuscripts, and most of her friends preserved her letters written to them.

The diary is now being published in its entirety, and with this volume we complete the publication of her surviving letters. Her autobiographical sketches, mostly written to amuse a few friends in the Memoir Club, her light-hearted play *Freshwater*, the drafts of some of her novels, *Anon* itself, have all been rescued from the oblivion to which she apparently condemned them. So Virginia Woolf, who guarded her privacy carefully and sometimes with ferocity, refusing interviews and hating to be photographed, is now totally exposed to public inspection. How much would she have minded?

Hesitantly I suggest that she would have been indifferent. "Let posterity burn or not", she wrote to Ethel Smyth in the letter from which the title of this volume is taken. She had no belief in an after-life, so why should she worry about something over which she had no control and of which she would remain for ever unaware? One can also imagine something a little more positive. She must have known that her fame as a writer would endure. She was called a genius in her lifetime. The lives and personalities of all writers of a certain magnitude attract posthumously a legitimate curiosity. She had herself written (Letter 743), "I am in the middle of 2 huge volumes by Mr Shorter upon the Brontës, which rakes up every scrap of paper they ever wrote upon, so that it is something like a realistic novel, and, as usual, absorbing." Life in Bloomsbury was far more interesting than life at Haworth. She knew that she and her friends would be endlessly written about, and may have hoped that they would be. How much better, then, that all the facts should be known about the growth of their friendships, their values, and her own struggles as a writer, than that these things should be left to rumour and guesswork.

Nor would she have much minded, I have persuaded myself, the publication of letters over which she took so little trouble, scarcely re-reading them before posting, although no writer took more pains about anything she intended for print. The haste with which she wrote her letters does not make them artless. They gain, like a garden, from not being too tightly planned or controlled. Her ideas bred other ideas profusely, she loved starring them with similes ("Nessa's Committee sat for 2 hours, on very few eggs"; "Ankles like the thick end of asparagus"), and delighted to describe people and scenes precisely, partly for her own amusement, partly to give it. Her long letter to Vanessa of 1 October 1938, written at the height of the Munich crisis, is an excellent example of her style. It is a string of small incidents, linked by "then, then . . .", cumulatively creating a picture of fear, chaos, exhilaration of a sort, relief, shame and absurdity. It is a *tableau vivant*, every character in a large cast delineated by a few strokes. How could Virginia have resented the publication of even so personal a letter, when it reveals brilliantly an important facet of her gift?

Any total correspondence, however, must to some degree be a betrayal of its author. Virginia could write to Ottoline Morrell after a visit to Garsington in 1919, "How happy you made me, and how the time seemed to lapse like the Magic Flute, from one air to another", and to Janet Case, about the same visit, "The discomfort is considerably worse than mere boredom". In this present volume (3165) she can write to Ethel Smyth that only Leonard and Vanessa prevented her from seeing her, and then tell Vita Sackville-West, "I could not face her, though she was passing our door". Such white lies are rare. She was ingenious in suggesting her true opinions (especially of friends' books) without causing them pain. She was often pugnacious but seldom angry: irritated, yes, usually by her own conduct in submitting too meekly to social interruptions when she wanted to write, and she would work out her annoyance by describing her visitors more unkindly than she felt. A letter was a wine-glass to hold her delights, or a sump for her despair.

She was a truthful woman, but her letters gave little away that was not already known to her friends. There was no person in whom she wholly confided, except Leonard, but she wrote to him seldom because they were rarely apart, and never consulted him about her writing until it was in more or less a finished form. Her letters to Vanessa were filled with chaff and gossip, teasing admiration and affection, but there is hardly a passage in them in which she openly expresses a profound emotion, knowing that Vanessa would be unlikely to respond. In writing to Ethel Smyth, Virginia could be tart, jocular and strict, but after her first flush of confidences, she became wary of her, warned by her outpouring of autobiographical books that she, Virginia, might present too tempting a subject for the next. "You can confess so openly what I should have hidden so carefully", she wrote to her (3615). From Vita there was never a comparable menace. Vita's trustworthiness, the value she placed on her own privacy, her lack of conceit or spite, were the qualities that Virginia most adored in her, and it is touching to find in the second half of this volume how tenderly their friendship ("a warm slipper relationship") revived. But again, their correspondence was not intimate in the sense that Virginia's diary was.

The letters, then, betray little that she would have wished to keep permanently private, and they do her almost no discredit. The exceptions are her tendency to xenophobia, her surprising lack of sympathy with the poor in mind, spirit or fortune, her mocking belittlement and sometimes jealousy of contemporaty writers, and cruel remarks about people of whom she was fond, against which one must place her kindness to them when they were in trouble, like her letters to Janet Case when Janet lay dying in 1937. Looking back over these six volumes, one is conscious above all of Virginia's courage, vehemence and racing mind, of her gift for impromptu comedy by which she triumphed over constant trouble, her heroic self-knowledge, her lack of self-pity, indeed her self-mockery of a mental condition which she knew to be precariously balanced. The letters reveal all this even better than the Diary. "They revolve like Catherine wheels", Noel Annan has written, "sparkling, spluttering, dangerously explosive. To read them is to listen to her talk."

In one of her essays Virginia called letter-writing "the humane art, which owes its origins to the love of friends". This is the second justification for publishing them. They add immeasurably to our knowledge of Bloomsbury. They record its growth and gusto, illuminate it, defend it, and consciously claim for it, as in her remarkable letter to Benedict Nicolson, for which we also happily possess her very different draft (3633-4), a significant role in social and intellectual history. "We ask a good deal of life, don't we?", she had said in 1904 when Bloomsbury began. "Perhaps we shall get it." Well, they got it. It is the context essential to an understanding of Virginia's personality and art. "How do we exist", she asked Molly MacCarthy, "save on the lips of our friends?", and how will they continue to exist save in their books, paintings and letters? No other group of friends has been more articulate or more candid about themselves, and perhaps never will be. One can scarcely imagine today the existence of a Memoir Club, meeting regularly to recall and record, in essays read aloud and preserved, the fun, follies and opinions of their youth, refreshed by the knowledge that their mutual liking had survived success, love-affairs, new friends, separation by war and travel, different careers, different interests. This is what we were, they said, and this is what we have become. They were self-conscious, with a touch of arrogance and self-congratulation, but Bloomsbury remained as cohesive, vibrant and fruitful as it had always been. Virginia's letters monitor what happened, as it happened, over a period of nearly forty years.

In these final years of her life, 1936-41, she published *The Years*, *Three Guineas* and her biography of Roger Fry, and wrote *Between the Acts* which was published after her death. She also wrote *Anon*, which has recently been published in *Twentieth Century Literature*. Her letters about some of these books are a little more informative than previously. "I cannot write if people talk to me about what I write", she cautioned Ethel Smyth (3223), but her struggle to finish *The Years* so damaged her peace of mind, driving her to the edge of insanity, that she could not suppress groans of anguish. Leonard praised it beyond what he felt to be its merits, fearing to tip the balance of her mind. On reading *Three Guineas* he was reserved, as were many of Virginia's friends, but about *Roger Fry* he was openly censorious, telling her that she had chosen the wrong method: "It's merely analysis, not history" (AWD. p. 328). Virginia was pleased by the reception of *The Years*, which sold more copies on publication than any other of her books. She was indifferent to the critics of *Three Guineas* because she had much wanted to write it, and felt sure of it. She was so relieved to have finished *Roger Fry* (how euphemise his love-affairs? how cope with the discipline of endless facts?), that she barely noticed the comments of anyone except Vanessa and Roger's family, who unanimously approved it. As for *Between the Acts*, she "enjoyed writing almost every page" (AWD. p. 359).

The decision to sell her half-share in the Hogarth Press to John Lehmann in 1938 relieved her of tedious work, but she continued to read manuscripts for the Press, and Lehmann himself has said that her retirement was little more than "a technical formality". Nor did she give up, till war came, her busy social life. There were whole weeks in London when she dined out, or gave dinners, every night, and Monk's House continued to offer its modest hospitality to a succession of visitors, welcome or less welcome. She ceased to see a few friends like Gerald Brenan and Rebecca West, and others like Ottoline Morrell, Ka Arnold-Forster and Janet Case, died, as did Leonard's mother at the age of 90. Virginia was never a recluse. She resisted the temptation to retire to the country until London became almost uninhabitable. If in her later life Bloomsbury friends were less in evidence than formerly, and some of her main correspondents, apart from Vanessa, were people who had only a marginal connection with it (Ethel, Vita, Hugh Walpole), Bloomsbury was still central to her life, including its allies and successors like T. S. Eliot, Elizabeth Bowen, Stephen Spender, Raymond Mortimer, William Plomer and John Lehmann. With her nephews and nieces she continued a brisk correspondence, seeing them as a new generation who would challenge, if they dared (and they did), the attitudes of her own.

One of them died terribly. Julian Bell was killed in July 1937, driving an ambulance in Spain. His motive for going there was something that Virginia never completely understood. Was it anything more than a sense of purposelessness in his life, a wish to identify himself with a cause even if he did not completely believe in it, "a wish to be in the thick of things", as she put it to Vita, an instinctive, irrational determination to prove himself in battle, a yearning for excitement, perhaps glory, to compensate for a youth spent, but not wasted, in talk, teaching Chinese students, and passionate though sometimes awkward writing which he was in too much of a hurry to publish? He reminded Virginia of Thoby, her brother, who had died slightly younger, his promise also unfulfilled. She could not help admitting that there was a kind of grandeur in Julian's death, but it was unnecessary, cruel to her, and crueller to his mother; not ignoble, but futile. In consoling Vanessa she grew closer to her, and her voice, as Julian's brother has written, was the only thing that "kept life from coming to an end". Vanessa told Vita, finding it impossible to say it to Virginia herself, that her only comfort was her sister's love. "When she is demonstrative, I always shrink away." No sentence that Vanessa ever wrote reveals more about their relationship.

Julian's death came at the very moment when Virginia was writing *Three Guineas*, a passionate condemnation of war and men's responsibility for it. In her mind, though not in her book, she drew on his experience as an illustration of what she meant. The young man of whom she was most fond had thrown his life away in the manner which she most deeply deplored. She tried to be rational about war, but her emotion got the better of her logic. Hating Fascism, she denounced warlike preparations to resist it. She signed anti-Fascist petitions and joined anti-Fascist committees, but regarded the petitions as useless and the debates as otiose. "I am always being warned that the end of civilisation is just about to come", she wrote with weary disbelief (3120). Her pity for the Basque refugees alternated with ridicule for gatherings in the Albert Hall to support them. During the Munich crisis of 1938, she felt relief that Britain and France shirked the final step, but could not help exclaiming to Jacques-Émile Blanche (3451) that "we were so afraid and so ashamed". She was only intermittently a pacifist, and never brought herself to the point of declaring, like Clive Bell, that "a Nazi Europe would be, to my mind, heaven on earth compared to Europe at war". She hotly denied to Vita that she had a grain of patriotism in her nature, but when war came, she naturally hoped for the victory that could only be achieved by methods which she had constantly derided. Now she could write to her niece (3570), "I'm more and more convinced that it is our duty to catch Hitler in his home haunts". She admired Churchill for his pugnacity and historical sense, and the ordinary people of London and Rodmell for their endurance. The war was hateful to her, but rather exciting. When the air-battles reached over the Channel to embrace her own village and bombs fell close enough to Monk's House to break the windows, she was physically courageous and even, at times, emotionally elated. She minded less the damage done to one of her houses in Bloomsbury, and the total destruction of the other, than she did the battering suffered by the City area between St Paul's and the Tower, Orlando's London, not Mrs Dalloway's. It represented to her the kernel of England's history.

It was not the war that drove Virginia to suicide, as most people assumed when her last letter to Leonard was published at the Inquest. They mistook her words "another of those terrible times" to refer to both wars, not to her previous attacks of insanity. The war often imposed on her bouts of numbness and depression, but it did not by itself make life seem intolerable to her. Indeed, in the autumn of 1940 she appeared at times almost euphoric, enjoying her writing, and an existence at Monk's House more restful, in spite of the threat of invasion, than she had ever known in peacetime.

Leonard has described in his autobiography how sudden was the mental attack that led her to take her life. Yet it did not come wholly without warning. In late January 1941 she entered 'a trough of depression' which seemed to pass; but she told Vanessa on 23 March that 'the horror' which was soon to kill her had begun several weeks earlier. It seems extraordinary, reading her last letters, that her mind could have oscillated between suicidal melancholia and cheerful plans for the near future. At least two more books were shaping in her mind, and she told Vita, Ethel, Susan Tweedsmuir and Nellie Cecil that she was hoping to visit them shortly, at the very moment when she had made up her mind to die. There can be several explanations. Either we have dated her last letters wrongly, and her suicide was not firmly premeditated by more than a day (the chronology is discussed in Appendix A). Or Virginia, having once decided, and made a first attempt, to kill herself, became quite calm, and wrote letters to her friends in order to conceal her intention, or because, as is more likely, she saw no reason not to write them, impelled by the momentum of her natural friendliness and courtesy.

She expressed clearly her motives for suicide. She believed that she was about to go mad again, and would not recover. She was hearing voices. She wanted to spare Leonard the anxiety and terrible responsibility of caring for her. If she killed herself, he would be able to work in peace. He must not reproach himself for her death. She insisted on absolving him from guilt, and felt none herself. To Vanessa she wrote more or less the same. "I have fought against it, but I cant any longer."

Leonard, at the time and on later reflection, added little to this. He believed that her suicide was due to the strain of finishing *Between the Acts*. He had read the book and praised it, and normally his verdict would have convinced her. This time it did not. She instructed John Lehmann (3709) to postpone publication until she had completely revised it again. As Octavia Wilberforce wrote to Elizabeth Robins after a visit to Monk's House on 12 March (her letters are in the library of Sussex University), she was feeling "desperate—depressed to the lowest depths, had just finished a story". On 21 March Virginia told Octavia that she could no longer write. "I've lost the art." This sentence is perhaps the key. It was not merely her usual reaction on finishing a book, but something more terrible, a conviction that her whole purpose in life had gone. What was the point in living if she was never again to understand the shape of the world around her, or be able to describe it? To end her life at this point was like ending a book. It had a certain artistic integrity. And she would cease to be a burden to herself and those closest to her, particularly, as Vanessa not too tactfully reminded her, if invasion came.

Was this insanity? No, it was a combination of fantasy and fear. She would have recovered, as she had before. She was not mad when she died. When Leonard visited her garden-hut that final morning, 28 March 1941, he saw nothing in her behaviour to make him hesitate to leave her alone. Her handwriting, even of her last note, was firm and normal. But she *feared* madness, and the fear of it was enough to justify the Coroner's verdict, in the kindly formula of his profession, that she killed herself "while the balance of her mind was disturbed", but he meant by it more than the facts prove. Her suicide, as Susan Kenney has suggested in her careful analysis (*University of Toronto Quarterly*, Summer 1975), was her "last desperate act of free will". Many people who take their own lives do not choose to die, but are impelled to it by their mental illness. Virginia Woolf chose to die. It was not an insane or impulsive act, but premeditated. She died courageously on her own terms.

NIGEL NICOLSON
Sissinghurst Castle, Kent

Abbreviations at foot of letters

Berg: The Henry W. and Albert A. Berg Collection of English and American Literature in the New York Public Library (Astor, Lenox and Tilden Foundations).

Sussex: University of Sussex Library, Brighton.

Texas: The Humanities Research Center, The University of Texas, at Austin, Texas.

King's: King's College Library, Cambridge.

Letters 3092-3117 (January–March 1936)

Virginia was immersed in the revision of the manuscript, and then of the typescript and proofs, of her novel The Years, *which she had been writing since 1932, and the labour imposed on her so great a strain that for days she lay in bed with severe headaches, and on many others could work for scarcely more than an hour. On 24 March she wrote in her diary, "I must very nearly verge on insanity, I think . . . Find myself walking along the Strand talking aloud." But by 10 March she had advanced the book far enough to send its first section to the printers. Her opinion of it varied. Sometimes she would consider it "a full, bustling, live book", but on 16 March her diary records, "I have never suffered, since* The Voyage Out, *such acute despair on re-reading". To add to her distress, the political situation was grim. Hitler invaded the Rhineland on 7 March, and Virginia was involved with Leonard in protest meetings of British and French intellectuals. At the same time she was continuing to read the letters of Roger Fry for her biography of him, and toying with ideas for* Three Guineas. *Although she refused most invitations in order to rest herself and concentrate on her book, there were occasional parties and visits to the theatre.*

3092: TO STEPHEN SPENDER   *Monks House, Rodmell,*
                                             Lewes [Sussex]

1st Jan. [1936]

Dear Stephen,

I enjoyed your story[1] very much, and would have written before to thank you, only Christmas has been such a hurly burly. If I were to criticise the story, I should say—but I'm sick to death of criticism; so I wont say anything. You must come and dine again and then we will go into the whole matter—prose, poetry, fiction, biography, Henry James and so on.

I hope Bruce Richmond will get you to do the Coleridge,[2] but I'm rather

1. The title story from the collection *The Burning Cactus*, 1936. Stephen Spender, the poet and critic, was then aged 26. He had first met Virginia in 1931.
2. Sir Bruce Richmond (1871-1964) was editor of the *Times Literary Supplement*, and one of Virginia's earliest patrons. The 'Coleridge' was *Selected Poems of Coleridge* (reprint) selected by Stephen Potter, and reviewed in *TLS*, 29 February 1936.

I

afraid he'll think some elderly gentleman now drinking tea at the Athenaeum safer—Anyhow, it isn't till July I think.

Best wishes from us both.

yrs sincerely

Virginia Woolf

Texas

3093: To Ethel Smyth

Monks House. [Rodmell, Sussex]

Sunday [5 January 1936]

Very sorry you've been so bad. I hope you're better. I've been in and out of bed all the past week with a d--d headache, so wont attempt to write.

Yr account of G. and V. is full of interest. Yes, I cant understand this leaving the family business.[1] She's coming to see me in London—so's Harold, he says.

But we shall stay here as long as we can, and I must say I dont want to be within range of the telephone again.

But no more at the moment. The pain is gone off, but oh the stupidity! And do lie warm and snug and rest on your laurels.

Yr voice was perfect[2]

V.

Berg

3094: To Lady Ottoline Morrell

Monks House, Rodmell [Sussex]

Sunday [5 January 1936]

Dearest Ottoline,

What a wretch I am—here I've been flaunting in your lovely colours [silk scarves] and brightening the perpetual mud of the landscapes, and never thanked you. But I've been in and out of bed with a headache—all through trying to keep a promise to a publisher [*The Years*]—and so stupid I couldn't write. But now I've gone out, in your colours, and the rain has stopped, and there are floods reflecting an extraordinary tropical purple sky all across the marshes. I've never seen them so lovely—like lakes in dreams, with the trees standing round. But what I was going to praise was not the

1. Gwen St Aubyn (later Lady St Levan) was the younger sister of Vita Sackville-West's husband, Harold Nicolson, and had been living for some years at Sissinghurst, the Nicolsons' home in Kent.
2. On 27 December 1935 Ethel had broadcast *I Knew a Man—Brahms*. The talk was recorded by the B.B.C. and repeated on 2 January, when Virginia heard it.

landscape, but you, for the gift with which you fish these silks out of drawers in shops where nobody else ever finds them. I wish I had that gift—it would be so much more satisfactory than dipping into inkpots, and think how radiant to dress as you do (this is a memory of seeing you come in that night at Aldous's [Huxley]).

I'm sceptical—but don't say this aloud—about Lotte Wolff.[1] Its true she made some very wonderful shots, but still more wonderful misses. But I'm not a fair test, because I only lent my hand because Maria [Huxley] asked me to, and was much more curious to investigate her than to have her analyse me. And I thought she flattered one too much. All the same she's got a great scent for a character—only isn't it merely that and nothing to do with marks on one's palm, and shouldn't we all—all that have a nose for character—know as much if we chose and had to make a living by it? But I liked her.

We shall be back at the end of the week I think, and then I must go to the Chinese again[2]—my one visit was as usual ruined by trying to dodge old friends (not you). And I've just been reading about the Chinese in some letters of Rogers [Fry]—he did all his off hand art criticism in letters, and I think its sometimes better than the printed—so fertile, so suggestive. But I must stop.

yrs VW.

Texas

3095: To Ethel Smyth   52 *T[avistock] Sqre. [W.C.*1]

Saturday [11 January 1936]

Yes, Ethel dear, that would be very very kind of you, to lend me the Daudet book.[3] If you could put it in a parcel and send it me, I'll return it honestly. A French memoir's my idea of bliss; I can read French when my own English has gone—as God knows it has gone—flat as last Sundays last muffin. D'you know what I'm reading—merely to pacify myself—all Borrow.[4] And very good too. For instance he has just gone up to the top of Snowdon with his daughter in the year 1854 and she says, That plant is Auricula Genesta, Papa: (No, I cant convey the flavour) upon which he bursts

1. Dr Charlotte Wolff, the German-Jewish palmist. Virginia's hand was twice read by her in December 1935 (see Vol. V of this edition, p. 452). Dr Wolff was expelled from Germany by the Nazis, and came from Paris to London at the invitation of Aldous and Maria Huxley (see Sybille Bedford, *Aldous Huxley*, 1973, I, p. 314).
2. The exhibition of Chinese art at The Royal Academy.
3. *Lettres de Mon Moulin* (1868) by Alphonse Daudet (1840-97).
4. George Borrow (1803-81). Virginia had been reading, among other of his books, *Wild Wales*, 1862.

into a few strains of Welsh song, and meanwhile they are surrounded by ordinary English tourists. And there was a little booth on top of Snowdon where refreshments were served—But this wont amuse you as much as it amuses me. But Lord, how I wish I could write that particular racy English eccentric East Anglian nonconformist style. It enchants me as Hardy does—another refuge in time of headache—his Trumpet Major [1880]—the worst book in the language—I finished without stopping t'other night—

As you see, we are in London, and I'm keeping myself to myself as they say. A merciful calm spread about the New Year as about the new moon—a space of silver light; and I ride my chariot like the witch with a broomstick in the picture, bidding Sybil Colefax avaunt.[1] Did I tell you how she insulted me, and was found out? No—And nows not the time either. Theres a Madame D'Erlanger[2] who gave a party. But no, I wont spoil the story. I'm amused about Vita—I don't think she will ever come back, wholly: I think G. [Gwen St Aubyn] answers to something deeper in her than I ever did. Partly the senses. Is your book[3] done and your cold finished? Oh I'm so spineless—but, as for the heart, thats gold.

Yr V.

Excuse these holes: meant to take notes on; cant find a proper page.

Berg

3096: To Elizabeth Bowen   52 *Tavistock Square, W.C.*1.

Sunday [12 January 1936?]

Dear Elizabeth,

Thanks ever so much for sending the flowers which are in a great bunch in front of me. But I wish I could have seen you, lovely as pink and yellow tulips are. I had a little influenza, which landed me in the usual cursed headache, so that I am kept in bed. But I am much better today and able to dip into about 20 different books, a thimblefull at a time between draughts of sleep. This is my usual method of recovery.

I hope to be up and about in a day or two; and would like to see you. Only as these headaches hover about, I cant make fixed dates, and dont like to ask you and then put you off. If you are up, and Thursday were possible, would

1. Lady Colefax, the London hostess, whose frequent invitations, and self-invitations, were almost more than Virginia could endure.
2. Baroness Catherine d'Erlanger, wife of Baron Emile d'Erlanger, who became a British subject in 1891.
3. *As Time Went On*, 1936.

you ring up? Only I cant be sure, so please do as you like—I mean dont let me interfere with anything you have to do, as I'm uncertain.

And thank you for the great bunch.

Yr VW

Texas

3097: To Ethel Smyth   52 *Tavistock Square, W.C.1.*

Monday [13 January 1936]

Ethel, could I ask of you a very great kindness (but in, God's name, only if you have time and aren't tired)—that is to scribble down roughly a translation of the enclosed maundering?[1] As you see, the woman begs me to get it translated by a German scholar—Aldous Huxley who is dabbling in psychology and so on, asked me to let this according to him inspired palmist read my hand: which I did very reluctantly; still more reluctantly paid her 2 guineas (but she's driven out of Germany—a Jewess) and now find that she wants to include what I suspect is sheer and mere drivel in a book of hands. But only do this if so inclined: I can get some other scholar easily.

Yrs in haste
V

Could I anyhow have it back?

Berg

3098: To Ethel Smyth   52 *T.[avistock] S.[quare, W.C.1]*

Thursday 16th Jan. [1936]

You are an angel, there's no doubt about it—this refers to your noble kindness in translating that magic statement [by Charlotte Wolff]. It reads to me a little too like the kind of lecture on the Novels of Virginia Woolf that earnest young men sometimes deliver at Huddersfield. But she'd only read—without knowing it mine—Mrs Dalloway. I gave her two seances though; and I imagine, though she denied it, some information filtered through from the Huxleys—Anyhow its a brave effort to earn 2 guineas, and I suppose she must publish it, and earn more. And when we meet in Heaven—how does your religion envisage Heaven?—I shall pick a stem of asphodel, and put it in

1. From Dr Charlotte Wolff (see p. 3, note 1). In her book *Studies in Hand-Reading* (1936) she reproduced a print of Virginia's left palm, and commented: "The hand is full of real and apparent contradictions . . . a desire to escape reality. . . . This over-stress of the imagination forces her to adopt a defensive attitude."

5

your button hole by way of thanks. Please inform me, by return, if asphodel and buttonholes will be recognised there. (I'm dipping into a man called McTaggart, a philosopher:[1] and am surprised to find how interesting mystic Hegelianism is to me) But to come to facts. About your visit: yes please come; only this is my regime at present: I must work from 5 to 6 or thereabouts; the book [*The Years*] must be sent off in the middle of Feb: and this means you get home so late. And some days I try to go on inserting commas, marrying and separating sentences—oh the drudgery—think of my 130,000 words!—till 7. I wd. arrange tho' if I knew. Not this week. Anyhow, a gifted sincere and I think rather charming young woman, Marchesa Iris Origo,[2] daughter of Lady Sybil Lubbock (Villa Medici Florence) wants more than anything to meet you. She's coming on Tuesday 28th. Could you come about 5? If so it would give her enormous pleasure. She's read your books. And theres another, Rosamond Lehmann,[3] (wrote Dusty Answer) also asks can I bring you together? She's a beauty in to the bargain.

Yr V

We have accepted Dr Gordon's second version of the L. of L:[4] L. has read it: I've not.

Berg

3099: To E. M. Forster   52 *Tavistock Sqre.* [*W.C.*1]
Sunday, 19th Jan. [1936]

My dear Morgan,
      I was very glad to hear about you from Leonard, though I'm afraid its an awful bore waiting.[5]

1. John McTaggart (1866-1925), the Cambridge Hegelian philosopher and a friend of Roger Fry.
2. Iris Origo (b. 1902) was the daughter of W. Bayard Cutting of Long Island and Lady Sybil Cuffe (later Scott, later Lubbock). In 1924 she married Marchese Antonio Origo, and lived in Val d'Orcia, near Siena. She is the author of several books of essays and historical studies.
3. Rosamond Lehmann, the novelist, sister of John, the Woolfs' ex-employee and future partner in the Hogarth Press. Among her best-known novels are *Dusty Answer* (1927), *A Note in Music* (1930) and *Invitation to the Waltz* (1932).
4. Mary Gordon, *Chase of the Wild Goose: The Story of Lady Eleanor Butler and Miss Sarah Ponsonby, known as the Ladies of Llangollen* (Hogarth Press, May 1936). The 'Ladies' were mid-18th century Irish women who declared their love for one another, and made their house (Plas Newydd, in the valley of Llangollen, Wales) a gathering place for intellectuals and free-thinkers of the day.
5. Forster was suffering from a bladder disorder, and had one operation in December 1935. Now he was awaiting the second, in February. Both were successful.

Charles Mauron[1] has just written to ask about you. We missed them when they were over, which I was sorry for, as though I always think him a formidable man—partly because of his eyes not seeing—I admire him, and have a sort of acquaintanceship now through Roger's [Fry] letters. What an odd pair—Roger and Goldie![2] Roger always so tactile and prehensile and Goldie up in the air with Goethe. I am still plodding on—reading—but less and less able to see any end.

We have been driving solemnly round Regents Park in the snow with Miss Crabbe. Who is she? Well, she's our travelling clerk, and Leonard is teaching her to drive. Her great topic is the King; but when I said would you rather he died—for the sake of the excitement? she was shocked, and said she understood from a man in sandals last night in a Bloomsbury café that if he died there would be a bloodless revolution.[3] This you see is the Bloomsbury we dont know. Miss Crabbe found 2 bugs in her tea cups the other day, and really had to break the tea cups and throw them away—Couldn't drink out of them afterwards.

I am plodding away trying to finish my book; and I gather Aldous has finished one [*Eyeless in Gaza*], also Rosamond Lehmann [*The Weather in the Streets*]: but it is yours I shall really enjoy.[4] This is not flattery—partly I'm so sick of fiction (my own too) partly, after reading Edith [Sitwell], St John Ervine and Mr [Geoffrey] Grigson just now in the Sunday Times,[5] I long for someone civilised. What a dirty ink pot they live in! like Miss Crabbe's tea cups, it ought to be smashed. I am re-binding all my Shakespeares—29 vols—in coloured paper, and think of then reading one of them. But there are so many interruptions, for example, Sibyl Colefax. Hoping to see you soon, and with both our love.

V.W.

Berg

3100: TO ETHEL SMYTH   52 *T.*[*avistock*] *S.*[*quare, W.C.*1]
Thursday [23 January 1936]

Thanks very much for sending, or asking your sister to send, the book: Daudets copy hasn't come—I've just begun, and shall continue till sleep falls.

---

1. Mauron (1899-1966), the half-blind French writer and chemist, had translated Virginia's *To the Lighthouse* and *Orlando*, and collaborated with Roger Fry on his translations of Mallarmé.
2. Goldsworthy Lowes Dickinson (1862-1932), historian and philosopher, and lecturer in moral science at Cambridge.
3. King George V died the next day, 20 January, after a short illness.
4. His collection of essays, *Abinger Harvest*, 1936.
5. See p. 10, note 1.

which wont I think be very long. We stood in the Sqre to see the hearse:[1] all London suddenly in an access of loyalty and democracy jumped the Sqre. railings, old greybearded ladies taking them at a flying leap, and though some stalwarts held the gates, the mob was on us, and Leonard who is a democrat was squashed between 5 fat grocers. This shows how enthusiastic Woburn Place was: and it all went by in 2 minutes, the crown glittering blue and white, and the long yellow leopards stretched over the coffin. In fact it was in its way, as they say, rather a magnificent, perfectly simple sight. Then there was a pause: then a vast royal omnibus in which sat an old woman clasping a parrots cage. How English!

But this is drivelling—we go to Canterbury via Rodmell this weekend. L. has to speak to a meeting of young men [The Workers Educational Association]. I shall take a wander in the sacred—d'you call it edifice [cathedral]? Then back here. Then on Tuesday the tea party for the woman who wants to meet you [Iris Origo]: to which Colefax has now invited herself. I make no plans of any kind save that I must stodge on, on, through this incredibly dreary mass of typed sheets: and then there'll be the proofs! Never again, oh never again. And what about yours! [*As Time Went On*] And when shall I read them? And do you still wheeze?

V.

I'm so sorry for Ly Balfour.[2]

Berg

3101: To Julian Bell   52 *Tavistock Square, W.C.*

Typewritten
30th Jan. 1936

Dearest Julian,

I'm so furious—an empty envelope arrived yesterday addressed to me in your handwriting. It was a large envelope, completely ripped open, with a note from the post office to say it had been found so. Nessa says she thinks you were sending me your thing about Roger—if so, God grant that you have kept a copy.[3] But there was no letter for me; and I'm very disappointed, as its such an age I heard from you. I wrote several scraps of diary for you,

1. The body of King George V (who had died at Sandringham) was being taken through London to lie in state at Westminster Hall.
2. Elizabeth, widow of the 2nd Earl of Balfour, a friend and neighbour of Ethel at Woking. Her mother, Countess of Lytton, was dying.
3. Since October 1935, Julian Bell, Vanessa's elder son, had been teaching English literature at Wuhan University, China. Virginia had asked him to write his memories of Roger Fry, to help her with her biography. Julian did so, hoping that the Hogarth Press might publish it separately, but they declined it.

but I think lost them at Monks House. This I will send though, even if its a scrap, in order to tell you about the empty envelope. Please be very careful and get some strong paper and cant you seal your letters? For though the officials may have tampered, as they did before, this one was so thin, and so all to bits, that I cant help thinking it was the fault of the paper not of the post.

We have been, as everyone will tell you, deluged in tears and muffled in crape for the past ten days.[1] The British public has had a fit of grief which surpasses all ever known. It was a curious survival of barbarism, emotionalism, heraldry, ecclesiasticism, sheer sentimentality, snobbery, and some feeling for the very commonplace man who was so like ourselves. But it's over today thank God; the sun is shining; prize fighting has begun again; there's a splendid murder—a mans body found in a field with five shots in it —and we are all cheering up. We had a completely aquatic Christmas at Rodmell; and I kept my head down so low upon my desk trying to finish my book, that I hardly saw or spoke; in fact laid it at last on a pillow and groaned. Leonard however went the usual round, and now here we are again, involved in the usual uproar of politics, society, Indians, niggers, poets, Ethel Smyth,—from which racket I except Ann,[2] who stumped in looking like a rugger blue the other night, and Christopher Strachey, whom you ought I think to elect to the Society.[3] At least he seemed to me a bubbling Strachey, with all their brains and the Costello guts; who might turn out much to the point, Ann too,—but L. says the Society is doomed, for he's had the sacred books [minutes] on his table since June and only yesterday did the Archangel [Secretary]—is that his name—write and ask if they were lost.

About the Roger [Fry] book—I am getting on very slowly, in the crannies of other writing (my novel has to go to America in Feb) and have made notes and extracts of all the Helen [Anrep], Vanessa, Goldie letters. Margery[4] said with emphasis that Charles [Mauron] would not let me or anyone read his letters. However he has now written to offer them to me in bulk—so there is another huge dossier waiting I imagine. Lord, how I wish you were here! So many things crop up I would like to discuss with you. But I see it will be a long job, if I do it properly; the letters are crammed with interesting things,

1. For the death and funeral of King George V. He was buried at Windsor on 28 January.
2. Ann Stephen, daughter of Karin (*née* Costelloe) and Adrian, Virginia's brother. She was then an undergraduate at Cambridge.
3. Christopher was the son of Rachel (Karin's sister) and Oliver Strachey. The 'Society' was the Cambridge Conversazione Society, better known as 'the Apostles'.
4. Margery Fry (1874-1958), Roger's sister, who had invited Virginia to write the book. She was Principal of Somerville College, Oxford, 1926-31, and promoted the Howard League for Penal Reform.

9

one could make a whole and manysided picture—if one chose; if the Frys—etc etc.

The literary world, or rather back kitchen, is amused every Sunday by the violence and vulgarity of Mr Grigson and Edith Sitwell.[1] You dont see the Sunday Times I imagine? Well there they befoul each other weekly—and St John Ervine[2] joins in; its about nothing but themselves as usual. Grigson I gather has pretty well denounced all of us—you included—in some little pamphlet; to which Herbert Palmer[3] takes exception. "Why call Edith an old Jane? Why call Osbert fat? and why lump me with them?" he asks, but then hes a Grigson himself. I think you're lucky, starting life in China away from all this pother. When you come back, you will start fresh and I hope bring a strong new bristly broom to sweep the stable with. Dadie has asked us to Cambridge to hear his Frogs; Lydia is bringing out her Ibsen; Maynards book is upstairs on Leonards table; Duncans and Nessas pictures are about to go to Glasgow; and Morgan is producing a large volume of essays.[4] So old Bloomsbury is active you'll agree. Morgan by the way has to wait a month before his second operation. So far he's very well. Are you writing any poetry? Are you writing any prose? Now I must go up to lunch; and I expect I have left out any news that might be interesting. We're going to Cambridge for the day to see Ann [Stephen] and deliver the sacred books [Apostles' Minutes] tomorrow; I'll try to pick up a few twigs and send them to you in a diary.

In fact this letter is only to ask for news of your empty envelope, and to beg you to buy others and write as soon as you can.

I am told on the very best authority that the new King [Edward VIII] is a cheap second rate little bounder; whose only good points are that he keeps

1. The public quarrel between Edith Sitwell and Geoffrey Grigson (then literary editor of the *Morning Post*) was mainly concerned with the merits of the new poets, Edith championing Eliot and Dylan Thomas, her protégé, against Spender and Auden; but it stemmed from Grigson's earlier charge that Edith had plagiarised Herbert Read in her *Aspects of Modern Poetry*.
2. The dramatist, novelist and critic.
3. The poet, ex-schoolmaster, and literary critic, 1880-1961. Geoffrey Grigson (b. 1905), the poet and critic, never wrote such a pamphlet. He suggests (in 1980) that Virginia might have been referring to a pamphlet written by Wyndham Lewis about Bloomsbury, but it was extremely libellous and was never published.
4. Dadie is George Rylands, previously employed by the Hogarth Press, and then a Fellow of King's College, Cambridge, where he produced Aristophanes' *The Frogs*; Lydia is Mrs Maynard Keynes, who was to appear in March as Hilda Wangel in Ibsen's *The Master Builder*; Keynes's book was his *General Theory of Employment, Interest and Money* (1936); the pictures by Duncan Grant and Vanessa Bell were their panels for the liner *Queen Mary*, then being fitted out on Clydeside; Morgan Forster's book was *Abinger Harvest*.

two mistresses and won't marry and make a home; and that he likes dropping into tea with the wives of miners. But this is from Iris Origo who danced with him several times; those who are more remote say on the contrary he has every virtue though not every grace; and was daily so insulted by the King that when the King died the only thing Edward could do to show his feelings was to have all the clocks put back half an hour.[1]

Love
Virginia

Quentin Bell

3102: To V. Sackville-West   52 *T.[avistock] S.[quare, W.C.1]*

Friday [31 January 1936]

Dearest Creature,

I'm fearfully sorry. You know how I hate that you should have this anxiety. But I do hope it will go well. Give Gwen my love.[2]

No of course you're not 'in disgrace' with me, and never will be. Surely thats as plain as a pikestaff and needs no saying? Chuck me as often as you like, and dont give it a moments thought.—as I should you. And if I can be of any use—or this house—but that goes without saying too

Love from us both.

V.

Berg

3103: To Ethel Smyth   [52 *Tavistock Square, W.C.1*]

Sunday [2 February 1936]

Could you very angelically send me the name of the man at St Leonards who does your typing? Is he good at corrections: can he be trusted to copy a badly typed script? I'm in such a rush that I must try and feed two of these monsters—Oh such a rush—and it becomes doubtful if I shall get it done [*The Years*].

Yes you were divine the other night, and it is a side I admit that I adore—Sh^re [Shakespeare] at his bawdiest, and also subtlest. [Iris] Origo I'm afraid has already gone back.

1. The fact, but not the implied motive, was correct. King George had always kept the clocks at Sandringham half an hour fast. The first decision of the new King was to restore them to Greenwich time.
2. Gwen St Aubyn had an operation on 27 January.

I hope Ly Sackville will now absolve Vita from any more shockers.[1] Cant write, think, or spell. and still 50,000 words and more to copy.

What about your bantling [*As Time Went On*]—your dropsical, but not so dropsical as my, bantling [*The Years*]?

V.

Berg

3104: TO HUGH WALPOLE   *Monks House* [*Rodmell,*
                                                    Sussex]
8th Feb. [1936]

My dear Hugh,

Your portrait with the dog is on my table, and it came at Christmas, and I've never thanked you.[2] But as you know, letter writing is one of the gifts which was kept back when fairies stood at my cradle and gave me a dumb but affectionate heart.

How are you? What about your arm? What about your life altogether? Have you invented a new art—is fiction bundled into the waste paper basket —as it deserves? I wish you'd sit down and answer all these questions at some length. Silence seems to have fallen on the press too—you never seem to write articles now. Every now and again there's a paragraph saying that you're in New Zealand or in Hollywood; but where you are on this very fine cold morning I can't imagine.

Theres a raging wind; some of Leonards crocuses are up,—the church-yard is full of snowdrops, and old Mrs Mockford [Rodmell woman] was buried yesterday. This is said to bring back the sense of England. But I ought to add that Lady Sackville is today being strewn on the waves at Brighton, by her own wish—Vita and Harold have hired a steam launch and are at this moment tossing up and down in the Channel. Its all as it should be, I feel: and I hope the poor old wretch who always reviled me has gathered her ashes together and is having a happy time at last. Of all lives that seems the least to be envied. I must stop these funeral reflections however, because I dont want

1. Victoria Sackville, Vita's mother, died at Brighton on 30 January, aged 73. In her later life she had become increasingly eccentric and quarrelsome.
2. This photograph of Hugh Walpole, the novelist (1884-1941), is reproduced opposite p. 161 of Quentin Bell's *Virginia Woolf*, Vol. II. Walpole had been in Hollywood since the previous August, working on the scenario of *Little Lord Fauntleroy*. While he was there, he was knocked unconscious by a wrestler flung from the ring into his lap.

to run on to the King and Mr Kipling,[1] whom I suspect that you knew. How I wish you were in London and would come and gossip about it all!

We still gather together in the intervals of burying our Kings and have a gossip. I saw William last week—very rubicund, save that his mother is dying.[2] Morgan Forster too has been having an operation. But I hope its all over well. And everyone is about to bring out a book—even I. I cant pretend you see to write a coherent and continuous account of life in London, because its neither one nor the other. I should like to be off abroad, but cant till I've finished my proofs: and the script is still on my table.

I was tempted to go to South America, but as a speech would have been exacted by the Buenos Aires PEN[3] who offered to pay my fare, I couldn't face it. Aldous Huxley is going—and there's another novel (his), about to be published. English literature is at the moment badly in want of good books; and it would do the critics a lot of good to have something to attack—as it is they never cease scratching and pawing each other. But I dont want to squirt our dirty ink—I mean all the squabbles in the Sunday papers—across the Atlantic.

I'm reading David Copperfield for the 6th time with almost complete satisfaction. I'd forgotten how magnificent it is. Whats wrong, I can't help asking myself? Why wasn't he the greatest writer in the world? For alas—no, I won't try to go into my crabbings and diminishings. So enthusiastic am I that I've got a new life of him:[4] which makes me dislike him as a human being. Did you know—you who know everything—the story of the actress?[5] He was an actor, I think; very hard; meretricious? Something had shrivelled? And then his velvet suit, and his stupendous genius? But you wont want to be discussing Dickens at the moment.

I too must fling my clothes into a bag and drive up through the villa residences to London.

You meanwhile are sitting with vast blue plains rolling round you: a virgin forest at your back; a marble city [Los Angeles] gleaming at your feet; and people so new, so brave, so beautiful and so utterly uncontaminated by civilization popping in out of booths and theatres with pistols in their hands and aeroplanes soaring over their heads—sometimes you find a bleeding corpse in the street but nobody thinks much of that—Well, I've no space to

1. Rudyard Kipling had died, aged 70, on 18 January, two days before the King, and was buried in Westminster Abbey.
2. William Plomer (1903-73) had published several novels with the Hogarth Press, including *Turbott Wolfe* (1926) and *Sado* (1931). His mother did not die until September 1939.
3. The international society of authors. The invitation was due to Victoria Ocampo.
4. *Life of Charles Dickens*, by Thomas Wright, 1935.
5. The actress Frances Eleanor Ternan (1802-73) formed an intimate friendship with Dickens which lasted for many years, and contributed to his estrangement from his wife.

describe Hollywood to you, and so must leave you to your cocktail. When are you coming back?

yrs aff
V.W.

Texas

3105: To Lady Ottoline Morrell

52 *Tavistock Sqre.* [*W.C.*1]

Monday [10 February 1936]

Dearest Ottoline,

I am a wretch never to have answered, but I know you are one of the few charitable people who don't expect answers. I got out of seeing Madame Hepp [*unidentified*], I'm glad to say. What do these prowling hyenas want of one? I could spend all my time answering their idiotic questions. As a matter of fact I've been so overwhelmed with all the drudgery of correcting type writing that I've had no time for anything. I try to keep my eyes on it for 2 hours in the evening: so that I couldn't suggest a night for our owling. But if you ever were free about 5.30 it would be very nice to stop correcting the innumerable blunders of this long and dreary book. Perhaps though you keep at home these bitter nights. And endless societies come and meet here— political I mean. So you see how cross grained, ill tempered, and altogether rough coated I am. (This is because I've had the whole afternoon wasted by an egotistical author.[1])

yrs
V.W.

Texas

3106: To Lady Margaret Duckworth

52 *Tavistock Square, W.C.*1.

11th Feb. 1936

My dear Margaret,[2]

I've been away, or I would have written before. I can't tell you how much I like the photographs. Some of them I remember—others are quite new to

---

1. John Graham, author of *Good Merchant*, published by the Hogarth Press in 1934. See Letter 3198.
2. The daughter of the 4th Earl of Carnarvon, she married George Duckworth, Virginia's half-brother, in 1904. He died in 1934, she in 1958.

me. Thank you very much for sending them. It was so strange how they brought back St Ives again.[1]

I should like very much to come and see you, if you'd let me come some time in March. We are going away a good deal at the present moment but shall be in London then.

Your affate

Virginia Woolf

Vanessa came in just now, and I showed her the photographs. She was as delighted with them as I was, and wants me to ask you if you could possibly let her have the negatives so that she might have more prints taken from them. It would be very good of you. She keeps a family album. Her address is 8 Fitzroy Street, W. We think we have made out all the people.

Henry Duckworth

3107: TO PERNEL STRACHEY   52 *Tavistock Sqre.* [*W.C.*1]

23rd Feb. 1936

Dear Pernel,[2]

I have painfully typed a letter to you in your other capacity. How nice and grand to have 2 selves and 2 addresses!

But there are all sorts of questions I want to ask; and gossip we must have; so if I'm in Cambridge may the star come to tea and the worm be eaten by the thrush? You see, I have two names also: the worm however is the one I know better than the star.

Just back from a wet weekend, and so dazed at having to drop snowdrops —no they were rarer, out of the greenhouse,—at Sybil Colefax's widowed mansion[3] that I can't even do justice to my wormhood. I doubt if we can face the Greek play [*The Frogs*],—though, not to be modest about it, the Provost of King's [J. T. Sheppard] did wire and ask us to stay. Thats more than the Provost of Newnham ever does: perhaps now I'm a patron, I shall be asked to lay a brick. You see, the worm idea goes on curling. A worm laying a brick—

What do you make of Ann [Stephen]? We had meant to come and see her,

---

1. Family photographs taken of the Stephen and Duckworth children at St Ives, Cornwall, where they spent all their summer holidays until Virginia's mother's death in 1895.
2. Pernel Strachey (1876-1951), the fourth of Lytton's five sisters, was Principal of Newnham College, Cambridge, from 1923 to 1941.
3. Her husband, Sir Arthur Colefax, K.C., died on 19 February. She continued to live for a year in Argyll House, Chelsea.

but I got some passing fever, and so didn't. Isn't she rather a strapping and stunning Giant Venus?

Love
VW

Strachey Trust

3108: To Elizabeth Bowen   52 *Tavistock Sqre.* [*W.C.*1]

Sunday [23? February 1936]

Dear Elizabeth,

I wish we could come and dine. But I've been in bed with a cursed headache, and have had to promise not to dine out for a week or two—till March when this dreary long book [*The Years*] will either be done or dropped into the wastepaper basket. Might we come then? We shall be here till Easter; and we want to come very much.

I'll ring up and ask you for a cup of tea next time I'm walking round the [Regent's Park] lake. Or would you drop in here one evening?

I'm sorry about Rose. I hoped that the apology in the Spectator had settled that mans hash—a monstrous affair I think.[1]

Yours
Virginia Woolf

Texas

3109: To Ethel Smyth   52 *T.*[*avistock*] *S.*[*quare, W.C.*1]

2nd March [1936]

I've just met the uncastrated cat [Ethel] at a concert where they played a long bad quartet, and she said to Arnold Bennett "If this goes on I shall be taken short." Do you remember this remark? It sounds genuine; and is now in print.*[2]

Well if youre at your Index I'm at my preface—so we go on. This is only

---

1. In December 1935 Lord de Clifford was charged with the manslaughter of a fellow-motorist by driving in a reckless manner on the Kingston bypass. He was tried by his peers in the House of Lords (the first such trial for 34 years) and was unanimously acquitted. Rose Macaulay, the novelist and essayist, was scandalized, and wrote a *Spectator* article attacking the verdict. De Clifford sued her and the journal for libel, and won. *The Spectator* paid £600 in damages, and printed an apology (see *Rose Macaulay*, by Constance Babington Smith, 1972, pp. 136-7).
2. Arnold Bennett, *Letters to his Nephew* (Richard Bennett), 1936. The remark was made on 3 February 1930 when Bennett and Ethel, who was sitting in front of him, were listening to a string quartet at the Aeolian Hall.

the greeting that one cat gives another over the garden wall. Next week I shall make a trip to Weymouth for a treat, if I can. I want to see the shore where I played my joke on the Dreadnought.[1] Horace de Vere Cole, as you may have seen, died yesterday: he was our interpreter. I'm glad you enjoyed my sister: she did you. And now I must turn to my vomit.

And I saw Lady Oxford on private and exciting business.[2] God be with you, as you would say; with me its a mere caterwaul.

V.

* See AB. letter to his Nephew

Berg

3110: To Ethel Smyth   52 *T.[avistock] S.[quare, W.C.1]*

Tuesday 10th March [1936]

Yes of course—this refers, at some distance, to your question if I want to see your proofs.[3] But when could I? I'm so steeped in my own ink at the moment that I daren't give an uncoloured opinion of anyone else: indeed have had to stop reading the Press MSS. But the worst pressure wont last beyond the next 2 weeks—pray God. I've sent off a large batch to the printer today.[4] So tell me what you want to do. Is Elizabeth[5] going to India? Oh but I want to see her before she goes. Please tell her so: and lets try to manage it.

I dont really get quit of my script till dinner: work from 10 to one: then 5 to 7. if work it can be said to be: anything more dreary cant be conceived. And the book itself disappears; I suspect its bad; but what do I care, once I can write End: and never look at it again. Forgive this egotism. Still more, forgive this dulness. I've been seeing no one. My friends die or fall ill.

1. The famous hoax, organised in February 1910 by Horace de Vere Cole (d. at Honfleur, France, on 26 February 1936). Virginia, Adrian and four friends paid an 'official' visit to H.M.S. *Dreadnought* in Weymouth harbour in the disguise of the Emperor of Abyssinia and his suite. See Adrian Stephen, *The Dreadnought Hoax*, Hogarth Press, 1936.
2. At the end of February Margot Oxford, anticipating her death, wrote to Virginia asking her to write her obituary: "When I die, I would like you to . . . say you admired my writing, and thought that journalists should have made more use of me." (See *Am I a Snob?* in *Moments of Being*, ed. Jeanne Schulkind, 1976.) Margot Oxford, who was born in 1864 and did not die until 1945, was the widow of the Prime Minister, Herbert Asquith. She published four scintillating volumes of autobiography and several other books, including one novel.
3. Of her new autobiographical volume, *As Time Went On*.
4. The first 132 pages of *The Years*. See *A Writer's Diary*, p. 266.
5. Elizabeth Williamson, Ethel's great-niece. She was then aged 33, and had been teaching astronomy at London University.

Sybil Colefax is now a widow—poor woman—still wants to come and dine —I read only solid history or Dickens to ease my mind of commas. Love seems a thing I've never felt or hope or faith either. Why, I ask does one do this sort of task? and who sets it? Whats the point? A 3 month sitting in a cellar. When the sun sinks I go owling round to Nessa. There we tell old tales by the light of a candle. Harold asks me to meet Lindbergh[1]—no I cant. [Lady] Oxford asks me to meet [Mrs Wallis] Simpson—the new Royal harlot—cant again. I meet Max Beerbohm[2] in the dusk—cant face him . . . so how shall I ever pluck up my feathers and ruffle them in the old tiger cats [Ethel's] rosy and lovely phiz [face]? But I should like to read you. I often have a sip of you when I'm feeling faint. Oh and politics go on all day, every day. L. is entirely submerged. I might be the charwoman of a Prime Minister. But we will come out of the tunnel one of these days, in the sun, on the grass —can I believe it?

Yes inky and bitter and old

V.

Ink you know dries bitter like gall.

Berg

3111: To Julian Bell   52 *T[avistock] S[quare, W.C.*1]

Typewritten
11th March 1936

Dearest Julian,
At last, two days ago, I got your letter written in the train from Pekin. From what you say, I gather that you have not yet sent me your paper on Roger, so that the empty envelope that I told you of must have contained something else.[3] I only write now by way of passing the time, for I'm so pressed with this more than accursed book—its now being sent to the printers;—I have to keep them going; have to re-type, correct, re-write all at the last moment—that my wits are wandering and my eyes are dim. I suspect it is a complete flop; that I've tried to do all the things nature never meant me

1. Harold Nicolson had known Charles Lindbergh, the American aviator, when he was writing the life of Mrs Lindbergh's father, Dwight Morrow, in 1935. The Lindberghs had now rented Long Barn, the Nicolsons' house near Sevenoaks, Kent, in order to escape Press persecution in America.
2. Max Beerbohm, the essayist and novelist, was then aged 64. He and his wife normally lived in Italy, but had taken temporary lodgings in Tavistock Square while he supervised the dramatisation by Clemence Dane of his book *The Happy Hypocrite*.
3. See Letter 3101, para. 1.

to do; but unless one flies in her face with a large duster there's nothing for it but to moulder in ones own dung. (Excuse the image.)

We've sold about seventy copies of your book;[1] so far that's not bad; its only had the one Lit. sup. review yet; the weeklies of course take their time with poetry. We'll send you them as they come out. I calculate it takes from three to four weeks before a book gets into the blood stream. Its always very trying—waiting, in dead silence. But you are I expect screened from those gnat bites in your august Chinese solitude.

Of domestic news there isnt much. Morgan [Forster] had his second operation last week [late February], and they said yesterday that he's going on very well. Desmond [MacCarthy] has been ill; is ordered to give up parties and cigarettes, which he finds impossible. I saw David and Rachel[2] a few days ago; and they say he cant be kept from dining out—the great ladies of London ring him up every moment. David wants to write about Lytton; David is now writing about Lord Melbourne. And Lyn Newman[3] came to tea. I doubt if she finds marriage with Max what one might call rapturous; they have a farm at Comberton [near Cambridge] but its too big; she has to work in the house; the baby however is nice; and the country would be nice, only they're under the shadow of an aerodrome.

As you can imagine, we are all under the shadow of Hitler at the moment[4] —even Nessa and Duncan start a conversation by saying, What is your opinion, Leonard, of whats-his-name? They ask intelligent questions about colonies. As for Leonard he works all day, drafting measures for the Labour party; answering that gaby Kingsley Martin,[5] who cant make up his own mind without tapping every other mind within a radius of twenty miles. He always interrupts our one resource against politics which is music. That's why I curse him.

But to return to Cambridge—Lyn [Newman] says Margaret Braithwaite[6]

1. *Work for the Winter, and Other Poems*, published by the Hogarth Press in early March.
2. David Cecil, the critic and biographer, had married Rachel, Desmond Mac-Carthy's daughter, in 1932. His book on Lord Melbourne, the Victorian Prime Minister, was published as *The Young Melbourne* in 1939, but he never wrote a book about Lytton Strachey, who died in 1932.
3. Lyn Lloyd Irvine, whose book *Ten Letter-Writers* was published by the Hogarth Press in 1932, married, in 1934, Maxwell Newman, Lecturer in Mathematics at Cambridge.
4. On 7 March Hitler sent his troops into the Rhineland in defiance of the Treaty of Versailles and the Locarno Pact. Britain and France took no action to force him to withdraw.
5. Editor of the *New Statesman* from 1931 to 1960. Leonard was still Secretary of the Labour Party's Advisory Committees on Imperial and International Affairs.
6. Wife of Richard Braithwaite, a Fellow of King's College, Cambridge, and University Lecturer in Moral Science.

is coming back to live there; and she hopes to find her congenial female society; otherwise there's none. Is she congenial? I've never met her. Sheppard[1] asked us to the Frogs, but it was such a damp dull week, and I'm so under the scourge of proofs that we couldn't face it. Then we met Maynard [Keynes] in the street, who says, Lydia is divinely happy, acting Ibsen. Only nobody will pay more than half a crown for a seat, and it takes London six weeks to know if a play's being acted; by which time its off. We went to Hedda Gabler last night with Nessa, Duncan and Mrs Grant—and oh what a show of peacock feathers and bright butterflies your [Chinese] silks made in the studio! I said I could see Angelica[2] grown old with white hair sitting in the chimney corner sewing at them. Nessa was in the seventh heaven of delight.

We're all very well; and I think Nessa seems more than usually cheerful. She's taken her own line in London life; refuses to be a celebrated painter; buys no clothes; sees whom she likes as she likes; and altogether leads an indomitable, sensible and very sublime existence. I won't go into the Duncan Queen Mary affair as I expect you have it first hand already.[3] And L. will put you wise one of these days when he gets a chink of time about politics. As for Clive [Bell], he's been to Paris; and then dines out, so that we seldom meet. And when we meet, theres a kind of straining to keep the two dogs from each others throats. Not that I mind a good row; but for all you say about the Apostles, your father is now such a flibbertigibbet one can't expect him to hit it off with L. who takes it all like doom and destruction. I think Clive got on Roger's nerves towards the end, and I expect he was hard on him. But it also seems to me pretty clear that Clive did pilfer a good deal without acknowledgement from Roger; and as Roger was half persecution mad—only he was far too sweet and sane to let the disease rip—he minded being pilfered far more than was reasonable. Then Helen[4] was inclined to rub the spot.

As for your Apostles, much though I respect them singly, I begin to think that these Societies do more harm than good, merely by rousing jealousies and vanities. What d'you think? it seems to me the wrong way to live, drawing chalk marks round ones feet, and saying to the Clives etc you can't come in.[5] However that may be a private whim of my own; nothing would make me take a feather of any dye to stick in my hat.

1. J. T. Sheppard (1881-1968), Provost of King's.
2. Angelica Bell, Vanessa's daughter, was then aged 17.
3. The panels which Duncan Grant designed for the lounge of the new Cunard liner *Queen Mary* had been rejected by the Chairman of the Company as unlikely to please the type of passenger he hoped to attract. Bloomsbury was scandalised. See Richard Shone, *Bloomsbury Portraits*, pp. 249-50.
4. Helen Anrep, who was married to the Russian mosaicist Boris Anrep, but lived with Roger Fry for the last years of his life.
5. While he was a Cambridge undergraduate, Clive Bell had been denied membership of the Apostles (the Conversazione Society), although he was a close friend of many of them.

I wish I knew what your work is really like. Interesting at all? Do you make friends with the Chinks—the students I mean? It all seems like a seraphic scene on a blue china plate to me. Here we never stop facing facts. Every day almost I get rung up to be asked to sign this, subscribe to that. . . . Society bubbles from society [*sic*]; and what good they do I don't know; but I sign and I protest and so on. Poor old Rose Macaulay has been fined £200 for making a mild and I think justifiable remark about Lord de Clifford and his motor car; Lord Hewart is completely down on her; the Spectator in which her article appeared paid £400 besides suppressing an issue and making an apology.[1] So now I've signed another paper to protest against the law of Libel. Now I must go and lunch. I hope next time to write a more consecutive letter—this is all jerks and jumps. But much love dearest Julian from us both.

Virginia

[*handwritten:*] L. has just heard that his brother in law, Southorn,[2] has been made Governor of Gambia. They come home in June.

Quentin Bell

3112: To Ethel Smyth   52 *Tavistock Square, W.C.1.*

Postcard
Thursday [12 March 1936]

Proofs arrived. Dedication exactly right and to my taste and fills me with pride[3]—When do you want E. [Elizabeth Williamson] to have them? No chance to read yet. or to write.

V.

Berg

1. See p. 16, note 1. Lord Hewart, the Lord Chief Justice, had tried the case, and in his summing-up accused Rose Macaulay of a "disgraceful libel".
2. Leonard's eldest sister Bella (1877-1960) had married as her second husband (Sir) Thomas Southorn, who was Colonial Secretary, Hong Kong, 1926-36, and Governor and Commander-in-Chief of the Gambia, 1936-42.
3. Ethel's book, *As Time Went On*, was dedicated to Virginia with the following inscription:
   "To dedicate your book to an author in token of admiration is an impertinence. To do it from affection is better. But what if the book turns out badly? That dedication may cost you a valued friendship.
   "Therefore, avoiding seductive quagmires that begin with an 'a', such as affection and admiration, I step on to safe ground and declare that solely because this book was written at her suggestion do I venture to offer it to VIRGINIA WOOLF."

3113: To David Cecil   52 *Tavistock Square, W.C.1.*

Monday [23 March 1936]

Dear David,

I wish we could come this weekend—nothing would be nicer—but I'm fated to deliver up a manuscript on the 10th—needless to say it's not ready; and I must stick at it till its done, and ware not the devils but the angels, behind me. But may we come later?

This is why I never thanked you too for your Jane Austen.[1] I've been reading it with great pleasure. I think its very good. For one thing, you pack so much into such a shapely nutshell: and then, besides making clear what one knows already, you set one asking questions (my test of criticism) about what one doesn't know at all. I now want to begin on Jane Austen again in order to verify and explore. Persuasion I thought last time I read it was my favourite, and I remember wondering what would have happened had she lived say another 10 or 20 years and developed that vein. But I mustn't run on: you see how much your nutshell holds. And how difficult it must have been to give a new fold to that so often neatly folded—what figure do I want? I'm so sleepy I can't think; but I'm dreaming of a lovely little toy that used to lie in a workbox: a nut, full of green silk.

How is Desmond [MacCarthy]?

And may we come another time? I had meant to implore you to write on Lytton: for one thing for his sake: for another in order to exercise your pen on the moderns: but have no more room: and thirdly for the sake of the Hogarth Press.

Yrs V.W.

David Cecil

3114: To Elizabeth Robins   52 *Tavistock Square, W.C.1.*

24th March [1936]

Dear Miss Robins,[2]

I don't know if you remember me, but we met some years ago, and I hope very much that we may meet again. I am writing however because I have had a letter from Maynard Keynes, in which he says "Lydia is extremely anxious for Elizabeth Robins to see the Master Builder . . . do you think it

1. His Leslie Stephen lecture, 1935.
2. The American novelist and actress (1862-1952) had been a friend of Virginia's parents. She lived at Brighton with Octavia Wilberforce, who became Virginia's doctor in the last month of her life. She was largely responsible for introducing Ibsen to the British stage, and the Hogarth Press had published her *Ibsen and the Actress* in 1928.

would be possible to get her to come?" So I said I would write and ask you. Lydia is Madame Lopokova and they are acting 4 of the Ibsen plays at the Criterion. They would give you tickets for any performance you liked to go to. And would you send a line, if you would go, to Mrs J. M. Keynes, 46 Gordon Square, W.C.1. (excuse these blots) and of course don't acknowledge this letter.

Yours sincerely
Virginia Woolf

Sussex

3115: To Ethel Smyth   52 *T.[avistock] S.[quare, W.C.*1]

Friday March 27th [1936]

I ought to have written to you: but then happily 'ought' is not all it might be with you. In fact I've been in bed 2 days with headache, just at the worst moment. But I meant to say, I told E[th] [Williamson] to tell you that I gave her your proofs as I wont touch them till my mind is clear of this incubus. I hope she explained. As she was coming, I thought it foolish even to begin— save for 2 glimpses—one, dedication; one by chance the Lyons party.[1] Has she read it? What does she think? And how did the dust cover settle itself? I believe a plain sheet would be best—but its an indifferent matter anyhow.

London's becoming rapidly so intolerable I think I shall fly for peace. Tell me what I ought to do about the conglomeration of old family friends who have been making my life a mere spasm this last week? When Mrs Grosvenor[2] says shes old and was my father's friend—when Miss Elizabeth Robins says she was my mother's friend—when Gerald Duckworth[3] says he's very melancholy and was my half brother—must I oh must I run hither and thither and see them all? And then—all within this week—in comes an antiquated Indian cousin, whose son's I gather rapidly going to the devil.[4] And why do I attract them? I cant unriddle this riddle: but it unravels my days; and makes me plan flight: the truth is I cant resist the telephone, and so spoil my days. Meanwhile, here I am at the last lap [of *The Years*], and mercifully entirely anaesthetised, and dont know or care if its the worst book

1. The party given for Ethel in a Lyons teashop after the concert of her music in the Albert Hall on 3 March 1934. (*As Time Went On*, p. 287.)
2. Mrs Norman Grosvenor, the novelist and painter who founded The Colonial Intelligence League for Educated Women. Her daughter, Susan, was a friend of Virginia, and married John Buchan (Lord Tweedsmuir).
3. The publisher of Virginia's first two novels, and son of Virginia's mother by her first husband, Herbert Duckworth.
4. Sir Harry Stephen (1860-1945) and his son James (b. 1908). See p. 204, note 3.

or the best. I'm sorry about Edith S's brother:[1] we live in such a world of horror its odd how a murder seems all in the usual run.

V.

Mrs Grosvenor says she meets you at the doctor, and knew you years ago.

Berg

3116: TO ELIZABETH ROBINS   52 *Tavistock Square, W.C.1.*
Sunday, 29th March [1936]

Dear Miss Robins,
    (I wish I could cease to be "Virginia Woolf" and become Virginia)
    I haven't been able to see the Keynes's; so I am only writing for Leonard and myself to say that we shall be delighted, I needn't say, to come to tea on Tuesday 14th April at 4.30. But you must put us off if as so often happens our visit suddenly becomes a penance. Our address, after the 3rd April, is Monks House, Rodmell, Lewes: and our telephone number there is Lewes 385. We went to the Master Builder last night. No—I didn't think it right, but I have no reason, except my own vague fancy, for saying so.
    It was very good of you to come here the other day. I re-read your essay on Ibsen[2] with great pleasure as soon as you were gone. And I hope you'll tell me some time, about my mother and father, among other things.

Yours sincerely
Virginia Woolf

Sussex

3117: TO MRS G. E. EASDALE   52 *Tavistock Square, W.C.1.*
Monday March 30th [1936]

Dear Mrs Easdale,[3]
    The daffodils came this morning—quite fresh and very lovely. I think I know the valley they came from—I remember picking daffodils there one

1. Vice-Admiral Boyle Somerville, brother of Ethel's great friend Edith Somerville, the writer and painter, was murdered on 24 March by Irish Nationalists.
2. *Ibsen and the Actress*, 1928.
3. Virginia had come to know her as the mother of the young poet Joan Adeney Easdale, whose early poems were published by the Hogarth Press in 1931-2. Virginia had previously described Mrs Easdale (Vol. V, p. 95) as "an incredible goose and chatterbox, but simple-minded and rather touchingly idiotic".

24

spring long ago when we had a house at Lyme.[1] Thank you so much for sending them.

I agree about the Cow. Why kill it? Still, what one could do with a swimming cow I dont know. It might have taken to other practises if you had it. I'm trying to finish my proofs, and hope you will like the book, if it should ever come out, which I begin to doubt. But I'm afraid its too long and too ambitious and a failure.

I'm sorry you should say the same of your book,[2] but I dont agree. If you had used proper names, I daresay the public interest would have been excited. They like personalities, not ideas.

Excuse this rambling letter—my eyes are so tired, after reading proofs, and my brain too.

Yours very sincerely
Virginia Woolf

University of London

1. Leslie Stephen rented a house at Lyme Regis, Dorset, for two weeks in April 1901.
2. *Middle Age 1885-1932*, Mrs Easdale's autobiography, published by Constable, 1935.

Letters 3118-3151 (April–July 1936)

The effort of revising The Years *had strained Virginia's health and mental stability to the point where Leonard feared a complete breakdown, and he took her to Rodmell to recuperate. The proofs of the book arrived, but she did not look at them for over two months, postponing publication till* 1937. *For days on end she lay in bed at Monk's House with torturing headaches. Then Leonard suggested a holiday, perhaps in western Scotland, but in early May they drove to Cornwall for ten days, staying for part of the time with the Arnold-Forsters at Zennor. On her return, Virginia was better, and was able to work on her proofs for an hour a day. However, a short visit to London renewed her headaches, and her doctor advised complete rest. They returned to Sussex for the summer.*

3118: To Ethel Smyth   *Monks House [Rodmell, Sussex]*

14th April [1936]

Dearest Ethel—oh no, you dont like formal addresses, I remember. And I only intended sympathy. I'm so sorry yes genuinely—about Pan.[1] Yes, I feel your feeling: but dont I pray you go on to infer that you can lightly extinguish, as you hint, that beaming Shakespearian character, whom I love. And indeed need. I refer to E.S.

Oh I'm so becalmed, befogged, utterly vacant and vapid. Lying on 2 chairs: leaving the 2 chairs for bed: and so on. I finished my typescript 5 days late: now hear from America they cant possibly produce before October. Thank God! So I've stuffed the proofs—all of which have not yet been sent me—(Easter in Scotland—[2]) away in a cupboard; and shant look at them for 4 weeks. Then I daresay I shall tear the whole thing up. I've not even once read it through!

But now I get 4 weeks absolute holiday, and beg of you not to mention that book, or any book except your own, till June 20th.

Thank Heaven, I never looked at your book. Do you know I cant even read the newspapers—cant even form letters. But all this passes off with miraculous speed, so long as I neednt read or write. So, my dear termagant— but tender termagant—please write me long letters wh. I love, and dip into—

1. Ethel's sheepdog, which was seriously ill.
2. *The Years* was printed by R. & R. Clark Ltd. of Edinburgh.

5 minutes at a time. You cant think what a rush London was—how some of my friends fished for my poor brain with pointed hooks, and tore it, and tortured it—not you. The first day we got here, Sibyl Colefax arrived: the widow: plucky but so arid, so hard, so dust strewn—all the graves have added nothing to her but dry dust. And now theres Elizabeth Robins the actress walking round the garden with L. and being told, no Virginia cant see anyone. A familiar situation: Very cold—very harsh. Very lovely in a flying way this country from my window—No dear Ethel please keep your light burning and be alive and souse yourself in salt and vinegar and battle with all the horrors for the sake of V. who thought by the way you regretted your dedication[1] because you despised her. and is so glad its the other way

V.

Berg

3119: To Ethel Smyth   *Monks House* [*Rodmell,*
                                        Sussex]

April 20th [1936]

So glad you have better news of Pan—I hope it continues.

No, dont send me the book till it comes out. I've had to take to my bed again, rather collapsed into a bad bout of headache—cant shake it off—so have to yield to it, and we shall stay on here indefinitely.

Yes—that was what I meant—we have had to put off The Years anyhow till the autumn; the Americans asked us to.[2] Also, I've never once read it through, and shall probably have to cut and revise considerably when I can tackle the proofs. But the printers have only just sent the last lot, so anyhow this summer was out of the question. I've completely forgotten what its about at the moment: do nothing but look at a starling in the rain.

Letters much appreciated. But keep your book please till I have something better than a damp piece of blotting paper in my forehead. Then I shall rejoice in it.

V.

Monday [20 April]

So glad of dedication Yes, my belief was genuine—that you had repented

Berg

1. See p. 21, note 3.
2. *The Years* was published by the Hogarth Press in March 1937, and by Harcourt, Brace in New York in the next month.

Monks House, Rodmell,
Lewes [Sussex]

21st April [1936]

My Violet,

I'm ashamed not to have answered your letter, which was very welcome, before, but it came just as I took to my bed with a violent headache, and I'm only now putting my head out of the blankets and beginning to look round. This was the result of a racket—what with politics, letters, Hogarth Press— life in London is very agitated—before Easter: however, though it still pours and the wind is like a scythe, I'm now so happy in the country I never want to leave it.

Its odd you should mention Sybil Colefax. She came here the other day, and I couldn't see that she was any different as a widow; but this no doubt is to her credit. Only I dont feel at my ease with people who take the deaths of husbands so heroically. They say its the good result of training in society— stoicism.

Why, in Heavens name, did you burn your memoir of the Stephen family?[1] I find that now we're grey and old, Nessa and I never meet but we crouch over the fire and tell old stories. Your view would have been fasci- nating—George, Gerald [Duckworths], Father—Hyde Park Gate. Cant you re-write it and send it me? If you will, you shall have a photograph. (heres one just come, from an American paper—you see, I'm turning black; save for a white patch on top, and look rather like a saucepan lid. But the time for photographs is over)

Holtby[2] I only saw 2 or 3 times—nice enthusiastic woman, but feather pated I thought. I couldn't help laughing to think what a story she could have told had she known the true Virginia.

Gerald I saw, for the first time these 20 years, the other day. I think he did well in his wife,[3] but her task in keeping that lethargic alligator in being must be heroic. He had been ill. I rather think as you say he has the same affection for the bottle that George[4] had for roast duck and spinach. But this is very uncharitable—also dull and disjointed; but then Leonard has turned on the wireless to listen to the Budget speech, and tells me there's another 3d on the income tax. I refuse to go into politics—for one thing I cant grasp

---

1. Violet Dickinson (1865-1948) was Virginia's most intimate friend in her early youth, although seventeen years older. She had known the Stephen family well, but there is no previous reference to this Memoir in Virginia's extensive corre- spondence with her.
2. Winifred Holtby, the novelist (*South Riding* etc.), published the first biography of Virginia in 1932, and died in September 1935.
3. Gerald Duckworth, Virginia's half-brother and first publisher, had married Cecil Scott-Chad in 1920.
4. Sir George Duckworth, Virginia's other half-brother, had died in April 1934.

them; only am always being warned that the end of civilisation is just about to come. I hope Welwyn [Violet's house] will escape—our garden here wont.

So write your memoirs as a little defence against the flood, and forgive this stammering but affectionate scrawl.

Love from us both—

V.

Berg

3121: To Ethel Smyth   *[Monk's House, Rodmell, Sussex]*

Thursday [23 April 1936]

About Pan:—

Leonards brother who has a passion for dogs thinks very highly of a doctor who, though a human doctor, X rays dogs and has made great discoveries: diagnosing diseases. If you think it worth trying, write to Harold Woolf Laleham on Thames, Middlesex who would be delighted to give you all information: The point is, no vet uses X rays: but this man treats dogs as if they were humans and puts the vet. on the right lines.

V.

Berg

3122: To T. S. Eliot   *Monks House, Rodmell, Lewes [Sussex]*

Thursday [23? April 1936]

My dear Tom,

What a base receiver of treasure I am!—never to have thanked you for your book.[1] But it proves the depth of my trust in your ancient goodness, that I don't think it matters if I thank you or not. I've been cursed with headaches, and so have had to sleep them off. That's one reason why I didn't write—the other, the chronic, is that I can't summon faith enough in my own judgment to criticise your poems to you; either to praise, blame, or discriminate. I've been lying in an arm chair in front of the fire with your book open, and such a radiance rises from the words that I can't get near them. So the first bee of summer feels for the first flower. I expect its what the Lit. Sup. critic would call enchantment, incantation—there must be a critic's word: but I'm too sleepy to find it—and so must merely testify to the fact: I'm held off from understanding by magic. Now you will have had enough. One of these days I hope to begin to understand again and then I shall cut the book into ribbons with a thousand pocket knives—so I hope. Because I

1. *Collected Poems, 1909-35.*

adore this exercise when I'm awake; and want, even now, to go into a thousand questions with you, about your plays in particular. But again, enough.

We are staying down here, and perhaps attempting a cruise in Scotland: but I'm still awfully cursed with headache as these lines show, and when my headaches go, as they are going, sleep rushes in, and I am now going to shut my eyes with affectionate thoughts of Mr Eliot and the Yorkshire terrier and the wild duck in Russell Square,[1]—wish he would come to tea—How pleasant to see Mr Eliot—how very nice that would be (This line was found in the margin of my copy)

Yr affec
V.W.

Mrs T. S. Eliot

3123: To H. H. Beecham

*Monks House, Rodmell,
Lewes [Sussex]*

23rd April 1936

Dear Mr Beecham,[2]

Your letter has been sent on to me here. It is very good of the English Club to ask me to read a paper to them. I am afraid that I must refuse, because I so much dislike lecturing, but I should be glad if you would thank your Committee on my behalf for their kindness in asking me.

Yours sincerely,
Virginia Woolf

Alan Gill

3124: To Ethel Smyth

*Monk's House, Rodmell,
Lewes, Sussex.*

Postcard
Sunday [26 April 1936]

No, no no—dont I beg of you mention my book or my writing to me till I give you leave. I want only to forget entirely about it. And then wake and tear it up I daresay. Until then. Sleep and silence. But I'm better. Fine here today—I've been out in the garden. Hope for better news of Pan. And

---

1. 24 Russell Square, Bloomsbury, was the office of Faber and Faber, the publishers, of which Eliot was a Director.
2. The writer of the invitation which Virginia here refuses was a *Miss* Beecham, of Somerville College, Oxford.

there's your book lying unread but it will be soon read at this rate. I'm forcing myself to hold back.

V.

Berg

3125: To Katherine Arnold-Forster

Monks House, Rodmell
[Sussex]

Typewritten
May 1st [1936]

Dear Ka,

Your very well typed letter was sent on here, where we've been spending three or four weeks, I, mostly in bed, trying to cure the usual old head ache. Now I'm up again, and we talk of going for a tour next week in the West—but its all rather vague. Should we come your way may we look in and claim the platter of cream that good bears always keep in the larder.[1] We thought of the Scottish isles; but in this weather, the West is more tempting. I can't resist the West.

About Rupert's letters. I'm all in favour of printing them and giving some sort of correction to that impossible sentimental fashion plate of Eddies.[2] If Gwen, Dudley, and you (—what about Noel though?[3]—) all contributed, that should be wiped out. I hadn't heard of the Bryant scheme;[4] but Morgan [Forster] talked to Leonard about your suggestion that he should write something. From what he said, I dont think there's much chance that he would do it, even if he were free. I suspect he feels too much outside—temperamentally as well as in fact. But of course I would talk to him, if you liked. But do you think that any writing, save a few dates and facts, that could be supplied by you or Gwen or Dudley, is needed? I rather doubt it. What would be interesting and a real reviver, would be an essay, preferably by one of the younger generation, on his work. He got so much into his letters, judging from the few I have, that they alone would blast Eddy [Marsh] effectively. Is there much to be told that isn't in them or hasn't already been said? However we must meet and talk about it. I wish very much

1. Katherine Arnold-Forster, *née* Cox, had been an intimate friend of Rupert Brooke and had known Virginia since her youth. She lived with her painter husband, Will, at Eagle's Nest, Zennor, in western Cornwall.
2. *The Collected Poems of Rupert Brooke, with a Memoir* by Edward Marsh, 1918.
3. Gwen Raverat, Dudley Ward, and Noel Olivier, all friends of Brooke. No full edition of his letters was published till 1959 (ed. Geoffrey Keynes).
4. Arthur Bryant (b. 1899), the historian and essayist. There is no record that he wrote about, or edited, Rupert Brooke.

that it could be done, for I can't help feeling that he has been smothered and castrated, and there he is, quite different, and memorable, could we disinter him. Is there any chance you would consider the Hogarth Press—theres nothing we should like better. But this is random and jerky; and I dont type as well as your son [Mark, aged 16].

We go to London tomorrow; then possibly on our drive. I've just been sent a collection of old snapshots of St Ives and my mother sitting on the lawn just as she used to sit surrounded by dogs and children and innumerable visitors and the old postman and the fishermen and the Sandreys and the Curnows [Cornish families]—so I feel much in spirit with the old lady who remembered her.

Leonards love; he is glorying in his garden, and thanks from both of us to Will for recommending a rhododendron now flowering on our table.

V

King's

3126: To Julian Bell   *Monks House* [*Rodmell, Sussex*]

Typewritten
2nd May 1936

Dearest Julian,

I'm afraid I've been very bad as usual, or worse than usual, about writing. Only for the past four weeks I've been so stupified with headache that I've practically not touched a pen. I've slept like a hog; and now I'm rather clearer in the head. What a bore it is—I hope you haven't inherited through your great grandfather, through your grandfather, [Leslie] Stephen I mean, this cursed irritable head piece.

So of gossip I have very little. We've been down here vegetating all April; and for the most part wrapped in quilts and furs. The Charlestonians have been in and out; Clive at his most affable, by the way; not a single quarrel between him and L. Dear old Quentin so manly and imperative, so political minded now, one might think him sixty. The Potteries have certainly changed him, I think for the better.[1] Charming he always was; now he's a responsible very forcible, though with a layer of dreaminess, citizen. Dont hand that on to your pupils as a model of English prose. I feel instinctively that China is a little like a blue pot; love a little flowery; learning a little scented. Old Bloomsy. may have more blood in it than you think.

I get the most astonishing elaborate letters from poet [T. S.] Eliot; who is now the titular head of English-American letters since the death yesterday of

1. In October 1935 Quentin Bell, who was 25, went to Stoke-on-Trent to learn the craft of pot-making.

Houseman.[1] Did you know him? Do you like his Muse? I dont altogether; why, I cant say. Always too laden with a peculiar scent for my taste. May, death, lads, Shropshire. But they say he was a great scholar, and I can remember when his Manilius [1903] came out Thoby [Virginia's brother] going about shouting out a sentence of abuse from it. But old Tom has issued all his poems in one vol, which he gives me. But theyre all known to you. Where he fails is when he takes on him to be a burly Englishman, with our gift for character drawing. Not a touch of Dickens or Shakespeare in him. Last night I read Midsummer Nights Dream. Well there you have it—all England, all May in a song or two.

Nessa by the way at last disgorged your Roger;[2] and at last I sent it to be typed before I read it being so bemused with headache. And now Mrs [Alice] Jones says she has a rash or something so cant type it. I am waiting to read it still therefore. But as I cant tackle that job yet, I dare say its as well to put it by. Save for Charles's [Mauron] letters, I've read and extracted the whole lot, and as soon as I'm quit of my book (proofs not looked at—I expect a hopeless failure but never mind) I shall solicit the muse of biography to help. How to do it, having read a great many worthless or merely meaningless lives lately, I dont know.

Leonard was in London at the Labour Party last week, but he tells you his politics so I wont. Its not at all pleasant,—our state; I have never dreamt so often of war. And whats to be done? Its rather like sitting in a sick room, quite helpless. Mr Hancock is not going to stand again, and they want to sell their cursed ugly house.[3] Why did they build it then? And Loder[4] has become a peer, so there will be another election. No, L. says it will be uncontested. I'm reading Murry on Shakespeare; much though I hate him, I think he has a kind of warm suppleness which makes him take certain impressions very subtly. Also I'm reading a life of Labby; also one of De Quincey, but all so drowsily and lazily I dont think I'm a judge of them.[5]

Nessa and Angelica came over to tea the other day—A. very ravishing in a new striped cloak made in Lewes. Her passion for clothes is one of the oddest of our phenomena. Its like a craze for drink; compare Ann [Stephen] in that respect. I dont know how far she will take her acting, but at present

1. A. E. Housman, the classical scholar and author of *The Shropshire Lad*, died at Cambridge on 30 April.
2. See p. 8, note 3.
3. F. Hancock stood as Labour candidate for the Lewes constituency in 1931 and 1935, both times unsuccessfully. He had built a disfiguring house on top of the Down above Rodmell in 1931. (See Vol. IV, Letter 2436.)
4. John de Vere Loder, Conservative M.P. for Lewes 1931-36. He now succeeded his father as 2nd Lord Wakehurst.
5. The three books were: Middleton Murry's *Shakespeare*; Hesketh Pearson's *Labby: The Life of H. Labouchere*; and Edward Sackville West's *A Flame in the Sunlight: The Life and Work of Thomas de Quincey*. All 1936.

she is set on it, but then with all her gifts any one of them may catch the wind and sail her away. Also, marriage; love;—by the way how is that going in China? You see how discreet I am.

Lydia and Maynard [Keynes] propose to spend most of the summer here, cultivating the farm; Lydia burst in on L. the other day asking his opinion about what new play to act. He said try Tchekov; but she wont. So I daresay it'll be Lady Macbeth. Your friend M. Raine[1]—Madge—is that her name?— has sent us a book. In strict confidence, its not very very good; yet interesting; prose poems; not good enough I'm afraid and difficult to sell of course. But I've only glanced through. John has been in and out of the Press, but I gather he's collecting works for John Lane's now—New Writing or some such title.[2] I think we shall be here off and on this summer, and Quentin says he means to retire to Charleston, and there'll be the Opera with all its flock of bright birds. But I wish you were here. Have you made your boat? I shall sail ours if I can get Q. to bring it over. Now I am going to beat L. at bowls, on a fine blowing evening with the children playing with their dolls in the meadow, all the trees in blossom, and some heat in the sun for a wonder. I hope to get a letter from you.

We are thinking of trying your Falmouth [Cornwall] for a fortnight driving down and pottering round. Again I wish you were with us. Love from us both, and I shall write oftener now

V.

Quentin Bell

3127: To Elizabeth Bowen   *Monk's House, Rodmell*
                                            [Sussex]
May 2nd [1936]

Dear Elizabeth,

I wish we could come and dine either of those nights, but I'm afraid we shall be away. I've been spending the last 3 or 4 weeks down here mostly in bed, trying to cure a succession of headaches. Now we're going for a fortnights driving in the West, and then I shall be in robust health and shall hope to see you.

---

1. Kathleen Raine, the poet whom Julian Bell had recommended as an employee to the Hogarth Press (see Vol. V, p. 245). The Press neither employed nor published her. Her first book was not published till 1943. She married Charles Madge, the poet.
2. John Lehmann had ceased to work for the Hogarth Press in 1932, though he was to return in 1938 as Leonard's partner. He was now editing *New Writing*, a bi-annual anthology of current literature, which was first published by the Bodley Head and after 1938 by the Hogarth Press.

I shall be in London this next week, but you say you're going to Ireland.

I told Julia Tomlin[1] by the way that you might possibly let her a room— She's an independent, secretive character, if you dont know her.

How do you manage to cope with London? I feel less and less capable— but let me know, when you're back, if you'll come and see me.

If we're down here, perhaps you'd come?

Yrs
(very stupid)
VW

Texas

3128: To Victoria Ocampo   *Monk's House, Rodmell,*
                                 Lewes, England

Typewritten
May 2nd [1936]

Dear Victoria,[2]

It was very nice to hear from you, and from such a romantic place, compared with our little suburban country, daily breaking out into a new villa.

I am sorry I'm not coming [to Argentina] this summer; but I've been ill all this month, too many people in London, too many political meetings taking place in our house and I havent the strength of mind to resist dining out. Hence nothing but headaches and lying in bed—that's a familiar way I have of spending my time. But I'm all right again now. I've had though (since you ask about it) to put off my book till the autumn; and even then I'm afraid its too ambitious, too dull, too long, too slovenly, for its not my line a very long book—to be worth anyone, reading. However, its taught me much about my own art and limits. Enough, though, of egotism. I hope you are leading a far more adventurous and exciting life. I hope you are making new friends and finding new things to make hum and buzz in South America. Here we live under the shadow of disaster. I've never known such a time of foreboding. Even the artists mope and pine and cant get on with their pictures.

1. Julia, daughter of Oliver Strachey, had married Stephen Tomlin, the sculptor, in 1927, and in 1932 the Hogarth Press published her *Cheerful Weather for the Wedding*.
2. Victoria Ocampo (1890-1979), the Argentinian intellectual, and founder-editor of *Sur*. Virginia had first met her in November 1934 in London.

I'm so glad you've done The Room;[1] I want to write many more books on all kinds of subjects. And are you also writing? Lecturing?

Forgive this rapid and random scribble.

Virginia Woolf

Estate of Victoria Ocampo

3129: To Grace Higgens[2]   *Monk's House, Rodmell, Lewes, Sussex*

Typewritten postcard
[4 May 1936]

Many thanks for the delicious cake which we both enjoy every day at tea. Could you be so good some time as to write out the recipe, as I cant get any cakes made except yours that I like to eat? We go to London tomorrow.

V. Woolf

Mrs Walter Higgens

3130: To Sibyl Colefax   *52 Tavistock Square, W.C.1.*

6th May [1936]

Dearest Sibyl,

I'm so sorry we are off tomorrow for a fortnight driving in the West (cant face Scotland) so I shant be back till after the 21st. But I would like to come later if I may. Still better I should like to sit with you in the garden [at Rodmell] and watch the cows and then cook our own dinner and talk and talk. London,—Bond Street, Wigmore Street, Holborn—seems to me detestable. Crowded, arid, sordid, unhuman—why do we all go on tapping these pavements?

Love. V.

Michael Colefax

1. The Spanish edition of Virginia's *A Room of One's Own*, translated by Jorge Luis Borges, and published by *Sur* in Buenos Aires, 1936.
2. Grace Higgens (*née* Germany) had been employed by Vanessa Bell as her maid since 1920, and remained with Duncan Grant after Vanessa's death until her retirement in 1970. She married Walter Higgens in 1934.

3131: To Ethel Smyth   [*Monk's House, Rodmell,*
                                        Sussex]
Telegram
[8 May 1936]

Reviews brilliant Am enthralled by book[1] Off to Cornwall
                                                    Virginia
Berg

3132: To Vanessa Bell   *Becky Falls, Dartmoor*
                                        [*Devon*]
Monday May 11th [1936]

Here we are, with the rain pouring, in the lodging where Leonard stayed
with Lytton and Moore in the summer of 1912.[2] The old lady says she remembers Lytton very well, as he used to sit in the garden painting, and once
stayed here for some weeks with his son.[3] We rather think this may refer to
Duncan—if so, will he clear up the matter. There's no need for secrecy now.
But the old lady seems rather doddering.

Its been roasting hot and fine: this is, after we left Weymouth, and came
to Lyme Regis [Dorset]. Till then it was sepulchral, like crawling under a
grey umbrella; very cold and colourless. This was disappointing, as I rather
think Weymouth is the most beautiful seaside town in Europe, combining
the grace of Naples with the sobriety of George the Third. Why are all the
West country towns precisely as they were in Jane Austens day? Yesterday
we had tea in an inn with an Adams fireplace and a ceiling the very image of
the one at 44 Bedford Square.[4] We were extravagant and stayed at the best
hotel in Lyme, in which the very pots were seasoned with camphor, and
Ethel and Nan[5] could scarcely have added another touch. I find the company
most refreshing: L. gets into touch with all the robust spinsters by means of
their dogs. They begin to snore; this leads to questions about spaniels snoring
and then we're off. Anyhow, I dont see how civilisation can be splitting

1. Ethel's *As Time Went On.*
2. In the summer of 1911 (not 1912) Lytton Strachey rented part of Becky House,
   near Manaton, Devon, a large cottage beside a waterfall. He was joined there
   for a week by two old friends, G. E. Moore, the Cambridge philosopher, and
   Leonard Woolf, who had just returned from seven years in Ceylon.
3. Lytton Strachey never painted, and he never married.
4. Ottoline Morrell's London house from 1907 to 1915.
5. Ethel Sands and Nan Hudson, both Americans and both painters, who divided
   their time between their Chelsea house and Auppegard in Normandy, where
   Virginia had visited them.

when theres not an arm chair without its old couple and all so urbane and kind. You see, without my telling you, how dull I am. Dull but content— save that there's no dolphin [Vanessa] to talk to, and that selfish marine monster wont write. My only letter is from Ethel S [Smyth]: which begins with a quotation from the Mass and goes on to say that Pan [dog] was put to sleep under the laburnum tree after breakfast. I had just sent her a wire to congratulate her on the terrific enthusiasm about her book in all the papers. I think you ought to read it. Considering she writes like an old turkey cock scattering the gravel with its hind legs, the picture of Ponsonbys and Vernon Lees and H.Bs[1] is rather amazing. Showers of gravel fly, but there they are. I shall try to imitate her technique when I write my memoirs. Theres a waterfall here; and it roars louder and louder. Also Mr [John] Galsworthy lived in the next village. I went into his church, but no one remembered him; except the postman. Tomorrow we go to Falmouth. Write good Brute

B[2]

Any news would be welcome. Is D. [Duncan Grant] back? What about the Q. Mary—Christabel? letter to the Times?[3] Eddy Sackville?[4] life in general? We called in at Ringwood, and I showed L. the house, a dismal place, where Thoby galloped round the courtyard—the summer The Rasponis stayed with us.[5]

Berg

1. Lady Ponsonby, a former Lady-in-Waiting to Queen Victoria; Vernon Lee, the pseudonym of Violet Paget, the novelist and critic; and Henry Brewster, the American poet and philosopher, whom Ethel had loved for many years. All were main characters in *As Time Went On*.
2. For 'Billy', derived from 'Goat', Vanessa's childhood name for Virginia.
3. The liner *Queen Mary*. Duncan and Vanessa had been commissioned to decorate two of the ship's lounges, but when the first of Duncan's panels were put in place, Sir Percy Bates, the Cunard Company's Chairman, rejected them. Letters of protest were addressed to *The Times*. Christabel Aberconway, whose husband Lord Aberconway was Chairman of John Brown & Co., which built the liner, felt obliged to support Cunard's decision publicly, which further outraged Duncan's and Vanessa's friends.
4. Edward Sackville West (1901-65), Vita's first cousin, the novelist and music-critic. He became 5th Lord Sackville in 1962.
5. In August 1898. The house was the Manor House, Ringwood, Hampshire. Thoby was Virginia's brother, who died of typhoid in 1906. The Rasponis were Rezia, Guido and Nerino, who lived in Florence and were childhood friends of the Stephens.

3133: TO ETHEL SMYTH

Becky Falls, Manaton,
Dartmoor [*Devon*]
also
Budock Vean, Falmouth
[*Cornwall*]

May 11th and 13th [1936]

Well Ethel, I finished your book[1] last night at Lyme Regis, and must write under difficulties, in a lodging house sitting room, to say I think its a triumph, and if I go halfway down the road to immortality it will be because my name is on your title page [dedication]. How you do it, God knows—I mean I cant see how its done—how face after face emerges, when there is apparently so little preparation, no humming and hawing, all so inconsecutive and unpremeditated,—all roads winding this way and that—streams running, winds intersecting,—how then do all these people stand and live in their own element with the life of their own time rushing past, as might be fish caught in a net of water: living, breathing and about to shoot on—the whole torrent pouring past, nothing frozen and final as happens with the usual skilled hack? Lady P. [Ponsonby] comes out sharper and clearer than I thought, and shaded too, a masterpiece, I think; but then so does the glimpse of Vernon [Lee]—how you convey her in a phrase—and H.B. [Brewster]— and you yourself preside—if it weren't truer to say that you encircle, like some rush of air and sun—(for you're very genial, as well as searching). But I'm not at all (witness this sentence) articulate, after driving all day and putting up at this lodging in the rain above a torrent which comes down from the moors. I think its far the best thing you've done since the first immortal volumes[2] (which by the way brought me to your spiritual feet long before I set eyes on your 4 cornered hat). Its partly the volume, and continuity, so that the whole seems larger and richer, even if the details arent more brilliant than they were in the other books. What you must do is *to continue.* You cant, in justice to posterity and the present, let your great fountain bottle itself up— to tell you the truth, I'm obsessed with the desire that you should paint me:[3] not a thing I often feel; but what a revelation it would be, painful no doubt: but like seeing the true soul, picked out from its defacing shell, its confining and twisting convolutions, by the silver sharp pin, or sword, of Ethel's genius. Forgive this scrawl—now taken out and finished at this absurd hotel

1. *As Time Went On.*
2. *Impressions That Remained,* 2 vols., 1919, which Virginia had greatly praised in print before she met Ethel.
3. But see Letter 3443 where Virginia says, more characteristically, that the idea of Ethel writing about her appalled her.

near the detestable town of Falmouth. No need to expatiate on my sympathy about Pan.

V.

Berg

3134: To V. Sackville-West   *Budock Vean, Falmouth*
                               [Cornwall]

May 14th [1936]

Dearest Creature,

It was very nice to see your blue envelope in the pigeon hole at Falmouth. I've been so cursed with headaches since Easter that I've hardly stirred my pen even to address a letter to the torrents of Coign.[1] I wish God had screwed my head to my spine rather better—its such an infernal nuisance, dillying and dallying in bed and out. As for that book [*The Years*], I'm so thankful not to be able to look at the proofs—anyhow the Americans wanted to put it off, and I should be delighted to tie a stone to it, and drop it into the Atlantic. But I'm ever so much better.

If all the old ladies and gentlemen weren't pattering and chattering round me—I'm writing to a foxtrot in the Lounge—I should fill at least 30 pages entirely with descriptions of Cornwall. My word—what a country! Why do we ever spend any part of our short lives in Sussex Kent or London? We dribble from bay to bay, and have discovered an entirely lonely virgin country—not a bungalow—only gulls foot prints on sand. Here and there a castle, and an old man fishing in his river with the sea breaking behind ilex groves, and a rim of green hill. Who owns Caerhays Castle?[2] Why dont you? You must come and see it—its far better than the Lands End—We're just in from Coverack and the Manacles [Lizard peninsula]. However, what I am writing to say is: for goodness sake choose your subject; whichever you will; and let us have it. What a generous and exemplary author you are compared with—but I leave a blank for fear of libel. L. says I'm to tell you we want another volume of poetry. Falmouth has a row of Penguin Edwardians.[3] Do they pay? do they sell? because I was asked to give them Orlando and in my

1. Ethel Smyth's house at Woking, Surrey.
2. Caerhays Castle, in Cornwall, belonged to John Charles Williams, Lord Lieutenant of Cornwall since 1918.
3. The paperback (Penguin) edition of Vita's best-selling novel *The Edwardians*, first published by the Hogarth Press in 1930.

hoity toity way refused.[1] I only want to write poetry about the Atlantic. We get back next week. Any chance of seeing you?

V.

Berg

3135: To Clive Bell   [*Falmouth, Cornwall*]

Postcard
[14 May 1936]

This (see X) [Kynance Cove, Lizard, Cornwall] is where we quarrelled in the year 1909 or 10.[2]

V.W.

Quentin Bell

3136: To Katherine Arnold-Forster

Monks House [Rodmell,
Sussex]

21st May [1936]

The post has just brought us the pipe and the book—more tokens of our demands upon Bruin's [Ka Arnold-Forster] charity. But what a good kind brute she is—to take us in, keep us so long, treat us so well. It was astonishingly nice of you and Will, we both thought.[3]

Now you'll be glad to hear I can hardly tolerate the smug suburbanity of Sussex. I think of you at this moment seeing the sun set, and perhaps a raven or a badger. Without exaggeration, I would rather live at Zennor than anywhere in the habitable world. But not at Sennen.[4]

We had a perfect evening at Coverack, and saw the notice of Will's speech in the Post Office. The only people in the hotel were purple-faced majors from Hong Kong, and rather dishevelled, slightly vinous ladies, who told the stories of their private lives in loud voices, to my delight. One of their husbands had committed suicide. Still they weren't the sort to go to lectures.

Well, I won't run on, and cut into your labours. Look on the envelope and see how impressed I was by them. I have added 'etc' to J.P. [Justice of the Peace].

1. *Orlando* (1928) was republished by Penguin Books in 1942, after Virginia's death.
2. In April 1908. It was the period when Virginia and Clive were flirting, not quarrelling.
3. Virginia and Leonard had stayed for three days with Katherine and Will Arnold-Forster at Zennor during their tour of Cornwall.
4. A village near Land's End, which they had visited.

It was very nice seeing Bruin padding round her lair so firmly wisely and decorously. How clean and capable she is—as well as all the other things.

Both our loves to you and your husband.

V

Let me know if I can do anything about John Sparrow.[1]

Mark Arnold-Forster

3137: TO ETHEL SMYTH   52 *T.[avistock] S.[quare, W.C.*1]

Wednesday [27 May 1936]

Your letter just come Yes of course I'd like to meet Madame de P.[2] *quietly* (quite selfishly, not on Nessa's behalf—indeed I dont much believe in the efficacy of that) but I dont see how to suggest anything definite—We go to M. H [Monk's House]—for Whitsun; shall stay a week I think. Perhaps longer. I saw the Dr. yesterday who wants me to spend the whole summer in the country and orders me not to work more than $\frac{3}{4}$ of hour daily. So God knows how I'm even to do my proofs. I'm all right, so long as I do nothing, And shall probably come up and down.

Vita to lunch today. Very solid, physically and mentally. I dont find any corruption or change: but then my relations have never altered: always affectionate.

Excuse this scrawl.

V.

Berg

3138: TO VIOLET DICKINSON   52 *Tavistock Square, W.C.*1.

Wednesday [3 June 1936]

My Violet

But why were you so foolish as to buy a copy of that book?[3] I would gladly have given it you, except that I've lost my copy which I could never

1. John Sparrow was then 29, a Fellow of All Souls College, Oxford (of which he was Warden 1952-77), and was practising at the Chancery Bar. His *Sense and Poetry* had been published in 1934.
2. Princesse de Polignac, Winnaretta (Winnie) Singer, the daughter of the American sewing-machine millionaire. She married as her second husband Prince Edmond de Polignac in 1893. They were friends of Marcel Proust and leaders of Parisian intellectual society. Ethel had been in love with her, and Virginia had met her with Clive Bell in December 1935.
3. Either *Virginia Woolf: A Study*, by Ruth Gruber, 1935; or *Le Roman Psychologique de Virginia Woolf*, by Floris Delattre, 1932.

get through. Poor Miss [Winifred] Holtby, who died immediately after the effort, wrote a much more readable, though wildly inaccurate book, which I have lost too. If only my vanity were flattered! But everybody writes books about everybody else. All the same, I would give £100 in gold to have your book.[1] That might get a nib between the ribs, if you merely set down a few plain facts. 22 Hyde Park Gate, for instance, Why dont you?

We are both alive and Leonard [is] holding a meeting to protest against something at this moment in the next toom; and as they will talk so loud, I cant write sense.

Nellie Cecil came here the other day which I thought extremely nice of her; and we pretty well fixed it that it was your back I saw in a garden 2 years ago, when I was too shy to come up.[2]

But shy and silent as I am, I remain devoted, grateful, humble and

Eternally yr

Sp.[3]

Berg

3139: To Ethel Smyth   *Monks House* [*Rodmell, Sussex*]

Thursday [4 June 1936]

I'm awfully sorry not to have written, but I've been rather bad again— the result I suppose of those 4 days in London. Sleep this time—seems to have gone: and as you know this leaves me very melancholy and restless by day. Seeing Vita* that lunch time [27 May] made me have to take chloral: but I now refuse to touch it. The detail I give you to show I must resist talk: so must not try to see you or M^m de P. [Polignac] If I can lie out all day and drowse then the nights are better. I'm not very happy—partly because I worry L.—so won't write. But if you ever would write, so much the better: * Of course dont tell her—no of course you wouldn't.
The Dr. said I must expect ups and downs for at least 2 months more. This is a down; but an up will come. Forgive me for being so egotistic. How are you and yr sister?

Berg

1. See p. 28, note 1. But Violet's only published work was her edition of the letters of Emily Eden, 1919.
2. In the garden of Leonardslee, Sussex, in June 1933. (See Vol. V, p. 190.) Lady (Robert) Cecil had for many years been a friend of Virginia, and both had contributed to the book reviews of the *Cornhill Magazine* in 1908.
3. 'Sparroy', the affectionate name used by Virginia solely in writing to Violet.

3140: To Ethel Smyth   *M.[onk's] H.[ouse, Rodmell, Sussex]*

Saturday [6 June 1936]

Yes, do send on the dog story.[1] We probably go up on Wednesday, so send here, to reach on Tuesday. We will give an honest unprejudiced verdict.

I'm afraid I wrote a wail to you—No—I'm not feeling "at an end" at all. Rather the other way. Heres my brain teeming with books I want to write— Roger, Lytton, Room of ones Own[2] etc etc—and I can only just manage one wretched ¾ hour proof correcting [*The Years*]. Thats my plaint. If only I could be free from this recurring nuisance! But its much better. Never trust a letter of mine not to exaggerate thats written after a night lying awake looking at a bottle of chloral and saying no, no, no, you shall not take it. Its odd why sleeplessness, even of a modified kind has this power to frighten me. Its connected I think with those awful other times when I couldn't control myself.[3] But enough, as Lady P [Ponsonby] (was it?) would say. I'm ever so much better today, and making up unwritten books at a great rate. My folly was I would do all the Fry papers in between times up till Easter: made 3 stout volumes of extracts: which takes thought.

I rather think I shall try a few days in London. I'm longing to see you, to talk, to dine out, to go to operas, ballets, pictures, to walk in Bond Street— but no.

You understand that if I dont ask you to come it is simply that I dare not get another bout and see my poor L. look as if we were both standing on the gallows. He has been most perfectly angelic—but eno' as Lady P. wd. say

Let me hear about the puppy.

V.

Berg

3141: To Lady Ottoline Morrell   *Monk's House, Rodmell, Lewes, Sussex*

Sunday 7th June [1936]

Dearest Ottoline,

I'm so sorry I didn't answer your letter before. We were driving about

1. *Inordinate(?) Affection*, Ethel's book about her dogs, published by the Cresset Press in November 1936.
2. *Roger Fry*, on which she was already working; Lytton Strachey, which she never began; and a sequel to *A Room of One's Own* which she was contemplating, and which eventually emerged as *Three Guineas*.
3. In her diary of 11 June, Virginia wrote: "I can only, after 2 months, make this brief note, to say at last after 2 months dismal and worse, almost catastrophic illness—never been so near the precipice to my own feeling since 1913—I'm again on top" (*AWD* pp. 268-9).

44

Cornwall for a time and then going up and down from London here. (I've been a good deal plagued with headaches, and the dr won't let me do any writing—thats why the book was put off). About Ireland—The place *not* to go to is Waterville: the place where the landlady gave us such a display of Irish charm was Glen Beigh (near Tralee). She was ugly, but so enchanting we sat up till one listening: and kept quite a good semi-country house Inn. We liked Glengarif very much. But we only whisked through. All that coast and the hills behind, seemed to me of unsurpassed loveliness. And I remember a grey stone field full of gentians opposite the Aran Islands. Elizabeth Bowen is not I think in the best part: but with a car, there's always loveliness, and complete solitude, and bays like Greece, untrodden, round the corner. It's a melancholy country though: partly poverty, the sense of inferiority, and for some reason the villages are like slices of South Kensington and the White-chapel Road.[1]

I hope we shall meet when you're back and I'm back. At the moment I cant bring myself to face London. It was like a parrot house and a bear garden—never a moments peace, what with politics, meetings, and the insane traffic of "seeing" people, whom there was no point in seeing. Here it rains, but its lovely in the garden; Leonard's flowers suddenly light up in the evening. I'm reading all Macaulay with rapture, and 9 volumes of Flaubert's letters[2] with complete delight—better I think than his novels. Otherwise I am very sleepy, and sit over a log fire and wish I had your memoirs to read.[3] So write some more, please.

yrs VW.

Texas

3142: To V. Sackville-West   *Monks House [Rodmell, Sussex]*

9th June [1936]

Dearest Creature,

They only sent on your book[4] from the Press yesterday, so I've not read it, and shant read it till I can get a clear space and a clear mind, when I shall fall upon it like a ravening tiger and if you want my opinion (not that I have much mind to give to opinions at the moment) you shall have it. At present,

1. All this refers to the journey which Virginia and Leonard made to Ireland in April and May 1934, including a visit to Elizabeth Bowen's house in County Cork.
2. Gustave Flaubert's *Correspondence* (1830-80), published 1926-33.
3. In the early 1930's Ottoline began to write her Memoirs, but they were not published until after her death, when they were edited in two volumes by Robert Gathorne-Hardy (1963 and 1974).
4. *Saint Joan of Arc*, published by Cobden Sanderson, 1936.

this is only a humble and grateful heart thanking you for your present. Its a very handsome looking book, anyhow: and Lord, how I envy you—collecting all those facts among the doves in your pink tower. I've been rather cursed again with sleeplessness, so we stayed on; and I have hardly put my nose beyond the garden, and so did not ring up 50 Sissinghurst. We go up tomorrow for a time, since there's so much to see to, for Leonard anyhow, in London. But I hope to come back again soon, and drowse away most of the summer down here. London seems to me a parrot cage—a lion house—all thats roaring, glaring, cursed, and venomous.

But what I wanted to say was about Eddy. I was touched that he should want to make up the quarrel.[1] Of course, I am more than willing. Will you convey this to him, should you see him. (I take it from you that it *is* a genuine desire: not merely, though this sounds vanity on my part, a snobbishness: I mean its affection, not wish to dine in Bloomsbury.)

Only I shant be back till October. If he would like to come then, I shall be delighted.

I am doing my little 3/4 hour daily at proofs; at this rate, it'll take me about 6 years.

And is it worth it? Oh Lord! I've so many letters to write. Ethel: Mme de Polignac is on the rampage: so are those idiotic societies: André Gide:[2] and Prof. Grierson.[3] Are you writing for his book? I really cant. Thanks again for Joan.

V.

Berg

3143: To Ethel Smyth   52 *Tavistock Square, W.C.*1.

11th June [1936]

Mainly on business:
(1) *Dog Story*
    But why not send us the story[4] *and* publish it in G.H. [*Good House-keeping*]? If it seems possible to the Press, there's no drawback in the previous publication. (by 'possible' I dont mean anything defamatory)—

1. Virginia and Edward Sackville-West had quarrelled in 1932 concerning the 'cheapness' of her remarks about 'his behaving like a gentleman' (see Vol. V, Letter 2591).
2. André Gide (1869-1951) was a member of the group of French and British intellectuals who met periodically to discuss the worsening international crisis.
3. Sir Herbert Grierson (1866-1960), the scholar of English literature, editor of Walter Scott's letters, authority on Donne etc. Virginia had been invited to contribute to the volume published in his honour, *Seventeenth Century Studies*, 1938, ed. J. Purves, but neither she nor Vita made contributions.
4. *Inordinate(?) Affection.*

provided that G.H brings it out this summer, and we keep it till Christmas. And you'd increase yr. profits: and we cd. print the photos of you in the Coachman's hat. So send it if you think good to.

(2) RM—is Raymond Mortimer this time—on you I mean.[1]

Yes, theres no fixity or standard in taste.

Why cant I relish yr. Beecham?[2] Why you not my Flush? I now sort my public into

1. R. of ones Own: Flush: 2 Common Readers:
2. The novels.

Neither has any validity in the eye of God—of final judgment, I mean. And God doesnt read. I see you universally praised. Listener just in.[3] I'm glad your in a 2nd edition. Wasn't I scrupulous to let Longman have it! Its a point of honour not to bag Golden Geese.

Back yesterday. Keeping very quiet. Refused all invitations. Gnats swarming—Sit within like light or lantern. (This is my new telegraphic style to save mental strain)

And how are you? And are you fond of me? Reading Joan [of Arc] in a drowse. Why 20 words where 2 are enough? Better: did ¾ hr proofs today: then lay down. Duck for dinner. Wish you'd write another book *instantly*

V.

Berg

3144: To Ethel Smyth   52 *Tavistock Sqre.* [*W.C.*1]

Thursday [18 June 1936]

Well, my dear,—thats a new form of address. I leave it, queer though it sounds. Here we are, and I have been exercising a control which I can assure you is heroic—like the iron clasp of a statue on a horses reins—by which I mean I have worked every day for one hour without a headache—But its a dismal, suppressed contorted life, and only my own profound self esteem, and the delight of correcting finally 2 pages daily (out of 600) keeps me to it.

And what about your sister? The puppy? The story? Mrs Simpsons pinks?[4] One of these days I'm going to ask you to come and see me between 5.30 and 7. I daren't suggest it to L. at the moment. So far he has been justified. But my spirit is mounting. And my word, what a treat to read my book

1. Raymond Mortimer (1895-1980), the literary critic, reviewed Ethel's *As Time Went On* in the *New Statesman* of 23 May.
2. Ethel's *Beecham and Pharaoh*, 1935.
3. Robert Hull reviewed Ethel's *As Time Went On* in *The Listener* of 10 June.
4. Ethel's youngest sister, Elinor (Nelly), the widow of Colonel Hugh de Crespigny Eastwood, was dying; the puppy was Ethel's new sheepdog, again named Pan; for 'the story' see preceding and following letters; 'Mrs Simpsons pinks' was a dianthus, *Mrs Sinkins*.

of an evening—Flauberts letters and Macaulay. I was saying, I havent read so much since I was a child. As a child d'you remember sitting with ones book on the sofa reading? So I lie on my sofa. And the gnats tap on the pane. No allusion to you. Even so, I've not yet read Vita [*Saint Joan of Arc*]. One's invalid taste is so pink fleshed and fastidious. I read slowly and roll the words. You see I've no news, and not much fluency, and not much play of mind, but if you could see my heart it would be like a gold pincushion glowing with love. The words E. . . L.S.th [Ethel Smyth] are traced there; can you interpret the meaning? Well, I'm going to lapse again into Macaulay whom I find so engrossing it almost tears me to wake to 1936

V.

Berg

3145: To Ethel Smyth   52 *Tavistock Square, W.C.*1.

[23 June 1936]

I have read it[1] with (laughter)
                        (tears   )
                        (pleasure)
                        (pain   )
complete medley of feelings. So has Leonard. In fact we both read without stopping. But we both felt the same doubt—Could the Hogarth Press deal with it? So we submitted it to our Manager [Miss West], Now she has given her opinion emphatically that the Press would bungle it. She thinks our public would be puzzled: it would not sell; in short, both for your sake and ours advises us against it. Of course, theres no denying that these small books are fearfully tricky to deal with. Therefore we feel that as the Cresset [Press] has made you a firm offer, you ought to close with them. As you see, the judgment is not literary but commercial, and it has more weight because you are a friend. I mean, if it didn't sell we should feel guilty. But I'm sorry and so's Leonard. It produced the oddest confusion of feeling in me—partly for psychological reasons: as a revelation of an unknown or little analysed feeling that is. And neither of us were, as you anticipated, shocked: no: not one bit. (I will get them to send it back tomorrow)

Oh the flowers! All mine were dried and yellowed: suddenly in comes your parcel—how touched I was by the thong of grass binding them, and to think of your stooping in that heat—and all my room blossomed and became like a spring meadow. There they still are—my only flowers.

Oh damn the Cresset Press! Still if they can make a good job of a small booklet, they must be brilliant publishers. . . . I rather suspect though they've worked up that particular market, and shall hope to hear its made their

1. The typescript of Ethel's book, *Inordinate(?) Affection*.

48

fortune. How did the other book [*As Time Went On*] do? Have you heard? Yes, I should like Colette and Eth's letter.[1] Did another hour today

V.

Berg

3146: To Ethel Smyth   [*52 Tavistock Square, W.C.*1]

[25 June 1936]

Heres the Colette and Elizabeth.

I'm almost floored by the extreme dexterity insight and beauty of Colette. How does she do it? No one in all England could do a thing like that. If a copy is ever going I should like to have one—to read it again. and see how its done: or guess. And to think I scarcely know her books! Are they all novels? Is it the great French tradition that lifts her so serenely, and yet with such a flare down, down to what she's saying? I'm green with envy: (all the same I've just done my first batch of proofs: considering my head was mostly like a boiled pudding laced about with red hot nerves this is to my credit as a woman—bad though the book is as a book)

We *go down today* till Wednesday. So deposit Simpkins [dianthus] on an altar, and sit there in the cool and think of . . .

But we must meet soon—I do want to hear the authentic voice. (I've had a whole week, doing 1 hour daily, and no pain—thats why I'm so cock a hoop. But I cant do a minute over the hour.)

I saw my Dr. [Elinor Rendel] She says in 10 years they'll be able to cure me completely by injecting hormones. At present she says its too risky. Its all the glands in back of my neck she says—And what about the Cresset and Pan?

V.

Berg

3147: To V. Sackville-West   *Monks House* [*Rodmell, Sussex*]

Monday 29th June [1936]

What a time I've been thanking you for your book! [*Saint Joan of Arc*] But my brain is an engine that only runs 10 minutes at a time. Now I've just done it, and if you want my opinion, worthless as I feel it considering the lump of putty where there should be a brain, I think its a solid, strong, satisfactory, most reputable and established work; stone laid to stone; squared, cemented, and all weather tight, roofed in and likely to last these many years. My only criticism is that you've been so damned fair that one

1. An article about Anna de Noailles by Sidonie-Gabrielle Colette (1873-1954), and a letter from Ethel's great-niece Elizabeth Williamson.

feels now and then a kind of wrench towards the middle of the road, not quite enough rush and flight to make Jeanne angular: to make her I mean rise up identical above all these facts. I see the difficulties. And I expect this was the better way. Only as there is so little one can know for certain, I wished sometimes you had guessed more freely. Thats all; and no doubt its a perverted and personal criticism. Whats interesting is the whole, however, not the parts. I keep speculating—which is what I enjoy most in all books: not themselves: what they make me think. How I wish you'd write another chapter on superstition: what the French peasant at that time believed. I cant help thinking the general state of mind was so different from ours that voices, saints, came, not through God, but through a common psychology: why was everyone able to write poetry: to carve statues; paint pictures?— then, and not now. So that they believed where we cant. Or rather, our belief is hardly perceptible to us, but will be to those who write our lives in 600 years. Therefore ... but I've no sense to follow this out. I agree, we *do* believe, not in God though: not one anyhow. And I cant lay hands satisfactorily on your 'unity'. Perhaps I mean, belief is almost unconscious. And the living belief now is in human beings. For example, to whisk off a little, how angelically you behave to the Hogarth Press! Generous, humane, honourable. In Jeanne's time none of those qualities existed. *Therefore* they heard heavenly voices for no doubt the human vessel is so limited that it can only contain a few exalted detached and impersonal feelings at one time. As a psychologist Proust is far in advance of Ronsard. My perception or your perception is far finer that any 2 womens in 1456. On the other hand, the Rodmell church bells rouse in me nothing but antipathy to the Xtian religion —more especially as they set Miss Emery's dogs barking.

But what I meant to say was I think its a massive and wholesome work; and entirely to the credit of the pink tower and the doves, also of the solitary bull. (Oh how I liked that poem—the best you ever wrote—to V.W.[1]) All I could wish is that you hadn't been haunted by the ghost of Lytton into avoiding all his faults and some of his merits. But then the facts—the swarm of facts. How can anyone lift a pen freely among them!

Yes, you're an angel about the Press: and, to contradict my own theory of contemporary humanity, not one of our authors ever treats us as kindly as you do. No theyre a pack of lily-livered money haunted mercantile midgets. who take all, and give nothing

Look at this: I did it myself.

[*stamped:*] Virginia
        Woolf
        Virginia
        Woolf

Berg

1. Vita's poem *Sissinghurst*, 1931, which she dedicated to Virginia.

Wednesday [1 July 1936]

Back here again.

Yes, I remember Nurse McKechnie well,[1] and with affection, though God knows I could hardly bring myself to see her, so hideous was the time when I last had intercourse. Oh how odd that she should turn up again—there was a fearful row with another nurse [Traill], and poor M. was vanquished, and left my father just before he died, and went to Lady P. [Ponsonby] I think she caused a good deal of rather satiric comment among some of Lady P's friends (Dickinsons I'm thinking of [Violet and her brother Ozzy]) who said Lady P. spoilt her, petted her, let her give herself airs, and get out of her proper station. She used to tell me about the P's long before I met them—a nice gentle, sensitive creature, whom my father liked much better than the one who supplanted her. But oh what an unhappy time that was. M. crying in my bedroom, I remember. I heard from Maurice[2] about some pestilential Frenchman he wanted me to see. I hope he's not as bad as his handwriting makes out.

I am badgered by all kinds of politicians at the moment, and have just written a firm letter to resign my only office,[3] on the ground that my husband does all that for two—or even one dozen. Buzz buzz buzz goes the telephone. But I'm slowly correcting.

V.

Berg

Friday [3 July 1936]

Only to say I'm sorry about your sister:[4] needless to say.

No, I didn't mean for a moment that M.B. [Baring] tried to make me see the Frog: only handed on a request, and was highly sympathetic.

Ozzie and Violet Dickinson: they used to laugh about Nurse M. [McKechnie] who was said to give herself airs. I dont think they were more snobbish than most of their generation—only amused.

1. McKechnie was a nurse who cared for Leslie Stephen until three months before his death in February 1904.
2. Maurice Baring (1874-1945), the novelist and essayist, was an intimate friend of Ethel Smyth, and in 1938 she published a biography of him.
3. The committee of Vigilance, an organisation of anti-Fascist intellectuals, of which Virginia and Leonard had been members.
4. Elinor Eastwood, who had just died.

I will endeavour to bring back the Coachman hat [photograph] next week. But must insist on return.

V.

Yes, I'm better, but still a molly coddle.

Thanks for sending on Colette. Very good of you. Whats her real name—address? Never mind: I'll thank through M^m de P. [Polignac]

Berg

3150: To Lady Ottoline Morrell

52 Tavistock Square, W.C.1

[6 July 1936]

Dearest Ottoline,

Fate seems perverse—I have been stricken with what seems violent toothache and have to go to the dentist tomorrow at 4.30. He may keep me, or I may be incapable—but I will come if possible. Only dont wait, and dont put off anything you have to do. I'll take my chance.

And let me come another time if this is doomed.

yrs
Virginia

Texas

3151: To Ethel Smyth   52 *T.[avistock] S.[quare, W.C.]*1

[8 July 1936]

Well you are a bold woman! This refers to Vita. I shall be eager to hear the result. But d'you think opinions have any power to alter? Anyhow you've done your duty by that character. Oh dear, I'm laid up again—had a tooth out. Result, all the old demons out of their lairs. But better again today. And I had thought I was 2 miles outside the wood, and could walk to Wimpole St. and back on my own feet: We go to M.H [Monk's House] tomorrow till Tuesday And I would like to see you, if only for ½ hour before we return, thank God to MH for the summer. But only if it can be done without adding to your preposterous labours. Think of sitting to Neville L:[1] He's not the man to do you. As I last knew him, he painted fading landscapes, one moor, one lake, one cow, on silk: but not a terrific sun rising a ball of fire

1. Neville (later 3rd Earl of) Lytton (1879-1951). He painted Ethel in the robes of a Doctor of Music, and the picture now hangs in the Royal College of Music. For Virginia's relationship with him, see Letter 3153.

from the ocean bed. Tell me too, if you will, about Rocks and D.W.[1] who has just sent me her poems, with a fanfarronade by Yeats.

Excuse scrawl—on my back, but Lord be praised better tonight. No proofs this week though.

Yr
V.

How's Maurice [Baring]?

I've written and thanked Colette C/o Polignac—very much pleased, I am.

Berg

1. Dorothy Wellesley (later Duchess of Wellington), the poet. She had edited and subsidised the Hogarth Living Poets series, and lived at Penns-in-the-Rocks, Withyham, Sussex, where she often entertained her friend and admirer W. B. Yeats.

Letters 3152-3179 (July–October 1936)

A week in bed at Monk's House somewhat restored Virginia's strength, but her recovery was painful and slow. She began again to work on the proofs of The Years, *and by mid-September could boast of "a burst of health", but the proofs were still unfinished by the end of the summer. As few visitors as possible were invited to Monk's House. Among those repelled was Ethel Smyth, with whom Virginia, her nerves taut, quarrelled momentarily over Bloomsbury and Maurice Baring, but soon forgave her with the endearing phrase, "I adore your broad human bottom". Among those admitted was Bertrand Russell, whom Virginia had not met for many years. Absence from London meant a relief from politics, and in her letters she did not once mention the outbreak of the Spanish Civil War in July.*

3152: TO LEONARD WOOLF   *Monk's House* [*Rodmell, Sussex*]

Tuesday [14 July 1936]

A very good, though very dull day. No headache this morning, brain rather active in fact: but didn't write—did nothing but lie in bed and read Macaulay. Then there was a telephone, to which I flew, thinking it was you: but it was only a wire from Ethel 'dont forget Coachman's hat'[1]—the photograph she means, which I must now send her. Then I lunched—Louie[2] very friendly and attentive—listened to a little dance music—took half an hour's stroll in the marsh—saw a grass snake—came back—lay in bed—slept over Blunt[3]— had tea, and am now listening to the Mcnaghton 4 tet (daughters of Malcolm)[4] playing Haydn. But they play too slowly.

Percy [Bartholomew, gardener] is mowing the lawn in front, having mown the Croft this morning. So thats all my news. Its not a nice day, though fine; hot and windy with black clouds; and when I've posted this I shall take another little stroll. No letters; but my cigars.

1. A photograph of Ethel Smyth wearing a tricorn hat which she had given to Virginia in 1935. It is reproduced in Vol. IV of this edition, opposite p. 362.
2. Louie Everest came to Monk's House in 1934, and remained in the service of the Woolfs (and then of Leonard alone) for nearly forty years.
3. *My Diaries* (1919 and 1920), by Wilfrid Scawen Blunt, the traveller, politician and poet.
4. Malcolm Macnaghten (1869-1955), a barrister, who married the daughter of Charles Booth, a friend of Leslie Stephen.

The fact is its damned dull without you, dearest M:[1] and if you didn't come back I should have to take to writing by way of fillip. I cant help thinking I can now—if I dandle my brain a bit and have frequent lie downs.

Could you bring some *cream?* Thats all I can think of to worry you with. But of course make Mabel [Haskins, cook] get it 1/- worth. Oh how we adore you! how angelic you are to us—I say its sentimental to say this, and that you know it already but the M's insist, and say a Bird in the bush is worth 2 in the hand. Indeed you cant think how like a widow bird I am, all makes a frozen sound; and how I miss Sally [dog] and Mitz [marmoset] too. But you most, dearest of all Ms. Take care: dont sit up to all hours: dont let the Bore [Kingsley Martin] entirely exhaust you and come back safe tomorrow. Lord how nice to hear you!

M.[1]

I hope you'll ask Elly[2] about your prophylactic.

Sussex

3153: To Ethel Smyth   *Monks House [Rodmell, Sussex]*

Tuesday [14 July 1936]

No, I hadn't forgotten the Coachman [photograph]. But only send it on the understanding you return. Why arent you here this moment? I'm alone. L. gone to London for 2 days. We came on Thursday meaning to go back yesterday, but I was so done up, I decided to make an end of London altogether and try a complete summer here. In fact, the last few days were useless, and I found I'd lost half a stone since Easter; now I've had 4 days in bed, and feel the sap in my brain again, and mean to set to work and live like a hermit till I've done the proofs—if I dont tear 'em up. Its odd—I always swore I'd never try a long book, as I always crack up in the middle of a book; and just was saying to L. well this once I've got through, when I smashed. Never again—never another long book for me. Half of this one wants cutting still—and heaven knows how much I oughtn't to re-write, if its to be presentable. Thats what comes of dashing ahead in a glory and a soaring delight. without forcing oneself to re-read and correct as one goes. Never again. Yet it gave me some superb months of fun, and I daresay there are flashes of virtue in it, amid a waste of trash.

I heard from Elizabeth [Williamson]—a very nice long traveller's letter [from India]. Please thank her. I'll write when I'm less of a mush. But tell

1. Virginia called Leonard 'Mongoose'; she referred to herself, but only in writing to him, as 'Mandril'.
2. Elinor Rendel, daughter of Lytton Strachey's elder sister, also Elinor, and Virginia's doctor for many years.

55

me: (oh I wish I could see you—even hear you on the telephone): first: about Dottie [Wellesley]. Did she discuss Vita? No, I daresay not. I had a letter—but always the same kind cool calm, and complete modesty which I adore. Says I've shown her all the faults in her book [*Saint Joan of Arc*]. Then: about N. Lytton.[1] Please scribble off a history and a portrait, as you alone can. Lying in bed, I've been reading Blunts memoirs, and recalling how my incestuous brother [George Duckworth] was in love with Judith: how she confided that she was in love with Victor: how he was in love with Pamela; and then, why I dont know, she married Neville,[2] who used to come to a Club we had, called the Friday Club,[3] infinitely distinguished and effete. After their marriage, I never saw them, and long to know why he left her: what he did: what she did: and whats up now. So do tell me. And I'll write, and come and stay in October. But you will come here.

V.

Berg

3154: To Ethel Smyth   *Monks House. [Rodmell,*
                                        Sussex]
Monday 20th July [1936]

Well, Ethel dear, I take my pen instantly as you see to answer your questions.

1 About the publishing: L. says that if you publish [*Inordinate(?) Affection*] after Oct. 31st you must lose the Xmas trade, because all the shops are stocked and wont buy more. (I've just had this applied to me. If I cant do my proofs by Sept: the book must wait till after Xmas—so be it) But surely G.H. [*Good Housekeeping*] could be made to listen to the argument, and stretch a point in your favour. Tell them the facts, and I'm sure they could squeeze it in now.

2. The sales of Time [*As Time Went On*] seem to us neither one thing nor the other. I should call them good for that priced book: but then your publicity and repute are such—not a bad review and all out in a flock on the day of publication—would make one dream of 5,000. Still, its astonishing, if our cupboard gave up its skeletons, how small the sales of books are. L. has just been saying how good it is when one of our books sells 600.

1. See p. 52, note 1.
2. Wilfrid Scawen Blunt's daughter Judith (who succeeded her mother as Lady Wentworth) married Neville Lytton in 1899 and divorced him in 1923. Neville's elder brother Victor (2nd Earl of Lytton) married Pamela Chichele-Plowden in 1902. The connection with Ethel was through Elizabeth Lady Balfour, her great friend and Woking neighbour, who was the sister of Victor and Neville.
3. In the period 1905-12. It was a society founded by Vanessa for the discussion of the fine arts.

So we come to Vita and my letter [No. 3147]. I went into no details—merely said I thought her Joan lacked outline and angularity: was tied down by a myriad of tiny threads of fact; and never thus lifted herself off the ground: but praised V's fairness, in intention, though told her she sat too firm on the hedge for any picture to emerge. C. St. John I thought very much to the point (though carefully muffled) and should myself have said much the same.[1] Vita entirely agreed—with me, I mean. And then—what other question was there? Oh my health. I won't boast, but I think my week in bed has done the trick: that is, I've worked one hour daily; and without falling flat after it on a sofa. But if I were to tell you the history of the past 3 months —if I were ever proud of myself, it would be that I did not—well, well. I dont want to go into it. You cant think what a legacy insanity leaves behind it—how the spectres come out on a sleepless night. But thats over.

Berg

3155: To Vanessa Bell   *Monks House* [*Rodmell,*
                                          Sussex]

Wednesday [22 July 1936]

What a stingy wretch you are! No letter, and yet there you are at the hub of the universe, a hum of wings round you. And me forgotten, I suppose.

I don't think I've any special news: nothing to compare with Lady Oxford and Christabel[2]—about whom I pine for information. We lead a very peaceful lonely life, which becomes extremely soothing. I work most of the morning; so does Leonard; and we walk and play bowls and cook dinner. Voices sometimes reach me from the outer world: [Sibyl] Colefax wants to dine; Stephen Tennant[3] wants me to drive in his Victoria with him, talking intimately; and then Nurse McKechnie has turned up, through Ethel—not in person, I'm glad to say, but remembering old days. She wrote to Ethel because of her sketch of Lady Ponsonby. Thats about all. On Sunday, as I daresay you heard, Quentin brought his menagerie over; but it was windy

1. Christopher St John (Ethel's future biographer, and Vita's adoring neighbour) had reviewed *Saint Joan of Arc* in the *New Statesman* on 15 July. She wrote that Vita's 'inability to make up her mind what line to take has impaired the clarity of her narrative. . . . I have not been able to discover her personal opinion of "poor Jeanne" '.
2. Christabel Aberconway (1890-1974), wife of the 2nd Lord Aberconway. She was a patron of the arts and a leading London hostess.
3. The painter (b. 1906), a son of Lord Glenconner. The Woolfs had lent Monk's House to him for a week in the summer of 1935.

and rather distracting (I hope Angelica's cold vanished) Janie[1] I thought a trifle gone dry like a cherry hung too long—like all Stracheys: doesn't she snap a little? But she's all that she ought to be fundamentally, and as gay as a Jerboa[2] physically. I think thats what[s] odd—the French chic with the Strachey bite. She abused Rosamond's book[3]—but I've not read it; and doubt whether I'm really jealous. Should I be? You see, what a water logged driftwood I am, asking you for literary gossip. On Saturday all the Wolves[4] come—hundreds of them, and then I change my skin, and inhabit an extra-ordinary world. They talk incessantly. Whats its about God knows. And nothing sticks to them. And at last my mother in law rather likes me. But I lie awake at nights imagining what they do at Bexhill. They never go out without meeting some one from Hong Kong, and if they go over an old house, a door opens, and out comes the owner, who turns out—this is fact not fiction—to be foster mother to Miss Beeton, the granddaughter of the Cook [Isabella Beeton, 1836-65], and Bella's oldest friend. So they establish what are called links, and it is thought that I'm going too to Bexhill to be introduced to the owner of Dixter,[5] Bellas old friend, and the descendant of Oliver Cromwell. When the Queen [Mary] came there she was put out by the Cromwell relics, and said Oh No. I'm sure those were stolen from Charles The First. No, the Queen's visit to Miss Beeton's foster mother was not a success. But why should you be told all this, living as you are on the height, on the thick; of fame pleasure and society? I gather Lady O [Oxford]: entirely succumbed, and so did Christabel [Aberconway] I daresay. Never mind. Here, in our garden, jealousies and strifes, competitions, Queen Maries, all vanities are less than the slug on the Zinnia. The garden is full of Zinnias. The Zinnias are full of slugs. L. goes out at night with a lantern and collects snails, which I hear him cracking—upon which Sally strays, then there's a stampede—for she's on heat you must know, only her love for Leonard is more than any carnal lust—if, indeed, as I suspect, she doesn't love him as carnally as any bitch ever loved any dog; so she only goes to the gate, looks up the road at [H.W.] Nevinsons white terrier and then returns. All the lights are extinguished, and silence reigns.

So you see what a blank my life is—unless I told you all about Honoria

1. Jane Bussy, the daughter of Dorothy (*née* Strachey) and Simon Bussy, the French painter. They lived in the South of France, and Jane had taught Virginia French in 1934.
2. A north-African jumping mouse.
3. Rosamond Lehmann's *The Weather in the Streets*, 1936.
4. Marie Woolf, Leonard's mother, aged 86, Bella, his sister, and her husband, Thomas Southorn, and Harold Woolf, another brother.
5. Great Dixter, Northiam, Sussex, a 15th-century manor-house enlarged by Sir Edwin Lutyens, which belonged to Mrs Nathaniel Lloyd, widow of the architectural historian.

Lawrence, mother of Sir Alick of Alenho.[1] But that I cant go into. Its a book
—So's Macaulay. So's Shakespeare. So's   [2] I'm alone, as L. is in
London, and have just listened in to the Children's hour and the history of
Big Ben. And here's a letter from Katherine Furse[3] asking us to dine to meet
Dr Cabot,[4] descendant of the discoverer of America, whose wife is dead,
which, Katharine says, has softened him. And I'm glad to hear it, for he was a
dry old dog, and told me the Cabots could only marry Lowells.[5] Now they
cant, since she's dead. And I had a visit, long long ago from Tom Eliot,
whom I love, or could have loved, had we both been in the prime and not in
the sere; how necessary do you think copulation is to friendship? At what
point does 'love' become sexual? Now I could run on for hours, but as you
never read what I write,—does it matter? Writing or non writing is all the
same to you. Next time I shall take a sheet of foolscap and make my mark. X.
And yet I have a thousand interesting things to say. Tell me what you think
of Lady O[Oxford]: of life: of sex: of art: and if Clive's back [from Paris]:
and have you seen any of my friends? I'm forgotten. But happy. And must
now cook mushrooms for my dinner.

B.

Berg

3156: To Ethel Smyth   [*Monk's House, Rodmell,
                                          Sussex*]

Saturday [25 July 1936]

Heres the [Alphonse Daudet] letters back. Well, I wish one of these days
you'd explain why you relish praise—its psychologically so interesting to
me—your need of it. Or am I wrong in thinking that you want it more than
most people? I dont think its like my vanity—its different—this desire for

1. Virginia had been reading *Honoria Lawrence: A Fragment of Indian History*, by
   Maud Diver, 1936. Her son, Sir Alexander Hutchinson Lawrence (1838-64)
   was 'his mother's treasure', and died in an accident in northern India.
2. Blank in original.
3. A daughter of John Addington Symonds and younger sister of Madge Vaughan,
   a great friend of Virginia in her youth. Katherine married Charles Furse, the
   painter, in 1900, and he died of tuberculosis in 1904, aged 36. For her future
   career see p. 429, note 1.
4. Richard Clarke Cabot (1868-1939), Professor of Clinical Medicine and Professor of Social Ethics at Harvard University. His wife, Ella Lyman Cabot, died
   in 1934. Virginia had met them in London in 1932.
5. "And this is good old Boston,
       The home of the bean and the cod,
   Where the Lowells talk to the Cabots,
       And the Cabots talk only to God."
       John Collins Bossidy (1860-1928), *On the Aristocracy of Harvard*.

reverberation: (not that Daudets letter is a good example of what I mean) It may be that you are an externaliser. I'm thinking out certain problems for my next book [*Three Guineas*]: thats why this comes pat.

Yes, if you're at Wotton[1] of course we may contrive to hide behind a hedge and see each other. My head—oh thank whatever Gods there be—remains so firm screwed I'm getting along fast with the disgusting paring and fiddlefaddling which I've got to go through with, and am entertaining 4 Wolves to tea. No: psychologically I think you were wrong about my being "happy" when you mentioned time of life. It was I think nervousness at the imminence of that season—which however came and passed, as gently and imperceptibly as a lamb, 2 years ago. So I dont think my headaches are due to that—indeed I cursed the Dr the other day, who always said, as they all say, you'll be much better then. So why these headaches now? However I admit I earned a far worse dose than I've had. Did I tell you of my great political shindy, in the worst too, of my coma, when I was drowsy and painful as a crushed snake? How I was hauled out to Committees[2] and meetings and abused and rooked and at last resigned, and now will never sign a petition or even read a report let alone attend a conference again? Still though I withdraw, Leonard doesn't. Last winter the bray and the drone of those tortured voices almost sent me crazy—meetings in the next room. And did I ever tell you of the visit late one night of the starving woman?[3] No—one cant, alas, entirely withdraw. But why am I droning on? Because lunch is late

V.

Berg

3157: To Jane Bussy

Monks House, Rodmell,
Lewes, Sussex

July 29th [1936]

What a good friend you are my dear Janie, to remember that book.[4] It has come at the very nick of time when I've nothing to read. And it looks—for I've only just cut the pages—full of the most entrancing, wicked, underworld Bohemian life, and just after my taste, though I still can't think how Colette being what she is, to look at, ever sent me her discourse with that cryptic message. She makes me feel so dowdy. The French always do.

That reminds me—my old mother in law was here with the Governor and Governoress of Gambia [Southorns] the other day. And she's practically

1. Wootton Manor, near Polegate, Sussex, which belonged to Ethel's friend, Alice Hudson.
2. Of Vigilance. See p. 51, note 3.
3. A girl, fainting from malnutrition, came down the steps of 52 Tavistock Square to beg for a glass of water. (See Quentin Bell, II, p. 188.)
4. *Mes Apprentissages*, a memoir published by Colette in this year.

blind. We got talking about France, and she said was there any chance that the delightful lady whom I liked so much, who talked French with me would talk French with her? I said I doubted it! But then Bella (of Gambia) the daughter, asked me privately if I could arrange something in the autumn; could it be possible, d'you think to find a French woman (not another Janie —no) who would, for a fee, go and talk to her (aged 86—but spry as a throstle) in her hotel in Earls Court? Should you think of anyone, let me know.

And come and stay. When? In September? The deuce is I must now work 6 hours daily: yes, I'm plodding along: but its hopeless to think of finishing in time for the autumn: so, when I've made this plain to my publishers, I shall feel free to ask you to stay. At present, so unsociable is literature, I plod on with my nose to the page, and say to all tempters and temptresses Avaunt. In another life there'll be another Virginia who never writes, but always talks and talks and talks and talks to Janie. So happy will that woman be: why must there be this one, who writes? Answer me that problem. You can't have your cake and eat it too, I suppose. But then painters do. I would like to take another page to discuss this and other matters only I would never have done: there's Quentin coming to tea: I must boil the kettle: but my dear Janie, what an angel you are to send me this book, over which I shall pore tonight in the rain. And do, while, as our Aunt [Fisher] said, taking plenty yourself, give my love to your mother.

V.

Texas

3158: To Hugh Walpole   *Monk's House, Rodmell, Lewes, Sussex*

1st August [1936]

Dear Hugh,

How very nice to see your rather illegible, but not so illegible as my, hand again! I was just looking at a picture of you and your dog.[1] But here we are, I'm sorry to say, until October, so there's no chance of tea at the moment —unless you are passing our way and will look in? Its much more likely, I'ᵣ afraid that you're off to Hollywood, or Bermuda—but do let us meet ⸝ that happens: there's a mass of things to talk about.

We came down here early, because I knocked up in Londᴏ think what a din and a hurly burly London was this sᵣ meetings, politics, societies, all I think of the utmost ᶜ come down here, and lie in bed for a month; with thᵣ vast pile of proofs to correct, and must keep mᵧ

1. See p. 12, note 2.

the moment however I'm going to wade through the water meadows in a mackintosh.

Love from us both.

yr V.W.

Texas

3159: To Ethel Smyth   *M.[onk's] H.[ouse, Rodmell, Sussex]*

[3 August 1936]

Oh dear me! I entirely misled you—about L. and politics. He never never made me go to a meeting in my life: Certainly not this summer. No: what I meant was, I was pressed by E M. Forster to be on a Committee [Vigilance]: then they bothered me to take part: endless correspondence: I refused to budge: finally resigned. But it was harassing. A woman called Ellis Williams[1] ran amok. Gide and other famous French abused me. But no: not Leonard. What is true though is that we have C[ttees] in the next room— his C[ttees]: I hear them droning. Thats all. And thats inevitable. Thats L's hobby. and passion. As for M Baring as author, I long to read your article;[2] hope it may open my eyes, which are sealed to the merits of that delightful man as novelist. How you can once more compare him to Stendhal seriously winds me—What common scale can we have in literature? And I tried M B. again the other day, and still blindness prevails.

No more. The 5 Wolves did for me next day; but my mother in law was so delighted and so blind and so touching in her gratitude that I couldnt think my headache ill earned.

No more, once more

V.

Berg

3160: To Ethel Smyth   *Monks House [Rodmell, Sussex]*

Aug. 13th [1936]

I send back the Baring article; but I'm not going to say what I think of it, for two reasons. First, I should have to write some serious criticism, for which my brain is at the moment unfit (I'm such a prig, I cant bear to write

She means Amabel Williams-Ellis (*née* Strachey), wife of Clough Williams-
[El]lis, the architect, a woman and writer of great energy in social and political

[articl]e by Ethel (in the *Quarterly Review* for October 1936) about Maurice

62

frivolously about books) Second: you'll be amused to hear, you made the blood come to my head the other day by some remarks of yours in a letter on "Bloomsbury" Now here on the very second page I think you say "important—to use the great Bloomsbury word" and again the blood rushes. To explain would take too long. But I daresay you'll twig from the following quotation. A young man the other day sent me a book in which he perpetually used "Bloomsbury" as a convenient hold all for everything silly, cheap, indecent, conceited and so on. Upon which I wrote to him: All the people I most respect and admire have been what you call "Bloomsbury". Thus, though you have every right to despise and dislike them, you cant expect me to agree. Moreover, to use a general term like this, without giving instances and names, so that the people you sneer at can defend themselves, seems to me a cowardly subterfuge, of which you ought to be ashamed. Anyhow, never come and see me, who live in Bloomsbury, again. (Maurice I see talks of Bloomsbury too)

And as you have once more trodden on that toe—I admit all the cheap journalists, ever since Roger and Lytton died, have been jumping on it,—I see red: which colour is not favourable to criticism: an art that should be impersonal; and so I wont tell you what I think of your article, for this second reason too. The first however, is the more important (to use a Bloomsbury word) I've read almost all Baring; and to sum up our differences would, as I say, use more time and brain power than are mine.

Lord! how I loathe Wokingism.

Yr V.

Berg

3161: To Vanessa Bell [*Monk's House, Rodmell, Sussex*]

Friday [14 August 1936]

Might we come to tea on Thursday next—20th—which is I think Quentin's birthday[1]—instead of this Sunday?

I've been rather headachy, and as we have Graham tomorrow, and Sally Graves[2] coming on Monday, I think I'd better draw in my horns and have a dull Sunday.

Unless stopped, we will come on Thursday; to which needless to say we look forward with great pleasure.

1. He was 26 on 19 August.
2. John L. Graham, whose *Good Merchant* was published by the Hogarth Press in 1934; and the niece of Robert Graves, the poet and novelist, later Mrs Richard Chilver.

I sink deeper and deeper in Lynn Linton[1]—and am entirely enthralled.

B.

I suppose you wdn't come over and paint one afternoon?

Berg

3162: To V. Sackville-West   *Monks House* [*Rodmell,*
                                                  Sussex]
Thursday 20th Aug. [1936]

I've been meaning to write and send a cheque for The Foundlings.[2] Now L. tells me he has done both. I wish my cheque had been larger. At the moment I'm rather cheese paring, as I've earned so little this year. However I'm getting along at last, and I daresay next year I shall have no excuse for stingyness.

But oh Lord the number of letters that come—(not as much to the point as yours) about the imprisoned, the insulted the injured the builders, the putters down—all wanting money from devils.

Here's a letter from old Ethel. I get one daily. This time she says she has been asking you why I'm enraged about the abuse of Bloomsbury. God knows what a tale she mayn't have pitched. The truth was she kept on sniping at By [Bloomsbury] for not admiring M. Baring; after which I let fly, all the more because I wanted an excuse to say nothing about her article, a bad one, on that great master of fiction. And now she seems to think I complain of abuse. Not a bit—not a bit—only of young men who insist upon coming to dinner, and then go away and send me articles in which they deride By: but haven't the courage to name names. So I daresay, as this had just happened, I wrote too strong; and she'll have got it wrong; but I can trust to you not to let her make mischief between us.

If Bloomsbury could only smell so strong that nobody would come near Tavistock Sqre, I should be oh so happy. I've been oh so happy down here. And we've only 7 weeks left.

I wish we could come over—perhaps we may later. At the moment I'm coddling, because when I have to talk,—and people will drop in—then my head aches; and my publishers are as you can imagine publishers would be—jerking my chain a little. That reminds me: did I ever tell you what a magnifi-

1. Elizabeth Lynn Linton (1822-98), the novelist and writer about women. Her most remarkable achievement was the *Autobiography of Christopher Kirkland* (1885), a 3-volume fictionalised autobiography in which she changed her own sex and that of many of her friends, in order better to disguise the story. Her biography, *Mrs Lynn Linton* (1901), was written by G. S. Layard.
2. The Foundling Hospital, established in Bloomsbury in 1739.

cent subject I think your Spanish one?[1] My mouth waters: I'm green with envy. And yet I'm so placid and water blooded down here, with long spaces lying out, when its fine, in bed, when it rains, that I feel the oncome of such benignity you wouldn't know me. Also Bertie Russell has sent us an amazingly interesting memoir in 280,000 words, of his family:[2] which I have to read in 2 days, and to which I must return. Tell me about old Ethel. She is impending—next week, she threatens.

V.

Potto's[3] old and unaltered affection

Berg

3163: To R. A. Scott James   *Monks House, Rodmell,*
                                     Lewes, Sussex
20th Aug 1936

Dear Mr Scott James,[4]

I'm afraid I cant manage the article as you suggest for October. I was ill and unable to work this spring, and am now so much behindhand that I cant take on anything more at present. Many thanks for asking me; and best wishes for the Magazine.

Yours sincerely
V. Woolf

Texas

3164: To Ethel Smyth   [*Monk's House, Rodmell,*
                               Sussex]
Saturday [22 Agust 1936]

Yes, I've no doubt I wrote too violently (this refers to By. [Bloomsbury]) and if I'd thought a moment I would have held my pen. I entirely agree that being abused is a compliment. And for the most part I dont turn a hair, accepting it for such (tho' now and then they rile me about Lytton, whom they pelt with broken bottles persistently). The thing that set me off though

1. Vita's *Pepita*, a biography of her grandmother, the Spanish dancer, and of her mother, Lady Sackville, published in October 1937 by the Hogarth Press.
2. *The Amberley Papers*, edited by Bertrand and Patricia (his third wife) Russell, published by the Hogarth Press in March 1937. There were two volumes, of 552 and 581 pages. Lord and Lady Amberley were Russell's parents.
3. Potto was Virginia's name for herself in writing to Vita. A potto is an African lemur.
4. Editor of *The London Mercury*.

was the young man [*unidentified*] who forced himself on me, in the middle of the morning: talked endlessly: then went off and wrote not only a sneer at By but an account of my dog, chair, cactuses, monkey, in one of the cheap papers. "Queen of Bloomsbury".

What would interest me though wd. be to know how that word, has crystallised in your aloof and independent mind into the symbol of all you despise: as for example: "I have just been told by . . . Oh *we* think M. Baring no good at all."! I said "Do you mean by *we* Bloomsbury?" He said "Well you can put it like that—if you like." "Good God what a "clever" place By. must be, I said. Do they believe in God?" And he said "Why? *do you?* (a snigger) ES. Yes, but then I dont live in By. So know no better." I dont think I locate my prejudices so accurately. But enough: enough: What I wanted to say—no time though—is that yr. article raised so many questions about the art of writing I can't dig them up without a pickaxe and patience— Both lacking. So will only ask one simple and material question: why do you write of MB. [Baring] as if he stood in need of recognition, when in fact, as I hear, his sales are large, his reputation great, and his public devoted? I thought the permeation of that protest as if you were special pleading on his behalf, coloured the article rather too strongly. Now I wont say, as I have it on the tip of my tongue, that "recognition"—no I wont say it, more especially as L. is waiting to take this to the post. Abuse By. as much as you like, and I take this second sheet—a proof of health, for I've scarcely written a letter—all cards—mostly illegible—to say how you grow on me. Isnt that odd? Absence; thinking of some one—then the real feeling has room to expand. like the sights that one only sees afterwards: Is that peculiar to me, or common to all? Anyhow, lying in bed, or listlessly turning books I could hardly read, over and over again I've thought of you; and dwelt on your affection—Lord, how that pleased me, what you said to Dotty [Wellesley]—as if it were a red sun I could see and feel hot through the mist. And what a superb friend you are! telling all those people not to bother me! So many of my friends insist that I ought to do this and that—you, on the contrary accept me, and dont fritter and fuss me. And then how I adore your broad human bottom—how it kindles me to think of you, worried and bothered, yet lunching at a party of 12, and I'm convinced keeping the table in an uproar; and plunging like a blue Italian Dolphin into all the nets of the Sitwells; always battling and battering—and with it all keeping a mushroom sensibility intact. But enough: as—who was it?—would say. What I should like would be that you should come one of these days to Wotton [Sussex], and let us meet calmly and quietly—The packed visit is what gives my brain a screw. Still I'm so much better, I daresay it could stand a screw.

Now what else? Oh if you've time some day tell me about Dotty. I've always wondered how the Vita affair went with her. My relations were a good deal obscured by Vita—I mean, she left Dotty originally, I think, mostly on my account.

A dull letter this: but its the first I've written with any flow these 3 months.

V.

Here is the post: a letter from Colefax inviting herself to dine in August: but so harried, selling her home [Argyll House], one can't but pity her.

To show theres no black blood between us, restore the remark in the article. Please—This is a serious request. The remark about By word important.

Berg

3165: To Ethel Smyth   *Monks House [Rodmell, Sussex]*

Wednesday [26 August 1936]

I was horribly sad— this is genuine—and reluctant, when L. wrote you that post card. (It was the result of an argument: I wanted to see you: Nessa and Leonard both argued against me).[1] The fact is, I'd been straining to finish a wad of proofs, and thus brought on another bout. the very day your wire came.

I said, and I think truly, that to see you for a short time would do me nothing but good. But then as they said, suppose it brings on another headache, whats the good of that? Still, I believe I'm right.

But we must leave it. And I know, Ethel dear, that you understand my position without my saying it—how I have to consider the appalling nuisance I am to L: angel that he is.

If I should overcome him, before Sunday, I'll telephone: but I wont try to over persuade him: Anyhow we've made our peace about By. I should never have fired up into a fury if I hadn't been on the strain. And what was the use of the strain?—for its clearly impossible to be done by mid September: so the book must wait till after Xmas.

I think myself you greatly exaggerate, as far as I am concerned, the effect of Maurice's religion.[2] I read him purely, as I hope I read everybody. After all, does Dante's religion make any difference, or Miltons? No I think all convictions, if honestly held as M. holds his, strengthen the brew; what would L's writing be without his fanaticism? It works itself into the fibre, and one cant exclude it, isolate it, or criticise it. It becomes part and parcel of the whole. No, I should never feel any grudge against Ms. religion in his novels;

1. But see the second paragraph of the next letter.
2. Maurice Baring was received into the Roman Catholic Church when he was a young man, "the only action in my life", he wrote in his autobiography (*The Puppet Show of Memory*, 1922), "which I am quite certain I have never regretted".

and indeed, until you laid that emphasis on it I had swallowed it down unconsciously. It is Maurice as an artist, seer, creator, that escapes me. Still, as I've long known, I'm always in blinkers about contemporary work. I cannot widen my eyes sufficiently from my own preoccupations; the glare of my own wretched little farthing candle is always in my eyes. I hardly trust my view as reader of novels to the Hogarth Press now. Think how little I appreciate [D. H.] Lawrence;—I give way to you completely. and only register the fact of my blindness. Of course the autobiography [*The Puppet Show of Memory*] I enjoyed immensely: but thats different: that doesn't come across my line of vision. I see it as it is. Oh when this book is over (or torn up) I shall do nothing but see my friends. I long for human intercourse. Yes, you'll have too much of me. And to think I might be seeing you today! Without flattery (trust me) there are few things I should like better, Ethel dear. And perhaps I shall before you go.

V.

Berg

3166: To V. Sackville-West   *Monks House* [*Rodmell, Sussex*]

27th Aug [1936]

Bless my soul—how little you know me. Witness: "I had just been thinking how much I wanted to write to you"—and you refrained, because you thought my old fashioned manners wd. make me answer. What in the world should I like more than letters—daily letters, long letters—letters written on the top of the Pink Tower with the swans circling? Lord love you, as Rupert Brooke used to say—no it was Lorlovaduk,—I wont answer. So do pluck a swan, and dip its feather in green ink. Do. do: and dont accuse me of being a frozen fountain if I dont answer.

Oh Ethel! I could not face her, though she was passing our door. Her letters sound as if she was in a furious droning mood, like a gale, all on one note— Every morning I get one. Now she's battering away about Maurice Baring, with odd shots at Bloomsbury; but Maurice Maurice all the time. The wind may change, but it always blows now. Deafness I daresay. Its the solitude; she cant get rid of her mind in talk: or rather, isn't checked.

I'm better: but drove myself into another headache trying to finish proofs: failed; so thank God, cant send them in time to print this autumn. But never again will I send a long book straight to the printer without reading the type through. The mess, the repetition, the diffusion, the carelessness were, and still are, inconceivable. At my age, to try these freaks—however, I'm slowly pulling up weeds.

Yes, I think we must come over [to Sissinghurst]. And you will write to counteract Ethel. Excuse scrawl: lying down.

V.

I'm sunk in the Russells. Do tell me about any relations of yours. 1700 pages, but fascinating[1]

Did you ever hear tell of the Amberleys—Bertie Russell's parents? I'm as bad as Ethel and her Barings. Any old gossip? She's a fascinating problem—was a Stanley[2]

Berg

3167: To Vanessa Bell   *Monks House [Rodmell, Sussex]*

Monday. [31 August 1936]

Here is this.
Congratulations to all the actors last night. We thought it the most brilliant of all the performances.[3] If anyone wants to come and play bowls, the garden is open.

B

Berg

3168: To Vanessa Bell   *[Monk's House, Rodmell, Sussex]*

Wednesday [2 September 1936]

Many thanks for Julians letters which we will return.
Would you like to bring the Bussys [Dorothy and Janie] to tea on Sunday? If so, tell Quentin; and remind him that he's dining with us tomorrow. I think my head has completely recovered, owing to the party.
About the cheque:[4] I can easily afford it. Should I have to scrap my book, or should it be a complete failure, I would give you warning. But I've lots of other ideas for books up my sleeve. All I mean is, I would always give you

1. See p. 65, note 2.
2. Bertrand Russell's mother, Lady Amberley, was the daughter of the 2nd Lord Stanley of Alderley and Henrietta Maria (daughter of Viscount Dillon).
3. A play by Quentin Bell, *A Guided Tour*, of Charleston in 2036.
4. An annual allowance to Angelica.

six months warning if I found I couldn't manage it. But as I say, my head piece has now revived. so I hope to go on.

B.

If you've finished Holman Hunt[1] would you bring it, sometime: no hurry

Berg

3169: TO ETHEL SMYTH   *Monks House* [*Rodmell,*
                                                     Sussex]
4th Sept. [1936]

About Maurice Baring—the article I mean: no of course I wasn't in a fit state to judge, therefore only hazarded an opinion, I'm sorry you handed it on, in any form, to him. But perhaps you didn't: I hope not. Of course, too, I recognise, even I, his merits, and probably was sincere, if rather titivated up for an author's ears in what I wrote to him about C.[2] The thing is, I think he's a very difficult case: and I should want a great deal of time and patience were I to disengage my true opinion from my flurry of surface feelings. Thats all about MB. But please dont let him think for a moment that I'm hostile. No: not in the least. (And him personally I always particularly like—find him curiously refreshing and sympathetic.) Again, thats all.

Well I lay low, saw nobody and am better again—much better: indeed, when this book is done, I expect a year or two of the highest health: I generally get a spurt on after one of these collapses. Thats what pulls me through—And psychologically they have their advantages—one visits such remote strange places, lying in bed. If I can tho', I shall plod on this month; and finish, if I can, down here.

Droitwich[3] must be the very hell. I had a halfbrother [George Duckworth] who used to visit it after the London season; when he'd earlier drunk every night too well But thats not your case. A very nice letter from Vita, who asks me to S^{ht}. [Sissinghurst] And if I can I may try a day there. And Joyce is engaged . . .[4]

It was an effort to think I might have had a good brush with you and did not. No grammar in that sentence. No cohesion in my mind. And are you fond of me? And tell me how you feel, physically.

V.

Berg

1. A. C. Gissing, *Holman Hunt: A Biography*, 1936.
2. Baring's novel, *C*, 1924.
3. In Worcestershire. It was famous for its brine baths.
4. Joyce Wethered, the women's golf champion, whom Virginia had met with Ethel at Woking. She married Sir John Heathcoat-Amory Bt. on 6 January 1937.

3170: To Vanessa Bell   [*Monk's House, Rodmell,*
                                          Sussex]

6th Sept. Sunday [1936]

We were very sorry not to see you, but the rain was terrific, and kept
Hugh Jones[1] away, though not the Wolves.

We should be delighted if you would all come on Thursday when Jones
is coming (not Mrs) We go to London on Tuesday. I hope Quentins all right.
Here is the wicked brats [Angelica] cheque: Why wicked? Because she didn't
help me out with my brother in law the stockbroker [Herbert Woolf] who
looks like the figure of the pale horse, and doesn't even whinny. When Jews
are glum the effect is something prodigious. And the cistern leaked, and the
frigidaire went wrong, and the meat has gone bad today and had to be
buried. And Louies [Everest] child has been bitten by a dog.

Look at this from the Sunday Times. I think they might have mentioned
us as they put in George.[2]

                                                            B.

Berg

3171: To Dorothy Bussy   *Monks House, Rodmell,*
                                         Lewes, Sussex

11th Sept [1936]

My dear Dorothy,

Is there any chance that you could give us a night here before you go—
the tea was so transient. Monday 21st is the day that would suit us best. I wish
we could ask Simon [Bussy] too—not that I suppose he'd come—but at the
moment we have only one spare room—and thats a very small one: and our
cuisine is supplied by a daily woman, I warn you. Still if you'd face these
disabilities, it would be a delight to both of us to see you again. (I'm sup-
posing you're not here in October: otherwise we could fix a later day.)

                                                            yr aff
                                                            V W

Texas

1. Philip Hugh-Jones (b. 1917), son of Philip Morrell and Alice Jones. His mother
   had been secretary to Morrell in the First War, and later assistant to Leonard
   when he was Literary Editor to the *Nation*. In 1936 he was a medical student in
   Edinburgh.
2. There is no mention of George Duckworth in this issue of the *Sunday Times*.
   Virginia may have sent Vanessa a news-item which describes an alligator called
   George at the London zoo which "resumed his old aggressive attitudes towards his companions", and was removed to a solitary pool where he remained
   motionless for days, "as though sulking".

Monks House [Rodmell, Sussex]

15th Sept [1936]

1.   Yes, I should be sorry, very, if Ethel died.

2.   Might we come over on the 24th? Sometime in the afternoon? At least, might we plan this, and if necessary, I mean if the cursed headache should descend, put you off?

I'm ever so much better, in fact in robust health six days out of seven. Only the seventh might be the 24th. I'm pulling rather a long face to Ethel though, as I find these strenuous interviews, and she cant help it, the devil. Dont let on, I mean, that I am all right: dont draw too rosy a picture, or I shall be abused, in sheet after sheet, . . . no, perhaps thats unfair. She's been extraordinarily considerate, and warm hearted.

3.   The Amberleys *are* ducal. Amberleys father was Lord John Russell, son of a duke of Bedford. And I come across some Lady . . . Sackville West, his cousin.[1] But Bertie [Russell] is lunching here, and I shall get all the family gossip.

Oh I've so many books in my head that I want to write. Every morning, as I turn wearily to my proofs, I think of a new one, and curse the old.

So dont suggest that I should take on your masterpiece [*Pepita*], fascinating though it sounds.

Let me have a card, if not a letter, about 24th.

V.

How is Sibyl [Colefax]?

She invited herself here that week end; and I lied to her.

Berg

Monks House [Rodmell, Sussex]

18th Sept. [1936]

Yes, I've been a beast not to write, but then thats a compliment to you, for I feel, anyhow Ethel won't mind. She'll ponder the obliquities of Virginia with an understanding mind. I've had such a burst of health this past 10 days, I didn't know myself; and used every ounce of it on proofs [*The Years*], in the wild belief that I might yet finish in time for the autumn. So I didn't write a single note. Now though marvellously fresh, I've used up my fiction vein; cant see a word I've written clearly, and so must stop again. (What interrupts more than anything is the pressure of other books I want to write. Thats the curse of my brain: it's either dry or flood—no medium). But you asked a practical question, which I will put to L. the moment I can catch him. I'm always losing him in the garden. He's up a tree, or behind a hedge.

1. Lady Elizabeth Sackville-West married the 9th Duke of Bedford in 1844.

I've not been to Vita, but plan to go next week, for the afternoon; a plan that can be broken. What else? O The Prelude. Have you read it lately? Do you know, its so good, so succulent, so suggestive, that I have to hoard it, as a child keeps a crumb of cake? And then people say he's dull! Why have we no great poet? You know thats what would keep us straight: but for our sins we only have a few pipers on hedges like Yeats and Tom Eliot, de la Mare—exquisite frail twittering voices one has to hollow one's hand to hear, whereas old Wth [Wordsworth] fills the room. Now theyre mending the church. Tap tap tap . . . it drives me wild, the care of your religion. As irony will have it, my garden room is immediately below the spire.

I read, in a casual way, masses of books. Did I tell you Bertie Russell has sent us, to publish, his fathers and mothers old letters[1]—sweepings of old desks—2,000 pages: so fascinating and tragic, I live almost as much with the Amberleys in the 80ties as here and now. Oh this tap, tap. . . . And are you better? I can see you floating in a scurf of white brine, unable to sink; but has it unstuck your joints?[2] Last night, being wakeful, I had recourse to Queen Victoria (you, I mean, on the hearthrug) and the immortal lady in the train,[3] who made me laugh aloud in the moonlight. What a gift you have! This is not titivated, nor am I, to you, I think; but genuine. By the way, I was asking myself also, how can Ethel like anything I write? It seems to me, (I am waiting for Leonard) that you cant wholly and truthfully, apart from me as a personality, get anything from those little books. Not if you didn't know me. When you've time one day, tell me honestly about this. It would interest me enormously. Criticism—I honour and respect; but never get, only braying and caterwauling. Whats wrong—whats right.

Here's L. Yes, he thinks you're right as far as he can tell. It seems fair. he says.[4]

Oh what a mist is coming over the marsh, and tap tap tap . . . The Lord must have his house even if V.W. has to pay for it.

Well what a dull distracted letter! But I'm so happy, so well. And you?

V.

Tell me: did you go to Stratford? I thought it almost, perhaps quite, the most moving emotion to be had anywhere—in any place.[5]

Berg

1. See p. 65, note 2.
2. Ethel was taking a cure at Droitwich.
3. Ethel's story *An Adventure in a Train* and her essay *Two Glimpses of Queen Victoria* appeared in *Streaks of Life*, 1921. The 'hearthrug' was at Balmoral. When the Queen was standing on it, the rank of the others in the room could be determined by how close to the rug she permitted them to approach.
4. The publisher's contract for Ethel's book on her dogs.
5. Virginia had last been in Stratford-upon-Avon in July 1935.

3174: To Elizabeth Robins   *Monks House, Rodmell,*
                                             Lewes, Sussex

20th Sept [1936]

Dear Miss Robins,

The Hogarth Press have sent me on your letter, and will let you have a copy of the book[1] as soon as it is out. I have been wanting very much to ask if I might come over, or if you would come here. But the summer for various reasons has been very much cut up and distracted, and I have always had to put it off.

Now we are going back again but perhaps you would come and see us in London? Anyhow, we shall be up and down: if I may, I will suggest a time for coming to Brighton on the chance it suits you.

I get to feel so much what you say—that everyone is always interrupting everyone—so that you must say no if it bothers you. Writing is an unsocial occupation; but I respect it in you and very much want to read the results. I read your Ibsen[2] the other day again and enjoyed it immensely. I've not read 'Our Freedom' but hope it is worth reading.

                                             Yours ever
                                             Virginia Woolf
Sussex

3175: To Stephen Spender   *Monks House, Rodmell,*
                                             Lewes [Sussex]

23rd Sept [1936]

Dear Stephen,

I was much amused by your post card of the two novelists;[3] and have stuck it in my album.

We are still down here and hope to stay at any rate till the beginning of October, as it is very much nicer here than in London.

I had rather a smash up, largely owing to the uproar of that town, in June, and spent most of July in bed. However, I'm all right now.

Leonard wants me to say that he is very glad that you confirm him to some extent in the great hotel food question. On the whole I think he got the worst of it—but he still holds out. We found Cornish cooking very good this spring. I hope we shall see you when we're back.

                                             yrs
                                             V.W.
Texas

1. *Our Freedom and Its Results, by Five Women*, ed. Ray Strachey, Hogarth Press, 1936.
2. *Ibsen and the Actress*, Hogarth Press, 1928.
3. Virginia and Stella Benson.

3176: To V. Sackville-West   *Monks House* [*Rodmell,*
                                             Sussex]
Thursday [24 September 1936]

Mitzi is perfectly well and sends her love. We didn't bring her because
she had been feeling the cold.[1] so L. said. She confides all symptoms to him.
Today she has eaten 40 worms, and turned head over heels. It was a great
treat seeing you—and Lord! what a setting! This house seemed like a snail-
shell afterwards. And, far from being tired, the jaunt set me up. I feel heavenly
well, like a horse thats had a holiday out at grass. L. and Percy have been
planting your poplars. How you shower, like a goddess, from your cornucopia! Oh Lord I cant write, but am very fond; so's Potto and lets have many
many jaunts.

Send me a card from Skye [Scotland].

Pipe lighter still the joy of my life.

                                                        T.O. [turn over]
I came back to find 6 pages from Bob Nichols to say "You are Stevie Smith.
No doubt of it. And Yellow Paper is far and away your best book."[2]

Berg

3177: To Ethel Smyth   *Monks House* [*Rodmell,*
                                             Sussex]
Sunday [4 October 1936]

Yes, I continue very well, and I hope you do too. I began a letter—cant
finish. Showers of letters have descended which I must answer. We go back
I think next Sunday   Press is becoming exacting. Apple's being picked.
Very fine: have done a good deal of work

                                                        V.

Berg

3178: To Violet Dickinson   *Monks House, Rodmell,*
                                             Lewes [*Sussex*]
6th Oct [1936]

My Violet,

     What a treat—to get a letter from you. Unexpected, unsolicited. I was
thinking of you, and even saying aloud that Bowyer Nichols[3] had been in

1. Mitzi was Leonard's marmoset. Virginia and Leonard had been to tea at Sissinghurst on 22 September.
2. Robert Nichols, poet, 1893-1944. Stevie Smith ('Stevie' was the nickname of
   Florence Margaret Smith) had just published her *Novel on Yellow Paper*.
3. John Bowyer Nichols (1859-1939), the writer on art, and father of Robert
   Nichols, the poet.

love with you, and wondering if he were alive or dead. This was because of a letter—a cracked crazy letter from Bob Nichols: and so I wish you would finish the story, and tell me if Bowyer was in love with you, and if he is alive: or dead. Better still, sit down this instant and write your memoirs.

Last summer I was walking in the churchyard behind your house [Mortimer Street], and wondering which was your window; the one in the drawingroom where we sat.

Bobby Dugdale,[1] whom I've been skipping, certainly ought to be annotated by you, and served up by Leonard; but when I showed him the book, he gave one sniff and returned to his apple trees. Its a bumper crop this year, and even I have been standing in the middle of a tree, with the trug [Sussex garden-basket] beside me.

I've been having a holiday from novel writing, and all writing, to ease off those infernal headaches, which kept coming back the moment I tried to correct a proof: now we're going back to London very vigorous; but there doesn't seem much point in novels, with the whole world gone crazy.

Yes, Fritham was a school; and the ponies did nibble; and there was a deer killed outside the house. Weren't you there? with Theodore Ll. Davies, who fell off his horse? Oh dear how long ago it all is, and father's famous cup of coffee![2]

Love from us both
Sp.

Berg

3179: To Lady Ottoline Morrell   *Monks House, Rodmell,*
                                          Lewes, Sussex
Oct 9th [1936]

Dearest Ottoline,

It was very nice to see your brown ink again. Its an age since we met, as you say. We were in Cornwall; then you were in Ireland; and then in the middle of July we came here. I never knew London more fiendish than last summer. Our room seemed to be the centre of all the howling winds, and distracted and vociferous politicians, till at last I could stand it no longer, and was almost submerged by headache—only mine aren't headaches, but enraged rats gnawing the nape of my neck. I went to a doctor, at length; but all the comfort I got was that in 20 years, when I'm dead, and dont want a head, they will be able to cure them—its a gland that gets tired, so they say—by injections. At the moment, the cure is too risky, so I had to fall back on old

1. Blanche Dugdale's life of her uncle, A. J. Balfour, the statesman, 2 vols. 1936.
2. Fritham was in the New Forest, where the Stephen family stayed in 1900, 1901 and 1902. Theodore Llewelyn Davies (1870-1905) was one of Margaret Llewelyn Davies' brothers.

Savage's[1] prescription—dont write or read or do anything you like doing. This I did all through August, and I'm now perfectly well again. But what a waste and a bore it is!

Now I must set to and correct the proofs of a novel; and start if I can some sort of life of Roger [Fry]. I've been going through all the letters, but how to make a life of him I cant conceive. I hope some flash will come: with luck. No, I haven't read Aldous, or Rosamond, or your friend, the white and voluble slug—Morgan.[2] Have you? Tell me what I must begin upon: if any. I've heard as usual contradictory reports, but not much praise.

We've been seeing Bertie [Russell]—he suddenly sent us 2000 pages of his parents' memoirs. We found them absorbing and are going to publish a vast book of them in the spring. So Bertie came here to discuss it, and we went there to his Tower on the downs and made the acquaintance of Peter.[3] I hadn't seen Bertie for 20 years. What an entrancing mind—but I must leave all this till we meet. We go back next week. And I do hope your headaches are better. But doctors know nothing. I'd far rather have typhoid, appendicitis and influenza than that long drawn misery with all its retinue of despairs and excitements. Perhaps though without our headaches we should be duller. But dont lavish yourself on slugs.

yrs V.

Texas

1. Sir George Savage (1842-1921), who specialised in mental diseases, and was doctor to the Stephen family for many years.
2. Huxley's *Eyeless in Gaza*; Rosamond Lehmann's *The Weather in the Streets*; and Charles Morgan's *Sparkenbroke*. All 1936.
3. Bertrand Russell was now living at Telegraph House, his brother's house, near Petersfield, Hampshire, with his third wife Patricia ('Peter', *née* Spence) whom he had married in January 1936, after living with her for several years. Russell and Ottoline Morrell had become lovers in 1911, and their affair had continued through most of the First War.

Letters 3180-3206 (October–December 1936)

Leonard pronounced The Years *to be "extraordinarily good", and a load was lifted from Virginia's mind. She completed the proofs on her return to London, cutting them from 700 to 420 pages, and was finally rid of the book just after Christmas. Almost immediately she began to write* Three Guineas, *while intermittently she read more of Roger Fry's papers, and resumed some journalism, notably a bi-centenary article on Gibbon. She also felt well enough to write, at short notice, a paper for the Memoir Club, to visit Ethel at Woking, and to read manuscripts for the Hogarth Press. The Abdication crisis of early December caused her considerable amusement.*

3180: To Ethel Smyth   52 *Tavistock Square* [*W.C.*1]

Monday [12 October 1936]

Yes, dear Ethel, or Ethel dear, I'm back again. But I must be crazed. I wrote you a long account—a fairly long account—of seeing Vita, and then tore it up, thinking for sure I had written it to you already. And now its stale. But shan't we some time meet? Why not? I'm having a holiday.

But of course I'm pestered with various things.

Glad Eh. [Williamson] is back: and glad you're better. and I've been seeing all the Wolves, some about to go to Gambia as Governors, and Lord it was hot and noisy and so many different cakes; and now I'm dropping off to sleep. Yes—yes yes. sleep.

Berg

3181: To Ethel Smyth   [52 *Tavistock Square, W.C.*1]

Thurs: [15th October 1936]

I rang up last evening and Mary [maid] told me you had fallen and hurt your ankle. The masseur was with you. I'm so sorry, and wont ring up, as I suppose you cant move. Dear, what a bore; and then you've rheumatism!— Still what I mean to say is, shant I try to come down [to Woking] and see you one afternoon, or lunch next week—as you mustnt come up—and I could

78

have tea *or* an hour or two and come home, I shd like it and want to see you.
So let me know.

V.

Perhaps Monday?

Berg

Saturday [17 October 1936]

Yes, I will come—if you would find it acceptable.

I see there's a train that gets in at 12.58. Does that hit a bus? Would that reach you in time for lunch?

Then we could talk; then we could be silent; then we could, if you can, walk: if I could be home for dinner.

No champagne needed: no wine at all;

Dear me, yes, how nice (what a niminy piminy little word that is) it'll be—seeing you again. Excuse my clothes though: I've only one dress, and thats full of holes burnt by cigarettes.

V.

Berg

Tuesday [20th October 1936]

Do you mean London on the 2nd: Liverpool on the 3rd? I hope so: because Monday 2nd would suit: the 3rd I cant manage (mother and brother in law coming). But let me know which. I did enjoy our expedition; sitting in the summer house [at Woking] in the livid storm while you relieved nature—oh and all the rest—Only I rather deplore my egotistic depression—I'm always like a reft mother bear when I'm not writing. And so am already boring my way into Fry papers. But I exaggerate my depression too—tho' it's bad, when my head aches, it lifts when it stops. But I dont exaggerate my pleasure, so soon as the 6 months mould had melted, in seeing you—I caught my train and was home almost punctually, a great achievement as we ran it fine: Oh and the champagne! how I liked it. Let me know the day

Berg

3184: To Ethel Smyth   [52 *Tavistock Square, W.C.*1]

Wednesday [21 October 1936]

Re Umbrella Mystery

I went to Burlington Gardens at 3.20. found umbrella which is no more my umbrella than the planet Jupiter. Went to gallery: walked 4 times round; could not see you. Left *my* umbrella (as I still think it, tho' I admit to have found a small rubber ring at top) so am now umbrella-less. I remember I left my umbrella on the ledge of the bookcase in the sitting room; also that I noticed the twin in the hall; therefore was careful to take mine, as I thought. But am now entirely perplexed—for can you have still another cane umbrella —but determined if I go without for ever, not to be landed with that horrid and indeed indecent monstrosity which you left for me: so whats to be done about it? And where were you? I saw Ottoline.

V.

Berg

3185: To Ethel Smyth   [52 *Tavistock Square, W.C.*1]

Thursday [22 October 1936]

Re Umbrella

This gets worse and worse. I left the monster in the rack with the label round it on which I had written a note to you. Now you say "the monstrosity was gone, and the other there". Someone must have taken it—and my note. Considering the label was addressed to me this seems pretty cool. But it was such a brute I dont grudge it them. What steps do you wish me to take? Enquiries for it at Burlington Gardens? Further, for curiosities sake, where is your umbrella?

But enough of umbrellas. What can I have said in my hasty note to make you think that my stammered and inadequate description of a very to me exciting experience[1] was all grudge? Of course I meant it. But at the same time, when I come back and find I cant work, depression does seize me; and I thought I had emphasised this, and minimised the sublimity of t'other experience (since of the two depression is the simplest to make other people feel) and thus apologised. But oh dear me, t'other is the real one.

No, I'm not starting any new work; only taking a week by the drawing room fire and ruminating this and that for the future, since I must have a break before reading that vast shuffle of exhausted sentences which I must now mother, alas. And now I think of Roger: now of a Room; now of criticism. But all must wait. More egotism! I'm still torpid like a snake—ah

1. Her visit to Ethel at Woking on 19 October.

but nothing shall ever again rid me of my moonlit night last August—
nothing. That was far more solid than any Room or Roger or Years—I can
assure you.

V.

Berg

3186: To Ethel Smyth   [52 *Tavistock Square, W.C.*1]

Monday [2 November 1936]

Yes I liked it very much—thought it very well Tossed, and a difficult
pancake (thats an unsought pun) to turn without breaking. One phrase
seemed to me so good. I should have marked it, if I ever marked books. And
now I cant find it—about marble—I liked the word 'marble' in that context.[1]
But thats a detail. Now and again it wobbled but righted itself. No 5th wont
do, because we're going down to Lewes to see the fire works.[2] Always meant
to, never have. A gorgeous affair, and we're joining one of the processions.
But I'm sorry. Oh dear, how unhappy you sound in that book, and how very
cold and distant other people are. But not me—not altogether.

V.

Umbrella statement enclosed.

Re Umbrella.

You said that I had taken yours.
Would I bring it to B. G? [Burlington Gardens]
You would leave mine in the rack.
Although certain that my U. was my U, I was slightly dashed by your
mention of an india rubber band: which I had not known of, but found.
Off I went therefore to BG with my U. Directly I saw the U in the rack I
knew it was none of mine.
Therefore I took both upstairs to confront you with them. I could not
see you.
So I came down, wrote a statement on the label, left my U. and the false
one in the rack, so that you might see for yourself.
You, meanwhile had come down, and seeing only one U—with a cane
handle—in the rack, had assumed it was the one I had left for you, and gone

1. *Inordinate*(?) *Affection* had just been published. The pun referred to Ethel's dogs,
   all called 'Pan'. Speaking of the "shades of the dead who once loved you",
   Ethel wrote (pp. 94-5): "the recollection of your harshness, your lack of sympathy with them when they were on earth (and perhaps being exceedingly
   trying) would be unbearable but for the burning hope ... no, the marble
   belief, that somehow or other they know you are sorry."
2. The annual Lewes fireworks display on Guy Fawkes Day (5 November).

off with it. This you sent me by post. I then realised that you had taken a strangers, and therefore returned to the BG. with the stranger: was told a gent. [Mr Cohen] was very angry and had gone to the police; but recovered both my U and the monster. Then I took the monster to Mr Cohen in Fitzroy Sqre. and retained what I had all along known was my own U.

Did you get yours?

And what has happened to Mr Cohen's?

Berg

3187: To Molly MacCarthy   52 *Tavistock Square, W.C.*1

8th Nov. [1936]

Dearest Molly,

What a devil you are! Of course I'm delighted that there should be another meeting¹—I dont mean that. But why should I read? Its not my turn. I'm almost memoirless. Can't you persuade yourself or Desmond [Mac-Carthy] or Maynard [Keynes]? However, since I see you're in a fix and fury I'll try to read some brief, rough notes, if I can find any.² Only someone else *must* form the staple joint.

And will you and Desmond dine here first? *7.30 Dec. 1st.* We shall expect you.

But if I give tongue this time, I shall remain silent till my 70th birthday, which is not far off. Those are my terms.

In Haste,
yr V.W.

Mrs Michael MacCarthy

3188: To Ethel Smyth   52 *T.[avistock] S.[quare, W.C.*1]

Thursday [12 November 1936]

Of course come to lunch on Saturday if you're up. The nuisance is, not that we've people, but that we're going out almost at once—say 2.30. But lunch could be at 1. Let me know.

1. Of Bloosmbury's Memoir Club, founded in 1920, of which Molly was Secretary.
2. On 1 December Virginia read to the Memoir Club her paper *Am I a Snob?* reprinted in *Moments of Being* (ed. Jeanne Schulkind, 1976). It begins: "Molly has very unfairly, I think, laid upon me the burden of providing a memoir tonight. . . . It is not my turn."

I'm entirely vegetable at the moment After a long walk—all over London
—alone; then political discussion; man here; then sleep.

Sorry about the dog.

V.

Glad about the wine.

Berg

3189: To Julian Bell   52 *Tavistock Square* [*W.C.*1]

Typewritten
14th Nov. 1936

My dearest Julian,

I dreamt of you so vividly last night that I must take my typewriter and
write, though its not my turn. No. Its *your* turn. But then I get news of you
from Nessa; and so I wont stand on rights. Why does it become so difficult to
write, when one dreams? And lord how charming you were in my dream—
you had come back; and we were all sitting in the studio. Soon that will be a
fact. And I wish it were one here and now. Because how can I tell you all the
news?

Let me see—since we came back we have been on the run and on the talk
almost incessantly. I have seen the young poets—Spender and Plomer, and
been induced to subscribe to the young poets paper, The Left review.[1] That
shows you that politics are still raging faster and fiercer. I've even had to
write an article for the Daily Worker on the Artist and politics.[2] Aldous
[Huxley] is on the rampage with his peace propaganda; and Leonard is trying
to convince the labour party that the policy of isolation is now the only one.
Berties book[3] convinced him. But then when it comes to making a practical
suggestion, which will convince Mr Gillies,[4] Berties book is not much use.
However, I leave this out of my letters—that and Spain,[5] which is now the
most flaming of all the problems, since no doubt you'd rather hear gossip
from me.

George Barnes[6]—d'you know him? He came to tea, for they want us to

1. A monthly, which ran from October 1934 to May 1938.
2. Virginia's article *Why Art Today Follows Politics* was published in the *Daily
   Worker* on 14 December. (Reprinted as *The Artist and Politics* in *The Moment*,
   1947.)
3. Bertrand Russell's *Which Way to Peace?*, 1936.
4. The Secretary of the International Department of the Labour Party.
5. This is the first reference in Virginia's letters to the Spanish Civil War.
6. George Barnes (1904-60) was head of the B.B.C.'s Talks Department, later
   Director of Television. In 1927 he had married Dorothy Anne Bond.

help them—the BBC that is—to keep in touch with intellect. They've asked me to give them a potted version of Spenser. I liked him;—Barnes—but couldn't remember his private life, save that Ann loves Dadie [Rylands], and is now desolated at being cut off from him. George seemed to me a dour, honest fellow; pausing over his sentences; old fashioned; 19th century; earnest. No mention though of Dadie or Ann. Charles Mauron is now over, on business with the Intellectual libertarians. He will dine with us tomorrow. And by the way I think Rogers and your Mallarmé is a masterpiece.[1] I think Maurons introduction one of the best pieces of criticism I've read this blue moon. He's so clear, so subtle and so witty all in one. I'm sure all the bother has been worth while, for its a fascinating book—and Roger's case about Mallarmé seems to me proved. I shall read it carefully; now I've only dipped. The Times lit sup; praised it highly yesterday. And the translation reads admirably. K. John has been highly intelligent as far as I can judge.

That brings me to the present state of literature; which in my case is to the effect that I've cut down my book [*The Years*] from close on 700 to 420 pages; its pretty bad; but I can't help it; and though doubtful (genuinely) if its worth publishing, shall publish, on Leonard's advice.[2] I'm so sick of it I can't judge. Now I'm free, almost, to tackle Roger, and shall try to get the papers in order.

What are you writing? What are your plans altogether? Quentin told me you mean to stand for Parliament. I dont see how any one can keep out of it as things are. Except Nessa and Duncan all our friends are in it—even Adrian, who deprecates it, but still marched all through the East end the other day with Karin in the anti-fascist procession.[3] As for Quentin he seems to have mastered the art of debate, and much impressed L. the other night when he gave an address to the Rodmell labour party. What a charming, detached, well poised dark horse with a whole bran pie of interesting buried objects in him he is! I like my nephews and nieces. Ann [Stephen] is so strenuous with meetings that she can't see us any time this term she says; but I hope to get her to stay at Christmas. And Judith [Ann's younger sister], Bertie Russell says, has a real solid strong philosophical mind.
Monday   Charles [Mauron] dined with us last night, and talked about you.

1. Roger Fry's translations of Stéphane Mallarmé's poems, published posthumously in 1936, with a commentary by Charles Mauron. Julian Bell had helped edit them, and together with Katherine John, translated a few of the poems.
2. On 5 November, Virginia had written in her diary: "L. put down the last sheet about 12 last night, and could not speak. He was in tears. He says it is 'a most remarkable book'—he likes it better than *The Waves*—and has not a spark of doubt that it must be published." (AWD, p. 272.) But in *Downhill All the Way*, 1967, Leonard confessed: "To Virginia I praised the book more than I should have done if she had been well."
3. Adrian Stephen, Virginia's younger brother, and his wife Karin.

He says for Gods sake don't leave China and come to fight in France[1]—in which I think he is right; but no doubt he has said so already. So I wont go on. I liked him very much. He's a real humorous vigorous little man, and we talked about Roger and he's going to let me have all his letters—over a hundred, he says. Today—a dull drizzling day—Lord Cecil[2] is coming to tea, to talk about Spain I think. He too is a nice man—there are many nice men; why are men in the mass so detestable? This morning I got a packet of photographs from Spain all of dead children, killed by bombs—a cheerful present.[3] Privately we keep up our spirits. I take tea with Nessa—my great resource; and old Duncan stumbles over his words and Angelica takes the winds of March with beauty. But lord, what a career—acting. Sally Graves is marrying a dull man called Chilvers;[4] and you should have married her.

Yes—tell me, what your amorous entanglements are? I swear I wont reveal them. What about the Chinese ladies? Are you wanting to come home? What about a book on China? We're having a bad season; no one buys fiction. L. is getting on with his second volume,[5] and I think of a new book daily. Peter Lucas attacks Tom [Eliot][6] as usual, but he says for the last time. And Yeats praises Dotty.[7] We are all very well, and look forward to Christmas. And I will write again, and so do you, if you can. A Chinese envelope is a very nice sight, even though your pen is—well, a great black spider. L. has written he says, and we both send our old loves across the many seas.

Virginia

Quentin Bell

1. Julian had heard in China of the possibility that the Fascist uprising in Spain might spread to France. He was hoping to take an active part in resisting Fascism, not merely as a politician in England. (See *Journey to the Frontier*, by Peter Stansky and William Abrahams, 1966, pp. 286-7.)
2. Viscount Cecil of Chelwood (1864-1958), formerly Robert Cecil, third son of Lord Salisbury. Having represented Britain for many years on international conferences, he was President of the League of Nations Union, 1923-45.
3. See *Three Guineas*, pp. 20-1, where she refers to these photographs.
4. Richard Chilver, a civil servant in the Air Ministry. Later she became Principal of Bedford College, London, and of Lady Margaret Hall, Oxford.
5. Of *After the Deluge*. The first volume was published in 1931.
6. F. L. Lucas (1894-1967), the poet, novelist and scholar, and Fellow of King's College, Cambridge. His attack on Eliot was contained in his book *The Decline and Fall of the Romantic Ideal*, 1936.
7. W. B. Yeats had just edited and published *The Oxford Book of Modern Verse*, in which he included eight poems by Dorothy Wellesley and praised her extravagantly in his Introduction to the volume.

Typewritten
19th Nov. 1936

My dear Mr Wells,[1]

It is very good of you to send me the copy of my father's article "The Study of Literature."[2]

I agree with you in thinking it a very good one. We have often considered whether it would be advisable to reprint some of the articles you mention. We have a box of them, which were not included in his published works. But as he went through them all, when he was deciding which to publish, and rejected them, we have always thought that it was better to respect his own judgment. He may have been too severe; but the fact is that he did not wish them to be reprinted. Nor should I wish to reprint my Times article on him.[3] It was rather a formal piece of work, done rather against my own wish.

But I am glad to think that you are interested in his work, and make it known to your students. Although the sale of such books as his must be small, it continues to be considerable over here, seeing how long ago my father wrote.

With many thanks for your courtesy,

yours sincerely
Virginia Woolf

I should of course be delighted to see your bibliography,[4] if you have a spare copy

Carlton Wells

1. Carlton Frank Wells was Professor of English Literature at the University of Michigan at Ann Arbor.
2. *The Study of English Literature*, which Leslie Stephen gave as a lecture at St Andrews University in 1887, and published in the *Cornhill* in the same year. It was not re-published until 1956, when it appeared in *Men, Books and Mountains* (ed. S. O. A. Ullmann, University of Minnesota Press).
3. *Leslie Stephen, The Philosopher at Home*. Published in *The Times*, 28 November 1932. Reprinted in *The Captain's Deathbed*, 1950.
4. Carlton Wells may have compiled a bibliography of Stephen's works for his students, but if so, it was never published.

3191: To R. W. Chapman   52 *Tavistock Square, W.C.*1

20th Nov 36

Dear Mr Chapman,
     Many thanks for sending me the Persuasion chapters.[1] I am very glad to
have them.
     I have often thought of writing an article on the coarseness of J.A. The
people who talk of her as if she were a niminy piminy spinster always annoy
me. But I suppose I should annoy them.

                              Yours sincerely
                              Virginia Woolf

Sold at Sotheby's, July 1978

3192: To Violet Dickinson   52 *Tavistock Sqre.* [*W.C.*1]

24th Nov. [1936]

My Violet,
     Yes of course—what are the letters?[2] It sounds most exciting. Do send
them—anytime: and we will read them with eagerness. Letters and memoirs
are my delight—how much better than novels!
     I saw Lord Bob [Cecil] the other day, but not Nelly [his wife]—and he
said you were going to stay with him. Isnt he a charming man—and now so
mellow and rubicund. And I often think of you and Beatrice[3]—and wish I
could send my love to her through the air so as not to embarrass her. She
too—what a nice woman—but I mustnt run on.

                              Looking forward to the letters.
                                        Sp.

Berg

1. R. W. Chapman, Fellow of Magdalen College, Oxford, 1931-47, Editor of
   Jane Austen's Letters and novels, 1932, etc. He sent Virginia his edition of the
   manuscript of two chapters of *Persuasion*.
2. See Letter 3195.
3. Beatrice Thynne (b. 1867, d. unmarried 1941), was the daughter of the 4th
   Marquess of Bath. She was one of Violet's intimate friends, and through her,
   Virginia had seen much of Beatrice in her youth.

3193: To Quentin Bell   [52 *Tavistock Square, W.C.*1]

Typewritten
[late-November 1936]

Dearest Quentin,

I forgot to give you this the other day.[1] But I should be very grateful for any criticisms. It is very cramped and limited; but the difficulty is that I suppose one can't write at any greater length. If you would note any thing that could be said more emphatically, in the margin, I wish you would. And would you send it back, as I haven't got a copy. I would willingly re-write it, if you could block out a different line of argument.

V.

Quentin Bell

3194: To Ethel Smyth   52 *T*[avistock] *S.*[quare, *W.C.*1]

Sunday [29 November 1936]

1) I was much impressed by Mme de Polignac:[2] thought her reserved, distinguished, not an oyster to open with one flick of the knife. And so handsome.

2) N Boulanger[3] (this is secret) was the one who most interested me: wanted to talk to her: but couldnt:

3) C. St John *has* written to L. about the book.[4] And he's told her we must wait to see if the series fails. Its been a very bad year with the Press (dont say so, tho')

4 But I didnt 'hate' V's book. I thought it good hack work. L. says her St Joan done for us is quite admirable for its purpose.[5]

4) No I cant be in on Tuesday:

5) I'm reading all Gibbon, to see if I'll do his centenary for the Times[6]— and other jobs: and multitudes and multitudes of people

Oh yes I did enjoy hearing you hold forth—I like your spoken English so much. And your great hat and your great head. Mlle Boulanger seemed to

1. Virginia's article on the artist and politics for the *Daily Worker*, published 14 December 1936.
2. See p. 42, note 2. Virginia had lunched with her at Claridges on 27 November.
3. Nadia Boulanger (1887-1979), the French composer, conductor and teacher, come to London to conduct the Royal Philharmonic Orchestra.
4. Christopher St John published no book between *Christine Murrell, M.P.* (1935) and *Ethel Smyth: A Biography* (1959).
5. A shortened version for children (80 pp.) of Vita's *Saint Joan of Arc*, which was published by the Hogarth Press in their *World-Makers and World-Shakers* Series, 1937.
6. *The Historian and 'The Gibbon'*, *T.L.S.*, 24 April 1937.

me a thoroughbred. Shabby wh. I like Too much food I thought. And is old Ronald[1] really—well, d'you find him interesting?

No more. In a devils own rush

V.

Berg

3195: TO VIOLET DICKINSON   52 *Tavistock Square, W.C.1.*

2nd Dec 36

My Violet,

This is just and only to acknowledge the great parcel which I found in the hall yesterday. I was in the devils own rush, had only time to snip it open, took out the Peacock[2]—has the bird brought back memories!—and then, expecting the letters of some 18th Century Eden, found my own![3] Oh dear, oh dear! I've only had time for one dip and no reflections, but hope for a quiet country week end and will write then.

Only I ask you, why send back the one thing I ever gave you? The Peacock? As for the letters, how could you have the patience to bind and keep all those childish scribbles? Is she nice, that flyaway girl? I can barely bring myself to look; but will soon.

Dear dear, what can I give you in return?

But I'm so weighed down with various bothers—letters, MSS and so on—tonight that I'll wait. This is only to say that the parcel came safe and thanks; as usual

Sp.

Berg

3196: TO ELIZABETH ROBINS   52 *Tavistock Square, W.C.1.*

3rd Dec [1936]

Dear Miss Robins,

I am afraid tomorrow is impossible—we go down to Monks House directly after luncheon. Then we have a nephew [Quentin] staying and a

---

1. Sir Ronald Storrs (1881-1955), formerly Governor of Cyprus and Northern Rhodesia, and author of the widely praised *Orientations* (1937), his memoirs.
2. A model peacock in silver.
3. Typescript copies of some 350 letters, bound in two volumes, which Virginia had written to Violet in her youth, including more than half the letters published in Vol. I of this edition. The copies now belong to Quentin Bell, but the originals are in the Berg Collection, New York Public Library. Violet published only one book, the letters of Emily Eden (her great-aunt), 1919.

Labour Party meeting and come back early on Sunday. But we shall be down for 2 or 3 weeks at Christmas. Might we come over then? Or will you suggest another day here—which I would do everything to keep free?

You said you were sending me something to read—I still wait.

yrs
Virginia Woolf

P.S.1 A man who was mending our gramophone said something about a Miss Robinson ringing up—you, I suppose.

P.S.2 I wrote this on Thursday night and forgot to send it. Here are the stamps—because I telephoned.

Sussex

3197: To Violet Dickinson   52 *Tavistock Square, W.C.*1
Dec. 6th [1936]

My Violet,

It was extremely good of you to keep and bind up so much better than they deserved all those scattered fragments of my very disjected and ego-tistic youth.[1] Do you like that girl? I'm not sure that I do, though I think she had some spirit in her, and certainly was rather ground down harshly by fate. I'm glad Angelica hasn't to go through all her Aunt did by her age. At points I became filled with such a gust from her tragic past, I couldn't read on. Letters seem more than anything to keep the past—out it comes, when one opens the box. And so much I'd forgotten.

All I beg of you is dont let anybody else read those letters. Should I ever write my own memoirs there are some scenes and a few sentences I should like to quote: but I don't suppose a memoir-writing fit will fall on me. As John Bailey[2] must have said, letters aren't written nowadays: compare these with the 18th Century: what jerks and spasms they come in.

But one thing emerges whole and lucid—how very good you were to me, and how very trying I was—all agog, all aquiver: and so full of storms and rhapsodies. Shall I get the Press to do them up soundly and send them to Burnham Wood?

On dear me, the Silver Peacock perches on my book case, and makes me think I have no right to it. Was it a present from George? [Duckworth]—and now George is underground [d. 1934]. But I'm glad you're on top; and still holding in your kind yet searching eye the memory of Hyde Park Gate and its family.

1. See p. 89, note 3.
2. John Cann Bailey (1864-1931), the critic and essayist.

I'd altogether forgotten those old drawings.[1]

Well, thank you for everything—if I were to write out all I mean by that, I should need many many pages.

Sp.

3198: To Lady Ottoline Morrell

52 *Tavistock Square, W.C.1.*

Dec. 8th [1936]

Dearest Ottoline,

The young man, John Graham,[2] whom I told you about, would, of course, be overjoyed if you let him come and see you, or to a teaparty: but I in no way committed you. This is only to give you his address:

10 Burgess Hill
Hampstead

He is nice, and modest, not immensely intelligent—a schoolmaster at the moment—wants to write, was a soldier and a champion runner, but has turned literary. Thats I think all. There I leave it, having done my Christian duty by him at least. And please don't take any sort of trouble—or answer this.

yr V.W.

3199: To Lady Ottoline Morrell

[52 *Tavistock Square, W.C.1*]

Postcard
[10 December 1936]

We will send you a copy of John Graham's book, but dont trouble to acknowledge—its about his cigarette making in South America.

Many thanks. Yes I agree about the lovers.[3]

V W

This is what we saw in Holland.[4]

1. Drawings done by Virginia in 1904-5, which Violet bound into the typescript volumes, together with photographs of Virginia, Vanessa, Thoby, etc.
2. Author of *Good Merchant* (Hogarth Press, 1934).
3. This is the first reference in Virginia's letters (though there is much more in her diary) to Mrs Simpson and the drama of Edward VIII's abdication, which took place on this day.
4. A picture of tulips and windmills was on the reverse of the card. Virginia and Leonard had been to Holland in May 1935.

3200: To ELIZABETH ROBINS   52 *Tavistock Square, W.C.1.*

Dec. 13th 1936

Dear Miss Robins,

Of course we shall be delighted to read your typescript.[1] Please send it as it is, and dont wait to have it done in triplicate. We will read it and give you any advice we can with great pleasure. If you could see the three foot wad of manuscript I have this evening been tumbling through, you would understand that the prospect of reading something by you—something written by a human hand—has its seduction!

We go down to Rodmell next Friday I think and shall be there if we can 2 or 3 weeks; so we hope to come over and see you at Brighton. Then we can discuss the book by word of mouth. The page you have sent interests me very much: and I am, genuinely and sincerely, anxious to read the whole.

Yours
Virginia Woolf

Sussex

3201: To JOHN H. THOMPSON   52 *Tavistock Square, W.C.1.*

Typewritten
[17 December 1936]

Dear Mr Thompson,[2]

Many thanks for your letter. I am afraid that I cannot accept your invitation to contribute to Signatures as my book will be out early this spring.

Yours sincerely,
Virginia Woolf

J. Howard Woolmer

3202: To ETHEL SMYTH   *Monk's House, Rodmell,*
near Lewes, Sussex.

Christmas Eve [1936]

Well Ethel thats a surprise—shows how purblind I am—I mean I thought you must have hated that stiff cold little lunch—All my fault. I ought never to ask people to lunch, or to lunch out. My brains are so addled by one o'clock after a morning in the basement [Tavistock Square] among my verbiage I neither see nor hear: and felt guilty, since I think you came out

1. Of *Both Sides of the Curtain*, published (but not by the Hogarth Press) in 1940.
2. Thompson was co-editor (with John Malcolm Brinnin) of *Signatures,* a periodical of which three issues were published in Detroit, Michigan, in 1936-7.

of your way. And then you say you "enjoyed" it! No, tea or dinner; as long as lamps are lit, and my illusions cover tea pots with an inch of running water —thats all right. Not the implacable prose of midday—Yes: I'm very sorry about the dog.[1] So's Leonard. And I've little else to say. I'm deep in Gibbon: have to read him, and then write him, and should like then to dash off a whole covey of little articles. Its as cold as an ice house, and as bright as a fairy palace. Which reminds me, for the image is theatrical, did you, or did you not, know Elizabeth Robins? Actress, suffragette? about 70 I guess: a woman with a past, who's just again, after 20 years, bobbed up: and I think she's rather a thick scored interesting volume: and I must go to Brighton and dine with her: and would like a few hints beforehand. But I think I asked you this before. She has—how nice and encouraging!—a very high opinion of me.

Again: is it to you I owe a mysterious present—a book about elephants? —It came unheralded; and the writing on the cover might be yours. Only can it be? These odd gifts always come this time of year. But I'm off to see Gibbons grave in a Sussex Churchyard.[2] Do you, like me, when you're writing about some one, entirely forget all else; and ferret out every token even 30 miles away? Yet 2 weeks ago I never gave him a thought. Now I think and dream and live in the august shade. If only I could write like that too! Or dont you admire him? No telling—you admire M.B. [Baring] of course—my most shadowy writer—his page is like a nice white sheet across which a fly has gently meandered with legs in the ink. This I put in from a wholly Christian wish to annoy. I like making cats roar. Now roar. And also you admire Dottys [Wellesley] poems! Oh my God!

V.

Berg

3203: To Janet Case   *Monks House, Rodmell*
                                        [Sussex]

Christmas Eve 1936

My dear Janet,[3]
    I was very glad to get a letter from you, but very sorry to hear that you're lying on a sofa, ill. I'd not heard of it—following you in the Manchester Guardian I thought you were up and about. I'm so distressed to think of it. But please do get well, because I want to drive over and see you.
    Last May we weren't so very far from you, driving to Cornwall, through

1. Her new puppy, Pan V, had died.
2. Edward Gibbon (1737-94) was buried at Flitching, Sussex.
3. Janet Case (1862-1937), the classical scholar, had taught Virginia Greek in her adolescence, and now lived with her sister Emphie in the New Forest, where she wrote Nature Notes for the *Manchester Guardian.*

Ringwood, only I said to Leonard, Nothing is more hateful than visitors dropping in, also we had to push on: also after a long grind in London—oh so many people—fretful authors—distracted politicians—and a vast wad of proofs of a novel [*The Years*]—I had the familiar headache and sleeplessness, which dont lead to pleasant habits in callers. So we spent a very vegetable summer, mostly down here, I lying in the garden. Now I've done the book, but as I had to cut out 200 pages, with a head like an old dry sponge, its a very bad book, much too long still, and I dont advise you even to look at it. But I'm ashamed of these grumbles, considering how much you've had to stand: and still do—as I remember without a grumble at all.

And I've been thinking so much of you this past month, that if thought were visible you'd have seen something luminous in the middle of the laurel bush. (is it laurel? I forget.)

Old Violet Dickinson, whom you may remember—the 6ft 2 woman, with a lot of chairs and dogs—suddenly sent me 2 huge volumes of my own old letters, from Hyde Park Gate mostly; and there your name so often occurred, and I could see you coming up to my room at the top of the house and saying You've not done any work! However, in spite of that, how very kind to me you were! And what a bore I must have been, besieging you at Windmill Hill [Hampstead], and telling you about my proposals of marriage! I think the young now have easier lives than we had, but then I don't believe they have such affection as I had, and have, for Janet Case. Nessa's Angelica, aged 17, told me the other day that she thought we—Nessa and myself—had had much more interesting lives than she has, because she has always had everything she wanted: I wonder if its true. Anyhow she's a lovely sea-nymph, and going to be an actress.

You see I'm wandering on, sitting over a log fire with Leonard reading history for his book [*After the Deluge*], and the black and white spaniel [Sally] in its basket beside him. I'm glad to hoick him away from his eternal meetings—Labour party; Fabian Research, Intellectual Liberty, Spanish Medical Aid—oh dear, how they poach on him—what hours he spends with dirty unkempt, ardent, ugly entirely unpractical but no doubt well meaning philanthropists at whom I should throw the coal scuttle after 10 minutes if I were in his place.

Now we have three weeks off, and he prunes his trees, and I read Gibbon, because I'm going to write an essay on him, and ramble over the downs for hours and hours.

How's Margaret,[1] I wonder? We wanted to go there this summer, but I couldn't get about much. I liked her house, and in particular a tree outside

1. Margaret Llewelyn Davies (1861-1944), formerly General Secretary of the Women's Co-operative Guild. Virginia had known her for many years, and had written an Introduction to her anthology of working-women's essays, *Life As We Have Known It*, 1931.

where she sits—a perfect place we thought, and both of them[1] seemed settled in happily.

Now I must stop and read a huge bundle of manuscripts. Every boy and girl who can buy a fountain pen and a ream of paper instantly writes a novel, ties it up and sends it to us. How I loathe novels! Why shouldn't you write, not a novel, but your reflections—on your life, or your great Aunts life—anything? Do. and then I shall be happy to read it.

My love—both our love—for L joins in—to you and Emphie.

yr
V W

Sussex

3204: To Lady Ottoline Morrell

Monk's House, Rodmell,
Lewes, Sussex

Dec. 26th 36

Dearest Ottoline,

What a remarkable woman you are—to send me something I shall really use and like. There it lies on my table or my chair already doing what it can to keep my letters tidy: and it gives an air of magnificence to the room. Didn't you give one like it to Lytton? I seem to remember seeing him writing here in the garden with a red leather case on his knee, which he said you had given him. You are a great giver. And then, wanting to find a little book for you, my usual old shop proved faithless—for one thing the electric light had failed and I couldn't see—so in despair I pulled out a mild little 18th Century poet whom I rather like from my own books and sent it. But this is only makeshift: next time I'm in a book shop I shall look again.

Yes I too carry the picture of Whitehall that afternoon in my head—you advancing with feathers, like a Stuart princess in mourning, and the Life Guards, and then old Bob[2] rambling and ruminating. Its odd how England suddenly takes shape—not that I have any patriotic pride—only a visual lust, and a sense of Shakespeare.

You were angelic to let [John] Graham come. There's not much inside him I'm afraid—we thought he might improve, but I doubt it. His anxiety to know writers touched me—its no longer mine: and now you've more than gratified it. No, I've not read Nightwood[3] yet, but I have written the name

1. And Lilian Harris, who had been her assistant secretary. They lived in Dorking, Surrey.
2. R. C. Trevelyan (1872-1951), the poet and classical scholar. Virginia had by chance met him and Ottoline walking in Whitehall during the afternoon of 10 December, Abdication Day.
3. By Djuna Barnes, 1936.

down, and shall read it, as soon as I've cleared off a heap of slippery manuscripts, all novels, all mediocre—how I get to hate fiction: but Tom said this was a remarkable book, so I must summon courage and plunge. Novels go so slow, and they drag in so many dull facts; but thats their business—yes, I will read the Woman in White[1] too. Yes—you see I write with your letter in the red case on the arm of my chair—I did read MacKenna,[2] and wondered what sort of man he was. I think a very queer mix: I liked him, but then his slang worried me—but I liked his life. I like scholars. I dont like freshmen as a rule. Ethel, that reminds me, has fallen in love with Dotty—I think (maliciously,) that Dotty's wine is so good and the beds so soft,[3] she owes her ascendancy to them—if you're old and luxurious and poor with only one maid and hash for dinner like Yeats and Ethel.

Its very lovely down here: I can still find a primeval down in 10 minutes; but yesterday we spent with Maynard and Lydia [Keynes] and all kissed and danced under the mistletoe.

This is mere maundering over the log fire—our old plum tree [cut down and cut up]: and I must stop.

Yrs
V.

Julian Vinogradoff

3205: To Katherine Arnold-Forster

Monks House, Rodmell
[Sussex]

Boxing Day [26 December 1936?]

My dear Ka,

We have this moment finished gloating on a delicious dish of fresh Cornish cream—but without a name; so I attach yours. I can't think there are two such friendly brutes in Cornwall—the rare old English bear is said to be extinct, save for one specimen at Zennor [Ka's house]. If however it was really sent by that eccentric lady [*unidentified*], d'you remember—the wife of the man who had read all the Classics—but this happened years ago, and you'll have forgotten: nor was she his wife, now I come to think of it—but if it was she who sent it to me, then you must give her my thanks—only I suspect and hope that they're both long dead.

I am rambling on because Duncan and Mrs Grant [his mother] have been here for Boxing Day tea, and stayed so late gossiping about the Pophams,

1. *Women in White*, by Peter Delius, 1934 and 1936.
2. Possibly Stephen MacKenna, the translator (1872-1934), *Journals and Letters*, edited by E. R. Dodds, 1936.
3. Dorothy Wellesley lived at Penns-in-the-Rocks, a lovely Queen Anne house at Withyham, Sussex.

Hugh and six children by 2 wives,[1] who now live next Mrs Grant at Twickenham, that I'm half asleep. Who is Mrs Popham—now? I had a Christmas Card from my god daughter, Noel's Virginia.[2] How old it makes us, or rather me, feel. And Asheham[3] where we used to sit in the sun is all cement works, but in fact rather fine lit up at night. Needless to say it is pouring wet. Nor did I ever thank you for a letter you wrote: but I could see no chance of coming to Cornwall since, as you know, I am now in the thick of the political world, and seldom get an evening without someone asking me to tell them what is likely to happen in Poland, Abyssinia, or some such area. Excuse this drivel. L. wants me to send his love.

yrs V.W.

Do you know Angus Davidson[4] and Miss Swinshead Smith [*unidentified*], both of whom live, but not together, at Sennen? Do you want to know them?

Mark Arnold-Forster

3206: To V. Sackville-West   *Monk's House, Rodmell,*
                                    near Lewes, Sussex

27th Dec [1936]

Well that is a pleasant kindly well meaning dauphin vulgaire[5]—d'you think its the very same that got caught and hung in the fishmongers shop at Sevenoaks [in 1925]? I rather think so. There's something—what they call ingenuous, a little foolish in its expression, that hints it might well have been netted. And then we stood and looked at it, and it winked at you in your pink jersey and white pearls.

How on Earth did you find it and pack it and send it to come on Christmas day when, as you told me, you have 175 presents to give on that day, not counting dog's presents, presents to swans and old men who sleep under sacking in the Barn? A miracle.

We will go to a sweet shop when you're in London; and you shall choose

1. A. E. (Hugh) Popham and his wife Brynhild (*née* Olivier) had three children before they divorced in 1924, one of whom, Anne Olivier, was to marry Quentin Bell in 1952. Popham then married Brynhild's cousin Rosalind Baynes (*née* Thornycroft) who already had three daughters, and Brynhild married F. R. G. N. Sherrard.
2. Virginia Richards, third child of Noel (*née* Olivier) and Arthur Richards. She was six years old.
3. The house, one mile across the River Ouse from Rodmell, which Virginia had leased from 1912 to 1919.
4. Davidson (b. 1900) worked at the Hogarth Press from 1924 to 1928.
5. A fish which Vita had sent Virginia for Christmas.

whichever sweet you like, out of a huge jar. Thats something for you to look forward to.

I've just been walking on the marsh: a winter sunset; and I was thinking, what do Kingfisher's do in winter, when lo and behold, one shot out under my feet, skimmed the river, and caused me about as much pleasure as an angel . . . no . . . I dont care for angels.

Now I'm sitting over my logs, and should be reading Gibbon. The other day I found to my surprise that this year for the first of many years I've not earned a penny:[1] and I must. So that accounts for Gibbon. Only when I read other people's articles I cant see any cause to write more. Lord, how I hate the weekly papers! Then why write articles? Because I must make 500 pounds.

Ethel's new dog is dead. The truth is, no dog can stand the strain of living with Ethel. I went down one day and found it on the verge of nervous collapse, simply from listening to her conversation. Never shall I forget a walk all round Worplesdon [Surrey] Golf Club in the rain—she lame, also taken short, not to put a fine point on it, in the pavilion. Well, well—if we all weather as red and roaring, we shant do so badly.

Are you coming up in January? Are we going jaunting? Yes, we're going to a shop with huge jars of pink yellow and green sweets. You shall have a pound in a paper bag. Excuse poor Potto's drool: I have just caught him a cuff on his tail and sent him back to Gibbon—a weighty author.

V.W.

Congratulate Harold on the success of his Sibyl fund.[2]

Oh I've been seeing Mme de Polignac.

Berg

1. But in 1936 she earned £721 from royalties on her past books, apart from journalism. In 1937 she earned £2,466. (See Leonard's *Downhill All The Way*, p. 142.)
2. Harold Nicolson had organised a subscription to buy a new car for Lady Colefax.

Letters 3207-3247 (January–May 1937)

The Years *was published on* 15 March, *the culmination of a five-years effort which had pushed Virginia to the edge of madness. The days of waiting for the critics' reaction were "dull, cold torture", but all except very few of the reviews were superlative. Already she had begun to write* Three Guineas, *which went smoothly, and at intervals continued her reading for* Roger Fry, *as well as writing occasional journalism and a talk on the use of words which she broadcast on 29 April. For a few weeks she was involved more than usual in the routine work of the Hogarth Press, following the sudden death in January of the Manager, Margaret West. Virginia's health was good, but she feared for Leonard's, who was examined for symptoms of diabetes or prostate, both found negative. Julian Bell returned from China, determined to play some part in the Spanish Civil War.*

3207: To Dorothy Bussy   52 *Tavistock Sqre.*, W.C.

Dec. 15th [1936]

My dear Dorothy,

I take up my pen to answer the letter you dont want answered—what a mercy!—(thats why I take up my pen). But at any moment the bell will ring and in will come Miss [Inez] Pearn who's engaged to Stephen Spender; then there'll be another ring and Tom Eliot will come in, with a thick green muffler round his livid cheeks. This is drawn from life—I met him in Russell Square . . . I put in these facts to give you a taste of the quality of life at this moment in Bloomsbury.

After dinner, to continue, there's a meeting to discuss Spain at Adrian's, —an Intellectual Liberty meeting[1]. . Shall I go? Its a bitter cold day but fine. Though this scarcely counts as news, the stir of the abdication still agitates our bosoms. Have you seen Mrs Simpson?[2] If so, do tell me—heres Tom— here he came in—

1. A British society of anti-Fascist intellectuals, corresponding to Vigilance in France.
2. When Wallis Simpson (soon afterwards Duchess of Windsor) left England a few days before the Abdication, she stayed with her friends Herman and Katherine Rogers in their villa near Cannes, not far from Roquebrune, where Dorothy and Simon Bussy lived with their daughter Janie.

[To Dorothy Bussy *contd.*]

Monk's House, Rodmell

Jan 1st 1937

This letter dropped out from some papers just now. I dont think its worth sending, but as its the first day now of the New Year, I will just fill up the break from friendship. What did Tom Eliot say that evening? I cant remember: but I remember meeting Mr Priestley[1] the great novelist at Adrians; and how we glared at each other, and what a dismal drab dowdy affair it all was. And nobody now talks of the abdication. Then we came here; and here we are, Leonard and I, sitting over the fire, on a wild wet night; and in a minute I must go down and put our dinner in the oven. I liked very much hearing from you, and wish letter writing were still a habit.

That reminds me—I saw James[2] at last, and I think he's given up the idea of writing about Lytton—thinks the letters make it too difficult. I daresay he's right; but I'm sorry. I wish something could have been printed.

London was the usual scrimmage. I saw too many people—among them, tell Janie, La Princesse de Polignac, née Winnie Singer, but whatever she was born she's grown into the image of a stately mellow old Tory, and to look at you'd never think she ravished half the virgins in Paris, and used, so Ethel Smyth tells me, to spring upon them with such impetuosity that once a sofa broke. We lunched at Claridges—very grossly and not well (you like to hear about food I know—next year my cooking will be better) and I aired my little forlorn relics of French to a lovely young Polignac niece, and to a remarkable middle class Mlle [Nadia] Boulanger, a musician. That was my top light in the matter of aristocracy. Thats why I boast of it.

This page ought to be all politics, but I cant go into that. And on your rock [Roquebrune], why disturb your peace? However, even for Leonard happily there's been a lull; and we have another week here, which I shall spend writing about Gibbon: and last night we dined at Charleston, where all was in full swing—Quentin, Angelica, Duncan, Nessa, Clive—and so broody with domestic peace you could almost hear a kettle sing. Then there's Maynard and Lydia; a very fine turkey, pheasant shooting, many wines and still more comfort. In spite of what they say about Bloomsbury, I continue to like my friends.

By the way, are you Bloomsbury? And what are you doing this wild wet night? I did enjoy seeing you—crusty incorruptible that you are. Now those two epithets dont apply to Sybil Colefax—whose obsequies I attended; which means I was summoned to a farewell tete a tete among all the doomed

1. J. B. Priestley (b. 1894), the novelist, dramatist, and essayist, whose most popular novels were *The Good Companions* (1929) and *Angel Pavement* (1930).
2. James Strachey (1887-1967) was Dorothy's and Lytton's youngest brother. He was Lytton's executor, and soon after his death went through all his papers with a view to publishing a memoir of him, but came to consider that the letters were too malicious about his friends. See Vol. V, p. 45.

furniture.[1] There was a sale next day, and she, who is said to have cancer, appeared almost, not entirely, (I spied one crack), indomitable. But I cant go into that, and have indeed wandered on unpardonably. Why do you always make me chatter?—and so egotistically? Well, happy new Year to the Bussys; and please find a warm admiring very French phrase for that formidable woman, your daughter.

yr
VW

Texas

3208: To V. Sackville-West   *Monk's House, Rodmell,*
                                      near Lewes, Sussex

4th Jan 37

But oh God we're here and shant be back till next week, so the 7th and 8th are impossible.

But are those your only days [in London]—is your stay merely that? Because we shall be there all the rest of the month. And I had been planning jaunts—and then your bag of sweets. You must come up later—please. Why Clive and not Virginia? Why Mary[2] etc etc etc Sybil etc etc and not Potto?

In great haste and fury
V.

Berg

3209: To Elizabeth Robins   *Monk's House, Rodmell,*
                                      Lewes, Sussex

4th Jan. 37

Dear Miss Robins,

I ought to have written before—I must apologise—somehow Christmas has been full of interruptions.

But may we come over to tea on Friday next 8th? We could get to you about 4.30. If that should suit you, dont bother to write. Then we can discuss the chapters of your book,[3] so I wont begin here.

1. Lady Colefax (who did not die until 1950) was selling Argyll House in Chelsea, and Virginia had visited her there on 22 October 1936. She describes this visit at great length in her diary and *Am I a Snob?*, the paper she read to the Memoir Club on 1 December 1936. (See *Moments of Being*, p. 182.)
2. Mary Hutchinson (1889-1977), wife of the barrister St John Hutchinson.
3. *Both Sides of the Curtain*, 1940.

A niece [Ann Stephen] suddenly arrived on Saturday—but I ought to have said before that we were doubtful if we could come to Henfield.[1] Many thanks for asking us.

Yours
Virginia Woolf

Sussex

3210: To Ethel Smyth

Monks House [Rodmell,
Sussex]

8th Jan. 37

I know I have been in every respect save one vile, but that one—the loving heart—remains: otherwise why should I light the fire and spend this moment writing? Partly because I have to go to Brighton in ½ hour to see Miss Robins: for I dont think you want letters. I think you are so battling with books and quotations that all you want is to be left alone.[2]

That has been my state. I've spent all the morning, every morning writing; every evening reading. I had to dash through Gibbon[3] and get something evolved before we went back. Thats done, after a fashion:—only after a fashion. The devil of these articles is the fitting in quotations: fitting in a little slice here, another there, like a cabinet maker composing a neat commode.

Is the sun shining at Woking? Here there is frost under the hedge, and a sun strong enough to burn one's cheek the other side. I've seen a great many relations: answered their Christmas letters, written very painfully to old servants, and had a little most amiable correspondence with Vita. But I shall miss her in London—I who of all people she wants to see. So there.

Now alas, I must as I began by saying, catch my bus.

Back on Wednesday.

What—? no; no time to ask questions, and I dont suppose you feel inclined to write letters. Did you though make it up with Maurice?

Yr V.

Berg

1. Elizabeth Robins and Octavia Wilberforce lived in Brighton, but Elizabeth also owned a farm at Henfield in Sussex, which she converted in 1927 into a Home of Rest for over-worked professional women.
2. Ethel's next book was *Maurice Baring*, 1938.
3. See p. 88, note 6.

Monks House [*Rodmell, Sussex*]

Jan. 10th [1937]

Yes of course that will be perfect, Jan. 22nd lunch I mean: let us say one o'clock and I will keep the entire afternoon for any purpose.

The widow of Jo:[1] was my first love. a great flame of George's. I remember sitting opposite her at supper at the Savoy about 1908, between the acts of the Walkyrie and adoring her—so that shows how time passes and now I daresay she's an old whitehaired respectable—but why are you going to tea with her?

Excuse this the last and only scrap of paper near me.

V.

Oh I've been meeting another old lady—Elizabeth Robins, and Octavia Wilberforce.

Berg

52 Tavistock Sqre. [*W.C.1*]

Wednesday [20 January 1937]

I'm so glad that you're in luck about the dog [Pan VI]. I hope the stars will bless him. Just back to find Miss West desperately ill with influenza pneumonia,[2] also the 2nd in control [Miss Bevan] away with influenza. This means L. is doing all the main work. I have to help with odd jobs so far as I can. Hence I'm rather rattled at the moment—cursing the Press, correcting other people's proofs. I dont see any chance of being free this week. I think you must let me know when you would naturally be coming up next week, and see which we can fit in. But for God's sake dont expose yourself to buses and trains while this pest is violent.

Yes, so far as I'm a coherent entity I'm desirous to see you, in fact, in short, as Micawber would say, fond of you. And I've rashly undertaken heaven knows how much scribbling of articles, besides Gibbon:[3] and am

1. Mary, the daughter of William Endicott, the American judge and statesman. In 1888 she married Joseph Chamberlain, who died in 1914. In 1916 she married William Carnegie (1860-1936), sub-dean of Westminster Abbey. Virginia had known the Chamberlains in her youth when her half-brother George Duckworth was private secretary to Joseph's son, Austen Chamberlain.
2. Margaret West had worked at the Hogarth Press for several years as Manager, and died the next day, 21 January.
3. Virginia is exaggerating. Besides Gibbon, she wrote only two other commissioned articles this year.

fingering Fry papers nervously; and feel once more the various horrors and delights of book making. Only how does one square the relatives? How does one euphemise 20 different mistresses? But Roger every day turns out more miraculous. So you see I'm in a pother: but amazingly well. And you? Oh Lord, poor Miss West—its doubtful now if she'll live—anyhow 3 months away. I suffer.

V.

Berg

3213: To Vanessa Bell   [52 *Tavistock Square, W.C.*1]

Monday [25 January 1937]

On wicked wicked! I thought there was to be no present giving.[1] However, I admit the problem of teapots is forever solved. At first I thought it was a kitten in a basket. But it is devilish wrong to shower these extravagances upon a woman whom after all you don't love. However . . . its exactly what I want, as one used to say. But this time truly.

Pippa[2] came last night to discuss possible managers. So we couldn't come round. Have you done your paper? We went to a funeral—Miss Wests: and Christabel [Aberconway] has asked me to lunch.

B.

Berg

3214: To Ethel Smyth   52 *T.*[avistock] *S.*[quare, *W.C.*1]

Wednesday [27 January 1937]

What a dismal world we live in! Miss West is dead of pneumonia, and we're plunged at the moment in chaos. It means all L's time is taken managing, and we have to see authors whom she'd have seen. Thats what happens tomorrow. A perfect stranger is coming at 4.30 for a long business talk about her book.[3] I dont think there's much use anyone else hoping to get a word in. or only sideways in discomfort. So I should prefer another day, but only if you have to come up. Another clerk is ill, and we may have to put off the books (once more) till June. I'm sorry to be so distracted. Lord! we went to the funeral, and there was the poor old crone [Miss Howlett] with whom

1. Virginia was 55 years old on 25 January.
2. Philippa Strachey (1872-1968) was the third of Lytton's five sisters, and from 1914 to 1951 was Secretary to the London-National Society for Women's Service.
3. Francesca Allinson, author of *A Childhood*, which the Hogarth Press published in October.

she'd lived; and other miseries, in pouring rain, and fog; and nothing to be said, for in fact they killed her with their wild idiocy[1] and she was far and away the best of our managers; and now the whole of that dreary business of finding and teaching begins again. But I expect next week will be freer.

Yr V

Excuse this egotism. I'm feeling we'd better shut up shop. What about the new dog and his home—to turn to something saner?

Berg

3215: To Philippa Strachey

52 *Tavistock Square, W.C.1.*

2nd Feb: [1937]

Dear Pippa,

Many thanks for your kindness. Miss Lange is coming as manager, and you have pulled us out of our hole.

We both liked the looks of her very much. And I expect you took a lot of trouble—which is what I expect of you: and we both greatly enjoyed giving you a scrap of meat the other night—so please come again.

Yr
V.W.

Sussex

3216: To Ethel Smyth

52 *T[avistock] S.[quare, W.C.1]*

10th Feb: [1937]

I forget what our last form of greeting was. I forget if we ever got within the same postal district—But anyhow, thanks in part to my energy in letter writing and interviewing we yesterday installed a new manager, a nice duck faced woman, who was at Longman's [publishers] and says she used to see you.

So thats arranged. And then the underling [Miss Bevan]—oh dear what a viper's nest of malodorous feelings Miss Wests death uncovered—gave notice: and she's also been replaced. And now we hope to bring the books out on March 15th instead of putting them off till June.

Forgive this dull chronicle. One gets so absorbed in one thing after another. Hows the puppy? And the new house? I'm so hard at work with various bits of odds and ends that once more my pen wont write of an evening. Is MB. [*Maurice Baring*] on the up grade? The writing is what I

1. See Letter 3218.

like: not the reading. I'm reading Shakespeare: I'm reading Gibbon: I'm reading little scraps of Ethel Smyth. And then my poor old mother in law gets blinder. and I get kinder Yes I'm very kind to her—but oh the heat of the room, the sweet sticky cakes. None of this is news, none of this will interest you; and I'm so sleepy I'm half inclined to tear it up. Still by way of a flourish of a paw I send it.

Inarticulately
V.

Berg

3217: To Elizabeth Bowen   52 *Tavistock Square, W.C.1.*

Wednesday [10 February 1937]

Dear Elizabeth,

Its all very annoying—in the first place about dinner on the 16th—that weekend we're taking Tuesday off at Rodmell to travel our books in Sussex, and Leonard thinks there's no chance that we shall be back in time for dinner: but if we should get back earlier, might we come in afterwards? and leave it open. At the moment we have a good deal on our hands for the Press, as our manager died suddenly last month, and we have the publishing season on us, and a strange new woman who doesn't know whats what [Miss Lange]. So we have to help.

Then about the Cocktail on the 4th—that afternoon I've promised to go down to Chelsea to see old Ethel Walker who's done a picture of Vanessa;[1] and can't cut her, since her parties are solemn feasts. But if I can get away to you, of course I will. However, if you're free on Friday which is I suppose the 5th, wouldn't you anyhow come to tea here?—an old crones' talk over the fire.

Excuse the scrawl; and its all hums and haws.

Yrs VW

Texas

3218: To Edward Sackville-West   *Monk's House, Rodmell,*
Lewes, Sussex

14th Feb. [1937]

Dear Eddy,

This is disgraceful—I got your letter I don't know how long ago, and meant to write, but never did. The fact was that when we got back to

---

1. Dame Ethel Walker (1861-1951), a member of the New English Art Club, asked in 1933 to paint Virginia, but no such picture exists. See Vol. V, pp. 174-5. Ethel Walker's portrait of Vanessa Bell (entitled simply *Vanessa*) is in the Tate Gallery.

London we found the Press ravaged with influenza; Miss West, our manager, died; this led to other complications—some, as usual, of a sordid though psychologically exciting, kind (this refers to Sapphism and jealousy and the state of mind of friends whose hostility is suddenly revealed by death)—and then we had to beat up other managers and clerks: all of which I found distracting. Also, I suspect that my letter writing age is past. I detest putting a new nib in my pen, and in London someone always rings up or comes in. But mercifully for the first time for a month we are down here.

The Labour party met here last night, and if I had the time I would counter your shining youth with a picture of Mr Neil Lyons,[1] the dramatist, Mr Fears, the postman, and Mrs [Louie] Everest the char, discussing not so much the Labour party, as Mrs Simpson and the Archbishop.[2] London is indescribable—so many people, so much chatter. But I cant help a disposition to dance on the bubbles; which I excuse by thinking we shall retire here for good one of these days. Its a misty Sussex day, and very lovely from this top room which looks across to [Mount] Caburn, over the marsh.

I can't make up my mind to take seats for Glyndebourne[3] in advance, because it seems so expensive. In May I shall rush to the office and find all seats sold. There is Glyndebourne, just behind the mist—I'm reading the Countess Tolstoy's diaries, and his diaries,[4] and both their public diaries and their private: and wonder what the diary instinct is—since it caused them both infinite anguish. But how the Russians always triumph over us when they take up the pen!

No room for more. VW

Berg

1. Neil Lyons (1880-1940) was a neighbour of the Woolfs at Southease. He was not only a dramatist but a novelist and journalist.
2. On Sunday, 13 December 1936, the Archbishop of Canterbury, Dr Cosmo Gordon Lang, broadcast to the nation an unctuous commentary on the Abdication which included this statement: "He sought his happiness in a manner inconsistent with the Christian principles of marriage, and within a social circle whose standards and way of life are alien to all the best instincts and traditions of his people."
3. The opera house and company founded in 1934 by John Christie on his own estate, Glyndebourne, five miles from Rodmell.
4. *The Final Struggle, Countess Tolstoy's Diary, 1910*, with extracts from Leo Tolstoy's diary, translated by A. Maude and published in 1936.

3219: To J. D. Hayward   52 *Tavistock Square, W.C.*1.

Feb 15th 1937

Dear Mr Hayward,[1]

Of course I remember you, and often read you, and hear of you from Tom Eliot also. I wont send you a proof copy of the Years, as the one we have to send out is very imperfect—one chapter is missing, and my corrections aren't in it. But I will tell the Press to send you an advance copy. It will be published I suppose on March 15th in America, by Harcourt Brace.

My husband wants to be remembered to you, and we both hope we may see you soon.

Yrs sincerely
Virginia Woolf

King's

3220: To Ethel Smyth   52 *T*[*avistock*] *S.*[*quare, W.C.*1]

Wednesday [17 February 1937]

What I meant by my cryptic remark 'I like writing not reading': was that I like the writing of my own books, not the reading of them afterwards. Thats not very profound: but it happens to be a fact. And I wondered if you were enjoying the writing stage of Maurice, or had come to the reading stage and were disgusted. Yes—to continue answering your letter: I think your remark that you wont send me Maurice is sound. And I was about, without that, to say that I was going to follow it on my side, and not send you The Years, because I'm certain you wont get through it, and it always seems to me that if one's given a book by the author one feels committed to 5/8 worth of praise. I hardly give away even my 6 copies for that reason. And that shows what a conscience I have about telling the truth to authors: for at this moment I'm in agony: theres a presentation copy and I can't thank the author [*unidentified*] because I can't praise: yet civility requires.

I met Elizabeth [Williamson] at a picture gallery: and hope one day to see her. And I've been working with the usual rash joy, and have got committed to a Broadcast:[2] and so far the new manager is doing well; and I still regret

1. John Davy Hayward (1905-65), the literary critic, bibliographer, and anthologist. Virginia had met him as an undergraduate at King's College, Cambridge, in 1925. He contributed articles to the *Nation* in the 1920s when Leonard was its Literary Editor.

2. On 29 April Virginia broadcast in the B.B.C. series 'Words Fail Me'. Her talk, entitled *Craftsmanship*, was published in the *Listener* for 5 May 1937 and was reprinted in *The Death of the Moth* (1942). The tape of this broadcast is the only substantial recording of her voice, but Quentin Bell (II, p. 200) warns listeners that it does not give its true quality.

Miss West; and long for a holiday in the sun; and now must try to write that other cursed letter: or can one simply leave it undone? And hows the dog? And ... but Lord! I must stop

V.

Berg

3221: To Clive Bell   52 *Tavistock Square, W.C.1.*

Thursday [18th February 1937]

Dearest Clive,

Your card has just come. We left Rodmell yesterday, as Leonard was ill. The doctor yesterday was inclined to think it serious—possibly prostate gland. Today he's more cheerful, and thinks its probably some kidney infection. He is having an X ray tomorrow. If, as there's reason to think, its passing off, we shall come back to Rodmell. But of course it depends on how he is. How long are you staying? We should like very much to see you and Janice [Loeb]. Let me have a line here.

yr
Virginia

King's

3222: To Ethel Smyth   52 *T[avistock] S.[quare, W.C.1]*

Wednesday [24 February 1937]

Yes, Ethel dear, I'd like to see you. But whats the use of seeing you against some intolerable necessary bore—this refers to a French translator[1] who's wasted one of my rare solitary evenings. Nor must you come, in this dripping cold mutton weather, on purpose. Still put it in your mind and lets attempt it next week or the one after: I've been kept on the hop by a most ridiculous but agitating scare—a doctors scare that L. showed signs of diabetes. He was sent to a specialist [Dr Gledham]—I had an hour to walk up and down Harley Street—then a week to wait while tests were worked out: finally yesterday the decision that he is perfectly normal. Oh what torturers these doctors are! Anyhow, now I'm so glad perhaps its been worth while: an extraordinary physical relief, as if someone had been cramping me together and suddenly let go.

I saw Elizabeth [Williamson] one evening, against the highty [*sic*] elegant profile of Ethel Sands. I like Elizabeth. I like her mind. And Ethel,

1. Marguerite Yourcenar, who published her translation of *The Waves* in this year.

who's a connoisseur in these matters, exclaimed "How well she dresses!"—a compliment I'd give my eyes for.

Oh yes—about the BBC.[1] Theyve suddenly taken me up: want me to write them stories, read them poets, and deliver an address in May on Words. This last I've agreed to do: at a fee of £20 guineas: which is d—d mangy I told the man, considering that they print it in The Listener too. He said, Ah but do it only once: next time you'll be able to bargain. So from that I expect you'll get your £50. He told me, in confidence, that all the well known writers, like ourselves, are now holding out for more. So if you stick your toes in, you're helping the rest of us. Do tell me what comes of your toes sticking in the rock. Winston [Churchill] asks £300—but doesn't get it. That little bit of gossip has landed me in a fresh sheet, which I cant fill, since I must cook dinner tonight—this pouring night, and the clerk has just come in to say, Mrs Woolf the rains coming through—on to our new books?[2] I demanded. Well, not yet on to the books: into the Pritchard's[3] larder; so I must collect all the chamber pots when this is done and stand them in a row, to protect our books.

I'm reading Moliere aloud to myself: by way of tuning up my French accent: and was delivering a great speech of Alceste[4] when the clerk came in with the news of the rain, and then I must switch off to chamber pots, via Ethel Smyth. Youre a parenthesis between Misanthrope and the other thing and I wonder if anyone ever wrote a letter as quick as this. About Dotty [Wellesley]: yes I expect there's something inside that contorted nut; but not for me. I dont think, after Vita and so on, I shall ever crack it. But I like to hear of your discoveries. I expect a hammer blow, such as you deliver and I dont, is whats needed. But isn't she, after Yeats' praise,[5] considerably restored from her old bitterness? I always thought praise would do the trick. Oh here's a card from Colefax who's back and must see me in her new house.[6] And I'm in the thick of Fry's again:[7] and have so many things to write I can't attend to biography at the moment. You see how fitfully my brain works: 6 months of

1. See p. 108, note 2.
2. The printers had just delivered the first copies of The Years.
3. When the Woolfs moved to 52 Tavistock Square in 1924, the two bottom floors (apart from the basement, where the Hogarth Press was installed) were already occupied by a firm of solicitors, Dollman & Pritchard. The Pritchards were 'old Mr Pritchard', his sister, and his son George.
4. The main character in Le Misanthrope, produced in 1666.
5. See p. 85, note 7.
6. Sibyl Colefax had been in Paris, and was returning to 19 Lord North Street, Westminster.
7. Virginia had been visited by Roger Fry's son Julian (b. 1901), who read agriculture at King's College, Cambridge, and in 1923 emigrated to British Columbia, where he became a rancher.

sterile misery, then a sudden flush, like the rain. And hows the puppy? and the book? and altogether, how does the pulse of life beat at Woking?

V.

7 minutes and ½.

Berg

3223: TO ETHEL SMYTH   52 *Tavistock Sqre.* [*W.C.*1]

Monday [1 March 1937]

Yes Ethel dear, it'll be very nice to see you—I dont know why it comes into my mind to shut my book and say this into the air at the moment, except that I'm feeling rasped and raddled, and so, as usual, turn to the sun over the moor. D'you remember walking on the golf course in a storm, and I said this, and you promptly squatted in a pavilion and made water [on 19 October 1936]? How I loathe the publishing of books—especially books that are so bad that the wastepaper basket was their true goal, and so it should have been, save for Leonard. But its not *that* I mind—what I mind is being hooked and hauled to the surface when my natural dwelling is in the dark at the depths. I cannot write if people talk to me about what I write. Enough, as the convenient ghost of Mrs Pankhurst, or was it Lady P.[1] always says; when I'm in need.

What I would like to say, is how brave I think you. Why do I think so? When? At the dead of last night being sleepless I thought of you with a clap of admiration, exercising the puppy, writing the book—thought of you as a little tossing tug boat might think of a majestic sea going white-spread, fountain-attended dolphin-encircled ship—forging on and on. And I whip and tumble in your foam. Now I believe courage to be the greatest of human virtues, and the only gift we can impart. Do you sometimes think that—oh here's L. with a manuscript thrust on us by Viola Tree[2]—what was I saying? —that life is of a hardness that still fairly terrifies me. Yet this isn't my life I'm thinking of: no: of Miss Bevan's who was in love with Miss West. So I must leave this hanging, inconclusive, a wisp of cloud crossing the sun. I talked for 7 hours to Desmond MacCarthy on Saturday without a stop. Yes, I do like, I could say love, my friends.

Yr V.

Berg

1. Emmeline Pankhurst, the suffragette leader, and Lady Ponsonby, a former lady-in-waiting to Queen Victoria, had been great friends of Ethel, and she wrote about both of them at length in *As Time Went On* (1936).
2. In October the Hogarth Press published her book *Can I Help You?* Viola Tree (1884-1938), the eldest daughter of the actor-manager Sir Beerbohm Tree, had trained as a singer. The Press had published her reminiscences in 1926.

Sunday [7 March 1937]

Yes what a gloomy season to be sure. I liked your thing about Clothild—
oh how's she spelt?—in the Times.[1] You have a gift of words. I'm much
interested by your theory that I like you best in absence: also that I dislike
your presence because it drags me to the surface. No—there are 2 ways of
doing it: the reviewers way I hate; yours I feel on the contrary bracing and
invigorating. But then to explain the difference I should have to write several
rather involved pages of psychological analysis. I think Proust explains it,
but I cant remember where. Something I mean about the soul, how its
elements are united differently by different stimulants; shaken together like
those scraps of colour in a funnel [kaleidoscope] that we played with as
children. But I've been sitting by my mother in law's bedside—she has flu—
and feel like a rag just wrung by a washerwoman. Oh how she afflicts me,
lying there alone, blind. But she pleased me immensely by saying she loved
me best of all her daughters in law.

Now I must stop. No of course I dont want to make you come up in this
bitter blast. And everyone seems chirping at me to read their damned works
for them. And I want to sink into Proust; and I wish I had a new book by you
to read, and I'll tell you the sad story of Miss Bevan one day—it was our
West she loved; and killed. or is so charged by the other lover [Miss Howlett]
—and comes to me in tears, but now is gone.

So no more. Hows the Puppy?

V.

Why does everyone bother me about politics?[2] Six letters to sign daily—or
nearly so. Do you also have to trump up this meaningless nonsense, sign
books, sign letters perpetually?

Berg

---

1. Ethel had written (*The Times*, 4 March 1937) an 'appreciation' of Clothilde
   Fielding, the daughter of Ethel's lover Henry Brewster. She had died on 25
   February following a life of domestic content and almost complete isolation,
   though she had been trained as an architect.
2. For instance, Virginia together with six other writers (including Somerset
   Maugham, Hugh Walpole and H. G. Wells) had written a letter appealing for
   signatures on a petition to set up commissions to investigate the economic and
   political causes of international unrest. A copy of this letter is in the Humanities
   Research Library, University of Texas.

3225: To Clive Bell   [52 *Tavistock Square, W.C.1*]

Postcard
[12 March 1937]

I daresay thats all very true:[1] but what concerns me at present isn't Gibbon but the pheasant. How pleasant, that present, due, as so often too, to you.

                                                            V.W.

Quentin Bell

3226: To Ethel Smyth   52 *T[avistock] S.[quare, W.C.1]*

Wednesday [17 March 1937]

I listened in and enjoyed it:[2] though I was sympathetically distressed to hear your sore throat. By the way, a fruit grower in Kent [Nicholas Bagenal] also listened, the first night, and said your voice alone convinced him of your greatness: all character, all charm, all majesty, he said, were in it.: and he also immensely admired what the voice said. What an unreasonable woman you are! It was your idea—not giving your book [*Maurice Baring*]: and a good one; because then one don't exact praise. But lord love me, if you *want*, unbribed, to write,[3] what more cd. I wish? Only I wdn't, if I were you, bother with all the stuffing. Present day, the last chapter, has as much as one wants. And its all very bad, but well meant—morally.

I'm so rushed I cant write even my usual scrawl. We've been bothered about Julian,[4] Nessa's boy, wanting to fight in Spain: and have to stop him, which means seeing people—politicians.

But this by the way is confidential.

                                                            Yr V.

How are you?

Berg

1. On the reverse of this postcard was a portrait of Edward Gibbon, and on the message side a nine-line biography of him, to which Virginia is referring.
2. On 9 March Ethel broadcast, as part of a series called 'Scrapbooks', *Scrapbook for 1912: Scenes, Melodies and Personalities of 25 Years Ago*.
3. To ask for *The Years*, which had been published on 15 March.
4. Julian Bell had returned from China on 12 March, and Virginia met him for dinner at Charleston on the next day.

March 20th [1937]

Dear Naomi Mitchison,[1]

Thank you very much for your letter. I dont think I have read To the Lighthouse since I wrote it, and thus I dont know what I should think of it now. But I am very glad that you like it, and rather surprised—partly because once a book is published it seems to disappear, and that it should still exist is a shock—this time a pleasant one. Perhaps some day you will tell me what you liked in it, or disliked. But London being what it is, one never talks to anybody, and reviewing being what it is, one never gets any criticism. Is that a reason why we dont write better books?—but my husband has just been saying that you have written us a very good book. I shall wait to read it till it comes out. Many thanks again for your letter.

Yours sincerely
Virginia Woolf

National Library of Scotland

March 22nd [1937]

Dearest Janet,

This is only a line to say that of course we will come and see you.[2] We go to Rodmell on Thursday—What we suggest is that we should drive over, possibly on Thursday 1st April, reach you in the morning, ask Emphie for lunch, and get back that evening. But I will write again or ring up, and settle more exactly from Monks House. And then Emphie could say what time suits you best.

Then we will have a good talk, so I wont write now, being stupid in the head, but in spite of stupidity—so many people in London—please know and understand with what affection I always think of you. How unhappy I was, and how you helped me, and still do, dear Janet, and so we both send our love and shall come and see you. Love to Emphie.

VW

If you want a copy of the Years, you've only got to send me word on a card

1. The Scottish novelist, born in 1897. In June the Hogarth Press published *Socrates*, which she co-authored with R. H. S. Crossman for the children's series *World-Makers & World-Shakers*.
2. Janet Case (see p. 93, note 3) was dying in her house at Minstead, in the New Forest, where she lived with her sister Emphie.

and a copy shall be sent—I didn't, because owning books is such a bore in a small house.

Sussex

3229: To Shena, Lady Simon   *Monk's House, Rodmell,*
Lewes, Sussex

March 27th [1937]

Dear Shena,[1]

It was very nice of you to write, and I would have thanked you before, only I too have been in bed, and couldn't write.

I'm so glad you enjoyed the Years—impossible though it sounds to me. But then one gets so sick of one's own books.

As for thinking that I should have exhorted you to go to a marriage service, I can only say last time I went to one I had much ado not to stand up and cry out on the disgusting nature of it. So next time you go, do this—One doesn't of course, through sheer cowardice. I went, forced to, to a burial service [of Margaret West] the other day, and that seemed if anything worse; because more solemn.

But we're down here, forgetting all these horrors, and as I'm still rather done up, I wont maunder on.

How is your history of Manchester? I think work at drains is not all narrow or selfish—in fact, how you do it I cant conceive. One of these days I want to come and see.

Yours ever
Virginia Woolf

Sussex

3230: To Stephen Spender   52 *Tavistock Sqre.* [*W.C.*1]

7th April [1937]

Dear Stephen,

I never got a letter from you from Valencia,[2] so I didn't write, or send the book [*The Years*]. Now I suppose from the card I got the other day that you're back in London. If you still want a copy I'll send it you.

1. Lady Simon, whom Virginia had known since 1933, collaborated fully in the work of her husband Ernest Simon (1879-1960), who became 1st Lord Simon of Wythenshawe in 1947. He was an expert on housing, education, and local government, particularly in Manchester, where they lived. Lady Simon was the sole author of *A Hundred Years of City Government* (*Manchester, 1838-1938*), which was published in 1938.

2. Spender had gone to Valencia as a journalist, not as a combatant, and stayed only a short time.

I said I'd write about it, but I've been so plagued by the usual spate of reviews, even more contradictory than usual—oh why haven't we got a single decent critic among us?—that I've almost forgotten the book. But what I meant I think was to give a picture of society as a whole; give characters from every side; turn them towards society, not private life; exhibit the effect of ceremonies; Keep one toe on the ground by means of dates, facts: envelop the whole in a changing temporal atmosphere; Compose into one vast many-sided group at the end; and then shift the stress from present to future; and show the old fabric insensibly changing without death or violence into the future—suggesting that there is no break, but a continuous development, possibly a recurrence of some pattern; of which of course we actors are ignorant. And the future was gradually to dawn.

Of course I completely failed, partly through illness—I've had to leave out one whole section which I could not revise in time for the press[1]—partly through sheer incompetence. The theme was too ambitious. However I enjoyed the writing immensely, though not the revision; and am longing to go on to something else. I expect I muted down the characters too much, in order to shorten and keep their faces towards society; and altogether muffed the proportions: which should have given a round, not a thin line.

Julian is thinking of going to drive a lorry. I wish you could talk to him before he goes; but I daresay you're busy, and he is all over the place, inter-viewing Labour party, communists and so on. Your letter came in the nick of time to set him against the CP.[2]—we of course kept your name and confidence intact: it was most interesting.

Excuse this scrawl. I'm in a rush, partly owing to the usual fret and bother of the publishing season, and cant form my letters, let alone my sentences, so must leave you to make what sense you can; and hope we may meet.

Your affate
V.W.

You say your wife would like a copy of the Years. Of course I'll send her one: but where to?[3] And dont let her say she likes it if she doesnt: I dont give

1. Virginia was probably referring to the second of the two unpublished episodes printed and discussed by Grace Radin in "*Two enormous chunks*": *Episodes Excluded during the Final Revisions of THE YEARS, Bulletin of the New York Public Library* (Winter 1977), pp. 221-51.
2. Julian Bell never joined the Communist Party, but he considered that it was his duty to go to Spain. Knowing what distress his decision would cause his mother, he agreed to go not as a soldier in the International Brigade, but as an ambulance driver for Spanish Medical Aid. The 'letter' to which Virginia refers contained accounts of the Communist-led International Brigade written by Spender's friend Jimmy Younger, who had joined it in Spain and become terribly disillusioned.
3. Inez Spender was now in Brussels, where she was studying Spanish manuscripts.

copies, for this reason—people think they must thank. But free criticism is always welcome.

Texas

3231: To Violet Dickinson   52 *Tavistock Square, W.C.1.*

Wednesday [7 April 1937]

My Violet,
     How nice to see your little bird's claw again!
     I dont see why you should lavish copies of that book [*The Years*] on Europe—if I'd thought you wanted one I would have sent you one myself. But it cost me so many headaches I thought it would cause them in those that read it.
     Anyhow we shall make enough to go off for a month in France, and heaven knows, what with one horror after another, Leonard at any rate deserves a rest. He's had to bring out the books—the Amberley papers,[1] which I hope you've ordered from the Library—was a great venture—almost off his own bat, as our staff collapsed. And then, at the critical moment, a rash broke out. The clerks started scratching. Bugs! the daughter of the bus driver had caught them at home.
     Last week I went over to Lyndhurst [New Forest] to see old Janet Case who is I'm afraid slowly dying; and she asked after Miss Dickinson, who'd been so kind about the duchesses and other things: and said would I remember her to you. So I do. If you're at Fritham again, perhaps you might call. But she's on the sofa; very gay, with an old sister; and some disease that kills slowly.
     I'm scribbling half asleep. Here's Leonard in from the House of Commons. Sends his love, must take his spaniel round the Square—hopes some day we may meet—so do I—have just cut a French book with the paper knife.

Sp.

Sussex

3232: To Ethel Smyth   52 *Tavistock Sqre.* [*W.C.1*]

Wednesday [7 April 1937]

     Yes. Ring up on Friday. I think it'll be all right. I had to go to Lyndhurst to see my old Greek teacher who's dying and asked me to come. Thats what set the pain off again—but its gone very quick this time. What a nice letter

1. *The Amberley Papers: The Diaries and Letters of Lord and Lady Amberley:* edited by Bertrand and Patricia Russell.

117

from Maurice! I liked it. I was so entirely and honestly convinced that the book was a complete failure that I still feel anaesthetised—cant believe anyone can like it. Its a comfortable numb sensation. Yet I get the usual, or more than the usual letters—from the oddest people—which I should answer at this moment. But I cant write at all.

Here's Maurice—yes, I do like it—I've just read it again The Palsy—would the man cure L. do you think?[1]

Yr V.

Oh I'm cursing the BBC—have to speak on the 29th—haven't a word in my head to fling at a dog and Gibbon [*TLS*] to finish for the 27th And what about your sack of coals, MB I mean?[2]

Berg

3233: TO JANET CASE   52 *Tavistock Sqre.* [*W.C.*1]
April 8th [1937]

Dearest Janet,

I know if we had been well mannered we should have written a Collins after our call. Wasn't it a nice visit? We enjoyed it immensely. Its odd what a charm you and Emphie, the blue china and the old furniture have, and have always had, for me. And where does one thing begin and another end? We had a lovely drive home too, by Winchester, a longer but a much nicer way. And when I got home, there was a letter from Violet Dickinson, who—such things do happen—had been staying at Fritham,[3] which has been bought and improved by one of her, I think titled, friends. So I wrote and gave her your message. She stayed with us at Fritham [in 1902] she said and I drove her to a meet of the stag hounds at Stony X. Would you like her to call in next time?

We came back here last Sunday and went to see Angelica act Ariel in Midsummer Nights Dream up at Islington. It was all very gay and youthful, and she was dappled with brown leaves and wore small horns—was lovely certainly, but whether thats enough I dont know. And Lady Oxford, the old skinflint, doesn't mean to give me *her* book—says its out of print[4]—only to scrounge (if thats the word) a free copy of mine. Emphie says you would like

1. From Maurice Baring's letter Virginia learned that a Dr Alexander had been treating him for palsy, and she now proposed to seek his help for the trembling of Leonard's hands, which affected him all his life.
2. Ethel's biography of Maurice Baring was not published until 1938.
3. Sir Timothy Eden's house near Lyndhurst. He was the brother of Anthony Eden, then Foreign Secretary. The Stephens had rented it for several summers at the start of the century.
4. One of Margot Oxford's four autobiographical volumes.

one—a very different pair of shoes. I'll send one tomorrow; I wish it were smaller and less of a dump in the shelf.

Who d'you think just's been to tea? The great novelist Hugh Walpole—immensely pink and fat and kind; but nourishing a sorrow that his books sell too well, and the intellectuals dont admire. So we all have our roseleaves under the pillow—do I mean peas? He is being paid £200 to describe the Coronation[1] for the Daily Mail, and given a seat. You cant have it both ways —thats what I tell him. This is old wives prattle; but I daresay you wont mind. Dont bother to write I'll scribble a line now and again if I may. And love to you both from us both.

V

Sussex

3234: To May Sarton   52 *Tavistock Sqre* [*W.C.*1]

9th April [1937]

Dear Miss Sarton,[2]

I must thank you for the flowers, and for the poems, which I have not yet had time to read.

It gives me great pleasure that you should like my books, and I am grateful to you for saying so.

Yours sincerely
Virginia Woolf

Berg

3235: To Violet Dickinson   52 *Tavistock Square, W.C.*1.

Tuesday [13th April 1937]

My Violet,

I've had a note from Janet Case—I'm afraid she's getting rather feeble. If you ever should be near, she says would you ring up and suggest a visit, but she's only able to see people for a short time, if they arrange it. Her address is Hewer's Orchard, Minstead, Lyndhurst, Hants. Telephone:

1. Of George VI on 12 May.
2. The American poet and novelist (b. 1912) was then staying in a flat at Whipsnade lent to her by Julian Huxley. Virginia later met her dining with Elizabeth Bowen, with whom Sarton was in love, and in her diary described her as "A pale pretty Shelley imitation American girl, who sat on the floor at my feet, and unfortunately adores and worships and gave me primroses one day in the winter and her poems." For Sarton's description of her early encounters with Virginia, see *I Knew a Phoenix*, 1954.

Cadnam 103: So should you be there, give her a ring. She would like a letter anyhow, I'm sure.

Oh the old Pattles! They're always bursting out of their casks. If you read the Amberley Papers you'll find them popping up again. And suddenly the other day a faded Pattle relic, aged about 90, wrote to me from Somerset, and said she had the china out of which my grandmother drank at Calcutta—the lovely one who fled from France.[1] And the relict lives with Hugh Lane's[2] sister—not I trust in sin.

Bugs turned into Nettlerash—after a terrific fuss: L. had visits from the Bus driver and the mother: undid their shirts and petticoats—proved themselves clean as eggs. Such it is to run a press. They said they had eaten mushrooms for the first time in their lives—and never again. Do mushrooms give one nettle rash? Perhaps if ones a bus driver.

So good night.

V.

Sussex

3236: To V. Sackville-West   52 *Tavistock Sqre.* [*W.C.*1]
Thursday [15 April 1937]

Yes, do come to lunch on Monday 1.30.

I'm perfectly recovered. We had the devils own time till Easter; the dr. said L. had diabetes.—which he hasn't, thank the Lord: then Julian arrived from China, said he was off to Spain to fight: then Bugs broke out in The Press, but proved to be Nettlerash—so that altogether I rightly earned a headache. Old Ethel was furious, because I wouldn't see her at Rodmell, and says of course its all sham and humbug—what a termagant the woman is. I'm rather glad Dotty supports half of that magnificent oak.[3] But this'll keep till Monday—I'm in a rush. And what d'you think we're doing on Monday

1. Virginia's maternal grandmother was Maria Pattle (1818-92), who married John Jackson, a doctor practising in Calcutta. Maria's father was James Pattle (1775-1845). He was said to have drunk himself to death in India, and his corpse was sent home in a cask of spirits which exploded during the voyage. The 'faded Pattle relic' was Marian Pattle, grand-daughter of General Thomas Pattle, James's brother.
2. Hugh Lane (1875-1915) founded the gallery of modern art in Dublin. He was an art collector and critic, and was drowned in the *Lusitania* when the ship was torpedoed in 1915.
3. Virginia meant that she and Dorothy Wellesley between them shared the burden of sustaining Ethel.

morning? taking Sally [the Woolfs' spaniel] to her bridals at Ickenham. But we'll be back before lunch.

V

Oh I never thanked you for a long nice letter from The Sahara,[1] where you were catching salamanders and eating a sheep roasted whole We've just been buying goldfish and daffodils. Did you bring the salamanders home?

Berg

3237: To Shena, Lady Simon   52 *Tavistock Square, W.C.1.*

21st April [1937]

Dear Shena,

I've got to Broadcast (very foolishly) on the evening of the 29th, and shall I know have to make my last touches at the last moment—so I dare not spend the afternoon as I should like—talking to you. But wont you be up again soon and suggest another time? I'm so sorry.

yr
Virginia Woolf

Sussex

3238: To Stephen Spender   52 *Tavistock Square, W.C.1.*

Postcard
Sunday [25th April 1937]

This week seems a hopeless muddle. But could you both come in on Monday 3rd May, any time after 9? The Grave's[2] are coming. I hope you can, as we go to France after that, and should like very much to see you both.

V

Texas

3239: To Lady Cecil   52 *Tavistock Square, W.C.1.*

Wednesday 28th April [1937]

Dear Nelly,

Oh dear—once again—we shall be in France, or on the way there, on Wednesday. We are flying for 3 weeks holiday to escape the coronation: but

1. In February 1937 Vita and Gwen St Aubyn had been on holiday in Algeria, where they spent a week in the ancient Roman city of Timgad on the northern edge of the Sahara desert.
2. Sally (*née* Graves) and Richard Chilver (see p. 85, note 4).

we're very sorry that this means also escaping you. Why do you and Lord Cecil always ask the woman he somewhat brusquely calls "The Old Frump" when she can't come? But we shall be back at the end of the month. May I come and see you then? Will you ask me?

David and Rachel [Cecil] have just left the room; a blooming sight for my old eyes—so young, so happy. Well, I enjoyed my youth too—especially some evenings on a green sofa in St John's Wood. D'you remember sitting there?

And its very nice of you to plod through those many years—I mean the printed ones. Will you one day hand me your censures? and I'm proud to think some scenes amused you, who have always been the source of so many delights to me. Do you know what torture I go through tomorrow? Broadcasting.[1] So I deserve my car drive in France: but as I began by saying I wish the Ancient Harridan could have lunched with you on Wednesday, and wrinkled her mouldy chops. So many thanks for asking us.

Yr aff
V.W.

The Marquess of Salisbury (Cecil Papers)

3240: To Stephen Spender   52 *Tavistock Sq.* [*W.C.*1]

Typewritten
April 30th [1937]

Dear Stephen,

Thank you very much for your letter. I'm very glad you liked the Years better than the other books; and that some part of what I meant to convey got through. I know I couldnt get the whole meaning expressed, partly because I left out one section, which was important; also because it was too big for me to encircle. I dont think I agree with you though that *all* the characters felt the unreality, the invalidity of their experience. Eleanor's experience though limited partly by sex and the cramp of the Victorian upbringing was meant to be all right; sound and rooted; the others were crippled in one way or another—though I meant Maggie and Sara to be outside that particular prison. I couldnt bring in the Front as you say partly because fighting isnt within my experience, as a woman; partly because I think action generally unreal. Its the thing we do in the dark that is more real; the thing we do because peoples eyes are on us seems to me histrionic, small boyish; However I havent got this expressed, and I daresay difference of sex makes a different view. Which is right? God knows.

But I'm very glad you saw that the tend of the book, its slope to one quarter of the compass and not another, was different from the tend in my

1. See p. 108, note 2.

other books. Yes, I am very anxious to develop it further; and almost tried a poetry section in this book; wanted to get some chorus; some quite different level. But once the narrative gets going the impetus is very heavy and difficult to interrupt, thats the horror to me of the novel. And in the Years I wanted to catch the general readers attention: perhaps I did this too much. But ever so many thanks for reading it so carefully. I've just been abused by the Dean of Durham[1] for irreligion and for saying that wrist watches were invented in 1880.

I'm glad your friend is in better circumstances.[2] You must tell us on Monday.

Julian has been up at Birmingham.[3] I feel that its a mistake his going to Spain, but its no good saying so. I dont suppose he would see my arguments.

Well till Monday.

yr aff
V.W.

Texas

3241: TO WILLIAM PLOMER   52 *Tavistock Square, W.C.*1

Friday 30th April [1937]

Dear William,

Yes, we would like very much to see you. The only time seems to be Monday next after dinner. The Spenders and the Chilvers are coming. We're off to France next week. I've never met Mrs Stephen [Inez Spender]: have you?

Ever since Christmas we have been rather battered and harried—for one thing our manager died, which led to a lot of worry—she was the perfect manager of course.

And I'm afraid you've had a bad time too.

What an incredible old ass Hugh is! Think of tagging a title to his quite respectable name![4] Why? If he had been Walter, I should have understood: because then he would have been in touch with the Wizard of the North [Sir Walter Scott]

1. Cyril Alington (1872-1955), former Head Master of Eton, had been Dean of Durham since 1933. On 15 April he had mentioned *The Years* in his broadcast *Book Talk*, and in the *Listener* for 28 April some of his remarks were printed: "The one thing from which I pray heaven to defend me ... is from the dreary adventures of men and women who are confronted with problems for which they can find no answer, because neither they nor their creators have any sure standard to which they can refer."
2. Jimmy Younger. See p. 116, note 2.
3. Canvassing for the Labour Party.
4. Hugh Walpole was created a Knight in the Coronation honours.

But do come on Monday night and let us have a good crack. If you're at Brighton you must come over and play bowls.

yr aff.
V.W.

Do not judge my character from this handwriting I beg: I'm in a rush, going off to Sussex in a minute.

Texas

3242: To Violet Dickinson

Monk's House, Rodmell,
Lewes, Sussex

May 1st 37

My Violet,

I wrote and told Janet Case that you might one day communicate. I hope you will; but I'm afraid she's not going to improve and theyre both [Janet and her sister Emphie] as young as foals.

Here we are, about to leave England for the Coronation. I suppose you're given a seat in the Abbey. If they gave me one, I would face London and its ribbons and hatchets, and no omnibuses:[1] but they wont give me one. So we're going driving through France, and whenever we come to an Inn which has paté de foie gras we shall stop. So you see to what we're reduced—mere gorgers and guzzlers.

And we've been walking in the woods this cold day looking in every nest for eggs, because Leonards marmozet has a passion for birds eggs. At last he found one, and sure enough she cracked it and all the juice ran on to Nessa's new carpet and I put an ashtray underneath to catch the drops. Nessa is having a show next week [at the Lefevre Galleries]; they say either all the world will come, or nobody. And should you be our way, in London, give us a call in June or July: after that, thank God, we shall settle in here.

Excuse this scribble.

Sp:

Sussex

3243: To George Rylands

*52 Tavistock Square, W.C.*1

Postcard
Sunday [2 May 1937]

Yes; Gibbon [*TLS*, 24 April 1937] was by your old friend. But I never thought to take in a real historian.

1. One of the decoration devices for the Coronation route was a line of silver hatchets mounted on poles. The Coronation coincided with a strike of London busmen.

You almost brought the Wolves to tears last night, reading Shakespeare so beautifully.[1]

V

George Rylands

3244: To V. Sackville-West   52 *Tavistock Square, W.C.1.*

Monday [3 May 1937]

But why, didn't you and Mrs Staples[2] ring up? I should have enjoyed it. No, I didn't think it was much good: first I had to shorten, then lengthen, and in the end I was bored stiff. It'll be in the Listener, but all in a muddle I suspect. I would have liked a crack with you, better, still, our jaunt; the sweets in a bag—d'you remember?[3] But Lorlovaduk, as Rupert Brooke used to say, shant I be thankful to be in a Courtyard in France, listening to a nightingale, drinking red wine, while you are curtseying and singing God Save the King. Oh the crush in the Tube this afternoon—there I stood, with my cake for Tom Eliots tea running chocolate down my legs. So farewell but come soon

V

Berg

3245: To Ethel Smyth   52 *T[avistock] S.[quare, W.C.1]*

Wednesday [5 May 1937]

I'm sorry I've been so dumb. But I've been forced to write I don't know how many letters and I cant make myself take up a friendly pen. On Friday we go to France, thank God, for our 3 weeks spin. I don't at this moment know where—except that we shall try to reach Montaigne's tower:[4] but any where, any where out of this world. I began this letter; meaning to rush out and buy shoes stockings vest: here's Desmond MacCarthy—says he must spend the whole afternoon and evening discussing a lecture on my father.[5] My God what do people think one's time's made of? Such a rush of things to do that even without him I couldn't summon any thoughts worth writing. Its the Leslie Stephen lecture, Desmond says. And aren't you his daughter. But must I write your lecture for you? And so on. Well excuse this gust of

1. On 1 May Rylands read selections from Shakespeare for the B.B.C. series *The English Poets*.
2. The Nicolsons' cook from 1926 to 1966.
3. See Letter 3206.
4. Michel de Montaigne (1533-92), the essayist, was born and died at the Château de Montaigne in Périgord, near Bordeaux.
5. Desmond MacCarthy gave the annual Leslie Stephen Lecture at Cambridge on 26 May.

temper. I will send a letter I hope from France. and if you should write, they would forward. Hope the book and the dog are doing well. I saw Vita the other day.

V.

Berg

3246: TO VANESSA BELL   52 *Tavistock Square, W.C.*1.

[6? May 1937]

I thought the show[1] a great triumph and wish I could express my critical perceptions with any clearness. I rather suspect that An McDougall was right and that you have penetrated to greater depths or heights than ever before.

At anyrate it gave me the greatest pleasure. I wish I could have seen more quietly, but everytime I began to look either the voice of Curtis or the bust of Stern intervened.[2] I did think the one I got a divinely lovely one—but there were several others I coveted, and shall have to go back and look again. "What a very gifted woman your sister is!" as an unknown lady remarked.

Yes, I'm jealous.

B.

What am I to say to Beton?[3]

Berg

3247: TO LADY OTTOLINE MORRELL
                                              52 *Tavistock Square, W.C.*1.
May 6th [1937]

Dearest Ottoline,

I'm so pleased and surprised that you liked my talk—it was such a bore doing it—first too long, then too short: finally I felt like an incompetent tailor making trouser legs that didn't match. But never mind, if you and Philip [Morrell] liked it. The sad discreet atmosphere of the BBC is very dismal: oh so proper, oh so kindly.

1. Recent paintings by Vanessa exhibited at the Lefevre Gallery. In an unsigned review in *The Times* of 13 May, the author wrote that her work "bears every sign of a maturing talent".
2. Minna Curtiss, an American, had been staying at Long Barn with Charles and Anne Lindbergh. 'Stern' was probably the novelist Gladys Bertha Stern (b. 1890).
3. Probably Cecil Beaton (1904-80), who had again asked to photograph Virginia, but she again refused.

I heard from Tom Eliot you weren't well—we sang a subdued nightingales duet in your praise the other afternoon—*that* might have been worth your hearing.

Now, early tomorrow, we fly to France for 3 weeks, to escape all this barrel organ braying. Wont it be nice to sit in a southern market place?—undecorated.

But I do hope you will recover quickly.

Old books: I've been reading Gibbon: the Autobiography, the history, with the greatest joy. And his letters.

Excuse this scrawl, and thank you once more, as usual.

yr
V.W.

Here is the article in the Spectator, which I dont want, and Philips article,[1] which I think he wants back. Please thank him. I was much interested: and enjoyed my last nights owling.

V

Walter Turner's protest may amuse you. Hayward had abused Yeats for exalting Dotty and Turner.[2]

Texas

1. Possibly *French Traveller in India a Hundred Years Ago*, by Philip Morrell, *Asiatic Review* (April 1937).
2. In the *Spectator* for 20 November 1936 John Hayward had reviewed W. B. Yeats' edition of *The Oxford Book of Modern Verse*, in which Yeats had praised the work of Dorothy Wellesley and W. J. Turner (1889-1946), with whom Ottoline had quarrelled in 1927. Turner wrote about Hayward: "His statement that it 'very rarely follows that the creator is also a critic' is simply untrue. In his obvious attempt to belittle Mr Yeats he has forgotten temporarily that our greatest critics—Dryden, Coleridge, Matthew Arnold, Keats—were all poets, but perhaps, according to Mr Hayward, not very good poets" (*Spectator*, 27 November 1936).

Letters 3248-3285 (May–July 1937)

Virginia and Leonard, with Mitz his marmoset, drove to the Dordogne, and as far south as Albi. On their way home they visited George Sand's house at Nohant. The holiday was a great success, not least because it spared them the Coronation celebrations in London, and once again they contemplated buying a small property in France. They were away from 7 to 25 May. On their return they found that Maynard Keynes had been more seriously ill than they had suspected, and that Janet Case was dying. Virginia sent her several cheering letters before her death on 15 July, and wrote her obituary for The Times. *Her main literary occupation was still* Three Guineas.

On 21 July they heard the terrible news that Julian Bell had been killed in Spain.

3248: To Vanessa Bell

Le Grand Hotel, Souillac
[*France*]

[12 May 1937]

Today is Coronation day, so I suppose it is 12th May; but so far we've not had a sign of it—but then we were at Rhocamadour in a cave when it was going on. This is not a letter: only to ask you on my knees to write: if you write on 17th or 18th and address to *Poste Restante, Guerét, Creuse, France* I should get it. I'm longing to hear about your show: has the Coronation affected it either way: what did Duncan see:[1] or any Royal gossip. Is Angelica back? And family news. In return I cant give much—save reflections on possible death in fog in channel. We stopped in the middle of the night and boats hooted all round: but nothing happened. We are now settled here for a few days—Roger came here I think—a lovely valley with hills not too near the Dordogne running past; a perfect small Inn I think: clean; pâté de foie gras at every meal, coffee and rolls: L. still says, to infuriate me that The White Hart [Hotel, Lewes, Sussex] is better.

The only drawback is wintry cold, thunderstorms, and a cultivated Englishman, who will I know turn out to be Harry Nortons[2] cousin. Why we dont live in France I cant think. The mere silence of the telephone is alone

1. Duncan Grant had a seat in Westminster Abbey for the Coronation.
2. H. T. J. Norton (1886-1937), the Cambridge mathematician whom Virginia had known since her twenties.

enough: no Colefax: no engagements. And we sat on the river bank last night in a vineyard and saw . . . no no: I will not run on, as dinner is about to ring. We have a lovely rose pink wine. Why arent you here? But then, you would have to tolerate poor Singe.[1] Theres a most remarkable church; its like Italy in many ways. And we went into a grotto and saw the stalactites dripping. red and green. How many pictures have you sold?[2] What criticism? I'm ashamed of this scribble, redeemed only by pure love.

Please write.
B.

Berg

3249: To Maynard Keynes   *Albi* [*France*]

17th May 37

Dear Maynard,

Here we are at Albi; and your biographies,[3] which at last reached me, have been giving me immense pleasure. I dont say that I understand every word, but great economists must surely be the most fascinating of men—or at least you make them so. Perhaps they're less hackneyed than the literary gents I attempt: anyhow in spite of every temptation to drowse over my Vin Rosé I've been lying on my bed engrossed by you. Why don't you do some more? I wish you would. Whole Lives.

The South is very seductive, in spite of Bank holiday and pouring rain at the moment. We turn back tomorrow. Leonard has recovered from his eczema, tell Lydia; so that her gloomy forecast of a marriage with me is not imminent. I hope you too are recovered[4] —

(1) Why do economists run to bibliophily?
(2) What is the way to bind pamphlets?

But I mustn't drivel on.

Love from us both.
Yrs V.W.

King's

1. See p. 152, note 1.
2. Vanessa had sold six paintings and made about £50.
3. Keynes' *Essays in Biography* (1933), of which he devoted the second section to the founders of Political Economy in Cambridge—Malthus, Marshall, Edgeworth and Ramsey.
4. Keynes had had a severe heart attack and was lying gravely ill at Cambridge, but Virginia did not yet know how ill he was.

3250: To V. Sackville-West   [*Chateauroux, France*]
Postcard
Friday 21st May [1937]

I think she (on the other side) is rather like you.[1] We've just visited the Chateau at Nohant—most romantic. A lovely journey, perfect country, the valley of the Dordogne. I mean to buy a house and live here. Did you enjoy the Coronation? Not a sign of it here.

                                                              V.W.

Jean Love

3251: To Janet Case   52 *Tavistock Sqre., W.C.1.*
May 26th [1937]

Dearest Janet,

I wonder how you are?—but I dont want to trouble you or Emphie to put pen to paper unless you have such a thing as a postcard handy—which I never have.

We have just come back from a drive through France, along the banks of the Dordogne, the loveliest of all rivers; and not a single tourist, and small inns, delicious food, nightingales, a hoopoe, innumerable churches, all as if 200 years ago—but why, you will ask, are travellers letters always dull? That's a question I've never solved.

So I must return to London—not that I have yet entered into life here, save for the telephone, and Desmond MacCarthy whom we found yesterday when we came back sitting waiting. Tomorrow he has to give the Leslie Stephen Lecture at Cambridge on Leslie Stephen—So dusty and hot as we were, with the marmozet chattering with rage—she came with us to France and enchanted crowds wherever we stopped—there we had to sit and hear his lecture. How I loathe lectures—all the same; always so emphatic.

That reminds me—why I dont know—why did you give away the bag, the only bag I ever made you? I would have signed a dozen copies of the Years rather than let a stranger have that clumsy tribute. Isnt it astonishing? The Years is a best seller in America,[2] and Leonard says we shall make enough to buy a new car.

But I want to know how you feel instead of gossiping on so idly. L. is at the Labour party: my actress niece Angelica is dining here: Julian is learning

1. A portrait of George Sand by Charpentier. She lived in the Château de Nohant most of her life and died there in 1876. It was a favourite resort of a remarkable group of intellectuals and artists, including Chopin, Liszt, Flaubert and Balzac.
2. By the end of May the American edition of *The Years* had sold 25,000 copies, and for weeks it remained at the top of the fiction bestseller list.

to drive a lorry in order to join the Ambulance Corps. And London is so hot and heavy and floppy with old streamers and banners, and people walking, that even I who love it long for the New Forest.

My love to Emphie, whom I think one of the nicest women I ever met. And to Janet too.

V.

Sussex

3252: To Maynard Keynes   52 *Tavistock Sqre.* [*W.C.*1]

May 28th [1937]

My dear Maynard,

We are very much upset to hear of your illness. Nessa wrote and told me when we were abroad. Are they sending you to Jack Hutchinson's and Ottolines retreat in Wales, I wonder?[1] If so, I have heard many amusing stories about it, and hope you'll add to them.

I'm waiting for Willie Robson[2] to come to lunch, and then, thank heaven, we're off for Leonards last week's holiday to Monks House. France came more than up to the scratch in food—its only one's own fireside thats lacking. The country is about 300 years behind England in bungalow growth—might be the age of Rousseau. By the way, I got into Nohant and saw the very piano Chopin gave George Sand, and the great ladies [*sic*] very pens—a fascinating faded house, full of the furniture of her grandmother, and the little theatre where Flaubert and Turgenev acted all set for a scene in the kitchen-quarters.

I'm grateful for the Browning Catalogue: if I dared I would go and bid. The Years is said to be a best seller in America—If I were certain what that meant I would plunge. As it is, no doubt Victor[3] will acquire the lot.

Lydia if very kind will tell us how you go on and if we may write—if

1. Keynes had gone to Ruthin Castle in North Wales to recuperate. Ottoline Morrell had been there in 1926.
2. William Robson (b. 1895), was Lecturer (later Professor) of Public Administration at the London School of Economics. In 1930 he founded with Leonard the *Political Quarterly*, and they were co-editors until 1959.
3. Victor Rothschild, who succeeded his uncle as 3rd Lord Rothschild in this year, was born in 1903, and in 1933 married Barbara Hutchinson, the daughter of Virginia's friends St John and Mary Hutchinson. At this time he was a Fellow of Trinity College, Cambridge. The 'Browning Catalogue' refers to the auction at Sotheby's on 7 June of the papers of Lt.-Col. Harry Payton Moulton-Barrett, which included important letters from Elizabeth Barrett to her younger brother and sister.

gossip from Tavistock Sqre. is allowed. Sally is gravid with at least 4 pups. And so we all send our love—heres Willie—

yr
V.W.

King's

3253: To Emphie Case

Monk's House, Rodmell,
Lewes, Sussex

June 3rd [1937]

My dear Emphie,

It was very good of you to write; and you must be having such a bad time.

But it does sound as though Janet [Case] might be now more comfortable. My father had the same operation.[1] If she can walk about, and look at her trees and birds, it will be an immense advantage.

Here we are, having a few days off, before we go back to London, which is all abuzz with the Opera, the season, the Coronation. How nice to think of you so much more sensibly and humanely employed with your blue china and salt cellars. I forgot to say how much the table at Hewer's Orchard [Janet's house] impressed me. It started me improving our kitchen—so if the new china cupboard and coal box are a failure, I shall blame you. I wish you'd walk in and look at them; and then we could have a gossip and say some truthful but flattering things about that very nice and good looking woman your sister. Shall I write to her? I'll try, in case she likes letters.

Please take care of yourself and accept both our very ancient and tender affection. L. is gardening.

yr
V.W.

Sussex

3254: To Shena, Lady Simon

Monk's House, Rodmell,
Lewes, Sussex

3rd June [1937]

Dear Shena,

I return your enclosure which has amused me very much, and also shocked me.[2] It seems incredible that there should be all this humming and

1. For abdominal cancer, in 1902.
2. Lady Simon had sent Virginia a confidential report of a meeting at Newnham College, Cambridge, protesting against the position of women in the University. Cambridge was the only university in Britain which still refused equal membership to women, who were given only titular degrees. This remained the position until 1948, when Newnham and Girton were at last accepted as full Colleges of the University.

hawing—about the university question I mean. I should have thought one could ask a plain question in a natural speaking voice without any fear of being squashed. But then, even less than you, do I know Cambridge. I am much tempted to write something off my own bat,[1] whether they ask me to lecture or not—and of course they wont. But no doubt I should have no effect, or a bad one. I never understand what "membership of the University" exactly means. You must enlighten me.

As for the gowns[2]—there we enter a world of such unreality that only a cave dweller can see the wood for the trees. Excuse these mixed metaphors. I'm writing in a hurry. How can human beings have got themselves into such postures!

I hear by the way that Maynard Keynes is better and going to Wales.

yr
V.W.

Sussex

3255: TO SAXON SYDNEY-TURNER   *Monk's House, Rodmell,*
                                          Lewes, Sussex

5th June [1937]

My dear Saxon,

Your letter was sent on here. Yes of course I should be delighted to dine to meet anyone you choose—the longer the notice the better. We have been driving about France during the Coronation celebrations, then finished with a week planting flowers here. But we go back tomorrow and shall be in London, save for weekends till the final holiday (that sounds like going to Heaven—but I only mean August.)

Have you ever seen Sarlat, Souillac, the caves with the drawings and Albi? Or are they too Latin for you?

yr
V.

Sussex

3256: TO LYDIA KEYNES   *Monk's House, Rodmell,*
                                   Lewes, Sussex

5th June [1937]

My dear Lydia,

It was very good of you to write, and we are much relieved to hear that

1. In fact, since December 1936 Virginia had been working on *Three Guineas*, in which she deals very fully with women's education.
2. The Newnham conference insisted upon the right of women to wear gowns, but in *Three Guineas* Virginia ridicules academic dress for men, and encourages women to refuse all such 'uniforms'.

Maynard is better. I hope he won't get stronger *mentally* as his normal strength in the head is quite enough for me. Now you must at once give him a kiss; from me; then he will at once give you a kiss, which will be from Leonard, and so it will be all fair and above board.

It's a pity we cant be kissing nose to nose this evening—The Cement works[1] are looking positively sublime in the evening light; it is a quarter to nine, but so hot we cant settle to our books—tell Maynard to read the Memoirs of George Sand by herself in 10 vols:—if he wants a soothing but enthralling bedfellow—and Leonard is engaged in putting his new tortoises to bed in the lily pond. They—we bought 3—are so active we cant keep control of them. I am perpetually being sent up the road in pursuit of the father tortoise—which reminds me that Sally is causing us great anxiety. We were certain she was pregnant, and indeed her marriage took 25 minutes, I mean the after marriage, that is the dovetailing, (I waited behind a wall at the breeders) and we thought she was swollen when we came back. But the swelling did not increase: last night Leonard dosed her for worms; at 3.PM. she voided some yards of tape, and is now virgin to all appearances. What are we to do?

We go to London, alas, tomorrow: my only consolation is that I'm dining with the Hutchinsons [St John and Mary] to meet Lady Diana and Duff Cooper, and hope to pump her about the Duke of Windsor;[2] anyhow I'm such a snob, that I shall enjoy my evening. No room for more. But here is Leonard who confirms the kiss. Love to Maynard.

V.

King's

3257: TO JANET CASE   52 *Tavistock Square, W.C.1.*

June 12th [1937]

Dearest Janet,

I heard from Emphie about your operation. I wont bore you by saying how sorry I was: but I hope you're back again in that nice room now, with the flowers outside; and feeling better.

A little worldly gossip is all I can supply. Would you like to hear about

1. Erected at Asheham in 1932. Virginia loathed them.
2. Diana and Duff Cooper had been guests aboard the King's yacht *Nahlin* when he and Wallis Simpson (now the Duchess of Windsor) went on a Mediterranean cruise in June 1936. Duff Cooper (1890-1954) was at that time Secretary of State for War, and one of the two cabinet ministers whom Edward VIII consulted during the Abdication crisis.

the beautiful Lady Diana—whom I rather think you once taught[1]—Duff Cooper she is now—married to a little puffed up robin redbreast of a man. Why? I cant think, and didn't like to ask though she was very free and easy and told me all about youth at Belvoir.[2] They had tin baths and large cans painted black with red spots. I said that in middle class households the cans were yellow. She said the nuisance was that her grandfather the old duke was such a democrat that people came into the house at all hours. But her brother [9th Duke] has changed all that. She is more beautiful I think than she was; less painted; more bone and hollow; and wearing a ravishing veil over her hair and a bunch of yellow flowers.

This is my only grand party since we came back from France. We had a time entirely without parties there; only looking at farms and churches and sitting on the banks of the Dordogne eating pate de foie gras—a lovely holiday.

Now in London there's a lot of telephone ringing: L. has all his politicians at him, and I have old Ethel Smyth who stumps in for what she calls ten minutes. Its really 2 hours; all one long harangue, to which I listen, because she's stone deaf, and her trumpet doesnt work, but what does that matter, since she has a supreme belief in her own divine genius, and if you get her off on that, and love, and music, and her sheep dog, there's no need to answer. I'm looking at boxes of Roger Fry's letters and wondering how anyone writes a real life. An imaginary one wouldn't so much bother me. But oh, the dates, the quotations!

This gossip is only by way of passing half an hour in your and Emphies company, which I always think preferable to other peoples. So let us come and see you again; and get better. Love to Emphie. The marmozet joins, and Sally.

V.

Sussex

3258: To Mrs G. E. Easdale   52 *Tavistock Square, W.C.1.*

Typewritten
13th June 1937

Dear Mrs Easdale,

I was amused by Joans article[3] which I return. Five guineas is quite a

1. Replying to this letter, Janet Case wrote that Lady Diana "used to come to her lesson like a nymph scarcely dry from her bath in a gauze wrap" (quoted by Virginia in her obituary of Janet Case, *The Times*, 22 July 1937).
2. Belvoir Castle, Leicestershire, was the home of the Duke of Rutland, Diana Cooper's (*née* Manners) father.
3. *Holes*, by Joan Easdale, in the May issue of the *Adelphi*. It was about appearance and reality in the physical world.

good sum; though Ive no doubt she worked hard for it. I never see the Adelphi, so I missed the other article. But I hope this means that she is getting work that she enjoys. I'm sure, hard as it is, writing articles is a good training at first; it makes one finish and compress.

We had a very good holiday in France, and missed all the Coronation riot. Do you know the valley of the Dordogne? We were much tempted to buy a farm and settle there; but cant manage it.

I am glad that you are back at Crouch [near Sevenoaks, Kent]; is Joan in London still, and does she find Mr Murrys establishment[1] satisfactory? But I must stop.

yours sincerely,
Virginia Woolf

University of London

3259: To Ethel Smyth   52 *T.[avistock] S.[quare, W.C.1]*
Tuesday [15 June 1937]

I wonder how many of my letters to you begin "I am a wretch . . ." Never answered and should have answered. Once more, I am a wretch. The slips[2] are a great discovery I think: I shall get some broader—so that I could type on them. and see if I cant cut down my labours by half; and thank you. L: is committed to 3 weeks of Dr Alexander,[3] who says he can undoubtedly cure him and make "a new man of him." L. thinks, after 3 sittings, there's undoubtedly something in it We had a long drive on Sunday and lunch with his brother after it. Normally he wouldn't have been able to cut his meat; and as it was, could hold his knife almost steady. But its too early to tell.

And why have you become so excessively tactful in your speech with me?[4] I dont like that particular virtue; perhaps I'm crotchety about it. Anyhow I refuse to be tactful myself; and say crudely and rudely, no I dont care for C. St John's article.[5] Why do you? Is it good criticism? Is it well written? Not in my eyes. So excuse

V.

Berg

1. John Middleton Murry (1889-1957), the critic, founded the *Adelphi* magazine in 1923 and continued as its editor until 1948.
2. Presumably for 'flagging' the Roger Fry papers.
3. See p. 118, note 1.
4. In refraining from asking Virginia about *Three Guineas*. When she received this short letter, Ethel wrote across the top of it: "After this I said 'This is so little pudding I can't eat it' "; and to Virginia she wrote on 18 June: "In my opinion you have got all you want, or can do with from me—that in a way our friendship has run dry" (*Berg*).
5. This article, if published, has not been traced.

3260: To May Sarton   52 *Tavistock Square, W.C.*1

June 16th [1937]

Dear Miss Sarton,

   Its very unfortunate—both this Friday and next Friday I shall be away. Monday 21st is the only day, but dont make a journey on purpose. Probably another Friday if thats your day in London would be free. But if you're going back, then make it Monday 21st at 4.30.

   But why should you have been frightened, considering that I am as tame and mild as a very old giraffe? I admit that the room looking onto the Lake[1] dazzled me; but only as a giraffe might be afraid of the lights.

   Please forgive this scrawl with people talking.

                                              Yrs sincerely
                                              Virginia Woolf
Berg

3261: To V. Sackville-West   52 *Tavistock Square, W.C.*1.

June 17th [1937]

   Yes, it would be better than nothing—lunch July 1st—one o'clock, so as to spin it out.

   Ah hah! (This refers to Curtis Brown).[2] But this business matter must be left for you and L. As for The Alsatians—no: no:[3] What have we spent the last days doing? Rigging up a lying in bed in L's study [for Sally]; the event comes off this Sunday. Thus we cant go to Rodmell. Dogs enough; if dogs there be. Some say she's still virgin. George (not an S)[4] certainly wasnt. Have you read her Memoirs? Do: But no more now—

                                              V.
Berg

3262: To William Plomer   52 *Tavistock Square, W.C.*1

Thursday June 17th [1937]

My dear William,

   You see from the above that we're in London—we dont go to Monks House till the end of July, except for odd week ends. But ask us then; and we shall be delighted.

1. Virginia had recently met May Sarton at Elizabeth Bowen's house which over-looked the lake in Regent's Park. See p. 119, note 2.
2. Vita's dispute with Spencer Curtis Brown, her literary agent, concerned the serialisation of *Pepita*, which the Hogarth Press published in October 1937.
3. Vita had offered one of her eight Alsatian puppies to Leonard.
4. George Sand. Vita had written 'Georges'.

You say you are up on Wednesdays: if you are free this Wednesday, 23rd that is, would you come in after dinner and help us through a mixed and completely haphazard evening when two unknown ladies said to be of the highest merit, and personal charm, and youth, one a Finn, the other the daughter of a man who edits Woodfords diaries are being sprung upon us by an aged eccentric.[1] Please do. If I had time I would invest the prospect with greater charm to tempt you. As it is I must depend on your good heart. Also, I've been meeting Tony Butts and hearing the story of the malignant Mary which I want to discuss with you.[2]

Have you any news of Wogan?[3] So you see to answer these questions and many more you must come. This week end we're cloistered here, attending the accouchement of Sally [spaniel], which takes place in Leonard's study.

Wd. you let me have a line.

yr V.W.

Texas

3263: To Margaret Keynes   52 *Tavistock Square, W.C.1.*

20th June 1937

Dear Margaret,[4]

It was very nice of you to write. It's so seldom any letter about one's books gives one pleasure but yours did; for one thing you liked some of the same people (in the book [*The Years*]) that I liked. Sally, for instance. I expect you're right about North—only the end had to be screwed up and he had to take more emotion than his share, by way of a finish. I thought it a complete failure when I'd done: it's a marvel to me that you find it not mere old wives gossip: I was very excited when I wrote it, I remember—only it was too long

1. This dinner party included Saxon Sydney-Turner (1880-1962), a brilliant, if eccentric and taciturn, member of Old Bloomsbury, who spent his career in the Treasury; Rosemary Beresford, who was an undergraduate at Cambridge; and an unidentified Finnish girl, who could hardly speak English. Plomer was absent, and the party was not a success. Miss Beresford's father, J. Beresford, edited the diaries of the 18th-century country parson, James Woodforde.

2. Anthony Butts, the painter, was one of Plomer's most intimate friends. They had travelled widely together and shared a house in London. Butt's sister Mary was a writer of fiction and autobiography. She had died on 5 March 1937 at the age of 44.

3. Wogan Philipps (b. 1902) was a painter and farmer. He married the novelist Rosamond Lehmann in 1928, and succeeded his father as 2nd Lord Milford in 1962. At this period he was driving an ambulance in Spain, where he was wounded.

4. Margaret (*née* Darwin) had married Geoffrey Keynes, Maynard's brother, in 1917.

and I was ill, and I couldn't pull it together. And oh, what a grind it was, cutting out, and trying to make a whole of it. But now your letter is a consolation.

I wonder if you've heard how Maynard is. Lydia only says he is going on well—but what the matter is, we don't know; or how long it is likely to take.

If you were ever free of an afternoon and would come in and have an old crone's chat over the tea cups, it would be a great pleasure. But I suspect you've no time—London is a bear garden. I often think of an evening in your garden, with the river and Rupert [Brooke], and you said the poplars were like ghosts. It was then I stole your book.

Yours ever,
Virginia Woolf

Your letter went to Rodmell and got stuck, unseen, under a bedroom door, hence the delay.

Sussex

3264: To Janet Case

Monk's House, Rodmell,
Lewes, Sussex

June 26th [1937]

Dearest Janet,

This is by way of continuing our conversation, and needs no answer—unless some day Emphie would write 2 words, to say how you are, on a postcard.

I have had no more experiences in the great world, unless sitting behind the Duchess of Atholl on the platform at the Albert Hall 2 nights ago can count. Oh what a bore those meetings are![1] We sat for 3 hours behind the Duchess and talked about Spain—I mean we listened; and they talked, but into megaphones, or microphones, so that not a word came singly but in a kind of double division to us behind. However, by hook or crook, really by means of a fat emotional woman in black velvet called Isabel Brown they collected £1500 for the Basque children.

That is the way London carries on. The nicest person I have seen lately has been my own niece, Ann—Adrian's daughter, the one learning to be a medical student at Newnham, a great big creature, like the figure head of an old sailing ship—shall we say the Aurora Matilda. She turned up with

1. The purpose of the meeting was to raise money for the support of the Basque children who had fled to England from Franco's forces in northern Spain. Among the speakers was Katharine, the Duchess of Atholl (1874-1960), Conservative Member of Parliament for Kinross and West Perth, 1923-38, and an articulate opponent of Franco and her own party's policy of appeasing the dictators.

Richard Ll. Davies,[1] and indeed they seem to be inseparable, but that dont mean marriage, as in our day. Is he nice? Is he good enough to marry my niece—should he want to? You see how family proud and exacting age makes me. But I was so pleased to be asked to supper in his lodgings—next week. How one prefers the invitations of the young to all the glories of the world— should they come our way. I'll write and tell you what Richard's supper in Brunswick Sqre. is like. It was in Brunswick Sqre. 24 [25] years ago that I became engaged.

Now Leonard can be heard through the open window clipping the yew hedge. Did I tell you we are gradually carving a recumbent peacock—year by year—now his tail, now his neck? But I wonder if you are back in your window looking at your garden and how you feel, and if you are more comfortable as I hope. Now I must go and pick a leaf full of strawberries for our dinner, which will otherwise consist of cold ham. Love to both Janet and Emphie, and I wish you were here to eat it with us.

V.

Sussex

3265: TO LADY OTTOLINE MORRELL   *Monk's House, Rodmell*
                                   [Sussex]
June 27th [1937]

Dearest Ottoline,
     That is very bad news—that you've been so ill.[2] I hadn't heard. When you last wrote you said you were going to Tonbridge Wells, only for a rest I hoped. Please dont wave your adieu just yet. I can assure you the world requires the presence of your golden wing, not its vanishing. But now all thats over, I hope; and we can owl for a moment—its as dark as midnight at the moment, with a storm coming up over Caburn.
     It was very stormy in France—otherwise perhaps it would have been too perfect. We roamed about in the Dordogne valley—Souillac, Sarlat, Treysac —do you know these little towns, on the river, near Cahors and Perigueux, but almost lost; no tourists; the loveliest farms, old houses that Montaigne's friends lived in and are now lived in by shoemakers—but I wont describe— England seems like a chocolate box bursting with trippers afterward. As for London, from which we've escaped this week end, I cant describe its horror— fascination too, since people are so odd—but how they swarm, and what a

1. A nephew of the Woolfs' old friend Margaret Llewelyn Davies. In 1937 he was aged 24. He married Ann Stephen, Virginia's niece, in 1938. His career was in architecture and urban planning, and he was created a life peer in 1964.
2. Ottoline had suffered a stroke and was now recovering at Dr Cameron's Tunbridge Wells Clinic, where she was also found to have heart disease.

din they keep up. If I had any sense I should only see the ones I like, but I lose my head, and in consequence see the ones I dont like.

Anyhow you are spared that. And illness is a very sublime state, if one can read; I'm so glad you liked my little Gibbon; I'm doing Congreve now.[1] If you want sheer joy read him; if you dont want anything so ecstatic, but broad and mellow and satisfactory, try the Memoires of George Sand. 10 little volumes; I'm in the 5th, and find it absorbing: We went to Nohant and saw her Chateau, her pens and desk and bed, all as she left them—the very wallpapers, and the table set for Flaubert and Chopins spinet and the little theatre where they acted, with Maurices [her son] dolls in a cupboard.

I must now pick a dish of raspberries for dinner, and cease to try your eyes. But if Philip [Morrell] some day would send a card to say how you are —no, I daresay he's too busy. Our love to you. L. is clipping his hedge.

V.W.

Texas

3266: To Ethyl Smyth   [52 *Tavistock Square, W.C.*1]
28th June [1937]

Just back from Rodmell.

1. Re St John article.[2] You told me it was a masterpiece from the point of view of style, and critical insight. It was thus that I judged it—not as a miraculously tactful statement of a point of view about which I can know nothing. I still maintain that I'm right in what I said from the only view point accessible to me.

2. L. goes every afternoon at 5, when he is free from other work, to Alexander. Thus he sees no chance of discussing him verbally with you— But should you wish him to ask any questions, he would willingly do so. I think theres no longer any doubt but that he's on the right track with L. He can hold a cup steady in one hand—more than he's done since 6 yrs. old. Alexander says he is certain of a cure: but wants him to cram in daily visits if possible.

Yes; I'm sorry about William[3]—Our last meeting was on the deck of the Dreadnought in 1910, I think; but I wore a beard. And I'm afraid he took it

1. Virginia was reading *Love for Love*, a comedy by William Congreve, produced in 1695. Her article (*T.L.S.*, 25 September 1937) was entitled *Congreve's Comedies: Speed, Stillness and Meaning*, and was reprinted in *The Moment*, 1947.
2. See p. 136, note 5.
3. Admiral Sir William Fisher, Virginia's cousin, died on 24 June. He was Commander-in-Chief of the Mediterranean Fleet, 1932-6. For the Dreadnought hoax, see p. 17, note 1.

to heart a good deal—so I've heard. So hot—so hot—and dining out; and must wash.

No I dont think 130,000 [*Maurice Baring*] a word too much—why, how can one enter into a mind in less? And we used to call William The Admiral when he was a Midshipman and made us a boat with a paddle that worked

V.

Berg

3267: To Elinor Castle Nef   52 *Tavistock Square, W.C.*1

Tuesday [6 July 1937]

Dear Mrs Nef,[1]

I have a message for you from my sister—that is, she has 2 or 3 sketches for the Q. Mary picture;[2] and will send them round to the hotel on Thursday, with prices attached. If you want to buy one, do: if not, dont, and send them back to her at 8 Fitzroy Street W.1. Telephone: 5596 Museum.

It was very nice seeing you and Mr Nef yesterday, and your flowers are still alive, and thank you for conveying Lady Colefax across London in yr. vast car.

Yours sincerely
Virginia Woolf

University of Chicago Library

3268: To Elinor Castle Nef   52 *Tavistock Square, W.C.*1

Postcard
[7 July 1937]

My sister also wanted me to tell you, but I forgot, that there is an exhibition [*Contemporary British Artists*] at Agnews in Bond Street which she thinks might interest you, of pictures by young artists: also old ones; chosen by Duncan Grant and Keith Baynes[3] and herself.

Please forgive this scrawl.

Virginia Woolf

University of Chicago Library

1. Virginia had first met John Ulric Nef (b. 1899) and his wife Elinor (d. 1953) in 1933. He was on the faculty of the University of Chicago, and later founded the Centre for Human Understanding. He was the author of many books bridging several disciplines. His wife had literary pretensions, but never published anything in her lifetime.
2. See p. 20, note 3.
3. A member of the London Group of painters, which also included Vanessa, Duncan, and Roger Fry. He was born in 1887 and died in 1977.

7th July [1937]

Dearest Janet,

But I never meant you to trouble to answer my letter—it was only by way of conversation—as this is: a gossip, when I would like to be on the chair by your side. By the way, if you ever would like to see me you've only to say: a days trip to the New Forest, and five minutes with you, and a sight of Emphie would be the greatest treat to me. And Emphie has only to say so with one word on a card.

Oh high life—thats what you like; and I wish I could provide you with anything higher in that line than Lady Colefax who came to tea yesterday and drove Leonard frantic because he says she's a damned snob; and there were 2 Americans [the Nefs] here, and until she had placed them, fairly high, rather rich, she wouldn't be decently polite. But then considering she has climbed from Onslow Gardens to Buckingham Palace—used to have the King to dine, let alone V.W.—how can I object? This little anecdote shows what a stew and a rush London in July is—we shovel them all into a black hole day: I buy a cake; find a pair of silk stockings; and L. comes in for all the world like a real English gentleman with his hand outstretched.

But today I've been so happy—rambling through Regents Park; and seeing Hampstead trees at the end of the Adelaide Road and thinking of Janet up at Windmill Hill. D'you know you see Hampstead from Gower Street? And now, six o'clock, what did I promise? To go to the Stracheys in Gordon Square and meet the great painter Matisse over a cocktail.[1] I cant abide celebrities and cocktails. So I say to myself, I would rather write to Janet. Let Matisse go hang. But he's the great god of the young; only so vain, so respectable, so slow, I'm told, in his wits that the entertainment is a horrid burden. He's over about a show of his pictures.

Leonard is at the Labour Party. And our maid is out. I wish it were 20 years ago and I could push through the garden gate and see you at the window. Richard [Llewelyn Davies] is a nice boy—he had bought us sardines, and he and Ann [Stephen] cooked a chicken and the asparagus was, by mistake, fried. But I liked them—with their canoe in a bag, about to float down the Rhone. What a life the young lead! No bother about engagement rings. Now dont answer, but let me write again.

Love V.

Sussex

---

1. Henri Matisse, 1869-1954. Dorothy Bussy (*née* Strachey) and her husband, the French painter Simon Bussy, were giving the party, but Virginia did not attend it.

Postcard
Thursday [8 July 1937]

I'm so sorry everything went wrong, but July in London is impossible.
However, the Whipsnade book[1] was beyond praise. On the other side are
the flowers I picked and was standing in—at Rodmell.[2]

V.W.

Berg

3271: To T. S. Eliot   52 *Tavistock Square, W.C.1.*

11th July [1937]

My dear Tom,
　　You would have met me at the Kettledrum if it hadn't been for some of
your compatriots—quondam I suppose you call them: do you know the Nefs
of Chicago and the Sartons of Boston? Well, dont then.
　　As for coming here, its high time you did. We suggest Sunday 25th at
4.30, since that seems the only hour to be slipped in between your activities
and our going to Rodmell. But, why shouldnt you come there this summer?
Or is every week end devoted to the Knights drains?[3] However, come on
Sunday 25th and we will have out our engagement books and try to rescue a
night from chaos. I didnt mean to make a pun; thats what comes of writing
to a poet.

yr aff
VW

Mrs T. S. Eliot

3272: To Margaret Llewelyn Davies

52 *Tavistock Square, W.C.1.*

July 11th [1937]

Dearest Margaret,
　　Yes. I know it must be very near. I heard from Janet herself only a few
days ago—not that she said anything about herself, but Emphie wrote too.
I felt when we went to see them, just after Easter, what you say—that one

1. A guide book to Whipsnade Zoo in the Chiltern Hills, where May Sarton was
   living in a flat lent her by Julian Huxley, Secretary of the Zoological Society.
2. The reverse of the card showed part of the Monk's House garden, with statues
   and a formal flower bed.
3. Eliot had been visiting Sir Bruce Richmond at Netherhampton, Salisbury, and
   had written to Virginia about 'his imperfect drainage' (8 July 1937, *Berg*).

was grateful to them both, for being as they were. And no one, not Leonard even, knows how much I have to thank Janet for.

I will try to write something about her, I dont know how one is to convey her peculiar charm. Still, if you think Emphie would like it, I will see if I can say something.[1]

We are both well—Leonard is going to a dr. [Alexander] whom Bernard Shaw discovered, and is—so we think—becoming cured of his trembling hand. Isn't that a miracle?

Our love to you both [M.Ll.D. and Lilian Harris]. We would like to come and see you very much—perhaps one day this summer, when we're at Rodmell.

I suppose there's nothing at all one can do for Emphie? You would tell me if there were—

yr Virginia

Sussex

3273: To Philippa Strachey   52 *Tavistock Square, W.C.1.*

Tuesday [13 July 1937]

My dear Pippa,

Yes my blood boils. Not a word could I find in any paper—however, I was glad to read your letter in the Spectator. But what a narrow shave![2]

I wish I could have had the volcano, or geyser or whatever you call it over me at Dorothy's;[3] but we've been so afflicted with Mr Mrs Nef of Chicago, and Miss Sarton of Boston, and Saxons Finns from, I suppose, Finland that by the time Wednesday came, my lips refused to function. But I'd much rather have seen you and Pernel, whom I never see, whom I heard was there, than the Finns and the Yanks and the Swedes. May we meet in a better world—perhaps the library in Marsham Street[4] over a cup of tea.

Yes Miss Douie was very prompt and to the point

Yr
Virginia

1. Janet Case died on 15 July, and Virginia's obituary, in which she calls Janet 'a noble Athena', appeared in *The Times* on 22 July.
2. On 9 July Pippa Strachey had written to the *Spectator* complaining that the press had not covered the parliamentary debate on the Contributory Pensions Bill, which unfairly distinguished between men's and women's pensions. The Bill was passed by only eight votes.
3. Virginia is referring to the party for Henri Matisse given by Dorothy Bussy on 7 July.
4. Virginia was a great supporter of the library at 29 Marsham Street, founded by the London National Society for Women's Service, of which Philippa Strachey was Secretary. Vera Douie was its Librarian, 1926-67.

By the way, do tell Pernel about Leonards man, Alexander. He swears he can cure asthma, and as last night we dined out and Leonard could drink coffee for the first time since I've known him without shaking, its clear he is curing him.

Strachey Trust

3274: To S. S. KOTELIANSKY   52 *Tavistock Square, W.C.1.*

Monday [19 July 1937]

Dear Kot,[1]

I have been away or I would have written before. This is our last week before going away, so it is very crowded. The only time possible for us both seems to be next Sunday 25th at 4.30. Would you come then? I think Tom Eliot, but no one else is coming. Then I could give you your book. But I'll send it if you cant come. However, I hope we may see you; which would be a pleasure. Yes, isn't it odd, that the Americans should like the Years?

yrs ever
Virginia Woolf

British Library

3275: To V. SACKVILLE-WEST   [52 *Tavistock Square, W.C.1*]

Wednesday [21 July 1937]

Dearest Creature

I wired to you because Julian was killed yesterday in Spain.[2] Nessa likes to have me and so I'm round there most of the time. It is very terrible. You will understand

V.

Leonard says if you could look in between 2.30 and 3 tomorrow he cd discuss the jackets [for *Pepita*]

Berg

1. Samuel Koteliansky (1882-1955) was an émigré from the Ukraine, who had several friends in Bloomsbury and collaborated with Virginia on translations from the Russian in the early 1920s.
2. Julian Bell went to Spain on 7 June as one of a team of ambulance drivers. He was attached to a British medical unit based on the Palace of the Escorial for the big Republican offensive to cut the supply route of the Nationalist forces encircling Madrid. Having survived great dangers, Julian was mortally wounded by a shell on 18 July outside the village of Villanueva de la Canada, and died a few hours later in the dressing station at the Escorial. He was 29 years old. (See Peter Stansky and William Abrahams, *Journey to the Frontier*, 1966.)

3276: To Ethel Smyth   52 *Tavistock Square, W.C.*1.

Thursday [22 July 1937]

Ethel dear Julian has been killed in Spain. Perhaps you saw this. I am with Nessa as much as possible, and we shall try to get her down to Charleston on Sunday if we can. It is very terrible: you'll understand.

                                                                    Yr V.

Berg

3277: To T. S. Eliot   52 *Tavistock Square, W.C.*1.

23rd July [1937]

My dear Tom,
    As you may have seen, Julian has been killed in Spain. I am with Vanessa as much as possible, and if she is able, we may go down to Charleston on Sunday. So we must put you off—but I'll write later and hope to see you. I know you will understand.

                                                                    yr aff
                                                                    V.

Mrs T. S. Eliot

3278: To S. S. Koteliansky   52 *Tavistock Square, W.C.*1.

23rd July [1937]

Dear Kot,
    As you may have seen, Julian Bell has been killed in Spain. I am with Vanessa as much as possible, and if she is able, we shall try to go down to Sussex on Sunday. So I must put you off. But hope to see you later. I know you will understand this.

                                                                    yr Virginia

British Library

3279: To Saxon Sydney-Turner   52 *Tavistock Square, W.C.*1.

[23 July 1937]

Dear Saxon,
    Would you thank Barbara.¹ Of course we would let her know if she

1. Barbara Bagenal, *née* Hiles (b. 1891) had been the first assistant at the Hogarth Press in 1917-18, and married Nicholas Bagenal in 1918 when Saxon Sydney-Turner was also much in love with her. He remained her intimate friend for the rest of his life.

could do anything. Angelica is acting every day till Monday and then we hope to take Nessa down to Charleston and A. would come too. She is a great help to Nessa.

Nessa seems rather better today. She is keeping quiet in bed, as the shock was terrible, but the effect is less today and she has taken food better. I will tell her what Barbara says.

V.

Sussex

3280: To Philip Morrell   52 *Tavistock Sqre.* [*W.C.*1.]

Friday [23 July 1937]

My dear Philip,

I was just going to write and thank you for your letter when we got this terrible news about Julian. I'm sitting with Vanessa most of the time, so I wont try to answer now. Only I'm so glad Ottoline is better. I know she'll understand what this means. Vanessa is still very exhausted and in bed, but rather better today and it is on the whole a relief to her to know at last how it happened. It was in The Times today.[1] Thank you for writing: I am always grateful to you and Ottoline

yr aff
V.W.

Texas

3281: To Margaret Llewelyn Davies
                                52 *Tavistock Square, W.C.*1.

Sunday 25 July [1937]

Dearest Margaret,

Thank you for your letter. I know you understand. It is so terrible to see what the suffering is; but she is wonderful. I told her you had written. We always think of Theodore and Thoby together, and now there is Julian too.[2]

She has been ill with the shock, and is still in bed, but better, and I spend the day with her, so have no time to write. But would you thank Mrs

1. *The Times* account gave these details: Julian Bell "died during the offensive on Brunete. He was in one of the British ambulances when it was hit by an insurgent bomb. The ambulance was badly damaged and a fragment of the bomb entered Mr Bell's lung. He died in hospital 8 hours later."
2. All three died as young men. Margaret's brother Theodore was drowned in 1905 at the age of 35, and Virginia's brother Thoby died of typhoid in 1906 at the age of 26.

[Rosalind] Nash for her letter. It was a great pleasure to think you and she liked what I said of Janet [Case].

Love from us both.

yr Virginia

Sussex

3282: TO MAYNARD KEYNES   52 *Tavistock Square, W.C.1*

Sunday [25 July 1937]

Dearest Maynard,

I thought I would tell you that Vanessa liked your letter. It said so beautifully what she had wanted someone to say. So thank you. Its been so terrible—now that she knows how it happened, the worst suspense is over. She's still in bed, and very weak. The strain ever since he went [to Spain] has been so great. But yesterday she slept without a sleeping draught, and tried to do some embroidery. I think now she only wants to go to Charleston—perhaps on Tuesday. I spend the day with her, and wanted to tell you your letter had been a comfort to us. Love to Lydia: and get well.

Yrs
Virginia

King's

3283: TO ROSAMOND LEHMANN   52 *Tavistock Square, W.C.1.*

Sunday [25 July 1937]

My dear Rosamond,

It was good of you to write. I gave Vanessa your letter, and she liked it and wanted me to thank you.[1]

No, there's nothing to be said. We've been through so much together, but this is the worst, except that she is always more wonderful.

Since she heard how it happened, from the Times, the worst suspense is over. She is better now, but still in bed. The strain before was very great. But if possible we shall go down to Charleston one day this week.

Will you tell Wogan [Philipps, her husband] I minded telling him like that in the street, but couldn't do anything else—he'll understand. I think she would like to see him some time. I'm just going round there.

1. Rosamond Lehmann had written to Virginia about Vanessa, "Does it help her to know he did what he wanted to do?" (23 July 1937, *Sussex*).

Yes, dear Rosamond, it does help, your understanding.

yr aff
V.W.

She likes to hear anything people say about him.

King's

3284: TO W. A. ROBSON   52 *Tavistock Square, W.C.*1.

26th July [1937]

Dear Willy,[1]

    I wanted to thank you today for your letter, but I couldnt. It was very good of you to write: I showed Vanessa your letter and she liked it, and wanted me to thank you. At the moment the private sorrow is so great one cant get anything clear in one's mind. He was a great joy to us; her children are like my own. But it had become necessary for him to go; and there is a kind of grandeur in that which somehow now and then consoles one. Only— to see what she has to suffer makes one doubt if anything in the world is worth it.

    Excuse this scrawl. Vanessa is still in bed, and everything has been so confused that I have not yet answered letters.

    Will you thank Juliette[2] from me, and say that I insist upon being Virginia, unless I am to call you Professor Robson. It was very good of her to write.

yr ever
Virginia Woolf

Sussex

3285: TO V. SACKVILLE-WEST   52 *Tavistock Square, W.C.*1.

[26? July 1937]

Dearest Creature,

    I was very glad of your letter. I couldnt write, as I've been round with Vanessa all day. It has been an incredible nightmare. We had both been certain he would be killed, and the strain on her is now, perhaps mercifully, making her so exhausted she can only stay in bed. But I think we shall drive her down to Charleston on Thursday.

    Lord, why do these things happen? I'm not clear enough in the head to feel anything but varieties of dull anger and despair. He had every sort of

1. See p. 131, note 2.
2. Juliette Alvin, the cellist, who married W. A. Robson in 1929.

gift—above everything vitality and enjoyment.[1] Why must he get set on going to Spain?—But it was useless to argue. And his feelings were so mixed. I mean, interest in war, and conviction, and a longing to be in the thick of things. He was the first of Nessa babies, and I cant describe how close and real and always alive our relation was. As for Nessa—but as I say I'm so stupid what with ordering the char to buy mutton, and generally doing odd jobs I cant think, or as you see write—so forgive this egotism. *Shall* you come over to M.H. one day? I should like to see you. And dear old Clive,—he is such a pathetic, and always honest, man. cracking his jokes. to try and make us all laugh—wh. I admire

Yr V.

Berg

1. Virginia analysed her feelings for Julian and his reasons for going to Spain in a memoir dated 30 July 1937. It is printed by Quentin Bell as an appendix to Volume II of *Virginia Woolf.*

Letters 3286-3321 (August–October 1937)

From late July until 10 October the Woolfs were at Monk's House, from where Virginia visited Charleston several times a week. As Vanessa wrote to Vita, Virginia's company was her major consolation for Julian's death, but her recovery from the shock was slow. Together they planned a volume of Julian's essays, letters and poems, published in 1938. Virginia found that she could do little work herself (mainly an essay on Congreve, which took her several weeks), but in August she resumed Three Guineas *and her reading for* Roger Fry, *and went on two daytime expeditions, to visit Margaret Llewelyn Davies at Dorking and the Nicolsons at Sissinghurst. Among the visitors to Monk's House were T. S. Eliot, William Plomer and the Stephen sisters.*

3286: To Vanessa Bell   [*Monk's House, Rodmell, Sussex*]

Tuesday [3 August 1937]

This is only to say that I'm coming over to tea tomorrow, which is Wednesday, unless you stop me—unless that is, you've had enough of your singe,[1] who adores you, and cant stay away from you. I find there are all sorts of trains and omnibuses and possible combinations, so that I can trot on my own toes.

Its a hazy hot day here; Leonard has been clipping his yews; I have been maundering over the downs, and trying to write Congreve, and theres not much village news, save that Louie [Everest] went in a boat yesterday for the first time in her life. How, being a mother at 14, she preserves this innocence of all other adventures I dont know. Then her friend, the Welshwoman, Mrs Polock, came to help in the house, and looks like the most sophisticated Bloomsbury Bunny,[2] only more competent. There's no doubt civilisation is beginning at the bottom, so that we shall all be overtaken, before long. No letters yet, but then thats Bank holiday; and Leonard is glad, because he can write his book,[3] but I like opening a letter, and thinking myself loved. I've written to Margery [Fry] to tell her to find more articles, and we'll bring

1. *Singe*, 'Ape', one of Virginia's childhood nicknames.
2. 'Bloomsbury Bunny', a phrase invented by Molly MacCarthy in 1917 for Carrington, Dorothy Brett and Barbara Hiles, who attended the Slade School of Art and wore their hair cropped short.
3. *After the Deluge*, Volume II.

them when we go up on Tuesday. I wonder if you've dipped into Helen's [Anrep] box. Monks House is like a green cave, no light to eat by in the dining room, so we dine in the kitchen: this comes of the romantic profusion of our Vine, which blocks all the windows. You'd say it was natural to Wolves—this dim leafage; and now I must stop chattering to my darling dolphin and go to the post, and hope for a letter and then play bowls, and then put the kettle on; but all the time adoring my lovely dolphin, and longing to see her.

B.

Berg

3287: To Vanessa Bell

Monks House [Rodmell, Sussex]

Thursday [5 August 1937]

This is only your Singe's morning kiss, and to enclose these letters. We can discuss Tom's this afternoon[1]—I mean tomorrow—when I shall turn up for tea.

I rather resented the presence of the spruce Jewess [Janice Loeb] yesterday, though there's no harm to her, and she only wants a ball of wool to turn her into a kitten. No, you'll say, she's not a patch on John Ruskin. We raced them as far as the halt, and Leonard then passed them, in sheer bravado; and I didn't altogether envy Clive boxed up for a month in that black beetle with that mild mixture. But I suppose there's no accounting for tastes, and the great thing is to have tastes.

I spent the evening binding my George Sand in Angelica's papers, which must be exactly what she wore the first time she met Chopin, so its most suitable; and conveys all the romance of Venice in the 30ties whenever I come into the room.

Otherwise the world of Rodmell is peaceful—roasting hot in my Lodge,[2] even with all the windows open, and the Downs are turning the colour of lions opposite. I wish dolphin were by my side, in a bath, bright blue, with her tail curled. But then I've been always in love with her since I was a green eyed brat under the nursery table, and so shall remain in my extreme senility.

Leonard has filled the house with oak logs bought off an old man with a waggon—they smelt of the essence of wood; and all the lilies are in the diningroom too; so it goes to the head like wine, and thus excuses poor Singes drivel, which is only by way of a morning kiss—dearest love, how I adore you

B

Berg

1. See Letter 3289.
2. The hut in the garden at Monk's House where Virginia normally wrote during the summer.

Monks House [Rodmell, Sussex]

5th Aug [1937]

No we only got down here last week end. Nessa was too done up to come before, and we wanted to drive her. And as you may suppose—damn the hair on the pen—I cant collect my wits to write a letter—cant get things into the right focus. So dont expect sympathy or understanding. I expect this sort of thing is fearfully bad for the character; I'm feeling wooden yet enraged. Most afternoons I go over to Charleston, one way or another, which takes most of the time, after the morning I mean, when I try to work. Next week I expect Nessa will begin painting; at the moment, someone coming is a distraction—all one can do.

Is it hot at Woking? Are you at Woking? I seem to have dropped out—cant remember where anyone is at the moment. And that reminds me—an intelligent girl, [Katherine John] writing a life of the Prince Imperial pesters me to meet you. I lent her your masterpiece on the Empress.[1] But shant tell her either to write to you or to ask to see you unless you say she may. And God knows why you should. Is the MB. [*Maurice Baring*] settled? When will it come out? And what line does he take?

Yr V.

Berg

3289: To T. S. Eliot   *Monk's House, Rodmell, Lewes, Sussex*

Typewritten
7th August [1937]

My dear Tom,

I showed Vanessa your letter, as I knew she was anxious to hear. She thanks you very much, and would I am sure like it if you would write to her some time yourself about Julian's essays. She is at Charleston, Firle, Lewes; —a good deal better, but still weak from the shock; and not able yet to work. She wants us to read the essays, only one of which, the Roger Fry letter, we have seen. Would you therefore tell whoever has them to forward them to me here as soon as convenient? Of course we would publish them ourselves,

---

1. The Empress Eugénie, wife of Napoleon III, had become in her widowhood a great friend of Ethel Smyth, who wrote about her extensively in *Streaks of Life*, 1921. Her son, the Prince Imperial, was killed fighting for the British in the Zulu War of 1879. *The Prince Imperial*, by Katherine John, was published in 1939.

but we feel rather that it would be better for someone outside the family to do it. But that can wait till we have read them.[1]

Yes, do come down. We shall be here till October save for an occasional day here and there. What week end would suit you? So far the only one engaged is the second in September. Therefore would you come the first week end or the third or late in August? I know Vanessa would very much like to see you, and so should we.

Grilling hot here; Leonard is yew clipping, I am drowsing over a book.

Yours affectionate
Virginia

Mrs T. S. Eliot

3290: To Vanessa Bell   [*Monk's House, Rodmell, Sussex*]

Sunday [8 August 1937]

This is only a nightjar's chuckle—that is to say, Could we come and dine with you on Tuesday?—That is to say if we're bringing Angelica back. Then I could leave some more papers on you—not that I've heard from Margery—still there may be some odds and ends; and I long—oh why are you the only person I never see enough of?—to see you again. Yesterday was such a medley—we thought we were free to bask in naked heat, when in stumped Mabel [cook at Tavistock Square], bored with Lewes races, as red as a tomato, as stuffed as a sofa, but she says she eats only cheese and junket, living in lodgings with Mr Sanford at Brighton. It occurred to me that she might do for you, failing the other woman for a fortnight. But this I could settle later. Then, no sooner had I given her some apples, during which I left the door open and Mitz escaped, and L. said Thats the last we shall ever see of her—not a bit of it—there she was on the kitchen table, nibbling a lettuce—Then, I say, as we recovered, a car stopped, out dashed John Graham,[2] in shorts, very personable, but condemned, by nature and fate, to be a schoolmaster at Hampstead. Not but what he has leanings to intellect. I have promised to go and disinter the iron age [camp] with him on Caburn. —Wont you come too! And he stayed, bowling with L. till dinner; and then at last we dined. This is a rigmarole: I ought to be tidying the drawing room, fetching the ice for the butter, and doing my hair, for L. will soon be back from Worthing with a cartload of very old blind ladies, one of whom was a

1. T. S. Eliot had been considering (on behalf of Faber & Faber to whom he acted as a literary adviser) the publication of some of Julian's essays, among them his 'letter' about Roger Fry, which the Hogarth Press had rejected. The essays, together with some of his poems and personal letters, were edited by Quentin Bell and published by the Hogarth Press in November 1938.
2. See Letter 3198.

hospital Nurse at Cannes and married his Uncle solely for the sake of his military bearing, for he was a bad lot, and she a complete ambient waxwork—like Traill,[1] only stupider, duller, and more entirely obtuse. Happily Q and A will I hope descend. So thats all my lovely Dolphin: let me know about Tuesday,—if that is you *dont* want us—wh. may well be—and if I can fetch anything in London for you.

B

If I dont hear, we'll bring A back and dine on Tuesday If I can I'll come over tomorrow to tea.

Berg

3291: To Vanessa Bell   [*Monk's House, Rodmell, Sussex*]

[August 1937]

Yes, I'll come tomorrow to tea, my own darling creature. You shant be rid of me for long. In fact I cant bear not seeing you. Heres the other lot of [Roger Fry] letters and 2 books that may amuse you. We've been bowling and its so late they must go. How have you slept. Bruce Richmond says a man called Lowndes in the office wrote the thing in the Times. Love from us, darling. Oh and Louie wanted to make you a loaf!

Berg

3292: To Vanessa Bell   *Monks House* [*Rodmell, Sussex*]

Thursday [12 August 1937]

I'm coming to tea tomorrow, Friday, as then Quentin will be able to drive me back. I wired to Judith [Stephen] to say you couldnt have Adrian, nor we Judith this week end; but would they come next week end. I wonder if you've heard from the [Charles] Maurons. I rather hope nobody will come this week end, since it means dolphin standing on her tail, and I think she ought to curl in a basket another week at least. This morning Faber at last sent Julian's essays.[2] I'll bring them tomorrow. And Ozzie Dickinson[3] wrote to say old Violet has fallen on a mat, broken her thigh, is in a nursing home, in plaster

1. Miss Traill was nurse to Leslie Stephen when he was dying in 1904, and later that year to Virginia when she was recovering from her mental breakdown. Leonard's aunt was called Ada.
2. See p. 155, note 1.
3. The brother of Violet Dickinson. He was at first a barrister and later Secretary to the Commissioners in Lunacy.

of Paris, and will I write to her and cheer her up. What human beings are to be sure! How can I cheer up Violet after a 20 years silence? One's jokes grow old. And he says she may never walk again. And I suppose shes 75 [72] at least. Then I had a cable from America, asking for a story—to which I replied, as you bade me, only if money is paid beforehand;[1] so I wait the result, but expect nothing'll come of it: and then you will be responsible. But I'm sure you're right all the same. And a great branch in the churchyard is cracked and hangs over our fruit. L. is at this moment writing to tell Mr Ebbs [Rector of Rodmell] that he must cut it. As its pendant, 100 feet (or so) high, how can a clergyman cut it? But as Mrs. Ebbs told us to mend our wall, they must cut the tree. I wish I were having tea with you: but you wdn't want me twice running I suppose. My love has always been fuller than your thimble. Heres an enclosure for Angelica. I'll subscribe for her if she likes. And the silk has come—a lovely evening beach colour, I mean the wet sand on a green evening. If Q. could take away the arm chair on Friday I wd. give it him: only its prodigious: solid however, and stuffed. How are you my loveliest of dolphins? Do you sleep?

B

Ethel Smyth threatens a visit

Berg

3293: To Violet Dickinson   *Monk's House, Rodmell,*
                                             Lewes, Sussex

13th Aug. 37

My Violet,

I was miserable to hear that you had fallen down and broken your leg. I only heard it two days ago, or I'd have written before. Not that unfortunately a letter will heal it. Still a little conversation would be a pleasure, to me: if I could only remember the names of flowers, and what Leonard is proud of this summer, it would be like one of old Miss Jekyll's[2] letters, minus the common sense.

We are safe in our garden, and its the most I can do to get Leonard to leave it. Can you make Ozzie walk? Thats the only relic I have left from my father. I still tramp off for 2 hours daily. Only he would have gone a whole

---

1. Virginia had been offered £200 to write a 1,500-word story for *Harper's Bazaar*. She wrote *The Duchess and the Jeweller*, which was published in the issue of April 1938.
2. Gertrude Jekyll (1843-1932), who is best remembered for the gardens she created with the architect Edwin Lutyens. Some of her letters were published in *Gertrude Jekyll: A Memoir* (1934) by Francis Jekyll.

day with a tin box of sandwiches, carefully packed by my mother. Is it a sign of age that I find myself thinking of St Ives [Cornwall] every summer?

Where did you spend your childhood? When did you begin to grow? And what did they say when you passed the 6 foot?[1] Am I right in saying that to be 6 ft tall in the Age of Q. Victoria was equivalent to having an illegitimate child?

I wish, now that you're stretched out, you would scribble me your memoirs—not necessarily for publication, as they say, but as a guarantee of old affection. Ethel Smyth wrote hers at my request: yours would, I swear, be much less egotistical. Please consider it. How you could describe the Duckworths, the Stephens, let alone the Thynnes [Lord Bath's daughters], and the ancient nobility of England! Do they all flock to your bedside? Coronets and garlands are strewn about you I'm sure. They always filled the hall in Manchester Street.[2] I wish you would do for my lovely niece Angelica what you did for her Aunt. She's lovelier far, and far quicker witted and more commonsensical than I ever was.

But I mustn't begin family praises. Dont try to answer. This is only a scrap and a scrawl with both our love:

Sp.

Sussex

3294: TO VANESSA BELL   *Monks House [Rodmell,*
                                          Sussex]
Tuesday [17 August 1937]

Quentin has just rung up; so I suppose the great muddle is more or less solved: And this is only by way of Singe's morning kiss. Helen [Anrep] wrote by the way to say if you dont like the hammock, it is to be given to me. So say you do like the hammock, because one telescope is enough for me.[3] There have been no great adventures to speak of, save that the Bridge[4] was open last night as we came through, in a storm of rain, a sailing ship passing, and all very romantic, and as usual I thought of you. Do you think we have the same pair of eyes, only different spectacles? I rather think I'm more nearly attached to you than sisters should be. Why is it I never stop thinking of you, even when walking in the marsh this afternoon and seeing a great snake like a sea serpent gliding among the grass? You were right about the American

1. Violet was 6 ft. 2 in. tall.
2. Violet's former London house.
3. Virginia had just been given a telescope by Elizabeth Williamson, Ethel's great-niece, who taught astronomy at London University. She didn't want to be 'telescoped' by a hammock.
4. Over the River Ouse between Itford and Southease.

magazine: they now say they will take my story if I wire a suitable synopsis —which is a sketch of the plot; so I've made up a story about a jeweller and a duchess, and cabled the plot—how he buys her pearls, for £10,000, knowing them to be false—thats not all of it by any means. Do you think, knowing the Americans as you do, that this will fetch them?[1] It means £200 if it does. I'm completely stuck on my war pamphlet [*Three Guineas*], so I may as well write about Duchesses. I'm always wanting to argue it with Julian—in fact I wrote it as an argument with him. Somehow he stirred me up to argue—I wish I'd got his essays to read—they might give me some ideas. I suppose Charles [Mauron] will discuss them with you; and I shant see you alone for ever so long. unless I creep over tomorrow, but I hardly think you'll want to see me so soon again. A letter from Tom [Eliot], who wants to come late in September: a letter from a lady who has described me in a French newspaper—"a noble lady with a great shock of white hair"—Lord, are we as old as all that? I feel only about six and a half. And now I must play bowls, be beaten once more, and then have out the scope and see if I can pry into your bedroom. If you notice a dancing light on the water, that's me. The light kisses your nose, then your eyes, and you cant rub it off; my darling honey how I adore you, and Lord knows I cant say what it means to me to come into the room and find you sitting there. Roger felt just the same. Have you noted any extracts in his letters? I think you must begin at the beginning with old Lady Fry [his mother]. So no more.

B.

I'll bring them from London next week.

Berg

3295: To Saxon Sydney-Turner   *Monk's House, Rodmell,*
                                       Lewes [Sussex]

18th Aug. [1937]

My dear Saxon,

    We are going to London on Tuesday and could then send Rosemary [Beresford] her MS.—if you would let me have the address. If however, she is in a hurry, I daresay you could find it if you went to the Press and asked them to take you to the flat. The MS. is in the cupboard (with a ship painted on it) attached to the tall green book case by the fire. Send me a card to say which you prefer.

    We're just walking over to Charleston. I go there most days. I think there's no doubt that Nessa is physically a good deal better. She is up all day and walks round the garden. This week end the Maurons and Helen Anrep

---

1. *The Duchess and the Jeweller.*

are coming. We are having Eddie Playfair[1] here—he wants to see Quentin and the Maurons. So you'll get news of her from him. She's reading Rogers letters and putting his papers in order.

Love from us both
Yrs V.W.

Sussex

3296: TO VANESSA BELL

[*Monk's House, Rodmell, Sussex*]

Friday [20 August 1937]

We didnt come over today because I expect you're too full of humans as it is. This is only to say we expect Quentin to lunch tomorrow, one, shall we say: and then we could all come over to tea. And then we can make other arrangements. God knows how my relics of 17th French will stand the battery.[2] I shant produce them in your presence anyhow. I'm half dazed at the moment, having wandered into Southease Church, and been fallen upon by the Rev. Thomas, who showed me round the frescoes with a long stick.[3] "See that mark? You'd think it a spider—Not at all. That is the Crown of Thorns. So Mr. Constable of the Courthauld[4] Museum says. All is done by the hand of God here. The electric heating is by Watts of Southwark. And Miss Humphries, a lady artist, has hung 10 water colour drawings, not as you or I would hang them, but as they hang them in the Royal Academy, half an inch off the wall. And that stain is a donkeys ears: for that is a fresco of our Lord on the Cross" Well it may have been: only it looks like a brown rat running in circles. I only escaped as another tourist came.

And a cable further stuns me, from New York, to say they cant make head or tail of my synopsis, so will I write the plot out at length—which means I fear they wont buy. And a letter from Saxon, about Rosemary's

1. Edward Playfair was Julian Bell's greatest friend at Cambridge. He had a distinguished career in the Civil Service, and later became Chairman of the National Gallery Trustees.
2. Charles Mauron and his wife were staying at Charleston. He disliked speaking English, and Virginia, who did not speak French easily, had been reading Molière.
3. Southease Church, a mile from Rodmell, was a 13th century building with faded wall paintings of the same date, including scenes from Christ's passion. They were rediscovered in 1934-5, and a local resident, Miss L. D. Humphrys, made sketches to identify the subjects of the original paintings. They still hang in the church.
4. William George Constable (b. 1887), first Director of the Courtauld Institute of Art, London University, and Slade Professor of Fine Art, Cambridge.

poems, and meeting Sidney Waterlow[1]—but as bare as a bone. And . . . oh here's Leonard to play bowls, so whats the use of sending this illegible scribble? None whatever. except that your Singe is never happy away from you, and when he sees a pen snatches it, and cant spell or write or think, what with Southease Church and having to give the Rev. Thomas 10/6 to buy a font with; but must kiss you all the same. How have you got on with the Frogs [the Maurons]? and the Hammock [Helen Anrep] and the Oaf [Igor Anrep]? and does Angelica control the whole boiling with her ineffable charm and her supreme tact?

B.

Berg

3297: To Rosamond Lehmann   *Monk's House, Rodmell,*
                             Lewes, Sussex

Aug 20th [1937]

My dear Rosamond,

Thank you very much. It was very good of you to write so fully. Archie Cochran and Philip Hart,[2] the dr., rang us up and offered to come down here the other day. We are going to see them in London next week; but I dont suppose they will add anything to your letter.

I showed it to Quentin, and he agrees that it is much better not to tell Vanessa anything about it. We are not telling her that we are seeing them, or that they are in London. I saw Portia Holman[3] from the hospital, a few days after Julian's death. She gave me rather a different, and perhaps less painful account—I mean it was less detailed, and I repeated this to Vanessa. She was greatly upset by it, though I think after the first shock it was a relief to her to know how it happened. But we dread opening the thing again, and there seems no reason to, since clearly from what you say there is nothing that she ought to hear. If she herself ever asked to see Archie Cochran of course it would be different. She is seeing Portia Holman next week.

We're very grateful to you for writing. It was good of you. I think one

1. Sydney Waterlow (1878-1944) had been an original member of Old Bloomsbury, and had once proposed to Virginia before he had been divorced from his
   first wife. He had been British Minister in Athens since 1933.
2. Both men were doctors attached to the Escorial hospital, and Archie Cochrane,
   an old friend of Julian at King's, was in charge of the receiving room there
   on the day Julian was killed, but it was Philip Hart who removed the shell
   splinter from Julian's chest.
3. She was a doctor, attached to the Medical Aid unit in the Escorial, and had
   known Julian at Cambridge. Later her career was in psychiatry, and for many
   years she was attached to the Elizabeth Garrett Anderson Hospital in north-
   west London.

day Nessa would like it if you wrote and told her things you remember about Julian—how he came when your baby was born and so on. She is better, I think, and takes more interest in other things. The Maurons are staying at Charleston this week end. The great thing I think is to help her to get back to family life and painting—as far as one can.

Thank you again, dear Rosamond. You have been a help.

yr aff
V.W.

I'm so glad Wogan is not to drive an ambulance again.

King's

3298: To Hugh Walpole   *Monk's House, Rodmell,*
                                          Lewes, Sussex

22nd Aug. 37

My dear Hugh,

I gave Vanessa your message, and she wants me to thank you. It was very good of you to write. Julian's death seems the most complete waste one can imagine. He was everything one could wish for: and now its all over.

I hope we shall see you in the autumn.

Vanessa by the way was saying how good you had been about their picture show.[1]

Yr affate
Virginia

Texas

3299: To Vanessa Bell   *Monks House [Rodmell,*
                                          Sussex]

Monday [23 August 1937]

I half sent a message through Angelica to ask if we could dine with you tomorrow, that is Tuesday? May we? We shall be coming back from London, and I'll bring some more Roger letters; and it would be a great treat to see you. But if you've had too many humans, you can prevent us by sending a tactfully phrased wire to Tavistock Sqre.

Oh I'm so furious! Just as we'd cleared off our weekend visits, the telephone rings, and there comes to lunch, late, hungry yet eating with the deliberation and mastication of a Toad, Mr Gillies of the Labour Party.[2] It's 5.30. He's still there, masticating. Half a plum cake has gone down crumb

1. The *Contemporary British Artists* exhibition at Agnews in June and July 1937.
2. See p. 83, note 4.

by crumb. Mercifully he was ceased [*sic*] with such a choking fit that I made off to my Lodge to write this. You cant conceive what the mind of a Labour party leader is like—George [Duckworth] is advanced, Saxon [Sydney-Turner] rash, and Barbara [Bagenal] wildly imaginative in comparison. And they scrape their knives on their plates. Never let Angelica marry a Labour leader: on the other hand dont tell Leonard this, for he lives in the delusion that they are good men.

Do you like Helen Anrep better than me? The green goddess, Jealousy alit on my pillow this very dawn and shot this bitter shaft through my heart. I believe you do. Its not so much the private wound I mind—its the deficiency of taste on your part. All the same I admit she has her moss rose charm: and in her breast instead of dew is a heart, I admit. I fell in love—this is to make you jealous—(but it wont) with Marie [Mrs Charles Mauron], whom I kissed as we exchanged roses under the mistletoe. She is a gypsy I'm sure. Once the paint cracks out comes the juice of the grape. Lord how I love writing to you. But I know you never read what I write. Heres Gillies: he's stopped choking alas: he's talking about the Labour Party Conference at Bournemouth. You see, theyre old maids wiping their china, gossiping about Sally and the policeman in the scullery. I liked Eddy [Playfair] too. I see I'm a snob. I really prefer Eton and King's to the elementary school at Glasgow, where Gillies took a prize.

here's L. so I'll discuss Eddie tomorrow if you'll have us

B

G[illies]. is going!!!

Berg

3300: To Vanessa Bell   [*Monk's House, Rodmell, Sussex*]

Thursday [26 August 1937]

I had hoped to come this afternoon, as Leonard thought of going to see cricket at Eastbourne—you know he goes to one match yearly: but he got too late to start, and is going tomorrow, so I'll come then instead. Oh dear, what a bore—because tomorrow and tomorrow and tomorrow there'll be Janie, and I want to see you without someone to distract you from me: jealousy pure and simple. Angelica's just rung up. I hope she'll bring Curtis[1] and Janie [Bussy] to tea on Saturday. and Quentin: for one thing the most enormous cake has arrived, from my mother in law. It is something like the Albert Hall; and has 3 garlands of leaves across it, one green: "As you were" (written in chocolate) one silver—"As you are." One gold. "As you will

1. Elizabeth Curtis, Headmistress of Angelica's former school, Langford Grove, Essex.

163

be—" Then 1912-1937[1]—Now the old lady thought this all out for herself: and then employed Lyons; and theyve done their best; only there's not a plum to be seen; which cuts Leonard to the heart. But as the course of our married life has been pure, so should our cake be. This idea I've been developing, with a whole gallimaufry of works to embellish it, at tea. What news of Edgar? Percy[2] says he's so often drunk in Lewes and then gets so quarrelsome, he always keeps clear of him, so had not heard. Dont you think we might send Maynard a Round Robin, all our names protesting in a circle, with the murdered white dog drawn by you in the middle? Our criminal [Rodmell robber] is still at large, and I thought I heard him in the garden last night but was too sleepy to lock my door. The police have arrested two farm hands; simply because they were sleeping in barns. So no doubt I shall be in prison—because if you're asked suddenly what is your name and what are you doing? you cant say. Louies [Everest] mother was asked her name in a shop the other day, and had to find her husband and ask him. So I shall ask you.

I dont like this very hot day: its extremely ugly. Old Miss Emery [Rodmell] has just been in with a basin of mulberries. An electric coffee maker, from my mother in law, has come; but the coffee, though made in ten seconds, is like very refined dish water; and a table has come from my brother in law, covered with great dragons. If you touch a spring 4 legs shoot out. Oh dear, what a thing real family life is! But I mustnt run on: and this is all dull.

So tomorrow.
B

Berg

3301: To Ethel Smyth   *M[onks] H[ouse, Rodmell, Sussex]*

27th Aug. 37

Its very good of you to go on writing, and I much appreciate your letters, seeing how little encouragement you get. But the fact is I'm not in a letter writing mood this summer; and also, practically speaking, dont get much time. One way and another, I've a good deal on my hands: not I admit that thats a real excuse. However, as one of your old ladies used to say, so be it.

Odd that you should be going to the Roman Wall: thats an old dream of ours.[3] We have it always up our sleeves. Do tell me, is it all we suppose? Can

1. 10 August was Virginia's and Leonard's silver wedding anniversary.
2. Percy Bartholomew, the Woolfs' gardener. Edgar Weller was the Keynes' chauffeur at Tilton, near Rodmell. He had shot a neighbour's dog.
3. The Woolfs visited Hadrian's Wall (A.D. 120) in the north of England in June 1938.

one walk a whole day along a rampart, surveying the border, the romantic borders, with the sheep cropping and the wild white moths? I'm amused at your swingeing of Elizabeth [Williamson]. What a censor of your kind you are! What an assurance you possess. Is it the solid legacy of the ancestral Colonels?[1] God and the Empire? Why attach such value to positive work? Theres Hugh Walpole, delivered of another 200,000 word book.[2] Do you therefore admire? Is there not a merit in contemplation? As for Vita, she's been stung on the ankle by a wasp and almost died but quite recovered. Asks me to go over, or will come here. No, I've heard nothing of Nigel on his Island, but Ben dined one night;[3] very like Vita at the chrysalis stage, as handsome, as indolent, as muffed. But this was long ago. A good many people haunt us; partly to take the load off Nessa. Oh dear—how can one ever make her happy again? Its a perpetual wound, and one cant stop it. Then your old lady says again enough. So MB [*Maurice Baring*] will be out this autumn. Well, according to our engagement, I'm not to have a copy or to express an opinion. [Dr] Alexander has certainly half-cured, and would whole-cure L: if he had time. So goodbye

V.

Berg

3302: TO MAY SARTON   *Monk's House, Rodmell,*
                                       Lewes, Sussex

29th Aug. [1937]

Your letter was sent on. I'm so sorry, I shant be in London again till October, when I suppose you'll be gone. If you're with Elizabeth [Bowen], will you tell her I'm sending her, at last, the book I promised. Best wishes for the novel.[4] Excuse this scrawl.

V.W.

Berg

3303: TO VANESSA BELL   [*Monk's House, Rodmell,*
                                       Sussex]

Tuesday [31 August 1937]

In wonder if you ever got my Sunday letter [*missing*]: as I've had no

1. Ethel's father was Major-General J. H. Smyth.
2. *The Joyful Delaneys*, a novel.
3. Vita's two sons were Benedict (1914-78) and Nigel (b. 1917). Nigel was spending a month on the uninhabited Shiant Islands in the outer Hebrides, which he had purchased in the previous year. Ben was an unpaid assistant at the National Gallery, the first step in his career as an art historian.
4. May Sarton was working on her first novel, *The Single Hound*, 1938.

receipts to the bills I paid then, I rather suspect the whole lot is stuck on the pillar box. I hope this wont, not that I've anything to say—except send this
No: here is the post, and a receipt, so perhaps yours alone stuck.
One of Julians essays came this morning. War and Peace—the letter to Morgan.[1]—I thought there were 2 others: perhaps they weren't being typed. Anyhow we'll read this at once.
No L can get the others from Q.
Letters, no news, save village gossip, demands for ladders to clip hedges, and Mr Wicks [Rodmell builder] out to plan Leonards new folly, another pond and a bricked garden. By the way, he said your figs were a far better kind than his own, darker, more passionate. This is an almost incredible admission, you'll agree.
Perhaps Q and A and Janie will step in from the heights of America,[2] but I doubt it, so I will trust this to the post once more. Any news of A's jacket?

B.

How I adore you! How astonishingly beautiful you are! No one will ever take the winds of March with beauty as you do.[3] Let me know about the letter as I must make a row.

Berg

3304: To Victoria Ocampo   *Monk's House, Rodmell,*
                                  Lewes, Sussex
2nd Sept 1937

My dear Victoria,
    I ought to have answered your letter before, but you will understand that I could not, for I had just had the news of my nephews death in Spain. He was killed driving an Ambulance near Madrid, and then my sister was ill and I have been with her, and not able to think of other things. He is a terrible loss;—but that you will understand. And I am furious at the waste of his life.
    Now however, I will answer your letter. Of course I am honoured and flattered and delighted that your long lecture[4] should have kept people interested, however we divide the honours between us.

1. *War and Peace: A Letter to E. M. Forster* was published in *Julian Bell,* 1938. In it Julian argues that "we have to choose war, not peace. I will not pretend this is anything but a choice of evil, not good, or that all my arguments are more in the end than 'it's an ill wind that blows nobody any good' ".
2. 'America Farm', a bungalow in the Downs above Firle rented by Elizabeth Curtis.
3. *The Winter's Tale,* IV, iii, 109.
4. In Buenos Aires about Virginia, one of several lectures and essays which Ocampo devoted to her.

I suspect you are one of the people—they are almost unknown in England—who can make a lecture exciting. Is it your Latin blood? I would rather sit in a cellar or watch spiders than listen to an Englishman lecturing. Of course I should like to read it, if you have a copy. I am here, Monk's House, till October: and thus though I'm told the Orlandos have come,[1] have not seen them yet. As for your passage from Orlando, it reads extremely well: I'm too rough, really with my French to compare it exactly with the English.

Your butterflies—do you remember the evening visit of the 2 mysterious ladies carrying butterflies?[2]—no—I do though—are hung over the door in Tavistock Sqre beside the portrait of my puritanical ancestor who disapproves of presents.

Come if you are in London, in the white chariot [car]. And forgive this late and quite illegible letter. My pen is like a rake this morning.

Yr Virginia Woolf

Estate of Victoria Ocampo

3305: To Vanessa Bell   [*Monk's House, Rodmell, Sussex*]

Wednesday [8 September 1937]

I'm afraid I shan't be able to come to tea till Friday when I hope you wont mind once more seeing your poor Singe.[3] Tomorrow damn it all, we have to go to Margaret Davies at Dorking and shall be too late to come round by Charleston. And on Friday there'll be Clive and [Janice] Loeb I suppose. If I cant come, would you tell Quentin we expect him to dinner at 7. But I shall do my best to come in spite of all drawbacks and disparagements, through sheer wish to see you, my lovely dolphin. That reminds me, we went to Brighton yesterday to look for a fountain for L's new pond, and there I bought a very nice shawl at Miss Acton's, she said Angelica, or rather Miss Bell of Firle had just been in and bought a muslin dress. However, we never saw Angelica, only Mrs Bradfield and another earnest worker, who dogged us through the lanes, or twittens as I prefer to call them. And no fountains of course, only a head of Aristotle which rather took my fancy, and a bust of Sir Walter Scott. Ask Q. to bring Julians other essays with him. I thought the letter to Morgan the best thing I've ever read of his; very like him, and at last I think I understand his point of view, which I didn't—about being a soldier I mean. I dont agree: from my point of view; however that may be my fault. But I expect you're right to send it to Chatto, and I should

1. A Spanish translation by Jorge Luis Borges.
2. See Vol. V, pp. 438-9.
3. Vanessa replied: "Please dont exhaust yourself by coming here if its too difficult—I really need not be visited like an invalid now" (9 September 1937, *Berg*).

think they'll certainly do them. Lord, how I wish I could argue the whole thing with Julian. Will you seriously consider doing a picture of Clive at his table for me? a serious commission? I feel I must get my Bloomsbury gallery started before we're all old and bald and bleareyed: but dont let Clive think he's going bald No, he'll wear his hair to the End. Any news of Adrian? A letter from Saxon about his old lady and the square, and he hears that Adrian is at Charleston recovering there from an illness: I suppose one of his mere romantic flights.

So goodbye my lovely dolphin

B

Berg

3306: To Vanessa Bell

Monks House [Rodmell, Sussex]

Friday [17 September 1937]

I had a letter from Margaret Davies, enclosing a letter from Maurice about Talland House,[1] which I was about to send you, but it seems to be lost. However it was a very dull letter—no Davies can write—all the virtues and all the graces but no gift with the pen. So I have no excuse for writing then, except to say I hope Quentin wasn't made really bad by that accursed English cooking.[2] It was the cheese I'm sure: it smelt like a skunk, and the old fogies [Sissinghurst servants] must have infected it with their funereal delay. Perhaps I could come over on Monday or perhaps Tuesday would be better, for you will be sated with conversation during the week end. I longed to ask Angus about Mary Butts,[3] but had just not enough wine in my head for the purpose. I hope you may. Vita was much impressed by the improvement in Angelica's beauty, which she said was purely Russian. It was a mercy not to find her Gwen [St Aubyn] there; and Quentin was completely master of all the intricacies of all the pots and pans. In fact they did me the utmost credit— I should say you, I suppose; but I intend to claim all their virtues in future. Dont do too much, my dolphin darling. But this sounds so much like Aunt Mary[4] I'm ashamed. I've just been wet through and almost clapped on the head by thunder on the marsh so excuse—

B.

Berg

1. At St Ives, Cornwall. It was rented by the Stephens for their annual summer holiday in Virginia's childhood until her mother died in 1895. Maurice Llewelyn Davies (1864-1939) was one of Margaret's six brothers.
2. On 16 September Leonard and Virginia, with Quentin and Angelica and Angelica's schoolfriend Eve Younger, visited Vita and Harold at Sissinghurst.
3. See p. 138, note 2.
4. Mary Fisher (1841-1916), the wife of Herbert Fisher, was the sister of Virginia's mother.

Monk's House, Rodmell
[Sussex]

Sept. 18th [1937]

Dearest Margaret,

Thank you very much for sending the extract from Maurice's letter. I am sending it to Vanessa, who will be interested, as I am. She remembers him coming, which I dont, and says that the first time she ever fell in love it was with your brother Harry, whom she only saw once, as a child, but thought him the most beautiful man she had ever seen. I enclose the photograph of Arthur, taken by George Duckworth, when he and Sylvia were staying at St Ives.[1] Was it on their honeymoon? I remember them very well. If you didn't mind sending it back, would you some time, as I keep a family album.

Ann and Richard[2]—how things repeat themselves!—should be here this very weekend; but she wrote from Dublin to say she was taking some anatomy course there, and would come and see us in London with him. She is a scholar at Newnham, taking a medical course, and wants to be some sort of public health officer, at Geneva, I think, in order to combine medicine with politics. As for the others, Angelica and Quentin, about whom you ask, here's a snapshot of them (if I might also have it back) sitting on a bank outside Rome with Vanessa 2 years ago. But its not good of her.

Yes I am snowed under with Roger Fry papers—boxes of letters and articles, but cant make up my mind whether to write anything or not. I think I'll try, as soon as I've read enough: and tear up if it seems, as I expect, hopeless. How can one write the truth about friends whose families are alive? And Roger was the most scornful of untruths of any man. This is all answers to questions—which shows that we ought to see you and Lilian [Harris] oftener. I wish we did. It was very refreshing to see you both again, and going home Leonard and I said how much we had enjoyed it and how glad we were we had come. The garden here is worth a visit—since its Leonards work I can say so at the moment truthfully.

yr V.W.

Leonard will write about the books you ask him about.

Sussex

1. Margaret's brother Arthur Llewelyn Davies (1863-1907) married Sylvia du Maurier in 1892. They had five sons, who were adopted after their parents' death by J. M. Barrie, the novelist and playwright.
2. Ann Stephen was Virginia's niece, and Richard Llewelyn Davies, Margaret's nephew. They were engaged.

3308: To V. Sackville-West   *Monks House, Rodmell*
[Sussex]

Sunday 19th Sept. [1937]

Here is the letter that concerns you.[1] Leonard thinks it is the writing of a maniac—but I cant make out if he's half serious or insulting. Not that it matters.

We did enjoy our afternoon. It was very good and kind of you and Harold to let us overrun you—dont I know how visitors interrupt and bore? But the children were tremendously impressed and amused; and its a great thing to give them a treat, so I'm grateful to you both.

Here it is dripping. I've been caught in a thunderstorm on the marsh, but managed to find a cap full of mushrooms. which I shall cook for dinner. Not yet have I had a moment for Pepita. Tomorrow I may: at this moment that old swan necked white lily Angus Davidson is expected; then we go to Lewes to attend the left book Club.[2]

But the trade paper says that Foyles have had to withdraw their first choice—Well's novel: owing to the uproar among booksellers, so we were well advised to back out.[3]

Yes I envy you Sissinghurst. Isnt that nice—being envied?

I swear I will go to Paris the 2nd week in October to a small new hotel I'm told of. If you're there, let us meet and discuss the Americans letter. Wouldnt that be fun?[4]

Now to answer Ethel's latest.

Y V.

Berg

3309: To Ethel Smyth   *Monks House, Rodmell*
[Sussex]

19th Sept 37

Well, are you still tramping the Roman wall? or have you come back South, and if you have come South what are you doing South? I shant be

1. Virginia had received a letter from an American asking her to write an article about Vita, adding that Virginia's 'affair with V. Sackville-West' should make her an authority upon the subject.
2. Founded in 1936 by Victor Gollancz, the Left Book Club sent their 60,000 members a left-wing book every month for 2s. 6d. They also published *Left News*, held weekend seminars and Russian language courses, and organised a poetry and a musicians' society.
3. The Hogarth Press, which had in the past published several works by H. G. Wells, refused his latest novel, *The Camford Visitation*, 1937.
4. Vita and Gwen St Aubyn went to Paris on 4 October, but Virginia did not join them.

told unless I ask, so, merciful heaven having provided a wet day, so that our visitors have put us off, I'm writing, though I've nothing to say. How was it that in such circumstances our ancestors at once wrote such letters as could be printed verbatim? Was it nice to get Horace Walpoles letters? Was it better than reading Hugh Walpoles novels? At Sissinghurst two days ago— we took Quentin and Angelica over—Harold was saying he more or less agrees with you about MB's novels. But when pressed to explain rather wobbled, so I thought. Gwen wasn't there—and oh the difference to me, as the poem says.[1] And the whole place was a magnificent proof of our old English aristocratic tradition. When I got back here I was positively ashamed of my middle class origin. It was a wet night and the kitchen was damp and my room all strewn with old clothes. But I recouped my spirits by saying L. and I wouldn't like to live at Siss[t]. Vita was perfect in her way and Harold in his. How I adore nice people. What else makes life worth living? Are you a nice woman? What do you think you live for? Of course, if one believed in God, as you do, it would make a very great difference. Tom Eliot is coming here next week end. I shall ask him, if I dare—but to ask him a question is like putting a penny in the slot of the Albert Hall—what he thinks about God. Audens Iceland[2] seemed to me mainly attitudinising, as if he were uneasy at heart, and must talk about himself in order to rid himself of some scabby itch: a kind of public scratching. I dont send this off as a specimen of a very good letter, but as a request for news. If I can I'm going to make a shot at seeing Paris before we settle in. Only its so difficult

V.

You remember the umbrella you stole?[3] Well I've just been walking under it through the marshes, and found some mushrooms.

Berg

1. She lived unknown, and few could know
     When Lucy ceased to be;
   But she is in her grave, and, oh,
     The difference to me!
                 Wordsworth, *She Dwelt Among The Untrodden Ways*.
2. W. H. Auden's *Letters from Iceland*, 1937, written with Louis MacNiece.
3. See Letter 3185.

3310: To Kingsley Martin   *Monk's House, Rodmell,*
                                            Lewes, Sussex
Typewritten
19th Sept. 1937

Dear Kingsley,

The book on Mass Observation[1] certainly sounds as though it ought to be interesting. But I'm afraid I cant do it, because I am full up with other work and dont want to do any journalism at the moment

Many thanks for thinking of sending it to me

                                            Yours
                                            Virginia Woolf

Sussex

3311: To William Plomer   *Monks House, Rodmell,*
                                            Near Lewes, Sussex
23rd Sept. [1937]

Dear William,

I'm sorry to have been so long answering: of course I am flattered to be asked to write an introduction to my father's book. But I'm afraid I cant; as I've nothing to say of any interest either about the 18th Century, or about his book. I cant remember at the moment which it is—lectures, I rather think. I'm glad its alive enough to be worth reprinting.[2]

We're going to visit an exhibition in Brighton on Thursday next and travel some books. Might we come to tea with you? Its the 30th. Meanwhile Tom Eliot is here this week end. If you'd come over to tea on Sunday we should be delighted. A vast niece of mine [Judith Stephen], aged 18, weighing 13½ stones, just about to go to Newnham, will be here: but not Mrs [Elizabeth] Curtis. But leave it open, as they say.

Yes, I remember Rene Janin[3]—if as I think he was the Frenchman who told me a fascinating story about coffee planting one night at Victoria Grove; which reminds me, I met Tony Butts, and discussed Mary's autobiography.[4]

1. *May 12th: Mass-Observation Day-Surveys*, edited by Humphrey Jennings, Charles Madge and Tom Harrison, 1937, a book about the opinions of ordinary people on Coronation Day, collected by means of interview. Mass Observation was organised in this year for the purpose of studying popular culture and public opinion.
2. Leslie Stephen's *English Literature and Society in the Eighteenth Century* (the Ford Lectures, originally published in 1903) was not reprinted by Plomer.
3. René Janin, the son of a French general, who settled in London in the early 1930s. He was a novelist and translator, and a friend of Plomer and Stephen Spender. Virginia had met him dining with Plomer in March 1932.
4. Mary Butts, *The Crystal Cabinet*, 1937.

But to go into all this would need another sheet or two, and I'm in a hurry: several squirrels in the basket as you'll see from my hand: in other words 3 letters to write before playing bowls. So I must hope to see you on Sunday.

Yrs VW.

Texas

3312: To Vanessa Bell
[*Monk's House, Rodmell, Sussex*]

Friday [24 September 1937]

I didn't come to tea today,—not that you probably expected me—because Clive rang up about coming here tomorrow: and I gather that he and Janis [Janice Loeb] are with you. So I shouldn't see you; had I come. But if you could stand it, I hope I will come on Monday; and hope too to find you without visitors. And hope also to be rid of my own. Oh to think of having Tom and Judith in the house for 2 days! Judith suddenly asked to come; so, as we'd put her off before, we agreed: how she'll mix with Tom, and perhaps William Plomer, and Clive and Janis Lord knows. Here's the letter from Margaret Ll. Davies. She has sent us a collection of Victorian photographs— some rather fascinating—which if I can I'll bring. And I've had a letter from Maynard, who wants to seduce me to buy rare books, saying he's coming next week, and hopes to see us. He will still lead an invalid life; but Ruthin's is an asylum.[1] however they say he can leave know. Thats about all, save for a demand from Chabrun[2] the man who bought my story, to see me, in London next Tuesday; which means I expect he wants to shuffle out of the Jew and the duchess [*The Duchess and the Jeweller*], as well he may. But I shall be as hard as flint. I've just come in from a walk all along the river to Piddinghoe— the river flooding, bright blue, barges going down the tide, and all so divinely beautiful I at last lay on the bank in the rushes and looked at it upside down. Then I wished you were with me, and reflected that no doubt you wouldn't like it, then I saw a Kingfisher, then I peeped over the wall and saw 3 elderly ladies of the worn Victorian elastic sided boot type meandering round an iron table on which was a plate of raspberries. Oh if I could have heard what they were saying! When do you go to Paris? Vita suggests that I should meet her and Gwen there: but no. For one thing I must finish my pamphlet [*Three Guineas*], and then, angelic though Vita is, Gwen is very stale milk in that cup o' tea. Lord how I miss Quentin and Angelica—I cant bear they're going. Judith wont make up at all. Angelica was so lovely the other night. She looked like an exquisite Jerboa making cigarettes with her front

1. See p. 131, note 1.
2. Jacques Chabrun, the New York literary agent.

173

paws. I shall be so jealous when she marries. But this is drivel and you wont read it

Yr one poor deviled B.

Berg

3313: To Elaine Robson
Monk's House, Rodmell, Lewes, Sussex

Typewritten (in capital letters)
Sunday. September twenty sixth [1937]

My dear Elaine,[1]

I liked your poem and your story very much indeed. I have not seen a rabbit washing his ceiling but yesterday I saw a hare who was making a warm bed for his winter lodging in the marsh. He had just laid down a nice blanket made of thistledown when he saw me and ran away. His bed was quite hot, and I put a mushroom there for him to eat. The marsh is full of mushrooms. I wish you and Daddy and Mummie were all here to pick them and then we would cook them and have them for supper. I also saw a kingfisher. His bed is in the bank of the river but I have never found it. Sally has had a thorn in her paw and we have had to poultice it. At last the thorn came out and her paw is only as big as a penny bun. It was as big as a soup plate. Mitzi had a macaroon for breakfast this morning. When you are in London will you come to tea with us and make a binding for your lovely poem and story. Do you like writing prose or poetry best. This typewriter cannot spell and sometimes uses the wrong type. xxxxxx Uncle Leonard sends his love: Sally has just barked her love also and Mitz bit me in the ear which means she sends you her love too.

Your affectionate Aunt Virginia

Elaine Robson

3314: To Maynard Keynes
Monk's House, Rodmell [Sussex]

Sept 27th [1937]

My dear Maynard,

Many thanks for the [book-sale] Catalogue. So far I have restrained myself from buying anything, because that would be the first step on the greasy plane to the workhouse. The collector in me is only just beneath the surface: another Catalogue, and the crust will be broken, Monks House sold,

1. The daughter (then aged six) of W. A. Robson and Juliette Alvin (see p. 150, n. 2). Elaine later studied biology at Cambridge, and became Lecturer in Zoology at Reading University in 1969.

Sally sent to the dogs home, and Leonard hawking geraniums in Covent Garden. Excuse these mixed metaphors (if such they be). I'm so sleepy after a weekend including Tom Eliot, and Judith Stephen, William Plomer, Clive and his Janis that my brain is like a broken watch with one Bee inside. Why werent you and Lydia here to support us under the weight of Tom? In fact he was as pliable as an old glove, very ridiculous, charming and affectionate. He asked that his love should be sent you.

We hope to see you soon. If Leonard could speak, but Sally's ear is laid across his mouth, he would send his usual greetings to your wife. In spite of Sally he kisses his hand to her (Lydia I mean).

Yrs V.W.

King's

3315: To V. Sackville-West   *Monks House [Rodmell, Sussex]*

Oct 1st [1937]

We have been so ridden with visitors that I never had a moment to write. In fact I was so touched by your letter that I couldnt. Isnt it odd? Nessa's saying that to you, I mean, meant something I cant speak of.[1] And I cant tell anyone—but I think you guess—how terrible it is to me, watching her: if I could do anything—sometimes I feel hopeless. But that message gives me something to hold to.

I doubt if I shall get to Paris at all. I want to finish a bothering piece of work in this comparative peace. If I'm there though when you are, perhaps we might scrape a dinner somewhere together. All the same, I doubt that threes company: and dont like, as they say, butting in. However, that too you'll understand. I thought the other day how comforting it was to see you: for without words you do understand.

Now I've left no time or room for Pepita. I read it like a shark swallowing mackerel. I think its far better than Joan, more masterly and controlled.[2] And I think you hold the innumerable threads wonderfully tight and yet easy. My only criticism, a personal deficiency I expect, is that I cannot altogether sympathise with your mother. There's something antagonistic in her. But no doubt my relations with her queer the pitch. This slightly impairs the

1. Vanessa had written to Vita telling her that Virginia had helped her after Julian's death more than she could say, and asking Vita to make Virginia believe this.
2. Vita's book about her grandmother (Pepita) and mother (Lady Sackville) was published by the Hogarth Press this month. Vita's *Saint Joan of Arc* had been published in 1936.

psychology of the character, especially towards the end. But thats all. Otherwise nothing but praise, if you care for that.

dining with Clive and his Jewess [Janice Loeb].

V.

I hope I've made clear how immensely I enjoyed Pepita: read it without drawing breath.

It must be a bestseller into the bargain.

Berg

3316: To Vanessa Bell   *Monks House* [*Rodmell,*
                                                        Sussex]
Saturday Oct. 2nd. [1937]

Thank you for sending Rees' letter.[1] I liked it. It gives me the feeling I had when Julian came back from China—also when I read his letter to Day Lewis[2] I think he had to go, and nothing could have stopped him. I wonder what you settled with Bunny about publishing.[3] I talked to Tom, and he agreed about the letter to Day Lewis, and thought it really important that it should be published, because it is different from anything that anyone else has written; and much more serious, we both thought, than any of the Audens and Spenders writings. He thought the letter about Roger [Fry] too confused as it stands, and hoped Charles[4] would either explain it was unfinished, or leave some of it out. I am selfishly rather glad that he feels this, as I've always wondered if I wasn't wrong.

Since you left we have been to Brighton, evaded Ethel Smyth here, had tea with William Plomer, dined with Clive, and have promised to go to Tilton tomorrow. Lydia rang up, and sounded, Leonard thought, rather depressed about Maynard, but we shall hear more tomorrow. Dinner at Charleston last night was rather subdued, but on the whole more to our liking than we expected. Janis subsided, but Clive left her to herself, and we

1. Sir Richard Rees (1900-70) edited *The Adelphi* from 1930 until 1936, and then went to Spain to join the British Medical Unit, where he spent some time with Julian Bell. He saw Julian's body in the mortuary at the Escorial. (See Stansky and Abrahams, *op. cit.*)
2. Cecil Day Lewis (1904-72), poet-laureate from 1968, had joined the Communist Party shortly after the outbreak of the Spanish Civil War, but left it in 1939. For Julian's letter to Day Lewis, see *Julian Bell, Essays, Poems and Letters* (Hogarth Press, 1938).
3. David Garnett contributed a memoir to Julian's posthumous book.
4. Charles Mauron also contributed to the book, but it was Quentin Bell who edited it.

had an amiable old world gossip without much showing off. The dinner included a jugged hare and a very good soup. But without you and Q and A and D. it lacked some splendour.

To my terror I was rung up last night from Paris and leapt to the conclusion, as they say, of some catastrophe.[1] But it was only Chabrun offering fabulous sums for a short story[2] which he wont take. And all it means is another interview, more telegrams: but I shant put pen to paper without a cheque.

Maurice Baring also has descended—or rather appeals for help, which means we must go over. Its a tragic story. [Dr] Alexander, he says, has taken him to pieces so that he can neither sit nor stand, but jerks perpetually, and has a heart that thumps till the bed jumps; which is different from paralysis, but is it any better? Do we think Alexander is killing him? Your friend Lady Lovat[3] is staying there; They are all gathering like the fowls to a feast; so if, as I suppose, we go over, I may revive myself by a sight of her beauty. But its a bore, as I want to work and finish my pamphlet [*Three Guineas*]. Did I tell you that Basil Williams[4] has got restive and made me send his letters back? So I must set to and do something or all the old fogies will be pestering me.

Now I must play bowls: it is a dull misty day, and I have fallen into a brook and am wet through. Leonard pulled out Mitzis front tooth—the very long curved one—this morning. But I must write a long letter about all that to Angelica.

I got their cards [Angelica's and Quentin's] this morning—a great joy.

I feel a lost old crone without you all: you cant think how I depend upon you, and when you're not there the colour goes out of life, as water from a sponge; and I merely exist, dry, and dusty. This is the exact truth: but not a very beautiful illustration of my complete adoration of you; and longing to sit, even saying nothing, and look at you. *Only dont* tire *yourself* (This is old Aunt [Mary] Fisher)

B.

I'll write about Maynard.

Remember to find out how long the pictures are open[5].

Berg

1. Vanessa was in Paris, with Duncan, Quentin and Angelica.
2. In response, Virginia wrote *The Shooting Party*, which was published in *Harper's Bazaar* (March 1938).
3. Laura Lovat (d. 1965) was the widow of the 16th Lord Lovat.
4. Arthur Frederic Basil Williams (1867-1950) was the Professor of History at Edinburgh University, 1925-37. He met Roger Fry in the 1890s.
5. An exhibition of *Chefs d'Oeuvre de l'art Français* at The Paris International Exhibition, 1937.

Monk's House, Rodmell
                                                          [Sussex]
Sunday Oct 2nd [3 1937]

Darling Pixie,

Heres one of the little sheets you like so much and adorn so beautifully. I was very glad to get the picture of George Sand and am sticking it in my self-bound edition.[1] I dont suppose art and society will leave you time for a full account of the exhibition. And to tell the truth, the pressure of Rodmell life is such that I cannot give you all the intimate details of our private affairs that I would—we are even now cleaning off the mud for tea at Tilton. However, Judith [Stephen] sent you, as they say, a million messages. She is a fine giantess with one spotted eye, like an old sheep dog, underneath, I suspect, like the mushroom, all gills and sensibility. Rather I think under the thumb—that is the beauty—of Ann. Thank God you haven't an elder sister to take the winds of March with beauty, as I had, and so force you to be a modest violet on a shady bank. But you should meet Judith. Tom was miraculous at bowls, dignified, supple, regretted you, and showed up well, Judith thought, beside William Plomer. On the other hand William much admired her. All this is too abbreviated to be of much value, psychologically. In the world of real life, Louie's [Everest] boy, aged eleven, rode his bicycle bang into his father's bicycle, and knocked out four front teeth, which nature will not replace. Also crumpled his father's bicycle. His father said, "Anyhow it didn't hit his brains": and teeth, he said, can be replaced. St Denis[2]—there's no visible connection—has sent me a full prospectus, as if he hoped I should become a play actor. Or is it that I may listen to you? If you should want a lodging next week, remember that 52 Tvis. Squre is at your service till Sunday anyhow; with Mabel to cook. Only warn me. And love me and give me my rights. Now I must face the Keynes', and to that end must strip and peel and wash. So give what is left of my love to Quentin, Nessa, Duncan, and tell Q. to come and dine. How did old Aunt [Mary] Fisher end [her letters]?

                                                          Old Aunt V.

Texas

Monk's House [Rodmell,
                                                          Sussex]
Typewritten postcard
Sunday [3 October 1937]

Many thanks for the card. This one will bring in the home note. Very

1. See Letter 3287.
2. Michel Saint-Denis, the theatrical director, who in 1935 founded the London Theatre Studio, where Angelica was a student.

damp and dismal here. I long for full news of pictures etc. and count that you will come over to any meal, hoping against hope for tiles.

Love Virginia

Quentin Bell

3319: To Vanessa Bell   *Monks House [Rodmell, Sussex]*

Wednesday. [6 October 1937]

I have told Mabel [cook] to be ready for Angelica—and here's Q. with Richard [Llewelyn Davies] and Ann [Stephen]—(so I cant write—theyre talking). Q says A went off this morning. I'm not very coherent, as they're arguing about Colonies. Q. arrived at tea, and the young couple are spending the night at Charleston. Very nice both of them, Ann rather fierce and tawny: Richard as smooth as silk. We had tea with the Keynes's. M. is looking much better—not so white and heavy. But Lydia seemed rather pinched, and said it would take a year before he was right. We talked about diseases mostly for an hour. He is now a medical expert. All London specialists were wrong about him. The only cure for all diseases is at Ruthin's. He asked a lot about you. Oh what an ugly home theyve made it—new cover, again. Then we had a day at Horsham travelling our books. But as you see I cant collect my wits; the argument about colonies is raging; it is getting late. I've got to cook dinner. It's only in way of a kiss that I send this scribble.

I told Mabel to look after Angelica. I'm sure she'll be solid and take her duties very seriously. We go up on Sunday. It will be a heavenly joy to see you. I'll try to write a better letter tomorrow

B

Edgar is talked of with the usual tender respect, so I suppose the incident is closed[1] It seemed more tactful to say nothing.

Berg

3320: To Donald Brace   *Monk's House, Rodmell, Lewes, Sussex*

9th Oct 37

Dear Mr Brace,

Many thanks for your letter. I am very glad to hear that the sales of The Years have been so good. I suppose now that they must slack off, but I am greatly pleased and surprised, that they have been so high. Many thanks for all the trouble you have taken on my behalf.

1. See p. 164, note 2.

I received the copies of the Modern edition of To The Lighthouse safely. I could wish (privately speaking) that the introducer did not think it necessary to drag in my private life.[1] I wish one could keep that out of writing and publishing. But I suppose one cannot complain, and people must make these guesses even if, as in the present case, the guess is wrong.

You will be glad to hear that Maynard Keynes is very much better, though still forced to rest.

It has been a perfect summer in the English style: and so fine even now that we regret going back to London tomorrow.

I hope you have recovered from your American summer.

With our kind regards
yours sincerely,
Virginia Woolf

Harcourt Brace Jovanovich

3321: TO ELIZABETH BOWEN   *Monk's House, Rodmell*
                                          [Sussex]
Oct 9th [1937]

Dear Elizabeth,

I'm so sorry I didn't write before, as I should have done, to say we wished we could come to you [in Ireland], but it wasn't possible. I didn't, as you'll understand, want to go far from Vanessa this summer. It has been very terrible, but you'll know that without my saying so.

Now I suppose you are back in London. So shall we be next week, and I hope you'll come and see me, or let me end one of my Regent Park walks in your house. I've just been walking over the downs, and now, like you, must wash my head. Only I wish I had done it and could sit on your steps and dry in the sun. Here it is pitch dark and dripping with mist from the Channel.

Tom Eliot came one week end, and we had tea with William Plomer in his bird cage [in Brighton], and lots of stray people strayed in. But I've not done much that I should have done. Have you? Finished your book?[2]

1. The Modern Library of the World's Best Books reprinted *To The Lighthouse* (originally published in 1927) with an introduction by Terence Holliday, in which he wrote, "It may not be impertinent to survey briefly here certain biographical material concerning her which is to-day available in any adequate library of reference." He went on to write of the "autobiographical element that pervades" the novel, especially in regard to the characters of Mr and Mrs Ramsay, their house (which he identifies as "on the western coast of England"), and the decay of that house in *Time Passes*.
2. *The Death of the Heart*, 1938.

entertained a great many starving scribblers? bought the house at Hythe?[1] despatched that goose May Sarton, who sent me a gentian picked by Julian Huxley—and so on. Oh and written in the loose leaf book. Well, I hope you'll come to tea, and thank you for asking us to stay. Another time I should like to.

Yrs V.W.

Texas

1. Although Elizabeth Bowen had loved Hythe in Kent for years, she did not buy a house there until the 1960s, when she acquired Carbery, Church Hill.

Letters 3322-3344 *(October–December 1937)*

Three Guineas *"pressed and spurted out of me"*, *Virginia wrote in her diary,* *and she finished the first draft in London on* 12 *October. Months of revision* *followed, in the intervals of further research for* Roger Fry, *a busy social life,* *and a visit to Cambridge.* The Years *continued to boom, specially in America,* *where it sold some* 40,000 *copies before the end of the year. Virginia's health* *remained on the whole good, but in December Leonard's suspected prostate* *caused them further worry. A major decision in the Hogarth Press was im-* *pending—to sell Virginia's half-share to John Lehmann.*

3322: To Vanessa Bell   52 *Tavistock Sqre.* [*W.C.*1]

Sunday [10 October 1937]

I'm rather vague, owing to Mabels vacancy, as to whether you're back yet.

There's a pair of shoes and a skirt belonging to Angelica so I hope she means to come and fetch them. We came up this morning and have spent the usual miserable day unpacking, seeing L's mother—at least he did. And had to break to her the news of her lovers death. She had a lover in Worthing, a doctor, aged about 66. Also the dachshund belonging to Edgar[1] has swallowed a ball of wool. So he has sat up 7 nights nursing it till the wool has been un-wound. The Wolves and their dogs are incredible. I'm longing to hear about Paris. not that I suppose there's much chance I shall go there; unless I make a dash.

In fact this is only to say I'm longing to see you. So if you should ever want to, send word. Not a single engagement in sight, thank God, so I could come any time.

We hear that Chabrun, my agent, is a suspected character. No hope of pay for my story I'm afraid.

I wonder if you saw the Keynes's. and if you're collapsed with picture seeing, and if you get up at 7 every morning and if you're fond of your adoring B.

Berg

1. Edgar Woolf, Leonard's younger brother and a stockbroker.

19th Oct [1937]

Well?—as Mrs Pankhurst used to say. I dont know where you are—Harrogate? Woking? or the Roman Wall?

I am in fact seated in the studio at Tavistock Square, surrounded by vast rolls of cardboard, which will soon, I hope, be wrapping the Autumn books —Vita's Pepita among them. We came back last week. I've been trying to clear my room; bought a book case to that intent; painted it elephant grey this moment. What I wished to lead to however, was Maurice [Baring]. I wanted to explain, he wrote to me about [Dr] Alexander: said could we advise him: was A. a quack who was killing him or not? (This was our last week at Rodmell) So L. gave his view, and we offered to go over and talk. Upon which Maurice scrawled a half legible note saying that he must decide for himself: but would love to see me. I felt this was one of an invalids chops and changes—for why ask our advice if he didn't want it?—and also felt, no, he doesnt want visitors. So did nothing. What I wish you would explain, if its worth it, is that if my going, or L.'s, one or both, would give him an instants pleasure, he's only to say so. We are there almost every other week end. I'm afraid he's horribly bad. Enid Jones[1] came over. She sees him it seems; they have a common grudge against Alexander, or rather suspicion; as her boy [Richard] goes to his school—fruitlessly, but immensely expensively.

There! That piece of business discharged, how can I now broach, I mean board, I mean beard, my uncastrated cat? Only an inch of paper and an ocean in my head. I've got Ronald Storrs from the Library:[2] there's an ocean, if you like!—but a little tumbled and tumultuous: I doubt I shall get to the end. There is no criticism though, as I'm not a serious student of Egyptian politics. Need I say that? Dont you know how little my skimp of a brain pan holds? No I never went to Paris: still think of it; but L. cant break loose, and I dont fancy an hotel alone. And your book? And Pan? And is Vaughan Williams[3] a great composer? If so, why does he sound so dull? A very ador-

---

1. Enid Bagnold, the novelist and playwright, who married Sir Roderick Jones, Chairman of Reuters, in 1920. They lived at Rottingdean, a few miles from Rodmell, and Maurice Baring was a neighbour.
2. *Orientations,* his autobiography, published in 1937. For Sir Ronald Storrs, see p. 89, note 1.
3. Ralph Vaughan Williams (1872-1958), about whom Ethel wrote in response to Virginia's question: "I have heard lovely things of his but he lapses easily into dullness" (21 October 1937, *Berg*).

able man I gather. And Jacques Blanche?[1] Do you know him? And ...
and ... and ...

V.

Berg

3324: To Violet Dickinson   52 *Tavistock Square, W.C.*1.
22nd Oct. [1937]

My Violet,
    Well, how are you? Have your legs mended themselves? I couldn't see from your letter anything wrong with your brain. And it is universally said, wherever people meet together, that your heart is as the purest unfractured gold. I was led to make these foolish remarks by tidying my bookcase: and out fell a very small red book,[2] in which you wrote A Tract for the Sp: fr. V.D. 1905. Now when so much has gone down the sink, see how affectionate I must be, and admiring of your writers gift—not the hand, which is slightly tied up—to have kept that and still read it after 32 years!
    But apart from that, I wonder if you are getting about again, and able perhaps to sit in the garden at Welwyn. At this moment I am scribbling in a rush because we're off, thank God, to our garden, via a Grocer's shop at Crawley, where Leonard is going to buy a leaden Cupid for his new water garden. He has a passion for ponds: and whenever the grocer has a cupid to sell, we buy it, to stand naked, with a tortoise balanced on the bow.
    So far as I remember, your garden, Ozzies garden, has ponds: but in every cranny you have some Himalayan gentian. We shall get to that in time, I daresay. But Lord, how I curse the builders! Bungalows on the very rim of the downs.
    It was sad my dear old Janet Case dying: we went to see her, and found her very humorous about it, and old Emphie the sister as gallant as could be. Dont, unless you can write lying down, answer this: which is only a tribute to Anthony Harte. I like his thoughts. You gave it me in the long room at Manchester Street overlooking the graves.
    Remember me to your husband,[3] and get well.

Sp.

Sussex

1. Jacques-Emile Blanche (1861-1942), the French portrait painter and writer, whom Virginia had met in 1927 through Ethel Sands. He wrote an article on Virginia, and for a short time maintained a correspondence with her (see Appendix B).
2. *These Thoughts Were Written by Anthony Harte.* Virginia thanked Violet for this gift in January 1905 (Letter 210). It is a tiny book, 5 in. × 3½ in., and only 18 pages long. It carries no date or publisher's imprint. The book is now in the library of Washington State University, Pullman.
3. An old joke. Violet never married.

184

3325: To Ethel Smyth

52 *T.[avistock] S.[quare, W.C.1]*

Tuesday Oct 26th [1937]

Of course the letters, our letters, crossed. What do you take me for? a parrot afflicted with aphasia that I should ask all the questions you'd just answered over again? Really, Ethel, I begin to think your boasted psychological genius is null; mine gigantic in comparison. Yet according to you its the other way round—No matter, as Mrs Pankhurst, Lady Ponsonby, and Archbishop Benson[1] would have said. I cant remember the questions I had to answer. Oh yes—the book [*Maurice Baring*]: postponing it to January: were you right? Yes. Leonard is inclined to think you were well advised. A book coming out in Nov^r^: doesn't have time to sink through impediments before Christmas. As for Pepita, the other question, is it good? Well, whats your standard? Boswell? Rousseau? or merely the current pitter patter? One never knows. I think it's of its kind whatever that means, admirable: as easy to read as velvet glove to slip into; and very skilful; and compact; and not a schoolboys essay like Joan: great fun; and should certainly sweep the market, break the Bank. The odd thing is, I detest Lady Sackville at the end of it: an insipid, selfish, rather stupid housemaid of amorous propensities jumped up into the Peerage. But Vita says she is adorable. So I'm no doubt wrong. And this hasty estimate is only for your own ears—Did you ever meet her? Oh I get so bored with her extravagances after the first fun! and the vanity and the illiteracy, and the magpie's claws.

We were on the front at Seaford during the gale. That's as near as I got to Paris. The waves broke over the car. Vast spouts of white water all along the coast. Why does a smash of water satisfy all one's religious aspirations? And its all I can do not to throw myself in—a queer animal rhapsody, restrained by L.

No news of Maurice. Alexander told L the other day he thinks him very bad; but then he wont do, A. says, what he's told. Did the nerve dr. help?

V.

Berg

1. E. W. Benson (1829-96). He was Archbishop of Canterbury, 1883-96, and the father of the three writers—A. C., E. F., and R. H. Benson. Ethel wrote: "Of the Archbishop I stood in deadlier awe than of anyone I ever met in the whole course of my life" (*Impressions That Remained*, Vol. II, p. 191).

3326: To Pamela Diamand   52 *Tavistock Sq.* [*W.C.*1]

Nov 3rd [1937]

Dear Pamela,¹

Thanks very much for your letter. If any of your mother's letters, or about her, should turn up, I shall be very glad to see them.

The more I read of Roger's papers the more impossible it seems to write a conventional 'life' of him: If I do write anything, I shall plunge and forget all relations and their feelings. I'm very glad to feel that you agree about this.

I'll suggest a visit when we are coming your way.

Yrs
Virginia Woolf

Pamela Diamand

3327: To V. Sackville-West

52 *T.*[*avistock*] *S.*[*quare, W.C.*1]

15 Nov. [1937]

Why 'once' Virginia? Why mayn't I answer your letter? That of course is the way to make me sit down at once and answer it. Why are you a dustbin? And why shouldn't we go for a jaunt? Why, why, why?²

Just because you choose to sit in the mud in Kent and I on the flags of London, thats no reason why love should fade is it? Why the pearls and the porpoise should vanish?³

No. I cant see your argument. In January I will take you to the place where we once had a glass of wine in a bow window overlooking the river.⁴ Also I'll take you to The Tower—I've just been there, this dripping Sunday; because almost every day I take my walk through the City. I like it better than Kent—Bread Street, Camomile Street, Seething Lane, All Hallows, St Olaves—Then out one comes at The Tower, and there I walk on the terrace by the guns, with the ships coming up or down—which is it? Last week [5 November] we went to Guy Fawkes at Lewes. Lordloveme, why

1. Pamela Fry (b. 1902) was Roger Fry's daughter, and married Micu Diamand, the Rumanian painter.
2. On 13 November Vita wrote to Virginia a very affectionate, nostalgic letter, beginning "my (once) Virginia", referring to it as "a thought of love from your Orlando," and closing: "a rather inconsecutive letter, I fear ... but somehow I always turn to you when I feel like the dustbin with fireworks inside it" (*Berg*).
3. This image, which is often repeated in Virginia's letters to Vita, refers to Vita's appearance as she stood in the doorway of a Sevenoaks (Kent) shop in December 1925 at the beginning of their love affair.
4. The Prospect of Whitby, a riverside inn in the east end of London.

didn't you come? Tossing torches all up and down the streets: people rigged up as courtiers, gondoliers, old farmers in black Spanish hats. Then we all trooped onto the downs, and burnt the Pope. It was the very image of an Italian picture of Calvary; crowds gazing up: the figure falling

As you say though, Spains burning and Hitler booming.[1] A french politician[2] is dining here: I have to cook the dinner, and cant, as you know, talk what you would call, French. (d'you remember the rough sea on the channel boat? and how skilfully I christened it?)[3]

So no more—But if your pen should again take to twisting, let it.

Because, my dear Vita, whats the use of saying '*once* Virginia' when I'm alive here and now? So's Potto if it comes to that

yr faithful old servants
and adorers
P and V

Berg

3328: To Shena, Lady Simon   52 *Tavistock Square, W.C.*1.

Thursday [18 November 1937]

My dear Shena,

Yes I shall be in at 4.30 on Thursday 25th; if you will come then.

I meant to write and thank you for your letter in [the] summer. It was a very nice one. But you said I needn't, and as you understand yourself, Julian's death seems to leave one with nothing to say. It was good of you to write as you did.

yr
Virginia Woolf

Sussex

3329: To Ethel Smyth   52 *Tavistock Square, W.C.*1.

24th Nov 1937

Well, Ethel?

This is the most perfectly dated and expressed letter ever written: as

---

1. 1937 was the 'year of no surprises' from the dictators, but Hitler was stepping up his claim for the return of the German colonies surrendered to the Allies after World War I, and he and Mussolini continued to intervene actively in the Spanish war.
2. There is no reference to him in Leonard's diary.
3. While crossing the Channel for their holiday in France in September 1928, Vita overheard Virginia asking a French sailor, "Est-ce que la mer est brusque?"

such I leave it and forebear to add so much as a sentiment by way of ending that might spoil its classic symmetry.

Well Ethel?

And it only takes 3 seconds to write,

Well Ethel?

Berg

3330: To Denys Kilham Roberts

52 *Tavistock Square, W.C.1.*

Typewritten
27th Nov. 37

Dear Mr Kilham Roberts,

Thank you very much for your letter of the 24th. As Mr Forster will have told you, the other letter that you speak of never reached me.

It is extremely good of you on behalf of the publishers to ask me to join the advisory committee which you describe.[1] I have thought the matter over, and regret very much that I cannot accept the invitation. I need not say that I think the idea very interesting, and that I wish it every success.

With thanks again,
yours sincerely
Virginia Woolf

Texas

3331: To T. S. Eliot

52 *Tavistock Square, W.C.1.*

29th Nov. [1937]

My dear Tom,

The woods decay, the woods decay and fall[2] . . . And why doesn't the old Possum (see poem)[3] come to dine?

1. Kilham Roberts, Secretary to the Society of Authors, had invited Virginia, E. M. Forster, Aldous Huxley and Hugh Walpole to advise Allen Lane on the choice of books for the Pelican paperback series, which Lane founded in this year.
2. "The woods decay, the woods decay and fall,
   The vapours weep their burthen to the ground."
   —Tennyson, *Tithonus*
3. On the reverse side of a letter dated October 1937 from the Secretary of St Stephen's Bridge Tournament, asking him to take a table or make a donation, Eliot had written the following poem and sent it to Virginia:
   "Among the various Middle Classes
   (who live on treacle and molasses)
   A custom has (for want of better)
   Been called the Bread and Butter letter

What about Thursday 9th at 8? And who would, or whom should it be, would you, or he should it be, like to meet?

Anyhow come, before all the vapours have wept their burthen to the ground.

Yr aff
Virginia

Mrs T. S. Eliot

3332: To Ethel Smyth   52 *Tavistock Square, W.C.1.*

Friday [3rd December 1937]

You say I'm not to pay attention to your letter, so I'll confine myself to the one word which you forbid, dont you? My love I mean: thinking of you and the dog.[1] I've been having the flu: and am still on sofa; but hope to get away tomorrow till Tuesday and be cured. Am practically all right today. Does 22nd mean Dec? Yes, of course: (I was dreaming we were still in Nov^r). Yes, I'll keep my word as a publisher: and thank you for letter.

V.

Berg

3333: To Helen McAfee   *Monk's House, Rodmell,*
Lewes, Sussex

Typewritten
6th Dec. 1937

Dear Miss McAfee,[2]
Many thanks for your letter. It is very good of you and Governor Cross[3]

But Mrs. Woolf would not rejoice
In anything that's so bourgeoise,
So what can poor Old Possum do,
Who's upper-middle through and through?
. . .
Whoever gives him their approval
He only hopes that Mrs. Woolf'll."
(copy at *Sussex*)

Eliot's most famous use of this persona is in his book of poetry for children, *Old Possum's Book of Practical Cats*, 1939.

1. Ethel's dog Pan VI had been killed on 28 November.
2. Managing Editor of the *Yale Review*, in which Virginia had published several articles since 1926.
3. Wilbur Lucius Cross (1862-1948), Dean and Professor of English at Yale till 1930, and subsequently Democratic Governor of Connecticut. For almost 30 years he was Editor of the *Yale Review*, assisted by Helen McAfee.

to invite me to send you something for the Yale Review. Since finishing the Years I have written a good many shorter essays; but I did not think of sending them to you because the subjects seemed unlikely to interest the American public. Here, as you know, we make a habit of celebrating centenaries, and reviewing new editions of old books. As I write chiefly for the Times Literary Supplement, I generally plan articles of this kind some time ahead for them, and have at the moment half promised to do something on [Samuel] Johnson's prose and something on Borrow.[1] But if an idea struck me that was more topical I would of course suggest it. At the moment however I am afraid I cannot propose anything definite. It is very kind of you to wish it, and I will certainly bear the suggestion in mind.

Many thanks for what you say of the Years. It has met with an extraordinary success in America—much to my surprise and delight. I need not say how glad I am that you found the book interesting. I was a great deal hampered by illness while writing it, and was afraid that the book had suffered in consequence.

My husband and I both send our best wishes for Christmas, which is already on us here. I am writing in a deep frost down in Sussex.

Yours very sincerely
Virginia Woolf

Yale University

3334: To Ethel Smyth   52 *Tavistock Sqre.* [*W.C.*1]
Monday 13th Dec. [1937]

Well I hope things are going as well as may be. Oddly enough, my mother in law was saying yesterday she had heard all about you and Pan from a stock broker called Smith (I think) who lives at Woking and greatly admires you.

But Vita is coming in to dine for a wonder—first time I should think this year—so I must hurry.

What I was going to say was that your gift of an inscribed copy [*Maurice Baring*] so much touched that flint my heart the other night that I didnt, as I ought, insist that I will only take it from you if you swear that you wont mind, and won't misinterpret, my silence. The truth is I've been so badgered all these years for opinions on books that I cant stumble out another, even if I like it. So I implore my friends not to give me their books, since I must, in the way of business, continue to read so many by force. And how could my opinion of what you say of MB. have any shade of value, coming from one

---

1. George Borrow (1803-81), the traveller and writer, whose special subject was the Gipsies. His best-known books were *Romany Rye* (1857) and *Wild Wales* (1862). Virginia wrote neither the Borrow nor the Johnson article.

purblind to the subject you're dealing with? As well ask a deaf donkey to criticise Mozart. And how did the BBC. do your concert:[1] No chance of hearing it, tho' there again my remarks wd. be worthless. Of course I'm longing to read your book: its only an opinion I cant give. Hilda was here, and gave Leonard a harrowing account of Dotty.[2] I wish I could send my sympathy; but I dont see how, my relations being queered as they are. So goodbye. Perhaps Vita will illumine this. She's coming to consult about some violent letters her Aunt is writing to the papers—her mothers sister— about Pepita.[3]

V.

Berg

3335: TO VANESSA BELL   *52, Tavistock Square, W.C.1.*

Wednesday [15 December 1937]

Will you give me the great pleasure of accepting what is *not* a Christmas present, but simply your due on the story which I sold entirely owing to you.[4] In fact its considerably less than your due. So do, good Dolphin; and buy a few little extras on the journey with it.

Also: Could you tell me any small thing Angelica wants? As its her birthday as well as Christmas: but I cant think what she wants—bag, stockings, brooch? Lord knows what. Barbara [Bagenal] has just been, with 6 bottles of mint jelly. A severe price to pay for mint jelly. And Lord lovaduk as Rupert [Brooke] used to say, Flossie [cook] has the bronchitis: what are you doing for dinner?

B.

Berg

1. *Dame Ethel Smyth, a Concert of Her Music*, performed by the B.B.C. Orchestra and Chorus and broadcast on 10 December.
2. Hilda Matheson (1888-1940) had been parliamentary Secretary to Lady Astor, Talks Director for the B.B.C., and was now working under Lord Hailey on the African Survey for the Royal Institute of International Affairs. Dorothy Wellesley, who had lent her a farmhouse on her Sussex estate, was becoming increasingly eccentric.
3. Lady Sackville's younger sister, Amalia Martin (*née* Sackville-West), wrote to the *Birmingham Post* on 10 December that Vita had "thrown mud on my mother's [Pepita] memory by raking up an old forgotten scandal that should have been allowed to die in the gutter whence it sprang".
4. Vanessa had advised Virginia to drive a harder bargain with her American agent on the sale of *The Duchess and the Jeweller*.

3336: To T. S. Eliot   52 *Tavistock Square, W.C.*1

Thursday [16 December 1937]

Dear Tom,

What a miracle—to come home and find your letter, after so brilliantly cutting each other in the alley. Still more miraculous that you should think of me and Portland together.[1] I'd just read Morgan's review, and asked for the loan of his copy. Naturally he's forgotten. Of course I should cherish a copy—just my line; to the very t.

Looking forward to Tom and Portland on Monday.

Yrs affate
V

Mrs T. S. Eliot

3337: To Duncan Grant   52 *Tavistock Square, W.C.*1

Thursday [Wednesday, 22 December 1937]

Dearest Duncan,

Here is a most inadequate cheque [for £35] for what I consider a masterpiece of the purest water. I am as tipsy as a bee with pleasure in it, and have just discovered a ship (not a sheep) in the background to make my pleasure complete.

Yrs
Virginia

with profound homage to your genius, and please express my amazement at her stitching to your mother.[2]

Estate of Duncan Grant

3338: To Maynard Keynes   *Monk's House, Rodmell [Sussex]*

23rd Dec. [1937]

Dear Maynard,

Yes. I liked the notice of Julian very much.[3] It is much what I felt—his extreme honesty, and something undeveloped. I think all Stephens are.

1. Eliot proposed giving Virginia as a Christmas present the Duke of Portland's recently published memoirs, *Men, Women and Things*.
2. See Letter 3343.
3. Keynes had written a brief obituary for the Annual Report of King's College, (13 November 1937) in which he said that Julian "had the utmost openness of

What would have happened, I wonder, if he had got his Fellowship [at King's, Cambridge]? But there's not much use in wondering.

Macaulay I had read, I must admit with great admiration. He has an odd look of Rose.[1] I wish you'd go on and do a whole portrait gallery, reluctant as I am to recognise your gift in that line when it seems obvious that nature gave me none for mathematics. Please consider it. Is portrait writing hard work compared with economics?—however I hope we may go into this by word of mouth. Leonard says, and I agree, that it would be very nice if the Keynes's came to Christmas lunch. William Plomer may be coming; but if it weren't too tiring you'd find a turkey

We came yesterday, and hope anyhow to see you some time.

Foot and mouth completely hems us in. Also Sally's on heat: also reputed pregnant after an hour's mating.

Love to Lydia.
Yrs aff.
V.W.

King's

3339: To Angelica Bell   *Monk's House, Rodmell, Sussex*

Christmas Day [1937]

Darling Pixy,

Since this is the very last hour of your birthday,[2] I must send you Old Aunt's Best Wishes, though Old Aunt's handwriting may be illegible. And for God's sake *answer* as I'm as solitary as a single sealion bereft of its mate in a cold ocean cave without you. As for Mummy, as she's forgotten she ever had a sister, creep gingerly on tiptoe, plant a kiss on her parting and sing or rather sigh "A present from Rodmell!", on which she'll jump like a cow stung by an adder.

Which reminds me, foot and mouth is still very bad: a fresh case at Black Cap:[3] so we cant walk.

---

character and purity of motive, simple and gentle, with truth and sincerity stamped upon him, and was gradually learning to form his character and to express it. He developed to maturity slowly and was still but a grown and clumsy child whose final accomplishment, now cut off, might have greatly exceeded his apparent early promise."

1. Rose Macaulay (1881-1958), the novelist and essayist. Lord Macaulay, the historian, was a cousin of her grandfather.
2. Angelica was 19, and was spending the Christmas holidays with Vanessa at Cassis in France.
3. A farm in the Downs halfway between Rodmell and Charleston.

The Keynes' came to lunch, and we put Maynard to bed on 2 chairs and talked and talked till he worked into such a fury about politics that Lydia called the car and off they drove. Theyve got a new chauffeur; a great mechanical genius, with whom Lydias in love, called Frank, Auntie's nephew in law, and a great improvement on Edgar. I was as tactful as an eel and said nothing to recall unhappy memories. And then Lady Colefax came to tea— in London. And *she* was tactful about Helen's party,[1] which, since she had been closeted with Duncan was, she said, all she could desire. Also HOW BEAUTIFUL HOW PERFECTLY LOVELY your niece is! she said. Beware. Beauty is only skin deep. It is sober worth that tells. And you'll be asked to North Street. Also she said Jane Clark[2] bought a picture. Also she told us the whole inside story of David and Wally Simpson.[3] It was thrilling. Wally is a perfect Lamb: David a man of genius—but as for the Duke of Kent[4]—Sybil almost cuts him when she meets him. But thats all I've room for. So darling Pixy good night, and dream of witches.

VIRGINIA

Please kiss Miss Campbell and Colonel Teed[5] on my behalf.

Texas

3340: To V. Sackville-West   *Monks House, Rodmell*
                                     [Sussex]
[26? December 1937]

Its not due to you that I'm alive today: I've eaten the whole pie practically myself!

Heaven above us, what immortal geese must have gone to make it! It was fresh as a dockleaf, pink as mushrooms, pure as first love. (but first love conveys nothing to the hardened and battered—this I put in by way of an aside) It was so divine, I could forgive any treachery. My word what a pie! Tom Eliot was dining with us the night it came. Complete silence reigned. The poet ate; the novelist ate; Even Leonard, who had a chill inside, ate.

1. A party given by Helen Anrep at which pictures were sold for the benefit of a proposed School of Drawing and Painting (later The Euston Road School), where Vanessa and Duncan taught without payment.
2. The wife of the art historian Kenneth Clark, who was at this time Director of the National Gallery.
3. The Duke and Duchess of Windsor. They had married on 4 June 1937.
4. George, Duke of Kent (1902-42), the youngest surviving son of King George V.
5. Teed was an ex-Colonel of the Bengal Lancers, who retired to Cassis, where he bought a lovely house called 'Fontcreuse', with a vineyard. He lived there with Jean Campbell.

Nothing of the least importance was said. Where do they come from? Could one send a card and have one at will? It seems incredible. And then Potto's collar arrived. Out I trotted with Virginia blazoned on my neck. Many people accosted me; others took the view that there was something sacred like a text from the Bible—about a woman with a name on her: others—oh did I tell you I'd been offered an Order?—I forgot—they thought I'd come from Buckingham Palace. A kind of Order of Merit.[1]

But Orlando, pink porpoise, isnt it against our Covenant to do this sort of thing? Dont you remember offering me Thackerays wine cooler or ash tray[2] or something in the days of the fishmonger and how I said: Unhand me Sirrah?

I'm not sure I shant send you a present: take care next time a rather heavy, thick malodorous packet arrives; a little oozy at the corners. The worst of owning Sisst. is that you can only be given liver, calves heads,—things that dont add to the value of the estate. Ethels in ecstasies over her pate. 12,000 copies of Pepita sold.

I'm thinking of buying a fur coat

V.

Berg

3341: To Ethel Smyth   *Monks House, Rodmell*
                                        [Sussex]
26th Dec. [1937]

The book came just as I was coming here: there it is: and here am I, silent, but grateful. I'll try, if I can find one, to read a novel of MB's [Baring] again. That'll be the best return I can make for the generous impulse which prompted the uncastrated cat—to whom, by the way, I listened in the other night, with great enjoyment;[3] partly I admit, of the human quality of the aforesaid quadruped's very friendly but not necessarily altogether approving voice. I like hearing your voice talking about the Kaiser, and supplying it simultaneously with quite other words. A harmless amusement you'll allow.

We're entirely marooned here. Foot and mouth to right of us, to left of

---

1. Meant humorously. She was never offered the Order of Merit. See p. 308, note 5.
2. Actually a silver paper knife which had belonged to Vita's ancestor the Duke of Dorset, reputedly the model for Lord Steyne in Thackeray's *Vanity Fair*. Vita offered it as a gift to Virginia on the night they began their love affair. Recalling the incident three years later, Virginia wrote: "The night you were snared, that winter at Long Barn, you slipped out Lord Steyne's paper knife, and I had then to make the terms plain: with this knife you will gash our hearts I said" (Letter 1976, 28 December 1928).
3. On 23 December Ethel had broadcast on the subject *Two Meetings with the Kaiser Before the War*.

us, foot and mouth all round us, so that if we want to step off the road we have to drive 5 miles. A murrain be on all farmers who cut me off my one wildest and purest pleasure! There are the marshes, and I cant walk there. So I cant think, cant read, cant write. However I've eaten the whole of one of Vita's Strasbourg pies. Blessings be on an inside that must be lined with felt and cased with iron. Leonard cant. . . . A man breaks in from the Cave where Christ was born. (BBC)[1] How repulsive the Xtian religion as conveyed by the Xtian clergyman is—But it has on this occasion the virtue of interrupting this letter. The man is actually on the stone where Christ was born—he is apparently chilly; he is also silly: a poem in its way—so, as Mrs Pankhurst used to say

No More—

V.

Berg

3342: To Vanessa Bell   *Monks House [Rodmell,*
                                          Sussex]
Tuesday, 28th Dec. [1937]

Your letter written on the 22nd only reached me yesterday—which shows what a time it takes. I'm horrified at your journey. Why on earth didnt you take my advice and travel first? However Leonard says its the usual incompetence of the Wayfarers[2]—when we went 3rd it was very comfortable. As a matter of fact it was a perfect summers day on Christmas day, also boxing day. One could have sat out. But all over the rest of England, you'll be glad to hear, it was black with fog. But thats our only good luck. Foot and mouth broke out at Blackcap just as they were taking down the boards here; so up they went again till the 8th, and we cant walk a step. But we've discovered some unparalelled beauties—East Chiltington in its way beats St Remi, to say nothing of Cassis—only 3 miles the other side of Lewes. The Keynes's came from Christmas lunch, as I told Angelica. It was Maynard's first outing. He said he had almost recovered from his setback, but could only creep upstairs with great difficulty and lie on chairs. However we talked incessantly till 3 or so, when he suddenly became very excited—almost in tears I thought—about politics and the Labour party and Lydia whisked him off. She was much more cheerful though: and we rang up yesterday and

1. This was the first occasion on which the B.B.C. broadcast live the bells of Bethlehem.
2. The travel agency patronised by all Bloomsbury. It was run by David Gourlay, who had married Janet, the daughter of Virginia's old friend Madge (Margaret) Vaughan.

he said it had done him good, and we're to go there. All the gossip was that Lydia thinks the N. Statesman hopeless; much prefers Night and Day;[1] M. has bought the site for a theatre in Lewes, but wont do more; investments are very bad; sport at Tilton very good; he's killings his pigs; has rejected Stephen Spenders play,[2] thinks Auden very dirty but a genius; and thats about all. Clive is probably coming down tomorrow, and if Janis [Loeb] is with him, wants to come over. However, I think we shall go up on Thursday to see L's doctor. His kidney is still rather a nuisance, and he cant garden, so as the 2 weeks are up, we shall see what Rau[3] advises. We've also got to see John, about the press,[4] so we shall stay a night, and then I expect settle in here again.

No, I've heard nothing of Helen [Anrep], but she was clearly so rattled and dithered and worried, as well she might be, that I thought silence indicated. Colefax, who at last forced herself on me, was all honey about the great party, though of course it had been very crowded, still she had had the joy of seeing Duncan alone, thought Angelica perfectly lovely, and swore that Jane [Clark] had bought a picture. after that she gave us a verbatim, hot from the Kings mouth, account of the Abdication: swore that he and Wally had never been to bed; says Wally is a simple good devoted soul, who implored the King to keep her as his mistress or let her go. "If you do" he said "I shall dog you to the ends of the earth in an aeroplane." Whenever S. goes abroad they ring her up and she stays with them. Unfortunately they refuse to take her advice—which is to go to South America—and are going to live in Paris, where no one will visit them, because of propriety. I gathered that Sibyl is going to act as liaison officer between them and the implacable Queen Mary, and I'm not at all sure that I'm not going to help David to have recourse to the classics—which, as Sibyl says, might do him a world of good. As for Wally, Leonard wd. feel perfectly at home with her. And so on, all in odds and ends, for 1 hour and 30 minutes.

Thats about all the London gossip that has come my way. Not much of interest I'm afraid. Yes it would be nice to be sitting in a vineyard with the frogs croaking and the yellow butterflies among the olives. The fog is creeping up this evening, and my only letter is a frantic appeal from Ethel Smyth to tell her what I think of her vast new book, all in praise of Maurice Baring—which God help me I cant and wont do. I see from The Times that

1. A humorous magazine published weekly from July to December of this year. Their announced intention was to amuse: "We shall try to do it intelligently; and without if possible being smart, fatuous, Bloomsbury or it-seems-there-were-two-Irishmen."
2. But Spender's verse tragedy, *Trial of a Judge*, was performed by the Group Theatre in 1938.
3. Dr Rau, an expert on tropical diseases.
4. See p. 200, note 2.

K. Clark is in hot water about his Georgiones again;[1] and that a subscription is on foot to buy one of Wyndham Lewis's pictures for the nation.[2] Old Tom [Eliot] actually signs this balderdash. He dined with us, but let on nothing; was in fact as genial and gentle as could be, and has mounted into the oddest world of antique respectability—for example, the Maxses, Leo's nephew, who's in the Guards; Algernon Cecil, widower of Gwen God-Osborne:[3] I suppose in order to cultivate society dialogue for his play [*Family Reunion*].

Mrs Grant [Duncan's mother] has sent me an exquisite square—the one I saw—infinitely lovely. And if I could find a rule I would measure for my glass. Duncan's picture arrived just as we left. I maintain its a masterpiece: all the sea in one shell. Thats all the art criticism you'll get out of me. I'm afraid tho' the shell is too big for the dining room.

Now good Dolphin, be careful; and warm; and eat and love

poor worm eaten
Singe

Berg

3343: To Mrs Ethel Grant   *Monk's House, Rodmell,*
                                  Lewes, Sussex
28th December [1937]

My dear Mrs Grant,

I cant tell you what a joy—quite undeserved though—your embroidery is to me. It hangs on a chair back at this moment, but no dog cat or human is allowed to sit on it. I dont think though you ought to give such sumptuous presents. Whenever I give Duncan even a twopenny halfpenny doll he bites me severely. And then you and he together produce this! Its exquisitely lovely.

I'm looking for a footrule with which to measure the space for the looking glass.[4] Its going to be in the sitting room here, as I'm so seldom in my bedroom. Can I look forward to it about Easter? And what about the rug?

1. Kenneth Clark, with the enthusiastic support of the Trustees, had purchased for the National Gallery four panels which he declared to be by Giorgione, but his attribution was challenged publicly by other scholars. The panels have not been exhibited since 1939.
2. Several pictures by Percy Wyndham Lewis, Bloomsbury's great enemy, hang in the Tate Gallery. It acquired his *Red Scene* in 1938.
3. The people mentioned are: John Herbert Maxse (b. 1901), a Captain in the Coldstream Guards; Leo Maxse (1864-1932), Editor of the *National Review* and an old friend of the Stephen family; Lady Guendolen Cecil (*née* Godolphin Osborne, d. 1933); and Algernon Cecil (1879-1953), the historian.
4. A looking-glass with an embroidered frame, which still hangs at Monk's House.

Will you really take a commission for that? The ex-blotter I shall make into a table cover, with glass on top, and you must really come and see us, and it, and Duncan's picture, which came just as we were coming here. A most exciting one.

I hope you were violently dissipated in Paris. Here foot and mouth hems us in, and fog, and every other horror of winter.

I hear from Vanessa that she and Angelica had an awful journey, owing to the Wayfarers' incompetence, but are enjoying Fontcreuse.

Thank you again.

Yr affate.
Virginia Woolf

Estate of Duncan Grant

3344: TO BEATRICE WEBB *Monk's House, Rodmell,*
Lewes, Sussex

28th Dec. 37

My dear Mrs Webb,[1]

We are deep in fog here and it seems rather foolish to suggest a long drive at the moment. I'm afraid January 29th does not suit us. So might we aim at March? Here again we cant ask you to keep a week end free, as our movements are rather uncertain. But if I might write and suggest a night in March rather nearer the time, it would be a great pleasure to us to come: and if it doesn't suit, perhaps you would suggest another.

I dont suppose that I, at least, should dare to disagree with you, and I am sure that even if Leonard dares, our common feeling is one of profound admiration.[2] But that does not happily, exclude argument.

Yrs sincerely,
Virginia Woolf

Leonard wants me to say that he looks forward to listening to your Broadcast.[3]

Passfield Papers, University of Lonhon

1. Beatrice Webb (1858-1943), co-founder of the Fabian Society with her husband Sidney Webb and others.
2. Mrs Webb had written to Virginia on 23 December: "We were so much interested in Mr Woolf's broadcast [*Does Education Neutralise Thought?*] the other day; it was admirable, alike in delivery and content. Though of course we did not agree with some of the assumptions in respect to individual liberty. In fact, I always find myself admiring the Woolfs without agreeing with them!" (*Sussex*).
3. On 4 February in the series *National Efficiency and Individual Liberty.*

Letters 3345-3401 (January–June 1938)

The year began with renewed fears for Leonard's health, but after many tests and the threat of a prostate operation, he was declared free of serious illness on 11 February. Virginia herself caught influenza. These weeks coincided with the negotiations which resulted in John Lehmann buying Virginia's half-share in the Hogarth Press, and he became Leonard's equal partner in April. It did not mean that Virginia ceased to take an interest in the Press (she continued to advise on manuscripts until her death), but it allowed her more time for writing. Three Guineas was published on 2 June, and uncharacteristically she faced publication-day with equanimity and scorned the few hostile reviews which she received. Already (1 April) she had begun to write Roger Fry, *and in the same month began her last novel* Between the Acts *(which she called initially* Pointz Hall*). Ottoline Morrell died on 21 April, and Katherine Arnold-Forster on 22 May. Ethel Smyth reached the age of 80, and Hitler invaded Austria.*

3345: To John Lehmann   52 *Tavistock Square, W.C.*1.

2. 1. 38

Dear John,[1]

I was sorry to have to turn you away on Friday, but I was in bed and not allowed to do anything. I shall be in bed for another week, and it is then hoped that I shall be all right.

You said something as you left which made me think that you meant me to consider a proposition which I had not understood you to make before.[2] I may have been completely mistaken, but I thought you meant that you

1. This letter is entirely written in Virginia's own hand, but was dictated to her by Leonard, who was ill at the time. Virginia probably had some part in composing it.
2. Briefly, the events which had led up to this point were as follows: In the summer of 1937 Virginia and Leonard once again considered giving up the Hogarth Press, and simultaneously John Lehmann (their previous employee) was looking for a new publisher for his biannual miscellany *New Writing*. At first the suggestion was that Lehmann, Spender, Auden and Isherwood might buy the entire Press for £6,000, of which Lehmann would put up half, but the other three could not raise their share. Leonard then conceived the plan explained in this letter. The agreement came into force in April 1938, with Lehmann as Manager and equal partner with Leonard. (See Lehmann's account in *Thrown to the Woolfs*, 1978, pp. 57-9.)

were prepared to come into partnership on your own into the Press, and to put £3,000 into it quite apart from the original arrangement succeeding or not succeeding. I have thought this over, and in principal it is attractive to us. That is to say, if we understood you aright, we should be prepared to consider further with you some such arrangement as the following:—

1. We should sell you a half share in the Press, for the sum of £3,000. Virginia would withdraw so that the other share would be owned by me alone, and the ownership would be a partnership between you and me.

2. You would be managing director with a salary of £500 payable to you before profits are divided in which case I would have a salary of £200 payable before profits are divided. You would undertake to act as managing director for two years at least, to be responsible entirely for the actual management of the office and staff, to attend the office for at least three days every week, except for the months of August and September and two periods of three weeks to be arranged during the rest of the year. I would normally do the work from Monk's House during August and September in the way in which I have done before, and if I were in England I would do the three weeks, but I would not pledge myself on this point.

3. Each of us would have an absolute veto against the publication of any book.

4. It might be advisable to turn the Press into a private company: in any case the terms of dissolution would have to be carefully considered. It might be possible to combine such an arrangement with a loose attachment to the Gang, in the shape of an advisory Board.[1] I should be willing to consider this favourably, though the working out of it might be difficult.

I shall certainly be in bed here until the end of the week, and could see you almost at any time if you rang up.

Yours
Leonard Woolf

George Spater

3346: To Ethel Smyth   52 *Tavistock Square, W.C.1.*

4th Jan. [1938]

Lord! What an inconsistent woman you are! There's a letter before me in which you say "*Of course* I dont want you to say anything about my book [*Maurice Baring*]. I'm giving it you simply because it pleases me to give it

1. The *New Writing* gang, i.e., Lehmann, Spender, Auden and Isherwood. The 'advisory board' was formed in August of this year, consisting in Virginia, Rosamond Lehmann, Spender, Auden and Isherwood. It never met as a board, but its individual members were consulted on books of special interest to them. Leonard invited Vita to join them, but she declined.

you"—and then when I stick to my side of the bargain you cry off. Never mind: I'll accept your inconsistency and write some time, not this moment.

I've been devilishly anxious. L. was taken ill at Monks House last week. We came up and saw the doctor who first thought it was prostate gland: then disease of the kidney. After an intolerable 5 days—X-rays, specialists etc—theyve put him to bed for a week, on strict diet, and will let us know the final verdict on Saturday—another 4 days. However the X Ray proved that there's no disease whatever; and the Dr. seems to think that it will pass off and leave nothing: he's much better already. But I'm a good deal distracted, I mean from reading serious books, or writing reports on them, as there's all the Press business to convey from the basement up here: and the letters to answer, and the dog to water. If alls well, we hope to get off to Rodmell next week; but that remains to be seen. Anyhow I'm glad to hear about your dog and that, for some mysterious reason, this harassed and ineffective woman [Virginia] (though so far I've shown, L. says, great common sense in the emergency) has been a prop to so magnificent a vine as the great Ethel. Yes, I'd very much like Saido[1] some time: not this moment. Ill write again.

V.

Berg

3347: To Harcourt, Brace   52 *Tavistock Square, W.C.*1

5 Jan 1938

Dear Sirs,

I have to acknowledge with thanks receipt of cheque for $5160.44[2] sent to me on Dec 20.

Yours faithfully,
Virginia Woolf

Harcourt Brace Jovanovich

3348: To Hugh Walpole   52 *Tavistock Square, W.C.*1.

5th Jan 38

Dearest Hugh,

I'm so glad you're going to be in London, and hope you'll come and see us. For the last week we've been having a bad time. Something wrong with one of Leonard's kidneys: the doctors dont know exactly what, but promise to be more definite in a day or two. So he's kept in bed, and our plans (we had been going away) uncertain: here, though, for the present.

1. *Sido*, Colette's memoir of her mother, 1930.
2. For *The Years*, U.S. edition.

Shall I like Maugham's Autobiography?[1] I'm sure I shall. And wish, to cheer me up, you'd add that youre not only reading his but writing yours.[2] I read read read—chiefly French memoirs [Chateaubriand]. Leonard who works works works in spite of a diet of rice pudding for lunch tea and dinner here looks up from his MS. and says you must come and see us, and we both send our love.

Now I must go and cook the rice pudding: maid [Mabel] being at the Movies.

Yr Virginia

Texas

3349: To Lady Ottoline Morrell

52 *Tavistock Square, W.C.1.*

9th Jan [1938]

Dearest Ottoline,

It is shameful that I haven't answered you or thanked you for the lovely green shell. This has become part of my washing table at Rodmell—a glorified soap dish.

I was beginning to haunt my old shops in search of a book, when Leonard was taken ill—something wrong with his kidneys, and we came back here. We have spent 10 days seeing doctors, he has been X rayed and so on: but they cant say exactly what is wrong yet. Probably we shall know if its nothing or something by the middle of the week. This is a great worry, as you'll understand: and the doctors spin things out so: one cant at the moment make plans, or I would hope to see you.

Nor have I read the Duke[3] which Tom [Eliot] gave me for a Christmas present. A lovely muslin picture of you. So you must excuse this scrap. I'll write again, and only send this now to assure you of my ancient affection; for its not worth anything else.

Yr V.W.

Texas

3350: To Vanessa Bell

52 *Tavistock Square* [*W.C.1.*]

Sunday 9th Jan. [1938]

I cant help thinking you owe me a letter—however, I had Angelica's, to my great content.

1. Somerset Maugham, *The Summing Up*, 1938. Virginia much admired it for its honesty and clarity (see Vita's letter to Harold, 3 August 1938, *Harold Nicolson's Diaries, 1930-9*, p. 350).
2. Walpole never wrote his autobiography.
3. The Duke of Portland, to whose memoirs (*Men, Women and Things*) Virginia was referring, was Ottoline's half-brother.

I've not written partly because I always hoped the doctor would say that L. was cured. However this wretched little bother—some pus or blood in his water—has gone on, so he's had to stay in bed. He got a temperature at Rodmell, and we came back. That went at once; but the other thing has gone on, and the dr. thinks it may be something wrong either with the kidneys or prostate. The X Ray only showed that one kidney wasn't working properly. And it may clear off and be nothing. But if it doesn't stop next week, we shall probably see a specialist. They can examine the bladder apparently and make sure if it is the prostate or not. Even so, of course there's no reason to think an operation would be necessary. He's certainly got better since he was in bed, and kept entirely on rice puddings.

But that explains why I've no news and write such a d-d dull letter. We've been back 10 days and the dr. Rau—who's a very intelligent man and quite skeptical of all medicine—says he must do every possible test, however inconclusive, so that most of my time is spent waiting for him to come or to telephone, and he generally forgets. Except for Judith, Harry Stephen[1] and Helen [Anrep] I've seen no one—Judith buying Duncan chintz's for the new house, and controlling Karins delirious excitement. It is now theirs. Then old Harry—77 so he says, but exactly the same. Dorothea[2] is lodged in England, and being X rayed, was found to have had consumption, but recovered. James has taken up singing, but remains at Toynbee, a Catholic.[3] Barbara thinks it a good sign that he sings without a collar—he is trying to pull himself together, she says. And Ethel Sands, of course, rings up and asks me to lunch; but I dont go. In fact London is still hibernating. Everyone away; and cold and rain most days, though nothing like the famous climate of the Riviera. My word you do sound cold! 4 inches of snow. I've just rung up Clive, in the hope of catching Quentin on his way back from the North, but he hasn't yet arrived, and may go straight to Charleston. Clive sounds cheerful, and is dining here on Tuesday; when I hope to get more mundane gossip. Hugh Walpole is coming to tea, and I'm to egg him on to buy a lottery ticket. Helen is only just emerging from the exhaustion of the party; which financially was a failure, that is they didn't get money for the Studio; but she's off again on the other schemes, chiefly in order to provide an

1. Judith, aged 19, was the younger daughter of Adrian and Karin Stephen, and now a Cambridge undergraduate. Harry was Sir Harry Stephen, 3rd Bt. (1860-1945), Virginia's first cousin, who had been a judge in Calcutta until 1914.
2. Dorothea Stephen (1871-1965), Harry's younger sister, had lived in India and was the author of *Indian Thought*, 1918.
3. Sir James Stephen (b. 1908) was the son of Sir Harry Stephen (whom he succeeded as 4th Bt. in 1945) and Barbara Nightingale, the daughter of Florence Nightingale's brother. In the year of his succession he was certified insane, and was not discharged from hospital until 1972. In 1936 he had become a Catholic, and was a resident at Toynbee Hall, the adult education centre in east London.

inaudible w.c. for the more refined pupils.[1] And of course Waley and de Zoete[2] were dining, and she had to go and cook dinner. Duncan's card was a great pleasure: the 2 hearts are shining on the mantelpiece.

I'm afraid I've droned on about medical details, but its a comfort to write to you, and I've told you all, so there's no need to worry. In fact, the dr: said this morning it might still clear up completely. But we cant know before Wednesday. I'll write, at once.

Now do be careful, and come back to your devoted Singe. L. sends his love. He works all day, and is quite unconcerned.

B.

Berg

3351: To V. Sackville-West   52 *Tavistock Sqre.* [*W.C.*1]

10th Jan. [1938]

Yes, certainly—19th dine. By all means. But we've been having the devils own time. Leonard's kidney got bad suddenly at Monks House: we came up ten days ago: since then he's been in bed, and we've had X rays, and all the other horrors: the dr. has just rung up to say the last report is favourable. Otherwise, he had suggested L's going to a nursing home for a complete examination. I hope now this is staved off, and all will be well. But as you see one cant be sure yet of our plans. I think if you didn't mind keeping the 19th free, I'd better send you a line later this week. They threatened the prostate —but as I say, now it seems over; and if thats so, he'll be all right by then.

Excuse this ungrammatical and unconnected jibber—they've kept us on the tenterhooks, as you may suppose.

Nothing settled about The Press: except that the scheme we told you of is off, and several offers have been made, and only one that seems likely.[3] But we'll keep that to discuss on the 19th—how nice to see you.

V.

Berg

3352: To Vanessa Bell   [52 *Tavistock Square, W.C.*1]

Monday 10th [January 1938]

I've just had a letter from you—the first for ever so long. You talk as if

1. See p. 194, note 1.
2. Beryl de Zoete (1877-1962). She was primarily an historian of dancing, and her publications included *Dance and Drama in Bali*, 1938, and *Dance and Music*, 1957. She lived with Arthur Waley (1889-1966), the orientalist and translator from the Chinese, from 1918 until her death.
3. See p. 200, note 2.

you'd never got a long letter I wrote from Rodmell just before we came back. Its quite likely—the posts have been so erratic.

However, this is only to add, as I wrote last night about Leonard, that Rau has just rung up to say the water is perfectly normal for the first time. This is a great relief, as we'd made up our minds that he'd have to go into a nursing home to be examined. Rau said if it stayed normal for 2 days we could consider the whole thing cleared up, though of course it may come back—or it maynt. Anyhow this is better than we had hoped for; and there seems no reason why it shouldnt stay normal now. Otherwise Rau says there's nothing wrong.

I didnt see Quentin. Clive said he'd gone straight back—nor have I heard of your adventure[1]—in fact I've had no news of you whatsoever, except from Angelica. Perhaps letters missed. L. says I'm to tell you he liked your jacket [for *Three Guineas*] very much—it was whisked off before I saw it. Owing to you, another story [*The Shooting Party*] has been taken in America, so good dolphin here's your Commission, and do for God's sake take *first class* this time. The cold sound[s] hellish. Here it is like the old underground, sulphur yellow and steamy. I've seen no one. I'll write again, but if you dont hear, dont worry: I mean, Rau keeps one waiting so long that I mayn't hear in time to tell you before you start. Lord how heavenly to see you again! L sends his love—

B.

I'm glad Charles' memoir is done.[2] Do bring all the things for me to read. Are you sending them to Chatto [& Windus]?

Berg

3353: To Molly MacCarthy   52 *Tavistock Square, W.C.*1.

Thursday [13 January 1938]

Dearest Molly,

Your letter has only now arrived. We are both desolated that you should be ill [gall stones]. Leonard is up today for the first time after 2 weeks in bed with kidney trouble—only rice pudding allowed. If he should be all right, we will walk into the hospital sometime tomorrow (Friday) afternoon. But not if its wet. May we leave it open? Only if you have a certain visitor, close with them, and shut us out, for its doubtful.

1. As Vanessa was driving from Cassis to Marseilles, where she picked up Duncan Grant, the car lights failed.
2. Charles Mauron's memoir for *Julian Bell*, which was published by the Hogarth Press in November of this year.

Lord what a year of incessant catastrophe—but that years over, so lets hope the best for this one.

And let us break up the frost of silence and meet constantly. Come and have pink cake again: soon. We go to Rodmell for one weeks breather on Saturday; the country has been wired off for foot and mouth for 2 months: then back here. Please get well and remember the old Guys, thats the Wolves, who both loll out their red tongues in kissing your hand. Gall dont matter; its what they make ink of. Kidneys I now know all about.

Yr Virginia

Mrs Michael MacCarthy

3354: To V. Sackville-West   *52 Tavistock Sqre.* [*W.C.*1]

Friday 14th [January 1938]

To our immense relief the doctor at last says that there's nothing wrong at the moment with Leonard.

So he's up and about, and for a month we're to forget it. Theyre not of course certain what it is after all this time, and say he may have another attack, or not. But oh the torture they put one to waiting for results, and then not knowing what they mean. Science is only half taught and completely untrustworthy.

But the result is that we shall dash down to Monks House tomorrow for a week, so must put off the 19th. But look here—do come up the next week— we shall be back on the 23rd.; and we'll keep any night you suggest. Only dont tell Sibyl [Colefax], who's pestering me to dine to meet you and I've said we shall be away. There's a mass of things to discuss with you, let alone the (purely aesthetic) pleasure your presence gives.

I'm so beside myself with relief—its like a flock of air balls tied to my shoulder instead of cannon balls; it was a damnable nightmare—

Potto

We had made up our minds to a nursing home and even heard of one— Roman Catholics in St Johns Wood.

Berg

3355: To Ethel Smyth   *52 T.[avistock] S.[quare, W.C.*1]

Friday. [14 January 1938]

This is only to let you know that at last the Dr. says L. is entirely normal and can get up and go about as usual. This is a tremendous relief, as they threatened a nursing Home. They wont say that its gone for ever, nor know exactly what it was. But for the present he's to forget all about it and consider himself cured. So we go off for a week to Rodmell tomorrow. Its been such a torture, waiting at the telephone end all this fortnight that I can only hold my breath and scarcely believe we're free to walk on the marshes. And foot and mouth is just over.

L. said you rang up and addressed him first as Leonard, then as Virginia.

So goodnight and as usual forgive scrawl, but I've had a mass of things to see to.

Hows the Book doing?

V.

and the dog?

Berg

3356: To Vanessa Bell   52 *Tavistock Sqre.* [*London, W.C.*1]

Friday 14th Jan. [1938]

This is only to say that the last sample was normal, so L. is now up and about. Its an amazing relief, as you can imagine. We were almost certain he would be sent to a nursing home. Of course Rau cant say anything definite. He thinks the trouble was probably caused by the prostate, and it may come back. But he advises us to do nothing about it for a month, and then see him again. Meanwhile to forget all about it. So we're off tomorrow to Monks House. I'm afraid we shall just miss you, unless you go to Charleston. I think we shall stay a week. Perhaps you'll ring up one evening. I long to see you. I've been so distracted I've practically no news. Molly [MacCarthy] is better: probably wont have an operation. Hugh [Walpole] is ready to subscribe £5 for a picture I think.[1] John Lehmann is probably becoming our partner. Clive dined and was very rubicund. I've not seen Quentin.

But I must post this: I got your letter this morning.

Lord once more how I long to see you!

B.

Kiss Angelica at once.

Berg

3357: To Molly MacCarthy   *Monk's House, Rodmell,*
                                Lewes, Sussex

16th Jan [1938]

Dearest Molly,

It was so wet and we were both so limp after being kept on tenterhooks

1. For the school of drawing and painting (later The Euston Road School).

for a fortnight by those infernal doctors who threatened nursing homes, and all the horrors, took photographs and couldn't explain them and so on— science has never been so dangerous as it is at present, I'm sure: but what I meant to say was that we didn't inflict our old damp limp bodies on you the other day: purely from love of you. But do send a line to say you're out of the Hospital, and Foss, or whatever his name is, is operating on Ellie's[1] liver not yours.

We're only down here for one week, flooded and battered, but so happy not to be in Harley Street we can do nothing but laugh. When may I come and have a gossip? Let it be over a crumpet over the fire. And we will slowly turn old Logan[2] etc. etc. on a spit and watch him melt. Owing to L's mysterious kidney I've not seen a soul, except Sir Hugh Walpole, Sir Harry Stephen and Clive Bell. James, Harry's only son, nephew of J.K.S. grand-nephew of Florence Nightingale, and my cousin, has turned Roman Catholic. I daresay this won't shock you, but it does me; and as for Harry, he wrinkles like a Baboon—the mandrill's behind is the very spit and image of his face— and says he'd far rather he [James] were dead. As it is, he's taken refuge in Toynbee Hall, and is succouring prisoners—I daresay an admirable conclusion, better than the Bar.[3] Clive has grown such a waistcoat that he eats only one meal daily. This is a fact. Nessa and Angelica are at this moment crossing France; Quentin is making pots at Charleston. Lydia and Maynard are lying very low but slightly recovering at Tilton. That's all my news, so you see I must come to tea and freshen my larder. And what did you think of Ethel Smyth and Mr Baring [*Maurice Baring*].

Yrs V. W.

Mrs Michael MacCarthy

3358: To Ethel Smyth   52 *Tavistock Square, W.C.*1.

Thursday 27 Jan. [1938]

So sorry I never answered—at least so I suspect. We came back on Sunday and I was at once seized with another influenza: from which I'm practically recovered (tho' not to the full use of my wits) today. L. you'll be glad to hear has really improved; and I feel much happier. We have to wait another fortnight for a final report. Its incredible—the cat and mouse of Dr. and patient nowadays. Also Vanessa is back from the South of France,

1. Elinor Rendel, who was Virginia's own doctor as well as Molly's. She was the daughter of Lytton Strachey's eldest sister, also named Elinor.
2. Logan Pearsall Smith (1865-1946), the American-born author of *Trivia* (1918) and other essays. Virginia's relationship with him suffered from an acrimonious exchange of letters in 1932 about Bloomsbury values, and never really recovered.
3. See p. 204, note 3.

which was under snow, and ravaged by mistral. Thats my temp. chart. And what is yours? In my debased condition I do nothing but read, Chateaubriand:[1] and see no one: hence should you require a picture of the great world, it cant be supplied.

Did the dog make a good week ender? The bitch, isnt it? No: you wont have bitches. Our bitch [Sally], mated for the 2nd time 5 weeks ago, again shows no signs of childbirth, like Princess Juliana;[2] and its laid to L's charge. Love for him they say, has turned her barren. Now I must fly to Ch^d. Memoires again; I left Napoleon retreating from Moscow. It seems to me a masterpiece, only a detestable sham Byronic man (C. I mean: not Nap.)

V.

Berg

3359: To Elizabeth Bowen   52 *Tavistock Square, W.C.*1.

Wednesday [January 1938?]

Dear Elizabeth,

That is a great relief to me—please thank your husband [Alan Cameron] for looking up the Terrace [?in connection with *Roger Fry*]. Now at least I shant get into trouble over that—if the book is ever written. It is a hopeless mess at the moment.

By the way, if you want to look at the stuffs, you can see them at Allan Walton's—100 Fulham Road, as he will send them to you.

I've got my new curtains up. Come again soon and see them.

Yrs
Virginia Woolf

Texas

3360: To Ethel Smyth   52 *Tavistock Square, W.C.*1.

31st Jan 1938

What a curse! Thinking I was cured, I went out after I'd written to you, to walk in Regents Park; came back to 101 again; so more bed; still befogged. I think I shall lie low this week, and be recovered next. I'm shutting my door on the world.

1. Vicomte François-René de Chateaubriand (1768-1848), *Deux Livres des Memoires d'outre Tombe* (ed. M. Levaillant), 1936.
2. Princess (later Queen) Juliana of the Netherlands married Prince Bernhard in January 1937. Between 1938 and 1947 she bore four daughters.

I'm glad the dog is so promising. And I saw somewhere that MB [Baring] is a best seller. So lets hope the tide is turning. Well cant write; but can read; *letters* as well as memoirs; hope to see you soon—

V.

Berg

3361: TO VANESSA BELL   52, *Tavistock Square, W.C.1.*

[3 February 1938]

I was so furious today not to see you properly dearest creature: I was thinking tomorrow is Julian's birthday and how I saw him in his cradle. You know I'd do anything I could to help you, and its so awful not to be able to: except to adore you as I do.

This doesnt want an answer:[1] its only Singe's kiss my own darling.

Berg

3362: TO PHILIP MORRELL   52 *Tavistock Square, W.C.1.*

Feb 3rd [1938]

My dear Philip,

Of course I am much touched, as well as flattered, that you should write to me[2]—and I would have written before, except that, like you and all the rest of the world, I'm in the grip of influenza. So excuse both handwriting and mind weakness. I cant conceive why you should be afraid of writing when you have such extremely nice things to say. However, I admit I often tear up letters myself: one cant, even at my age, believe that other people want affection or admiration; yet one knows that there's nothing in the whole world so important. Why is it? Why are we all so tongue tied and spell-bound? Why, as you say, do we live three streets off and yet never meet? I think human beings are fundamentally crushed by a sense of their insignificance. You and Ottoline seem to me to have everything: why should you

1. On 4 February Vanessa replied: "You do know how much you help me. I cant show it and I feel so stupid and such a wet blanket often but I couldnt get on at all if it werent for you—so you mustnt mind my being or seeming so grumpy.... Its stupid to mind dates isn't it—This one I cant help thinking of" (*Berg*). Julian would have been 30 on 4 February.
2. In 1927 Philip Morrell had fallen quite seriously in love with Virginia, and she regarded his advances as touching but pathetic. Now he had written to her again in the same strain.

care a bent farthing what I think or feel? Thats the line it takes with me: and to my surprise, apparently with you.

But merely as an author, that curious extension or excrescence on the original V.W—I'm delighted with—first: your liking Jacobs Room [1922]: my own favourite, the only one I can sometimes read a page of without disgust: second, that you should actually have read, still more marvellously have liked, Night and Day [1919]: a book written in half hour laps in bed, and so tedious to remember, and, I have always been told, a complete failure to read. Nothing will make me read it: but owing to your letter, a faint sunset glow surrounds it on the shelf.

I'm so glad Ottoline is better. I always hope you both realise what a part —and an unthanked part—you both played in the old civilisation. But why dont we renew it? Perhaps when I'm up and about you'll come to tea. Anyhow thank you for your letter, and excuse this feeble answer.

Yrs V.W.

Texas

3363: To V. Sackville-West   52 *Tavistock Square, W.C.*1.
Monday 7th Feb [1938]

Dearest Creature,

I am miserable to hear that you have been so bad.[1] It sounds the most hideous combination of diseases—Are you better? Isn't it frightfully painful? I, who am an Ostrich, and dont know what indigestion even means, always suspect that gastric inflammation must be the worst torture in the world. And jaundice added. Let me have one line, if you can, to say how you are. Anyhow, it can't be laid to my door: poisoning you with oysters, or stale cod; more likely. Was it Clives fault? You say your 'gay season' which is one night at K.B.W.[2] drinking cocktails with the ephemeral beauties of both sexes isn't it?

I would have written before, but the moment we got back from Rodmell I developed influenza: got up after a week; then caught it again; and so dribbled on, in my usual way; nothing to matter, only a head like the towel L. uses to wash Sally: damp; dirty; dismal.

Thank Heaven, nothing *seems* wrong with him; but all depends upon samples of his water: another is to be taken this week. If its innocent, we can forget all about it: if not, they suspect his prostate. Even so, it cant be very bad: only one would have possibly to consider an operation. But he seems so

1. Vita had been seriously ill at Sissinghurst since 30 January. Two nurses looked after her for a period of two weeks.
2. 4 King's Bench Walk, Inner Temple, Harold Nicolson's flat since 1930.

well, I cant help being sanguine. The doctor [Rau] admits that doctors know nothing.

Do they think your illness will pass off now completely, or shall you have to be very careful? I know nothing about it.

I've not seen a soul for 4 weeks, except in the way one does between doctors visits, telephone calls etc. Hugh [Walpole] came one day: his kidneys dont work either, but he looks like the sun in a fog. An old cousin of mine [Harry Stephen], about the sole remaining now Will Vaughan[1] has had his leg off and died in India, was crackling and bubbling at 77 with enthusiasm for Pepita, which is still selling: and we're taking John Lehmann as partner strictly under Leonard. Sales of Pepita to date, as they say in our trade, over 13,600

What about America?[2]

L. sends sympathy: so does Sally: and

Potto

Berg

3364: To T. S. Eliot   52 *Tavistock Square, W.C.*1

Wednesday [9 February 1938]

The Wolves hope that The O'Possum,[3] who is hereby created King of all Possums, and an Irish Monarch, will come to tea, 4.30, on Tuesday 15th: one Wolf has now recovered, it is hoped, from kidney disease, the other from influenza: recurring; and both would relish a little cheerful talk about ptomaine poisoning and laryngitis,—the Wolf who is holding the pen cant spell tonight or form her letters, but thats nothing to the discredit of her heart, which is true and tender as the poet says the North is:[4] and oh god what a good poem Venus and Adonis is compared with Mr—I forget his name but must now read his MS.

V

Mrs T. S. Eliot

1. William Wyamar Vaughan (1865-1938), Virginia's first cousin, had been head-master successively at Giggleswick, Wellington and Rugby, from which he retired in 1931. He went as a delegate to the Indian Science Congress in December 1937, and while visiting the Taj Mahal, he fell and broke his leg. It was amputated, and he died of pneumonia on 4 February 1938.
2. The American edition of *Pepita*, published by Doubleday.
3. See p. 188, note 3.
4. "Oh tell her Swallow, thou that knowest each,
   That bright and fierce and fickle is the South,
   And dark and true and tender is the North."
   Tennyson, *The Princess*, IV, 73-5

3365: To Ethel Smyth   52 *Tavistock Square, W.C.*1.

Friday, 11th Feb. [1938]

Hurrah! The report today says completely normal. So thats over. No surgeon shall fright me again. They did their best. I'm persuaded I was right, and the whole trouble was neither kidney disease, Brights disease, nor Prostate gland: but simply a blow in the back, as I suggested but I was poohpooed, from the handle of the car in October. Also, you'll be amused to hear, and as we're on medical subjects we may as well be quit of them, I submitted my abnormal temperature to the infallible Berlin Jew [Dr Rau], who at once declared it to be caused by an infection of the sinus: for which they now operate; but never as yet with any success. Result: nothing can be done; which is highly satisfactory. In his opinion this poison also causes my headaches. To be incurable is a great relief. I hear Vita's been ill with gastric inflammation; my cousin Will Vaughan is dead of a fall at the Taj Mahal: but now that Leonards well I'm as selfish as a hedgehog, and can only sink back in my chair with complete relief; the first time since Dec. 26th.

No time or room or even a pen that can write; so no more. We're in the thick of taking a partner [Lehmann], who's about to dine with us, and fill up legal documents. And the dog? And Ethel Smyth? What news?

I send this to catch Saturday post.

V.

Berg

3366: To V. Sackville-West   52 *Tavistock Square, W.C.*1.

Valentine's day [14 February 1938]

Its the greatest relief—at last, they say L. is perfectly normal. So thats over. I suspect it was a blow he had doing the car—nothing else. My influenza leaves a little tempe^re: the dr. says a Sinus infected: but nothing anyhow. As for you—Lord how bad you must have been! And the horror—2 nurses! And still one left. Poor wretched sheepdog; all mange and misery. But do say, seriously, is it serious still? Shall you get quite rid?

Now: the *only* day I lunch out, with Clive, curse him, is the 22nd. Could you make it 21st or 23rd or in fact any other day that week or month? Please do: I cant throw over Clive, as he's engaged me this 10 days, God Knows why.

And I have a lover [Philip Morrell]. The husband of a lady in high life. Wishes to meet me clandestinely. I put this in to see if I can rouse jealousy: one spark; or does jaundice forbid? And has time sealed the source? Anyhow, I make my bid. How odd, this red flower on a grey tree! (He's grey: so am I)

Well: tell me how you are: what the dr. says: and arrange another day please, or I shall elope

V.

Berg

3367: To V. Sackville-West   52 *Tavistock Square, W.C.1.*

Thursday [17 February 1938]

Yes of course: the 23rd. or any other day. Wait till you are certain and then send a card. And what food?

When I got your letter I said to L: who was feeding Mitz, Vita is the nicest of all our friends. Why? He said. Whereupon I explained how your modesty as an author is nothing to your fidelity as a friend. Isnt that a nice sentence? Whereupon, he agreed. Then Mitz wetted. Oh Lord—I meant to write a long letter, and here's the usual scrap: but Londons a tinkling caravan: although Sibyl is weekending in Palermo.

Yes, I'll tell you about the loves of the aged—how violent they are, and ridiculous, ending in The Reform Club of all places; where they cook beefsteaks.

But you dont say if the disease is going, or how you got it, or whether you love me.

And I've a green flame on the horizon: thats the tremor a new love rays up; and not male either: its seen by solitary watchers off Iceland and heralds gigantic Bergs: so mine heralds—

Well, why shouldnt it be Vita on the 23rd?

Now for a pack of dull letters. But that was exact, what I said to L. when he was feeding Mitz—about you minding his illness, and *his being well now*

V.

Berg

3368: To Lady Ottoline Morrell

Monk's House, Rodmell,
Lewes, Sussex

Saturday [19 February 1938]

Dearest Ottoline,

Yes—thank goodness, after keeping us on the tenterhooks for I don't know how long, the doctor declares Leonard normal. This is a great relief as you can imagine. I've been having influenza, of my own kind, which goes on dragging a miserable little temperature behind it: so we've been lying very low. But when you are back, and sunned, and all our germs are dried out —as they may be today—its like an early June morning here—birds singing and blue between the trees—then I hope we shall meet. Its an age since we came owling.

How beneficent of you and Philip to take down my old books again! I cant believe that any human being can get through Night and Day which I wrote chiefly in bed, half an hour at a time. But it taught me a great deal, or so I hoped, like a minute Academy drawing: what to leave out: by putting it all in.

I bought a book for 6d in the Penguins called William by E.H.Young,[1] and, for a wonder, enjoyed it greatly. She knows how to put in, and yet remain readable: so minute and yet so alive. And as its the kind of book I generally dislike, I think she must be a very good novelist, and wonder she's not far more famous than dear old voluble Hugh, and Wells and so on. Did you once say you knew her? or was it Ethel Mayne?[2]

Now I must put our rice in the oven. Then I shall read Chateaubriand; and fall asleep over the fire. I am surrounded, still, by Roger's papers, and as soon as I'm normal and collected, shall have to begin to burrow.

And how are your memoirs? The Duke's [of Portland] had a flash of the 18th Century: otherwise the self complacency seemed omnipotent and overwhelming.

Yr V.W.

Texas

3369: To Ethel Smyth   52 *Tavistock Sqre.* [*W.C.*1]

[24 February 1938]

Now there's so many things to answer, how can I begin?

Montaigne. Yes, one of my favourites, as they say in birthday books, or am I thinking of Lord Beaconsfield?[3] I mean if you intend to die, but dont do it for my sake, give me a last—oh I cant think of the word—a last shower of your brutal gentleness and wisdom—thats much in his line. But dont anticipate the date on my account.

The Years: Yes I thought you might one day come to like it better; but didn't give it you, so as not to prod a sitting hen. L. always maintains that it is the best but the most difficult of my brew. I loathe it and see a sweat stain, a tear stain, a gash—200 pages cut—on every existing page.

Temperature: Still up and down but next week, being the 4th, I always break the thermometer. Whats the use of being 99 pt 4? What the harm?

1. Emily Hilda Young (1880-1949) wrote novels about everyday life, including *William* (1925) and *Miss Mole*, for which she was awarded the Tait Black Memorial Prize in 1930.
2. Ethel Colburn Mayne (d. 1941), the novelist, translator and authority on Byron.
3. Benjamin Disraeli (1804-81).

Information wanted:[1] Are women allowed to play in orchestras? When was this, allowed, if so: and are they now musically, (as far as training goes) equal with the other sex? I've now got to produce, in the usual fury and despair and haste, what should have been a booklet, and has swollen to a book, in which this fact, or fiction, occurs, and I want it to be accurate, but have lost my note, so appeal to you.

Vita still too ill to lunch: has had 2 nurses. Have you any news, via Dotty or Hilda? You see this is a new kind of paper, and not so large as t'other: or I would discourse on Vernon,[2] whose letters I suspect are the best things she wrote—that is from the sample in your MB: a book I mean to read when I'm quit of proofs. And do you know Landouska?[3] She's asked me to stay.

So thats all for the present moment. But why doubt my love?

V.

Berg

3370: To George Rylands   52 *Tavistock Square* [*W.C.1.*]

Sunday [27 February 1938]

Dearest Dadie,[4]

Leonard thinks it almost certain he won't be able to come, because we've taken John as partner and he has to go through all the stock in the first week of March: also is on an Arbitration body[5] which is then sitting. But if we should find a day free might we let you know? And a thousand thanks for remembering the old Wolves who would love to see your Lear[6] (and you).

Your
Virginia

George Rylands

1. For the notes to *Three Guineas*, but Virginia added no more information to her statement in the text (p. 70) that the "educated man's daughter" in the 19th century "tinkled on the piano but was not allowed to join an orchestra".
2. Vernon Lee (1856-1935), the novelist and critic, whose real name was Violet Paget, had been an intimate friend of Ethel Smyth and Maurice Baring. In Ethel's life of Baring she included a large selection of the Lee-Baring correspondence.
3. Wanda Landowska (1877-1959), the Polish pianist, harpsichordist and composer.
4. George Rylands had been manager of the Hogarth Press from July to December 1924, and was now a Fellow of King's College, Cambridge.
5. In 1938 Leonard was nominated a member of the Whitley Council for the Civil Service, and remained a member for 17 years. The Council arbitrated on wage claims and working conditions within the Civil Service. See Leonard's *Downhill All the Way*, pp. 209-10.
6. Directed by Rylands for The Marlowe Dramatic Society at the Cambridge Arts Theatre (8-12 March).

3371: To V. Sackville-West   52 *Tavistock Sq.* [*W.C.*1]

Tuesday [1 March 1938]

Damn: I mean, I'm thankful you're better.

But: Monday the 7th I've said I'll take Angelica to a concert.

Could you conceivably change to Thursday 10th or Friday 11th? When we shall be alone?

If this is impossible, I, but not L. can manage Monday: I mean he could take Angelica. Only do let us arrange something. And how are you? In haste—

V.

Your letter, dated Sunday, only came this Tuesday morning

Berg

3372: To Vanessa Bell   [52 *Tavistock Square, W.C.*1]

11th March, [1938]

I never realised, till I bought a calendar yesterday, that it is already 11th of March. So I'm 10 days late [with Angelica's allowance].

I'm told that Angelica absolutely refuses to go to the Stephen's [Adrian and Karin] party tomorrow: and I dont suppose I shall dare.

I was going to inflict myself for tea upon you, but have to spend the hours between tea and dinner correcting what is absolutely the worst book I've ever written,[1] let alone that I shan't, when published, have a friend left.

But you wont have missed me.

Shall we come in on Sunday night?

My unfortunate mother in law has just been knocked down and seriously hurt by a maid running out of a bedroom. So we've got to go and see her tomorrow; or I hoped to suggest a jaunt

Thats all: except that Singe [Virginia] adores you

B

Berg

3373: To Ethel Smyth   *Monks House* [*Rodmell, Sussex*]

Friday [18 March 1938]

We came down yesterday, as we have to go to Oxford on Sunday; and

1. But in her diary for 11 April Virginia wrote that *Three Guineas* "shows industry; fertility; and is, here and there, as 'well written' ... as any of my rather skimble skamble works! I think there's more to it than to a *Room* [*of One's Own*, 1929]" (*AWD*, p. 289).

218

thus even had you been available, I couldn't hold up a finger. And oh Lord! how difficult, with this riot of horror drumming in at the window to make any engagements.[1] Leonard is in the thick of meetings; the telephone never stops ringing; agitated editors arrive with articles intended to prevent war— though I can do nothing, and scarcely now understand, my mind is all a ruffle and a confusion. But whats the use of passing this on to you, who know it already? So to return to private matters:—*Barnes*[2]—is that his name?—I've only met him on business, and we call each other punctiliously Mr and Mrs: so why Virginia so familiarly? *Vita:* she dined t'other night; and seemed rather aged, I thought: but still (in spite of Gwen) a perfectly modest and (in spite of Ethel) sincere human being.

Temperature: I feel less hot; less stale; so expect when next taken, to find it normal. *Work:* What are you doing? *Dog:* and how's he shaping? Dogs and daffodils alone retain their sanity. Yes, I'd like to see you again; often indeed think of you; and shall one of these days read MB [*Maurice Baring*]. Did I tell you, that, all these weeks the pressure of life has been increased by our taking John Lehmann as partner? a bold step; but one that will free Leonard from work; at present, what with interviews and lawyers, work is doubled. And a vast pile of MSS. lies on the floor.

But Ethel dear, in spite of this rigid and rudimentary scrawl, accept the affection of your distracted and inefficient

V.

I was thinking last night of the little book [*unidentified*] you gave me—And now L's old mother has been knocked down, seriously hurt, and we have to spend hours trying to cheer her. The Jews can lament: but how they cling to life!

Berg

3374: To Vanessa Bell   [52 *Tavistock Square, W.C.*1]

Tuesday, [22 March 1938]

I'm slightly worried to think that you're going to the Stephen Spender play.[3] I found it rather upsetting; and though I daresay its foolish to be upset

1. On 12 March German troops had crossed the Austrian frontier and entered Vienna unopposed. Austria was annexed to the German Reich, and Kurt von Schuschnigg, the Austrian Chancellor, was arrested.
2. George Barnes, Director of the B.B.C.'s Talks Department. See p. 83, note 6.
3. *Trial of a Judge*, produced at the Unity Theatre in London by the Group Theatre Company. Virginia thought that the mother in the play resembled Vanessa.

in that way,—theres a young man killed and of course one thinks of Julian—
I cant help wishing you wouldn't go. I expect this is silly: but I thought I'd
say so, so forgive

B.

Berg

3375: To Ethel Smyth   52 *Tavistock Square, W.C.1.*
Friday [1 April 1938]

Found after you had gone; and honestly returned; in gratitude for the
kind and inspiriting visit, which I would also return, but shant be asked: so
thats that.

But what about celebrating the 80th anniversary[1] together by eating a
really good dinner?

Berg

3376: To V. Sackville-West
                              52 *T.*[avistock] *S.*[quare, *W.C.*1]
Tuesday [5 April 1938]

No, I hadn't heard a word, and only got your letter late yesterday on
coming back from Rodmell. I am miserable to think how bad you've been;[2]
and going through all that torture of waiting for results. Are they sure they've
spotted it now? And why lead from Cider? Isn't it from painting a greenhouse?—But if you have a moment let me have a word. We both sit up like
begging dogs, with our paws up, sending our faithful humble sympathy.
And how do they de-lead you? And shall you be up again? Kew is very lovely.
I remember sitting there once in a livid storm with you [21 July 1927]. This
is no more than a mew: I'm incapable of writing, but trust you to divine my
intention—yes, it was kind of you to write, and not to make me also wait in
suspense, which is loathsome.

I've been to the Charterhouse[3] today. Where Col Newcome died saying

1. Ethel's 80th birthday was on 23 April.
2. Vita had been ill with lead poisoning, for which her doctor blamed the cider
   press at Sissinghurst. She spent five days (27-31 March) in a nursing home, and
   had lost two stone since her illness in January.
3. Near Aldersgate in London, on the site of a 14th century Carthusian monastery.
   In the early 17th century the buildings became a hospital for the poor and a
   school for boys, but the school was moved in 1872 to its present location in
   Surrey, and male pensioners continued to occupy the original Charterhouse
   which Virginia visited. For Colonel Newcome see Chapter LXXX of Thackeray's *The Newcomes.*

Adsum; and there he was [his portrait], in a white tie and black cloak at 3 pm. today; we collided.

But forgive my chatter and accept my homage and Pottos love and get well and did you ever read the Zincali: (Borrow)[1] and is The Pepita there (a prostitute gipsy) any relation of yours?

V.

Poor lean wizened brute—your coats what they call "staring" I suppose. 2 stone! Lord!

Berg

3377: To Ling Su-Hua   52 *Tavistock Square, W.C.*1

5th April 1938

Dear Sue Ling,[2]

I hope you have had the letter I wrote in answer to your first letter. I wrote only a few days after I had yours. Now Vanessa has just sent on your letter of March 3rd. I wish I could help you. I know that you have much more reason to be unhappy than we have even; and therefore how foolish any advice must be. But my only advice—and I have tried to take it myself— is to work. So let us think how you could fix your mind upon something worth doing in itself. I have not read any of your writing, but Julian often wrote to me about it, and meant to show me some of it. He said too that you had lived a most interesting life; indeed, we had discussed—I think in letters —the chance that you would try to write an account of your life in English. That is what I would suggest now. Your English is quite good enough to give the impression you wish to make; and I could change anything difficult to understand.

Will you make a beginning, and put down exactly anything you remember? As no one in England knows you, the book could be more free than usual. Then I would see if it could not be printed. But please think of this: not merely as a distraction, but as a work that would be of great value to other people too. I find autobiographies much better than novels. You ask what books I would advise you to read: I think the English in the 18th

1. George Borrow, *The Zincali, or an Account of the Gypsies in Spain*, 1841.
2. The wife of Professor Chen of Wu-han University and an intimate friend of Julian Bell while he worked there. She had written to Virginia that she was helplessly depressed by Japan's invasion of China and her refugee life in the western province of Szechuan. In 1947 she followed her husband to England, where he worked first with the Sino-British Culture Association and later with UNESCO. The autobiography which Virginia urged her to write was eventually published by the Hogarth Press in 1953 under the title *Ancient Melodies*.

Century wrote in the best way for a foreigner to learn from. Do you like letters? There are Cowpers, [Horace] Walpoles; very clear and easy; Scotts novels; (Rob Roy); Jane Austen: then Mrs Gaskells life of Charlotte Brontë: then among modern writers, George Moore's novels—they are simply written too. I could send you English books, but I do not know if you have them already. But from your letters I see that you write very well; you need not copy others, only find new words by reading quickly. I say nothing about politics. You know from what I said before how strongly the English are on your side but cannot do anything to help. We hear about China from friends here. But perhaps now there will be a change. The worst may be over.

At any rate please remember that I am always glad if you will write and tell me anything about yourself: or politics: and it would be a great pleasure to me to read some of your writing, and criticise it: so think of writing your life, and if you only write a few pages at a time, I could read them and we could discuss it. I wish I could do more. We send you our best sympathy.

Yours
Virginia Woolf

Ling Su-Hua (Mrs Chen)

3378: To Vanessa Bell   52 *Tavistock Square, W.C.1.*

Postcard
Wednesday [6 April 1938]

As it is Cranium[1] night tomorrow, Thursday, would you and Angelica dine with me; or might I dine, or come in after, with you? I rang up, but no answer; and so write tactfully, so that you can excuse yourselves. But would you ring up.

Berg

3379: To Ling Su-Hua   52 *Tavistock Square, W.C.1*

April 9th 1938

Dear Sue Ling,

I got your letter written on March 3rd a few days ago, and answered it at once. But stupidly I forgot to send it by airmail—so I write this to tell you that I have written. And the only thing of any interest I had to say was to ask you to write your autobiography, and to say I will gladly read it and give it any correction it needs. Now your other letter (March 24th) has just come, in which you tell me that you have begun to write this. I am so glad. Julian

1. The convivial society founded by David Garnett in 1925.

always told me that you had lived a most interesting life: and you say he also wanted you to write it down—simply, as it comes, not bothering about grammar at all. I also asked if you would like me to send you any old English books—18th Century ones perhaps—so that you could learn words. But you will find this in my letter. Let me know if I can do anything to help you in your work. I am certain work is the only way in which one can live at this moment. I will send this now, and hope you will get it soon.

We send our sympathy and shall always wish for news both of you and of your war, and politics.

Yrs
Virginia Woolf

Ling Su-Hua (Mrs Chen)

3380: To Ethel Smyth [52 *Tavistock Square, W.C.*1]

Monday [11 April 1938]

Well anyhow you might have sent the train list. After Easter, in the sun, your mood may melt—what with the warm womb stimulant etc. After Easter, I may be asked. After Easter—but I cant continue the list, being in a hurry and only write to say, if you've an exact account of the Bournemouth orchestra affair,[1] might I have it; in case I could use it: not that I suppose I can: but has the paper printed it? If its handy and no trouble post it me. And I'll write a long long letter all about love one of these days. Appropriate aphrodisiacs for your venereal state.

And the dinner? 80th birthday?

Monks House for a week on Thursday.

V.

Berg

3381: To John Lehmann *Monk's House, Rodmell, Lewes, Sussex*

Friday 22nd April [1938]

My dear John,

I am ashamed not to have answered your very nice kind and by all means welcome letter before. How can I write suitably now, because I am being badgered by Philip Morrell to write an obituary of Ottoline.[2]

1. The exclusion of women-instrumentalists from the Bournemouth Municipal Orchestra.
2. Ottoline Morrell died of heart disease on 21 April in Dr Cameron's clinic at Tunbridge Wells. She was 64. Virginia's obituary of Ottoline appeared in *The Times* on 28 April.

I'm full of sanguininity about the future: and thankful to lift the burden onto your back. Nor can I see myself any reason why we should quarrel; or why we should drink the Toast in cold water.[1] What about a good dinner (not English) at Boulestin or some such place? You are hereby invited to be the guest of Virginia Woolf's ghost—the Hogarth ghost: who lives let us hope elsewhere. Lets arrange it. We come back on Sunday: and then there'll be the usual uproar.

Much warmth of feeling in this bitter evening (sitting over the fire) from us both. And Lord! when I die, dont ask anyone to write a few words about me in The Times.

Yrs ever
V.W.

Please thank your mother for the invitation. May we suggest a day later? We should like to come down very much. And I forgot to post this.

John Lehmann

3382: To Ethel Smyth

M[onks] H.[ouse, Rodmell, Sussex]

Saturday 23rd April [1938]

I hope my wire conveyed, inadequately, loves and congratulations.[2] And it admitted my fault—I mean, looking hastily I skipped a week, and though it was *next* Saturday. At the same time, I dont think, considering the very modified joy with which you received the proposal (see postcards) that I was wrong in assuming that you'd be glad to be quit of the affair: hence your "bitter disappointment" surprised me. Still, if you *are* disappointed, and would like to celebrate the wrong day, whats to hinder? Oh dear, how mistaken I always seem to be! Only your postcards were very tepid, I assure you.

However, faults or not, here's my health to you in ink, surely since it was with that liquid that Shakespeare wrote the sonnets; ah but you'll say Sh^re

---

1. The agreement between Leonard and Lehmann (by which Lehmann bought Virginia's share of the Press) came into force at the beginning of April. After the signing Lehmann wrote to Virginia: "Leonard was very rugged the other day when I signed the Partnership Agreement, and to my proposal that the event be marked by a mutual health-drinking, replied that he only had cold water" (Lehmann, *Thrown to the Wolves*, p. 59).
2. On Ethel's 80th birthday, 23 April.

had a heart:[1] so have I: only not liquid; compact: congealed; stupid: solid however. Only at this moment rather lacerated by Ottoline's death: cant help feeling a queer loveliness departed: and much bothered by frantic appeals from Philip, to write about her in the Times—How I hate that!—but must, I suppose.

So once more, forgive: and dear Ethel continue to live and to forgive another 50 years for the sake of your distracted Virginia who will certainly require your living and forgiving as long as she lives.

Berg

3383: To V. Sackville-West   52 *Tavistock Square* [*W.C.*1]
May 3rd [1938]

I was awfully distressed (I wish there were any decent words for this sort of sentiment) to hear you had been attacked again. What the devil is lead poisoning? And when shall you be cured—idiotic questions, but then this letter writing business is such a fraud. And I cant ring you up, for your telephone isn't attached to the Pink Tower, where I hope you're thinking of Leonardo not of lead.[2] This is a mere drivel of affection: should you have a card handy write a fact about yourself on it, and dont confuse the most modest and least egotistic of women with that other former lover of mine— who by the way has just rung up to impose a visit with, I gather your [Winnaretta] Polignac in tow. Ethel I mean. I had intended an 80th birthday Boulestin party, and to ask you, but we were at Monks House, and I put it off, to her fury—not that you could have come. But will you face it one of these days?

We think of driving up to The Hebrides, the furthest seas—where the cuckoo calls—whats the quotation Im thinking of?—breaking the silence of the seas[3]—anyhow, thats what we mean to do in June. Oh I'm so sick of this blasted London; its perpetual drab, its drip today, its grey everyday, and all

1. Shakespeare died on this date in 1616.
    "Scorn not the Sonnet; Critic, you have frowned,
    Mindless of its just honours; With this key
    Shakespeare unlocked his heart."
            —Wordsworth
2. By this time Vita had fully recovered from lead poisoning and had returned to her tower-study at Sissinghurst, where she did not, however, write about Leonardo.
3. "A voice so thrilling ne'er was heard
    In spring-time from the cuckoo-bird,
    Breaking the silence of the seas
    Among the farthest Hebrides."
            —Wordsworth, *The Solitary Reaper*

these people. The Press however is now chained to John Lehmann, or will be in October; and I hope (not with great sanguinity though) to be quit of those eternal MSS. Six lie before me at this moment. And we've had such a good year and made so much money, and I cant help some pride when I think of the type in the carpet at Hogarth House;[1] and now they say its worth, The Press, £10,000. Much thanks to the noble daughter of all the Sackvilles.

My God, how does one write a Biography? Tell me. I'm fairly distracted with Fry papers. How can one deal with facts—so many and so many and so many? Or ought one, as I incline, to be purely fictitious. And what is a life? And what was Roger? And if one cant say, whats the good of trying? Yet its my favourite reading—short of shall we say Shakespeare and Sackville West: biography. I am reading for the first time a book which I think a very good book—Mandeville's Fable of the Bees [1714]. Only I must turn to Libby Benedicts Fable on Libby Benedict.[2] As I began by saying this is merely a fish without any bait for news. of you. I was at Ottolines funeral services.[3] I miss her; I mean Gower Street[4] looks to me dumb and dismal. I used to go round between tea and dinner, and now—so dont put the light out which as you remember lit up the porpoise at Sevenoaks.[5] And excuse so very mild a dribble—Its Potto's fault

V.

Berg

3384: To Margaret Llewelyn Davies

Monk's House, Rodmell,
Lewes, Sussex

Typewritten
Sunday May 8th [1938]

Dearest Margaret,

Yes it has been a horrid long gap since we were at Hillspur [Dorking, September 1937]. (I'm getting so illegible that I spare you my handwriting.) So much has happened, one way or another, that it seems useless to try to catch up here. And yet what happens is so incessant and so small—one thing then another—that its difficult to say what it amounts to. You ask about

1. Richmond, where the Woolfs lived from 1915 to 1924, and from which they launched the Hogarth Press in 1917.
2. The author of *The Refugees*, published by the Hogarth Press in March 1938. Virginia met her for the first time on this day.
3. On 26 April at St Martin's in the Field, Trafalgar Square.
4. Ottoline's house, 10 Gower Street, Bloomsbury.
5. See p. 186, note 3.

Angelica—well, she's just appeared as a dancer at her Studio theatre;[1] and Nessa rang me up in great excitement because she shows a brilliant gift— dancing a whole Spanish play mostly alone. We shall go and see her tomorrow night. I think this is the only comfort for Vanessa—otherwise, I sometimes feel as you can imagine, that life is very hard for her. She is painting however; they have a school in the Euston Road—she and Duncan—where they teach the young gratuitously.

I went to Ottolines service, Philip's rather formal but on the whole touching address was read by the actor Speaight who acts Becket in Tom Eliots Murder in the Cathedral—one of Ottolines friends.[2] And now I have the agitating prospect of an interview with Philip to discuss some memorial to her, and to choose one of her shawls. I had grown very fond of her—she was changed; so shabby and humble and humorous; I always saw her alone. The parties were a grind; and she was so deaf.

Ann and Richard brought your niece,[3] and we thought her so distinct and minute and on her own; though she was too shy to talk; and Ann and Richard talk nineteen to the dozen—all about politics, which as you say, are unmentionable. We have at last shifted half the burden of the Press onto a partner—John Lehmann, Rosamond's brother.

It has become so prosperous—isnt it odd, thinking how it began in the drawing room at Hogarth House. All Leonards time and more of mine than I like to give has lately had to be given to MSS and authors. After October I hope he will be free for his next volume. And if we can steal three weeks in June, we are going to drive through England up to the very tip of Scotland. This year France and Italy seem too red hot; but we long for seals and islands and bays and old country people. And no Press. Leonard is set upon here by the villagers, who have made him a School Manager and he runs the Labour party and the cowman [Hubbard] consults him about divorce—so the garden though flowering in every colour at the moment is not altogether a sanctuary.

Yes—when are we to meet? I did enjoy seeing you and Lilian [Harris]; but I know how exhausting friends visits are. You must let us know when you feel up to it. Its not a very difficult drive from here or from London. Leonard says there are 395 copies of "Life" . . . left.[4] I wish we could bring out another volume. The young are all on the side of the workers, but

1. The London Theatre Studio, Islington.
2. Robert Speaight (1904-77), the actor and author of many books on theatre and theology. He appeared in *Murder in the Cathedral* at the Canterbury Festival in 1935 and London in 1936.
3. Richard Llewelyn Davies's sister Catherine ('Kitty'), who later became a historian.
4. *Life As We Have Known It*, autobiographical essays by women members of the Co-operative Guild, was introduced by Virginia, edited by Margaret Llewelyn Davies, and published by the Hogarth Press in 1931.

naturally know nothing whatever about them. I'm always on the look out for a real Co-op autobiography; L. is in the house planning a [issue of the] Political Quarterly; and I must stop and dish up our lunch.

I wish you would come here—I have a garden room, cheek by jowl with the Church, and with a great elm tree over it.

But no more—

My love to Lilian
Virginia

Sussex

3385: To John Lehmann   52 *Tavistock Square, W.C.1.*

Sunday [15 May 1938]

Dear John,

I'm sorry that you and Leonard didnt manage to fix an evening for our dinner. Meanwhile this is only to say, as you asked me about a story [for *New Writing*], that I'm afraid its impossible, as L. says you have to make up your number early in July. I want to take a holiday in June, —so shouldnt anyhow have time. Many thanks for suggesting it, and excuse this scrawl, the result of driving through Surrey this evening.

Yrs V. W.

John Lehmann

3386: To May Sarton   52 *Tavistock Square, W.C.1.*

Typewritten
May 19th [1938]

Dear May Sarton,

This is only a scrawl to say, in answer to your letter, that though they sent me a bound copy of your book,[1] I have still not had time to read it. Every sort of MS. and other demand has been made on me partly through Ottoline's death and Philips wish to discuss her diaries and so on: and its no good sitting down to read a book seriously with a mind in a whirl.

Also, I have lost all belief in written criticism—anyhow my own. One screws out a few bald statements, is terrified of results and so I become more and more loath to write down what is only a shot in the dark. But if you're in London later and still want wild and random impressions verbally prob- ably we could arrange it. And as for feeling suspense about my judgment— that seems to me if I may say so absurd in the extreme.

1. *The Single Hound*, 1938.

I'm packing to rush down to Sussex; and have to sort out Roger Frys papers to take, so forgive both the typing and the matter.

Yours
Virginia Woolf

Berg

3387: To Viscountess Rhondda

52 *Tavistock Square, W.C.1.*

May 24th 38

Dear Lady Rhondda,

Your letter has given me great pleasure all day. I admit I am nervous about 3 Guineas[1]—not about making a fool of myself, but about being a mischievous fool, for the subject is a risky one. But if the extract you read pleased you, then it cant be such an empty gesture as I had come to think it. I wrote it partly to clear my own mind, and partly because I could not write anything else—And though I'm afraid that nothing can have any influence now, anyhow the fact that you liked what you read relieves me of some of my fears. So thank you very much for writing to say so. I wonder if we could really do anything with the outsider idea?[2] I've only skimmed the surface of that and many other ideas. But I'm very glad that you call yourself an outsider—the first to take the name! Thank you very much.

Yours sincerely
Virginia Woolf

Texas

3388: To Angus Davidson

52 *Tavistock Square [W.C.1]*

May 26th 38

Dear Angus,

I have just read your life of Edward Lear,[3] and must send a line to say how much I have enjoyed it. I think you have dealt with that very sympathetic and curious man most skilfully and have suggested much more than you say; a great tribute to your art and one most biographers dont deserve. I hope you will go on and provide us with many more such portraits.

1. A friend had read extracts from an advance copy of *Three Guineas* to Lady Rhondda, the Editor of *Time and Tide* and an ardent feminist.
2. In *Three Guineas* Virginia suggested the formation of the Outsiders' Society, an anonymous organisation for educated men's daughters who would work "by their own methods for liberty, equality and peace" (p. 193). Virginia at one moment thought of founding an illustrated journal called *The Outsider*.
3. *Edward Lear, Landscape Painter & Nonsense Poet, 1812-88* (1938).

Have you heard anything about Ka Arnold-Forster's death?[1] It is a great shock—I hadn't known she was ill. Christopher A-F.[2] wrote to me this morning. He says Will [her husband] is in Canada.

Yours ever
Virginia Woolf

Angus Davidson

3389: To T. S. Eliot   52 *Tavistock Square* [*W.C.*1]

Typewritten
26th May [1938]

Dear Tom,

Whichever Woolf it was, it wasnt this Woolf; but now it is this Woolf—which sounds like a passage from the works of the inspired Miss [Gertrude] Stein.

This is only to say in soberer language, that we go away for Whitsun on Wednesday; would therefore suggest tea on Sunday next at 4.30; failing that, tea on Tuesday next at the same hour; the snag then being an Italian woman[3] at five thirty who might cut into our great pleasure in unadulterated conversation. But from your engagements, and their lieu, it looks as if neither day would do; in which case, we must leave it to you. Perceive how I rhyme—how instinctively and in the manner of George Herbert!

I'm longing I needn't say to hear how the visit to the water closet at Netherhampton went off; if you met Miss Edith Olivier;[4] if she's as nice as she says she is; if Mr Stephen Tennant[5] (to me an incredible bore) is as she says Oscar Wilde incarnate; and so on and so on. Yes, I murmured 'I'm Mrs

1. Katherine Arnold-Forster had friends who rented a small moorland cottage near her house (Eagle's Nest, Zennor, Cornwall) and feared it was haunted. On the night of 22 May, in order to reassure them, she walked up the long and rough track to the cottage and kept watch with them for two hours. She then had a heart-attack and died without regaining consciousness. She was 51.
2. Christopher Arnold-Forster (1890-1965), Ka's brother-in-law. He was primarily a sailor, then a stockbroker, and rejoined the Navy to serve as Assistant Director of Naval Intelligence, 1942-5.
3. Not identified in Leonard's diary.
4. See p. 144, note 3. Eliot had been to Salisbury to speak on the poetry of George Herbert. He stayed with Sir Bruce Richmond, Editor of the *Times Literary Supplement*, and his wife Elena at Netherhampton House. Edith Olivier was the author of several books, and in 1938-9 was Mayor of Wilton, Wiltshire, of which her father had been Rector. She died in 1948.
5. Stephen Tennant (b. 1906) was the fourth son of Lord Glenconner. He was a painter, but he was known chiefly for his glamorous parties and charming appearance.

Woolf,' at Ottolines funeral; then in a bold loud voice BUT I REPRESENT
T. S. ELIOT—the proudest moment of my life; passing, alas, like spring
flowers.

Affectionately V. W.

Mrs T. S. Eliot

3390: To Lady Tweedsmuir

*Monk's House, Rodmell,
Lewes, Sussex*

Monday [30 May 1938]

My dear Susie,

I'm afraid village business makes the 9th hopeless. Leonard is a school
manager: the Clergyman's wife [Mrs Ebbs] has fixed the school board
meeting for Saturday 10th: so we must stay here: but it depends upon an
Archdeacon. I know you have these complications at Elsfield,[1] and know
how exacting they are, and how impossible to arrange, or re-arrange. So we
must wait till July. I shall be in the Hebrides—Skye I mean—from June
20-25th: I look forward to a silent rock and gannets, but at the same time
would like to see you. So please keep July in mind, and suggest a day if you
still have one.

Excuse scrawl

Yrs V. W.

Lady Tweedsmuir

3391: To V. Sackville-West

52 T[avistock] S.[quare, W.C.1]

1st June [1938]

Thats an angel—I mean the gift to the Library.[2] In return you shall have
all the autographs you want for all the Princesses in Europe.[3] But what does
it mean? autograph collecting? Something sexual, like the dukes Hat [*unexplained*] I expect.

The book comes out tomorrow. Its only a piece of donkey-drudgery,
and as it repeats in still soberer prose, the theme of that very sober prose The
Years, which, rightly, you didnt like, I hadn't meant to send it. But I will, by
way of thanks, and you need neither read it nor write and say you have. Both
those books are now off my mind, thank God. Why did I feel I must write
them? Lord knows.

1. Elsfield Manor, near Oxford, the house of John and Susan Tweedsmuir
   (Buchan), where Virginia had stayed in July 1935.
2. See p. 145, note 4.
3. Probably Princess Anne-Marie Callimachi of Roumania, who had become a
   friend of Vita and Harold.

When you left in your sweeping black car the other night I exclaimed (this is verbatim and would stand in a court of law with my hand on a Bible). I think Vita is the nicest person we know. And L. said yes. So your feeling about our house is very welcome to the old Wolves; and they hope there'll be as many evenings with Vita in future as the house will hold. Oh dear how grim life can be: and how merciful some moments are—About Ben [Nicolson]—I'm very glad you think he would like to come. That slippery little sandhopper, [*name omitted*], led me to think, by some insidious report he made, that Ben hadn't enjoyed it when he did dine here; so, very regretfully, I'd determined not to ask him again. (though in fact I suspected [*name omitted*] of spite) What is Ben's address? I'll remember, and he as mum as a mouse. And he's so like you I couldnt help liking to have him.

No sign from Edie.[1] There's a fate against my joining. But I mean to and would like very much to see the marionettes. So prod her from behind. Just off to M.H. where, Lord be praised, we stay a week; then here, then Scotland. Potto's autograph. He thinks you would like it [*squiggly design*].

Berg

3392: To Ethel Smyth   52 *Tavistock Square* [*W.C.*1]
1st June. 38

Ethel you're a trump. A heart of gold under a somewhat charming exterior. They will be overjoyed. And I've told them you might add a book or two. If you know which you want to shed, write the titles on a card and send to Miss Douie, Librarian, 29 Marsham St. SW1.[2] Theyre so cramped they have to choose which to house. I think its almost the only satisfactory deposit for stray guineas, because half the readers are bookless at home, working all day, eager to know anything and everything, and a very nice room, with a fire even, and a chair or two, is provided. So you were as usual, under your exterior, as wise as Goethe, and as good as gold. I'm rather distressed, all the same, at taking your money.   .

I will send you 3 guineas (the book only I mean) tomorrow. I hadn't meant to, as it only repeats The Years, with facts to prove it, not fiction; and is a hurried piece of work—though it was hard work collecting the facts—and you wont like it or agree with it.[3] So lets say no more about it.

I am also to thank you for the letter about Scotland. It comes in the nick

1. Edith Craig lived with Christopher St John in the house of her mother Ellen Terry at Smallhythe, Kent, where she organised a society for the production of plays in a converted barn adjoining the house.
2. See p. 145, note 4.
3. But Ethel replied: "Your book is so splendid that it makes me hot" (3 June 1938, *Berg*).

of time, as there are difficulties about Skye, and we think of confining ourselves to [mainland] Scotland. Your nephew is a very kind good man to have
troubled. Will you thank him? or shall I? Another friend [Ka Arnold-
Forster] has died suddenly on a Cornish moor. Oh dear me, I cant keep pace
with all these deaths. And so count on you to keep on the sunny side of the
grave a little longer. We are going to M. H. today, because L. has to inspect
the village school. There are too many things to do, on the sunny side, but
such is the . . . I cant finish what I meant to say, because L. says I must pack.
And I've all Roger's letters to tie up and take. But I will get a quiet evening
at Rodmell and write a long long letter. a love letter, one of the very sweet,
the very rare the very few and to you.

V.

Berg

3393: To Sibyl Colefax
Monk's House [Rodmell,
Sussex]

2nd June 38

Dearest Sibyl,

Late last night we drove down in a storm of wind—but oh how peaceful
it was—the garden at midnight even in a roaring gale after London! And
here we are for a week, and then dash off for our annual holiday—this year
in the Hebrides, if we can manage it. So think of me on a rock the nights you
ask me to dine, talking to gannets.

I'm getting so old and so drowsy I hardly ever dine anywhere except at
home. I dont think one ought to parade one's stupidity after dark any longer.
But I wish sometimes you'd drop in between the lights, or dine alone, or—
but then you're a firefly or bird of Paradise, whose natural element is the
fiery. Am I thinking of a salamander? That's what comes of writing over a
wood fire.

Only its very nice of you to go on asking me: and I wish we could ever
be in the same room at the same moment; only, as I say, I'm a bat and you're
a butterfly. And battishness grows on me. I shall nest in your hair. And
aren't bats covered with fleas?

Forgive this babble and do let us meet.

Yrs V. W.

Michael Colefax

3394: To Lady Tweedsmuir
Monk's House, Rodmell,
Lewes, Sussex

2nd June 38

My dear Susie,

How difficult these dates are—here we are for Whitsun, and shan't I think be in London till the 9th anyhow, and then I expect too late for you. After a week in London, we go to Scotland for a fortnight: back again the beginning of July till August. But what are you doing? I must leave it, and hope, if July is free, you will suggest a day. I hope Canada give you a holiday till August anyhow.[1]

You needn't apologise for not subscribing to the Library. I ought to apologise rather for adding another letter to the daily heap. I owe all the education I ever had to my father's library, and so perhaps endow libraries with more divinity than I should. But this one is far more my care than yours—who have all Canada to provide for 170,000 books! the thought staggers me, and makes me doubt if we ought either to buy more books or write them. Who can read 170,000? And who has written them?

I'm longing to be instructed on Canada, and all the rest of your doings since we met, and you were choosing a dress if you remember to match the Viceregal carpet. What is it like being Queen? and will you be relieved if I dont try to curtsey, etc. etc. etc—I've too many questions to ask and no room. So I hope we may soon talk instead.

Yr V. W.

Lady Tweedsmuir

3395: To Ethel Smyth   *M[onks] H.[ouse, Rodmell, Sussex]*

June 7th [1938]

I'm so relieved to find I'm not cut off, as I half expected, from all affection, now you've read 3 gs, that I must hastily (we're going out.) scrawl a line of thanks. I think your criticisms are most interesting. As you'll have guessed, that was largely the little creatures object: to rouse objections. And I shall be smothered with them, once the pens get to work. Not so good as yours, though.

1 There are some single points that occur to me. You say you're going to speak about (I suppose) the musicians expelled at Bournemouth.[2] I had hoped to use those facts, but I had such a heap—half had to be struck out of the notes in proof. to keep some slimness, and not repeat inordinately. It strikes me though that you would do well to lay your facts before the Council for Civil liberties. L and I both subscribe. L. doubts if it is within their province —I think it should be, and want very much to know what line Ronald Kidd, the secretary, would take. He gets my occasional guinea. Why not submit the story to him before you speak? Cold facts are the only weapon; and if I'm a judge, its a monstrous story: and the hiding of it blatant Hitlerism.

1. Lord Tweedsmuir was on leave from Canada, where he was Governor-General from 1935 until his death in 1940.
2. See p. 223, note 1.

234

2) I cant generalise about young men and war. I only know that my own nephew had a passion for the art; and a longing—instinctive and irrational—to fight himself. Yet why? And if you can, as in this village, beat up recruits from the farm, on the strength of red coats and pay, surely the instinct must be there, if mitigated in the more sophisticated quarter. But I do suggest that there's a strong turn against it—witness pacifism growing; only routed by the 'virile' conception. And suggest indifference.

3) Patriotism. My dear E ... of course I'm 'patriotic': that is English, the language, farms, dogs, people: only we must enlarge the imaginative, and take stock of the emotion. And I'm sure I can; because I'm an outsider partly; and can get outside the vested interest better than Leonard even—tho' a Jew.

4) Notes. Yes that was a question; bottom of the page or end. I decided for end, thinking people might read them, the most meaty part of the book, separately. Gibbon wished to do this, but gave way to friends. Pippa Strachey writes that she's glad they are at the end. I had a mass more and still have. Yes—very hard work that was

5) Alas, there wont be a 2nd edition in my lifetime. L. printed 15 thousand! —against my judgment.

6. The Times photograph[1]—damn them. They rang up and asked for me. Were given the stock reply. "Mrs W. doesn't want her photograph published"—whereupon they go to a shop and buy the Lady in the Lit Sup. who gave me a shock. No I dont think she's a beauty: but her nose looks sharp eno' to cut hay with. Why shd. I reflect "what a beautiful woman" I am? I'm not, and never think so. (This is true)

Here till Saturday I think, owing to a School Board meeting, and now I must rush

V.

The address is:
Ronald Kidd
National Council for Civil Liberties
320 Regent Street W.1.

I send back your Bournemouth budget

Berg

3396: To Vanessa Bell   [*Monk's House, Rodmell, Sussex*]

Thursday [9 June 1938]

The picture has just been nailed up—its perfectly lovely—What a great artist you are! Everything complete and entire, firm as marble and ravishing

1. The *TLS* on 4 June published one of the photographs of Virginia taken by Lenare in January 1929.

as a rainbow. How I wish I were a painter! Its as good as having a new oil painting. Do consider our plan—I'm sure it might be a howling success. No bill with it. Whom do I pay? *And have you brought the chair?*[1] Go to Heals. I have an account there. Also get a cover, included. I've just heard that Redpaths [upholsterer] mother is very ill, so she's had to to give up all work.

Q coming to tea and dinner. We shall be back on Saturday, but you wont be there. What about dinner on Monday at 52—you, Duncan and A?

Well your art does give me heavenly joy

B.

Berg

3397: To Viscountess Rhondda   *Monk's House, Rodmell,*
                                      Lewes, Sussex
Typewritten
10th June 38

Dear Lady Rhondda,

I ought to have thanked you before for your letter, and for subscribing to the [Marsham St] Library. I know what a multitude of such demands must be made on you, and was therefore loath to add another. But books have always been so prolific in my life that I can't help being shocked to think that there are those who go without.

I cant say how pleased I am that you should like Three Guineas. I know much of it is sketchy and wants working out; but I had not time. The guns sound so very close. But if it stirs up thought, that is what I wrote it for. And if someone like yourself feels that there is some scattered truth flying about in it then perhaps it won't be, as I so often feel writing to be, a mere bonfire of words.

As for patriotism, I expect I have it as strong in me as you. But I dont think its as strong in me as in an old half brother of mine [Sir George Duckworth] who shot and rode and owned several acres. This applies too to what you say of the echoes of pride vanity and combativeness.[2] There they are in us of course; I feel them pricking every moment. But again they have so little encouragement in us; surely, with the great example of what not to be blazing in front of us, we can damp them down before they get a hold. If we emphasise our position as outsiders and come to think it a natural distinction it should be easier for us than for those unfortunate young men

1. Virginia's birthday present for Vanessa, who was 59 on 30 May.
2. Lady Rhondda had written: "But in my heart I find, it seems to me, such echoes of all the pride, vanity and combativeness I ever see in men that I don't need to have it explained—I *know*. Still it is true that we don't do the actual killing—and don't want to" (2 June 1938, *Sussex*).

who are shot through the sausage machine of Eton—Kings or Christchurch. But I wont drone on.

What you say about the difficulty of running Time and Tide is very interesting. But isnt that too a proof of what I say—I mean, as a woman shut out from so many of the newspaper sanctuaries you have to fight to enter; and thus dont think, as those within naturally do, how to shut others out.

But I only took up my typewriter—to spare your eyes the difficulty of my now dissolute hand—in order to thank you, not to inflict more arguments. But I must repeat, it makes me so happy to think that you, with all your work on hand, have taken the trouble to read my book.

Yours very sincerely
Virginia Woolf

Texas

3398: To Violet Dickinson   52 *Tavistock Square, W.C.1.*

June 13th [1938]

My Violet,

What an Owl you are to buy 3 Gs! I'd have given you one with pleasure had I thought you would have poked your nose that way. As I remember it has a chip off the end of it. Only the village idiot ever writes to me about my books; but there are many villages well supplied; some with male some with female: all idiotic.

I'm much amused that Lord Weymouth[1] is laying down a cellar—is he as beautiful as Katie, or as remarkable as Beatrice? I think Clive meets him at the Club, and no doubt tipped him the wink. Oh dear what an age it is since I saw Beatrice save in print one day, opening a Donkey show or something.

And what about you? Why do you yield to these broken legs? Must you? And how are you? And do you lie in the garden—where the birds used to sing so loud, and I used to be all of a fizz coming down for the afternoon, and walking back along a field path. Only I was also very crazy then so my memories jigger.[2] Not of your infinite kindness though. And Nellie [Cecil]? Well, if you can write, do; and put in all the scraps you can think of. Heres Nessa coming in—we're bringing out a book of Julian's letters. Theres not

1. The eldest son (b. 1905) of the 5th Marquess of Bath who succeeded his father as 6th Marquess in 1946. Two of his aunts were Lady Beatrice Thynne and Katherine Cromer. Violet was a frequent visitor to their great family house, Longleat, Wiltshire, and Virginia had known them through her.
2. After Virginia's mental breakdown in the summer of 1904, Violet took her to her own house at Welwyn, where Virginia lived under the care of three nurses, but nonetheless attempted suicide by throwing herself from a window.

much solid happiness in the world, is there? But we are just going, driving, for a fortnight to Skye—thats a lark.

Yr Sp

Sussex

3399: To Saxon Sydney-Turner

52 *Tavistock Square, W.C.1.*

Tuesday [14 June 1938]

My dear Saxon,

The rumour about the Odyssey isnt quite correct: [Michel] Saint-Denis,[1] who taught Angelica, suggests that I shall help him with a version which he has had in mind for 4 years: a highly stylised version, I gather; and my part will only be to re-English somebody else's English.[2] But it has gone no further than talk, and I doubt, considering his engagements and my disabilities that it ever will. He wants, of course, to stage it: but has highly original ideas. So far I've merely glanced at Samuel Butler.[3] My favourite poem still—the O.

I'm so glad you like 3 Gs. If you would note misprints I would give you a clean copy—for I cant go through that labour again. And it swarms—But we've printed so big a first edition I'm afraid the 2nd won't be needed. Just off to the Hebrides. When we come back, will you dine.

Excuse this potty scrap. Packing: and so on.

Virginia

Sussex

3400: To A. G. Sayers

52 *Tavistock Square, W.C.1.*

15 June 1938

Dear Sir,[4]

Your letter about my book Three Guineas has given me great pleasure, and I am grateful to you for your generous approval. I am glad that you do not think me guilty of exaggeration. I have only myself experience of one profession, and in dealing with others had to depend upon books and hearsay —hence I might have gone wrong. The book is a mere outline, but I wanted

1. See p. 178, note 2.
2. The idea never came to anything.
3. Samuel Butler (1835-1902), the author of *Erewhon* and *The Way of All Flesh*, believed that the *Odyssey* had been written by a woman. He published a straightforward prose translation of it in 1898 and 1900.
4. A. G. Sayers was the senior partner in the London firm of chartered accountants, Sayers, Seaton and Butterworth.

to state the case as briefly as possible, for it seems to me of great importance. And I am very glad of your sympathy. I have made some readers very angry.

With regard to the work of Mr and Mrs Pethick Lawrence,[1] I have the greatest admiration for it, and it was mere chance that I used other quotations and made no mention of them. In fact I did not read Mrs Pethick Lawrence's book till I had done. But I regret that I said nothing; they deserve all the praise they can have.

Thank you for troubling to write and believe me

Yours sincerely
Virginia Woolf

A. M. Sayers

3401: To Shena, Lady Simon   52 *Tavistock Square, W.C.1.*

June 15th 1938

My dear Shena,

I must send one line—a very hasty one—to thank you for your letter. I'm much relieved that you like 3 Gs. It got on my nerves, that it would make everyone furious, and no good would come of it. I dont suppose any good will: but its a great pleasure that you enjoy it: and I'm glad I've not infuriated Pernel [Strachey]. It was such a grind, collecting and compressing the notes, slipping in facts and keeping up enough of a dance to lead the reader on so that I couldn't keep my eye on the general aspect, and was much in the dark as to the whole.

But of course you're an outsider.[2] Much more effectively than I am. I think its the only thing for us to be. I want to explore the idea—and many others—much further, only what I admire in those, like you, who do the things that I talk of. I'm getting a fair bag of the oddest letters: and some angry reviews: but oh I'm so glad to be quit of it for the moment. We go to Skye tomorrow: but back in a fortnight, and packing waits, so forgive this whirlwind hand and scamper of ideas: only I am so glad you liked the book.

Yrs V. W.

The [Marsham St] library to which you contributed so generously write in great joy and gratitude.

Sussex

1. Frederick William (later Lord) Pethick-Lawrence (1871-1961) and Emmeline Pethick-Lawrence (1867-1954), the leaders, with Mrs Pankhurst, of the women's suffrage movement. Mrs Pethick-Lawrence's book was *My Part in a Changing World* (1938).
2. See p. 229, note 2.

Letters 3402-3426 (June–July 1938)

From 16 June to 2 July Virginia and Leonard went on holiday to Scotland, spending a few days en route on the Roman Wall in Northumberland, and continued through the Highlands to Skye in the Hebrides, where they visited Dunvegan Castle. It was the only time that Virginia saw Scotland, apart from a brief trip to Glasgow in 1913. On her return, she resumed work on Roger Fry, *interviewing his relations and visiting his houses, and was interrupted by a heavy correspondence about* Three Guineas, *the men mostly protesting, the women mostly approving, except Vita, who accused Virginia of "misleading arguments", a charge which Virginia greatly resented. Intermittently she worked on* Pointz Hall, *first in London, then at Monk's House, where the Woolfs remained from late July until mid-October. A new library for Leonard, and a balcony, were constructed there during August.*

3402: To ETHEL SMYTH   *Lincoln*

Postcard
June 16th [1938]

We made a good start today—been to Croyland and the Thomas Abbey[1]—all in June weather—on to Corbridge[2] tomorrow. So Friday no good.
PTO. for a rough version of the real Leonard and Virginia.[3]

V.

Berg

3403: To VANESSA BELL   *The George Inn, Chollerford,*
                                                   Northumberland.
Saturday 18th June. [1938]

Chollerford, as you probably know, is a Roman Bridge (only one arch

1. Croyland (or Crowland), a market town in Lincolnshire. The abbey, in its present form, was built in the 12th century, during the archbishopric of Thomas à Becket.
2. In Northumberland. It has extensive Roman remains dating from the period when it was the main supply base for the garrison of Hadrian's Wall.
3. On the reverse of the card was a photograph of two medieval stone carvings depicting a man's head and a woman's.

left) over the River Tyne, at the bottom of the great wall [Hadrian's], which separates England from Scotland; and about 30 years ago, Waller took us to see it at Gilsland from Corby.[1] In fact, we're not very far from Corby. The country from the wall is precisely like the [Roman] Campagna.

Thats all I shall say by way of description.

However, I must rapidly add that we must all leave London at 7 on a fine summer morning: reach Peterborough at 12: then visit Thorney Island and Crowland Abbey. This last is the finest Church in England. It is in the middle of the Fens. And it is exactly like a Church in the Dordogne. Why it is so magnificent I cant say. But we could see all this—and the Fens—and have a thorough English lunch off fruit salad and cold beef and be back in London in time for Angelica's show (as we now call it) at 8. So do consider the matter. England is practically undiscovered and incredibly lovely. I will not describe the rose-red Italian Castle that we discovered in the back streets of Gainsborough:[2] out of Siena it has not its match. The grass grows round it; iron railings are of course included; orange peel, paper bags; one old gent. lives in one vast tower. Thats enough. . . . I hope John [Lehmann] has been submissive. He rang me up late on Wednesday, after L. had gone to the House of Commons, and was rather huffy at being told all was settled with Mrs Nicholls and we couldn't see him.[3] He said he had travelled post haste from Prague to see Leonard. I said, A misunderstanding. Then we shut off.

I could write at least 16 reams about life in the hotel here. There was an otter hunting party at breakfast this morning: the river runs through the garden. Old ladies of 70 appeared in tweed suits with the pads of otters or foxes mounted in gold pinned to their breasts. Last night I was shut up alone with two spinsters; who after welcoming me very kindly, turned upon each other with such ferocity over patience that the room rang. All reticence was forgotten. Their skirts rose over their long brown legs. And now they're reading opposite. But the key to their souls is Patience—I cant go into it fully.

B.

Berg

1. Corby Castle, which lies just east of Carlisle on the River Eden, was the home of Herbert Hills, the father of John Waller Hills. In 1897 John Waller married Stella Duckworth, the half-sister of Virginia and Vanessa, and in September of that year, after Stella's death, he took them there to stay with his parents.
2. The Old Hall, Gainsborough, Lincolnshire, one of the largest medieval houses in Britain.
3. Mrs Nicholls was the new manager of the Hogarth Press, following the departure of Miss Lange. Lehmann's major concern at this time was the editing of the memorial volume for Julian Bell, about which he disagreed with Vanessa and Leonard.

3404: To Lady Cecil

The George Inn, Chollerford,
Northumberland

[18 June 1938]

My dear Nelly,

Well you are a nice woman to write such a nice letter, when you might have cut up as rusty as a—now what? old razor blade, shall I say?—indeed many people have over 3 Guineas: so you're balm and dock leaves and the River Tyne itself—(Which is running past the Inn window: 5 old gentlemen are fishing in it, and a party of 40 adults spent the morning catching an otter in it.) But I was thanking you for being, as usual, so spirited and unexpected and altogether coming out on the right side of things, (which is mine) in spite of every temptation to belong to the other nation. The whole difficulty of writing 3 Guineas was to quote rightly: so you've said the very thing I wanted said. One flies along full tilt on one's own sail: then there's a loathsome lump of fact—some Bishop or Marquess or Mr [Stanley] Baldwin or Whitaker [Almanac]—to be worked in—thats the snag: full stop: curving round them: carrying them along, and then again and again and again. . . . I thought my wits would turn, merely quoting. But it is only a sketch for a book—a fling of my line (like the old gents on the Tyne) over a boiling and bubbling stream, so full of fish one cant pick and choose.

So—to write plain English—we must meet over a teapot, and discuss the question: I mean the million questions. I wish you would. One brain is only a teaspoon or a thimble; and we ought to combine. But the old ladies are now playing patience, and the rules of the game seem to rouse pugnacity. How, though, can women stick together as men do without money? without Clubs, Claret, otter hounds—only packs of patience at Inn tables, and such very cheap green—no brown—cotton stockings?

We are on our way to Skye; shall be back in a fortnight. The wrinkled hag, as he calls her, wishes to send her kind regards to Lord Cecil, as she calls him. And come and see me, or let me come and see you.

Yrs affly
Virginia W.

The Marquess of Salisbury (Cecil Papers)

3405: To V. Sackville-West

George Inn, Chollerford
Northumberland

19th June [1938]

We're only on our way to Skye—stopping to explore the Roman wall. Have you seen it? Anyhow, its no good describing it—we've been lying on the top all this afternoon. Of course I knew you wouldn't like 3 gs— thats why I wouldn't, unless you had sent a postcard with a question, have given it you. All the same, I dont quite understand. You say you don't agree with 50% of it—no, of course you dont. But when you say that you are exasperated by my "misleading arguments"—then I ask, what do you mean? If I said, I dont agree with your conception of Joan of Arc's character, thats one thing. But if I said, your arguments about her are "misleading" shouldn't I mean, Vita has cooked the facts in a dishonest way in order to produce an effect which she knows to be untrue? If *thats* what you mean by "misleading" then we shall have to have the matter out, whether with swords or fisticuffs. And I dont think *whichever we use*, you will, as you say, knock me down. It may be a silly book, and I dont agree that its a well-written book; but its certainly an honest book: and I took more pains to get up the facts and state them plainly than I ever took with any thing in my life. However, I daresay I'm reading more into "misleading" than's there. But oh Lord how sick I get of all this talk about 'lovely prose' and charm when all I wanted was to state a very intricate case as plainly and readable as I could. There is an otter-hunting party going on in the hotel at this moment, so I cant write, and I'm roasting after 6 hours in the sun. And I want to describe the view from the wall—miles and miles: but won't as there's no room. We shall be back in a fortnight. Anyhow (to return to 3gs) I'm delighted I've exasperated my dear old sheepdog.[1]

V.

Berg

3406: To Vanessa Bell   *Flodigarry Hotel, Portree,*
                                         Isle of Skye
25th June [1938]

Well, here we are in Skye, and it feels like the South Seas—completely remote, surrounded by sea, people speaking Gaelic, no railways, no London papers, hardly any inhabitants. Believe it or not, it is (in its way, as people say) so far as I can judge on a level with Italy, Greece or Florence. No one in Fitzroy Street[2] will believe this, and descriptions are your abhorrence— further the room is pullulating and popping with Edinburgh tourists, one of whom owns spaniels, like Sally, but "all mine are gun trained, the only thing they wont carry being hares"—so I cant run on, did you wish it. Only—well, in Duncan's highlands,[3] the colours in a perfectly still deep blue lake of green and purple trees reflected in the middle of the water which was enclosed with green reeds, and yellow flags, and the whole sky and a purple hill—well, enough. One should be a painter. As a writer, I

1. Virginia summarises more of Vita's offending letter in Letters 3421-2.
2. 8 Fitzroy Street, where Vanessa and Duncan had their London studios.
3. The Grants came from Rothiemurchus, Inverness-shire.

feel the beauty, which is almost entirely colour, very subtle, very changeable, running over my pen, as if you poured a large jug of champagne over a hairpin. I must here tender my congratulations to Duncan upon being a Grant. We've driven round the island today, seen Dungevan [*sic*], encountered the children of the 27th Chieftain, nice red headed brats:[1] the Castle door being open I walked in; they very politely told me the Castle was shut to visitors, but I could see the gardens. Here I found a gamekeepers larder with the tails of two wild cats. Eagles are said to abound and often carry off sheep: sheep and Skye Terriers are the only industries; the old women live in round huts exactly the shape of skye terriers; and you can count all the natives on 20 feet: but they are very rapacious in the towns, and its no use trying to buy anything, as the price, even of Sally's meat, is at least 6 times higher than in our honest land. All the same, the Scotch are great charmers, and sing through their noses like musical tea kettles. The only local gossip I've collected for you is about your Mr Hambro's wife[2]—the one who was drowned in Loch Ness. We met a charming Irish couple in an Inn, who were in touch, through friends, with The Monster. They had seen him. He is like several broken telegraph posts and swims at immense speed. He has no head. He is constantly seen. Well, after Mrs Hambro was drowned, the Insurance Company sent divers after her, as she was wearing 30,000 pounds of pearls on her head. They dived and came to the mouth of a vast cavern, from which hot water poured; and the current was so strong, and the horror they felt so great, they refused to go further, being convinced The Monster lived there, in a hollow under the hill. In short, Mrs Hambro was swallowed. No drowned body is ever recovered and now the natives refuse to boat or to bathe. That is all the local gossip. And I will *not* describe the colour.

I think John's [Lehmann] story utterly absurd. Poor old Leonard had been most careful to tell him not to come after 4: had waited in all day; and left all instructions in writing with Mrs Nicholls. John then rings up at 6.30 and makes no apology—in fact complains ... however, Leonard is writing to you himself. All I did was to repeat my orders. But he's as touchy as a very old spinster whose one evening dress has a hole in the behind. It was the way he behaved before. We hoped, and he declared, that life had taught him better. God knows how he'll settle down, if he's still so itchy. I'm glad you've talked to Clive. I feel he wants to talk, only cant, unless

1. Dunvegan Castle in the north of Skye was the hereditary seat of the McLeods of McLeod. The 27th Chief of Clan McLeod had died in 1935, and was succeeded by his daughter Flora (b. 1878). The 'brats' were her grandchildren, Robert, John and Patrick.
2. Winifred Hambro (wife of Ronald Olaf Hambro, Chairman of Hambro's Bank) was drowned in Loch Ness in August 1932 when her speed-boat exploded. All the other members of her family in the boat survived.

one starts him. Its such a mistake, letting one'self become snowed under. Also I'm glad he approves of the book [*Julian Bell*]. I quite agree that letters must be redundant—its the way you get the whole feeling of a character, and I only wish there was a complete account—childhood, Cambridge etc: after all, nothings so important as a person like Julian. However, I think there's enough to give an outline, and nothing seemed to me too private. Yes—writing lives is the devil. I shiver at the thought of Roger. And really mustn't begin a third sheet. but cant help hoping you may write another letter before we come back. I rushed to the office here: saw your envelope, tore it open, regardless of all questions.

That shows how your poor Singe adores you. Of course *both* chairs are my present.[1] And a very small one. This is absolutely understood, good Dolphin. If not, then cloaks, stockings and a pearl necklace will descend. The Clarks [Kenneth and Jane] asked us: thank God the party question is solved if one's in Skye.[2] When shall I see you? We start back on Monday and shall be home on Sunday. but I suppose you'll be at Charleston.

Very cold here, and all weathers; but, as I say, lovely—

B—

Flora Macdonald lived in this house.[3] The sea is beneath the window. Here came Prince Charlie dressed as a beggar. Possibly Dr Johnson and Boswell—but dont take this for a fact and boast of it

Berg

3407: To J. M. Dent   *Flodigarry Hotel, Portree,*
                                        Isle of Skye

25th June 38

Dear Mr Dent

As you see from the address, I am travelling, and your letter has only now reached me.

I had forgotten that Mr Forster's article did not mention The Light-

1. See Letter 3396.
2. Vanessa had written to Virginia about the pleasure of having decided that one should not go to parties. (*Berg*)
3. The Flodigarry Hotel has since been renamed The Royal Hotel, and a room is pointed out as the one in which Prince Charles Edward, disguised as a maid, said farewell to his benefactor, the famous Flora Macdonald, in 1746. Dr Johnson and Boswell stayed in the same inn during their tour of the Hebrides in 1773, and met Flora Macdonald at her house in another part of Skye.

house. I think Dr Hoare's article does admirably, and should make a very good introduction; and I hope Dr Hoare will allow it to be used.[1]

With apologies for the delay

Yours sincerely
Virginia Woolf

Carol Collins

3408: To Ethel Smyth   *Flodigarry Hotel, Skye*

26th June. [1938]

Well Ethel this is an heroic effort, writing in a lounge with the Old English sheep dogs,—the hearty hoary old ladies and gents. in tweeds— all a blowing and a puffing round me. So you will excuse the illiteracy. I am under the lee of a military man reading the Times: rain: outside; a divine sea: little islands: some sun; never was such a June; people popping in and out. "Of course my spaniels are all gun trained. They'll carry anything, except a hare ..." But to return: yes, we were 2 days on the wall: lay on top of it the one hot day; and saw the landscape that to me is loveliest in the world; miles and miles of lavender coloured loneliness, with one thread white path: dear me, were I a writer, how I could describe that: the immensity and tragedy and the sense of the Romans, and time, and eternity; and then the wild white hawthorn, and the sheep cropping, and 3 little white headed boys playing in a Roman camp. No I'm not (at this moment) anything but a drab dowdy middle class lady;—"Are you going to ... Well, its worth seeing. But the Inn to stay at etc etc ..." Yes, I never saw a country more to my liking than the wall: d'you know how suddenly a country expands an airball in ones mind—I mean states a mood completely that was existent but unexpressed, so that at every turn of the road, its like half remembering, and thinking it can't be coming, but then it does?—a feeling a dream gives? and also that it is oneself—the real Virginia or Ethel, the dormant, the eternal? Now thats enough about the wall; to which I shall return, if I live long enough. One evening we walked from Chollerford to Haughton Castle; oh me! the river running and the old Castle, and the grass path and the people—peasants, wandering along the bank, and talking to us, like something in the time of Elizabeth, so that I felt I was actually in Shakespeare, one of the northern ones. Again, I must stop; as theyre now reading extracts from the papers, just in. "How unlucky about the Kings visit to Paris! All the decorations will have to be

1. J. M. Dent & Sons published *To the Lighthouse* in their Everyman's Library on 27 October. The volume contained an introduction by D. M. Hoare. E. M. Forster's article about Virginia had appeared in the *Criterion* for April 1926.

removed . . ."[1] You must grant the English are a rocky race: this spring, the country, is somewhere within; but so impeded. Then we drove through the Highlands, and there was one lake, with trees reflected which I think carried beauty to the extreme point: whether its expressible, that rapture, I doubt: green and purple trees hanging upside down in the middle of a perfectly still lake, and green all round. Do you like descriptions of nature? or do you skip?

I cant at the moment get back to the land of fact; and have forgotten all about 3 gs. except, my vanity reminds me, that it is selling very well, tho' none of the shops at first would take it. Not a novel, they said, and the public won't touch anything controversial about women. And I'm getting the oddest letters, which I shall collect, as a valuable contribution to psychology. The reviews—poor devils, I was so hard on reviewers—and theyre so painstaking—they are better on the whole than I expected; more serious, less spiteful, tho' I'm glad to see that I raised the hackles of that mincing old pedant, that omniscient but altogether meretricious in the sense of lapped in book dust humbug: G. M. Young.[2] Otherwise I'm out of that mood and longing to be off on fiction:[3] which I must curb: for all the Fry papers wait me.

Only another week and we shall be back. But I feel as if I'd been ducked upside down, what with the hoary sheep dogs, the otter hunt, the ruins of Melrose and Dryburgh where I glutted my passion for Scott on his tomb[4]—like chocolate blanc-mange—so appropriately, with the wild syringa growing too, and Haig[5] all covered with red poppies in stuff whose colour had run next him. Now we are driving in this mixture of sun and mist round the island, so the scrawl of this inebriate hand must cease.

I'm longing to hear about the speech;[6] and will subscribe to the Band;[7]

1. King George VI and Queen Elizabeth had planned a state visit to France, but the sudden death of the Queen's mother, Lady Strathmore, on 23 June caused the postponement of the visit until 19 July.
2. George Malcolm Young (1882-1959), the distinguished historian, author of *Victorian England* (1936) etc. In his review of *Three Guineas* in the *Sunday Times* on 19 June he wrote: "I wish Mrs Woolf would resign herself to the necessity of being an Insider and not an Outsider: and let that spark fly freely among the moth-eaten feathers and tarnished *passementerie* of Edwardian feminism."
3. Virginia was turning over in her mind her new novel *Pointz Hall*, which was published posthumously in 1941 as *Between the Acts*.
4. Melrose (Roxburgh) and Dryburgh Abbey (Berwick) had strong associations with Sir Walter Scott. He was buried at Dryburgh in 1832.
5. Field Marshal Earl Haig (1861-1928).
6. Ethel was to make a speech of protest on behalf of the women members of the Bournemouth Orchestra. See p. 223, note 1.
7. Sir Henry Wood (1869-1944), best remembered for his Promenade Concerts under the auspices of the B.B.C., had proposed the formation of an all women's

and want to hear all about N. Boulanger,[1] who gave me a thrill—seeming, even at a lunch party, a genuine live fish, not a stuffed Inn trout. Whats up with her? And you?

V.

Berg

3409: To Duncan Grant   [*Isle of Skye, Scotland*]

Postcard
Monday [27 June 1938]

This is the nearest I could get to the Isle of Barra.[2] Skye is often raining, but also fine: hardly embodied; semi-transparent; like living in a jelly fish lit up with green light. Remote as Samoa; deserted: prehistoric. No room for more.

V.

Duncan Grant

3410: To Clive Bell   [*Isle of Skye, Scotland*]

Postcard
Monday [27 June 1938]

Its a good thing Clive and his sister-in-law didn't quarrel at this point [Duntulm Castle, Skye], or the mews [gulls] would have picked their bones. Skye is full of mews.

V.

Quentin Bell

3411: To Vanessa Bell   *Park Hotel, Oban,*
                                          Argyllshire
Tuesday 28th about [June 1938]

We are now in Oban, which is, as far as I have seen it, the Ramsgate of the Highlands. Only the Scotch having melancholy in their bones—thats where The Stephen's, as Julian said, get their black melancholy, turned to

---

orchestra which he would direct himself. Ethel was helping to raise funds for the project, but it never materialised.

1. For Nadia Boulanger, see p. 88, note 3.
2. On the reverse side was a photograph of Uig Bay in north-west Skye.

madness in some of us by a drop of French blood,—being entirely without frivolity build even bathing sheds of granite let alone hotels. The result is grim; and on every lamp post is a notice, Please do not spit on the pavement. We had a terrific drive yesterday in one of the worst known gales, over the wildest passes. Trees were hurtling; rivers simply cataractuous, but very beautiful, if the rain had stopped; but it didnt. Our petrol gave out; and the oil clogged the engine. But miracles happen, and suddenly an Inn appeared, in a black gorge; and on opening the door, there were 20 tables with cloths laid diamond shape, maids in white aprons, and 7 different cakes; including the best shortbread I've ever eaten. We were warmly welcomed by the 20 old fishing men and women—they're practically sexless, and I've often taken one for a dog and vice versa: Some had been fishing in the rain for days and caught one trout. They talk such a brogue I had to invent replies, so off the point that at one moment I was talking about the Queens mother's death [Lady Strathmore] and they were talking about the rarity of polecats or somesuch topic Then a garage mended the car. off we swept into the desert, and just as night was falling—that is a kind of cadaverous dawn, for the sun neither rises nor sets in the highlands—I saw 2 great deer, bounding from rock to rock Thats all the description you need skip.

I've had a wild raving letter from Will Arnold Forster, describing his feeling in an American forest while Ka was being buried. He is now coming back, and must see me at once. Shall I counter him with Pipsey [Morrell]?—the two widowers might cancel out. Will has all the [Hilton] Young phrases; oh dear, how stagey that group was: breezy, elemental, slangy, and manly: at the same time, gulping with profound emotion.

No more letters from you, which casts a gloom over me; for I feel so very highland and garish out of your radius. Today I bought woolen gloves and a waterproof hat—my only purchases, for there's a scarcity of civilisation you cant credit. Not a turnip grows, nor cabbage: but wild roses, and foxgloves; and though the weather is like a weathercock, one day is always fine for half the time, and then freezing. The food varies. Last night even you would have been tolerably content; simple and indigenous; fish is the trump card, Leonard says—haddock and herring divine, but I dont think fish a good invention any time. Then cakes. Leonard says they are unmatched; I dont like scones for breakfast, or ginger in the cake. Still the more frivolous sugar cakes are very good. And the porridge is a dream. Only I loathe porridge. Theres a good earthy soup—all vegetables unsorted. That I like, and the splendour of sausage, bacon, ham, eggs, grapefruit, oatcake, grilled ham for breakfast— The people are enchanting. Mr Cunningham the baker is sending me 6 tins of his own shortbread. He, wife, and children at Skye were beyond belief nice, and I adore all who live in hotels, but not so much as I adore you. Heres L. so I must explore Oban in the rain. No letter from John about Julian's book. We had, very tenderly, to reject his novel.[1] I suppose he's in a huff. Have you settled with him? Back on Sunday. Oh how I long to see you, Angelica and even Highland Duncan.   B.

L. is picking ticks out of Sallys head. but sends love.

Berg

3412: To Margaret Llewelyn Davies

52 *Tavistock Square, W.C.1.*

Typewritten
4th July 38

Dearest Margaret,

Here we are, back again, having dashed through Scotland, Skye and Kirkby Lonsdale.[2] I suppose you will think us exaggerated, but Kirkby Lonsdale seemed as lovely as any place we saw—I longed to take an old grey house I saw to let on the road. It was a perfect morning, after violent storms, and the moors looked magnificent, and the town so dignified, and an old woman said she remembered your father, and I could hardly bear to drive away. But I mustn't run on about places we saw, or I shall bore you to death.

There's so much to say—where am I to begin? If only you were still at Reigate we might call in on Friday; Leonard always stops at Reigate to buy worms for his marmoset. Worms—German worms—are the staple product of Reigate. But now you'll be home again.

I've had a sad letter from poor Will Arnold Forster who is in Canada. Ka died suddenly out on the moor above Zennor—a death anyone might like; but she was younger than I am, and was so devoted to the boy.

Its very good of you to attempt my book [*Three Guineas*]. I felt it great impertinence to come out with my views on such a subject; but to sit silent and acquiesce in all this idiotic letter signing and vocal pacifism when there's such an obvious horror in our midst—such tyranny, such Pecksniffism— finally made my blood boil into the usual ink-spray. Yes, I had to choose

1. John Lehmann's novel was originally called *The Boy Who Disappeared*. He later rewrote it, and it was published by the Cresset Press under the new title *Evil Was Abroad*.
2. Margaret's father, the Rev. John Llewelyn Davies (1826-1916), had been destined for a high position in the Church, but a sermon which he delivered in the presence of Queen Victoria on the evils of imperialism so outraged the Queen, that he was sent to the remote living of Kirkby Lonsdale, Westmorland, in 1889 and re- mained there for 20 years. From the Vicarage Margaret organised the Women's Cooperative movement.

at random from such a mass of material that I knew I could have quoted better and more to the point. Thats always the difficulty—quoting rightly. And it was this partly that led to verbosity. One has to secrete a jelly in which to slip quotations down people's throats—and one always secretes too much jelly. But then I was writing for the very common, very reluctant, very easily bored reader—not for you. As for G. M. Young, I'm glad I roused his rage; if I had not been away, I might have answered. But I see that Time and Tide did it for me;[1] and proved, as I suspected from his bad temper, that he had got his facts wrong, and cooked others. But what's the use of taking reviews or answers to reviews seriously?

The Co-op; women as usual are magnificent. I had seen the resolution—they beat the Labour Party hollow. I gather that Ann and Richard are to be married[2]—so we shall be cousins in law—a great satisfaction to me, remembering so many childish and grown up days with Arthur and Theodore [Margaret's brothers]; and you.

Our love to you and Lilian.

Virginia

Sussex

3413: TO VANESSA BELL   [*Monk's House, Rodmell, Sussex*]

Thursday [July? 1938]

Many thanks for the jacket.[3] I think it is one of the best you ever did—quite lovely, and also practical, and so you've killed 2 birds with 3 cheques.

Quentin's coming to tea this afternoon—so's Maynard and Lydia And here's Mr Wicks to discuss the new room.[4]

We come up on Sunday—shall we come in after dinner?

B.

Berg

1. For G. M. Young's review see p. 247, note 2. In an unsigned note in *Time and Tide* of 25 June *Three Guineas* was called "A terrible sight. Indecent, almost obscene." Replying to these critics in the next issue, Renée Haynes defended the book strongly.
2. Ann Stephen was the daughter of Virginia's brother Adrian, and Richard Llewelyn Davies was the son of Margaret's brother Crompton. They were married on 21 July.
3. For the American edition of *Three Guineas*.
4. The Woolfs were planning to convert part of the roof space of Monk's House into a library for Leonard. The work began in early August.

3414: To John Lehmann   52 *Tavistock Square* [*W.C.*1]

Typewritten
[early July 1938]

My dear John,

It seems hopeless to arrange a meeting in which we can discuss anything except Press business, and so, as you asked me yesterday again about writing something for New Writing, I think I had better explain in writing.

You said that I'm an adept at getting out of things. And it's true that I dont at all want to get into things. I loathe having to keep to dates and so many thousand words. Indeed save for writing an occasional article for the Lit. Sup. and two pot boiling stories for America I've not written for any editor for years. Thats one reason why I dont commit myself to you.

The other reason is that I find the foreword to New Writing distinctly inhibiting. You say it exists particularly to "further the work of new and young authors". Well, I'm neither new nor young, alas. But it's what follows that bothers me—"whose aims are in any way in sympathy with its declared character". You may have sent some declaration which I've missed. If so, let me have it, and I'll consider it. But my instinct is to fight shy of magazines which have a declared character. Why lay down laws about imaginative writing?

Probably I'm an incorrigible outsider. I always want to write only for the Hogarth Press, and feel if I'm forced to commit myself to anybody else that I'm writing what I dont want to write and its sure to be bad.

But of course I'm very grateful (this is genuine) that you should ask me; and its because you've asked me so often that I go into detail, instead of saying as I usually do—and its true, God knows, with the whole of Roger waiting to be dealt with—that I havent the time.

I liked Herr [Martin] Freud; and it was a great comfort that you were there to lubricate his English.

Yours
V.W.

Texas

3415: To Ethel Smyth   52 *Tavistock Sqre.* [*W.C.*1]

Monday 11th July 1938

I know I am unpardonable this time. I have it on my conscience like a grain of lead that I ought to have answered some definite question about a definite day—Only the large hearted great minded Ethel will excuse me, when I say that though we've been back a week, not a moment has passed without some laceration. Now its a young woman who must talk about her novel [May Sarton]—now Freud's son [Martin], must be given a meat meal; now one of the Stracheys passing through London[1]—and then oh the letters, all asking different questions, abusive, inquisitive, idiotic intelligent—3gs. has let me in for such a swarm of these gentry: and I devote the time I usually read or talk to dealing with them. Some are heartbreaking though—But to turn to facts, thats why I've not answered you. And now dont know where you may be. About the speech—was it a success? Is there a report? And the Orchestra?[2] I never knew how many womens organisations there are till this moment: how poor; how clamorous. But tell me about this one. We shall be here now, in this very divided and tumultuous way—I mean "seeing" people, till the end of the month. So if you're up next week—but I haven't the face to propose plans. Nor any hope of a quiet afternoon. Still, still. ... I dont think I shall ever write a "controversial" book again—the racket is too distracting.

—Still I would like to toss you a kiss over the heads of my own rain beaten Mrs Simpkins [a dianthus]. All the roses in the garden were like dim lamps burning under grey veils—the mist, the rain, the fog.

V.

Berg

3416: To Benedict Nicolson   52 *Tavistock Square, W.C.*1.

Tuesday 12th July [1938]

We shall be in next Thursday, 14th, if by chance you were free and would come in any time after 9. Dont bother to answer or to change.

Virginia Woolf

Vanessa Nicolson

3417: To Sir William Rothenstein
52 *Tavistock Square, W.C.*1.

Typewritten
12th July 38

Dear Sir William,

I have been away, or I would have written before. Of course I am ready that you should quote those lines, if you think them worth it. I rather think

---

1. Marjorie Strachey (1882-1964) the youngest of Lytton's five sisters, who was a teacher and the author of a novel about Bloomsbury, *The Counterfeits*, 1927. Martin Freud (b. 1889) was a banker and took charge of the financial affairs of his father Sigmund Frend, whose works the Hogarth Press published in translation.
2. See p. 247, note 7.

the sentence should read "Why there arent more critics of painting I cant make out" rather than the other way;[1] but it doesnt matter.

By an odd coincidence I got your letter and a copy of the first volume of your memoirs to read again by the same post. I am trying, at the wish of Margery Fry, to write something about Roger Fry; and I remembered your account of meeting him in Paris. I wonder if you remember more than you say there? If so, I wonder further whether you would come one day and let me talk to you about him—the early visit to Paris is left very vague in his letters. But I daresay you have nothing to add.

In any case I am so glad you are going on, for I enjoyed the first two volumes greatly.

Yours sincerely
Virginia Woolf

Houghton Library, Harvard University

3418: To Sir William Rothenstein
52 Tavistock Square, W.C.1.

14th July [1938]

Dear Sir William,

It would be delightful if you would dine here on Monday next at 8. We shall be alone. I should be much interested to see any letters of Roger's.[2] I only knew, vaguely, that there had been some coolness,[3] but he never spoke of it to me, and always said that he admired your work.

If this suits you, please dont bother to write. And of course dont change.

Yours sincerely
Virginia Woolf

Houghton Library, Harvard University

3419: To Ethel Smyth   [52 *Tavistock Square, W.C.*1]

Friday, 15 July 1938

But I did read, not meaning to, being in a rush: and then cdn't stop—

1. Sir William Rothenstein (1872-1945), the portraitist and Principal of the Royal College of Art, had asked Virginia's permission to quote several sentences from her letter to him of 2 November 1932 (see Vol. V, Letter 2655) in the third volume of his memoirs, *Since Fifty* (1939). He did so without using the sentence to which she refers. His two earlier volumes, entitled *Men and Memories*, were published in 1931-2. Virginia quoted quite liberally from them in *Roger Fry*, when she was writing about Roger's visit to Paris in 1892.
2. Virginia published two letters from Fry to Rothenstein in her *Roger Fry*.
3. There was a temporary coolness between the two friends in 1912, when Rothenstein was unwilling to support Fry's second Grafton Galleries Exhibition of Post-Impressionist paintings.

this refers to the [Canterbury] lecture: so you see you've slipped the pill into me in the most lubricous way. I laughed aloud. But cant find an envelope so will send tomorrow. Yes, I'm having the most hardworking part of 3 gs now: when someone says Can you explain this? Will you see me and discuss that?—I feel that its part of my intolerable job. I think the sales have struck the rock of rage, and wont go any further. Oh I've made some so furious: And then a Quaker or governess makes up by thanking:

I see you say—in a hurried PS. that you *might* look in on Saturday. tomorrow 6. If so, would you ring up first? I think I shall be in—hope so; but there's a muddle about going to see E M Forster's play[1]—I dont think it'll be necessary, only should you be able to come make sure first—

and once more excuse this palsied hand.

V.

PS.

I must write this more clearly. I hope and think I shall be in tomorrow, about 6 Saturday, but will you ring up should you find you are able to come. There! Thats better.

Berg

3420: To R. C. Trevelyan   52 *Tavistock Square, W.C.*1.

Typewritten
July 22nd 38

Dear Bob,[2]

(Excuse this typing; which is to spare your eyes my illegible hand)—

I am trying, with great difficulty, to get something written about Roger, and I've now come to the time at Beaufort Street. I can find very little about it; and wonder whether you could write a few lines, for me to quote or paraphrase, about your life there. Anything that occurs to you; anything that gives a notion of what he was like then; and of the manner of life. . . . Do you know what papers he was writing for? And did you see a great many people? However I neednt particularise. Any scrap, the less formal the better, would be a great help; if its not a bother to you. We go

1. Forster had written an historical village pageant in support of the Dorking and Leith Preservation Society. Virginia did not attend it.
2. Robert Trevelyan (1872-1951) published several volumes of poetry with the Hogarth Press. He shared a house with Roger Fry in 1893-6 in Beaufort Street, Chelsea, where 'Harris' was their temperamental maid-of-all-work.

away next week, or I would have asked if you could come and talk. We havent met for an age.

Yrs ever
Virginia Woolf

[*handwritten:*]
"Harris" cuts a great figure in R's letters home—she seems to have drunk.

Sussex

3421: TO V. SACKVILLE-WEST

52 *T*.[*avistock*] *S*.[*quare, W.C.*1]

22 July [1938]

Leonard says you have sent a poem,[1] and would like to know what I think of it. Now I would like to read it and normally would fire off an opinion with my usual audacity. But I want to explain: constituted as I am (not as I ought to be) I feel I cant read your poem impartially while your charges against me, as expressed in a letter I have somewhere but won't quote, remain unsubstantiated. I feel, I mean, that you thought me dishonest in 3 gs: You said something about its being "misleading" and suggested that if only you weren't incurably clumsy honest and slow witted yourself you could demolish my specious humbug. You could knock me down with your honest old English fists and so on. And then you sicklied me over with praise of charm and wit.[2]

This is only a recollection: but anyhow it reverberates; and being imperfect as I am, I know that I should hear these growlings and mutterings distorting your poem. And with my (though you mayn't believe it) dogged belief in the absolute necessity of absolute honesty about poetry, I couldn't say what I thought; because I shouldn't be capable of pure thinking.

So come to lunch: and we need not, if you dont wish it, discuss either my prose or your poetry. being, as I maintain, quite fond of each other for other reasons. The porpoise and the pearls at the fishmongers for instance.

A rush of an unholy nature here, so I cant comb out this untidy letter. Dotty [Wellesley] rings up to ask us to go to meet Yeats. etc. etc.

Your old humbug
V.

Berg

1. *Solitude*, published by the Hogarth Press in November 1938.
2. See Letters 3405 and 3422.

Saturday [23 July 1938]

What on earth can I have said in my [preceding] letter to call forth your telegram?[1] God knows. I scribbled it off in five minutes, never read it through, and can only remember that it was written in a vein of obvious humorous extravagance and in a tearing hurry. However, I'll try to explain— but what a bore—what a fool I must be. What happened was this.

Leonard showed me a letter from you in which you said you'd like my opinion of your poem if I had time to read it. Now I've been in a rush and haven't had time. It came into my head, as I went downstairs that you have never answered a letter I wrote you from Northumberland [No. 3405] in answer to your letter about 3 gs. And I had a vague memory that you had said something which had slightly irritated me—you know how one gets a whole shower of letters when a book comes out and I was feeling a little harassed—because I thought you meant that I was not quite honest in what I said in 3 gs. And I should mind you to think that very much. I've now looked for your letter and this was the phrase: "You are a tantalising writer because at one moment you enchant one with your lovely prose and next moment exasperate one with your misleading arguments. . . . And far be it from me to Cross swords with you publicly, for I should always lose on points in fencing, though if it comes to fisticuffs I might knock you down. So long as you play the gentleman's game, with the gentleman's technique, you win." That was the phrase that slightly irritated me (whether rightly or wrongly) and I think in my letter from the North I asked you to explain what you meant by it. Well, you never did; and as I came downstairs I thought, "Oh Vita never answered my letter, so I suppose she did mean something. And I cant sit down and read her poem if she thinks me dishonest, or whatever it was that she did think me." But I was so hurried and took the whole thing so lightly, and had alas such implicit faith in my own power to convey this random hurried vague grievance in writing that I never bothered to see what you had said, and dashed off the letter which must have been a triumph of misrepresentation.

Its a lesson not to write letters For I suppose you'll say, when you read what I've quoted from your own letter, that there's nothing to cause even a momentary irritation. And I daresay you're right. I suspect that anything written acquires meanings and both the writers mood and the reader's mood queer the pitch

So let us leave it.

One reason for writing by the way was that I thought I shouldn't have a chance of talking when we did meet.

But, as I say, lets leave it: and I apologise, and will never write a letter

1. Vita had wired, "Horrified by your letter."

so carelessly again. And I've no grievance whatever; and you need say no more, because I'm quite sure, on re-reading your letter, you didn't mean that I was dishonest: and thats the only thing I minded. So forgive and forget

V.

Berg

3423: To V. Sackville-West

52 *T.[avistock] S.[quare, W.C.1]*

Monday [25 July 1938]

No I never got your Skye letter, as we didnt go to Sligachan. So that's explained—and for the rest lets wait to argue till we meet—if argue we must. (and of course, tho' I dont agree with your deductions, there are any number of possible, and natural, disagreements)

It was the feeling that you thought me shifty that I minded: but thats cleared up and this is only written, again in a furious rush, to say that its all over, and to explain that we went to Flodigarry [Portree] only—a much nicer place: and hearing nothing I was expectant.

So hope to see you on Wednesday lunch.

V.

Berg

3424: To R. C. Trevelyan   52 *Tavistock Square, W.C.1.*

Monday [25 July 1938]

Dear Bob,

Many thanks for saying you will put down what you can remember [about Roger Fry]—That is just what I want, and you wont mind if I leave things in or out. At the moment I can't see what scale the book—if it is to be a book—should take. But any thing you remember will be of the greatest help. The letters then are mostly to his mother; and that means a great deal is left out.

We go to Monk's House, Rodmell, Lewes tomorrow. Would you write there. We tried to get to Morgan's pageant [at Dorking]—I heard it was lovely; but another engagement prevented, most tiresomely.

Yours ever

Virginia Woolf

Sussex

Typewritten
27th July 1938

Dear Madame Sue Ling,

I have just seen Christopher Isherwood,[1] who gave me the lovely little box with the two little gifts from you. I need not say that I am much touched that you should have got them for me, and I shall keep them on my table—not as a memory of you, for I have never seen you, but all the same I think of you often. Thank you so much. I heard from him how much they had enjoyed seeing you. But he was only here for a moment, and I did not have time to get much information from him. I hope however that you are going on with your work. I am sending you two little books, one is the [Mrs Gaskell] life of Charlotte Brontë, the other Lambs Essays. I think Lamb wrote very good English prose—but do not bother to read it as an exercise; only for pleasure—The life of Charlotte Brontë will perhaps give you a feeling for the lives of women writers in England in the 19th century—their difficulties, and how she overcame them. And it is a very interesting life in other ways. But I will send other books from time to time, on condition that you do not think you must thank me for them. And certainly you must never think of paying for them. They are so cheap in England. I can buy them for a few pence. Tell me the names of any you think you would like.

We are just going down to Sussex, and I hope to have more time there. London is so crowded. There is a quiet time here politically for the moment. That is to say we are waiting for what Hitler may do next. People are tired of talking about war; but all the same we do nothing but buy arms. The air is full of aeroplanes at the moment.

I hope some day you will write again and tell me how you are getting on with your work. And please remember how glad I shall be to give you any help I can in reading it and correcting any mistakes. But write exactly as you think—that is the only way.

With my love, good bye. Please call me Virginia. I do not like being Mrs Woolf.

Virginia Woolf

Ling Su-Hua (Mrs Chen)

---

1. Isherwood and W. H. Auden had been to China to write about the Chinese civil war for their book *Journey to a War*, 1939.

28th July 38

Dear Bunny,

I have signed the paper—is that right?—with pleasure. Here it is. I have never heard of the Wilsons, but thats to my discredit, and it seems a monstrous case.[1] Yes: we keep your offer in mind, like a dock leaf among nettles. That is, London is a hurlyburly: I'm packing to go to Rodmell; smuts descend; telephone rings; pens wont write. Oh and what about Westmoreland? Your cottage in that paradise?[2]

No time for more.

Yr affate old harridan
V.W.

Berg

1. Garnett was trying to obtain a civil pension for the widow of Professor Charles Wilson (1848-1938), for fourteen years Professor of Persian at University College, London. Garnett's appeal was rejected.
2. The cottage which Garnett rented from 1934 to about 1946 was not in Westmorland but on the edge of the moor overlooking Swaledale in Yorkshire.

Letters 3427-3458 (August–October 1938)

The Woolfs remained a longer time than usual at Monk's House, return-
ing permanently to London as late as mid-October. The summer and early
autumn were clouded by Hitler's threat to Czechoslovakia and the apparent
imminence of war, which was averted at the last moment (29 Septem-
ber) by the Munich pact. Virginia kept Vanessa (then at Cassis) fully in-
formed of the development of the crisis, and its impact on their personal lives
and Leonard's political involvement in it. They were issued with gas-masks,
and considered moving the Hogarth Press out of London. Roger Fry was
Virginia's main solace during this acutely troubled period, and she was simul-
taneously working on Pointz Hall.

3427: TO LADY TWEEDSMUIR *Monk's House, Rodmell,*
Lewes, Sussex

1st Aug 38

My dear Susie,

I ought to have thanked you and your husband before this for sending
me the books. It was very good of you, and very good of him. Will you
thank him from me, and say that as soon as I have despatched certain
dreary tasks I'm going to read his Scott first. This is self indulgence because I want to get his advice which of the Waverley novels to re-read. I
have them all here, and must cure myself of the habit of reading the same
over and over again. And then I shall read Oliver Cromwell.[1] That'll be to
see how biographies are written—I'm finding my own attempt incredibly
difficult.

But it was good of both of you on your holiday to remember to send
me these books. And I'm so glad to find my name in them.

Now you've brought 10 volumes of George Sand[2] on yourself—and a
copy I have pasted over with scraps of leather so that its garish. The original binding was tidy but ugly. I rather think I stuck a picture in too. But

1. The two books which they sent to Virginia were John Buchan's (Tweedsmuir)
   Sir Walter Scott, 1932, and his *Oliver Cromwell*, 1934.
2. *Histoire de Ma Vie*, 1856. Virginia had rebound the volumes in blue and green
   morocco leather with hand-blocked, paper-covered boards and handwritten
   labels.

if you disregard this amateurish bookbinding, you'll find—at least I did—
that she's a magnificent old woman. Anyhow, do try her when the winter
is white and the wolves howling. This Wolf is so hot after walking on the
downs, she cant write. But do some day tell me if you like G. S.

Yrs aff V.W.

Sold in April 1978 by Bertram Rota Ltd., London

3428: To Ethel Smyth   *M[onks] H[ouse, Rodmell,*
                              Sussex]
Sunday. Aug 7th or 8th [?] 1938

Oh you old Cross Patch! What d'you think I'm made of? hands, like a
centipedes feet, each holding a pen and one that'll write, which is more
than most will? I'm still 10 down on my 3 guinea letters: earnest requests for
enlightenment—now what did you mean by this?—reach me daily. No
secretary. Must sometimes walk. Sometimes talk. The great thing to remember about friendship is that it hangs like fruit on a bough, ripening,
not rottening, nor falling. However, I break off this meagre twig, only its
with a brain sodden with Roger, and apprehensive of more, and more
necessary, letters. For if one writes books that incite Headmasters, one
must take the consequences. Reply. My dear Sir, In answer to your enquiry...

Roasting hot till today; and old Mrs Woolf comes over and spends 4
hours remembering the coffee cups and overmantels now stored: says she
wants to know, would I like, when she dies, either a drawing room chair,
or a silver 1870 sugar caster? Which shall it be? Telephone rings: I'm the
lady who broadcast your praises in Dublin[1]—Will you see me at 2.30
tomorrow?—thats all I'll tell you of facts. Vita came. Heavenly good:
sound and sweet as an apple. Loves Gwen as much as ever. But to my
pleasure would like to see me too.

I'm deep (when I can dive beneath chatter) in art history. I think I've
mounted a barren nightmare in this book (R.F.) but shall finish the dreary
round and then dismount and see what's the use of it. Odd what a grind
biography is. This is my favourite reading: what hard writing. L. has
broken his pen too. Foxes bark outside the window at night. Oh and to
our dismay, found workmen making a library in the attic—meant it for the
Autumn. Hammer hammer all day for 3 weeks. L. has invented a roof
verandah.[2] 6 doz: French white wine just arrived. Rain today. I must put
on a sou-wester bought in Oban and trudge. How is Crosspatch feeling

1. Coralie Anderson, born in New Zealand. She had telephoned from Newhaven,
and Virginia invited her to tea, but she did not come.
2. This led off one end of the projected library and formed a small open-air platform
on which Leonard and Virginia intended to sit on hot summer nights.

now? And where shall I send this? What about Roman wall? and the Opera?[1] When? Toscanini? And Henry Wood?[2] I'm avid of all news, and all letters, that dont ask, now what did you mean on p. 172?

Yr
V.

Berg

3429: To ANGELICA BELL   *Monk's House, Rodmell,*
Lewes, Sussex

7th Aug 1938

Dearest Pixie,

I was so glad to get your scrap on top of the circular. And I've invented this bold black big hand which the man in the moon can read without glasses.

To fix the mind on facts:—we have arranged in the family to come next Saturday and see the Gammer.[3] So when the moon rises, look for me: there in the magic circle green winged I'll be. Quentin has just been to tea: practically naked; had to borrow Leonard's shirt which looked like a handkerchief on a hippopotamus.

We've workmen dinging and donging: we are making our library, but it has suddenly given birth to a balcony and a verandah. I can't explain now. Come and see.

Vita was here for a night—and brought a bottle of her mother's best wine—which you must help to drink. We had also several Wolves[4] God help us, have to go with them to see Alsatian police dogs rescuing babies at Uckfield [on 15 August]. And to London to see John Lehmann. And its raining. So Goodbye, lovely witch. If you want any cash, let me know.

Virginia Witcherina

Texas

3430: To R. C. TREVELYAN   *Monk's House, Rodmell,*
Lewes, Sussex

7th Aug 38

Dear Bob,

Many thanks for your letter. It is exactly what I wanted and freshens up

1. Possibly Ethel's opera *The Wreckers*, which was performed in April 1939.
2. His proposal for an all-women's orchestra. See p. 247, note 7.
3. *Gammer Gurton's Needle* (written in 1566). Angelica was taking part as a member of the London Village Players, a company formed for the summer only by former students of Michel Saint-Denis.
4. Leonard's mother Marie Woolf, his younger brother Edgar, and Edgar's wife Sylvia.

the whole of the Beaufort Street time. I shall certainly hope (if I get on with the book [*Roger Fry*]) to quote some of it; and only wish there were more. Could you, do you think, give some sketch of Helen[1]—how she struck you to look at, talk to, and so on. I never saw her; and get confused accounts, naturally, from Roger's sisters.

Indeed, if you had the time, and could put down anything you remember of Roger it would be a great help to me to have it by me. Roger told me at various times a good deal about Helen's breakdown. There was a mysterious story about a doctor who had poisoned a friend. Was this partly the cause of her first breakdown—2 years after they married? But of course I shan't need to give details.

We both like the poem on Goldie[2] very much indeed. I found it very moving myself: so simple, and yet enclosing him in real poetry. Will it be printed in your book?—I think I saw that you are bringing out complete— I mean up to the present complete—poems. And this ought to be among them.

Many thanks again: and if you should think of more notes, please let me have them here, where we shall be till October.

Yours ever
Virginia Woolf

Sussex

3431: To Benedict Nicolson   *Monk's House, Rodmell*
                                     [Sussex]
Sunday 7th Aug [1938]

Dear Ben,

I've had a wire from Vita to say that you would read and annotate Roger Fry's articles. That is extremely good of you: but I have only a selection of them here, and I'm finding them so important at the point I've reached that I think I must keep them and anyhow read them myself. But there's a mass of his lectures, unpublished, and more articles in London. I'm sure that anyone with knowledge of art could make a fascinating book of

1. Helen Fry (*née* Coombe), whom Roger married in 1896. After a struggle of several years, she became permanently insane and died in 1937. The 'mysterious story' in the second paragraph refers to a doctor who, according to Helen, had killed a patient by prescribing the wrong medicine. Helen saw this doctor while on holiday, and believed that he intended to kill her too. Roger quickly removed her to another hotel, but told his children later that this incident was a first symptom of her persecution-mania.

2. Goldsworthy Lowes Dickinson (1862-1932), the historian and philosopher, and lecturer in Political Science at Cambridge. Trevelyan's poem "To G.L.D." appeared in his *Collected Works*, 1939.

extracts. Would it interest you to consider doing this?[1] I should have of course to consult his sister, who is his executor.[2] If you're in London in October before going to America would you come and talk it over? Meanwhile, many thanks for your offer of help.

Yr ever
Virginia Woolf

Vanessa Nicolson

3432: To Vanessa Bell

Monk's House, Rodmell,
near Lewes, Sussex.

Sunday [14 August 1938]

As the usual confusion has arisen as to what the final arrangements were, this is to say that the Wolves expect to dine at Charleston on *Sunday* next not Wednesday. They hope that Quentin, or anyone, will come to tea and bowls any day except Monday or Friday. And we're very grateful for the lift last night and hope you weren't exhausted.

By the way, with reference to the Chicago show, and my introduction, it strikes me that it would be possible to use Rogers article on you, and also his article on Duncan,[3] much more effectively than anything I could write. They would only need a little introducing—And this would relieve me of the crime and discomfort of Nepotism (for meaning of this word, consult Quentin)

Berg

1. Ben Nicolson worked on this plan, but never completed it. However, during his 30-year editorship of the *Burlington Magazine* (which Fry had helped to found in 1903), he wrote frequent editorials and articles on Fry's contribution to art history.
2. Margery Fry (1874-1958), who had shared a house with her brother in Dalmeny Avenue, London, from 1919 to 1926, when she became Principal of Somerville College, Oxford.
3. The two Fry articles were *Vanessa Bell and Othon Friesz* (*New Statesman*, 3 June 1922) and the Introduction to *Duncan Grant* (Hogarth Press, 1924). There is no record in Chicago of any exhibition which included paintings by Vanessa and Duncan.

3433: To William Plomer

Monk's House, Rodmell
Lewes, Sussex

Aug 18th [1938]

Will you come over to tea this Sunday and bowls; and stay to dinner?
I've been enjoying Kilvert[1] greatly.

Virginia Woolf

Texas

3434: To Mrs Ethel Grant

Monk's House, Rodmell,
Lewes, Sussex

20th Aug. [1938]

Dear Mrs Grant,

Duncan brought the mirror; I have painted it with creosote (or something); it has been hung. And I am now sitting under it in a state of such gratified content—not that I can see myself—its not that which gratifies me—that I must write and thank you.

What an extraordinarily clever woman you are! Naturally you have a son of the same cast: and the result is the loveliest looking glass I've ever seen. Also it exactly fits the place, which is miraculous. I wish you could see it. There are some yellow begonias; and some fine white dahlias at the edge, to give a dash of colour in the corner. But I wont describe it all to you, since you must know the pattern by heart.

How is the carpet doing? We have 6 workmen in the house making the new room. They say it will be done next week—thats to spur you on, for of course it wont be done.

Please give my love to Duncans adventurous Aunt[2] who goes to Sweden. And please tell me what I owe—in cash I mean: for the other debt is about £1,000,000.

Yrs V.W.

Estate of Duncan Grant

3435: To Ethel Smyth

Monk's House, Rodmell,
near Lewes, Sussex

29th Aug [1938]

I dont know, or indeed care, whose turn it is to break this long silence—last time you wrote from Harrogate: and did I answer, or didn't I? I cant

1. The diaries of Robert Francis Kilvert (1840-79), the Vicar of Bredwardine on the Wye. They were discovered by Plomer and edited by him in three volumes (1938-40).
2. Mrs Grant's sister, Violet McNeil.

remember what we were talking about. Operas? Workmen? Thats the curse of letter writing—Why should you be agog to hear how the new room's going on—how L. suddenly invented a balcony and a verandah— how there are sheets everywhere: dust falling—hammer and nails— workmen peeping in at me breakfasting in bed. You will skip all that. As for politics, I feel as if we were all sitting downstairs while someone slowly dies. So why write letters? Nevertheless, here we've been to Sea-ford today to mate Sally, in spite of the politics. She wouldn't mate. Leonard has gone to fetch her after 2 hours further solicitation. And I've been walking; found a dead tortoise on the top of the downs; also several clouded yellows [butterflies]. All the morning I work my brain into a screw over Roger—what did he do in 1904—when did his wife go mad, and how on earth does one explain madness and love in sober prose, with dates attached? I saw Vita and I saw Gwen. Vita has written a long poem [*Solitude*], L. says very good: I've not read it. That I think I told you. And you now—now drop your trumpet, which by the way is upside down, and tell me: about the opera; about the orchestra: about Mary [Ethel's maid] and Woking and the Balfours.[1] Why is the aristocratic mind invariably middle class when the body is divine? Just finished Lady Fred Cavendish's diaries:[2] no vigour, no insight, no originality. All as drab and dowdy as Mabels Sunday best (Mabel is our maid of all work.) Explain this to me. And such damned condescension to artists. Yet all else is fine and flowing and thoroughbred—only the mind cluttered with curtains and ferns. I want to settle in and read some entire pure classic to rid me of the infection. But instead I play bowls with fanatic fury like yours for golf. So we approach, you and I, from different points of the compass. Here I cook dinner, so must stop, just, it happens, as a flock of fine feathered ideas perches on my wire. No I dont like Harolds BBC manner,[3] oh and every day I get a packet of abuse or ecstasy. Letters, I mean from that hysterical and illiterate ass the Public.

As I said before I must cook dinner, and wait the return of the Bride [Sally]. I had tea today at Seaford with the bastard son [Philip Hugh-Jones] of Philip Morrell. Did you know that ante-chamber to Ottolines drawing room? Now Ethel, answer.

V.

Berg

---

1. Lady Elizabeth Balfour, a daughter of the Earl of Lytton who married the 2nd Earl of Balfour in 1887, was Ethel's friend and neighbour at Woking.
2. *The Diary of Lady Frederick Cavendish*, edited by John Bailey in 1927.
3. Harold Nicolson was doing regular B.B.C. talks on current political affairs.

Typewritten
30th Aug 1938

Dear Mr Brace,

I have just received the American copies of Three Guineas. I think it looks very attractive, and I hope for both our sakes that your forecast of success may come true. I was afraid it might be too much concerned with English problems to interest American readers.

Thank you also for your letter. It is very encouraging to write for so appreciative a publisher! It is not the first time that I have felt this, but this time I am specially grateful. There are many things in my book that I know may irritate people—yet I felt them to be important, and did not write it merely to annoy. It has roused a good deal of interest here—both anger and approval.

At the moment things are so bad here that one can hardly think of books. But I hope before this reaches you there may be some improvement.

Many thanks again, and kind regards from us both.

Yours sincerely,
Virginia Woolf

Harcourt Brace Jovanovich

Typewritten
31st Aug 38

Dear Bessie,

Many thanks for your letter about Helen Fry.[1] It is a help, because it bears out the vague feeling that I am getting from her letters. I think the dread of insanity must always have been in the background, and probably made her morbid and afraid of people. It is a terrible story, for at times one gets too so clear a sense of her brilliance and a curious individuality. But of course, if I do get anything written—and the difficulty increases as one goes on—not much in detail can be said of her. But I want an outline, and what you and Bob have told me is very helpful. Thank you so much for writing.

I hope we may see you and Bob when we are back in the autumn.

Yours affectionately
Virginia Woolf

Trinity College, Cambridge

1. See p. 264, note 1.

3438: TO ETHEL SMYTH   M.[onks] H.[ouse, Rodmell,
                                        Sussex]
Sept 2nd [1938]

About Wednesday 7th—by all means come to Lewes about 4, and L.
will meet you—But he can't take you to Polegate,[1] flowering or not, as
there's a Labour Party meeting here at 7. So would you as you suggest, get
Miss Hudson to fetch you. The workmen, though, are in the house—
every room occupied, save the dining room: but this may be mitigated by
Wed: 4 weeks has now spread to 8. Let me know train. and any details.
for which I have at the moment no time owing to the imminence of Post,
and the presence of a charming man in a white smock who's ladders touching my nose.

                                                        Yr
                                                          V

Berg

3439: TO ANGELICA BELL   *Monk's House, Rodmell*
                                        [Sussex]
5th Sept 38

Dearest Pixie,
    Nessa says that you are now of an age [nearly 20] to manage your own
money affairs. I quite agree. So I am writing, as legibly as I can, to suggest
that in future I should pay the £100 which I have sent her in the past to
spend on you direct to you. She thinks it would suit you better if this were
paid quarterly instead of half yearly. So I am sending £25 now, and will
send again the first day of every other quarter, trusting you to remind me
should I forget. All I have to add is that I hope to be able to do this regularly
and lifelong: but as the money has to be earned, I might at some time not be
able to make it. I will give you six months notice, if I find I cant manage it.
Meanwhile I count on you to spend it to the best advantage, on clothes and
other enjoyments, and to let me know (as we agreed) if at any time another
dollop would come in handy.
    Thats all: and I hope you admire both the clarity of the handwriting and
the businesslike style in which the statement is made. An acknowledgment
of cheque enclosed herewith will oblige, and I beg to remain without
further ceremony, your faithful and obliged humble servant
                                        Witcherina Maxima
Texas

1. Wootton Manor, Polegate, Sussex, which belonged to Ethel's friend Alice
Hudson.

3440: To Sibyl Colefax   *Monk's House [Rodmell,*
                                          Sussex]
Monday [5 September 1938]

Dearest Sibyl,
    Yes delighted *Thursday 8th*, but:
        (1) View is ruined
        (2) No room for chauffeur in house
        (3) The smallest possible doghole for you
        (4) Village char is cook
    Let me know if you are daunted. If not, whether we shall meet a train:
if so, which.

                            Yours in haste (not hate) Virginia

No clothes but nightgowns worn here.

Michael Colefax

3441: To Ethel Smyth   *Monks House [Rodmell,*
                                          Sussex]
Sunday [11 September 1938]

    Yes, a very nice letter from that interesting attractively shabby woman.[1]
What a sonorous language French is, and how on occasion they know how
to roll it out! This is not an occasion when I can attempt the same with my
mother tongue; because there's a swarm of people about.
    I dont think that your insight is faultless where L[eonard]. is concerned;
but would not in any case analyse other people's so complicated relations. I
think if you were ever a day alone together the mists would disperse. As a
matter of fact, the day you came happened to be a distracted day for him—
the funeral, then the will,[2] and then, the moment you left, our local candidate [Mr Black] arriving—to early dinner, and a speech; and a meeting in
the dining room, which needed whipping together. So he was brooding a
dozen things at once. Oh what a dismal little man, a collector of match-
boxes, he turned out—this Labour party Champion—like a mouse, which
indeed his daughter breeds and sells for 6d a head to the mousebreeder of
Seaford. And it is thus that the L.P. counters Hitler. Well, the situation
this morning makes everything completely visionary—I cant feel that

1. Perhaps Nadia Boulanger.
2. Of Mr Thomsett, a Rodmell farm worker and husband of Annie, who lived in a
   cottage which belonged to the Woolfs and periodically worked in Monk's House.
   In his will, which Leonard had drawn up for him, he left all his property to his
   daughter Doris and nothing to his other children.

there's as much as a mouse involved: yet all the guns may be pulled by that insignificant insect.

How was Maurice [Baring]?

Here, like yourself, I tear up 6 pages of the most acute psychological investigation. I analysed your feeling, and mine, and what I thought as we sat down to tea, and then again as I got up to put the kettle on for your very spruce Chauffeur [Miss Hudson]: and now destroy it all—as—you did. 6 pages, Ethel, ... One day we'll talk them. Not now

V.

Meanwhile, yes, I like laying my furry head on your magnanimous breast.

Oh I've had such a drubbing and a scourging from the Cambridge ladies—the professors of Eng. lit: at Cambridge for 3gs.[1] I'm a disgrace to my sex: and a caterpillar on the community. I thought I should raise their hackles—poor old strumpets.

Berg

3442: TO R. C. TREVELYAN   *Monk's House, Rodmell,*
                                            Lewes, Sussex

Sunday 11th Sept 38

Dear Bob,

Thank you again for your notes. I am very glad of them—especially for the picture of Helen [Fry] which I think is very vivid. It will help to make her real—and I'm encouraged by what you say, to go on. There's such a mass of documents and letters—the difficulty is to choose whether to speak oneself or let him speak—and how to combine the different voices. But of course its immensely interesting.

Will you thank Bessie [his wife] too for sending me the amusing note of Roger's early art criticism? It was very good of her.

Morgan [Forster] is spending the weekend. I'm so sorry to hear that Bessie's eyes have been bothering her. We agree by the way in all liking your Goldie poem[2]—and send our greetings and hopes that we may meet.

Yr ever
V. W.

Sussex

1. In the September issue of *Scrutiny*, Q.D. Leavis wrote a vitriolic review of *Three Guineas*: "Mrs Woolf's latest effort is a let-down for our sex ... this book is not merely silly and ill-informed, though it is that too, it contains some dangerous assumptions, some preposterous claims and some nasty attitudes ... It seems to me the art of living as conceived by a social parasite."
2. See p. 264, note 2.

M.[onks] H.[ouse, Rodmell,
Sussex]

Sat. 17th Sept. [1938]

1. We were on the Great Wall about the first week in June this year.
2. The illegible word was FURRY[1]—applied to myself in sympathetic reference to Pan.
3. That was one of my jokes—I mean, pretending I'd written 4 pages and torn them up.[2] I did no such thing. Had I written, I would have sent.
4. Of course you dedicated Time Went On [1936] to me. But why not 2 books—Vita does, to Gwen, and again to Gwen[3] But I agree: its better not.
5. No, of course again, I never dreamt except in some visionary rhapsody of your writing about me.[4] As for publishing a description during my lifetime the thought appals. When Margot [Oxford] asked me to write about my youth, I saw, if I did, I should cease writing altogether. And its the same with being written about. I must be private, secret, as anonymous and submerged as possible in order to write. So never think of it as you dont.
5 [sic]. Lets leave the letters till we're both dead. Thats my plan. I dont keep or destroy but collect miscellaneous bundles of odds and ends, and let posterity, if there is one, burn or not. Lets forget all about death and all about Posterity.

When do you go? And for long? And I envy you, I, chained to my R F [Roger Fry]. who is, in himself, magnificent.

Yr
V.

Berg

3444: To H. A. L. Fisher

*Monk's House, Rodmell,
Lewes, Sussex*

17th Sept 38

My dear Herbert,[5]

Of course I shall be delighted to send a copy of Three Guineas to Mr Nowell Smith.[6] It will take a few days, as I havent got one here to sign.

1. See the postcript to Letter 3441.
2. See the last paragraph before the signature in the same letter.
3. Vita dedicated *The Dark Island* (1934) and *Solitude* (1938) to Gwen St Aubyn.
4. Virginia had once tried to imagine what it would be like to be described in print by Ethel. See Letter 3133.
5. The historian H. A. L. Fisher (1865-1940) was Virginia's first cousin. He had been President of the Board of Education, 1916-22, and since 1925 Warden of New College, Oxford.
6. Nowell Charles Smith (1871-1961), formerly Headmaster of Sherborne School, and Chairman of the English Association 1941-3.

May I come and see you one day quietly? I should so much like to, but am always afraid that you and Lettice are overdone with people. Tell Mary[1] that if she ever wants a meal in London there is always one for her at Tavistock Square—at least after this month.

I hope you are better.

Yr affate
Virginia Woolf

Bodleian Library, Oxford

3445: TO VICTORIA OCAMPO

52 *T[avistock] S[quare, W.C.1]*

27th Sept 38

Dear Victoria,

I am spending the day in London and found your letter. We are now going back to the country—Monk's House, Rodmell, Lewes, Sussex. I dont know whether we shall be up again next week—it depends upon this cursed Hitler. But if I can do anything to help your sister,[2] write to me there. Its been such a turmoil I had no time today for anything. But let us meet if possible and forgive this scrawl. I am just off.

Yr Virginia Woolf

Estate of Victoria Ocampo

3446: TO VANESSA BELL

Monks House [Rodmell, Lewes, Sussex]

Wednesday, 28th Sept. [1938]

I was very glad to get your cards. I dont know whether you are at Cassis, or if this will reach you but write on the chance. At the moment we're waiting to hear the Broadcast of Chamberlains speech in the House this afternoon, so dont know for certain if we're going to war or not. It looks like it: anyhow you'll know by the time you get this, so there's nothing to be said. We were in London yesterday and there everyone took war for granted. They were digging trenches in the parks, loud speakers were telling one to go and be fitted for gas masks, and of course there was the usual buzz and ... Here the BBC. announced that Hitler has asked

1. Mary Bennett (b. 1913), the daughter of Herbert and Lettice Fisher. She became Principal of St Hilda's College, Oxford, in 1965.
2. Victoria Ocampo had brought her sister to England for medical treatment.

Chamberlain to Munich![1] Its an immense relief. Leonard has rushed out to tell Percy [Bartholomew, the gardener] and so on. However you'll have heard this. We think it must mean that there's going to be a compromise. God knows what. I was saying London was appalling yesterday. Kingsley Martin[2] suddenly rang up the morning before and said the Labour Party wanted L. to come up at once and try to arrange a liaison with the Liberals. So we had to go for the night. Of course it was one of KM's hysterical outbursts. There were endless meetings, telephones and so on: and nothing done.

We're staying here for the present. John takes over the Press on Monday. It may of course have to close down, as he moved to Fieldhead[3]—but all's now in the melting pot. We've had innumerable visitors—Noel Olivier, Judith, Clive, Raymond, Janice:[4] no, we're too near London for peace. Not much gossip, only eternal war talk. Noel very solid badgerly and dependable: my goddaughter [Virginia Richards] a nice little elf. The Charleston atmosphere is metallic and brittle: as for Janice she never commits— not even a nuisance. Raymond I cant cotton to though his virtues are as prominent as his nose. Tomorrow we go to Sissinghurst to discuss politics with Harold.[5]

So you see I regret you immensely: and the loss of you which I meant to use in work, I've spent chattering. Please let us know your plans, and if we can help in any direction. We had meant to travel our books in the West, then make a flying visit to S. Remi[6]—Well, it looks even possible again.

1. This was the Munich Crisis. Hitler threatened to occupy Czechoslovakia, on the pretext that the Sudeten Germans on its western borders were oppressed. On 15 September the Prime Minister, Neville Chamberlain, had flown to Germany, and agreed in principle to the secession to Hitler of these areas. On 22 September Hitler increased the pressure, and five days later the French army and the British fleet were partially mobilised. At the last moment, while Chamberlain was describing these events to the House of Commons on the 28th (and while Virginia was writing this letter), he received from Mussolini the proposal for a conference at Munich the next day to settle the crisis.
2. Editor of the *New Statesman*, 1931-60.
3. The house of John Lehmann's mother at Bourne End, Buckinghamshire. The Press was not moved from London until September 1940.
4. Noel Olivier (1892-1969), the youngest of the four daughters of Lord (Sydney) Olivier, who qualified as a doctor in 1917 and married Arthur Richards in 1921; Judith Stephen, younger daughter of Virginia's brother Adrian; Clive Bell; Raymond Mortimer (1895-1980), the literary critic and journalist; Janice Loeb, Clive's lover.
5. Harold Nicolson had been Member of Parliament for West Leicester since 1935. He was not at Sissinghurst when the Woolfs came, as he was kept in London to discuss the crisis with Churchill and others.
6. In Provence. Roger Fry had been to St Rémy in 1923, and in 1931 bought a small house (Mas d'Angirany) which had been owned by Marie Mauron's parents. Fry shared it with the Maurons.

But our excitement—here's the carpenter come to talk it over—may be ill founded. I dont suppose you'll get this: so end.

> And count on a letter
>
> B.

Julian's book[1] is doing unexpectedly well in the shops, L says. considering the crisis

Berg

3447: TO VANESSA BELL   *Monks House* [*Rodmell, Sussex*]

Typewritten
1st October. [1938]

Your letter has just come. I scrambled off a very hurried letter to you last Wednesday, half thinking you'd be marooned somewhere, and thus not get it. Now still in a hurry and therefore typing to save your old eyes I will continue the narrative. I daresay its an old story now; but no doubt you will excuse repetitions. Never never has there been such a time. Last week end we were at Charleston and very gloomy. Gloom increased on Monday. It was pouring. Then in the morning Kingsley Martin rang up to insist that L. must come to London at once and make a desperate attempt to unite labour and liberals—to do what was not obvious. But he seemed desperate, and so we flung a nightgown into a bag and started. In London it was hectic and gloomy and at the same time despairing and yet cynical and calm. The streets were crowded. People were everywhere talking loudly about war. There were heaps of sandbags in the streets, also men digging trenches, lorries delivering planks, loud speakers slowly driving and solemnly exhorting the citizens of Westminster Go and fit your gas masks. There was a long queue of people waiting outside the Mary Ward settlement[2] to be fitted. L. went off at once to see K.M. I discussed matters with Mabel [their maid]. We agreed that she had better go to Bristol—whether she has or not I dont yet know. Then L came back and said Kingsley was in despair; they had talked for two hours; everybody came into the N. S [*New Statesman*] office and talked; telephones rang incessantly. They all said war was certain; also that there would be no war. Kingsley came to dinner. He had smudges of black charcoal round his eyes and was more melodramatic and histrionic than ever. Hitler was going to make his speech at 8. We had no wireless, but he said he would ring up the BBC after it was over and find out the truth. Then we sat and discussed the inevitable end of civilisation. He strode

1. *Julian Bell: Essays, Poems and Letters* was to be published by the Hogarth Press in November.
2. An education centre at 36-7 Tavistock Place.

275

up and down the room, hinting that he meant to kill himself. He said the war would last our life time; also we should very likely be beaten. Anyhow Hitler meant to bombard London, probably with no warning; the plan was to drop bombs on London with twenty minutes intervals for forty eight hours. Also he meant to destroy all roads and railways; therefore Rodmell would be about as dangerous as Bloomsbury. Then he broke off; rang up Clark, the news man at The BBC;[1] "Ah—so its hopeless . . ." Then to us, "Hitler is bawling; the crowds howling like wild beasts." More conversation of a lugubrious kind. Now I think I'll ring up Clark again . . . Ah so it couldnt be worse . . . To us. No Hitler is more mad than ever . . . Have some Whiskey Kingsley, said L. Well, it dont much matter either way, said K. At last he went. What are you going to do? I asked. Walk the streets. Its no good—I cant sleep. So we clasped hands, as I understood for the last time.

Next morning Tuesday every one was certain it was war. Everyone, except one poor little boy in a shop who had lost his head and was half crying when I asked for a packet of envelopes (and he may have been in some sort of row) was perfectly calm; and also without hope. It was quite different from 1914. Every one said Probably we shall win but it'll be just as bad if we do. I went to the London Library to look up some papers about Roger. I sat in the basement with the Times open of the year 1910. An old man was dusting. He went away; then came back and said very kindly, "Theyre telling us to put on our gas masks, Madam" I thought the raid had begun. However, he explained that it was the loudspeaker once more addressing the citizens of Westminster. Then he asked if he could dust under my chair; and said they had laid in a supply of sand bags, but if a bomb dropped there wouldnt be many books left over. After that I walked to the National Gallery, and a voice again urged me to fit my gas mask at once. The Nat Gallery was fuller than usual; a nice old man was lecturing to an attentive crowd on Watteau. I suppose they were all having a last look.

I went home, and found that L. had arranged that the Press was to go on; but the clerks to go away into the country if they liked. Then Miss Hepworth the traveller said the shops were mostly refusing to buy at all, and were mostly going to close. So it seemed we should have to shut down. The clerks wanted to go on, as they had no place in the country; and of course no money. We arranged to pay wages as long as we could— but plans were vague. Mrs Nicholls said she should prefer to lie in the trench that was being dug in the square; Miss Perkins preferred to sit in the stock room, which she had partly prepared with mattresses etc. Then, after lunch, an American editor[2] arrived to ask me to write an article upon

1. John Beresford Clark (1902-68), Director of the B.B.C. Empire Service, 1935, and Assistant Controller of Overseas and European Service, 1939.
2. Miss Moir of the *Forum*, New York, for which Virginia had written before.

Culture in the United States. We agreed however that culture was in danger In fact she said most English authors were either in Suffolk, or starting for America. In Suffolk they were already billeting children from the East end in cottages. Then Rosinsky[1] came; he thought he had a visa for America and was going to try to go at once. Then Mrs Woolf rang up to say she was going to Maidenhead if she could get rooms. Then an express arrived from Victoria Ocampo who had just landed from South America, wished to see me at once, was trying to fly to America and what could she do with a sister who was ill—could we advise a safe retreat? Also Phil Baker[2] and others rang up Leonard. With it all we were rather harassed; what should we need if we were marooned in Rodmell, without petrol, or bicycles? L. took his mackintosh and a thick coat; I Rogers letters to you, and a packet of stamped envelopes. Then we had to say good bye to the press, and I felt rather a coward, as clearly they were nervous although very sensible; and they had no garden. But the Govt; asked all who could to leave London; and there was John [Lehmann] in command. So off we went.

It was pouring terrific torrents; the roads packed; men nailing up shutters in shop windows; sandbags being piled; and a general feeling of flight and hurry. Also it was very dark; and we took about three hours to get back. At ten oclock Mr Perkins knocked and entered with a box of gas bags which he fitted on us. No sooner had he gone. than Mr Jansen came with another box. He said that children were arriving from the East End next morning. Sure enough, next day,—but I wrote to you and told you how we had the news of the Prime Ministers sensational statement—we thought it meant anyhow a pause—well, after that, Mr Perkins came and said the children were coming—9,000 had to be billeted in Sussex; fifty in Rodmell; how many could we put up? We arranged to take two. By that time, the nightmare feeling was becoming more nightmarish; more and more absurd; for no one knew what was happening; and yet everyone was behaving as if the war had begun. Mr Hartman [of Southease] had turned his barn into a hospital and so on. Of course we thought it was ridiculous; yet still they went on broadcasting messages about leaving London; about post cards with stamps being given to refugees who would be deposited safely, but they must not ask where. At any moment the fifty children might arrive. Also the Archbishop would offer up prayers; and at one moment the Pope's voice was heard ... But I will shorten; and skip to Sissinghurst; where we

1. Herbert Rosinski, author of *The German Army*, published by the Hogarth Press in 1939, and—with Werner B. Ellinger—*Sea Power in the Pacific, 1936-41* (1942).
2. Philip Noel-Baker (b. 1889), Labour Member of Parliament for Derby, and formerly a member of the League of Nations section of the British delegation to the peace conference, 1919. In 1954 he was awarded the Nobel Peace Prize for his work on disarmament. Virginia knew his wife Irene Noel, and visited her at her father's estate in Euboea, Greece, in 1906.

went on Thursday; and heard that the Italian King had saved the situation by threatening to abdicate. Harold had seen the PM grow visibly ten years younger as he read the message which was handed him.[1] It was all over. And I must play bowls. Leonard sends a message to Q[uentin]; in his opinion we have peace without honour for six months.

I'll write again. Maynard comes tomorrow. Plans vague; but we write here, where we shall probably stay at present. [*handwritten:*] No time to read this through.

Post going,
B.

Berg

3448: To Ethel Smyth   *Monks House* [*Rodmell, Sussex*]

Oct 3rd [1938]

I never tried to write even; I did try to read Sido[2] got halfway; then off we went to London—that was a remarkable experience, but as its all in the papers, why write it out again? We left our clerks, some to take refuge in trenches, others in the Stock Room. I felt very craven to be flying back here—where a man with gas masks awaited us, and another man telling us to be ready to receive two refugees. This is already a stale story, nor have I yet sorted out the various emotions, of which the residue is now anger and shame, on top of sheer cowardly relief. Well, no more of that. And I must begin to read Sido again.

This is to salute you before you retire to the Roman Wall. And what are *your* feelings?

Here we stay, for another 10 days or so; for I must try to work; and want, if I can, but no doubt I cant, after so many distractions, to take 10 days holiday at S. Remy partly to see Rogers little Mas there: a barn he lived in.[3] But I believe politics will bring L—now, today, a free man—free from the Press that is—to London. And I've not the spirit to pack up and go without him. Aint I a craven?

I think I shall now read Troilus and Cressida. Its a roaring, raving evening, apples pelting down, and the marsh like a widow tearing her hair. A Victorian widow in a white veil.

Write a line, do: Oh and I went and saw Gwen and Vita at St: ostensibly for L to see Harold, who was kept in London.

V

Berg

1. See p. 274, note 1
2. Colette's memoir of her mother, 1929.
3. See p. 274, note 6. Virginia did not, after all, got to St Rémy.

Typewritten
Monday, October 3rd [1938]

Ive just got your second letter, from Cassis. You say you would like gossip about the inner history, so I'll use my fragment of time before lunch —I've been trying to describe the first PIP show[1] without success—to go on with my scrambled and inarticulate story. Everything is still incoherent; but you'll excuse . . .

Well, I think I broke off at Sissinghurst last Thursday. We found that Harold had been kept in London, to arrange a counterblast to Chamb[erlain]. with Eden, Churchill etc. He had just rung up Vita and said she was to show us his diary.[2] This was very interesting. They had all been convinced that war was inevitable. The cabinet had tried to control Chamb— the younger members that is. They were certain he was going to sell us. However off he flew [to Godesberg]. When the House met that Wednesday [28 September] they all believed it was to announce war. He spoke very wearily yet precisely, like a business man making a statement. Then they saw the note [from Mussolini] handed him. He lit up, looked ten years younger, made his announcement; whereupon they all went mad, threw hats in the air, rushed about the lobbies shouting. That was all he knew when he wrote. Then Vita showed us the great barn with windows covered with frames that didnt fit and doors half sealed. Thirty people were to sleep there. I forget how many children were to be put up in hop oasts. The farmer [Ozzy Beale] arrived to ask what was now to be done.

Then Gwen St Aubyn arrived from Lewes; she had been taking her daughters school [Frances Holland] from London to Stanmer Park [near Lewes], which Lady Chichester had given over; and sixty girls were already lying in the picture gallery on mattresses, and blackboards were ready for next days lessons. Miracles of organisation had been performed by everyone. The roads, she said were crowded with lorries full of escaping schools. Vita said it was known for certain that London was to be attacked at twenty minutes intervals for twenty four hours with gas and bombs. Also that Mussolini had been stiffened at the last moment by The King of Italy who had said he would abdicate. Hence his pressure upon Hitler; which had turned the tide at the last moment. We came back, half expecting to find our refugees waiting us at Monks House. Mercifully there was no one.

Then next day we all turned rather cynical, and were sure of peace with dishonour. Then the BBC kept on saying that nothing was safe; we were

1. The First Post-Impressionist Exhibition, organised by Roger Fry at the Grafton Galleries in November 1910.
2. It was later published (ed. Nigel Nicolson) in 1966. For Harold Nicolson's account of the Munich crisis, see pp. 356-76 of that volume.

all to go on expecting war; until finally Chamberlain arrived; and we heard him read the terms from Heston;[1] frantic cheers; hysterical cries from old ladies; then the Archbishop praying; then bells pealing; while here at Rodmell a service was hastily got up; our bells made a perfectly infernal din; Mrs Ebbs in vain tried to whip up the villagers to some excitement; but one and all they remained perfectly sure that it was a dirty business; and meant only another war when we should be unable to resist. Of course the country was much calmer than London. Leonard was amazed by the sagacity of the old gaffers. The Postman stayed and talked good sense for about half an hour. The BBC however still announced that all reptiles would be shot at the Zoo; and any tiger that escaped killed at sight. I think they were so proud of their organisation that they wanted to air it, though it began to leak out that the air defence had been found full of holes; and that the carnage would have been immense in London.

Yesterday the Keynes came to tea. Maynard had already summed up the situation in a very good article which he read us; I'll send you the N.S on Friday in which it appears.[2] His view is that the whole thing was staged by Chamb.; that there was never any fear of war; that he never even consulted Russia; that it was a put up job between him and Hitler; that he would now call a general election; that our business is to fight Chamberlain; that we are sure of peace during our life time; that Hitler wants the Ukraine; that he'll get it; that Italy will be wiped out; that we shall do a deal with the colonies; that Chamberlain is a mere Birmingham politician; and so on. We all analysed our complexities of shame, and fear; Lydia said Maynard had really been a great deal alarmed; and excited. Of course the truth was that one felt all along that Chamb. had something up his sleeve; only one couldnt say how much. Also the feeling of despair and coming death was very genuine in London, however irrational. I am proud to say that my last words on leaving the Press were "There wont be war" but I was hooted down. I suppose everyone, except Kingsley Martin, chopped and changed. For instance some of the Gordon Square pundits—friends of Maynards— refused to agree to trenches being dug in the square and held out that war was impossible. On the other hand, the whole Royal Society has fled to the country; and Cambridge was so disorganised—all the colleges fitted up as hospitals—that it has had to put off term for some days. If it was all a piece of stage management on Chambs part, he took in a great many authorities. But you'll have had enough of this; and I expect I am sending, as you

1. The London airport where Chamberlain returned on 30 September, bringing with him a declaration signed by himself and Hitler early that morning in Munich, by which Britain and Germany pledged themselves "never to go to war with one another again". From the windows of Downing Street he assured the cheering crowds that he brought back "peace with honour".

2. *Mr Chamberlain's Foreign Policy* (*New Statesman*, 8 October 1938).

would say, coals to Birmingham. Duff Cooper, much to Maynards surprise and admiration, has resigned.[1] There is now going to be a great reaction against the terms; and I'm afraid L. will be drawn in. Already John wants us to go to London to discuss plans for the Press tomorrow. But we mean to stay here at all costs this week. The hubbub is incessant in London; and one simply repeats the same thing, and is exposed to all the bray of all the donkeys.

The weather has completely broken up; we have gales and tremendous pelts of rain. Its been very difficult to settle down to work, even here; I wish I could get to S. Remi, but I feel I ought to work hard here for a week or two, as I'm at rather a critical point. Also we had promised to travel the books in the West—happily we're free from the Press today; John has taken over. So theres no need to make any fixed plans.

Ann has just rung up to ask if she and Richard may come for the week end. Its death having people to stay but I suppose we must. Now I must go into the house through the rain and the falling apples to lunch. The tweeds have just arrived. I will keep them. And its pelting with rain—marshes all a mist, cows sheltering, aeroplanes still booming; cold mutton and apples for dinner. I'll add a less frantic line before I send this.

[*handwritten:*] But I dont think there's anything to add—except, tell Q., that Mrs Larter, the [Rodmell] schoolmistress, has left the Labour Party and turned Conservative—so she told Louie. The K's are off to Lydias flat at Cambridge. I'll write again. Immense relief that youre safe. France must have been in some ways worse than England. Please write here

B

Berg

3450: To Victoria Ocampo   *Monk's House, Rodmell,*
                                          Lewes, Sussex
Postcard
4th Oct [1938]

I have just had your telegram; and write, in a haste to catch post, to say I shall be in London after 16th and hope to see you. I doubt if I shall be up for more than an hour or two before. Let me know to above address.

V. W.

Estate of Victoria Ocampo

1. Duff Cooper (1890-1954) was First Lord of the Admiralty in Chamberlain's Cabinet. On 3 October he delivered his resignation speech, which concluded with the words: "I have ruined, perhaps, my political career. But that is a little matter; I have retained something which is to me of greater value—I can still walk about the world with my head erect."

Monk's House, Rodmell
Lewes, Sussex

5th Oct 38

Dear Mr Blanche,[1]

I was very glad to get your letters. It is odd to think that for the first time in my life I could not answer letters, because of the state of Europe. We were so angry here in Sussex, and so afraid and so ashamed. But I will not try to describe. I am only explaining how it was that I could not answer.

I have not a copy of the Common Reader here; and cannot remember what I said in my article.[2] No doubt, like most articles, it was too short and too positive. Only I had been told by Madame de Polignac (née Singer) that Proust lived a great deal with them, and took notes of their life, which she used, at his request, to correct. Probably he was often wrong; and of course I can see that his love life is wonderfully truthful. But I think there is less division between classes in France.[3]

Last night we had a meeting, to discuss politics here. The villagers all sat silent. The middle classes talked. Our young writers have a sentimental and emotional love for "the poor". They know nothing and care nothing— that is snobbishness partly—about the great. Now that Lady Ottoline is dead, perhaps there are no salons where the classes meet.

But I accept your correction, adding once more that these little articles are always like snapshots, too black, too white, too elementary altogether. I look forward to reading your memoirs. I am very dependent upon French memoirs. Having finished Chateaubriand, I am now reading 15 volumes of Madame de Sévigné [1626-96]. Has anyone written a life of her?—a real life?

But I must not begin upon Madame Sévigné or you would have a whole

---

1. See p. 184, note 1. His memoirs were published in several volumes—*Les Cahiers d'un artiste*, (1914-19) and *Mes Modèles*, 1928.
2. Blanche had disputed the comment which Virginia made about Proust in *The Niece of an Earl* (*The Common Reader, Second Series*): "At all times the great families of England and France have delighted to have famous men at their tables, and thus the Thackerays and the Disraelis and the Prousts have been familiar enough with the cut and fashion of aristocratic life to write about it with authority."
3. On 18 September Blanche had written to Virginia that he was astonished by her remark that people of her class did not understand working people. He wrote: "I have often talked to the plumber and his wife and every sort of workman in town and country, and it is easy to descend to their level" (*Sussex*).

new volume of the Common Reader, solely devoted to her, upon your hands!

Thank you again for writing.

Yours sincerely
Virginia Woolf

George Lazarus

3452: To Amabel Williams-Ellis   *Monk's House, Rodmell,*
Lewes, Sussex

Typewritten
7 October 1938

Dear Mrs Williams-Ellis,[1]

We are willing to sign the letter to Dr Benes. My husband has two points: (1) Are you quite certain of the accuracy of the statement that Benes proposed to cede the German-speaking territory to Germany and was overruled by the Allies?[2] (2) The word loutish though accurate reads a little oddly in a document of this kind.

Yours sincerely
Virginia Woolf

University of Illinois

3453: To Victoria Ocampo   *Monk's House, Rodmell,*
Lewes, Sussex

7th Oct 38

Dear Victoria,

What bad luck! I had hoped that this [Munich] Peace would mean that you stayed on in London: I'm trying to work, and must stay, save for one day up, till next week. Let me know, in time, the next chance there is of meeting.

Meanwhile: V. Sackville West lives always in the country. Her address is, Sissinghurst Castle, Kent. If you write there, she would tell you about translations. Pepita, I suggest. I will consider the other books you want to hear about—Send me your address. Its useless cramming into this sheet,

1. Amabel Williams-Ellis (*née* Strachey), the wife of Clough Williams-Ellis the architect, was a prolific author and journalist, mainly on political subjects.
2. Leonard was right. On 18 September the French and British Governments proposed that the German speaking areas of Czechoslovakia should be handed over to Hitler, and Benes (President of Czechoslovakia) accepted the plan under their strong pressure. The letter to Benes was organised by H. G. Wells protesting that Chamberlain had betrayed the Czech democracy.

with this stiff pen, all I want to ask and hear. Your butterflies hang over my front door[1]—always brilliant; wings stretched, flying, like you: but pinned; unlike you.

Yrs
Virginia Woolf

Estate of Victoria Ocampo

3454: TO VANESSA BELL   *Monks House* [*Rodmell,*
                                                          Sussex]
Typewritten
Saturday Oct 8th [1938]

Your letter has just come; and I at once answer, moved by flattery partly—for I dont think you like reading my letters; and Im very modest at the moment; also, if I dont start. I shall get swamped; Davies[2] arriving: then London; household supplies—partridges, hare, possible goose—all imperfect. Lord, what a scrimmage—But to facts.

You say you want details. England has now settled down to the usual cat and dog; I mean, I told you so, its your fault no its not; Kettle yourself; pot yourself; or whatever the phrase is. Trenches were dug because if you lie at the bottom of a sloping hole, a shell will burst at either side and miss you. Two workmen were buried alive making them. As for gas masks, many have died through testing them on the exhaust pipes of cars. Govt; has now issued an edict that theyre not to be tried on gas pipes as they dont work. Black boxes are being issued to keep them in against the next war. Some grateful owners have paid the Treasury one guinea apiece. Ours lie on the drawing room table. I did not say the press was fortifying my studio; I said the stock room [Tavistock Square]. This is a firmly built stone lined compartment behind the front room; most suitable, therefore as Miss Perkins [Hogarth clerk] said. Lined with books and mattresses practically impregnable. However as I told you Mr Higham wouldnt issue the key of the square [central garden] to non-residents, so our trenches were useless for Mrs Nicholls [Hogarth manager].

Next Clive Bell. Here I draw attention to a curious psychological incident, which the United brains of Cassis can analyse—if I can get time to explain. We asked Keynses to Sunday tea, and told them to fetch Clive, also invited. Lydia rang up to say "Janice [Loeb] is there; we will not have Janice." I said, "Settle it yourselves—Ive asked Clive." They came shame-faced and sheepish. "Clive is not coming." Have you told him the [that] you

1. See Letter 3075 (Vol. V). The case of South American butterflies still hangs at Monk's House.
2. Ann and Richard Llewelyn Davies.

wont have Janice? 'No.' 'Then what happened?' He will not come. I said 'She will bring him'. 'No he will not come.' Sure enough he didnt come. Now what had Lydia really done about it? Anyhow he neither came nor answered; so I've not heard about the Beefsteak club.[1] Tilton [Keynes] agreed to take six children [Munich crisis]. I am sending the N.S.[2] Q's [Quentin] letter has never come; rumour says he used it to wipe the bottom of a goose; but rumour is a strumpet.

Oh the vintage [at Cassis]! Just what my eyes crack to see. The one thing in the world I was born to describe. The one scene I need for my book. But consider my predicament. Owing to one thing and another, bowls, crisis, native sloth, I'm only at 1911 in Roger; I cant increase the appalling muddle of that book by darting off a chapter about S. Remi; I'm flummoxed entirely how to deal with your own letters. I shall be ready in December. Then no vines. Marie has just sent me her novel.[3] No time yet to read it. I wish youd find out when we could go for a week or so to their Inn.[4] If theres a room to write in. If they would have us peacefully. L; says its no use till middle of March owing to Mistral. Is this true? But as I was saying, how am I to write this book? What am I to say about you?[5] Its rather as if you had to paint a portrait using dozens of snapshots in the paint. Either one ought to dash it off freehand, red, green, purple out of ones inner eye; or toil like a fly over a loaf of bread. As it is I'm compromising; and its a muddle; and unreadable; and will have to be used, like the letter, to wipe a gooses rump. But Roger himself is so magnificent, I'm so in love with him; and see dimly such a masterpiece that cant be painted, that on I go. Also, reading his books one after another I realise that he's the only great critic that ever lived. For instance Cezanne [1927]—a miracle. [Characteristics of] French Art [1932]—another. Why did one only read his little articles? So, as you see, on I go; and grumble; and sweat; and sometimes get so hot in the head I roll in the cabbage bed. Do give me some views; how to deal with love so that we're not all blushing.

Shall I send you books? I am writing with your letter before me, and thus hop from twig to twig. Theyre bringing out a book on John Cornford next week, practically identical with Julian's poems, essays etc.[6] Shall

1. A men's luncheon and dining club in Irving Street, near Leicester Square, of which Clive Bell was a member.
2. Keynes' article in the *New Statesman*. See p. 280, note 2.
3. Marie Mauron's latest novel, *Le Quartier Mortisson*, 1938.
4. Near the Maurons' house at St Rémy, of which Charles was Mayor, 1945-59.
5. Roger Fry and Vanessa had fallen in love in 1911. In the book, Virginia simply referred to 'their friendship'.
6. *John Cornford, a Memoir*, by various authors. Cornford, the son of F. M. and Frances Cornford, and the great-grandson of Charles Darwin, was killed fighting in Spain on his 21st birthday, 27 December 1936.

I send it? I'll give L. the addresses. At present, John [Lehmann] is more worry than help; incessant questions; we have to go up for the day on Tuesday; then back for four days; then I think settle in for the winter and work. at 52. We get snatches of divine loneliness here; a day or two; and sanguine as I am I said to L. as we strolled through the mushroom fields, Thank the Lord, we shall be alone; we'll play bowls; then I shall read Sévigné; then have grilled ham and mushrooms for dinner; then Mozart— and why not stay here for ever and ever, enjoying this immortal rhythm, in which both eye and soul are at rest? So I said, and for once L. said; Youre not such a fool as you seem. We were so sane; so happy; and then, I went in; put the kettle on; ran up stairs looked at the room; almost done; fireplace lovely; wood wrong stained; but still felt floating on the wings of peace. Made tea; got out a new loaf; and honey and was about to call in L from the ladder on the high tree—where he looked so beautiful my heart stood still with pride that he ever married me; and then. . . . A face at the window. A voice. May we come in, Virginia? A jersey; trousers; bright red cheeks; glassy blue eyes. [Name omitted]. An interval of sheer horror; of unmitigated despair; my life crashed; my soul broke; my tongue faltered; and there was [her husband].

So we had them both for four hours by the clock. Lodging with Mrs Curtis they had tried to find you; were told by the pistmas (I mean postman) Charleston was empty; so came without the decency of a card or a telephone; planted their dismality on me. Such crude brutality, such denial of all human decency seems to me so unthinkably bestial that after they'd gone— and we had to drive them to Firle—I let fly; and for hours L. and I argued; he thought me too harsh; I thought him deplorably sentimental. But we both agreed that the poor [names omitted] are in the lowest rung of life; water blooded; blowsy; grumpy; servile; their eyes all flies; one drip drip drip of complaint from [her], [her daughter] such a trial; no friends; boys so stupid; cant pass exams; no money; no servants; no friends; and of course none of it said rhymically [sic] like this, with some arch to the back; but all verified and stated in words like hard boiled eggs; so that there I sat staring. L. took [him] round the garden. [He] too giggles. Not a drop of hope or health in them; and so we settled like creeping flies on [a friend] who at least excites [her] bitterness; she has found him a flat in Greenwich; why wont he face the fact that he must live there? Wont have money to go to the Opera. Has the eczema on his hands. Over eating. Yes, [he] moaned—hes terribly greedy. Eats grouse alone. Not a grouse had come their way these ten years. And why should it? And theyd no milk, nor eggs; had picked twenty dead mushrooms by way of gift; and I had to explore Itford Farm in the twilight with [him] to furbish up their miserable larder. But enough. Poor things—its a death to your door; the refrain was always Nessa and Duncan—Angelica and Quentin, as if you had obsessed them and dispossessed them. Tell Angelica that [their daughter] considers her the only friend she has; "But of course Angelica never invites her now. . . ."

Oh God, god, what world is there dispeopled, solitary, sane, where I could merely sit down, take my Bellows [French] dictionary and even write a letter to J. E. Blanche, who complains, like them all that Vanessa Bell was lunching with Miss Sands and they didnt ask him. Ive a letter from Will Rothenstein too, from Herbert Fisher also; and yesterday we had tea with the Keynesa [*sic*] (you see thats a word that cant be spelt on a type-writer) our friends at Tilton; and L. read them his play;[1] They seemed rather impressed; they think the Group [Theatre] may do it. I thought it rather good too; but who am I? I never get any praise for what I write. [Raymond] Mortimer praises Elizabeth Bowens new novel.[2] But I'm not jealous; too far sunk into fritters, with Ann and Richard [Llewelyn Davies] coming, to feel more than a drowned cat feels when it has been pulled from the ice by a policeman. However we have a grouse for lunch.

Maynard is a great man, I rather think. They had caught three mice in one trap; this excited him to the verge of hysteria. Now thats true great-ness; combined as it is with buying a whole flock of sheep; ditto of cows; he had been also dictating a letter to the Times;[3] is overcoming the innu-merable actors and actresses who wont act Phedre; they will act Phedre;[4] had also a complete knowledge of Tuberculosis in cows; meanwhile gave permission for Auntie to drive with Edgar [chauffeur] to Lewes to buy stockings; all details are referred to him; yet he remains dominant, calm; intent as a terrier to every word of L's play; spotted at sight things Id never seen from sheer vacancy; and left me crushed but soaring with hope for a race that breeds men like Maynard. And I kissed him and praised to the skys his Memoir Club paper;[5] by which, most oddly to my thinking, he was really pleased. D'you ever feel such a worm as I almost always feel? Or are you always as beautiful as I thought you the last night at Charleston, when I could hardly breathe for fear of unsettling the magnificent human Camberwell beauty [butterfly, i.e. Vanessa] who was, I suppose, mending socks? Nothing to add at the moment which is pouring; electric light off; storms universal.

[Name omitted] told me Pamela had been almost mad from suspense about

1. *The Hotel*, by Leonard Woolf, was published in 1939 and republished by the Dial Press in America in 1963. It was never produced.
2. *The Death of the Heart*, 1938.
3. On foreign trade (*The Times*, 7 October).
4. Racine's *Phèdre* (1677), produced for the Cambridge Arts Theatre, which Keynes endowed in 1934, and whose activities he supervised closely.
5. The Memoir Club had met at Tilton on 11 September to hear Keynes's paper on Cambridge and G. E. Moore.

Micou being a Roumanian being interned in late crisis;[1] but [*her*] almost mad means mere common sense.

Write Dolphin; and tell the young Dolphins to follow in your blue wake. Q and A. that is. Old father Dolphin by whom I indicate the real Duncan might one would have thought have turned his brush to a better use for old sakes sake.

And then when I hear Ill once more scribble.

B

Berg

3455: To Elizabeth Bowen

Monk's House, Rodmell, Lewes, Sussex

Oct 9th [1938]

Dear Elizabeth,

What a nice woman you are to send your book [*The Death of the Heart*] to this grudging old grump in a battered garden! By grudging, which I cant spell, I only mean that I'm thanking you before I've read it, because I've not had time—too many people in Sussex: and also, as you know, I'm incapable of writing criticism. As soon as I get 2 days free, I shall fall on the book, devour it and then—we come back next week—do come and see me, and let us talk about it for hours and hours.

So far the only reviews I've seen have been enthusiastic, but meaningless. That is they've not told me anything I wanted to know. But anyhow they all praise, and that whatever one may say is warming to the cockles of the heart.

I can hardly see to write, though its midday: the storm is battering me so in my garden room.

Your Virginia

I forgot to post this, and now cant remember your address: [Clarence] gate? or terrace? so must take it up and look in the telephone book tomorrow, on a dash to London.

Texas

3456: To Ethel Smyth

Monks House [Rodmell, Sussex]

Oct. 13th [1938]

Now that was nice of you to write that letter. It came so pat. A damned headache;—too much Roger: nephew and niece staying: a dash to Lon-

1. Pamela Fry (b. 1902), Roger's daughter, had married Micu Diamand, the Rumanian painter.

don—in short a headache that knocked the pen out of my hand and left me prone for any fly—angry letters from enraged readers of 3 gs.—bothering demands for sympathy and criticism will I read this and that, sign this and that, and I say all this pricked me as I lay prone: and your letter gave me a lift. "So I havent been an entire and utter failure from start to finish if Ethel likes me"—that was my reaction: I fastened specially on the word "staunch". Of course I like praise of my books—to me just now so futile, so intolerably airy and off the point; but I like praise of my friendship much better, being in that mood. Years ago, after a long and interrupted friendship, a man,[1] one of my oldest friends, said suddenly I was the most *faithful* of friends. Never have I forgotten that word, and here underline it against my practise; I was so proud.

Well I cant further expatiate as I'm still stupid. And it drizzles and blows. And I cant moon off to the river and let my head drift on the stream, nor sit in the garden; nor pester myself to read, nor even think of that cursed biography. I'm sorry you're delaying the [Roman] Wall. It should be a hot still day with the sheep cropping and a little boy playing in the ruins. Also a white thorn tree.

We go back on Sunday but now we have a partner [Lehmann] I dont intend to be fixed in London any more.

So thanking you for your letter and blessing the new book[2]—what a treat to look to!—

V.

We both thought Elizabeth's [Williamson] letter very fine, and wish to congratulate her. A remarkable letter. May others follow suit!

Berg

3457: To Ling Su-Hua   *Monk's House, Rodmell,*
                                        Lewes, Sussex
Typewritten
15th Oct. 1938

I am typing this, so as to save your eyes, for my writing is so hard to read. At last I have read the chapter you sent me[3]—I put it off, for one reason and another. Now I write to say that I like it very much. I think it has a great charm. It is also of course difficult for an English person, at first, there is some incoherence, and one does not understand the different wives;[4]

1. Probably Lytton Strachey.
2. Ethel's last volume of autobiography, *What Happened Next*, 1940.
3. See p. 221, note 2.
4. Su-Hua's father had several wives, and was Mayor of Peking.

who they are; which is speaking. But this becomes clear after a time; and then I feel a charm in the very unlikeness. I find the similes strange and poetical. How far it can be read by the public as it stands, I do not know. That I could only say if you would go on sending me more chapters. Then I should get the whole impression. This is only a fragment. Please go on; write freely; do not mind how directly you translate the Chinese into the English. In fact I would advise you to come as close to the Chinese both in style and in meaning as you can. Give as many natural details of the life, of the house, of the furniture as you like. And always do it as you would were you writing for the Chinese. Then if it were to some extent made easy grammatically by someone English I think it might be possible to keep the Chinese flavour and make it both understandable yet strange for the English.

One of the reasons why I did not read it or write before was that we have been so uneasy in England; we were almost sure of war. Everything was ready, even the gas masks served out, and orders given to house children from London. This atmosphere made it difficult to fix ones mind on books. Now for the time at least that strain is over.

Please forgive me then for having been so long in writing. Next time you send me more chapters—soon I hope—I will write more quickly. We are just going to London. The houses there are still protected many of them with sand bags. But in China I know things are far worse. I find the only relief is to work. And I hope you will go on, writing, for it might be a very interesting book.

Did you get a letter I wrote in August [No. 3425], and a parcel of books? Tell me, for if they came safe I will send more. It is easy to get books cheaply in London. Please never think of paying for them. It is a great pleasure to me to send them. Tell me what you like. It is difficult to know. I am keeping the manuscript you sent. I can read your writing quite easily, so dont bother to type.

Yours with love,
Virginia Woolf

Ling Su-Hua (Mrs Chen)

3458: To Sir William Rothenstein   *Rodmell, Lewes*
                                        [Sussex]
Postcard
15th Oct [1938]

Many thanks for your card. We are still down here, but I hope to see your pictures[1] when we are back next week.

V. Woolf

Houghton Library, Harvard University

1. His one-man show, *Fifty Years of Painting,* at the Leicester Gallery, 5-22 October.

Letters 3459-3474 (October–December 1938)

The Woolfs returned to London on 16 October, and remained there till Christmas, apart from fortnightly weekends at Rodmell. Roger Fry *had now become "that cursed biography", but Virginia struggled on with it, alternating it with* Pointz Hall, *which she enjoyed far more, and with stories and articles like* Lappin and Lapinova. *In London there was "a perpetual fizz and fritter", like a party given by Sibyl Colefax at which Virginia met Max Beerbohm. Echoes of* Three Guineas *continued to reverberate, mainly through strangers, but Virginia noticed that her friends scarcely mentioned it. She was unexpectedly worried by her loan to Helen Anrep of £150, which she could well afford. Jack Hills, the widower of her half-sister Stella Duckworth, died on Christmas Eve, on the same day as Leonard's marmoset Mitz.*

3459: To Quentin Bell   52 *Tavistock Square* [*W.C.*1]

Typewritten
Tuesday Oct 18th 1938
(I put the date as it may be a piece
of news to you)

Dearest Quentin,
    An anonymous post card has just come: The Colonel is engaged—
Not Cory,[1] I take it? Then it must mean that Teed has at last consented to make an honest woman of Miss Smith and her seven children;[2] it cant be that Angelica—? No I refuse to dream, even, that a blood niece of mine has married a vine. Wine would be a passport to my heart, its true. Still, the bridegroom seems a little past bearing—a good vintage I admit. When does the marriage take place? In the vineyard? nuptials to be consummated I suppose in the butts—caves, what do they call them.
    Well this has rather dashed my sober political style. En revanche as they say, I enclose a cutting from last nights paper.[3] L says no man survives the third stroke. Meanwhile I'm pending a letter to Mary [Hutchinson]—if

1. Colonel Cory Bell, Clive's brother. He had married in 1903.
2. Colonel Teed had been living for years with Miss Jean Campbell, not Miss Smith, at Cassis, where he owned a vineyard.
3. About the illness of St John ('Jack') Hutchinson, the barrister. He did not die until 1942.

only I had command of Nessa's style in these matters. What cant be mended had better be ended, and so on.

Yes, we are back, in the full tide of human existence; of which I will try to send you a brief epitome before lunch. Jack you see has dropped down; and Kingsley Martin is on the telephone. London is strained: sand bags still in situ quo: the scavenger stops me in the Square to say 'in my opinion maam ther'll be war in February.' The pundits are all devising schemes for foreign policy. Kingsley is all for being a third class power in servile isolation; Cole[1] is all for fighting to the last gasp. Its not a nice place, London. We were not hysterical, at the worst; only like a pack of spaniels on the leash, now fawning, now foaming. No; Sally [spaniel] is not pregnant. Mitz [marmoset] almost died of the chill that cold drive home; but is quite well again, tell Angelica . . .

Here Leonard comes in. John [Lehmann] is upstairs. A board meeting! I made a brilliant pun. But puns apart, John is a little crowing over your rather imperfect index.[2] He says that he had several omissions to fill in; misquotations and false attributions. He also says that the printer[3] who is a personal friend of his, objects at the last moment to printing bugger, fuck, balls and piss. John offered to put initials. The printer holds out for dots only. This matter is still in dispute. Of course they make the objection at the very last moment, with the page proof about to be printed off. And its all John's fault for employing a friend who's a notorious prude. We had the same row over one of Plomer's books. L. is holding out. But the crisis—political—for some reason has meant a fortnights delay. We shant publish now till the 27th—hence any delay is very undesirable. So far Julian's book has done much better than was expected. All the shops have taken a good deal of interest in it. I dont know what the figures are—but I was told I could say it had been well received by buyers. I suppose the crisis will damp the whole season inevitably. So they all say.

Privately, what gossip is there? Joan Easdale the daughter of the mad woman, Adeney, is engaged to Jim Rendel. I rather think he's Jill's brother. Helen Anrep dines here tomorrow. Theres some gloomy business at work in Charlotte Street I gather from Mabel. "Mrs Anrep says she dont want Flossy [maid] any longer. She says the children have to manage for themselves. If I were her I should say the same"—this is the silent Mabel's report. Helen on the phone sounded pessimistic, over blown, over grown, distracted;[4] Roger's first proofs[5] had arrived; she was off to correct them

1. G. D. H. Cole (1889-1959), the author of many books on social and political theory. At this time (1925-44) he was a Fellow of University College, Oxford, and University Reader in Economics.
2. Of *Julian Bell*, which Quentin edited.
3. A member of the firm of Hazell, Watson & Viney.
4. For Helen Anrep's domestic difficulties, see next letter.
5. *Last Lectures*, introduced by Kenneth Clark, 1939.

with Margery [Roger's sister]. So I chipped in, and said, Come and dine with us—that is with me, as L. is discussing Labour politics with Dalton.[1] Here she groaned like a sea monster just arisen from the briny. Everyone groans. We had Ann and Richard [Llewelyn Davies] to stay; I like him; I think he has a head piece; as well a—codpiece is suggested; but that not what I meant. I mean I think he has guts as well as charm; is not near so scatterbrained as Ann; who has shot into a beanstalk; is now hideous, now lovely; a leggy colt, whereas Richard is trim and solid and about twenty years more mature. But how I hate week ends! If we could only solve that problem, why dont we all retire to Sussex? The room is finished; but where's your and Nessa's bill?

I went to the Tate yesterday; but was harassed by Herbert Read.[2] At the same time I liked the impressionists; why are they so much quicker off the palate than old masters? I can souse myself in them like a puppy in a bath. They've got a show together. Oh do tell Nessa to write and tell me how I'm to deal with Roger—here I am, obsessed, and quite futile. Cant stop; yet plunge daily deeper into despair. Writing is far too concentrated to be a human activity. I've not seen Clive; but have read his pamphlet— Warmongers.[3] I wont say what I think till you do. L. wont even read; but will say what he thinks without reading. We cant go on our western tour as none of the books are ready for travelling; I cant come to S. Remy because I'm stuck at 1911. Marie [Mauron] has sent me her novel. Oh do give them my love; also do buy me any picture postcards of the place.

And I'm positively longing to see the new pictures by the Dolphin family [Duncan and Bells]. I long to see pictures of vineyards. Are they very good? Shall I . . . another interruption. A man called Philip Rose wants to know if I'll help him to write a book on Stevenson;[4] he seems to think I am Stevenson's grandaughter.

And now it is one; and I have not somehow rivalled Sévigné—no, dearest Q; but I could do better with encouragement; letters; love; sympathy; When do you come back? Rodmell is seething with excitement; there was a great burglary at Northease;[5] a safe was exploded with dynamite; but the ruby necklace was not found.

Write V.

Quentin Bell

1. Hugh Dalton (1887-1962), Member of Parliament for the Bishop Auckland Division, Durham, and Chairman of the National Executive of the Labour Party, 1936-7. He became Chancellor of the Exchequer in 1945-7, and was created a life peer in 1960.
2. Herbert Read (1893-1968), the poet and critic of literature and art.
3. *Warmongers*, published in this year by the Peace Pledge Union. Clive had written that "A Nazi Europe would be, to my mind, heaven on earth compared with Europe at war . . . the worst tyranny is better than the best war."
4. Philip Rose wrote no book on Stevenson or any other subject.
5. Northease Farm, half a mile from Rodmell on the Lewes road.

Typewritten
24th Oct [1938]

Your letter I may tell you very nearly had fatal consequences. I very nearly rushed off to Cassis, so intoxicating were your words; and the sense of heat; and vines; and beauty; and freedom; and silence; and no telephones. You very nearly had me on you; and then what a curse you would have found it! Only the timely revelation of the complete failure of our marriage prevented it. Only just in time to stop me taking my ticket. Its an awful confession—if I werent so hurried I would conceal it; but the fact is we are so unhappy apart that I cant come. Thats the worst failure imaginable—that marriage, as I suddenly for the first time realised walking in the Square, reduces one to damnable servility. Cant be helped. Im going to write a comedy about it. But if I had come your perfect globe would have been smashed; you know how careful I have to be, too, to bait my hook with little minows [*sic*] and other tit bits to disguise my rapacity for your society with whats acceptable to you. Had I come the hook would have been bare; all this winter you'd have had nothing but the rusty steel to grate your teeth upon. Also, its a good thing that Wolves and Bells should be separated sometimes in order that each may inspissate their identity. Enough. No News of Clive.

London is appalling, but also I admit fascinating—in its meretricious way. Also Exmouth Street Market, with a black corpse of a horse among flowers and cheap glass has its appeal; also Hampton Court[1] where we went yesterday in the balm of a perfect summers day was worth all your black visaged spectacular south. We roamed the park, smelt the flowers, and mooned along the galleries where, thanks Roger, I'm now seeing in chairs pictures tapestries a remote world of inexplicable significance. I think the art of painting is the art for ones old age. I respect it more and more. I adore its severity; its bareness from impurity. All books are now rank with the slimy seaweed of politics; mouldy and mildewed. I wish I could settle to pure fiction; indeed had to rush headlong into a novel [*Pointz Hall*]; as a relief; but am now back at Roger and the compromise of biography again. That reminds me; please will you and Duncan write something quick about the Borough Polytechnic.[2] Any facts. Who were the artists?

1. Roger Fry had worked intermittently for several years, beginning in 1910, to restore the Mantegna paintings, *Triumphs of Caesar*, in the Royal Collection at Hampton Court.
2. In 1911 Roger Fry was commissioned by Basil Williams to decorate the students' dining-room at the Borough Polytechnic, London. Roger, with the help of young artists (Duncan, Frederick Etchells, Bernard Adeney, Macdonald Gill and Albert Rothenstein) did scenes of the amusements of London. Fry had painted a scene at the Zoo. Two of Duncan's murals are now in the Tate Gallery.

What were the subjects? Does the dining room still exist? Can one see it? Do answer this. I'm toiling in a maze; and no one so far has thrown me a single bone of help.

Now to gossip. Jack Hutch, youll be glad to hear was let blood copiously, and has recovered. Mary [Hutchinson] says it was a slight attack. He is at work again. This was imparted to me as I sat talking to [Sibyl] Colefax. You see I get from people what you get from vines. These distorted human characters are to me what the olive tree against the furrowed hill is to you. Colefax is an essential part of the composition; wrinkled I admit. I was led, by a spirit in my feet, (that is Shelley)[1] to denounce her life to her; her snobbery; her falsity; her damned dressed up dinner party society. I will only dine with you, I bellowed, (without you V. B. I become so vehement,) if I may walk out of my own house, as I am, to your door. "Done!" she cried. Today I'm invited to meet Max Beerbohm and Lord Ivor[2] without washing; and will I bring Isherwood on the same terms? What am I to say? Why do I seek to change society, when it means that one has to act on ones words? L. says I can rat.

I'm in a rush; so what news is there? Desmond's [MacCarthy] mother is dead, of cancer. Then we had tea with Margery yesterday to meet deaf Agnes.[3] But deaf Agnes was involved in a street accident. Margery much upset. At last deaf Agnes very fluttered arrived. Walking with Lady Lawrence[4] in Chelsea, suddenly she saw Lady Lawrence, wall eyed Bob's wife, flat on the ground, pouring blood with her face cut open and an omnibus advancing. Deaf Agnes was surprised. To cut a long story short—I had to write on a paper all my questions—Lady L. was carried home; Dr Quackenbosh summoned; and a nurse. So we proceeded to discuss Sir Edward's[5] views on Darwinism; this had to be gingerly done, as she disapproves of any truth told about the Frys. But she was a charming apparition, wild eyed, flying haired, magnanimous; walled still in the 19th century; shouting like a lost sheep in a gale.

Helen Anrep was there—by the way I had a long evening alone with her; and I'm in rather a distress about her. *This is highly confidential.* She has dismissed Flossie and does all her cooking and cleaning herself, being battered and altogether scatterbrained, because she has an over draught

---

1.   "And a spirit in my feet
       Hath led me—who knows how?
       To thy chamber window, sweet!"
                    Shelley, *The Indian Serenade*
2. Lord Ivor Churchill (1898-1956), youngest son of the 9th Duke of Marlborough.
3. Agnes Fry (1868-1958), Roger's sister, was deaf nearly all her life.
4. The wife of Sir Alexander Lawrence, 4th Bt. (1874-1939), formerly Chief Assistant Solicitor to the Treasury.
5. Sir Edward Fry (1827-1918) the judge, and father of Roger, Margery and Agnes.

[*sic*]; In fact she seems in very low water. Oughtnt one to help?[1] Ive no doubt I could lend her or give her something towards the overdraught; on which she's paying interest. What do you think? But then theres the horror of her toadies and claimants. Is it hopeless to insist that she has a maid? She told me to tell you that owing to Rogers proofs she can't come to Cassis yet. But she is coming later. Meanwhile of course Preece[2] is preying on her; and the female oaf[3] is utterly intolerable. Analysis which costs £100 is useless; yet she must be analysed so Helen must do the cooking. . . .

Now Rose Macaulay is ringing up; also Stephen Tennant. I tell you this not to impress you; but only to show the meretricious fascination of London. Thank God we're off for two days on Wednesday to M. H. and to travel our books. Then back to a vast family dinner given by Mrs Woolf; who is aging and decaying so rapidly that the leaves seem to drop in to the tea cups. Everyone loathes the idea; she insists. A dinner at a club. And you in bliss. Ive no room for more.

[*handwritten:*] Theres a rush at the Press—John all over the place. I cant get time to write, so send this, in default of better. The drop drop of fascinating postcards continues to keep me on edge. What a torturer Q is! I hope to see him. and when shall I see you? But no doubt you prefer Helen Anrep. Why?

B.

L's play [*The Hotel*] is being considered by the Group [Theatre, London].

Berg

3461: To Ethel Smyth   52 *Tavistock Square* [*W.C.*1]
Tuesday [25 October 1938]

I'm sorry, but we must start at dawn—should the sun rise—tomorrow, and travel our books on the South Coast: ending at nightfall at Monks House. There we stay till Saturday when there's my mother in laws 89th birthday party—her last I suspect.[4]

I'm glad you saw the [Roman] Wall in a tempest, and Humshaugh[5]

---

1. Virginia cleared Helen Anrep's overdraft with a loan of £150, of which Helen repaid £25 in 1941. Later it was discovered that Helen's accounts had been muddled, and the overdraft was largely imaginary.
2. Patricia Preece, herself a painter, had lived with Stanley Spencer, and married him in 1937 as his second wife.
3. Anastasia, one of the children of Boris and Helen Anrep.
4. It was her last. Mrs Woolf died on 2 July 1939.
5. Virginia was thinking of Haughton Castle, a few miles north of the Wall. See p. 246.

[Northumberland] I found afterwards we could have been shown over—I want to hear the story. Oh must I read Enid Bagnold?[1] For my sins, I thought Velvet a fake: but you know what an irregular critic, how independable I am, especially about living fiction,

Berg

3462: To V. Sackville-West   *Monk's House, Rodmell,*
                                     near Lewes, Sussex
27th Oct [1938]

Yes, Mrs Nicholls [Hogarth Press] has handed me a copy of your book [*Solitude*]: which I certainly consider my due, with an inscription. I dont believe you care a damn what I think of it. However, I'll tell you when I've read it, if you want to know. Yes, so far as I know, Novr. 17th will suit perfectly: the whole day if you like. If you cant spend the whole day junketing pick out any portion of it: lunch, dinner, tea: all three. We're down here, thank the Lord, but only momentarily; yesterday we travelled our books in Horsham, where Shelley worshipped:[2] tomorrow its Hastings— who lived there?[3] I cant remember. Anyhow I've stolen a walk in hot sun along the river which was brimming blue, a kind of winter summer, trees bare, sky blue: but you'll have seen all this for yourself. We plan to retire here for ever: in which case I should sink as deep in solitude as even you could wish. As it is, back we go on Saturday to my mother in laws 89th birthday party, and Sybil and Max Beerbohm—But let me know some time about the 17th.

                                                      Yr V.
Berg

3463: To Hugh Walpole   52 *Tavistock Square, W.C.*1
Sunday [30 Oct 1938]

My dear Hugh,
    I dont see why you accuse me of nocturnal habits. We were up in

1. *The Squire* (a novel published in America as *The Door of Life*), 1938. 'Velvet' was Enid Bagnold's most popular novel, *National Velvet*, 1935.
2. Shelley was born at Field Place, near Horsham, Sussex. When he was 19, he was sent down from Oxford for circulating his pamphlet, *The Necessity of Atheism*, 1811.
3. Byron, Keats and Leigh Hunt lived briefly in Hastings, but the literary figure most closely associated with it was the poet Coventry Patmore, who had a house on Old London Road from 1875 to 1891.

Keswick:[1] asked for Sir Hugh: and were told he's invisible—I suppose in London. Come to tea—or why not come in on Thursday next, 3rd Nov, after dinner—Stephen Spenders dining, hence no room at the table for more? anytime after 9.

Yr Virginia W.

Yes, Leonard is all right. Water pure as—What is pure? too hurried to remember.

Texas

3464: To Vanessa Bell   52 *Tavistock Sq*[*uare, W.C.1.*]
Typewritten
Nov. 2nd [1938]

You are a good dolphin to write, and the facts about the Boro. Poly;[2] will come in very useful. Now that we're on facts let us stick to them. About Helen. I think her overdraft is about £200.[3] So she said the night she dined here. And she promised to find out exactly and tell me; as I think she was then ready to let me lend it her. I heard no more; so wrote and asked and have had no answer. Mabel says Flossie goes twice a week to clean; but last time she went Helen was away. I'll ring up and see if I can get any facts. but you know how vague she is—didnt know what she was paying, but thought the interest came to £10 yearly. And she certainly seemed weighed down and altogether rather under the weather or water or whatever the phrase is.

About houses—we actually went over one in Endsleigh St [No. 6, Bloomsbury] yesterday, being struck with the dream of buying a large freehold, housing ourselves and the press and having rooms to let. But it was hopeless; all the top rooms cut in two and mere garrets. Our lease lasts till 1941; so unless we can get a freehold, and sublet this we shall have to stay on. But we're much inclined to your plan of country living with a room here. I suppose you and Clive could move any time. And we shall have the Press to house which complicates matters. But with John in charge, we are, or shall be, free from London; and I agree with you, it grows intolerable. One party lasts me at least a month. The perpetual fizz and fritter is inevitable and if only Sussex werent so accessible, I would willingly domesticate myself there. So I'll keep my eyes open for large houses that could be let out in rooms. Thats the facts;

1. Hugh Walpole lived at Brackenburn, near Keswick in the Lake District, where the Woolfs stayed on their way back from Scotland at the end of June.
2. For the Borough Polytechnic, see p. 294, note 2.
3. See p. 296, note 1.

My Colefax party was perhaps worth going to, as I didnt dress, and sat next Max [Beerbohm], and we talked writers shop. He's a charmer; rubicund; gay; apparently innocent; but in fact very astute and full of airy fantasies. He invented obituaries, and has an extraordinary gift for telling little stories that he makes up on the spur of the moment. When we went to Hastings the other day an old man stopped me in the street and said. 'Have I the honour of addressing Miss Edith Sitwell?" "I'm Mrs Woolf," I said. He then swept off his hat and said "Not my old friend Leslie Stephen's daughter?" "Who have I the honour of addressing" I said. "Somebody whose name youve never heard," he said. . . . "Coulson Kernahan!"[1] I told Max this; and he instantly told me the whole history of C.K.'s life; how he'd written a book called God and the Ant; sold one million copies; also one called Celebrities I knew—how he visited Lord Roberts "who rose from his chair and looked at me with eyes—were they blue? were they hazel? were they brown? No they were just soldiers eyes" He also wrote a book called Celebrities I did not know. Max Beerholm .. for one. . . How much was true and how much invented I dont know. But it was very amusing as he told it; but I cant record it. Then there was Somerset Maugham. a grim figure; rat eyed; dead man cheeked, unshaven; a criminal I should have said had I met him in a bus. Very suspicious and tortured. But youve met him. And Lord Ivor [Churchill]; and Lord de la Warr;[2] and Christopher I[sherwood]. who seemed all agog with amusement; but is a shifty quicksilver little slip of a creature—very nimble and rather inscrutable and on his guard. I had no talk with him; but he said he had heard of you and would come and dine. Will you come and meet him?

Oh what a joy to think you're coming back! I feel like a very old sponge that hears water dripping at the thought. I get so pulverised without you; youre somehow the breath of life; did I say water? Well, as usual I'm mixing my metaphors writing in a hurry, after my mornings work. We have the Spenders to dine tomorrow and Joan Easdale, now Rendel; and Bunny [Garnett] I think. And on Friday we go to Rodmell; and Q. dines— that I shall enjoy—I long to see my nephews and my nieces; but theres a L. P. [Labour Party] meeting; and then theres Guy Fox;[3] and Q. says Clive and Janice [Loeb] are to be down; so doubtless we shall all meet. But whats the point, when you and D. and A. arent there?

1. Coulson Kernahan (1858-1943) the writer and soldier. Max Beerbohm's summary of his career is accurate, except that Kernaham wrote no book entitled *Celebrities I Did Not Know*. One of his books was *An Author in the Territorials*, with a foreword by Field Marshal Lord Roberts of Kandahar (1832-1914), the hero of the Afghan and South African wars.
2. 'Buck', the 9th Earl De la Warr (1900-76), President of the Board of Education in Chamberlain's government, and Vita's cousin.
3. The Guy Fawkes festival at Lewes on 5 November.

Julians book [*Julian Bell*] comes out on Monday, and we sent the copies as you said. The reviews will begin next week I suppose, I'll send them. Ive been looking at it, and am sure it was a good thing to print it. He comes out so much of a whole. And the letters are so unself-conscious that nobody could feel them too personal. Also I think it makes something rather important, and not a mere scrap book—I mean though there are so many different people writing, they all fall into line. It is a far more solid book than the John Cornford.[1] Theres been the usual rush and chaos here; Miss Strachan away; ill; John talks and talks . . . Mrs Lehmann [John's mother] appeared; the Sunday Times book show on us this week;[2] indeed I had to take to doing up parcels again; and L. worked in the press till eight. But this is only the after effects of that damnable [Munich] crisis, which L. is discussing once more with K. Martin, as I write.

[*handwritten:*] I sent a New Statesman to enlighten you.

[*typewritten:*]   *After tea;*

I got on to Helen [Anrep], at last. She never got my letter. She says her overdraft is £150; Ive arranged that I will pay this myself. We can discuss later about subscriptions; but as Ive got the money, I thinks its much simpler for me to do it. The thing is—can you tell me what my commitments are to the Studio school?[3] I thought I promised to guarantee £50 a year for 2 years. Do you think this will be wanted? I told Helen I'd find out from you before saying for certain that I can pay the £150. So could you let me have a line—I should like to pay her as soon as possible. I gather she's rather anxious to have it settled. I said I was telling you.

Well this is a dull dismal interrupted letter. In between paragraphs I've been to Selfridges; ordered a goose; walked across the Park; come home to find John [Lehmann] to tea; and am altogether more in favour of a country life than ever. Lord! wish you were back, and were coming round. Its as bright as June here; no mistral; but I admit we have fires. I'll write to Angelica to curse her for her absolutely exacerbating, infuriating, intriguing and preposterous system of post cards; ones missing; I cant make it all out; and have scratched a hole in my head worrying to connect the Colonel [Teed] with his private parts.

[*handwritten:*] Theres an account of Cousin Isabel and Adeline[4] in Benson.

Berg

1. See p. 285, note 6.
2. The Hogarth Press rented a stand at the annual *Sunday Times* Book Show.
3. The School of Drawing and Painting (later the Euston Road School). See p. 194, note 1.
4. Lady Isabel Somerset (1851-1921) and her sister Adeline, Duchess of Bedford (1852-1920). They were first cousins of Virginia's mother Julia. E. F. Benson devoted a chapter to them in *As We Were* (1930). He said of Isabel: "She was one of the pioneers who have won for their sex liberty and the right to work."

Wednesday I think 9th as I saw the Lord Mayors [procession] coach.
[9 November 1938]

No I'm not such a fool as you think.

I know a good book when I see one, but I have to see it over and over again before I see it. In fact thats how I know a good book—that I have to see it 4 times at least. This refers to Sido [Colette] which I've only read once. And once isn't enough—except to show me something gleaming, like an iceberg of which the roots are underwater. Its a shape I haven't grasped. But I'll send it back. For at the moment I'm driven. I'm working and worried. So whats the use of thinking I can begin again? Can one buy it? I'd like to read it over and piece it together. What a born writer! and how infinitely delightful that is to me, a new combination—always a thrill: and to me the only way of learning myself how to write—a lesson I much need at the moment when biography is still as a frozen field on my pen.

I'll send it one day very soon.

A rush here, owing to publishing: the crisis has tangled us in a muddle. Whats the use of sending this scrawl—to my old striped tiger cat, with her growl and her claws and her soft fur? I couldnt go to Londonderry House[1] to hear Nadia [Boulanger], as invited; but heard her on the wireless. Cant bear music mixed with peerage. and a supper at the [French] Embassy.

Oh and thanks for Somerville[2] who cheered me after a fine dust up with one of the dons.

Yr
V

Berg

Thursday [10 November 1938]

I dont think this will reach before you leave [Cassis]. So its only to wish you a good journey. And I'll write to Paris. and keep any gossip till then. Your letter only came yesterday. So I told John to keep the books [*Julian Bell*].

1. The great house in Park Lane, which the 7th Marquess of Londonderry and his wife Edith made into a centre of political and cultural society.
2. Edith Somerville (1858-1949), the novelist, who with her cousin Violet Martin (pseudonym 'Martin Ross') wrote several successful books, the best known of which was *Some Experiences of an Irish R.M.*, 1899. She was a great friend of Ethel, and it was perhaps some of her letters to Ethel that Virginia had just read.

Dont be rash at corners and come home and *kiss* me but no more till Paris.

Berg

3467: To Duncan Grant   52 *Tavistock Square, W.C.*1

14th Nov. 38

Dearest Duncan,

I was greatly pleased to get a letter from you, and only wish you would take to the pen oftener. Like all painters, your sense of words is plastic, not linear, and I am on the side of the plastic myself. But this is not the time to broach that—only to welcome you back to civilisation; its a bear garden, and I'm entirely of your advice that we should rusticate. That reminds me, Ethel Sands has written to ask,—on behalf of Nan [Hudson]—whether Nan can come over from Aix to visit you. I've said she'll find the nest [Cassis] empty. Yes, Ethel is on the tapis: lunch, tea, dinner etc: but so far I've slipped out. And there's Mary [Hutchinson], and Colefax and Eddie Playfair and Helen Anrep—ever so many buzzing round; like the flies round Nessa's lamp.

However I will keep all gossip till we meet. Tomorrow we dine with Clive. By the way Adrian says he thinks Janice [Loeb] is tiring of him—so I've let slip one piece of gossip. No more. We go to Rodmell on Friday. Do you come to Charleston? London is extremely beautiful at the moment, blue as June, soft as down. Think of my idiocy—I walked from Marble Arch to Horse Guards admiring two divine young men. So beautiful were they I circled round and round to hear what they said. In vain. Like young gods, with small chins, blue eyes, perfect hips and shoulders. Ouida[1] would have adored them. The sky like a Canaletto. By the way there's a new Rembrandt.[2] But I did not go to Will Rothensteins show, or to his son's.[3]

I've lots to say but this paper cuts it short. Not however my affection, or the desire I have to see you. "You" in this context stands for the two divine women [Vanessa and Angelica] also.

V.

Estate of Duncan Grant

1. Louise de la Ramée (1839-1908), the popular novelist who wrote under the name Ouida. Splendidly elegant guardsmen were frequent characters in her flamboyant novels.
2. A portrait of his wife in 1635, entitled *Saskia as Flora*, recently acquired by the National Gallery.
3. Michael Rothenstein (b. 1908). His show was at the Matthiesen Gallery, London

Typewritten
Monday Nov 21st [1938]

My dear Shena,

Forgive this typing, but my hand is getting worse and worse and worse. Thank you very much for telling me about the Fabian meeting.[1] I'm surprised and delighted that fifty intelligent people should think it worth while to talk about 3 gs. As we were saying the other day, I dont believe anyone reads what one says; they only skim off enough to blow soap bubbles on their own. Still, thats something. I cant myself conceive any position more positive than an outsiders, if one could put it into practise. One cant— thats the difficulty, owing partly to the vileness of one's own nature and partly to poverty. As for war and capitalism, Leonard says that is the invariable Fabian argument. But who are the capitalists? not women. Every day I'm having that proved to me. But I wont begin all over again ... it was very good of you to take my part; and I'm sure you did it much better than I could have done. Because for one thing you do practise what I merely preach. And the people of Manchester however much they may wrap themselves up in gold lace probably know it in their bones—if they have bones. How amusing that the dress charge rankled![2] Of course it goes very deep; and we shan't be free to discuss it for at least a century. So I wont bore you at the present moment.

I saw Hugh Walpole the other day, and he was very nice, in spite of his floods of verbiage in writing. People generally are, in themselves.

No, I dont type much better than I handwrite.

Yours Virginia Woolf

Sussex

3469: To Ethel Smyth   52 *Tavistock Square* [*W.C.*1]

Friday [25 November 1938]

A bitter, black cold day, and to tell the truth I was feeling very miserable. I was walking down Regent Street, thinking how can I face Leonard, who sent me out to buy myself suspenders, since my stockings came down in the Square; and the horror of shops, especially intimate underwear shops, holds me so fast that I cannot go in. But this grave weakness seemed in the gloom, Ethel, in the spare brown failing November light, still unpricked

1. The Fabians were a socialist society founded in 1883. Among its leading members were G. B. Shaw, Sidney and Beatrice Webb, Sydney Olivier, Graham Wallas and H. G. Wells. It had affiliated branches at the major universities, including Manchester.
2. The absurdity of scholars wearing academic dress (see *Three Guineas*, p. 39).

by the lamps and stars, so profound in my soul, that . . . well I hadn't a bone to throw to a dog, or a Bo to say to a goose; when suddenly from a bye street there marched out, ahead of me, you yourself. You were wearing a spongebag suit, and a grey felt hat. You were striding along at first I thought with another woman. So I followed. I did not like to interrupt. And then I thought, well old Ethel wouldn't mind if I did break in: And old Ethel would put the fear of God in me and the courage of a Cavalry Regiment. And I should buy my suspenders. So overcome with love and reverence for Ethel, and sure that she would solve all my problems, I dashed after you. And oh God it wasn't you! No, only a stranger. A mild elderly suburban woman.

This sad true story is scribbled down, in all humility. What did I do next? Took a bus home; and here I sit, over the fire, cursing the ghost. Not you. But why wasnt it you? Or did you send a spirit to Regent Street to hearten me to buy suspenders; about 4 this afternoon?

And did you get Sido [Colette] safe?

And have you ever read Chaucer?

V.

Berg

3470: To Margaret Llewelyn Davies

52 *Tavistock Square, W.C.*1

Typewritten
27th Nov 38

Dearest Margaret,

It was very nice—yes theres the silly word again—of you to send me the letters;[1] and to write. We missed seeing you this summer, for though we were in Tunbridge Wells one day, selling books, we didn't like to break in on you. But we suggest that possibly one day before Christmas we might come down to tea; tell us some suitable days; and then Leonard will shove aside some of his innumerable committees with pleasure. Theres too much to say in a letter. About Vanessa—she is just back from Cassis, where they spent two months, painting hard. Her lovely daughter has decided, to our joy, against the stage, and is becoming a painter. She liked the work; but the life horrified her; cadging parts off managers, waiting about endlessly, and then acting some nonsense. I think Vanessa is better; happily she has much to do; and she is glad that Julian's book is out. It was what she wanted; though to her the publishing was difficult.

Ann and Richard [Llewelyn Davies] stayed with us for a week end. A charming couple; he much more mature than she is; and she referred to

1. Letters from Maurice Llewelyn Davies describing his visit to Virginia's parents at St Ives in the 1880s, and their replies to him.

you—"You were quite right about Margaret; I liked her very much". You see, I had sketched a very remarkable new Aunt for her. And the young are shy of praise, so I thought it a high compliment. They are coming here this week again.

Leonard is working hard at a second vol, of the Deluge;[1] it should be out next autumn. Also he is writing a book on Civilisation for Gollancz, the Left Book Club;[2] and has finished a play [*The Hotel*]. So having a partner is a success so far. I told you I think that John Lehmann is now half the Hogarth Press. Its odd to think what a business has grown out of the type in the Hogarth House drawing room. There are now seven clerks.

I have read hastily the old letters you sent. I wish they could be kept, a bunch like that creates a whole world. But its difficult to see how and I suppose I must tear them up. I send back your Uncle's. As for Ottoline, I heard that Philip is writing an account of her;[3] indeed he asked me to contribute, but no—I have enough with Roger Fry—I am toiling, rather hopelessly, among masses of his papers; and hardly see how to make a book out of him; for he was in touch with every kind of idea, and emotion and human being; and left a huge glow, but one that is impossible to make visible in ink. At least, so I begin to feel. But I have a passion for biographies; hence my distress that you should be tearing up old papers.

This morning we walked all over Hampstead Heath. It was like a June day, and Leonard told me he had once walked with you there. And how often I used to go and see Janet [Case] at Windmill Hill! We had meant to drive to Harrow, and sit on Byron's tomb;[4] but half way a fog came down; and we turned back; and then Hampstead was as clear as glass.

I will get L to finish this page; which I hope will be talked out soon at Dorking [Margaret's house].

Virginia

Sussex

3471: To R. A. Scott-James   52 *Tavistock Square, W.C.*1

Typewritten
7th Dec 38

Dear Mr Scott James,[5]
    I would have liked to write about the reviewing question. But I dealt

1. *After the Deluge*, Vol. II, 1939.
2. *Barbarians at the Gate*, 1939.
3. This project was never completed.
4. It was not Byron's own tomb (he was buried at Hucknall-Torkard, Nottinghamshire), but the tomb of John Peachey, known as the Peachey Stone, on which Byron used to sit for hours, composing poetry, when he was a boy at Harrow School.
5. Editor of the *London Mercury*.

with it as far as I am able in Three Guineas; and do not want to repeat what I said there. Nor do I think I have anything fresh to add to it.[1]

But again it is very good of you to ask me to write; and please accept my thanks.

Yours sincerely
Virginia Woolf

Texas

3472: To HELEN McAFEE   52 *Tavistock Square, W.C.*1

Typewritten
Dec 12th 1938

Dear Miss McAfee,

I have been reading the Yale edition of the Horace Walpole letters with great interest, and was prompted to write a sketch of the characters of Cole and Walpole, whose letters are printed.

Would you care to use it? You were so kind as to say that you would like an article from me sometimes and so I send you a copy of this.[2] I should be glad if you would let me know as soon as you can if you wish to print it, so that I may arrange for publication to suit you over here.

We have been having, as you can imagine, a very agitated time here politically; and I found myself turning to the Yale Walpole by way of a respite. I hope you in America are less distracted. But the politicians are very gloomy on this side as to the future.

With kind regards
yours sincerely
Virginia Woolf

Yale University

3473: To DUNCAN GRANT   52 *Tavistock Square, W.C.*1.

15 Dec. 1938

Dearest Duncan,

I enclose cheque for £40. The carpet will be a lifelong joy; will you thank your mother and tell her how much I admire her astonishing skill and her son's genuis.[3] And its very cheap considering both. I only hesitated

1. But in the next year Virginia wrote *Reviewing*, a long essay published separately by the Hogarth Press.
2. An essay-review of *Letters of Horace Walpole to the Rev. William Cole*, eds. W. S. Lewis and A. D. Wallace, and published by Yale University Press in 1937. It appeared in the *Yale Review* for March 1939 under the title *Two Antiquaries*.
3. Mrs Grant had worked a carpet to her son's design.

because I've been rather extravagant, but the Americans in the nick of time have asked for a story.[1]

By the way, how can I get the carpet? Shall I fetch it in the car? Or could it be brought? I would like to try it here up on the landing where nobody sits and theres no furniture before settling on Monks House.

Yr grateful and devoted

V.

Estate of Duncan Grant

3474: To V. Sackville-West   *Monks House, Rodmell*

[Sussex]

Xmas day 38

Well that was a princely thought—the pate, and better than a thought, it practically saved our lives; pipes frozen; electric fires cut off; nothing to eat, or if there were, it couldnt be cooked; and then behold the parcel from Strasbourg! So we dined and then lunched and then dined off that—I can eat it for ever—I could have been content to freeze almost, if I could eat such gooses liver for ever. But what an extravagant Prince you are! How tremendously in the vein of the pink, and the pearls and the fishmongers porpoise this pink cream with the black jewels imbedded is—or was. Oh yes! and then what about Love—to which you so tantalisingly refer?[2] Suppose you write it down, and then I will go into the matter. I can't (you'll be glad to hear) now; just in, all snow scattered from walking—the downs rose red and bright blue in the snow: wild duck circling; and now off to Keynes' Christmas cake and Nessa for dinner.

And my poor old brother in law Jack Hills[3] is dead: and Mitzi died in the night of Christmas Eve. It was very touching—her eyes shut and her face white like a very old womans. Leonard had taken her to sleep in his room, and she climbed onto his foot last thing.

But enough—dont die—

Please,

Yr V.

Leonard says: Thank you for the pate, Merry Christmas. Have you heard from your solicitor about the letter?[4] Love to Harold.

I'll write a proper letter soon about all sorts of things.

Berg

1. *Lappin and Lapinova*, published in *Harper's Bazaar*, April 1939.
2. Vita had written on 19 December: "And to think how the ceilings of Long Barn once swayed above us! . . . and dolphins sported on the marble slabs" (*Berg*).
3. John Waller Hills, who had married Virginia's half-sister Stella Duckworth, died on 24 December at the age of 71.
4. Vita was arranging to raise a mortgage to purchase a small sailing-ketch for Harold.

Letters 3475-3518 (January–June 1939)

The Woolfs returned from the country to London on 15 January, to lead a very active social life, including a visit to Sigmund Freud, one of the many Austrian refugees now living in London whose plight engaged much of Virginia's sympathy and time. She had completed the first draft of Roger Fry and was steadily revising it, using Pointz Hall as a relaxation from biography. She read many volumes of French memoirs, and visited two of Charles Dickens's houses, already contemplating, perhaps, her future book on the history of literature which emerged (unfinished) as Anon. The international crisis was renewed with Franco's final victory in Spain, Hitler's occupation of Prague, and Mussolini's of Albania.

3475: To Angelica Bell

Monk's House [*Rodmell, Sussex*]

Jan 2nd 1939

Dearest Pix,

Heres the cheque[1] almost to the Tix.

Nessa might like to see this from old Sophie.[2] But give it back on Wednesday. Also a chamber pot. And Saint Simon.[3] What a lot!

[Elizabeth] Curtis sends her love, by post from Newhaven.

And the Raven says Oh never more cursed bore.[4]

V.

[*Added on back of envelope:*] You see in today's paper that I refused the O.M.[5] Leonard has given me the O.F. Guess what it means.

Texas

1. For Angelica's quarterly allowance.
2. Sophie Farrell, the Stephens' cook at Hyde Park Gate, who later worked for Lady Margaret Duckworth, the widow of Virginia's half-brother, George.
3. A short version of the *Memoirs du Duc de Saint-Simon* (1675-1755), which Lytton Strachey had urged Virginia to read in 1908.
4.   "Take thy beak from out my heart, and take
         Thy form from off my door!
       Quoth the Raven, 'Nevermore'."
              Edgar Allan Poe, *The Raven*
5. Virginia was never offered the Order of Merit. On this day the award of the O.M. to Sir James Jeans and Lord Chatfield was announced, but Virginia's 'refusal' was a joke.

Monks House, Rodmell
                                              [Sussex]

9th Jan 1939

Its time I know that I scratched a few words; only my brain gives out of an evening, and my hand. I'm trying to "work hard" at Roger; for me, working hard is 3 hours; and thats all. But then I come in and read—oh the packets of old letters that still remain! And then I fall asleep, and when the post comes, and theres nothing from you, it occurs to me, The old devil wont write until I pull the string. So having an evening off, rather feloniously, for we come back on Sunday and then there'll be no evenings for old letters, I scratch a few words. Its old news about the frozen pipes, frozen w.c.; and no fire; for the grid broke. So thats despatched. I've also lost a brother in law, Jack Hills: him you never knew, so I cant go into that. Mitz the marmozet is dead. But you never liked her. I forget what else has come my way. I'm sociably inclined tonight, but there's 60 miles between us and a gale blowing from the Channel. My mother in law (you asked) has once more bobbed to the top. As she longs to live, at 88, why not? The family begin to treat her as a cricketer doing a record score. All grievances silenced. Can she make 100? I daresay. Vita I've not seen, but ate a giant paté sent by her. Fields too wet to walk in. How I should like a talk! My eyes swim with reading. Cant relish Sévigné or Chaucer. Percy [Bartholomew] is talking about frozen roots in the garden. Sally [spaniel] snoring. How's your book—the one you're writing for me [*What Happened Next*]? I must cook dinner—maccaroni cheese with a bacon fry. But, perversely, I long for the Ivy [Restaurant] and champagne. Too many souls and bodies to be satisfied: the Puritan and the Harlot. Mixed marriages result in this mixed Virginia. how were you mixed? So this is a little worm dangled to catch a letter—a long one.

                                                              V.

Berg

Monk's House, Rodmell,
                                                 Lewes, Sussex

12 Jan 39

Dear Victoria,

No I am not at the moment in London; but I shall be there next week; and expect to be there, with occasional absences, till the spring when, if theres no war, we shall drive about France. So let me know, from this vague sketch, what chance there is of meeting. Thank you for offering a room in Paris—if I can, I would enjoy coming very much.

About V. Sackville West: she told me she was lecturing in Paris: I dont know when. But your best plan would be to write to her direct:

Sissinghurst Castle Kent.[1] I'll explain to her—only I expect she knows—
who you are, what Sur[2] is: then you could meet in Paris. A bientôt.

Virginia Woolf

Estate of Victoria Ocampo

3478: To V. SACKVILLE-WEST   *Monk's House, Rodmell,*
                                     near Lewes, Sussex.

Friday [13 January 1939]

A woman, Victoria Okampo, who is the Sybil (Colefax) of Buenos
Aires, writes to say she wants to publish something by you in her Quarterly
"Sur". She is in Paris, has heard you are going there to lecture—I presume
wants to meet you. I've told her to write to you: but that I would explain.
She's immensely rich, amorous; has been the mistress of Cocteau, Mussolini—Hitler for anything I know: came my way through Aldous Huxley;
gave me a case of butterflies; and descends from time to time on me, with
eyes like the roe of codfish phosphorescent: whats underneath I dont know.
        Going back, damn, on Sunday

V. and P[otto].

Berg

3479: To V. SACKVILLE-WEST   *52 Tavistock Square, W.C.1.*

Tuesday 17th Jan. [1939]

Yes that is Okampo; I think she wanted a poem: also, had wind you were
coming.

Marmozet: What about a Bush Baby?[3] but Sally likes being the only
one.

Margery Fry: Now I'd never have guessed that! Lovely! no. Humorous
yes. But I'll tell you more when we meet. Not that I've anything but good,
so far as I know of her. And how did you meet her?[4]

Dinner. The 3rd is a Friday and we go to Rodmell. Could it be the
2nd.? Thursday. Either here (when L. would be here) or at a place you will
choose (and I pay my fare) if alone. And I mean a restaurant.

1. Vita met Victoria Ocampo for the first time on 26 January in Paris, where Vita
   was lecturing about *Pepita*.
2. The name of the publishing firm in Buenos Aires and of the literary review
   founded by Victoria Ocampo in 1931, both edited and directed by her until her
   death in 1979.
3. A small African tree-climbing lemur, related to the potto.
4. On 6 January Vita had met Margery Fry lunching with Freya Stark.

The disgusting obscurity of all this needs no excuse to one who knows the turmoil of Tavistock Sqre. on coming back after 3 weeks So goodnight; and watch the stars from your tower and when one dartles, thats me.

V.

Berg

3480: To George Davis   [*52 Tavistock Square, W.C.*1]

Typewritten
18 January, 1939

Dear Mr Davis,[1]

Many thanks for your letter. I am glad you like the story. We shall probably be in London during February and will look forward to seeing you then.

I presume that the fee for the story [*Lappin and Lapinova*] will be the same as before, $600.

Yours sincerely
[*unsigned*]

Sussex (carbon copy)

3481: To Ethel Smyth   52 *Tavistock Square, W.C.*1.

Tuesday 24th Jan. [1939]

I knew I didn't deserve a letter, as I never answered the long one—the charming one—the one that jumped and tumbled and wandered in and out of corners that you wrote the other day. But ... well you know my habits as a letter writer, so I'll say no more.

Its no good Madame de Polignac asking me to dinner, because, last time I dined out, I found the moths had eaten a hole in my dress, and I'm not going to buy a new one, it was,—it is,—my only one. But she's not written—should she ever wish, in sober truth, not in the radiance of your generosity, to see me, why dont you both come to tea? Quiet talk in the twilight suits me best as a human being. I cant arrange things, so leave it, as the cab driver does, to you. Politics are coming much too close. Wretched Austrians[2] to tea—What can one do for them? German lessons? But they cant even teach; Home Office wont allow it. Even I have to write letters, try to be "kind". Then the police discover 300 cartridges hidden behind the

---

1. The Editor of *Harper's Bazaar*, New York.
2. Mela Spira and her husband, who had fled from Graz in Austria after the Anschluss with virtually no possessions or money, and were temporarily lodging in Hampstead.

gardeners hut in the Square.[1] And Leonard's out once more talking—talking—Whats to be done; Oh dear Ethel, why did our parents conceive us so that we saw this particular stretch of time? I have such an immense capacity for sheer pleasure up my sleeve; and shant use it this side of the grave. So I burrow into Roger. And what are you doing? The same, I expect: Anyhow we artists have that anciliary—whats the word?—other world outside the real world I mean. If this is real. I am reading Sévigné; that leads to Michelet;[2] that to Saint Simon; and I see Rabelais at the turn of the corner. We're going to see the great Freud on Saturday.[3] Tell me, should I like Lady Desborough?[4]

V.

Berg

3482: To Vanessa Bell   [52 *Tavistock Square, W.C.*1]
Wednesday [25 January 1939]

Of course you've given me[5] what I'd rather have than anything. And you know, darling love, how I thank you.

Berg

3483: To Elizabeth Bowen   52 *Tavistock Square, W.C.*1
Sunday [29 January 1939]
My dear Elizabeth,
    No, alas, I dont think Thursday is possible. We are taking 2 or 3 days at Rodmell, for a treat. The Wolves troubles—well, they haven't been

1. A reporter questioned Leonard about them, and he suggested that 'one of the Irish rebels' who lived in the neighbourhood might be responsible.
2. Jules Michelet, the 19th century French historian. Among Virginia's books were Vols. XII and XIII of his *Histoire de France*.
3. This was Virginia's only meeting with Sigmund Freud, whose works the Hogarth Press had been publishing in translation since 1924. He was now a refugee from Vienna, and had taken a house in Maresfield Gardens, Hampstead, where he entertained Leonard and Virginia to tea. Leonard describes the meeting in *Downhill All the Way*, pp. 168-9. Freud was very courteous (he ceremoniously presented Virginia with a narcissus), but was suffering from the cancer which killed him eight months later at the age of 83.
4. Ethel's friend, Ethel ('Ettie') Grenfell (*née* Fane, 1867-1952), whose husband William became 1st Lord Desborough in 1905. Her house, Taplow Court on the Thames, was a centre of Edwardian society.
5. For Virginia's 57th birthday.

spectacular, like poisoned thumbs: only moth powder in Leonard's pyjamas! Dont sprinkle Alan's [Cameron, her husband]. I'll tell you why, if you'll come. About the man with the Irish name,[1] I've never read him, but am sure he's nice: only Tuesday next, 31st, is my only free day. Would you come to tea with him, with me, 4.30? Or next week—but then he's only here, you say, this week. Do let me know.

I'm bemused with acting the part of Cleopatra in a mask last night in Regents Park.[2] The gloves (blue, yours, wool) saved my life. I told you this I hope, but am as you gather, no mistress of my thoughts; things bob up disorderly, if one's been up, with Tom Eliot as Crippin, till—well, it was only 12.30: but it seemed somehow very very deep in a very long night.

So forgive and tell me if you cant come, when you can.

Oh and dont bother about the stockings.

V.

Texas

3484: To Ann McKnight Kauffer

52 *Tavistock Square, W.C.*1

31st Jan 39

Dear Miss Kauffer,[3]

I remember your coming to the Press, and Miss West introducing us. I am glad that you have taken to writing poetry, and that you think it one of the important events of your life. That means that you are going to take it seriously: so you don't mind if I tell you to put these poems away and write a great many more and re-write them before you try to publish them. I have never written poetry myself, so my advice isn't much use; but as you have sent me your poems that is what I should advise you to do. I like them: I think you have a feeling that makes you write; but there is a lot of work to do before one can make a poem express one's feeling completely for other people. So you must go on, and dont care what I say or what anyone says.

Yours sincerely
Virginia Woolf

Mrs Ann Rendall

1. Sean O'Faolain (b. 1900), the fiction writer and biographer, best known for his many volumes of short stories.
2. At a fancy dress party given by Adrian Stephen, where T. S. Eliot appeared as the American-born Dr H. H. Crippen, who was hanged in 1910 for the murder of his wife.
3. Daughter of Edward McKnight Kauffer, the artist. She had been taken to Tavistock Square by her mother to visit Margaret West, manager of the Hogarth Press, and Virginia later used one of her designs for an advertising poster.

Typewritten
2nd Feb 39

Dear May Sarton,

I was glad to get your letter, in spite of the request you make in it; and in spite of the fact that I have no time to answer it. (I am rushing down to the country; and snatch ten minutes off what ought to be my work). About the MS. for the Refugees society. I am sure it is a good society; but my repulsion from societies is great; still greater my hatred of encouraging writers in their idiotic vanity about their own little doings. I tear up my manuscripts when I have any; but in fact I make such wild sketches in hand writing alter so completely on the type writer that a manuscript of mine is mostly nonsense. And I dont like to sell nonsense; nor do I think it would sell; for no sane person could make head or tail of it. Still, I promise that I will rout among my papers and see if there's some page not too incoherent. If so I'll do violence to my horror of this groping and send it to the address you give.[1]

I'm glad that youre writing poetry; also that youre teaching it. I have no recollection of hearing from Mrs Swift or that I ever had a book from her.[2] Please apologise for me, if she accuses me of not thanking her, as I fear she well may. But I think you know, among other objectionable characteristics, my hatred of thanking writers for their books. One cant say what one thinks; But its rude—uncivilised; a futile protest against the immense reciprocity required by civilisation. This will help to explain my dumbness about your own poetry; which I will read, and say nothing about. In fact, since we had a partner in the Press, two months ago, I gave myself a license to read no modern writing of any kind for one full year. I have been so steeped in modern manuscripts that I was losing all sense that one differed from another. I am reading Chaucer and hope in a year to have recovered my palate. At the moment Auden reads like Spender; Spender like Auden; and neither mean anything. So if I did read you I should only get another confused note in the general clamour; but I hope this will have sorted itself out by next January. As you can imagine, there are so many other things dinning in one's mind here—war, politics, and an infinite number of different people. I shall be seeing Elizabeth [Bowen] and a young man called Sean O'Faolain next week; which I shall enjoy; and hope to see you when youre over. I'm ashamed to let this scribble cross the Atlantic; but

---

1. In fact, Virginia sent the manuscript of *Three Guineas* for sale on behalf of the refugees. See Letter 3493.
2. Elizabeth Townsend (Mrs Rodman) Swift had written a book on the psychology of women, which May Sarton had sent to Virginia in the hope that the Hogarth Press might publish it.

if I dont, then you will give up your last relic of belief in me, which I have some vague wish to preserve.

There are half a dozen snowdrops out in our garden; and we are now driving through the bitter east wind to see them. Best wishes and thanks and apologies.

yrs
Virginia Woolf

Berg

3486: To Ethel Smyth   *Monk's House, Rodmell,*
                                near Lewes, Sussex

Monday 6th Feb. [1939]

Well Ethel dear, how nice to think that you're as I hope, alive. This lyrical outburst is inspired by the extraordinary June weather; my elm trees, the two I see from my window, are at the moment irradiated with the sun, and about 5000 starlings are netted there: why do I always want to find a phrase for what I see? Its not a net; its rather like the edge of a veil thick with black spots. But as you're in Woking, you wont be seeing Mount Caburn across the flats, between the branches.

We took 2 extra days off; very sensibly: and have been walking the cliff at Birling Gap.[1] I saw Winnie [Polignac]; she climbed my stairs; panted, gasped and had to consume 2 tabloids. Then recovered; was very gracious; something like an old manor house with the sun in its windows; and I'm glad I saw her privately, not gobbling chickens soaked in cream at Claridges. I like people singly not in glittering chains. Oh and she sent me, of course, handsome presents—Beethovens Cavatina. Should you be in London on Friday about 5.30 come to tea: no, not tea, nothing; but I've an old friend [Marjorie Strachey] coming; and you say you like that way of breaking ice. But you wont be in London on Friday.

I've been reading David Cecils Melbourne;[2] a very composed well set up biography; I enjoyed it. I've not met Etty [Desborough]; I've not done any of the things I should have done. As the paper nears its end, I always add, And you? Winnie said you were "very brilliant." How I adore, among the rest of your gifts, that quite useless delight.

So no more. The starlings, you may like to know, have flown, and the suns sunk

V

Berg

1. On the Sussex coast between Eastbourne and Seaford.
2. *The Young Melbourne and the Story of His Marriage with Caroline Lamb,* 1939.

3487: To Elaine Robson   *Monk's House, Rodmell,*
                                    Lewes, Sussex

Typewritten (in capital letters)
February sixth [1939]

My dear Elaine,[1]
    The type writer is going to try and write you a letter to thank you for yours. We are sitting in hot sunshine and can almost hear the snow drops growing. There are several white patches and one or two very small yellow noses. These I think must be young crocuses. We come back to London tomorrow. No we have no new monkey, partly because Sally says she likes being the only animal. Yesterday Leonard saw a kingfisher and I saw an old rook asleep on a stake. It winked at me but it did not move. And I stood and watched it and it seemed to be thinking about something. I could have caught it, but it had a long sharp beak. So I left it. I like your journal very much indeed. It tells me all sorts of interesting things. I hope you write it every day and will let me read it when you have done enough. Please put in some poems. Now we are going to drive over the downs and see if we can find a fox. One was barking at dawn under my window. We are going to sit on the cliff and I wish you and Philip [Elaine's brother] were coming.
                        How are the fish?
                              Virginia, Leonard, Sally

Elaine Robson

3488: To Helen McAfee   *52 Tavistock Square, W.C.1*

Typewritten
7th Feb 1939

Dear Miss McAfee,
    I return the proofs[2] herewith. I have made scarcely any corrections, and accept your's I think in every case. I spell 'draught' like that; but if 'draft' is your way—I wasn't certain—of course keep it.[3]
    I am so glad that you like the paper, which seems very far away from the world of London at the present moment. Bullets, Irish I suppose, have just been found in our Square. But let us hope for better times.
                        With kind regards,
                              yours sincerely
                              Virginia Woolf

Yale University

1. For Elaine Robson see p. 174, note 1.
2. Of *Two Antiquaries; Walpole and Cole* (*Yale Review*, March 1939).
3. "He sat secluded, wrapped up from the least draught . . ."

Sunday [12 February 1939]

I dont think this next Wednesday will be any use, as, so far as I can see the week is already chock full and running over. But the unexpected may happen—if not, what about the week after? Oh dear, I sympathise with the toe, more almost than with the head. For if one hurts a toe, one cant walk, and that would be, vagrant rambler that I am, the worse hell of the two— the other being not to think. Witness this fact—just back from a jaunt to Rochester, to see Dickens's house at Gadshill[1] and stretch our legs. Its as exactly Dickens as David Copperfield—the house, the conservatory, the steps, the underground tunnel and the grove in which he had a chalet— d'you remember he was writing there one summer evening when he felt ill, came into dinner, through the tunnel and died? I wonder if these things affect you as they do me. I'd been reading Great Expectations and wanted to see the Marsh—d'you remember again? Well we saw it all, and lunched in the Bull Inn,[2] where, so they say Queen Victoria slept in the same bed as Dickens and Pickwick. But this chatters away far from your toe, and your cold: and it was a bitter East wind down at Gadshill, and I've to go to hear Auden's play[3] But before putting the chicken in the oven, I snatch this interlude to send—no you object to love—Thats what you call helping you across the road. Lord what a buffet I got the only time I tried that! Lord, again, how glad I shall be to see to the end of my Roger: but am appalled by all the re-writing that remains; swarm with ideas for stories; must batten them under: would like to see you; hope you're writing hard. Have you ever read Somerset Maugham? And which of Dickens is your favourite?

V.

Berg

Sunday 19th Feb [1939]

It is rumoured that a large shaggy sheepDog was lately seen in Piccadilly. On being questioned, it answered to the name of V. Sackville West.

I dont know why it came into my head to tell you this fact; except that I think its time V. Sackville West answered to her name. What happened in Paris? I never heard. Did you meet Ocampo? Did you effect any shall we

1. Dickens spent the last years of his life at Gadshill Place, outside Rochester, and it was there that he wrote *Great Expectations*.
2. Rochester, one of the most important settings for Dickens's *Pickwick Papers*.
3. *On the Frontier*, a verse play written in collaboration with Christopher Isherwood, and performed by the Group Theatre.

say intimacy with her? And did the speech electrify The Frogs? And what was it about?[1] I last heard from you as you were about to step on board The Channel steamer in a storm. In fact you wrote in Pencil. So shabby shaggy sheepdog, tell me true. We're basking in the sun; people always say that—but its true. Leonard is cutting off shoots, or grafting, or tying together—Lord knows what you gardeners do after tea in February. And I should be reading Roger Fry.

Old Ethel has a soft corn which keeps one leg perpetually in boiling water. What about Dotty and Yeats? Did she take him South? According to Ottoline, he cut a gland, in order to inject virility, woke to see Dotty, and died of the rush of virility injected. But this is malicious. I am sorry he is dead.[2] I wish someone would write me a poem.[3] Lord how bad the Auden Isherwood play was: so good in a dull way. But I wont read any new poetry for a year, nor meet new poets. I saw Freud the other day. I have fallen in love with . . . [dots in original]

So Vita its for you to finish the sentence, and I'll write no more and go no more a roving, a roving sweet maid.

You have a ladder: on which rung am I?

V.

Back in London tomorrow.

Berg

3491: To George Rylands   52 *Tavistock Square, W.C.*1

Tuesday [21 February 1939]

Dearest Dadie,

It's angelic of you to ask us.[4] I wish we'd known before. As it is this week is already so packed that there seems no chance of getting a day off. If there is, may I let you know, on the chance that you can have us—but you mustn't bother.

---

1. See p. 310, note 1.
2. W. B. Yeats died of heart disease in a small hotel near Roquebrune in the South of France on 28 January 1939. Dorothy Wellesley was living in a nearby villa and often saw him during his last days.
3. Perhaps a reference to Auden's poem *In Memory of W. B. Yeats*, which he composed immediately after Yeats's death, but which was not published until 8 March in the *New Republic* (NY) and again in the April issue of the *London Mercury*.
4. Rylands had invited Virginia to attend a performance of *Macbeth* which he was producing at the Cambridge Arts Theatre for the Marlowe Dramatic Society.

We had a young pupil of yours here last night—Peter Raleigh:[1] and talked of you with admiration, affection—as usual.

So let us put these sentiments into practice soon. Come and gossip.

Your affectionate
Virginia

George Rylands

3492: To Ethel Smyth   [52 *Tavistock Square, W.C.*1]

Monday [27 February 1939]

I think this [a glove] must be yours, not Madame [Mela] Spira's

No time for more. But will write a comment on your charming humble letter—as if the Lioness took to eating bread and milk out of a thimble.

Berg

3493: To Elizabeth Bowen   52 *Tavistock Square, W.C.*1

Tuesday [28 February 1939]

Dear Elizabeth,

Oh dear, I'm afraid I shant get off for a walk tomorrow. The rush at the Press has upset my days and muddled me. But I'm sorry; What about next Tuesday? I hope I've not upset your day. I did ring at your telephone, but no answer—Mrs Camerons out. So I scrawl.

I've a nice letter from someone called something Jones who bought 3 Guineas, I hope for a large sum.[2] Will you thank her, if you see her.

yrs V.W.

No sooner had I written this, than my niece Angelica rang up with this request: (I had told her that you have a lovely house) She says: Would Mrs Cameron lend her house for 3 nights, March 30th, 31st, and April 1st to the Artists Committee for the Spanish Relief.[3] That is they want to hang pictures, and invite the rich to a party and induce them to buy. As you can imagine they find great difficulty in getting the house. And I cant conceive, as I told her, that its a possible suggestion. Nor are they yet decided, as others are in view. But I promised to ask you in this tentative way. And

1. Malcolm Gordon Raleigh, then an Exhibitioner at King's College, Cambridge.
2. To aid the refugees. See Letter 3485. The manuscript of *Three Guineas* is now in the Berg Collection, New York Public Library. The first purchaser, Miss Jones, is unidentified.
3. On the previous day, 27 February, Britain and France had recognised Franco's new government.

finally must plague you to ring me up, if you would,—oh dear, what a bore I'm being: but as I told her, you're a very nice woman. I also told her I thought it out of the question. So forgive.

V

Texas

3494: To Elizabeth Bowen   52 *Tavistock Square, W.C.1.*

Thursday [2 March 1939]

Dear Elizabeth,

Thats angelic of you and Alan; but as far as I can make out, my brother has promised his house so there was no need to bother you. If there is any hitch, I'll tell Angelica to let you know.

Dear me—what a bore. I've a wretch of a German (unknown)[1] coming here on Thursday, and I've promised to take him on to John Lehmann's.

So let us arrange something when you're back; but fix it soon, as we shall vanish before Easter and I want to see you.

Please thank Alan; I think you are amazingly generous.

Yrs (in a rush)

V.

Texas

3495: To Hugh Walpole   *Monk's House, Rodmell, Lewes, Sussex*

5th March 39

Dearest Hugh,

How very nice of you to be reading the Common Reader—By the same post someone wrote and said that the Waves was my best book. Its seldom I get praised for my criticism and my fiction on the same day. One's always on top, and the other below; so I was very glad of your letter. I agree about Lady Dorothy. If I'd known her, I'm sure I should have liked her. It was a youthful spree on my part; and one's heartless (but clever) when one's young.[2]

What a life you lead! Covering (is that the word?—it seems a little improper) the Pope: hobnobbing with journalists; and laying violets on

1. Leonard's diary identifies him as Herr Podbieski.
2. *Lady Dorothy Nevill*, an article in *The Common Reader*, was first published in the *Athenaeum* in 1919 when Virginia was 37.

Keatses tomb with Alfred Noyes.[1] Come back before April 1st or we shan't be in London, and I long for your gossip.

I havent much news to send from the above address: only the cook's mother's baby is an idiot—but must live to be 80: and the rector's wife wont buy a piano for the school but will paint it; and the Labour candidate is suspected of embezzling party funds. Much the same goes on in Keswick, I suppose.

I should be dining with Sibyl [Colefax] to meet Max [Beerbohm]: but am crouching over the fire instead: a blackbird singing; a bonfire burning, and must now go on with Dickens. Do you read Dickens? I've just been to Gadshill in piety.

Yes, if you'll read them, I would like to write another 6 Common Readers.

Love from us both and excuse handwriting due to cold!

Yrs V.W.

P.S. Rome's the place I love best in the whole world. I put this in, on the spur of the moment: no room to say why. The Campagna ... the Gardens ... and then the sheepdogs ... the shepherds etc. etc. ...

Texas

3496: To Charles Douglas   52 *Tavistock Square, W.C.*1

9th March 39

Dear Mr Douglas,[2]

The poem[3] that you ask about has never been published. It was written by Charles Elton, a lawyer and historian; he made it in his sleep, together with one upon Sharing. These were his only poems. Lytton Strachey used to repeat them, and it was from him that I heard the one I quote. There are several verses, and I hope one day to print them in full.

Many thanks for your kind words about my books. Monday or Tuesday [1921] has been out of print for some time.

Yours sincerely
Virginia Woolf

Robert H. Taylor

1. The Hearst newspapers had sent Hugh Walpole to Rome to report on the funeral of Pope Pius XI, and a month later on the coronation of his successor Pius XII. On the anniversary of Keats's death, 23 February, Walpole had made a pilgrimage to the Protestant Cemetery with the poet Alfred Noyes (1880-1958).
2. Of The Leasowes, Barnt Green, near Birmingham.
3. *Luriana, Lurilee*, part of which Virginia quoted in *To the Lighthouse*, was written by Charles Elton (1839-1900). It was first published in full by Vita and Harold Nicolson in their anthology *Another World Than This* (1943).

3497: To T. S. Eliot   52 *Tavistock Square, W.C.*1

Tuesday [14 March 1939]

My dear Tom,

No, naturally you cant come the first night of your play.[1] I'd made a muddle.

What about the following Tuesday, that is 28th, dinner, at 8—and no need to change for the old woman of Tavistock Square.

I have just cut the string of Family Reunion, and have gratified myself by reading the inscription—for both I am deeply grateful, and beg to subscribe myself your much obliged, much touched, attached and humble servant, V.W.

Mrs T. S. Eliot

3498: To V. Sackville-West

                           52 *T.[avistock] S.[quare, W.C.1]*
14th March [1939]
                    A Begging Letter

Scene, sitting room after tea. V.W hoping to read Chaucer. Telephone rings.

V. Oh my God why do we live in London? (Tosses Chaucer on the floor)
Angelica. I'm Angelica.
V. I thought you were Sibyl Colefax.
Ang: Well I am, more or less. I want you to ask Vita . . . I want also to ask you . . . I want to ask you both . . .
V. Well, spit it out like a Briton—
Ang. To ask you both, whether, if—oh dear how am I to explain? Its The Village Players. You remember the people I went about with last summer, acting Gammer Gurtons Needle?[2]—
V. A very coarse play I thought it: but none the worse for that.
Ang: And they want to act again this summer. But Theyve no money.
V. Ohhh oh ohhh . . .
Ang: Now dont cry before you're hurt. I'm *not* asking you for money— I'm asking if you and Vita would—would—would—guarantee, suppose they cant pay their expenses, but they probably will—only theyre all as poor as mice—and its very important to keep the company together—and theyre acting old English plays—and Michel St Denis has promised to come and see them—and he might give them jobs in his company—and

1. *Family Reunion* opened on 20 March at the Westminster Theatre.
2. See p. 263, note 3.

the villagers love the plays—so would you guarantee them—well whatever
you can—and the chances are you wont pay a penny . . .

Well, thats very good of you: that a great help (I guaranteed £10: in
the hope it wont be needed)

And would you ask Vita?"

V. But I hate asking my friends . . . Vita has a million other bloodsuckers
after her. And if I do ask her I shall tell her to be as firm as The Monument
and as hard as stone.

Ang. But promise me you will ask her—

V: Oh Angelica—Angelica—

The telephone is cut off. I ask you, according to promise

And now return to Chaucer.

And there's no reason whatever that you should guarantee a brass
farthing

Berg

3499: To V. Sackville-West   52 *Tavistock Square, W.C.1.*

16th March [1939]

Oh dear, you are a generous, golden hearted woman, dog, or whatever
it may be. Angelica gave a jump of delight when I told her. She was altogether taken aback: all of a heap. Indeed it was good of you—no, its not
Virginia Isham;[1] but I'm handing on the suggestion that they might act at
Sissinghurst. I saw them at Midhurst, in a village Hall; and was greatly
impressed. They run about with a van, and rig it all up themselves.

Yes, of course, youre coming—thats a nice thought—on the 31st.
Come early and see me alone, dearest creature—once in a way. Anyhow,
I'll keep free: unless you want to see Hugh, who threatens, after covering
the Pope for the Daily Express in Rome, to come here.

I think it would be amazing fun to do Jane Carlyle. But instead of
Leonardo?[2]—And are you sure there's not a life? I rather think I've read
one.

What about George Sand? Did you see they've just discovered certain,
but unprintable proof, that she was a—I mean of the tribe of Sappho?[3]

1. Virginia's first cousin once-removed, who had hoped in 1933 to bring a group of
players to Sissinghurst, but the project had been abandoned.
2. Vita wrote nothing about Jane Carlyle or Leonardo.
3. In *Le Secret de l'Adventure Venitienne* (1939), Antoine Adam revealed that George
   Sand's two great passions were for Princesse Belgiojosa and the actress Marie
   Dorval.

Everything is explained; Musset, Chopin etc.
Such a rush.
Only meant for thanks.

V.

Berg

3500: To Angelica Bell   52 *Tavistock Square, W.C.1.*

Postcard
[16 March 1939]

Look, dearest Pix: here's Vita's letter. And I see she promises rather more
than I thought. Also what about acting at Sissinghurst? I think you should
write to her, thanking her, and answering yourself. You might wring more
out of her golden heart.

V.

Texas

3501: To Mark Gertler   52 *Tavistock Square, W.C.1*

Tuesday [21 March 1939]

Dear Mr Gertler,[1]
    Vanessa told me that she had been talking to you about Roger Fry. I
am trying to write something about him, and it would be a great help
if you could possibly write what you remember. Or if that is asking
too much, would you come and see me and talk about him? I'm very
anxious to get your account of the way he struck younger painters.
    Would you be free to dine with us on Saturday next at 8? We should so
much like it if you would.

Yours sincerely
Virginia Woolf

Luke Gertler

3502: To Elizabeth Robins   52 *Tavistock Square, W.C.1*

Wednesday 29th March [1939]

Dear Miss Robins,[2]
    Your letter has been sent on here. We dont go to Rodmell till next

1. Mark Gertler (1892-1939), the painter, had studied at the Slade School, where he
formed an intimate friendship with Carrington. He later exhibited with the London Group, whose membership included Vanessa, Duncan, and Roger Fry. The
dinner proposed in this letter was postponed until 14 May. On 23 June Gertler
killed himself.
2. See p. 22, note 2.

week—but then we shall be down for a week or two. Of course we should much enjoy seeing you, and if we can give you any help, so much the better.

I think we had better ring up and suggest a time later, I'm so sorry you have been ill, and so cant come over, though last time we were down there was no sitting in the garden, which we should like you to see.

Yours
Virginia Woolf

Sussex

3503: To the P.E.N. Club   52 *Tavistock Square, W.C.*1

Typewritten
1st April 1939

Dear Sir,

Josefa Frankl of Vienna has written to me to say that the English P.E.N. Club has asked her to give them English references, and she writes to ask if I will supply them.

I know nothing of her personally, nor do I know her books. She wrote to me some time ago asking me to find her a lodging in England, which I have tried to do without success. She refers me to Mr and Mrs Kantor, Hotel Vanderbilt, 76-86 Cromwell Road, but I do not know them.

It seemed to me best to put these facts before you.

Yours sincerely
Virginia Woolf
(Mrs Woolf)

Texas

3504: To Angelica Bell   52 *Tavistock Square, W.C.*1

Tuesday [4 April 1939]

Dearest Pixie,

Sorry to be late [with Angelica's allowance]. I forgot the day.

And now all the Birds of Paradise are warbling—Troratrou—so I cant condense my mind. Such a lot of gossip—Tom, Ann and so on. So must hope to meet. And what about your parties? And Vita? Oh curse Mrs Curtis and sink America [her house] to the deeps of Hell, and Kenneth Wood too.

V.

Texas

3505: To Ethel Smyth   *Monk's House, Rodmell,*
                                        near Lewes, Sussex
14th April [1939]

Yes, I was going to write to you, but then Leonard got influenza: then I got influenza: you know how that horrid little tick of a disease sucks my brain. This is my first attempt at a letter, and its to you, and that shows how deeply I trust you, for you're the only one of my friends who will take the trouble to read such a scrimp of a hand. (Why have I no pens—and why is my ink brownish? Have flies died in the pot? When I prod, some soft matter emerges). So I'm really asking for a letter from you. Isn't it odd too how difficult it is to write under this pall?[1] We turn on the wireless and so on. And put off living happily till its settled one way or tother. But its useless going on putting off. And now the war seems put off again for another week. I am reading Nicholas Nickleby. When woken by aeroplanes at night I read Ethel Smyth—Gleams of Memory.[2] So please have your new supply ready soon. For I can almost go on where I open—have to shuffle the pages to find a fresh paragraph. I'm toiling revising re-writing Roger. Friends go on discovering new packets of letters. Its like making a dress thats always having a new arm or leg let in in the skirt. But as drudgery its wholesome. I say Ethel what a happy life you had—in the very cream and marrow of the 19th Century. I had a glimpse too, but not a long look. I say Ethel ... well, we shall be back in 10 days and perhaps may meet. Only theyre already pulling down the house next door; the rats are escaping, and the dust settling. How can I do with that uproar?—Find me a garret somewhere. And think of Duff Coopers library![3] Why have the possessors so much added to them? I will write a long letter if you will answer this and wish it. And are you writing? playing golf? And the dog? And Mary [maid at Coign]?

                                                                    V.

1. In mid-March Hitler, in violation of the Munich agreement, invaded Czecho-slovakia and annexed it to the Reich. In early April Mussolini attacked Albania. The British and French governments announced that if Hitler attacked Poland (apparently his next victim), they would give the Poles 'all support in their power'.
2. Ethel wrote no book of this name, and Virginia is probably inventing it as a collective title for all Ethel's autobiographies, including *Streaks of Life,* 1921.
3. Duff and Diana Cooper had moved to 34 Chapel Street, where Rex Whistler was designing and decorating the great library. Virginia had visited them there in mid-March.

I open this to say that Maynard Keynes is being cured by your Plesch,[1] whom he says is the greatest genius that ever lived.

Berg

3506: To Ling Su-Hua   *Monk's House, Rodmell,*
                                        Lewes, Sussex
Typewritten
17th April 1939

Dear Sue,

I am so glad to hear that you have at last got my letter safely. I will always send them by air mail in future. I have heard several times from you, and I am keeping your chapters as they come. But I hope you keep copies, so that there may be no risk through the post. It is difficult to know what to advise you to do, except that I am sure you ought to go on writing. The difficulty is as you say about the English. I feel that the whole feeling of the book would be very much spoilt if some English were to put what you write into formal English prose; yet of course as it stands it is difficult for English readers to get at your full meaning. I suppose you could not dictate to an educated English person? Perhaps in that way the sense and the feeling could be combined. But it would depend entirely upon finding some-one who could be quick enough to understand and able to express. I must of course leave this to you, as I do not know what opportunities you have. Meanwhile, I think it is best to get together as many chapters as possible; and then to read them all through together. One cannot get a true impression if one reads in little bits. But I have seen enough to be interested and charmed. Publication would of course depend upon many things so that it is useless to think of it—things we cannot control. But please go on, and let us hope that it will become more hopeful for books later. At the moment we are finding it very difficult to continue our publishing for nobody will read anything except politics; and we have had to make plans for taking our press away from London, and of course have to face the prospect, should there be war, of shutting up our publishing house altogether. It is very difficult to go on working under such uncertainty. But I myself feel it is the only pos-sible relief from the perpetual strain. It has become worse here, since Italy also began to steal land [Albania]. We do not know if the American presi-dent's appeal will be heard.[2] If not, there is nothing can prevent war. We

1. Dr J. Plesch, who remained Keynes's doctor for the rest of his life, and became his close friend.
2. On 15 April President Roosevelt sent a personal message to Hitler and Mussolini asking them to undertake no further aggression for at least ten years. The dictators ignored it.

are spending Easter in the country; but all the time aeroplanes are crossing the house and every day we hear of some unfortunate refugee who asks for help. I am reading Chaucer and trying to write about our friend Roger Fry. Also Vanessa and her children come over and we play bowls, and try to go on with our painting and gardening as if we were sure of living another ten years. When I go to London I will see if I can find some books to send you. Only I find it so difficult to guess what you would like. Never mind; books are very cheap; and you can always throw them away.

I have not seen Christopher Isherwood as I had hoped but he and Mr Auden like so many people have gone to America. They dont like it, I hear; but at any rate there is more feeling of security there; and they can work better so they say. But I had wanted to hear more about you. It seems millions of miles away—your life, from this. It is full spring here; and our garden has blue, pink, white flowers—and all the hills are deep green; but very small; and our little river is about as big as a large snake; Julian used to wade across it; and sail a tiny boat. On the other hand, people crowd together. We are hardly ever alone even for a day. Would you like this change of proportion? I often envy you, for being in a large wild place with a very old civilisation. I get hints of it in what you write. Do you ever send Vanessa your paintings? Please write whenever you like; and whatever happens please go on with your autobiography; for even though I cannot help yet with it, it will be a great thing to do it thoroughly. I am giving you the advice I try to take myself—that is to work without caring what becomes of it, for the sake of doing something impersonal.

I will send this by air, and let me know if it comes safely. If so, I will go on if you dont mind these very scrappy letters; written in a garden house, after my morning working at my book.

Yours
Virginia Woolf

Ling Su-Hua (Mrs Chen)

3507: To ETHEL SMYTH   52 *Tavistock Square, W.C.*1

Monday [24 April 1939]

I'm having the usual after-influenza temperature, which makes me feel incredibly stupid. So I wired to say I wouldn't come tomorrow.[1]

But if I'm all right I'll come and risk getting a seat. I thought you might want to give it away. Yes, I gather from the papers The Wreckers has been a tremendous triumph. I'm proud and pleased—its your favourite work of

---

1. To a performance of Ethel's opera *The Wreckers* at Sadler's Wells. It was given three times.

mine. So I'd like anyhow to see it—but whats the use if one's shivery and all cotton wool in the head?

V.

Berg

3508: To V. Sackville-West   52 *Tavistock Square, W.C.*1

Tuesday [25th April 1939]

Well Sibyl Colefax,[1] this is a queer go. I'm addressing the lady who has an ancestor, and wants to write a book about him. The queer go is that the very same idea flashed into my head about 3 weeks ago—and I put it to Leonard and John at lunch; and it also had flashed in L's head. But he's writing to you on the morals of the case;[2] so I won't; only try, as you say, to get into touch with you—thats the other you, sheepdog Vita.

We came back, damn it, yesterday. And would have suggested coming over to St. [Sissinghurst], only 3 of our days went in my influenza—not Leonards: I have my own influenza; and this makes me hope you didn't catch his. So the time went, and now we're back; but hope to be down again, and not so tied to weekends, soon: when The Press accounts—a very dismal matter this year, Pepita the only bright spot,—are clinched, concluded—whats the word? D'you know they're pulling down the houses next door? We're shored up; and feel very transitory, like crows in a tree thats being cut down. Dust fills every cranny; and when the hammering begins I shall fly.

I've just had a letter from Ben about the Roger Fry papers—Yes, I think it an admirable idea; and will write to him. But Margery Fry, as executor, will have to be consulted.[3] Is Ben under Kenneth Clarke?[4] No I shouldn't like looking after Royal pictures—thats only my relics of re-publicanism: I suppose its a great chance, and a lifelong adventure. What fun to be Ben—I long for news of his encounters. And to see you. We've been given stalls for a 1st night of Wuthering Heights—a movie.[5] There I

1. Vita had signed herself 'Sibyl Colefax' in her letter to Virginia of 23 April.
2. Another publisher had offered to lend Vita his files on Thomas Sackville, 1st Earl of Dorset (1536-1608), Queen Elizabeth's Lord Treasurer and co-author of the tragedy *Gorboduc*. Vita wanted to write a book on Sackville, using the files, and wondered whether she could then properly offer it to the Hogarth Press. The book was never begun.
3. See next letter.
4. On Kenneth Clark's recommendation, Ben Nicolson had been appointed Deputy Surveyor of the King's Pictures, of which Clark was Surveyor.
5. With Laurence Olivier as Heathcliff and Merle Oberon as Catherine.

shall meet the real Sibyl. Shall you be up soon? Yes, I well remember buying rolls for breakfast at Vezelay [in September 1928].

Hows Gwen?

V.

Berg

3509: TO BENEDICT NICOLSON   52 *Tavistock Square, W.C.*1

27th April 39

Dear Ben,

I am very glad that you are still interested in the Roger Fry papers. I have a great mass of them here, and there are others scattered about. My own feeling is that a very interesting book could be made of them, but of course you could only decide this by going through them. Also, I should have to consult Margery Fry, Rogers executor, to give permission. And she is abroad at the moment.

I will write to her, and then perhaps you would come here and discuss it.[1]

Many congratulations on your appointment [King's pictures].

Yours

Virginia Woolf

Vanessa Nicolson

3510: TO W. S. LEWIS   52 *Tavistock Square, W.C.*1

Typewritten

30th April 1939

Dear Mr Lewis,[2]

I am delighted to think that my article upon Cole and Walpole[3] gave you pleasure. It is a very small return for the pleasure that your great work has given me. I felt indeed some impertinence in writing at all upon such a book, for I am a very casual and unlearned reader, and to express an opinion seemed foolish. But after all, as I reflected, you are doing the work to give pleasure to the foolish as well as the wise, and so I plunged. I heard about it from James Strachey, who told me fascinating stories of your manuscript hunts in England. With his brother, Lytton, who was a Walpole enthusiast, I used often to discuss Horace and his queer character. I only

1. See p. 265, note 1. The project was abandoned on the outbreak of War.
2. Wilmarth Sheldon Lewis, Fellow of Yale University and Editor of the massive Yale Edition of *Horace Walpole's Correspondence*, 1937-48.
3. In the *Yale Review* for March 1939.

wish he could have read the Du Deffand volumes.[1] I feel sure, though much in the dark, that Horace did not hurt her wantonly; but shall—if we are not all destroyed—enjoy the full story when you print it. And I hope that you will come and see us next time you are in London.

Yours sincerely
Virginia Woolf

Sussex

3511: To Elizabeth Bowen   52 *Tavistock Square, W.C.*1.

[3 May 1939]

Oh Elizabeth, d'you know what was put out of my head by Clive ringing up, and its been bothering me so much since that I must write it down—thats about Dickens. Not that I want to write about him—good Lord no: but the other day when I had the flu I read Nicholas Nickelby: and my brain teems with what I wish I'd said this evening. We went to Gadshill, and yesterday to Doughty Street[2]—yes my brain teems with the amazement of Dickens, and I'm about to begin Our Mutual Friend, but will say no more, and only scrawl this to rid myself of the absurd impediment which something unsaid leaves behind. So if you'll come another day we'll talk about Dickens, and I'll be Molly Grubious[3] about the house and the old wives croans no more.

So sorry I was grumbling today[4]

V.

Texas

3512: To V. Sackville-West   52 *Tavistock Square, W.C.*1.

4th May [1939]

No we hadn't gathered the facts about your Sunday: so as we cant come on Friday (owing to a meeting of the School at Rodmell) may we come on Monday—about 3.30 as near as may be. If this is wrong, ring us up 385 Lewes (for letters aren't delivered)

Nothing heard, we'll come.

1. Volumes 3-8 of the Yale Edition contained Walpole's letters to Madame du Deffand (1697-1780), about whom Lytton Strachey wrote an essay in 1912.
2. 48 Doughty Street, Dickens's London house for many years. Virginia had visited Gadshill, his house near Rochester, on 12 February.
3. Virginia's invention of a Dickensian name, perhaps based on Molly, Jagger's housekeeper in *Great Expectations*.
4. Elizabeth Bowen had been to tea with Virginia.

And then one day you'll come here; please Mrs Nicolson.
This is added by Potto [*squiggly design*]

Berg

3513: To Ethel Smyth   52 *Tavistock Square, W.C.*1
Sunday May 14th [1939]

I have been solacing myself this wet evening by reading Jeremy Taylor,[1]
and reflecting upon my lack of what you possess—faith; which lack has led
to this letter, by the way; for though he has his great moments—oh dear
me yes—he has also his dronings and hummings, like all other preachers;
and then I shut the book and write. I wonder how soon you would shut the
book?—how much more pervious to preaching your faith makes you than
my lack? I dont want an answer to that question. I dont want to invade
your privacy, upon which Taylor has a very fine passage.[2] Are you still
as you were immersed in the splendid solitude of disease? Can you read,
if you cant write? I hope your symptoms dont mean anything lasting I
rather count upon your presence on the earth—your effluence, even if I
dont come within the actual ray. Thats a compliment for you. I gather
youve had a glut of them. When will they do The Wreckers again—oh but
I mustnt go asking questions, or you'll seize your old staggering pen. In
fact, your hand is a Greek Goddess compared with mine. Dont you admire
the paper though?—I use it only for great occasions—
    I dont think I have much to say, and its sheer perversity to write to
you when I have a dozen addled eggs of letters—all over a week old—
wanting answers. But my head is still in that torpor which comes when the
influenza dares—as if my brains had coiled like sleeping adders or gorged
crocodiles, save that theyre empty. Thank the Lord, we're going to get 2
weeks in France—after Whitsun. Oh to drink wine in the sun! Yes, theyve
pulled the house down next door, and will begin hammering girders tomorrow. And we think of flitting to another Square if we can be rid of our
lease.[3]
    Why do I like boring Ethel with all this? Because of her candid smile.

1. Jeremy Taylor (1613-67), whose most famous works are *Holy Living* and *Holy
    Dying*.
2. Perhaps the passage from his sermon *The Marriage Ring*: "If single life hath
    more privacy of devotion, yet marriage hath more necessities and more variety
    of it, and is an exercise of more graces."
3. The Woolfs were already negotiating for the lease of 37 Mecklenburgh Square,
    Bloomsbury, to which they moved in August.

When I cant remember how your mouth goes, I can always see your innocent blue eyes. You, Max Beerbohm and Bernard Shaw all have the same eyes—as if you'd just awakened in Heaven—

And heres L. to take my letter—my yellow worthless letter

V.

Berg

3514: TO ETHEL SMYTH   52 *Tavistock Square, W.C.*1

Sunday [21 May 1939]

I've lost your letter in a heap—oh the American professors have started writing about my father now—in a heap of their demands for what they call intimate details: so cant be sure what you said about London. If Tuesday at 5.30 is any good, I shall be in. But dont fash your bones, as the nurses used to say. You said something about influenza, didnt you: but thats gone long since: only this knocking down of houses makes the base of my head more stupid than naturally. Also you said something about Mrs Lascelles and her tragedy. How I long to know—though why? Because I made up a story about it.

We're going to Brittany for 2 weeks. Never been there. I have made up another story out of the names Paimpol [north coast of Brittany] etc. and the fishing fleet from [Pierre] Loti, Renan, Chateaubriand—oh and above all, Les Rochers.[1] I'm writing about Sévigné[2]—Have you read her? And like a worm under a stone try to lift the weight of Roger. The stone is then firmly stamped down. So I've about 6 books in my head. Stella Benson's Life has been just sent me: a drivelling book, judging from 10 pages: but why choose Ellis Roberts to serve one up in cold dish water?[3]

So end in haste to cook Sunday dinner

V.

Berg

3515: TO VANESSA BELL   *Monk's House, Rodmell,*
                                     near Lewes, Sussex.

Monday [29 May 1939]

This small offering[4] is to be spent *simply and solely on Models* Duncan and Angelica are witnesses; and if a penny goes on any other subject (to

1. Madame de Sévigné's country house near Vitré in Brittany.
2. Published in *The Death of the Moth*, 1942.
3. Richard Ellis Roberts had been Literary Editor of the *New Statesman* until 1930. In 1939 he published his *Portrait of Stella Benson*.
4. Vanessa was 60 years old on 30 May.

333

wit, gas bills or boots) they will report; the cheque will be stopped: complete confusion will result. So, good Dolphin Be warned

B.

Berg

3516: To Victoria Ocampo   *Monk's House, Rodmell,*
                                            Lewes, Sussex
30th May 1939

Dear Victoria,

So it always happens! I'm going to France this week, just as you come to England. But I shall be back by about June 16th—either here or in London. Do write to Tavistock Square and let us hope that we can arrange a meeting.

Flying off again! How you range the world!

Yrs

Virginia Woolf

Estate of Victoria Ocampo

3517: To Elizabeth Robins   *Monk's House, Rodmell,*
                                            Lewes, Sussex
Sunday [4 June 1939]

Dear Miss Robins,

Yes, of course. I should like nothing better than to read the other book first, and then the R and I book.[1] I rather doubt my own capacity as a critic, but such views as I have I will certainly give you; and how exciting to read the book, and perhaps encounter Oscar Wilde and Widow Green[2] (so we always called her) and perhaps myself peeping round the door. I now remember the occasion. I wasn't purposely eavesdropping—(not that I should much have hesitated) but was accidentally reading my book and taking a nip of Widow Green behind one of the folding doors. After the Widow had gone. I went to my father and said, "Why does she say that Katherine Symonds[3] is becoming a Roman Catholic?" Upon which he

1. Elizabeth Robins had asked Virginia to read the manuscripts of her autobiographical volumes *Both Sides of the Curtain* (1940), and *Raymond and I* (published posthumously in 1956). In the latter she describes her search for her brother, who had joined the gold rush to Alaska.
2. The widow of J. R. Green, the historian (1837-83), whose letters Leslie Stephen edited. She was born Alice Stopford, and died in 1929 at the age of 82.
3. See p. 59, note 3.

334

started and said "Good Lord—I never knew you were there!" but was amused all the same. And Katherine (now Dame Furse), didn't become an RC so my surprise was justified. But I mustn't write my own memoirs— with a hand sticky from gardening and a pen like a shark's nose.

We were both very happy to see you and Cousin Octavia[1] here, and hope you'll come soon again.

I shall be in London about the 16th: so if you would send the exciting book there, it would reach me.

You left these scraps, which I enclose.

Yrs Virginia

Sussex

3518: To Ethel Smyth   *Monk's House, Rodmell,*
                                         near Lewes, Sussex
[4 June 1939]

Yes, the lady whose name I cant remember but think it was Leontine Lermontov[2] or something of the kind came: and in strictest privacy and most secret confidence, no, I didnt take to her.

She seemed to me underworld, if you know what I mean: I dont mean anything about birth, but something about mind and flesh: She was a little cringing and plausible, and wrote to thank us, which I thought excessive. On the other hand, she was as bright as a new pin and as brisk as a sand hopper. And L. thought she might pan out better in solitude. It was the quality of the flesh I didn't like: and the clothing and the fawning. So thats all . . . about Leontine Lermontov. And I am trying to make a bootbag for the journey and looking for nightgowns. These annual jaunts expire one's wardrobe.

A raging Mistral here: all beauty and joy destroyed. Miss Elizabeth Robins with eyes like pale cinders has just been over. Yes, all letters will reach me in Brittany. A hint to write: for I'm going to bask and shant have a thing to do but think of absent friends, and Madame de Sévigné Lord how I look forward to French food, wine, sun, and yellow houses. Yes, and we pass Combourg where Chateaubriand lived too.

V.

Berg

1. Dr Octavia Wilberforce, who lived with Elizabeth Robins in Brighton. Her family and Virginia's had been closely linked in the 19th century through the Clapham Sect, whose prime achievement was the abolition of slavery in the British Empire. Leslie Stephen's grandmother was a Wilberforce.
2. Miss Leontoneff, a friend of Ethel's great-niece Elizabeth Williamson. Virginia had met her at a party on 13 May.

Letters 3519-3549 (June–September 1939)

On 5 June Virginia and Leonard went on holiday to France, driving slowly through Brittany and Normandy, her last journey abroad. They returned on 20 June, and looked for a new London house, as 52 Tavistock Square (where they had lived for fifteen years) was threatened with demolition. They found 37 Mecklenburgh Square nearby, and took a ten-year lease of it with their solicitor-friends who had shared Tavistock Square, and began to move their belongings there during August. Leonard's mother died on 2 July. Virginia was still rewriting Roger Fry. On 25 July the Woolfs went to Monk's House for the summer, and were there on 1 September when Hitler invaded Poland, and two days later when Britain and France declared war on Germany.

3519: To John Lehmann   Hostellerie du Dauphin,
Vannes [France]

9th June 39

Dear John,

I finished the pamphlet about reviewing. It'll want some re-writing. Leonard disagrees with some of it: and is going to write a reply attacking. We thought of printing both together, and calling it (as its too hot to think) Reviewing: by Virginia and Leonard Woolf.[1]

Weather almost too fine. London broiling too I suppose. We've been sitting among the tombs at Carnac.[2] Lovely towns—rather dull inland. But its great fun so far.

Yrs V.W.

John Lehmann

3520: To Molly MacCarthy   Hostellerie du Dauphin,
Vannes [France]

Sunday, 11th June 1939

Dearest Molly,

    I began a long letter to you, and then Miss Elizabeth Robins inter-

1. The pamphlet was indeed called *Reviewing* when it was published by the Hogarth Press in November 1939, but the authorship was attributed to Virginia alone, 'with a note by Leonard Woolf'.

2. The celebrated group of megalithic monuments on Quiberon Bay.

336

rupted and the dog walked on it: It was only to ask how you are. This is to ask the same thing. But for God's sake don't think you have to answer, unless you wish. I shall hear from Nessa.

The Wolves are on tour as you see, and this is a very nice town, a real aristocrat, like Ottoline or the Duchess of Montrose compared with Lewes and Brighton who are merely Sibyl Colefax and Dora Sanger. However, I won't tell you anything about the druids and Carnac, or Les Rochers and Madame de Sévigné. You know I'm still midway through her; and was thus enchanted to see the chaise longue and the chamber pot she took to Court—like a soup tureen. But that's all. Travellers are the greatest bores out, and this one has a spasmodic fountain pen—now blotting, now costive. How I hate them!

Desmond will have told you all about the Memoir Club [30 March]; and how Clive got a bit restive, some old grudge against Roger raising his hackles and making Nessa as marmoreal as a stone. The stonier she, the more hackled he. We were well served for having it sans you, sans Desmond, and sans the Keynes's—who took it rather ill. So please arrange another, and stay at Monks House, which has been much smoothed since your fall. And read your Paper.

I won't now go on to say how often I think of you, as that's an old Fisher Aunt's phrase, and generally meant a snub following. But I always feel you meet crises such as operations infinitely better than I do. In short, I can't say how I admire you, and with what affection Leonard and I discussed you walking on the bank of a river last night when the green was so green that an old curé on a bench looked for some reason bright purple. Do you like being discussed? I do. And it's rare at our age. Yet how do we exist, save on the lips of our friends? So last night, between 6 and 7 you were absolutely incandescent.

Excuse this babble. It's raining at last and the little Brides—communiquées—are trotting along under gamps [umbrellas].

Let me come and see you as soon as we're back—10 days time. Oh, we're leaving Tavistock Sqre for Mecklenburgh.

Love from us both.

Yrs V.W.

Mrs Michael MacCarthy

3521: TO VANESSA BELL   *Concarneau [France]*

Tuesday [13 June 1939]

No letter from you. In spite of the fact that you're living in the hub of the universe. and I've only been meandering from town to town. We spent 5 days at Vannes, also saw Les Rochers, and came on here yesterday. Vannes is a most sympathetic dignified town, with a quay, blue ships, old walls, old women marching about in black velvet robes with white caps, and in short all that one needs. I wont say that L. is satisfied with the cooking. Sometimes we've struck very bad inns. The country isn't exciting, but there are lovely low sandhills and troops of pines and grey farms—also semitransparent green corn standing against the sea. The sea is mostly long lakes. And Auray is a lovely town. How I love reflections in water—fishing boats dripping blue, the green so green it seems to make every other colour either black or purple—is this an illusion? We discussed Mollys [MacCarthy] character walking by a river and the cuckoos were snapping—I cant get my words in hotels—all round. Yes, I dont think England can compare for amenity or space and composition with France. I rather suspect your brother brushes have spoilt the north. They're to be seen at the street corners. And the English have begun for the first time here. I wrote to Molly. Have you heard of her? I see Francis Acland is dead. Wasn't Hester Ritchie[1] in love with him? I think we've got 37 M. [Mecklenburgh] Sqre. but havent let 52 so please do your best or we shall be ruined. Les Rochers we saw in a livid broiling light, but I was greatly moved—an old farm—chateau made of silver oatcakes. And a shabby distinguished garden, all symmetrical. Not, to my mind, very good churches, but the common buildings are so aristocratic. And the colour everywhere so harmonious—all greys and biscuit whites. Cant form my letters, poor Dolphin. won't be able to read. Home, Rodmell on Tuesday. I see Simon has a show.[2] Are you engulfed in society? Are you painting from models? Now we explore Quimper.

Love to adorable Duncan and my fiendish niece.

B

We were broiled alive for 6 days—almost too hot to open one's eyes—now its cold.

Berg

3522: To John H. Simpson   *Concarneau, Brittany*
June 15th [1939]

Dear Mr Simpson,[3]

We are driving about France—hence the delay in answering.

1. The granddaughter of W. M. Thackeray and Leslie Stephen's niece by his first marriage. Sir Francis Acland (1874-1939) was a Member of Parliament, and held several junior offices in the government. He lived in his ancestral house, Killerton, near Exeter, Devon.
2. Simon Bussy's exhibition of his recent paintings, at the Leicester Gallery, shared with Jacob Epstein, Jacques-Émile Blanche and Doris Zinkeisen.
3. The author (under the pseudonym 'John Hampson') of *Saturday Night at the Greyhound* (1931) and *O Providence* (1932), both published by the Hogarth Press, which refused his homosexual novel *Strip Jack Naked* (1934).

I dont follow the [publisher] reader's argument altogether. Why is bugger worse than bitch? Why bog worse than W-C? However there is a special code about these things. I look forward to seeing what the innuendo about candle is, and if I can spot it.[1] But soon these words will have lost their force—a great boon—for I dont like to be held up in writing English, and the taboos inhibit me. This pen is such that I cant write more, but we hope to see you again in London, or in Birmingham.

Yours sincerely,
Virginia Woolf

I've just found this letter put away unposted in my bag. Rodmell—June 20th

Library of the University of California, Los Angeles

3523: To Elaine Robson   *Dinan, Brittany*

15th June 1939

Dear Elaine,

I had a lovely poem, every line except one, rhyming, from you the very day we left for France. And as we have been eating and drinking and walking and climbing up and down cliffs all day since I have not been able to thank you. I liked your poem very much. Could you write one in French? And make it rhyme too? Please try. I wish I were French and English as you are, like an ice that is half strawberry and half lemon. We had to leave Sally alone at Rodmell. She sleeps by herself in Uncle Leonard's arm chair. We get back on Tuesday at seven in the morning and she will wake up to find us. Will you come to tea soon. I will get another yellow cake if you will. So I must say Good Bye.

Next time I will try
To write a better
and longer letter
But now I must get a
French stamp and post this
To Elaine in London
    Without a Rhyme.

Virginia

Elaine Robson

1. " 'Miss McGuire complained about the candles again.' 'Did she, the bitch! Well, we all know why' " (*Care of 'The Grand'*, by John Hampson, 1939).

339

3524: To Vanessa Bell   *Bayeux [France]*

Sunday June? [18 June 1939]

I got your letter much to my happiness but its not much use trying to write save out of devotion (unrequited) because I'm sitting in a courtyard at an Inn table, with the Feast of St John going on—that is gipsies dancing, old men in black velvet suits with silver buttons, divine youths in mediaeval doublets, girls with lace caps like the Eiffel tower dancing and the usual merrygorounds. They're celebrating midsummer night—The din is infernal. And I'm half tipsy. We have been in great luck this last week, always striking the right Inn, and the food, though too shelly and fishy for my taste is so succulent that L. has had to succumb. The civilisation is astonishing—everyone polite, virtuous, happy, non-political. Bloomsbury at its best—I mean no logic chopping. And I'm even favourably impressed by the Roman Catholics—they strew the streets with branches and flowers, and we saw an archbishop—a man all clad in white samite[1] under a palanquin of gold and stars—blessing a fishing boat slung with roses today against a lead blue sea. Its certainly a great advantage to have a reason for dressing up. But its so dark I cant see. What a bore to come back to England, except that I shall be happier with you than here. Also Inns are oppresive after 2 weeks. Now theyre lighting a great triangle of Japanese lanterns and we must traipse about the streets.

I've no news, save that the Sidney Webbs want to see us, and Eddie Sackville. and Philip Morrell wants me to subscribe to a home for fallen women, to be called The Lady Ottoline home; in which her portrait, whether as example or warning, is to be hung perpetually.

We get to Rodmell on Tuesday and shall come up on Friday I expect. We've got 37 *M. Sq* I suppose rather rashly.

Dear me, this is a dull letter. Please believe that I'm more amusing in the flesh. and give my love to—here's the procession so I must follow.

Poor dear tipsy B sends love.

Berg

3525: To Ethel Smyth   *Bayeux [Normandy]*

Sunday, St. Johns Night [18 June 1939]

No we kept clear of St Malo, and went down to Vannes, and round to Carnac, Paimpol etc: and are now here, in the midst of crackers, fireworks, religious processions, and endless merry go rounds. The tobacconist, who

1. "Clothed in white samite, mystic, wonderful" (Tennyson, *The Passing of Arthur*).

says he's descended from the Bishop of Dublin, but cant remember the name, says they'll keep it up till 3 a.m. Its midsummer night, rather cold, but Lord how rapturous and civilised and sensuous the French are compared with us, and how it liberates the soul to drink a bottle of good wine daily and sit in the sun, and even the white robed clergy under Palanquins dont offend, but even induce in me regrets for our stony and grim Protestantism—Yes, I went to Les Rochers; also saw Carnac, which is somehow impressive, like an army of old washerwomen emerging from primeval times, each with a sheet on her head. Dear me, what a row the French do make—and no snobbery. And I'm reading Colette, "Duo" [1934]; all about love; and rather too slangy for my vocabulary, but what a born writer! How she walzes through the dictionary. I got your letters, and read them with greed. I dont want to come back to England, but we cross tomorrow. An old man in black velvet with silver buttons is playing a bagpipe such as the Druid shepherds must have played to Iberian goats. And now a youth in medieval scarlet has seized a girl with a tower of white lace in her hair and theyre dancing. Can you imagine Mr Piddinghoe so doing with Mrs Sidgwick[1]—and whats the use of logic and chaste Cambridge conversations if one cant do that?

However its growing cold, and I'm sleepy, having been to Caen, having done all sorts of exciting things. What? Well, I wont begin guide book writing at my time of tipsiness. Yes, I agree that The Poets Pub—Dotties and Yeats—is a sophisticated humbug.[2] The French figure at 60 does not lend itself to a jumper—the good lady in front of me is like a cottage loaf; but as tight and tidy as a pin or a mackerel.

Now the lights in our Hotel lanterns are about to be lit, and I must follow St John through the streets

Excuse this scrap and scrawl, which testifies to my devotion and is for that reason to be excused.

V.

Berg

3526: To Beatrice Webb   *Bayeux [Normandy]*

18th June, 1939

Dear Mrs Webb,

Your letter has just reached me here. We are much disappointed to have

1. Eleanor Sidgwick (1845-1936) and Leo Piddington had been neighbours of Ethel in Woking. They shared an interest in the occult (see Vol. IV, Letter 2500). Mrs Sidgwick was Principal of Newnham College, Cambridge, 1892-1910.
2. Soon after Yeats's death Dorothy Wellesley built a little temple in the garden facing her house, Penns-in-the-Rocks, and dedicated it "To the Poets who Loved Penns"—Yeats, de la Mare, W. J. Turner, Ruth Pitter, Vita, and Dottie herself.

missed seeing you in London, and hope you will suggest another visit later. We shall be at Monks House, Rodmell in August and September, and should be delighted if you and Mr Webb would visit us. In October we move to Mecklenburgh Square; and I will send you our new address, later.

It would be a great pleasure to us both to see you again.

Please give our greetings to Mr Webb.

Yours very sincerely,
Virginia Woolf

University of London (Passfield Papers)

3527: To Benedict Nicolson   52 *Tavistock Square, W.C.*1

23rd June [1939]

Dear Ben,

I wrote to Sissinghurst to ask if you would send back my key, but I expect you never got the letter, so I'm writing to St James's Palace; on chance. Could you send it, as I shall find myself one of these nights locked out. I'm afraid I've had to move some of your papers, as I'm starting work again.[1]

Perhaps you would look in some time and then we could see how to arrange things. Also theres a letter waiting for you, but I'm not sure where to send it.

Yours ever
Virginia Woolf

Vanessa Nicolson

3528: To Victoria Ocampo   52 *Tavistock Square, W.C.*1

26th June 39

Dear Victoria,

I am very sorry that you were annoyed the other day and thought that I didn't wish to see you.

Its quite true—I was annoyed. Over and over again I've refused to be photographed. Twice I had made excuses so as not to sit to Madame Freund. And then you bring her without telling me, and that convinced me that you knew that I didn't want to sit, and were forcing my hand. As indeed you did. Its difficult to be rude to people in one's own house. So I was

1. During their absence in France, Virginia had allowed Ben Nicolson to use her studio to sort out Roger Fry's papers. See Letter 3509.

photographed against my will about 40 times over, which annoyed me.[1]
But what particularly annoyed me was that I lost all chance of talking to
you. That you will agree is a proof that I did want to see you. And there
wont be another chance till Heaven knows when. And Heaven knows too
what is the point of these photographs. I can't see it. And I hate it.

Excuse this frankness; but if you're honest, so am I.

Yours
Virginia Woolf

Estate of Victoria Ocampo

3529: To George Rylands   52 *Tavistock Square, W.C.*1

Monday [26 June 1939]

High time that the old Wolves refreshed their memories of the Golden
Boy. Also the House is coming down and they flitting. So come on Tuesday
July 4th at 4.30 and rejoice.

Old Virginia

George Rylands

3530: To Elizabeth Robins   52 *Tavistock Square, W.C.*1

28th June 39

Dear Miss Robins,

Yes, France was very lovely but its over. And now we're back here, but
I'm afraid nothing has happened yet about the play.[2] Mr Priestley,[3] says that
he can't venture on a new play this season. However, we've just heard that
the Co-operative Society, of all people, is (or are) starting a theatre, and as
Leonard has a great name among co-operators we are going to try them. Or
to ask Peacock,[4] the agent, to.

About your book [*Both Sides of the Curtain*]—you ask what I should
say if you sent it me as you finish it. I should say its one of the very few

1. On 23 June Victoria Ocampo brought Gisèle Freund, the photographer, to see
   Virginia and show her photographs of some of her other literary sitters. Virginia
   reluctantly agreed to sit for Freund the next day. (See Doris Meyer, *Victoria
   Ocampo*, 1979, p. 128.) One of the resulting photographs forms the frontispiece
   of this volume.
2. Leonard's play, *The Hotel*. See p. 287, note 1.
3. J. B. Priestley acted as a Director of the Mask Theatre which produced plays at
   the Westminster Theatre, 1938-9.
4. Walter Peacock, theatrical agent, of 60 Haymarket, S.W.1.

books I should like to read, and that all my faculties, such as they are after struggling with a difficult biography all the morning, are at your service.

So I hope you will send it whole, or bit by bit. Save for weekends, we shall be here till the end of July.

Leonard is out coping with the Labour Party so I wont send his respects, but mine.

Are the [Swiss] mountains doing you good?—as I was taught by my father that they did?

Yours
Virginia Woolf

Sussex

3531: To Ethel Smyth   52 *Tavistock Square, W.C.*1

4th July [1939]

I think it likely that I owe you a letter. But you see why I didn't write— as soon as we came back, my poor old mother in law, with whom we'd had tea the day before, fell and broke 2 ribs. Then she was taken to a nursing home, and there lingered; finally died and was buried yesterday.[1] All sorts of family conclaves were held here—Now its over,—

Meanwhile, we've taken 37 M^burgh Sqre: and at the moment L. is measuring the book cases with a view to the move, in August.

Are you in Ireland? You said something about it, in the letter I got and read—oh such years ago—in a sunny market place in France.

Well this is only the waggle of a finger tip in your direction, which is uncertain.

Harold [Nicolson], I hear, says there's to be war on July 12th; which adds to the general mess.

So no more

V.

Berg

3532: To Angelica Bell   52 *Tavistock Square, W.C.*1

4th July [1939]

I think this [allowance] is due, and overdue.

We called in after the funeral[2] yesterday, but were told by a man that

1. Marie Woolf died on 2 July, but was not buried till 5 July. Even Leonard did not know her exact age, but she was about 90.
2. The removal of Marie Woolf's body to a private house (Laleham) before her burial.

344

Miss Bell was in her Bath. Now I hope Miss Bell is in her nest. Mary Hutchinson is dining with us so I must wash.

V.

Texas

3533: To ELIZABETH ROBINS   52 *Tavistock Square, W.C.*1

11th July 39

Dear Miss Robins,
    This is just to say that the MS. has arrived safely.
    My instinct is to gulp it down entire, once I am free, and then, I hope to talk it over with you as a whole. Of course I'll scribble criticisms in the margin, if you want them. But of what? Style, grammar, dates? But I dont suppose there's anything I could say about all that. If there's anything special, let me know—otherwise I'll gulp.

Yours
Virginia Woolf

Sussex

3534: To BENEDICT NICOLSON   52 *Tavistock Square, W.C.*1

Postcard
[13 July 1939]

    We should like very much to come in if we can on Friday and sit on the floor. [*See* p. 413.]
    We went on arguing till 1.30 the other night[1] about an epitaph for Ottoline, so I wish you had come. But anyhow you are dining on the 18th.

V.W.

Vanessa Nicolson

3535: To JOHN LEHMANN   *Monk's House, Rodmell,*
                               Lewes, Sussex

Saturday [15 July 1939]

Dear John,
    I enclose a letter from Geoffrey Agnew about a book on Sickert,[2] and

1. At 8 Fitzroy Street, with Vanessa, Clive and Duncan.
2. Possibly R. V. B. Emmons's *Life and Opinions of Walter Richard Sickert*, 1941. Virginia had herself written about the painter in 1934. Geoffrey Agnew was at this time Managing Director of Thomas Agnew & Sons (Fine Art Dealers). The book had no Introduction.

have said that the man—I cant read his name—had better get into touch with you.

Its magnificent down here, and I hope with you. My nose is not among the flowers, but on the grindstone. Moses had a very good show—I'm reading it.[1]

Love from us both

V.

Ben N. said that Graham Bell[2] is the best of the young critics,—in case the slimy toad WR [William Rothenstein] refuses, he might be worth considering.

John Lehmann

3536: To Ling Su-Hua   52 *Tavistock Square, W.C.*1

Typewritten
16th July 39

Dear Sue,

I am afraid that I have been very bad about answering your letters. It is partly that I am a very bad letter writer—after writing all the morning about Roger Fry, I hate the type writer. And then we went to France for a holiday, driving about Brittany; and directly after that my mother in law had an accident; was ill and died. And now we have to turn out of this house, which is crammed with books and papers and type and furniture and go to another. 37 Mecklenburgh Square will be our address in September. So I hope you will write there.

Also it is difficult to think of any news worth sending. One only caps stories of war—and you have enough of your own. Here they say it must come next month. That is what Harold Nicolson who is in Parliament told me two nights ago. By this time one is so numb that it seems impossible to feel anything, save that dull vague gloom. We are getting used, I suppose. But it will be different when it comes. Like you, I find work the best thing; and I have more than I can do. It is dull work—sorting letters, trying to

---

1. Katherine John's translation of Sigmund Freud's *Moses and Monotheism* was published in this year by the Hogarth Press.
2. Graham Bell was the South African-born painter who came to London in 1931, and with William Coldstream was the intellectual force behind the Euston Road School. He also wrote art-criticism for the *New Statesman*, and his pamphlet *The Artist and his Public* was published by the Hogarth Press in 1939. He was killed serving in the R.A.F. in 1943 at the age of 32.

find quotations; trying to fit them together. Roger Fry left such masses of papers; and they are full of interest; but full too of detail. I keep wanting Julian to help me. I am keeping all your chapters together.[1] As I told you, I shant read them till the book is done. And please go on with it, as it might be of such great interest. I am also sorry that I have never sent more books— I began to feel for one thing that books would never reach you. But I will get some cheap ones this week; chancing that you may like them. There again, I dont know what to send, whether new or old, poetry or fiction or biography. But tell me some time what it is that you would like.

Thank you very much for the red and black poster, which I liked. And you say you are sending something else to Vanessa. I am just going to dine with her. That is a great pleasure. And I wish you lived near and could come in. These little meetings are the best things we have at present. We talk about pictures not about war. I am so sorry for all you are having to suffer—but what is the use of saying that, all these miles away? Any time you want to write please do. The letter will be sent on. Next week we go down to Sussex, Monk's House, Rodmell, Lewes is the address. Will one be able to work? Will one have to fill the house with refugees? There are aeroplanes always round us; and air raid shelters—but I still believe we shall have peace. And there I will stop. With my love and believe in my sympathy, futile as it seems.

Yours
Virginia Woolf

Ling Su-Hua (Mrs Chen)

3537: To Shena, Lady Simon   52 *Tavistock Square, W.C.*1

20th July [1939]

Dear Shena,

I'm so sorry, we shall be away. We go on the 25th;—we shall be up again, off and on, because we're moving house, to 37 Mecklenburgh Sqre in the middle of August.

So you must come there,—but I wish it could have been sooner. And the chaos is already such that I doubt if there'll ever be a room to sit in.

This is being pulled down.

Yrs
Virginia Woolf

Sussex

1. Ling Su-Hua, from remotest China, was sending Virginia chapters of her auto-biography (*Ancient Melodies*), one by one. See p. 221, note 2.

3538: To R. C. Trevelyan   52 *Tavistock Square, W.C.*1

21st July 39

My dear Bob,

I ought to have thanked you long ago for my share in your collected poems.[1] But we were abroad—moving house, and so on.

I've been reading them again, at intervals; and I must thank you, not only for giving us the book, but for the poems. I didn't realise how much I liked them. They come through—so I feel reading them together—more than I'd remembered. Its as though all superfluities had been consumed and whats left is very satisfying. That is a quality I admire very much, and don't find often among the moderns. And often there's a special colourless (perhaps I mean unexaggerated, or impersonal) beauty that I find also lasting and possessing—not surprising, but stealing over one. Also, in the Letters especially,[2] I like to trace the character of the writer, the peculiar humour and idiosyncracy of his mind, a quality I find oftener in prose. I'm not getting the right words for liking your poems. Never mind; perhaps one can't, when poetry is good—it is too complete to break up into reasons. At least I find it so.

But I wanted to thank you, and take this occasion since I've just been made angry—tho' thats too strong a word—by a silly review by Stephen Spender.[3]

Leonard is out, or he would add his thanks too.

Yours ever,
Virginia Woolf

Sussex

3539: To May Sarton   52 *T[avistock] S[quare, W.C.*1]

Postcard
24 July [1939]

I'm so sorry—we go down tomorrow to the dew pond[4] on the other

1. Trevelyan had given Virginia and Leonard Volume I of his *Collected Works*, 1939. At the same time he published a second volume of his plays.
2. In 1932 Trevelyan had published with the Hogarth Press his *Rimeless Numbers*, which contained several poetic letters addressed to his friends.
3. Spender's review of Trevelyan's *Collected Works* appeared in the *New Statesman* on 21 July. He wrote: "The reader is often left wishing that Mr Trevelyan had never been to Cambridge, that he had been, perhaps, a shepherd or a fisherman, singing his simple ditties to the stars."
4. In the garden at Monk's House.

side of this card. So I'm afraid there'll be no more evenings at 52 T.S. But I hope you'll come to 37 Mecklenburgh Sqre.

V.W.

Berg

3540: To May Sarton

[Monk's House,] Rodmell
[Sussex]

Postcard
July 29th [1939]

Thanks very much for the poems, which I shall put into the 1940 cellar safe. On the other side you will find last Christmas.[1] I'm now making a cake.

V.W.

Berg

3541: To Vanessa Bell

[Monk's House, Rodmell,
Sussex]

Saturday [August/September ? 1939]

A brother of L's is coming to tea tomorrow. I tell you, in case you would curse me if you came: but I hope you will come. Especially as the wife admires yr pots and chair covers and would be a possible client for Q.

So wait in hope of a visit from some, any, all

B.

Berg

3542: To Donald Brace

Monk's House, Rodmell,
Lewes, Sussex

Typewritten
10th Aug 1939

Dear Mr Brace,

I have been reading in manuscript a book [*Both Sides of the Curtain*] which has interested me very much—the memoirs of Elizabeth Robins, who, as I expect you know, was the American actress who made Ibsen famous in England; and is also the author of The Magnetic North [1904].

These memoirs cover the first years of her life in London, (c. 1889-90)

1. A photograph of Monk's House in the snow.

and describe her dealings with Beerbohm Tree, Irving;[1] and give in particular a most interesting account of Oscar Wilde. However, the point to my mind is that she has written a fascinating book, apart from having known celebrities. So I told her that I advised her to send it to you; and that I would add a word from myself. But I feel sure that if you read it, you will not need any recommendation from me. I read it with excitement all through.

It is a long book; and she is at work on another volume. But what she has shown me is complete in itself, and could be published as it stands. I know she is anxious for an early decision,—she is well on in the seventies— and any help you could give in this way would be much appreciated.

With kind regards from us both,

yours sincerely,

Virginia Woolf

Harcourt Brace Jovanovich

3543: To V. Sackville-West
19th Aug: [1939]

Monk's House, Rodmell, near Lewes, Sussex

Isn't it nice sometimes to write a letter one doesn't have to write? So this is one. I've been walking on the marsh and found a swan sitting in a Saxon grave. This made me think of you. Then I came back and read about Leonardo—Kenneth Clark—good I think:[2] this made me also think of you. And in a minute I must cook some macaroni.

We're half way through our move—have no house at the moment— only boxes in vans. Lord what a mess; in a rage I tore up masses of papers. More and more and more remain. I've two nice rooms at the top,—I like them—there you'll come—one side is chimneys on a hill, I suppose Islington —t'other all green fields and the Foundlings[3] playing. So we'll sit in the window, and I shall say, which rung Vita—which rung am I on?

I had a visit from Eddie the other day: and really he wrung my heart— like a face tossed up from the bottom of the sea on a beach—one of those

1. Sir Herbert Beerbohm Tree (1852-1917), the actor-manager. In 1887 he became the successful manager of the Haymarket Theatre, at which he produced, among other plays, several by Ibsen. Sir Henry Irving (1838-1905) was the greatest Shakespearean actor of his day, and appeared for many years opposite Ellen Terry.
2. *Leonardo da Vinci: An Account of His Development as an Artist*, 1939.
3. The Foundling Hospital had moved out of Bloomsbury in 1926, and the buildings were pulled down. The grounds were rescued from development and became a children's playground, Coram's Fields, behind Mecklenburgh Square.

bits of wasted white wood sea eaten—a death mask. But whats it all about?[1] Three years of misery. Himself I suppose (being, though sympathetic, uncharitable.) Rebecca West[2] came over—but why so prosperous and fat? and why this dillydallying with the world and the flesh? No, I dont think one makes much headway—she's too distorted one foot on sea and one on land, as your ancestor sang.[3] I'm in a rage. That devil woman Giselle Freund calmly tells me she's showing those d—d photographs—and I made it a condition she shouldn't. Dont you think it damnable?—considering how they [Ocampo and Freund] filched and pilfered and gate crashed—the treacherous vermin. Do give her a piece of your mind if you see her. I loathe being hoisted about on top of a stick for any one to stare at. Shall you send me a book to read soon? Are you tackling the old ancestor—whats his name [Thomas Sackville]? Now I've enjoyed writing when I needn't; thats not to say you've enjoyed reading. And which rung are we on—my poor Potto and V?[4]

V.

Inez has left Stephen for Mr Madge a poet.[5]

Berg

3544: To John Lehmann

Monk's House, Rodmell,
Lewes, Sussex

Saturday [19 August 1939]

Dear John,

Could you come and stay next week end, that is 26th? Perhaps Morgan will be here—anyhow we hope you can. There is a lot of gossip besides the old H.P.—and more peace here than in the basement. What a turmoil! I hope its settling.

Yrs
V.W.

John Lehmann

1. Edward Sackville West's unhappiness was due to his constant ill health, the imagined failure of his books, unsatisfactory love affairs, and the approach of war.
2. The novelist, critic, and political writer (b. 1892), whose most recent book was *The Thinking Reed* (1936).
3. *To All You Ladies Now at Land*, by Charles Sackville (1638-1706).
4. Vita replied: "Virginia darling, you are very high up on the rungs—always" (25 August 1939, *Berg*).
5. Charles Madge (b. 1912), the poet and sociologist, first married the poet Kathleen Raine, and after their divorce, married Inez (*née* Pearn), ex-wife of Stephen Spender.

3545: To Ethel Smyth   *Monk's House, Rodmell,*
                                         near Lewes, Sussex
[20 August 1939]

Yes I know, though you have been forbearance itself that I have been the very opposite. Two days ago, perched in the ruins of Tavistock Sqre, I took up the pen: then the man came about the geyser [water-heater] ... So to 37 Meck[8]: so here; so back again for the last worst fight of them all on Thursday. Then we shall be installed. And I've two nice quiet rooms right at the top only at present they beckon like fields of Paradise across the river of Time—oh and my pen has a hair, so I cant finish the phrase.

In the intervals, we're down here, grilling in the garden—a forest of dahlias and zinnias; and of a morning I struggle to finish Roger—how to deal with love affairs—thats the particular problem now—then bowls, Leonard beats me; then reading—what? Oh Pascal now. and so to reflections upon theology. Miss Robins came over, remembers you at Hill House;[1] is writing her memoirs on a scale of one year to 500 pages. Its like following an insect across an ordnance map, but very fascinating. What about yours? Then there's the war—black outs: a man shot in the river where I walk; and the Labour party meeting here. I cant make a song of this, not a consecutive phrase, for I'm too hot. Its only to show you I've a loving heart. But that you never doubt. I was amused to hear of Drishane and the dilapidated Edith.[2] No, I never read their [Somerville and Ross] books. one of my vacancies, of which I've many, as you know. Did the visit end on a note of harmony? Yes, I think landscape a great support. Who prop in these dull days my mind?[3] Well the downs and the river Ouse, in spite of the man who shot himself and the sheep I found on its back. Can nature be called beneficent? I doubt it. So back to Pascal, and in hopes of your memoirs.

                                                              V.
Berg

3546: To Judith Stephen   *Monk's House, Rodmell,*
                                          Lewes, Sussex
Typewritten
Aug. 22nd [1939]

My dear Judith,
    Are you back? The last letter I had from you said that you were sitting

1. The country house (near Epping, Surrey) of Ethel's sister, Mary (Mrs Charles) Hunter, the Edwardian hostess.
2. Edith Somerville was then 81 years old and lived at 'Drishane', in the village of Castle Townshend, Co. Cork.
3.   "Who prop, thou ask'st, in these bad days, my mind?"
                              —Matthew Arnold, *To a Friend*

352

half naked in an Inn yard about to plunge into the Pyrenees. Since when no news. The other day I heard that Leslie Humphreys[1]—oh how does he spell it? had been to see over our flat. We'll let him have it cheap, if it's not taken already. But the thing I meant to say was that though, as Leonard decrees, we mustn't ask you to stay, will you ask yourself? And now we've a garden room of a sort and can put up two; so will you bring anyone you like—Leslie, if he's in London; or we could get old Tom [Eliot]; or William [Plomer]. Only not the weekend of 16th Sept. The middle of the week is also possible and less somnolent perhaps.

We are in an ambiguous position, without a house; that is, with two houses, but none to live in; but hope to settle a few chairs on Thursday at 37 Mecklenburgh Square; which is now our town address. But write here. And what's been happening? Here, as usual, the crisis is pretty thick; but lets leave that out, as its a bore croaking in concert. Rodmell has its suicide, and two escaped prisoners, by way of a private enterprise, and I only just missed the convict, and the man in a canoe who shot himself. Otherwise we have made some new improvements, and bowls are going strong; Quentin and I beat Leonard and Angus Davidson last night. Leonard is simply rampant; not a stroke but hits the jack.

A large Labour Party meeting [at Rodmell] discussed education two nights ago; Louie [Everest] read a paper; even Nessa gave tongue. But I mustn't drivel on; and there's so much to say I'm stopped like a bottle held upside down.

So lets try to fix a date, but of course its left entirely and completely to you as the younger generation.

Virginia

Nigel Henderson

3547: To Ethel Smyth   *Monk's House, Rodmell,*
                                  near Lewes, Sussex

29th Aug: [1939]

Just listened in to the Prime Minister, from which it seems that there's another day of peace anyhow.[2]

Oh what a bad Virginia psychologist you are! I leave this hanging in a vacuum, because though it arose from reading your last letter, the connections are broken.

1. He was briefly engaged to Judith Stephen, but she broke off the engagement to marry Nigel Henderson.
2. On this day Hitler proclaimed that Poland must surrender Danzig to Germany, but before the Poles had time to reply, Hitler launched his planned invasion of Poland on 1 September. Britain declared war two days later.

In fact thats the sum of the situation—here we are on a small sunny island—outside wastes of gloom and dark. I peg away at Roger Fry: L. arranges the now complete muddle of a Press, where no one will call to fetch books—all vans commandeered: and a flat entirely blocked with unpacked furniture—again, no vans to send unpackers. So there's enough, let alone transporting clerks here if war comes to engage all his magnificent powers.

And in betweeen times I read—what? A mixture of Gide, Pascal and the latest biography.

Thoughts of Ethel curl, like flames from an invisible fire, round corners. And now and then I walk off, miles away, into the downs, find a deserted farm wall, and lie among the thistles and the straw.

Thats about all I can put together of our state. Should you ever connect pen and paper, well you might remember me. But all's so dislocated, I cant hope it—nobody answers letters—everything hangs fire.

V.

We go up to tackle the flat problem [at Mecklenburgh Square] on Thursday.

Berg

3548: To V. Sackville-West   *Monk's House, Rodmell,*
near Lewes, Sussex
Tuesday 29th Aug. [1939]

Well, there's another day of peace—I mean we've just listened in to the P.M. I suppose Harold came back [from the House of Commons], so you didn't come [to Rodmell].

I cant help letting hope break in,—the other prospect is too mad.

But I dont think I'm philosophic[1]—rather, numbed. Its so hot and sunny on our little island—L. gardening, playing bowls, cooking our dinner: and outside such a waste of gloom. Of course I'm not in the least patriotic, which may be a help, and not afraid, I mean for my own body. But thats an old body. And all the same I should like another ten years: and I like my friends: and I like the young. That'll all go forever if—Meanwhile, not a van will come to unpack furniture or remove books at 37: all's held up: publishing and moving blocked. We go up on Thursday to see whats to be done.

Otherwise come at any time, and indeed, my dearest creature, whatever

1. Comparing her own reactions to the approaching war with Virginia's, Vita had written: "I think you are much braver than I am; or should I call it more philosophical?" (25 August 1939, *Berg*).

rung I'm on, the ladder is a great comfort in this kind of intolerable suspension of all reality—something real.

But isn't it odd?—one cant fold it in any words.

V.

Berg

3549: To V. Sackville-West   [*Monk's House, Rodmell, Sussex*]

[2 September 1939]

Yes, dearest Creature, come at any moment you like and share our pot. Alone today and what a mercy!

I did like your letter. And if I'm dumb and chill, it doesn't mean I dont always keep thinking of you—one of the very few constant presences is your's, and so—well no more. Yes, I sit in a dumb rage, being fought for by these children whom one wants to see making love to each other.

So come: and I'll write to you, if to no one else, when ever I've a moment free.

dearest creature, how I go on seeing you, tormented.

V.

Berg

Letters 3550-3577 (September–December 1939)

At the start of the war 37 Mecklenburgh Square was uninhabitable, and the Woolfs, having chanced upon the worst possible moment for moving house, were still sorting out their possessions when they spent their first nights there in mid-October. They had decided to stay most of the time at Monk's House, making only occasional visits to London, and were still able to entertain their friends in the country, among them Eliot, Plomer, Edward Sackville West and John Lehmann. Members of the staff of the Hogarth Press began coming there in rotation as a relief from the increasing inconveniences of life in the city. Virginia was now approaching the end of her revision of Roger Fry, made more difficult by new material which kept pouring in, and accepted several offers of journalistic work. The war entered a temporarily inactive phase after Hitler's conquest of Poland, and there were rumours of peace-moves which came to nothing.

3550: To RAYMOND MORTIMER

37 Mecklenburgh Square [W.C.1]

Typewritten

Thursday [7 September 1939]

Dear Raymond,

Many thanks for your letter. I've an idea or two at the back of my mind for a possible article—perhaps Gilbert White into whom I've plunged by way of a respite, or theres an obscure autobiography that I unearthed in the local library—theres an account of a party at Abbotsford that might be made amusing.[1] Shall I try these first; and if they dont work, then I'll ask you for Gray, but dont keep him if you want him done. About 1500 words I suppose. Is there any special date you have in mind? I'm horribly rusty, and distracted, so you must be severe and reject.

1. As Literary Editor of the *New Statesman & Nation*, Raymond Mortimer had asked Virginia for contributions. She sent him *White's Selborne*, an essay about Gilbert White (1720-1793) and his famous book *The Natural History and Antiquities of Selborne* (*New Statesman*, 30 September 1939); and later *Gas at Abbotsford*, based on an episode from *Sir Walter Scott's Journal*, Vol. I, ed. by J. G. Tait (*New Statesman*, 27 January 1940).

I'm so glad you think of trying a weekly article on old books. That would be a relief. And it would be fun now and then to re-read a classic. Like you, I've been steeped for months in memoirs—but French.

We're up for the day, unpacking furniture here; but its still uninhabitable. So excuse this relic of paper, and general mess. The war caught us on the move.

I hope we may meet. You won't be giving up the N.S. will you?

Yours ever

no pen, so I must type, Virginia Woolf

King's

3551: To V. Sackville-West

Monk's House, Rodmell, near Lewes, Sussex

8th Sept [1939]

Isn't it difficult to write letters? D'you feel it? Id like to know what you feel. Every now and then one seems completely cut off. Not in the body. That is, there's an incessant bother of small arrangements—2 Hogarth Press clerks [Mrs Nicholls and Miss Perkins] to put up; mattresses to buy, curtains to make; the village swarming with pregnant women and cottages without a chair or table to furnish out of scraps from the attic. So why does one feel inert, oppressed with solitude? Partly I suppose that one cant work. At least today I wrote ten sentences of Roger, but each word was like carrying a coal scuttle to the top of the house. Yesterday we were in London—seeing Stephen Spender, seeing John, laying carpets, half listening for the siren. I think I boasted too soon about not being afraid physically Anyhow I was glad when we were out on the road home again.

Oh yes, what you said about Julian was what's been on my mind all the time.[1] I must be naturally dense. At least, it took his death to make me—oh its no use trying to say how one goes on glooming. Mercifully, Quentin has been rejected by the Territorials—his old tuberculosis; and now has been given a job on the farm by Maynard.

This has been interrupted; and its not worth sending, save as Potto's kind of scratch at your door. Its broiling hot: I've been walking by the river, and came on 6 cygnets paddling in the brooks.

1. On 1 September Vita had written: "I keep thinking of Quentin as a young man and Julian already gone. Perhaps she [Vanessa] will now not feel so bitter about Julian's lost life because he did at least sacrifice it voluntarily for a cause he believed in, which is nobler than being conscripted against his will into a general holocaust" (*Berg*).

The week ends we have the clerks down; and so have so far escaped the women and children of Bermondsey.[1] Have you?

Yr. V.

13th Sept This got put away: and isnt worth sending save to draw an answer perhaps from you

Berg

3552: To Ethel Smyth

Monk's House, Rodmell,
near Lewes, Sussex

12th or 13th [September 1939]

Well Ethel, I know its quite impossible to write. At the same time I have a great wish to be written to. And I'm not going to tell you all the worries and bothers: the expectant mothers, curtain making, entertaining refugees—for the less we talk of these things and the more we talk of Plato and Shakespeare the better.

But can you read? Isnt it like being knocked on the head? I struggle out to my room, and cant believe I was ever writing a life of Roger Fry, or shall ever finish it. Then I try a story—no go. So to read Greek[2] with a crib. Happily, we have to arrange our horrid London muddle—electricians and movers and clerks: and shall we or shant we try to bring out our books? Its really a mercy to have a bone to gnaw. I didn't much like London though I admit. So silent, so hot, so brooding. And to think we've taken a 10 years lease of that mansion!

I rather suspect you have a method of your own for living out this kind of horror. My only relief is that Quentin is employed safely driving a tractor—rejected by the army. Its hard work talking to clerks. Thats been the only work I've done since last week. But you see my little tap already dries up.

I suppose Sussex is off, your visit I mean. We stay here till October anyhow: then I suppose London. Next letter I shall write about Plato and Shakespeare. So if you can move a pen, do try—I dont mean write to me about Racine or Montaigne—but about anything.

Excuse dulness—

Yr V.

Berg

1. The government had evacuated children from London, but many of them were homesick and returned to London after a few days.
2. The *Ethical Characters* of Theophrastus.

358

Monk's House, Rodmell,
near Lewes, Sussex

Tuesday 26th [September 1939]

Yes it was angelic of you to write. And I would have answered—but since Sept 1st this house has been a refugee haunt—always a clerk from the Press, or some fugitive, and God knows, though I've no cause to complain, since we escaped 3 East end children, visitors fritter one's day to shreds. The last went this morning. So until raids begin we shall be alone—save for raids from neighbours. We're exposed to neighbours. Thank God though I've made my head work in the mornings, and so am more or less calm. But no reading. All talk. Some of the clerks turned out magnificent. One a publicans daughter, another a greengrocers, a third a photographers, a fourth a sheer adventuress with a fatherless, I mean Bastard child, for whom all her concern was. Then we dashed to London, decided to go on publishing, brought out all our books yesterday—L's 2nd volume: a masterly work.[1] Pray God some one will buy it But the confusion in the trade is confounded—no one buys in shops, no bagmen. And so ruin stares us in the face; and I begin to be stingy. I'm seeing Vita tomorrow. Both the boys [Ben and Nigel] are in the army, and Harold in London. I'm sorry— oh dear how sorry, for I know what waiting about means. The garden is (now—6 o'clock) so ravishing I cant keep eye to paper. A great ash tree fell on a sunny evening. L. is now hatching it into fire wood for our winter evening. Plans are unsettled. Here till the 15th anyhow; and dashes up to see if 37 [Mecklenburgh Square] can be made habitable.

Why you old wretch—how I laughed at the love over the garden wall, and yet was jealous.[2] So you see there's green fire in me if not red. And I've taken to article writing too; and would like to see yours.[3] Now I must use my first free evening to do Fry papers.

V.

Berg

---

1. *After the Deluge: a Study of Communal Psychology*, Vol. II.
2. Ethel was still falling in love. In her letter to Virginia of 22 September she had described two new loves, one a 35-year-old American woman she met in Ireland, and the other a next door neighbour of 81: "She was to me a new type and has shown me you need not give up the ghost because you're over 80. But to be truthful I never thought you need, though one must always be prepared—and I am—for it!" (*Berg*).
3. Ethel's article was *England's Effort* (*Good Housekeeping*, October 1939).

Monk's House, Rodmell,
Lewes, Sussex

Typewritten
29th Sept 39

Dear Pip,[1]

I liked your letter so much that I kept writing to answer it until I had a free moment. Ever since the war we've been infested with refugees. And you know how they fill the place with odds and ends and how one has to ring up the butcher the baker the candlestick maker at all hours of the day and night. Ours were clerks from the Hogarth Press. At last they've gone— so I have a free moment.

I'm purring all over like an old Siamese cat to think that you liked some of my books. I rather suspected that you thought I was a complete fraud and that your mistresses were even greater nincompoops than you otherwise suspected for reading them and wanting to know whether poor Aunt Virginia smokes cigars or has a bald head. In fact most admirers are only fit for the infant school But then you're sensible; I dont know though that I agree with you. Must a book have a special meaning? Three Guineas was a pamphlet to make people angry and say irritating things. The Waves was written with no wish except to make something solid. But it was much harder to write than the others. I dont much like the Years; but thats not because its about disagreeable people; its because its too long, and too minute and I got sick to death of it; and took Leonards garden scissors and cut out patches and flung them on the bonfire.

I'm glad you liked Douarnenez.[2] It reminded me of Greece because there were trees growing by the sea; and no villas; and quite clean grass. When we were there the trippers hadnt come; in fact we thought it was a deserted island. Did you do any more painting? Or were you a snob, and determined not to look like one of the lady artists in your brilliant sketch? Do go on painting; because when you're very old you'll be happy if you do; and if you take to curing foot and mouth, you'll be left alone with an old sheep somewhere and will infuriate your neighbours by breeding dogs.[3] My neighbours enrage me by breeding Elk Hounds which bark just when I want to write.

What did you think of Brave New World? I much much much prefer

1. Philippa Woolf (then aged 15) was the first child of Leonard's younger brother Philip (1889-1962) and his wife Marjorie (*née* Lowndes). She married Maurice Hardman in 1951.
2. On the coast of Brittany between Quimper and Brest, where Philippa was staying with her family. Virginia had been there in June of this year.
3. At this stage of her life Philippa intended to become a veterinarian (to the despair of her parents, who hoped that she would be a painter). In fact she became a doctor.

War and Peace. But then Aldous Huxley has one blind eye; and he's stuffed with valuable facts; and has taken up Indian mystics; and all that seems to be a bore. But War and Peace is the greatest novel in the world; and if I'm not bombed I shall read that and Anna Karenina this winter.

Our new flat is a mere stickleback of chairs and tables on end. Will you come and see it soon? We shall try and sleep there in a fortnight. Only Leonard says he's coming back here, because he likes his fish better than his friends. And everybody quarrels; and if you go out at night, a man sticks a knife in you. They say London is like a dark drain with a few blind fish, and sharks, and only the blind can see. I've typed this so as to save your eyes, my hand being all gone to pieces.

Please write again if you've ever time. And give my love to all your mistresses too, but more seriously to Cecil, to Marie, and to your father and mother. Would you tell Philip I smoked his Rothschild cigar for about three hours; and enjoyed every single second.[1]

Oh dear, here are some more refugees so I must rush into the house and tidy

Yours affectionate

Sussex (copy)

3555: To Angelica Bell

Monk's House, Rodmell, Lewes, Sussex

1st Oct [1939]

Dearest Pixy,

Here is the cheque. Now I want to consider the future. I'm afraid its possible that I may have to send you less. Leonard says we shall be a good deal poorer, owing to taxes, not having let 52, the Press not paying etc. But of course we cant tell yet. What I'll do is to pay you next quarter for certain. Then we'll reconsider it. Anyhow, even if its less, I'll always pay something, unless bankrupt: and consider you come first after paying household bills. Only as I said I would give you six months warning I thought I'd better write now. What a damnable curse the war is.

We thought Judith's man [Leslie Humphreys] rather a bore—nice but dull: and wont be so nice in ten years and duller, and nothing to look at and very middle class Tunbridge Wells, so what does she see? And he makes her schoolgirlish. Oh dear.

V.

Texas

1. Cecil and Marie were Philippa's brother and sister. Her father Philip was the manager of the Rothschild estate at Waddesdon Manor, Buckinghamshire.

361

3556: To Ethel Smyth   *Monks House, Rodmell*
                                         [Sussex]
Monday, 9th Oct [1939]

Ahhah! This has never happened before—that I can truthfully say, I am writing out of the goodness of my heart, without being written to. Yet so it is. Cupid I suppose has shot his dart over the garden wall[1] and transfixed your pen. I am jealous, furiously: And have nothing to lure you back with. Am damp and dull. Am working like a nigger. Shall be in London but shant see you. (I leave out the "I's' in order to impress you with a sense of importance) There's a peace in the country which surrounds me as a mouse is surrounded with cheese. Nothing but the sound of my nibbling is to be heard. Reading writing I'm always at it.

As for Ethel Smyth, she's languishing in the violets and lavenders of lust: I suppose; gratifying the flesh. I may have gone too far. If so, I withdraw. Are you, then, more chastely, finishing your book [*What Happened Next*]? And when shall I read it? I daresay we both think the same about politics. I am reading Erasmus. I am reading Lewis Carroll.[2] Oh and I saw Vita—One never has a moment to oneself in the country. Yet the country is a vast Cheddar cheese. Oh how it rains and rains! Leonard is storing apples. No, we cant play bowls. And I have to cook a rice dish mixed with herbs for dinner

                                                            V.
Berg

3557: To Sibyl Colefax   *Monk's House [Rodmell,*
                                         Sussex]
11 Oct. [1939]

Dearest Sibyl,

I too often thought of you, but always with an impassable barrier. House-moving; war. Two days before the war 52 Tavistock started to move to 37 Mecklenburgh. It's still on the way.

We go up on Friday. How long we stay we don't know. But perhaps we might meet— Only how can one make engagements? All's such a distracted muddle.

But if not there, then here.

Oh and thank you for your letter. Yes, I find the copulation of 18th century frogs [Frenchmen] the only reality, anyhow comfort.

                                                            Yrs V.W.
Michael Colefax

1. See p. 359, note 2.
2. Virginia wrote a review of *The Complete Works of Lewis Carroll* for the *New Statesman*, 9 December 1939.

3558: To A. G. Sayers   *Monk's House, Rodmell,*
                                         Lewes, Sussex
11 Oct 39

Dear Mr Sayers,[1]

I have opened the book;[2] and I like some of the poems very much. Your son seems to get at things for himself; and so, in the midst of our present chaos, I find him refreshing and shall read on—thank you for sending it to me.

Three Guineas did very well, so far as sales went. Whether it made any impression, I don't know. I doubt that ideas ever do. But at least I haven't been sent to prison—rather, on the contrary, to Coventry.

Please express my gratitude to your son, and hope that he won't be darkened by the war. We, as publishers, are hoping that people must read; and so there must be writers. I'm interested to see that he dedicates his book to E. M. Forster, an old friend of mine.

                                         Yours sincerely
                                         Virginia Woolf

A. M. Sayers

3559: To Angelica Bell   [37 *Mecklenburgh Square, W.C.*1]
Monday [16 October 1939]

Dearest Pixie,

You cant think how difficult it is to write a letter in this doomed and devastated but at the same time morbidly fascinating town. Also there's a dearth of pens and a prevalence, indeed a pullulation of chamber pots. Oh and the books: all over the floor: oh and the pictures: all on their heads. Oh oh oh . . .

But to business, or I shant earn my living. My hook is baited with so much gossip it might catch a whale: Nessa to wit. I mean we've been seeing Will and Ruth Arnold Forster: and went into the question, the painful question, of my legacy. The little devils, keeping Duncan's picture because he's bought a chair-cover to match; so gave me Ka's old garnet necklace: which rained garnets into the soup: broke at once. The filling in of that story, and the story of Ruth, of Rupert's letter, of George Mallory's death on Mount Everest would fill oh the whole of the telephone book.[3]

1. See Letter 3400.
2. *Poems of Twenty Years*, by A. M. Sayers, privately printed, 1939.
3. After Ka Arnold-Forster's death in 1938, her widower married Ruth, the widow of George Mallory, who was killed on Everest in 1924. Ka had been the intimate friend of Rupert Brooke, but the story of his letter is not now recoverable.

Then we lunched with Mrs Drake[1] to meet Mrs Webb: and she was like a dead leaf spotted with fire—so crinkled so curled but invincible in spite of bladder trouble and cancer by the sheer might of disinterested intelligence. Another vol. required. Her nephew at the War Office says there'll be a raid tonight: (so this is no doubt my dying word) and the War will be over by Xmas, because its a fact that the German army is already in disruption. Hitler's last fling will be at our heads tonight and tomorrow.

Then there's Stephen and John. And their deadly feud, in which L. and I are now involved.[2] I'll leave that till we meet. Then there's Tom [Eliot] tomorrow. Colefax threatens also—you dont know what a queer place London is—Here we are running in and out of each other's houses with torches and gas masks. Black night descends. Rain pours. Vast caterpillars are now excavating trenches in the Square. Shops shut at 5 or so. Many windows remain black all day. The streets are a hurry scurry of people walking. Ambulances abound. Very stout women wear blue trousers. No one ever sits down. The buses are quick but rare. And in short—I've just pulled down the black blinds—rats in caves live as we do.

Thats all I can think of. And I hope you're recovered; and that Charleston remains as sane and sound as ever.

V.

Bobo[3] was very nice, as sleek as a yellow cat, and is coming over. It was the grandest house I've been in for years. Maids in caps. Four courses.

Texas

3560: To Hugh Walpole   *Monk's House, Rodmell,*
                                          Lewes [Sussex]

Friday [20 October 1939][4]

My dear Hugh,

We were only up 3 days this time, and they were crammed full. And I hunted in vain among my litter of books still unsorted for my father's

1. Barbara, eldest daughter of Daniel Meinertzhagen, and a niece of Beatrice Webb. She lived with her husband Bernard Drake (1876-1941), a solicitor, at 15 Sheffield Terrace, Kensington.
2. Stephen Spender had joined the advisory committee of John Lehmann's *New Writing*, but now agreed to assist Cyril Connolly in the editing of the new journal, *Horizon*. Lehmann feared that these two roles might conflict, as the younger intellectuals might be drawn away to *Horizon* from *New Writing*.
3. Beatrice Mayor (1885-1971), who was a younger sister of Barbara Drake.
4. At a late proof-stage in the production of this volume, it was noticed that the date of this letter should be 19 April 1940.

MS. But my brother Adrian is sending one, direct to the Red Cross[1]—which MS I dont know. I've written the enclosed note, as you wish.

We come up every fortnight—the 30th will be the next time: let me either then or later come to tea, with you alone—for lunch is a horrid unsociable hour: and I want to see your things if I may.

Oh no—I'm not a novelist. Always wanted to name my books afresh.[2] This continues our correspondence. But no time now.

yrs VW

Texas

3561: To Mrs G. E. Easdale   *Monk's House, Rodmell,*
                                     Lewes, Sussex

25th Oct 39

Dear Mrs Easdale,

I never expected flowers this autumn, so they were all the more welcome. Let us hope they will outlast the war. They are making my sitting room very bright at the moment. As usual, they come just as the garden is settling in for the winter. We are spending most of our time down here; when we go up it is to struggle with the miseries of house moving under war conditions. I am afraid this is affecting the reviewers too. But I hope Joan isn't disappointed.[3] They will come in time; and we are selling more books than we expected.

Thank you once more for the flowers.

Yours sincerely
Virginia Woolf

University of London

3562: To Edward Sackville West   *Monk's House, Rodmell,*
                                  Lewes, Sussex

25th Oct 39

My dear Eddy,

It was nice of you to write to me about the Waves. Its the only one of my books that I can sometimes read with pleasure. Not that I wrote it with pleasure, but in a kind of trance into which I suppose I shall never sink

---

1. Hugh Walpole had been invited by the Lord Mayor of London to be Chairman of the Books and Manuscripts Committee, which was organising a sale of manuscripts on behalf of the Red Cross.
2. Virginia often reflected that her novels could better be termed 'elegies' or some other term to suggest that they were not traditional fiction.
3. The Hogarth Press had recently published Joan Easdale's poems *Amber Innocent*.

again. And a word of praise from a reader like you almost persuades me that I could get back to that world in spite of the war. As it is, I cling to Roger Fry and facts.

What are you doing?—writing I mean? Did the diary ever take shape?[1] I wish it would. I want some fragmentary but natural voice to break into the artificial bray to which we're condemned. And I believe its your form, and you could use it.

We're just back from a visit to London—an incoherent and rather terrifying visit—the flat half furnished, and all our friends jangling like so many strained wires. I would have tried to see you had I known you were up. Could you come down here some time? I rather think we shall stay here mostly: leaving London was rather like drawing the curtains and finding it a fine day. The old man who brings the milk is far better company than Kingsley Martin and that ilk. My only comfort lies in the obvious horror we all feel for war: but then with a solid block of unbaked barbarians in Germany, whats the good of our being comparatively civilised? So I read poor bewildered Gerald Heard[2] and turn from him to Dickens. But I must stop and attend to black out for a Labour party meeting. Thank you for writing.

yrs
V.W.

Berg

3563: To Ethel Smyth   *Monk's House, Rodmell,*
                                           near Lewes, Sussex
26th Oct. [1939]

As you'll have gathered from my wire, we came down here, after a ravaging but in its way rather absorbing week in London—So many people to see; and all the time the telephone failing, the oven ceasing to cook, and workmen in to ask "Where d'you want the light in the lavatory?" —The W.C. I always correct them in the interests of democracy. So I left your letter in London, and cant remember what precise question I was expected to answer about your article.[3] Was it whether you were parodying your own style? Well, I think my observation would be that, writing I suppose for your favourite Everyman, you dissipate your forces a little to the distraction of that eccentric individual V.W. I see the attraction—I

---

1. Edward Sackville West never published his diary.
2. His *Pain, Sex and Time: a New Hypothesis of Evolution*, 1939. Heard was one of the outstanding British intellectuals of his day, a writer on scientific and philosophical subjects. He and his close friend Aldous Huxley spent most of the war in the United States.
3. *England's Effort* (*Good Housekeeping*, October 1939).

cant imitate it—of the personal style—"my heads too large for my hat—
my puppy . . . my" this that or the other. And I envy you the abandon with
which you can toss all your private—no, I mean personal—trinkets at the
readers feet. But it a little blocks the road to the final grasp on the theme.
The hat obscures Englands effort. And, absorbed in the humours of the
omnibus,—well, I mean one flies off at a tangent; which in a short article,
leaves one too little to perch upon. But then, cut out Ethel, and the broth
would miss its savoury. So I should advise concentration rather than
elimination. I suspect that the amateur author feels the drag of the public
more than the old hack: hence this skittishness: hence also this charm. But
is that true?—Do you I mean feel when you write that the curtain rises
and the stage is lit? and so increase, unintentionally, your gesticulations?
Anyhow I enjoyed it: rare in an article: and here return it, with apologies
for the random nature of these remarks, which probably miss whatever the
mark was you wanted me to aim at. And what does Alba[1] say about the
situation?

V.

Berg

3564: To Dorothy Bussy   *Monk's House, Rodmell,*
                                          Lewes [Sussex]

Nov 5th 39

My dear Dorothy,
     This being Sunday morning and Tom Eliot and Leonard playing chess
over the fire, I've just said that I'm going to write letters. So why not to you,
specially as there's no need to write to you, and I ought to be writing oh
dear me so many dull letters. I'm going to pretend that its the 18th century,
as indeed it is in many ways: and one wrote long long letters to friends in
distant parts. Only you must keep up the game your end. And now I cant
think how one does it, and my handwriting isn't what theirs was.
     Where did we break off? I believe with Tom Eliot in Tavistock Square.
Now T. Sqre is a myth, and 37 Meck Sqre is neither one thing or the other,
by which I mean theres a chamber pot in the sitting room, and a bed in the
dining room. Still we have spent a week there in mediaeval gloom, which has
its glory, for the return of nature, that is darkness and trees instead of taxis
bowling to parties has its charms. You see a spark and suddenly an old gent
looms up: then he's gone, and the wind howls and the leaves drop. But I
cant go into the war and the rest of it. Is Nice in the war too?[2] I suppose so.

1. The Duke of Alba was the Spanish Ambassador to Great Britain, 1939-45. He
   had met Ethel through his aunt, the Empress Eugénie.
2. The Bussy's were still living in Roquebrune on the French Riviera.

And do you sit as we do here on a magic carpet about 6 foot square with a bright lamp and a book?

Yes it was the book, among other things, that brought you to mind—Gides journals. All the intelligentsia is reading them, and out of snobbery I followed, and found you there: and then re-read Si Le Grain ne meurt with amazement at the frankness.[1] Why, if he can say all that, cant I come out with the comparatively modest truth about Roger and his affairs? Yes, I find Gide very bracing and drastic, and a little stringent. So very French: and here we're so very plumpuddingy. Thats the only word for the wireless ... but no, I will not broach politics, unless I can rouse the chess players to tell me some fact you'd like to know.

As for gossip, we've seen a good many refugees of sorts—they flock out of London; and the young are very quarrelsome: Stephen Spender and Inez have parted; Rosamond has one foot on sea—Geronwy Rees[2]—t'other on shore—Wogan; a new magazine [Horizon] is being started; publishing is bad but struggles on;—what else? we're driving to Charleston in this whirling gale to lunch with Nessa. There we shall meet Desmond; and Clive has (well I must take another page, as the chess players wont answer) Clive has had his hair cut, and looks like a very fierce little red bull: Quentin drives a tractor for Maynard; and looks like the rising sun; Angelica undulates over the world like a pearl pink cloud: and Duncan, well I can only at the moment see Duncan for ever hitching up his trousers which are of blue corduroy and for ever coming down. Also he goes to London to sit on a Committee. Nessa has bought 30 hens, some turned out to be cocks, others half bred pheasants, so the egg question which they were to solve remains I think in the air: she says not. Mrs Grant and Miss Whats her name—Aunt Violet[3]—have gone; to everyone's relief, theirs too, for its no use waiting any longer for raids which dont come. The other morning I roused the house, because of two wasps in my jampot which I mistook for the warbling.

I'm reading Little Dorrit; I'm reading Erasmus; I'm reading Plato; I'm reading Gide; I'm reading William Rothenstein's memoirs. So there—Does that make you think the worse or the better of me, for thats the real question I want answered, my appetite for compliments being undiminished. And of course it maynt be a compliment.

So give Janie [her daughter] my love.

1. Virginia was reading André Gide's *Journal, 1885-1939* (1939) and *Si le grain ne meurt* (1926), in which he openly discusses his homosexuality.
2. Goronwy Rees (1909-79) the novelist, had been assistant editor of the *Spectator* in 1936. He became Principal of University College, Aberystwyth, Wales, 1953-7. Rosamond Lehmann, who was married to Wogan Philipps, was in love with Rees.
3. Violet McNeil, Mrs Grant's sister.

V. "I'm writing to Dorothy Bussy"
Tom Eliot. "Please send my love"
V. "Any political gossip?"
Dead silence. I think Toms beat.
So I must end.
If you would write, what a treat.

V.W.

By the way, Leonard and his co-editor Robson, say you wrote a most brilliant review for the Pol Quart.[1]

And please remember me to M. [Simon] Bussy.

George Spater

3565: To Elizabeth Robins   *Monk's House, Rodmell,*
                                         Lewes, Sussex

8th Nov. [1939]

Dear Miss Robins,
    I was just going to write to you, but I am glad to find from your letter that its useless. What I was going to say was that Faber & Faber were anxious to be allowed to read your MS [*Both Sides of the Curtain*]. I'm so glad that Heinemann's are doing it. It shows their sense; the other people— I forget who it was—seem to me stone blind for rejecting it.
    With our congratulations,

yours
Virginia Woolf

Sussex

3566: To The New Statesman & Nation

11 November 1939

Sir,
    Grateful as I am to Y.Y. for his courteous article on my pamphlet, *Reviewing*,[2] may I express my regret that in his anxiety to convict me of burying the reviewer alive, he has ignored the resurrection service that followed the obsequies? Had I been, as Y.Y. asserts "contemptuous" of the

1. In the *Political Quarterly* for October-December 1939, Dorothy Bussy reviewed *France and Munich* by Alexander Werth and *France* by Wladimir d'Ormesson.
2. Y.Y., the pseudonym of *The New Statesman* essayist, Robert Lynd, said in his review of Virginia's pamphlet in the issue of 4 November that her attitude towards reviewers ". . . was surely the most contemptuous yet uttered: she tells them that they have ceased to be of any use to the world".

louse—Dickens' word, not mine—I should not have devoted several pages to an attempt, however feeble, to preserve him. I am a louse myself, and well aware of it; but if, as I infer from Y.Y.'s eulogy, the rest of my colleagues are gay little crickets chirruping about the house to their own content, the public good and under conditions that would delight a sanitary inspector, I withdraw every word and keep both contempt and pity for myself. In the same issue of *The New Statesman & Nation*, however, I notice that Mr John Mair begins his review: "What is a reviewer to say when faced with a batch of thoroughly dull novels? The conscientious critics of the national press crowd infinite boredom in a single column, and briefly outline the plots of a dozen books, say 'brilliant', and pass on to the next. Another, less responsible school, abandon at once duty and discretion, and, like the beaver biting off his stones . . ."[1] But I must not crowd all the animals in the Zoo upon your limited space, nor try again to remedy what is, so obviously, a completely satisfactory state of things.

Virginia Woolf

3567: To Mr Sutcliffe

Monk's House, Rodmell,
Lewes, Sussex

Typewritten
16th Nov 39

Dear Mr Sutcliffe [*unidentified*],

Many thanks for your letter and apologies for my delay in answering it. I know of course that I was only able to raise questions in my pamphlet, not to answer them satisfactorily. The whole question of reviewing is extremely complex. To touch on one or two points—I agree that we must have some way of knowing what is published. The T.L.S. supplies this admirably in its shorter notices. I find that I order books from the library from that rather than from reviews. But then I suggested that this should be kept for the reader. The "private conference" was for the benefit of the writer.[2] At present they have no way of discussing their work with competent people. I am aware of this from the number of requests for criticism that come to our office. They also insist (as authors) upon advertisements, which are largely wasted—or again, so it seems. I believe with you that a monthly or quarterly is the only way of keeping criticism alive; but then it seems to mean starvation both for those who write it and for the publishers. All this seems to prove that it is time the problem were discussed and, if possible,

---

1. John Mair reviewed, collectively, five new but insignificant novels.
2. In *Reviewing* Virginia had suggested that in place of the present system, an author might meet privately with an informed critic for an hour's consultation about his book.

without loss of temper. As I expected, my remarks have raised more anger than helpful criticism. I am the more grateful to you for taking the question seriously. There is so much talk of the value of freedom at the moment that it seems a good thing to put it into practice, or at least to try.

Yours sincerely
Virginia Woolf

Robert H. Taylor

3568: To Vincent Sheean   *Monk's House, Rodmell,*
Lewes, Sussex

Typewritten
23rd Nov. 1939

Dear Mr Sheehan,[1]

I need not say that I sympathise with the aims of the League of American Writers. I am very sorry that I cannot help by sending a manuscript as you suggest; but I seldom keep MSS. and those that I have, as I always re-type, are only a few notes, and thus of no interest.

But my brother and I should be very glad to give a MS of my father's, Sir Leslie Stephen, if you would care to have it. Should you wish it sent, will you write to my brother, Dr Adrian Stephen, 26 York Gate, Regents Park, London NW1.

Yours sincerely
Virginia Woolf

Houghton Library, Harvard University

3569: To Shena, Lady Simon   *Monk's House, Rodmell,*
Lewes, Sussex

30th Nov. [1939]

My dear Shena,

Yes, as it happens I'm in London next Tuesday. Do come if its not too dark, at 4.30. We are at 37 Mecklenburgh Square. Not far from Kings Cross station—5 minutes down the Grays Inn Road.

3 Gs still making enemies, anyhow. As an Outsider I've been attacking my profession [in *Reviewing*]—all reviewers have their knives in me. This suggests your disagreeable duty—to become Principal of Newnham. No time to explain these remarks, so I must leave them for Tuesday.

Yrs
VW

Sussex

1. James Vincent ('Jimmy') Sheean (b. 1899) was an American journalist and novelist who achieved great popularity in English society.

Monk's House, Rodmell,
Lewes [Sussex]

Typewritten
2nd Dec 39

Dear Judith,

I'm glad you've been reading Julian's book—how odd that you didn't come across it before. No, I suppose not; few people have read it. Its a great muddle I think—so many things he wrote in a hurry or left unfinished. But it's very like him. And I wish too you'd known him. I don't think he had worked out a system—in fact he was always changing. This was part of his charm. And he was young for his age, and full with theories and ideas. They make rather a whirlpool of his essay on Roger. It goes round and round, but it's very vivid, and Julian was a magnificent creature. What would he have done, I wonder? He had such an immense store of life in him, and God knows why he went and threw it away. But I daresay it was better in Spain than in Flanders.

What sort of creed are you coming to? As far as I remember, 21 was a devillish age; so intense; and so violently crabwise—this way, that way, and as you say back as much as forward. But it was amazingly exciting too. Never shall I forget arguing with Thoby [Stephen], Lytton, even old Saxon [Sydney-Turner], hour after hour about good and truth, and one's personal emotions as we called them.

I was asked to lecture the Cambridge English Soc. too, but really I've so often said lectures are damned things; also that no woman should give tongue in Camb. until Camb. has done its duty and made them members of the University—but what's the use of protesting? With this war on. However I'm more and more convinced that it is our duty to catch Hitler in his home haunts and prod him if even with only the end of an old inky pen.

I saw Adrian and Karin at 37 [Mecklenburgh Square] the other day; we had a turkey; and a gossip. And they thought they had found a tenant. But Karin seemed very dismal, and says she can't work. That's an awful state to be in. However, there's news of a possible family legacy, via Jack Hills, via Stella.[1] (I wish you'd known her too). But if it is a legacy, that'll be a very timely help in present troubles.

I will note your needs about the house. I think May or June will be the time for looking, as you only wanted a short lease. And if there are houses standing, I daresay one will be haddable. It's the dear time, though, July, August. Yes, you must get it, and be near enough to us to come over and do your duty by the old.

1. After Stella Duckworth's death in 1897, her widower Jack Hills gave to Stella's half-sisters, Virginia and Vanessa, the income from her marriage settlement. He continued these payments until his second marriage in 1931, and on his death in 1938, bequeathed the capital sum equally between Virginia, Vanessa and Adrian.

Here's Nessa, Duncan and Clive coming for a Sunday tea. Only bread and butter. It's raining too, and L. has just beat me on the sodden grass at bowls. So you see we keep the flag of culture flying. Write again and tell me about your future, and if it's settled or come undone. Ann [Judith's sister] has become to my delight a fertile letter writer. Perhaps we may all meet at Christmas.

VW

Nigel Henderson

3571: To V. Sackville-West   *Monk's House, Rodmell,*
                                     near Lewes, Sussex

Dec. 3rd [1939]

That was nice of you—to send me your book.[1] It really touched me. I've not read it (and I dont suppose you'd care a damn to know what I thought, if I thought about it considered as a work of art—or would you?)— but I dipped in and read about Saulieu [Burgundy] and the fair and the green glass bottle. The pictures are lovely; but oughtn't they to be a little sharper? Weren't they when we saw them that day in the office? (that reminds me: I owe you 1/2 for cigarettes). I shall keep it by my bed, and when I wake in the night—no, I shant use it as a soporific, but as a sedative: a dose of sanity and sheep dog in this scratching, clawing, and colding universe. The war makes one horribly bad tempered. Against that I set the country: no, I dont think I shall ever live in London again. Yesterday I saw a cormorant and a kingfisher together on the river in a storm and today I've been battling against the wind to the top of the downs, where there's a hollow— a windwarm hollow, as the poet, but which?—says.[2]

One day we were in Tunbridge Wells. travelling books Shall we meet there, before Christmas?

Tomorrow we have to go to London for 2 nights, and I have to give old Ethel lunch. So imagine me shouting while the ear trumpet dangles down her back.

1. *Country Notes*, 1939, a selection of Vita's articles on country matters, including an account of the journey she made through Burgundy with Virginia in 1928.
2. Perhaps a reference to *The Passing of Arthur* (from *Idylls of the King*), by Tennyson:

> "I am going a long way
> . . . . .
> Where falls not hail, or rain, or any snow,
> Nor ever wind blows loudly; but it lies
> Deep-meadow'd, happy, fair with orchard lawns
> And bowery hollows crown'd with summer sea,
> Where I will heal me of my grievous wound."

Dear me, I'm so tired of correcting Roger, and its so bad. But then how can one make a life out of Six Cardboard boxes full of tailor's bills love letters and old picture postcards?

With our deep love and respects

Potto and V.

Oh Eddie [Sackville West] came for a week end and was charming: so brisk and pointed, not a word of complaint—indeed very considerate and kind:

Berg

3572: To Philippa Strachey   *Monk's House, Rodmell,*
                                                Lewes, Sussex
[11 December 1939]

Dear Pippa,

Leonard says you said you would come and spend a weekend. Would you come this next weekend, 16th, or would you come for Christmas— Saturday to Tuesday? Remember, life here is primitive: very; but it would be very nice for us to have you. So if you will brave it do: and let me know: and then I'll look up trains. They're not so bad—trains: anyhow one good one still.

Yr aff
Virginia

The Fawcett Library, London

3573: To Stephen Spender   *Monks House, Rodmell,*
                                              Lewes, Sussex
Typewritten
Dec 16th 39

Dear Stephen,

Thanks very much for your letter. Leonard says he will answer his share of it himself. For my part, I think its very nice of you to want me to write for Horizon. But as you will understand, New Writing Folios, or whatever the new version is to be called, does make it rather difficult for me. Its not a question of hurting John's feelings,[1] but as its to be a Hogarth Press venture and as I'm taking a kind of sub-editorial part, I feel I must give them any help I can. The truth is I dont much want to do articles for anybody. As for doing one on "The Young"—well, I've already set all the reviewers against me by my pamphlet, and I dont want to set all the young

1. See p. 364, note 2.

against me too (more than they are necessarily and rightly). Is there any use in contemporaries writing about contemporaries—even if some are older and some younger? I can't see it; but if you can, come and explain it. That brings me to the point. We shall be up on Monday. Will you come in on Tuesday night, any time after 9.30. The St John Hutchinsons are dining with us, it would be very nice to see you again. I'm sorry your difference with John hasnt been made up. I've not seen him for some time to talk to, and so dont know what the state of things is. But it seems a pity.

Yours affectionately
Virginia Woolf

Drew Ponder-Greene

3574: To Shena, Lady Simon   *Monk's House, Rodmell,*
Lewes [Sussex]

16th Dec [1939]

My dear Shena,

I ought to have answered you before. I dont want to put any extra burden on you, but if you would some time write down any views you've come to about women and war I'm sure it would be a great help to me. I've promised to write something for America,[1] and the view of someone who moves and acts like yourself would prevent me from, what is a great danger now, living in the country—I mean becoming angular and eccentric. Its an appallingly difficult job anyhow. I'm encouraged, (I daresay my author's vanity is flattered, speaking more honestly) by two letters today, one from a soldier in the trenches who says he's read Three Guineas and "feels that its true;" and is apparently so "unspeakably bored" that he'll tackle any more views on the same lines: and another from a middle class provincial lady, who asks distractedly for help, and wants to start an outsiders Society among the women of Yeovil [Somerset]. She's shocked to find them all in uniform, greedy for honour and office.

And then America—I've never been there—How far are our problems theirs? You see, I'm going to sponge upon you, because all your doings, one way and another, have filled your sponge so much fuller than mine. So don't curse me—not even for scribbling this, half asleep, and ought to be cooking dinner, over a large log fire. It was very good of you to come through all that black the other night and I wish we'd had more time for talk.

Yrs ever
V.W.

Sussex

1. Virginia was contemplating an article for *Forum*, the American monthly review, but she never completed it.

3575: To Ethel Smyth   *Monks House, Rodmell,*
                                              Lewes, Sussex
22nd Dec 39

No, I never begin a letter Dearest Ethel, as my pen intended. And have been dashing about London so violently, and oh dear correcting MSS. so incessantly, that I never could sit down to write. Allow for the intermittency of the pen, and don't blame 'em on the heart. Maynard sayd he's cured by Plesch—are you? The last visit (yours to me) was broken off, if you remember, to visit him—Plesch I mean. Oh and I wanted to throw my cap over the rooster by way of shouting Hurrah to your Finis [of *What Happened Next*]. Isn't that a triumph—the last word, no matter what agony and drudgery have gone before. Never have I written it save with tears and sweat. Now when shall I read the whole? and shall I exalt it to the shelf where, to solace and support sleepless nights (I mean starts of terrified about nothing waking when even the stars through the apple trees mock and diminish)—the shelf where I keep Imps?[1] Yes, I expect so. And little though I shall carry across the Styx to justify my life here, that one bright deed shall shine like a medal, or a wound, to show that I, Virginia, kept Ethel at it. For, though you dont humour me much, you must admit that. Thank God, we're out of London, and in front of a fire, alone, this frosty night Your gibe about Eddy Sackville [West] and his week end fails to score. Did I ask him? No. He leapt at a vague hint and pinned me down. I never "ask" anyone. Sometimes very persistent people I've quarrelled with and half made it up with, like Eddy say Lets forget and be friends, But I shall be more sociable once I'm out of the wood, and have a resident maid perhaps, so that I neednt cook dinner and cut long arguments. to boil potatoes and bake pies. Oh yes, the waits are singing [carols], and so I wish you peace, virtue and love me another year or two.

                                                             V.

Berg

3576: To William Plomer   *Monk's House, Rodmell,*
                                              Lewes, Sussex
28th Dec 39

Dear William,

This is the only sincere letter of thanks I've written this Christmas, because your present was the only one that gave (and gives—its by no means finished yet) complete satisfaction: I didn't know chocolates like that still existed. My Grandfather[2]—an old man with a white head like the

1. Ethel's *Impressions that Remained*, 2 vols., 1919.
2. Her mother's father, John Jackson, who died when Virginia was five years old.

376

shavings people put in fireplaces in summer—used to give us them. So now I look upon you as a kind of re-incarnation of all goodness. It was, we both say, much too good of you. Yes—about the young men. We had them to tea. I thought it pretty sticky myself. John was haughty; Stephen suppliant. Leonard says it was a success, though. All this gossip we must have by word of mouth. We shall be coming up, and I'll write. This is only thanking you; and wishing you'd spent Christmas here. And what about Kilvert?[1] Vol. 3?

V.W.

Texas

3577: TO ANGELICA BELL

Monk's House, Rodmell,
Lewes, Sussex

Sunday 31st Dec [1939]

Dearest Pixy,

Here is the £25.

About the future—I'm afraid while the war lasts, I'd better be on the safe side and say I'll give £60 a year. The thing is I cant at the moment make money in America, and my life of Roger wont I'm afraid pay at all. But the moment the war is over, I'll reconsider it; and I may have a stroke of luck—in which case you shall benefit.

So forgive me my stinginess and apply at once to me if you're ever in a fix.

Witcherina Virginia

Texas

1. The 19th century country parson, Francis Kilvert, whose *Diary* Plomer edited in three volumes, 1938-40.

Letters 3578-3603 (January–April 1940)

During the cold and inactive winter of 1940 Virginia and Leonard remained at Monk's House, paying only a few visits to London. They scarcely used their new flat in Mecklenburgh Square. Until May, Virginia seldom mentioned the war in her correspondence, not even the German invasion of Norway in April. In spite of a prolonged attack of influenza in March, she was able to concentrate on the final typescript, and then the proofs, of Roger Fry. Vanessa and Margery Fry approved it, but Leonard was openly critical of its biographical method, which Virginia did not seem particularly to mind. On 27 April she gave a lecture to the Workers Educational Association at Brighton, The Leaning Tower, one of her few recent criticisms of contemporary writing.

3578: To Vera Brittain   *Monk's House, Rodmell,*
                                          Lewes, Sussex
2nd Jan. 1940

Dear Vera Brittain,

It was very good of you to send me your book.[1] I waited to thank you until I had read it. And now that I have read it I feel that, thanks to you, I know her much better than I did before. I was puzzled by something about her when we met—I think I only saw her two or three times. I felt that she was oddly uncertain about something important—perhaps you'll understand. I think I see now what it was. And having never read her books because I felt this, I'm now going to. I am very grateful to you for giving me this fresh insight. Its so seldom that a biography does that, but yours does. More than ever it makes me feel, as I did when I read a book of her letters,[2] that she was only at the beginning of a life that held all sorts of possibilities not for her only but for the rest of us.

Thank you again.

Yours sincerely
Virginia Woolf

Sussex (copy)

1. *Testament of Friendship*, 1940, a tribute to Winifred Holtby (1898-1935), the Yorkshire-born novelist, and author of one of the earliest studies of Virginia's work (*Virginia Woolf*, 1932). Vera Brittain (d. 1970) was also a novelist and the author of *Lady into Woman* (1954), a history of women.
2. Holtby's *Letters to a Friend*, edited by Alice Holtby and Jean McWilliam, 1937. The 'friend', who is addressed as 'Rosalind', was in fact Jean McWilliam.

16th Jan. [1940]

I'm sorry I didn't answer your question, and the second letter has gone round by M.H.: so thats why I'm late.

L. says that though the price of novels is being raised, this so far has made no difference to the author's royalties. Certainly you ought not to get less: indeed probably authors may in time demand more. So stick to what you had for the last—We're up for the usual 4 hectic days, and very cold, but not quite so cold as the country.

Are you trying Holtby? Well I said I would—South Riding[1] I mean; and will borrow your copy perhaps one of these days. But, tho' I wrote Vera [Brittain] a polite letter, I didn't somehow enjoy or wholly like her Life: too petty and that horrid little reviewer's gossip; she had a good deal more to her than V.B. saw, and was no more a writer (to my mind) than a barrel organ is a string quartet. But it was a scrambling gasping affectionate book: and W.H deserved a better.

Now Hugh Walpole is on me; so I must—but I break off to say I'm agog for your book.

Back to M.H. on Friday.

V.

Berg

3580: To SHENA, LADY SIMON   *Monk's House, Rodmell,*
                              Lewes, Sussex

Jan 22nd [1940]

My dear Shena,

I've had too many distractions to write—people staying here, London and so on. But not too many to read your paper. I find it useful, suggestive, and sound. I agree with most of your arguments. I wish we could meet and discuss them. What the Americans want of me is views on peace. Well, these spring from views on war. So I shall work on from your paper when the time comes.[2] Meanwhile, do cast your mind further that way: about sharing life after the war: about pooling men's and women's work: about the possibility, if disarmament comes, of removing men's disabilities. Can one change sex characteristics? How far is the women's movement a remarkable experiment in that transformation? Mustn't our next task be the emancipation of man? How can we alter the crest and the spur of the fighting cock? Thats the one hope in this war: his soberer hues, and the unreality, (so I

1. Winifred Holtby's best-known novel, 1935.
2. See Letter 3574. Virginia wrote nothing more for America until *Thoughts on Peace in an Air Raid* (*New Republic*, 21 October 1940).

feel and I think he feels) of glory. No talk of white feathers anyhow; and the dulness comes through the gilt much more than last time. So it looks as if sexes can adapt themselves: and here (thats our work) we can, or the young women can, bring immense influence to bear. So many of the young men, could they get prestige and admiration, would give up glory and develop whats now so stunted—I mean the life of natural happiness.

Excuse this scribble: pipes are bursting; a pool in the kitchen. All I mean is I am very grateful for your thinking; and shall embed what you say in what I may write.

Yr V. W.

Sussex

3581: To Vanessa Bell   [*Monk's House, Rodmell, Sussex*]

Wednesday [31 January 1940]

I've rung up, but find your telephone is broken. This is only to say weve had to give up going to London, and hope somehow to meet. God knows how.

Our worst day was Monday when the electricity failed and we had to cook on the fire. Yesterday only a hunk of bread remained, but providentially a leg of mutton arrived. I daresay you're worse off[1]— Ring up when you can.

V.

How did Duncan manage?

We've got Q's starter.[2]

Berg

3582: To Ethel Smyth   *Monk's House, Rodmell, near Lewes, Sussex*

1st Feb 40

Yes, I'd like to look at South Riding, if its no trouble to you to send it on. I think I meant that W.H. [Winifred Holtby] was a barrel organ writer. Vera [Brittain] is a scrambling and enthusing chatterbox, but of course very competent. I'm judging WH. only on her journalism—and she insisted to me that that was all she ever wanted to do—and the book on me, which I

1. The winter was one of the severest on record. Trains were late, mails delayed, services cut off.
2. Possibly an electric lamp to keep a car-engine warm.

felt to be a painstaking effort rather to clear up her own muddles than to get the hang of mine. But I didnt want to be written about (not personally) and so did more than whip through it with one eye shut. I dont like pulling out all the organ stops and 'humanising': I dont like regional novels: those are my prejudices; and I much prefer people who let all that settle down (like Hardy, like Tolstoy) and only write when the sediment is firm and the water clear. Therefore I'm not likely to be fair on W.H. And oh Lord how I loathe that scribbling business: 35 novels to be reviewed for Harpers Bazaar in one morning in a bungalow. So I'm not unprejudiced, but will try to be.

Here we are snow bound. All engagements in a muddle. We tried to go, but the car frozen, the roads impossible. I should be listening to Desire under the Elms[1] this moment. Never was there such a medieval winter. The electricity broke down. We cooked over the fire, remained unwashed, slept in stockings and mufflers. And what about you?

I'm using this frozen pause to confront a long last grind at R.F. Then it'll be done. but goodness knows when. The [Fry] family has to pass it. Endless objections I foresee. And its not a book, only a piece of cabinet making, and only of interest to R's friends, for whom I've tried to stick together an amalgamation of all his letters. And what a job to do! And its of no interest that I can see, except to his half dozen devotees. Never mind —I've learnt a carpenter's trick or two.

Reading Burke. Reading Gide. and I have to lecture on the moderns to the working classes at Brighton.[2]

V.

Berg

3583: To Vanessa Bell   [*Monk's House, Rodmell, Sussex*]

Sunday [4 February 1940]

I've just been looking at my birthday present by daylight. Its a lovely picture—what a poet you are in colour—one of these days I must write about you. And I do enjoy having a picture of my dear Quentin.[3] What a pleasure your brats are to me—I long more and more for Julian, whose

1. Eugene O'Neill's play, written in 1925.
2. On 27 April 1940 Virginia spoke to the Workers' Educational Association about the poetry of Auden, Spender, MacNeice and Day Lewis. Her lecture was later published as *The Leaning Tower* in *Folios of New Writing* (Autumn 1940), ed. by John Lehmann.
3. The picture, of Quentin Bell standing and reading, is still at Monk's House.

birthday it is today, and cant help just saying so, though I know you know it. My own darling I do think of you and him so much.

No answer—
B.

Berg

3584: To Ethel Smyth   *Monks House [Rodmell,*
Sussex]

7th Feb. [1940]

That was a nice long letter, and now the fat book[1] has come. I think (so far) she has a photographic mind, a Royal Academicians mind. Its as bright as paint, but how obvious, how little she's got beneath the skin. Thats why it rattles on so, I think. One's never pulled up by a single original idea. She's seen nothing for the first time, for herself. I feel, as I do when God Save the King strikes up, that I could sing the whole book straight through. But then I'd just finished Little Dorrit. And its not fair perhaps. He rattles along, but how muscular, how positive, and what a ripple of bone and entrail and sinew under that taut surface. But again thats unfair, and I've only read 150 pages; and enjoyed them, as one does a film. She's a ventriloquist, not a creator. Sometimes, of course, she has the very words on her lips. But they dont come from the heart. Well—this is scribbled, by way of a rest from correcting Rogers French—thats scribbled too, no accents, and I daresay the wrong genders; and as my own French is as mouldy as the dining room carpet—the waters oozing from the bricks now,—oh damn this thaw—the howlers will cry aloud, and make poisoned darts in all the furious and vindictive old men. We've been entertaining the local gentry—a mild eyed, sheep witted Major [Gardner], who proses on about Singapore and loves rats, which he feeds, and his daughter (painter) and son (bank clerk) and now we have a meeting to debate socialism. I rather at times long for the dry and glittering streets and even old Ethel. A joke that, in bad taste. So, as my written jokes are bad, I will stop—

V.

Berg

3585: To Ethel Smyth   *[Monk's House, Rodmell,*
Sussex]

20th Feb: [1940]

We lead a distracted life—one week in London, the next here. As you can imagine I leave there what I want here, and t'other way about. But

1. Winifred Holtby's *South Riding*.

here's your Laski card. He's a little drop of brown quicksilver—the cleverest imp that ever was—was Lord Morleys confidant—then, I think, [Arthur] Balfours—no, not Balfour, but some other P. Minister.[1] He's the great unknown behind politics; consulted, influential, anonymous. I like him; but then he thinks 3 gs. the greatest book since Mill. However, he cant read my novels. L. says he's an influence rather than a writer. If I can find L— who is fitting up an electric stove, ordered 4 weeks ago, just come with the thaw,—I'll ask him about the book to read.

London is packed from morning till night; here there's complete solitude, save for the Bells, and stray callers—a good diversion. Now I'm sending my MS (oh—I must correct the typing all day tomorrow) to Margery Fry, and feel like a small boy showing up an exercise. Whats happened about Nina? I read the scratched out story and was enthralled.[2] What a rackety race you Smyths are—Bankruptcy, Sapphism, hunting, suicide, all in one gulp. How then did you keep so d—d military upright and brass buttoned? Explain. And about your book. Oh I have to lecture at Brighton next week[3]—to the working classes.

V.

Berg

3586: To Donald Brace

*Monk's House, Rodmell,
Lewes, Sussex*

Typewritten
Feb 21st 1940

Dear Mr Brace,

I think I told you, when we last met, that I was working at a life of Roger Fry. I write to say that I have now finished this, and we hope to publish it over here in the late spring. In about a month's time I expect to have the proofs, and will send you a copy. It will make a book of between 90 and 100 thousand words I expect.

1. Harold Laski (1893-1950), the political theorist and Labour Party leader who for 30 years taught at the London School of Economics. Among his many distinguished friends were John Morley (1838-1923), the statesman and biographer of Gladstone, and Ramsay MacDonald, the Prime Minister. His books included *The Crisis and the Constitution* (1932) and *Law and Justice in Soviet Russia* (1935), both of which were published by the Hogarth Press.
2. Nina Hollings, Ethel's younger sister who married Herbert Hollings in 1886. She was a great eccentric (see Ethel's *What Happened Next*, 1940, pp. 121-3). The 'story' was probably about Nina and Lady Helena Gleichen. See p. 389, note 1.
3. Her lecture to the Workers' Educational Association was postponed until 27 April.

All our publishing is carried on under great difficulties, as you can understand; but I will not go into that. So far we have not done so badly as we expected. We are living half here, in the country; and half in London. Our new address, 37 Mecklenburgh Square, W.C.1 will always find me.

With kind regards from us both,

yours sincerely,
Virginia Woolf

Harcourt Brace Jovanovich

3587: To STEPHEN SPENDER

Monk's House, Rodmell, Lewes, Sussex

Typewritten
7th March [1940]

Dear Stephen,

Yesterday, tidying up, I came upon this envelope of your poems. Ought I to have sent them before? What I expect happened was that you said youd come round and we'd talk. Well, alas, we cant do that. I wish we could. I like some very much; others not—but I cant write criticism, only talk it. So I send them by way of an excuse for asking you to write me a letter. Someone said you were teaching in Devonshire[1]—someone else that theyd seen you in London. How vanished every one is. Here we exist on our little plot of ground, sometimes like solid emerald; at others a damp fungus. Various people buzz about. At this moment we're off to Brighton where L. lectures on Common sense in Politics. So I must stop.

Not seeing ones friends is very depressing; not knowing what point theyve reached; whether as I hope youre in the middle of a great book. Poetry? Autobiography? Fiction? That brings me back to my demand for a letter—an immense long letter.

Yours ever
Virginia Woolf

I note that Mr Connolly upbraids L and V Woolf for not writing for Horizon.[2] Well, if you like to suggest a subject, I'll certainly try.

Texas

1. Spender was teaching at Blundells School, Devon, but he hated it and left after one term.
2. Cyril Connolly was Editor of *Horizon*, and Spender his Assistant. In the issue of February 1940 he described Virginia as one of "the ivory tower dwellers", together with Proust and Joyce, but there is no reference to Leonard. Later in the article he implies that he is "baiting the trap" for her.

Monks House [*Rodmell, Sussex*]

12th March [1940]

Oh what a pleasure to get your letter! And how odd!—I was saying to L. I felt that you felt we were out of touch: as for myself, I *never* feel out of touch with Vita. Thats odd but true. And whats made it happen with you? Politics, religion, patriotism? what are the "various reasons" you, dear old sheep dog, talk of? I long to know, for I've divined them thro' the door.

Here I am in the week of influenza—cant get normal, but hope to be up by the end of the week. A d—d sore throat.

And this is the only scrap of paper I can find

But my dear how nice to get your letter! How its heartened me! And how I long to hear from your own lips whats been worrying you—for you'll never shake me off—no. not for a moment do I feel ever less attached. Aint it odd? And so I didn't write but waited— Yes, do, do come. What fun, what joy that'll be.

Y
V.

Berg

Monk's House, Rodmell, near Lewes, Sussex

Friday [15 March 1940]

Your letter has made me so happy.[1] I've been so haunted by the fear that you wouldn't like it. I never wrote a word without thinking of you and Julian and I have so longed to do something that you'd both like. As for thanking me—well, when you've given me Julian and Quentin and Angelica—

L. says the typing in the last part is awful and some passages make complete nonsense.[2]

Perhaps you and D will come over.

V.

Berg

1. Vanessa had read *Roger Fry* in typescript, and sat down at once to write to Virginia: "Since Julian died I havent been able to think of Roger. Now you have brought him back to me. Although I cannot help crying, I cant thank you enough" (13 March 1940, midnight, *Berg*).
2. Leonard strongly criticised *Roger Fry*. In her diary on 20 March Virginia wrote: "At last he was almost angry that I'd chosen 'what seems to me the wrong method. It's merely analysis, not history. Austere repression. In fact dull to the outsider. All those dead quotations.' . . . It was a curious example of L. at his most rational and impersonal: rather impressive" (*AWD*, p. 328).

3590: To V. Sackville-West

Monk's House, Rodmell, near Lewes, Sussex

March 19th [1940]

Dearest,

I have a horrid little fear, as you've not written, that I said something idiotic in my letter tother day [No. 3588]. I dashed it off, I was so glad to get yours, with a rising temperature, and perhaps said something that hurt you. God knows *What*. Do send one line because you know how one worries in bed, and I cant remember what I wrote.

Forgive what is probably the effect of the flu. I've got what they call the recurring kind, I suddenly jump up to 102, and so am kept in bed till the end of this week anyhow, and as its the 4th week, one gets rather mopy and broody. However I'm normal today and expect its over. I got a little bronchitis too and wheeze like an old bagpipe. This is to show why I'm being, as I expect, foolish and exacting. It also shows how much I depend on you, and should mind any word that annoyed or hurt you. One line on a card—thats all I ask.

And come soon and lets talk.

V.

Berg

3591: To Ethel Smyth

Monk's House, Rodmell, near Lewes, Sussex

19th March [1940]

Ever so many thanks for remembering your decrepit friend. No sooner had I sent you that card than another attack developed and the Dr. now calls it recurring influenza with a touch of bronchitis. So I've been in bed again since Friday and stay there till Friday next. Then, if theres no more rise, I'm to get up. And I'm normal today. These disgusting details are only to serve as bait for a letter. Oh dear, this is my 4th week of noncomposity— and I'm so sick of turning over library books and biting a crumb out of Shelley and then going asleep over Havelock Ellis.[1] A letter's about my length—an Ethel letter. Yes, I dipped into Time Goes On: and wish it had a twin. May you say? Oh but I shall be in full feather long before that. Did you kill poor Longman?[2] (a very bad joke) Well I'm glad you pegged your guineas down first. Just heard that Margery Fry approves of R.F.

1. *My Life*, 1940. His *Studies in the Psychology of Sex* was published in six volumes between 1897 and 1910, and a seventh was added in 1928.
2. Sir Hubert Longman (b. 1856), member of Longmans, Green & Co., publishers, died on 16 March. He published most of Ethel's books, including *As Time Went On* (1936) and *What Happened Next* (1940).

But there's any number of corrections: and how, with a brain like old macaroni, can I make them in time for this season? So I suppose its put off till the autumn: if there is to be an autumn. Its a bore—I'd get it all done if it hadn't been for this cursed germ. And my Lecture put off too. Dont bother to write unless the champagne in yr. blood has begun to fizzle. I've ordered Lady Helena Gs book[1]

Berg

3592: TO HUGH WALPOLE   *Monk's House, Rodmell,*
                                         Lewes, Sussex
19th March 40

My dear Hugh,
    I like some of Roman Fountain very much: I dislike some very much. Oh to disentangle these questions with you by word of mouth— how that would interest me! Its my belief we could do each other a lot of good by word of mouth—honest word of mouth. Meanwhile, I've had the sensation of Rome, Strong, and the colour, and the sound of water; and as Rome is the place I adore of all places, I'm humbly thankful. And how good the pulley is—and the smoke is[2]—but here I stop, for I'm in my 4th week of whats called recurrent influenza, bronchitis being added, which means up you get up for 3 days: then the shivers seize you: back to bed: and there I stay this week; but the dr says next week I shall be well.
    So excuse—I'm not asking for a draught from Hugh's well known Elixir—sympathy: but should he have an impulse to write a letter, what I call a real life letter, you know, all about what seem to me so miraculous, facts—well do write it. Only not if its a bore. One day (to return to R. F.) will you show me your treasures: oh for a sight of pictures and rare books![3] Thats a passion of mine I've had to repress. But reading you revives it. I should like to tumble your Cezannes, Renoir, first editions through my

1. Lady Helena Gleichen (d. 1947), the painter and author of *Contacts and Contrasts*, 1940. See p. 389, note 1.
2. *Roman Fountain* (1940) is an account of Walpole's visit to Rome in 1939, interspersed with reflections on past visits. The 'pulley' was the device which lowered the body of Pope Pius XI into the crypt, and the 'smoke' that which signalled the election of Pius XII.
3. In his book Walpole described the paintings he had collected, complaining that certain visitors to his London flat were more appreciative than others. He also owned many rare books, including Charles Lamb's copy of *Don Quixote*, to which Virginia refers in her letter to Walpole of 28 March.

aging claws. After Easter, please lets discuss the works of Hugh Walpole. And do write more autobiography.

Yr V. W.

Texas

3593: To V. Sackville-West   *Monk's House, Rodmell, near Lewes, Sussex*

22nd March [1940]

(1) Yes do tell me when the French Broadcast is to be.[1] We'll listen with all our ears pricked with pride.

(2) Yes, do come any time I think after the 7th. I've got if possible to finish off my R. Fry book and send by that date—the only chance is to work every day so I wont ask you till the horrors over.

(3) Yes. All L's plants are yellow. But he's making a new rock garden which he longs to show you.

Potto here licks the page in love of you [*squiggly design*]

Berg

3594: To Vanessa Bell   *Monk's House, Rodmell, near Lewes, Sussex*

22nd March [1940]

Here, good Dolphin: I've at last found my cheque book under the bed. I'm making it £40, because I include a frame for the picture of Quentin. Aint that grasping? Its dirt cheap I consider, looking at the masterpiece of L. and Sally which will be a source of eternal pleasure.[2]

I hope D. [Duncan] is better and that you'll come over.

Margery [Fry] wants to come on Wednesday I hope you sent off the chapter [of *Roger Fry*] to Helen [Anrep], as I must get it back as soon as possible.

V.

I enclose Margery: cd. I have it back

Berg

1. Between March and May Vita recorded several broadcasts in French for Radio Paris at a secret radio station in Renby Grange, near Tunbridge Wells. She was invited to do this by her friend Hilda Matheson, who was now working in the propaganda branch of military intelligence.
2. This picture is now in The National Portrait Gallery.

3595: To Ethel Smyth

Monk's House, Rodmell,
near Lewes, Sussex

27th March [1940]

Well if you have fibrositis in the back, I've something more glutinous in the head. Yet what an amusing letter you wrote!—the Brewster one, culminating in the sanitary towels which made me hoot like an owl with ecstacy. The influenza has receded; leaving what dont matter and cant be cured, my old friend an evening rise of temp.—like the trout after the fly. Oh I'm working so hard—8 days to sending in: and Margery Fry has very reasonably spattered me today with some 100 corrections; all to be entered; some to be contrived; and yet her kindness and reasonableness is such that I cant ignore. Yet why is filial love so deucedly persistent? And erratic? I cant even guess what she allows and what she forbids. I'm blind with accent inserting, and to relieve me write to you.

Do, if you've time, continue the Nina-Helena saga. D'you know, I liked Helena's book;[1] was it all humbug? Hasn't she something rapid and racy and high handed, as well as the Hun and the miser? So I thought. And such a mixup: the spooks: and old Lemon whom I knew; and the aristocratic love of the direct: and the brutality of the aristocrat; and the naivete; and the courage: and I suppose all sorts of horrors, not hidden, but ignored— in herself. However it passed me a whole day in bed amusingly. I heard of them all from the Thynnes, years ago, and like the rebels side, which Beatrice T.[2] carried further.

Well, I'm fixed to my shoemakers board all this week and then—oh glory to be quit of corrections till the proofs come! And to do nothing— and to let my cistern fill—and perhaps see a friend or two, and waste my days in talking till the sun goes down the sky.[3] Why must one ever again lift the load on one's shoulders? Vita says she's coming—Has Gwen left her? Is V. now Catholic?[4] Can I plunge into all this? You would.

V.

Berg

---

1. *Contacts and Contrasts* by Helena Gleichen (1940). 'Nina' was Ethel's sister, Mrs Herbert Hollings. 'Old Lemon' was Arthur Lemon, the painter, and Helena was his pupil. Helena's book was mainly about her experiences during World War I, when she and Nina ran an ambulance unit on the Italian front. Afterwards they lived together in Gloucestershire.
2. Beatrice Thynne, daughter of the Marquess of Bath.
3.   "How often you and I
          Had tired the sun with talking and sent him down the sky."
                    —William Johnson Cory, *Heraclitus.*
4. Gwen St Aubyn had moved from Sissinghurst to London. She was converted to Roman Catholicism, but Vita never was.

Monk's House, Rodmell,
Lewes, Sussex

28th March [1940]

But my dear Hugh, I must have said something I didn't mean at all if you think as you say that "its my excitement which irritates you all". Your excitement is the quality I like most of all. Every one of my friends has been excited—most of them have had collections. So dont, I beg of you impute to me what may be the incredibly idiotic opinions of other people. No, no, no what I objected to in Roman Fountain wasn't *that*—but what it was I'll only tell you by word of mouth. And perhaps not then. For whats the use? None I suspect when Hugh and Virginia remain at opposite ends of the bloody stick.[1]

I only send this P.S. by way of removing a misunderstanding. Aint I always agog myself? Quivering at the garden this moment.

And mayn't I one of these days come and look at your lovely things which make my mouth water? Did I ever tell you of my Jane Austen find?[2] Oh and to see Lamb's Don Quixote, and the Scott MSS.

Never mind answering this rapid scrawl, when I should be copying all the corrections of all the Frys (angelic as they are) into my biography.

The 4th influenza seems to be the last. Thank God its gone.

and so farewell
V. W.

Texas

Monk's House [Rodmell,
Sussex]

Typewritten
6th April [1940]

Dearest Margaret,

What a time I've let your letter go unanswered, and it was such a nice one. But I had five weeks of influenza, and then had to set to and finish off

1. Hugh Walpole had written to Virginia: "As for my writing, you and I are the opposite ends of the bloody stick. You are the supreme example of the aesthetic —conscience—there has never been such another in English fiction. But you *don't* write novels. What you write needs a new name. I am the *true* novelist—a minor one but a true one. I know a lot about the novel and a lot about life seen from my very twisted child-haunted angle" (*Sussex*).

2. In October 1936 Virginia bought from a Bexhill bookseller Jane Austen's copy of Ariosto's *Orlando Furioso*, translated from the Italian by John Hoole, 1783. She gave it to Maynard Keynes, and it is now in King's College Library. In 1933 Virginia also bought Jane Austen's copy of the works of James Thomson in 4 vols., now the property of Mrs Quentin Bell.

my life of Roger Fry, so as to bring it out if possible this summer. Now thats sent off, so its possible to turn into a human being again. I suppose Leonard told you how we live now—partly here, mostly here, but partly in London. The new flat is in a lovely quiet square, and we've set up house as in Tavistock, with our old solicitors [Dollman & Pritchard] as tenants, the press in the basement, and ourselves perched on top. By a stroke of luck we had taken John Lehmann as partner just before the war, so Leonard is quit of most of that burden and can spend his time writing all the morning, digging all the afternoon. If it weren't for the war, it would be a perfect life. But of course he's drawn in, and what can one do? As you say, how make peace terms now? Still, he collects other enthusiasts. Will Arnold Forster and so on, and they try to put some brains into that fat timid sheep the labour party. I'm becoming, you'll be amused to hear, an active member of the Womens Institute, who've just asked me to write a play for the villagers to act.[1] And to produce it myself. I should like to if I could. Oh dear how full of doings villages are—and of violent quarrels and of incessant intrigues. The hatred for the parsons wife [Mrs Ebbs] passes belief. We're thought red hot revolutionaries because the Labour party meets in our dining room.

Ann sometimes writes to me—I think she's happier living in the hospital in Dublin, but its a great breakup for them—how one pities the young—and I hope Richard may get some job.[2] He was dreaming of going to the Fiji islands at one time. Ann sent me, not Sean's novel,[3] which she said was a very queer work, but a long letter, which was much to the point I thought, as a private document. But can one write novels about Mrs Smith and Mr Jones if one sits over the fire with ten Greek dictionaries and refuses to see a soul? I liked her so much, and found her so attractive and individual when she came in one night.

What a lot of neighbours you must have—the Trevys [Trevelyans]—yes, I like old Bessie, and adore Bob because he's the greatest bore in the world, and I like anyone who takes their own line so regardless of other people's fancies. I've been in touch with Ralph Vaughan Williams too—over a poetess; he was as nice as could be in his letters. De Lisle Burns we used to meet, at the 1917 club, and his son is a friend of Judith's.[4]

1. Virginia wrote no play for Rodmell, but Miss La Trobe writes and produces a village pageant in *Between the Acts*.
2. Anne Llewelyn Davies (*née* Stephen) and her husband Richard married in 1938, but the marriage was dissolved, and in 1943 he married Patricia Parry. His later career was as an architect (particularly of hospitals) and town planner. He was created a life peer in 1964.
3. Sean O'Faolain, *Come Back to Erin*, 1940.
4. Ralph Vaughan Williams (1872-1958), the composer, married Virginia's cousin Adeline Fisher; Cecil Delisle Burns (1879-1942), the social philosopher; the 1917 Club, of which Virginia was a member, was a left-wing club with premises in Soho.

I hope you're now better, and perhaps sitting at the window with the lovely view [near Dorking]. Isn't the country ever so much nicer than London? Please give Lilian [Harris] my love, and tell her how often I chuckle over the stories she told of her family. Is she really reading old G. M. Young on Gibbon? I cant help feeling that he's packed his egg—I mean head—too full of facts and its addled. At least I stuck in the Victorian book. But do tell me how he and Mona carry on[1]—and if you've any gossip to impart. There are lots of things I want to ask; but must wait till we meet. Heres Leonard back from a school meeting and a fight with the parson's wife. I stuck all your photographs[2] into a great book and called it Eminent Victorians. Nessa's children and I gloat over it.

We both send our love to you both; and so often find ourselves talking about you, dearest Margaret.

Yr V. W.

Sussex

3598: To V. Sackville-West   *Monks House, Rodmell*
                                     [Sussex]
Thursday [18 April 1940]

Shall you be coming on Tuesday next as we hope?
I sent a card, but all answers go wrong now.
So let me have a line to Rodmell
O Lord London's gloomy.

V and P

Berg

3599: To V. Sackville-West   *[Monk's House, Rodmell,*
                                     Sussex]
Friday [19 April 1940]

Yes of *course* you are to stay the night—2—3—4—5—if you will. Certainly Tuesday night. Shall expect you between tea and dinner: Potto all a quiver on the look out.

Yes—Flaubert[3]—but no time now. Letter just sent on to discuss. here—London—just off.

V.

Berg

1. G. M. Young published his *Life of Gibbon* in 1932 and *Victorian England* in 1936. He lived with the writer Mona Wilson at Old Oxyard, Oare, Wiltshire.
2. Of Virginia's childhood at St Ives.
3. What Virginia meant by this reference cannot now be determined, but Vita may have asked Virginia to suggest to John Lehmann that the Hogarth Press publish a book on Flaubert, and that Vita might write it herself (see Letter 3602).

Monks House, Rodmell
                                              [Sussex]
22nd April [1940]

I told you, Ethel dear, I'm perfectly well—whats more I dashed off Roger—so it may come out with luck in June. But its only a book for old Crones so dont set your teeth in it. Now I have to write my lecture [*The Leaning Tower*], or rather to re-write it—An hour, for 30 typists—well its cost me more trouble than 2 Common Readers. Thats what comes of yielding to the damnable importunity of a wretched little man who lives on tinned tomatoes on top of a hill. My swan song—positively my last public misery.

Now take care, when all your joints have been loosened, how you cross the floor. There's John Lehmann's mother stretched senseless—broken thigh—all for a slip on her rug; and my very old venerable cousin Herbert Fisher killed by a Lorry.[1] Please Ethel dear look to the right and left and dont come out behind a Bus.

I'm amused that your brother thinks my Gleichen sketch[2] was intuitive. That is my gift—like it or lump it—No heart you say: how then do I transfer these images to my sensitive paper brain? Because I have a heart. Yes, and its the heart that makes the paper take, as they say. I beg you to consider this theory in the night watches.

I often consider you, when I draw my curtain about dawn and survey the sky. Otherwise how remote the stars would be. If you think of someone when star gazing their horrid little stare is outfaced. So please send me, no publish—for I'll buy it—your book, so that I may have something to counter the stars with. Two swallows seen today; and a cuckoo calling.

I'm reading Sydney Smith—his life—with only one wish in the world: that I'd married him: Isnt it odd when the rumble tumble of time turns up some entirely lovable man?[3] And did you ever know Clara Novello Davies?[4] I'm reading her too. Not lovable I guess: but tell me.

                                              Yr V
Berg

---

1. H. A. L. Fisher died on 18 April 1940, several days after being hit by a lorry. He was on his way to preside at a tribunal for conscientious objectors to the war.
2. See Letter 3595, paragraph 2.
3. Virginia was reading Hesketh Pearson's *The Smith of Smiths* (1934), a life of Sydney Smith (1771-1845), the clergyman, author and wit.
4. Dame Clara Novello Davies (1861-1943), the Welsh choral conductor and author of several books, including her memoirs, *Voice Building*.

3601: To Hugh Walpole   *Monk's House* [*Rodmell,*
                                          Sussex]
Tuesday [23 April 1940]

My dear—oh curse the hair in the pen—Hugh,

Very well: very nice, tea, 4.30 or so the 30th—don't be alone, unless you wish to be alone. All I meant was I'm damned unsociable at lunch. And I do want to hold [Lamb's copy of] D. Quixote in my hands—and I was invited to meet you on Monday at Sibyl's—Cant. And I dont think to the L.[1] is a novel. Do coin me a word for the next.

Oh I've got to lecture—upon you among others—to the Brighton working classes on Saturday. Modern trends they want to hear about.

It costs me agony: how does one lecture! "Hugh Walpole," I say is an aristocrat.[2] Thats as far as I've got—and it lasts one hour.

Aristocrat intellectually, I add. And what comes next? Aldous Huxley I suppose: T. S. Eliot I suppose. Auden. Spender.

Heres Vita, so no more of this drivel.

                                                    Yr V. W.

Texas

3602: To V. Sackville-West   *Monk's House, Rodmell,*
                                         near Lewes, Sussex
Sunday [28 April 1940]

Oh Potto was so glad to huddle upon the Rung again.[3] Yes, it was a great treat having you. In fact, isn't it a duty, in this frozen time, to meet as often as possible? so that even in the cold night watches, when all the skeletons clank, we may keep each other warm? So, next time, we're going up by train; so will save petrol; so shall come to Sissinghurst and oh my God—do fix it up with the Sidneys.[4] I dont want to see *them*: but have a passion to see the house.

Nothing was said about Flaubert. The gold box [with Vita's saccharine tablets] is safe. Shall I send it registered in a tin?

I lectured for an hour yesterday: 200 betwixt and betweens—you know how they stare and stick and won't argue. Well thats over. And now I'm

1. *To the Lighthouse.* See p. 365, note 2.
2. In *The Leaning Tower*, Hugh Walpole's name appears in a list of people who wrote some of the best books of the period 1910-25, and were educated at public schools and universities.
3. Vita had written on 24 April: "Your friendship means so much to me—in fact it is one of the major things in my life" (*Berg*).
4. On 14 June Virginia, Leonard and Vita visited Penshurst Place, Kent, the ancestral home of the Sidneys (Lord De L'Isle and Dudley).

going to plunge into proofs, and then into poetry; so you must swim ahead.

Please write the book for me. I assure you its far and away the best, I should say the better, idea—I mean the one most fitting your ins and outs—than any of them.—no cant get it right.[1]

Here I must stop and take tea with Mrs Chavasse, the dr's widow, in order to discuss the village plays.[2]

Please dearest Vita, come soon again. You've got a hoard [of petrol] in your tank.

and you love your

Virginia

Another invitation from Sybil [Colefax].

Berg

3603: To Elizabeth Robins   *Monks House, Lewes,*
                                           Sussex

Sunday [28 April 1940]

Dear Miss Robins,

We couldn't get to you yesterday—we got kept by the young woman in Wards' [book] shop. Also I should like to see you when I'm not flustered with trying to lecture. It was extraordinarily nice of you and Octavia [Wilberforce] to come—but it wasn't meant for the likes of you. You cant think how difficult it is—speaking to the W.E.A.—that must be my excuse.

We shall have to visit the bookshops again—so may we postpone our visit till then?

I enclose the letters about your book.[3] I'm so glad that my opinion has been confirmed. I was certain I was right. And so, shall continue to worry you for a second volume: then for a third: then for a fourth.

Was that splendid bunch of carnations—it suddenly struck me—from you? I remember another splendid bunch you once gave me. Anyhow, they are now ablaze in my room, and until I hear that I'm wrong, I shall thank you.

I hope you are really better,

Yrs ever
Virginia Woolf

Washington State University, Humanities Library

1. Vita's next major book was not about Flaubert, but *The Eagle and the Dove* (1943) about St Teresa of Avila and St Thérèse of Lisieux.
2. See p. 391, note 1.
3. *Both Sides of the Curtain* (1940).

395

Letters 3604-3642 (May–September 1940)

For Virginia's reactions to the defeat of France and the threatened invasion of Britain, her diary is a better guide than her letters (in which, for example, she referred to the retreat from Dunkirk simply as "What a lot of disagreeables!"), but the sustained cheerfulness of her correspondence concealed the strain of these months. Rodmell now lay very close to the front line, and air-battles often took place over her head. London was not yet seriously attacked, and the Woolfs were safer there during their fortnightly visits than at Monk's House, now their base. Virginia was taught elementary first-aid and fire-drill. Other diversions were more enjoyable. As German planes streaked across the Channel, she played bowls. G. E. Moore and Desmond MacCarthy came for a weekend, and Virginia lectured to the local Women's Institute on the Dreadnought hoax of 1910. With Leonard and Vita she visited Penshurst Place on the very day (14 June) when Paris fell.

Roger Fry was published on 25 July. Friends and reviewers praised it greatly, and when Ben Nicolson attacked Roger's "failure to combat Nazism", Virginia replied with a searing and exceptionally careful counter-attack (Letters 3627 and 3633-4), and then invited Ben to Rodmell.

3604: To V. Sackville-West   *Monk's House, Rodmell, near Lewes, Sussex*

[early May 1940]

Yes: Saturday 11th.[1]—Probably we must come by train. Will meet you in The Pantiles [Tunbridge Wells], at 1.30.

Leonard makes a stipulation: not to meet the Earl.[2] If its a social function he wont come. (aint that like him?) I'll bring [saccharine] box. What a dream I had of you! A cow flew over us and crushed your nose—It went black. I had tapioca pudding handy, and applied it. The nose gradually blew out like a toy pig. Whats the interpretation? Horror and guilt both strongly present.

V.

Berg

1. For the visit to Penshurst, later postponed until 14 June.
2. The 4th Lord De L'Isle and Dudley (1854-1945). He was not an Earl, but his nephew (6th Lord) was created a Viscount in 1956.

3605: To V. Sackville-West   *Monk's House, Rodmell,*
                                  near Lewes, Sussex
Tuesday [7 May 1940]

Forgive me for my wire, and the intolerable nuisance I am. But The Press has suddenly put a pistol at my head; and say they cant bring R. F. [*Roger Fry*] out this summer unless I send final proofs this week. That means I must work every day and cant take an afternoon off. Even so, I think its doubtful—

So, will you forgive? Whats more, can we put it [Penshurst] off to another Saturday? About a fortnight later? Well,—I know its my fault, but the Frys have sent so many last minute corrections, and it means much more re-writing than they know. and I'm so slow and get so muddle headed. . . .

Would you also tell Ben [Nicolson] that I waited for him to ring me up again (at 37) and hoped to arrange something. I do want to see him. Whats his address?

I'll write and suggest a dinner next time we're up.

                                  Your wretched drudge—
                                  oh how I want to come on
                                  Saturday!—
                                                    V.
Berg

3606: To Rupert Hart-Davis   *Monk's House, Rodmell,*
                                  Lewes, Sussex
May 8th [1940]

Dear Mr Hart-Davis,[1]

Many thanks for telling me about the book, which I shall certainly read. Nothing comes more welcome than a book to read in these days. That reminds me, I dont think I ever said how much I liked another book— William sent it me.[2] I've forgotten, as usual the name—by an old man, in the manner (with differences) of Jane Austen. Anyhow, I liked it, and hope it reached the public; though I suppose not.

I was so glad to see you again; and hope the war won't make another meeting too difficult.

                                  Yrs sincerely
                                  Virginia Woolf
Rupert Hart-Davis

1. Rupert Hart-Davis (b. 1907) was at this time a director of Jonathan Cape. Later he founded his own publishing company and wrote a biography of Hugh Walpole (1952).
2. William Plomer, who was a reader for Jonathan Cape, had sent Virginia *He and His* by R. C. Carter (Cape, 1940).

3607: To Benedict Nicolson   *Monk's House, Rodmell,*
                                   Lewes, Sussex
Sunday 12th May [1940]

Dear Ben,

I just missed you the other day, and didn't know how to get hold of you.

Will you dine with us at 37 [Mecklenburgh Square] on Thursday 23rd? at 8. We shall be up that week, and it would be very nice to see you in any clothes.

We come up every other week, normally, and any time you're in our neighbourhood, please come without waiting to be asked.

I wonder how you like your job.[1]

                                   Yr ever
                                   Virginia Woolf

Vanessa Nicolson

3608: To T. S. Eliot   *Monk's House, Rodmell,*
                                   Lewes, Sussex
Typewritten
15th May 1940

My dear Tom,

No, alas, we're not coming up till Tuesday: which is the 21st. If by chance we do come up this Friday, 17th, then I'll ring up on the chance again. Its all on the chance.

I cant help hoping that your Italian venture may be put off.[2] In that case, will you dine with us on Tuesday 21st—at 37—at 8?

This week end is over occupied with Desmond MacCarthy; and old George Moore, the philosopher;[3] or I would have chanced that.

All my spring was decimated by four attacks of influenza; spaced out, they laid waste six weeks; that's why you didn't have me pestering you to drop in.

But I did, by heroic efforts, buy the copy of the paper with your poem in it;[4] and I liked it. Dear, how I'd like to discuss poetry with you! And not with the WEA at Brighton. I'm reading Coleridge through; and have a

1. Ben Nicolson was then serving as a lance-bombardier in an anti-aircraft battery at Chatham, Kent.
2. See Letter 3610, second paragraph.
3. G. E. Moore (1873-1958), the Cambridge philosopher whose *Principia Ethica* (1903) greatly influenced the young men who were the original nucleus of Bloomsbury.
4. *East Coker*, published in *New English Weekly* (21 March 1940).

theory that contemporary Pickering editions reveal new aspects; and so am going on to Shelley, 1839.[1] You see how through diabolic shyness I swerve from your poem; isn't it odd, how difficult it is to talk of writing—I mean one's own; or t'other persons? Thats not true of Stephen [Spender]; whose latest I don't like; but can't say so.

Consider Tuesday 21st dinner; but if I don't hear I shall conclude you're off. But if you're back on 12th June keep the very next day for your old and affect:

Virginia

Mrs T. S. Eliot

3609: To Ethel Smyth   *Monk's House, Rodmell,*
                                        near Lewes, Sussex

17th May 40.

I've not written, for one thing because, till 2 days ago, I was almost blind, entering 3 different Frys comments into the edges of proofs, and altering my own words to admit theirs Now thats done. And I dont suppose its any use, all that labour: we shall have to postpone What does Longman say about your book [*What Happened Next*]?

Its a good thing to have books to believe in—and any number of little drudgeries: food to order: a village play to rehearse; and old Mrs West and her idiot boy—they took an hour this afternoon. We shant I suppose be killed; but I think of Montaigne, let death find me planting cabbages.[2] A disease has struck our gooseberries. Percy [Bartholomew] is mowing the lawn, and I have just forced myself to answer a lady who wants to know—what, dont matter. Still, in this numb and prosaic state, I should like a letter. Dont you owe me one? Oh about [Winifred] Holtby—yes, the letter I answered was from a Weaver at Hull who knew her by sight. I'll return [Holtby's] South Riding. I see its my own limitation: but, I could no more return to the page where I stopped than to last years Tatler: its already an out of date picture paper. I repeat—this is my own obliquity. D'you know what I find?—reading a whole poet is consoling: Coleridge I bought in an old type copy tarnished cover, yellow and soft: and I began, and went on, and skipped the high peaks, and gradually climbed to the top of his pinnacle, by a winding unknown way. So then I bought a Shelley: tea stained, water marked; but also no edited anthology cabinet piece. Him too I'm going to explore in the same sauntering under the bramble way. I

1. Both Coleridge and Shelley were published by William Pickering (1766-1854) in his 53-volume Aldine Press Edition of the English poets.
2. "Let death seize about me whilst I am setting my cabbages, careless of her dart, but more of my imperfect garden" (*To Study Philosophy Is to Learn to Die*, Book I, Chapter 19, Montaigne's *Essays*).

find the poets and Ethel Smyth very effective when I wake between the worlds—3 and 4. Well—I'm drivling, and wish only to say I hope we may once more meet. But when I'm in London, youre not. Next week I shall be there—only to get through the Press business

V

And what about Nina [Hollings] and Helena [Gleichen]?

Berg

3610: To Judith Stephen

Monk's House, Rodmell,
Lewes, Sussex

Typewritten
May 29th [1940]

My dear Judith,

Are you through your exams [at Cambridge]? And have you got a first? Old George Moore, the great philosopher, was here last weekend, and said the tripos was then on, I hope by now its off; and is there any chance of seeing you? We shall be in London, 37 Meck. Sq., next Tuesday till Friday; and then back here; where there's always more or less of a bed, should you ask for it. As you remember, Leonard won't let me at my age ask you at yours. Its an age, though, since you and Leslie [Humphreys] came—wasn't it in the snow? Or was it the apple-picking day? And dear me—what a lot of disagreeables have happened since![1] However let us say nothing about that; and rack our brains for a pennyworth of gossip.

I saw old Tom [Eliot] last week, and William [Plomer] too. Old Tom was about to start for Italy, to lecture on contemporary poetry and so persuade Italy to remain neutral. But on the very edge of the boat train he was stopped; and so dined with us. Then we had old [G. E.] Moore, and Desmond MacCarthy. I forget—did you ever read the book that made us all so wise and good: *Principia Ethica*? That reminds me—what about Bertie?[2] And Ann [Judith's sister]? Once she wrote to me, but then she lapsed; and so I don't know what's happened to Richard [Llewelyn Davies]. Did he get a job? Well I can't, even I, go on asking questions. And perhaps you're still up to your eyes in work. Have you—oh here's another question— settled what you're going to do, to be? What about America? What about anthropology?

I can't give you all the gossip of Rodmell, because it would need a ream. We're acting village plays; written by the gardener's wife, and the chauffeur's wife; and acted by the other villagers. Also we're doing this that and the

1. The evacuation of the British Army from Dunkirk began on 27 May and ended on 3 June.
2. Bertrand Russell, author of *Principia Mathematica* etc.

other about an air-raid shelter. And Leonard is up in London organising the Fabians. And we've played ever so many games of bowls, some I win; more I lose. Quentin is still ploughing; and Angelica has gone up north. And Duncan has been painting battleships at Plymouth;[1] and Leonard has finished a book for the Labour Book Club;[2] and the Press is living like a cat on eggs. So you see here's the end of the page. You must turn up one of these days, for we would like so much to see you.

Your old Aunt,
Virginia

Nigel Henderson

3611: To V. Sackville-West

Monk's House, Rodmell, near Lewes, Sussex

Sunday 9th June [1940]

Is there any chance that next Friday, 14th, would suit you for a visit to Penshurst? If so, we'd meet you in The Pantiles at 1.30: and lunch somewhere. And I'd bring your golden box—and lord what a treat to see you! —and I believe Penshurst is open to the public every day. Except Monday— —or was last year. So need you bother to tackle the Earl?

Let me know, and we'll come either by car or train.

Our telephone is 385 Lewes.

Potto's love,
V.

Berg

3612: To Ethel Smyth

Monk's House, Rodmell, near Lewes, Sussex

9th June 40

I was up last week, but Wednesday was my only free day; and I thought that was earmarked for Lady Balfour, so I didn't suggest it. Also, it was such a grill that I wouldn't have let you come anyhow. I'll write and suggest a Thursday next week, if we come up. But at the moment,—well, at the moment one cant plan for certain. So dont put yourself about: I'll ring or write nearer the time.

I expect its right to bring out your book; and we incline to do the same. Only Longman has a big staff, and ours is very small. I hope anyhow, for yours. I read myself into a state of immunity. And, as you know, I

---

1. Duncan Grant had probably been given this official commission.
2. Leonard's book was *The War for Peace* (1940), but he published it with G. Routledge & Sons.

find your drug very potent. I dont think I was alone for 3 days for one moment; and each brought a little jab of the war—each time the door opened or the telephone rang it was war and war—and "still we danced forward." D'you remember that quotation? [*not traced*]

My brain hums with scraps of poetry. Some of them were desperate; others hopeful; and some "plucking the flower while they may"[1]—thats my niece Judith boating on the Lake in Regents Park, having just done her tripos. "We never talk about war at Cambridge" she said. "We leave that to the dons". Then in came Kingsley Martin and Rose Macaulay, and there we sat in the hot evening, till the stars came out, never lighting a lamp, and gradually Kingsley Martin sucked every drop of lifeblood to feed his great purple vampire body. The searchlights are very lovely over the marsh, and the aeroplanes go over—one, a German, was shot over Caburn, and my windows rattled when they dropped bombs at Forest Row. But its like a Shakespeare song today—so merry, innocent, and very English.

Oh Holmes[2] and my father. No, I dont know of any pamphlet: only that they climbed [mountains] together, and Holmes was a great charmer, and lunched with us. There were éclairs—and he pointed to one, and said "Why éclairs?" A question I've never answered: a beautifully urbane, witty, over cultivated American.

All right: dont send me your book; and I won't send mine. But I will return South Riding [Winifred Holtby].

V.

Berg

3613: To G. B. Shaw   *Monk's House, Rodmell, Lewes, Sussex*

Typewritten
13th June 1940

Dear Mr Shaw,

It was only last week that I was in London and saw the Roger Fry picture that you sent me.

It is one of his best I think, and to have it from you adds to its beauty. One day I hope you will come and see it hanging in my room. And if ever you had time, and a half sheet of paper, and would write upon it that it was your picture and that you gave it me, my debt of gratitude to you would mount, if possible, higher. But I'm not going to bother you any more.

---

1. Virginia's adaptation of Herrick's famous line, "Gather ye rosebuds while ye may" (*To Virgins, to Make Much of Time*).
2. Oliver Wendell Holmes (1809-94), the American poet and essayist, best remembered for *The Autocrat of the Breakfast Table* (1858).

This is only to thank you for sending it, and to assert the affection which, though suppressed, is always alive in the heart of yours gratefully.

Virginia Woolf

Texas

3614: To ETHEL SMYTH   *M.[onks] H.[ouse, Rodmell, Sussex]*

Sunday. [30 June 1940]

This is only a letter of thanks for what I am about to receive. The book [*What Happened Next*] came yesterday, and I've only looked at the pictures. As we go up tomorrow for our 5 days of incessant interruption, I shall read no more, if I can resist it, till next weekend, when, please God, we may be alone. At the moment a great God like niece [Judith] is talking to me—about emigrating to America.

I saw the Times Lit Sup^t review—very cordial for that milk and water paper.

Oh you never looked back as you turned the corner of Meck. Sqre the other night—so you never saw me waving. It was thus that I endeavoured to thank you for coming all that way in the heat.

My gratitude, and indeed love, was lost upon your grey coat and straw hat. What a pity there's no wave language—for then you would have gone home with the sound of song in your ears.

No more now. Too hot: but there's the book—Can I resist the temptation? Shall I put it in my bag?

Yr

V.

Berg

3615: To ETHEL SMYTH   *Monks House, Rodmell, Lewes. [Sussex]*

Typewritten
9th July [1940]

My hand has staggered into the stages of illegibility; so put up, for old sakes sake, with this typed gabble.

I did put off reading till this week end, and now only put down flying impressions as they rise—I am talking about your book [*What Happened Next*]. And you never signed my copy—damn you.

First: no; its not so *brilliant* as the other;[1] because of course you bagged

1. *Impressions That Remained*, published in 1919, was the first element in Ethel's nine-volume autobiography. The series continued with *Streaks of Life* (1921), and ended with *What Happened Next* (1940).

all the high lights for that; but its richer; more luminous; and to my mind more sequacious.

2.... One always compares 'I' reading to 'I' writing. On the whole as read, Virginia comes off very badly compared with Ethel, cant think how Ethel ever liked me, such a new moon slip of a life, compared with her full orange harvest glow.

How when shes picked every plum off the tree, can she have fingered my crude little unripe apple?

Those are two rapid and rather devastating impressions. Theyre quite genuine and I think interesting. For what impresses me in this book more than in the others, is your ripeness. In fact I did wish, had I had a pencil, and no scruples about marking margins, to mark down some of your half conscious wisdom. And then it pulls together, the whole drag net of your various trophies; oh how many people youve known; but that I always realised. What I never before did justice to was the humility, which I like better than the brilliancy.

3.... but I wonder how it feels to do it. I mean to be so candid; and convinced that the public will be enthralled. I couldnt do it; but then you can. How? By having some kind of settled conviction? Its a curious light on your psychology; that you can confess so openly, what I should have hidden so carefully. And of course as I see, youre absolutely right. Yes, I get a great deal more of Ethel this way than any other.

4.... "Mum chance" ... what a good word; how that expresses your rapid, random, but after all very carefully aimed English. Oh and then finally—but I'm writing against time, so this isnt finally; only a string of perfectly inconsequent exclamations—how rightly and soberly it closes. D'you know for the first time H B[1] comes home to me? That end is so moving. His silence when he knew he had cancer. And yours too; as if the lights lowered and yet one saw everything.

But one thing I must protest; it isn't the end. Oh no. When youve got all the themes alive and combined you dont end them here. You go on. There must be artistically as well as humanly another volume. Really I cant argue the question; for its as if you had got us all listening; and promised us that we shall have the final harmony. You cant then stop; without breaking faith.

Lord how I envy you, compared with my tethered and literal rubbish-heap grubbing in R F. [*Roger Fry*], this complete and free handed and profound revelation.

Heres lunch; and rations to weigh out.

So I'll send this not as a statement but only as a huddle of little chirps.

V.

Berg

1. Henry Brewster, the Anglo-American poet and philosopher, with whom Ethel was intimate until his death in 1908.

3616: To Angelica Bell

Monk's House, Rodmell,
Sussex

12th July [1940]

Dearest Pixy,

What a joy to get your letter![1] But O Lord—I'm 12 days late in sending this, so your letter struck splinters of fire through my heart. First I lost my cheque book; then I still lost it and Mummy gave me your address, and I lost that. Heres Leonard's cheque. And please dearest Pix, cash it—I mean send it to the Bank—at once, or the whole structure of our fortune topples.

What with the company we keep and the fire lectures and the Gas lectures,[2] and old Miss Green aged 60 letting herself down out of the Rectory window in shorts to show us how, when we're on fire, life has left me no time for anything. I jump off my bicycle to find Judith and Leslie jumping off theirs: the engagement is announced;[3] she's got a ring; they've taken the Greens cottage; all August we shall be ringing and raging with the young. As there's only one young (called Angelica) I want to ring with, I'm a little grumpy. On Monday we go to Lewes to hear Jack Hutchinson try the case of a woman abortionist out of whose cupboard at Brighton dropped a dead girl. Two more were found in a ditch. This is sober truth: you'll see it in the paper.

On Tuesday I lunch with Lady [Margot] Oxford, who says she's dying, and wants me to write a eulogy:[4] on Wednesday, my old love Pipsy has asked me to tea. He's dying too.[5] I throw these hints of gaiety at you to draw another lovely, delicious, tipsy, lyrical and also literary and also— how I liked the description of the white calf—agricultural letter.

As you can't read a word of this, my hand being palsied, I stop. But will write if written to. And will love even if not. And hereby claim all my rights[6]—at compound interest too. Any facts or emotions I devour. By the way, Louie [Everest] caught us a hare; the cat ate it. No tea, no marg: how do you and Brock badger it out in your Charte hovel?[7]

V.

Texas

1. From Richmond, Yorkshire, where Angelica was on holiday with David Garnett.
2. Virginia and Leonard were attending first aid courses at the Rodmell rectory as a precaution against enemy air attack or invasion.
3. See p. 353, note 1.
4. See p. 17, note 2.
5. Philip Morrell did not die until February 1943.
6. Virginia's 'rights' with Angelica consisted in embraces and kisses (on the eyes, the nose, etc.) which Virginia claimed each time they met.
7. 'Brock' or 'Badger' was Virginia's new name for David Garnett, and The Chart was the wood surrounding the house of his mother (Constance Garnett) in Surrey, where Angelica sometimes stayed.

3617: To Ethel Smyth   *Monk's House, Rodmell,*
                                          near Lewes, Sussex

24th July [1940]

I'm here at the moment—here being a place much visited by German
raiders. Its odd, rather satisfactory, how soon one gets accustomed, at least
to their neighbourhood, and the sound of a bomb or two dropping over
Brighton. If they dropped in the garden, doubtless this facade would break;
and out would tumble a coward.

I wish I hadn't let a whole week of incessant human voices—London
last week—come between me and your book. However, it survives: and in
answer to your question, about sequacious (a word Coleridge uses) it
means connected; and I used it[1] to indicate a quality of currency, flowing-
ness, in this book, which, though I didnt find it so crested and high
stomached, as some of yours I liked. For so the characters come together,
more subtly: thats I think why I grasped H B more firmly this time. He
was too quiet and many tinted to survive the abandonment—emphasis of
the other books. Here you let him grow. I never agree that one book is
"the best". Unless of course one's Shakespeare—and how few of us are!—
I believe every book is only a fragment; and one may be a brighter or a
bigger fragment; but to complete the whole one must read them all. Certainly you got things said in this one that you didn't in Imp [*Impressions
That Remained* 1919]: and t'other way about. Thats, partly, why I want
you to continue. Because you *do* continue, being, thank God, not a finished
precious vase, but a porous receptacle that sags slightly, swells slightly,
but goes on soaking up the dew, the rain, the shine, and whatever else falls
upon the earth. Isn't that the point of being Ethel Smyth? Now Vernon
Lee, I daresay, completed her shape, and was sun dried and shell like. Well,
I mustn't run on inordinately.

No, I shan't send you R.F: because, dear Ethel, its no more your book
than Maurice Baring was mine.[2] And I don't like to think of you rubbing
your spectacles and screwing up your forehead. No, Let it lapse; and one
of these days I'll write something you'll take to like a duck: or so I hope.

I cant say what I'm doing next week: alls a vast leap in the dark. So I'll
leave it to the moment and the telephone, as before.

Now its clouding over: is there time for a game of bowls? Thats my
passion.

                                                              V.

1. In the third paragraph of Letter 3615.
2. Ethel's biography of Baring, published in 1938. *Roger Fry* was published the
   next day, 25 July. For Ethel's comments on Virginia's book, and her reply, see
   Letter 3631.

I spoke to the Women's Institute yesterday about the Dreadnought hoax.[1]
And it made them laugh. Dont you think this proves, beyond a doubt, that
I have a heart?

Berg

3618: To Mrs Lehmann

24th July 40

Dear Mrs Lehmann [John's mother],

Your letter gave me so much pleasure that I must answer it, in spite of
the fact that you forbid me. I was so afraid that I hadn't been able to convey
anything of Roger Fry, that it is a great relief to me to find that you, who
didn't know him, feel his great charm. I only hope that there will be more
readers like you—anyhow, its a great comfort to have you. I never found
any piece of work so difficult.

Its a bad time to bring a book out, and I'm specially sorry on John's
account. Its been so hard on him, beginning his work with the war. All the
same, both Leonard and I feel that the partnership is turning out a great
success, at any rate from our point of view. Its years since Leonard has had
such a free time, and I'm sure, when the war ends, John will make a great
success of it.

I do hope you're better. I was so sorry that you had to have another
operation.

Thank you again for writing.

yrs very sincerely
Virginia Woolf

John Lehmann

3619: To Sir William Rothenstein

24th July 1940

Dear Sir William,

I am anxious to send you back the Roger Fry letters which you were so
very kind as to lend me.[2]

But people move about so much now that I want to be sure of sending

---

1. In February 1910 (see p. 17, note 1). Three pages of her talk are printed as an
   appendix to Quentin Bell, *Virginia Woolf,* Vol. I.
2. See p. 254, note 2.

them to the right address. Would you let me have a line to say where this is?

I ought to have asked your leave to quote from some of your memories. But I took it, I hope rightly, that you would not mind.

Thank you again for letting me have the letters.

Yrs sincerely
Virginia Woolf

Houghton Library, Harvard University

3620: To John Lehmann   37 *Mecklenburgh Square, W.C.1.*

29th July 40

Dear John,

I handed on your message to Leonard, and we're both very sorry you couldn't come to Monk's House, and that your mother's ill again: please give her my sympathy. We could have offered you a great variety of air raid alarms, distant bombs, reports by Mrs Bleach who brought a stirrup pump[1] (installed, needless to say in my bedroom) of battles out at sea. Indeed its rather lovely about 2 in the morning to see the lights stalking the Germans over the marshes. But this remains on tap, so you must propose yourself later. And let me know if you want to meet the Major [Gardner] and hear about—what was it?—why the crab walks sideways?

Leonard's tackling Mrs N [Nicholls, Hogarth Press]. downstairs— showers of confidences and complaints, also children's letters make the room almost uninhabitable he says; and he's teaching Miss Griffiths how to mark off [for printing]. I'm quite pleased with the sales of R. F. so far—L. is binding more.

Don't bother to read it now, but some day I should value your opinion very much. Its no good reading other people's books when one's writing one's own. I hope your Penguin is a fully feathered bird by this time,[2] with a vast throat to swallow all the sprats. I'd like you to print the Leaning Tower,[3] if I can bring myself to revise it, which I loathe. Also, when would you want it—also, what about America? I mean can I print simultaneously there? But at the moment I can't stop reading Coleridge—thanks to you, I'm lured back into the ancients, and read a William Morris,[4] chants for

1. For extinguishing incendiary bombs.
2. Penguin Books published in 1940 a selection from *New Writing*, edited by Lehmann.
3. Virginia's lecture to the Workers' Educational Association. Lehmann published it in *Folios of New Writing* (Autumn 1940).
4. The poet, designer, and socialist (1834-96), whose *Chants for Socialists* (seven poems) appeared in 1885.

socialists, with immense pleasure. So I can't bring myself to do anything I ought to do.

Forgive this long letter,

Yr V. W.

John Lehmann

3621: To J. B. PRIESTLEY   *Monk's House, Rodmell, Lewes, Sussex*

Typewritten
2nd Aug 1940

Dear Mr Priestley,

I shall be glad to join the general committee of the Authors national committee.[1] Many thanks for asking me. Your letter has been following me about, or I would have written before.

Yours sincerely
Virginia Woolf

Texas

3622: To V. SACKVILLE-WEST   *Monk's House, Rodmell, near Lewes, Sussex*

6th Aug [1940]

Oh yes do come—I've been in such a pelt that I couldn't write before. So now merely suggest, emphatically, *Friday 16th*[2] ... stay the night and its understood that means all Saturday—no evasions about lunch, or someone waiting at Sissinghurst.

Great lorries are carrying sandbags down to the river: guns are being emplaced on the Banks. So do come before its all ablaze. At the moment, the flowers are doing their bit. This jargon from my first aid practice, and the Womens Institute.

Oh dear how nice to see you—and there's the gold [saccharine] box, only one or two tablets pilfered, on the table.

1. A committee organised by the publisher Stanley Unwin, and joined by Priestley, Hugh Walpole, Geoffrey Faber and A. P. Herbert. They waged a campaign against the inclusion of books in the proposed Purchase Tax. The proposal was eventually dropped by the Government.
2. Vita, after all, did not go to Rodmell on that day. A later arrangement for 30 August was also cancelled because of the constant German air-raids on Kent and Sussex.

Louies [Everest] father is being buried in state; so I have to wash up and must now descend to the sink.

V.

I did all the peas; potatoes; and made a pie.

Berg

3623: To Desmond MacCarthy   *Monk's House, Rodmell,*
Lewes, Sussex

6th Aug [1940]

Dearest Desmond,

Your article[1] made me so happy that I must write and thank you. I was afraid I had made an awful hash of Roger. It was the very deuce to do. So bless you for seeing with your affable but hawklike eye[2] what I was at. I'd just been reading that venomous and malignant little man Herbert Read in the Spectator.[3]

Yr Virginia

I'm afraid your mystic voice must have meant Armistice Day 1941 [*unexplained*]. Nessa and Duncan, by the way, did supply an account of Roger's painting, anonymously, in an appendix [to *Roger Fry*].

Mrs Michael MacCarthy

3624: To Clive Bell   *Monk's House, Rodmell,*
Lewes, Sussex

Tuesday [6 August 1940]

Dearest Clive,

Your letter gave me very great pleasure. I valued your opinion so much that I didn't send you a copy so as not to influence you even to the extent of 12/o. But its at your service if you want it. But it isnt only my author's vanity thats pleased. I've been haunted by the fear that I'd not brought out Roger's qualities. Now that you approve I dont care a snap what anyone

1. In the *Sunday Times* (4 August) Desmond MacCarthy wrote that Virginia had presented a completely convincing portrait of Roger Fry, and he only regretted that she had not felt qualified to make more of his painting.
2. MacCarthy's pseudonym was 'Affable Hawk'.
3. See next letter.

says—the only detractor so far is Herbert Read who's voided all his spite against Roger in the Spectator.[1] What, I wonder, was the cause?

I didn't myself feel that the first part was dull, nor did I think the break so marked, but one gets so immersed in detail and I was also so fascinated by Roger's progress, that I felt I couldn't judge. Of course the great difficulty was not to intervene oneself, and yet not to be colourless. I've never done anything so devilishly difficult—Well this is only to thank you for writing. I dont know when a letter gave me (and not my vanity) such satisfaction. And there's a heap of things I want to talk to you about.

Yr V. W.

Quentin Bell

3625: To V. Sackville-West   *Monk's House, Rodmell,*
                                     near Lewes, Sussex
12th Aug. [1940]

1. What about Friday 30th?—same condition: Saturday lunch.
2. Leonard must admit that he *had* this gadget[2] already; but is none the less grateful:
3. Country notes idea enthusiastically accepted:[3] good news already sent to John: who will communicate officially.
4. Why dont we some day meet at Sheffield Park and see Gibbons home?[4] I throw this out as a plan to be considered when you come. So let me know that you *do* come: and isn't this a plain direct business like letter.
5. Love. Rather pestered by niece [Judith Stephen] and her young man [Leslie Humphreys]: nice niece; dull young man:
    so must stop—

V.

Berg

1. Read praised Virginia and the book, calling it "honest, sympathetic, understanding and . . . objective in its design and workmanship"; but he gave Roger Fry himself a bad review: "It [Fry's sensibility] gave him immense joy and stimulated him to endless intellectual research; but it could not prevail against the Inheritance—against the pettiness and the protectiveness of the Ivory Tower, against the benevolence of the Liberal outlook, against the intellect's pretensions to the final word."
2. A gardening tool costing 4d.
3. A further volume (the first had been published by Michael Joseph in 1939) of Vita's articles from *The New Statesman and Nation*. It was called *Country Notes in Wartime*, and was published by the Hogarth Press in the autumn.
4. The historian Edward Gibbon (1737-94) lived most of his life in London and Switzerland, but he often visited his friend John Holroyd, 1st Earl of Sheffield (1735-1821), at his home, Sheffield Park, near Uckfield, Sussex. See Virginia's article *Reflections at Sheffield Place* (*New Statesman*, 19 June, 1937).

411

3626: To R. C. Trevelyan   *Monk's House, Rodmell,*
                                             Lewes, Sussex

12th Aug 1940

Dear Bob,

Your letter gave me very great pleasure. You knew Roger long before
I did, and in many ways must have known him better. I was terribly afraid
that my portrait of him wouldn't seem to you a true one. Its a great relief
to me that you and Bessy like it.[1] The difficulties, as you say, were immense. Often I almost gave up in despair. I was so hampered by family
feelings (though the Frys have been very kind) and then the mass of letters
was bewildering. But I'm glad now, if you think its given something of
what Roger was, that I went on with it. I'm specially pleased that Julian[2]
was interested—Roger would have liked to attract the younger generation.

We're having—much to our surprise—to print a second edition. I'm
sending some of your corrections, but doubt if they'll be in time. If you
could let me have the others, I would keep them, in case there should ever
be a 3rd edition. Dear me, how careless to let so many creep in: Margery
Fry, Leonard and Vanessa, all read the MS: and I hoped it was unusually
accurate.

We would very much like to see you. In the autumn we shall be in
London, at 37 Meckg Sqre, every other week, so we could easily arrange it,
if you'd let us know when you're up.

I'm so sorry about Bessy's eyes. I enjoyed a thing she wrote in the
Abinger Chronicle so much.[3]

What are you working at?

Leonard and I send our love—and again it was a pleasure to get your
letter.

                                             Yr ever
                                             Virginia Woolf

Sussex

1. See Letter 3641.
2. Julian Trevelyan (b. 1910), the painter, was the son of Robert and Elizabeth
   ('Bessie') Trevelyan.
3. *The Foreigner in the English Landscape*, by Elizabeth Trevelyan, published in
   the *Abinger Chronicle* in the issue for March 1940. The *Chronicle* was founded in
   December 1939, and was the local monthly journal of Abinger Common,
   Surrey.

3627: To Benedict Nicolson

Typewritten
13 Aug. 1940

Dear Ben,

Just as I began to read your letter, an air raid warning sounded. I'll put down the reflections that occurred to me, as honestly, if I can, as you put down your reflections on reading my life of Roger Fry while giving air raid alarms at Chatham.[1]

There goes that damned siren, I said to myself, and dipped into your letter. You were making extracts from Roger's letters as you listened. "Returning slowly through France he stopped in many of the towns and villages...." I began making extracts from your biography. "Returning slowly from Italy with Jeremy Hutchinson, Ben Nicolson reached Venice in May 1935 ...".

Here the raiders came over head. I went and looked at them. Then I returned to your letter. "I am so struck by the fools paradise in which he and his friends lived. He shut himself out from all disagreeable actualities and allowed the spirit of Nazism to grow without taking any steps to check it...." Lord, I thought to myself, Roger shut himself out from disagreeable actualities did he? Roger who faced insanity, death and every sort of disagreeable—what can Ben mean? Are Ben and I facing actualities because we're listening to bombs dropping on other people? And I went on with Ben Nicolson's biography. After returning from a delightful tour in Italy, for which his expensive education at Eton and Oxford had well fitted him, he got a job as keeper of the King's pictures. Well, I thought, Ben was a good deal luckier than Roger. Roger's people were the very devil; when he was Ben's age he was earning his living by extension lecturing and odd jobs of reviewing. He had to wait till he was over sixty before he got a Slade professorship. And I went on to think of that very delightful party that you gave in Guildford Street two months before the war. I remembered Isaiah Berlin[2] discussing philosophy—not Spinozas—[G. E.] Moores—with Leonard; Stephen Spender flirting with a young Freud; Cressida Ridley[3] and all the rest of the young talking exactly as we used to talk at Bernard Street.[4] Then I looked at your letter.. "This

1. See p. 398, note 1.
2. Isaiah Berlin (b. 1909), the philosopher and Fellow of All Souls College, Oxford. He had a great influence upon Ben Nicolson's and subsequent generations of Oxford undergraduates. Ben's party was on 14 July 1939.
3. The daughter of Sir Maurice and Lady Violet Bonham Carter, who married Jasper Ridley in 1939. He was a close friend of Ben Nicolson at Oxford, and was killed in the war.
4. 48 Bernard Street, Bloomsbury, Roger Fry's house from 1927 until his death in 1934.

intensely private world which Roger Fry cultivated could only be communicated to a few people as sensitive and intelligent as himself . . ." Why then did Ben Nicolson give these parties? Why did he take a job under Kenneth Clark at Windsor? Why didn't he chuck it all away and go into politics? After all, war was a great deal closer in 1939 than in 1900.

Here the raiders began emitting long trails of smoke. I wondered if a bomb was going to fall on top of me; I wondered if I was facing disagreeable actualities; I wondered what I could have done to stop bombs and disagreeable actualities . . . Then I dipped into your letter again. "This all sounds as though I wish to say that the artist, the intellectual, has no place in modern society. On the contrary, his mission is now more vital than it has ever been. He will still be shocked by stupidity and untruth but instead of ignoring it he will set out to fight it; instead of retreating into his tower to uphold certain ethical standards his job will be to persuade as many other people as possible to think and behave in the same way—and on his success and failure depends the future of the world."

Who on earth, I thought, did that job more incessantly and successfully than Roger Fry? Didn't he spend half his life, not in a tower, but travelling about England addressing masses of people, who'd never looked at a picture and making them see what he saw? And wasn't that the best way of checking Nazism? Then I opened another letter; as it happened from Sebastian Sprott,[1] a lecturer at Nottingham; and I read how he'd once been mooning around the S.Kensington Museum ". . . then I saw Roger. All was changed. In ten minutes he caused me to enjoy what I was looking at. The objects became vivid and intelligible . . . There must be many people like me, people with scales on their eyes and wax in their ears . . . if only someone would come along and remove the scales and dig out the wax. Roger Fry did it . . ."

Then the raiders passed over. And I thought I cant have given Ben the least notion of what Roger was like. I suppose it was my fault. Or is it partly, and naturally, that he must have a scapegoat? I admit I want one. I loathe sitting here waiting for a bomb to fall; when I want to be writing. If it doesn't kill me its killing someone else. Where can I lay the blame? On the Sackvilles. On the Dufferins? On Eton and Oxford?[2] They did precious little it seems to me to check Nazism. People like Roger and Goldie Dickinson did an immense deal it seems to me. Well, we differ in our choice of scapegoats.

But what I'd like to know is, suppose we both survive this war, what

1. W. J. H. ('Sebastian') Sprott (1897-1971), a friend of Maynard Keynes and Lytton Strachey, was Lecturer in Psychology at Nottingham University. For Virginia's reply to his letter see Letter 3629.
2. Ben Nicolson was at both. His mother Vita was a Sackville. His father's aunt Hariot married the Viceroy of India, Marquess of Dufferin and Ava.

ought we to do to prevent another? I shall be too old to do anything but write. But will you throw up your job as an art critic and take to politics? And if you stick to art criticism, how will you make it more public and less private than Roger did? About the particular points you raise; I think if you'll read some of last articles in Transformations [1926] you'll find that Roger got beyond the very classical and intellectual painters; and did include Rembrandt, Titian and so on. I've no doubt you're right in saying that his attempts at the sort of Berenson[1] connoiseurship were lamentable. I've never read BB, so I cant say. I did read Roger's last Slade lectures[2] however; and was much impressed by the historical knowledge shown there. But of course I'm not an art critic; and have no right to express an opinion.

Well, the hostile aeroplanes have passed over my head now; I suppose they're dropping bombs over Newhaven and Seaford.

I hope this letter doesn't sound unkind. Its only because I liked your being honest so much that I've tried to be. And of course I know you're having a much worse time of it at the moment than I am ... Another siren has just sounded.

Yours ever
Virginia Woolf

[*handwritten:*]
I'm not sure, on reading this letter over, that I'm right to send it. It sounds too severe. I've been discussing it with Leonard. He says he thinks everybody's to blame for the present condition of the world, but the difficulty is to see what anyone—or in a particular case Roger Fry—could have done, which would have made the slightest difference to what has happened. Equally, I think you'll understand I'm not blaming you, and so send it.

Vanessa Nicolson

3628: To Sibyl Colefax   Monk's House [*Rodmell,
                                    Sussex*]

14th Aug [1940]

Dearest Sibyl,
What a faithful friend you are—reading your friends' books, when you have so many friends who write books. I'm delighted that you heard the voice of Roger. I never thought that anything would come through those innumerable cardboard boxes stuffed with bills and love letters. It's a great consolation to me that it has. I only dip into London now for a few

1. Bernard Berenson (1865-1959), the art historian who in his early life specialised in attributions of Italian paintings.
2. Fry was appointed Slade Professor of Fine Art at Cambridge in 1933. His *Last Lectures* were published posthumously in 1939.

distracted hours—no time to get to Westminster. So you must take us on one of your owling flights over the fields. But we're almost daily shot at—it's not what they call a healthy neighbourhood. If you hear that Virginia has disarmed 6 German pilots you wont be in the least surprised, will you?

                                              Yrs V. W.,
                                                    with gratitude
Michael Colefax

3629: To W. J. H. Sprott   *Monk's House, Rodmell,*
                                          Lewes, Sussex
15th Aug 40

My dear Sebastian,

I was so glad to hear from you that you liked my life of Roger. It wasn't an easy book to write, as you can imagine; there were so many feelings to consider, and such a mass of odds and ends out of which to make a whole. So I'm very glad that it has brought him back to you. Oddly enough, its being successful.

I never meant to be severe on critics, as you say I've been: only on the reviewers who ought to grow into critics instead of remaining sprats and minnows. It struck me, going through Roger's papers, how I wished he had done fewer articles, and more books.

I'm sorry you are so immersed in fat squat little men at Rotary Clubs [in Nottingham]. We are now living a betwixt and between life—half in the midst of our village—which must be typical of all villages—and half, or less than half, at 37 Mecklenburgh Square. Air raids are now twice daily here. Nobody pays them much attention so far.

If life continues in the autumn, wont you come and see us in Mecklenburgh Sqre? We should like very much to see you again: and both send our love.

                                          Yr ever
                                              Virginia Woolf
King's

3630: To Sir William Rothenstein
                                          Monk's House, Rodmell,
                                          Lewes, Sussex
15th Aug 40

Dear Sir William

Many thanks for your letter. I am so glad that you find my life of Roger Fry on the whole a fair portrait. I did my best to make it so; but of course there were great difficulties. I am not sure what phrase of mine led you to think that I asserted "that those of us who did not follow Roger have been left behind." What I think I said was that when Roger spoke of those who, like Professor Tonks[1] for example, saw nothing in Cézanne, he conveyed the impression that in his opinion they "had receded into the background." I did not express any opinion of my own, for naturally it would have been worthless. And of course I should not think of giving my opinion as to what had or had not influenced the work of John, Steer, and Sickert.[2] No doubt, as you say, Roger had no influence upon them. But many of the younger artists have told me that Roger's influence upon their work was very great. That, I think, it was right to state. But I should be incapable of saying—and certainly did not say—whether he did or did not "deter some of the younger men from following their natural bent." That of course must be left to experts to decide. And I hoped that I had made it plain that I have no such qualification.

I am sorry for the delay in returning your [Fry] letters. They were in London, I found; but I had them sent yesterday, and I hope they have reached you safely.

Thank you again for allowing me to use them.

Yours sincerely
Virginia Woolf

Houghton Library, Harvard University

3631: To Ethel Smyth   *Monk's House, Rodmell*
                                         near Lewes, Sussex

16th Aug. [1940]

My opinion of you as a critic has gone up almost to fever height. I suppose I wronged you, but I thought, Ethel will never see what I've been at. She'll say this is a dull meticulous book about a dull pedantic man. And then you go and pick up the trail at once—well, at second reading—and follow it with your nose to the ground and pounce upon the heart and centre of the book as though I'd stuck red and green lights at every point.

Of course I dimmed those lights deliberately. That was my intention—to lead my reader on, till without my showing him, he (in this case she) saw. Now Vita didn't see: but your letter I thought a miracle of discernment. It was an experiment in self suppression; a gamble in R's power to transmit himself. And so rich and to me alive and various and masterly was he that I was certain he would shine by his own light better than through any painted shade of mine. Lord! how I sweated! But to my amazement, its succeeded.

1. Henry Tonks (1862-1937), the painter, and from 1918-30 Professor at the Slade School. For Fry's opinion of Tonks see Virginia's *Roger Fry*, pp. 168-9.
2. Augustus John (1878-1961), Philip Wilson Steer (1860-1942), and Walter Sickert (also 1860-1942).

That is, its selling; the public does see Roger plain: in fact we're printing a second edition—and now a third is to be ordered—Heres an air raid siren. . . .

Then Mrs Ebbs come to borrow my table for a village play. Then my niece Judith and her young man to borrow bread. I'm afraid, in this racket, theres no chance of writing coherent thanks: all the same I was very happy, reading your letter. And amazed once more, at the surprises you hold under your 3 cornered hat. Oh yes, send me your marginalia—please do—and any further comments—about Roger, or about the invisible V—the submerged V. I rather respect her, for going under. . . .

V.

Berg

3632: To R. C. Trevelyan   *Monk's House, Rodmell,*
                                  Lewes, Sussex
18th Aug [1940]

Dear Bob,

Many thanks for sending the corrections. I'm sending them, or the most important, for some I think dont matter—off at once. The book is selling extremely well, much to our surprise, and we are having to reprint a third time. I'm very pleased, as I thought nobody would read it at the present moment. And it shows that Roger does come through and excite interest. Of course it would have been much easier, for me, to write a fantasy about him, as Arthur Waley I think suggests,[1] I should have done. But then I dont feel his letters dull; and I wanted him to speak for himself. So many people are interested that I think it was the right way. Anyhow, I felt it was.

I'm glad you're writing poetry. I like yours better and better whenever I re-read them. I think thats the only test. And I read more and more poetry now. I wish I could read Latin and Greek easily:[2] so as I cant, I shall like to have your translation. How I envy you, being able to do that! Latin always floors me.

Yrs ever
Virginia Woolf

Sussex

1. Arthur Waley reviewed *Roger Fry* in *The Listener* of 15 August.
2. Trevelyan had made many translations from the Greek and Latin, most recently *Translations From Horace Etc, With Two Imaginary Conversations* (1940). For Virginia's reactions to this book see Letter 3667.

3633: To Benedict Nicolson   [*Monk's House, Rodmell,*
                                              Sussex]
Draft of Letter 3634, typewritten[1]
[24 August 1940]

Dear Ben,
    My letter [No. 3627] was also written very hastily; no doubt I mis-
interpreted what you said, though I didn't mean to. To be frank, I doubt if
I've got your meaning in your last letter. But I would like to understand
your point of view; and if possible make you understand mine. So I answer,
in the hope that the sirens will remain silent.
    "My quarrel" you say "is not with art but with Bloomsbury." What do
you mean by Bloomsbury? It is rather as if I should say, My quarrel is not
with art but with Mayfair, meaning by Mayfair Ben Nicolson, Vita, Eddie
Sackville, the Sitwells, Stephen Tennant and David Cecil. You would feel
I meant something vaguely abusive, but you would find it very difficult to
say what. Apparently you mean by 'Bloomsbury' a set of people who sat
on the floor at Bernard Street saying "More and more I understand nothing
of humanity in the mass" and were content with that, instead of trying to
make humanity in the mass understand and appreciate what you know and
say. It was Roger Fry who said "I understand nothing of humanity in the
mass." I did not say that: if you impute that to me, then you must also
impute to me his saying "More and more I dread the imprisonment of
egotism." You must make me responsible for teaching elementary school
children in the black country how to dress, for setting up the Omega, for
decorating the walls of the Boro Polytechnic.[2]
    But in fact I am not responsible for anything Roger did or said. My own
education and my own point of view were entirely different from his. I
never went to school or college. My father spent perhaps £100 on my
education. When I was a young woman I tried to share the fruits of that
very imperfect education with the working classes by teaching literature at
Morley College; by holding a Womens Cooperative Guild meeting weekly;
and, politically, by working for the vote.[3] It is true I wrote books and

----

1. Virginia worked on this letter more carefully than on any other private letter of
   which we have a record. First she typed it. Then she added and altered a great
   deal in manuscript, including one whole page which amounts to a second
   draft. Then she retyped it (Letter 3634). About one-third of the draft and
   its inter-lineations have been omitted because they are repetitive of the final
   letter.
2. For 'children' see *Roger Fry*, p. 206; for Omega, p. 182 ff.; for Borough Polytechnic, p. 173.
3. Virginia taught evening classes at Morley College, south London, from 1905-7;
   she held Guild meetings at Hogarth House, Richmond, from 1916-20; and in
   1910 she worked for Women's Suffrage.

some of those books, like the Common Reader, A Room of One's Own and Three Guineas (in which I did my best to destroy Sackvilles and Dufferins) have sold many thousand copies. That is, I did my best to make them reach a far wider circle than a little private circle of exquisite and cultivated people. And to some extent I succeeded. Leonard too is Bloomsbury. He has spent half his life in writing books like International Government, like the Barbarians at the gates, like Empire and Commerce, to prevent the growth of Nazism; and to create a League of Nations. Maynard Keynes is Bloomsbury. He wrote the [Economic] Consequences of the Peace. Lytton Strachey was Bloomsbury. His books had a very large circulation and certainly influenced a wider circle than any small group. Duncan has made a living ever since he was a boy by painting. These are facts about Bloomsbury and they do seem to me to prove that they have done their very best to make humanity in the mass appreciate what they knew and saw.

To return to Roger Fry himself. You say that his "interpretation of art was too sophisticated, too private for the general public." Yet he could fill the Queens Hall with two thousand listeners from all classes when he lectured. Can Herbert Read do that, or Berenson, or Kenneth Clark?

But you say "You must educate your public. Taste and appreciation can never improve until attitudes of mind are changed ..." There I agree with you. I cant answer for what Roger felt. But I do feel myself that I ought to have been able to make not merely thousands of people interested in literature; but millions. Why have I failed to do that? The other day [27 April] I went and lectured to the WEA at Brighton, and felt that it was hopeless for me to tell people who had been taken away from school at the age of 14 that they must read Shakespeare. It is impossible so long as they are educated as they are. Now my own education (alone among books) was a very bad one. Yours too, at Eton and Oxford was I think tho better than mine a bad one. What is the kind of education people ought to have? That it seems to me is the problem we have got to solve. Until we do, we must have people like Roger Fry talking only to thousands instead of to millions. I dont think he was wrong in the way he taught them; but I think it was impossible for them to learn. We must have Mayfair (your group) and Bloomsbury (my group,)—But can the Roger Frys change the education? Isn't that for politicians?

My own feeling is that Roger Fry did the best he could, given his education, given the society in which he was brought up. (He gave his own views on the artist and society by the way in Vision and Design [1920]). But the best he could was limited by the society. My puzzle is, ought artists now to become politicians? My instinct says no; but I'm not sure that I can justify my instinct. I take refuge in the fact that I've received so little from society that I owe it very little. But thats not altogether satisfactory; and anyhow it doesn't apply to you. I suppose I'm obtuse, but I

cant find your answer in your letter, how it is that you are going to change
the attitudes of the mass of people by remaining an art critic.

Sussex

3634: To Benedict Nicolson   *Monk's House, Rodmell,*
                                     Lewes [Sussex]
Typewritten
24th August [1940]

Dear Ben,
     Thank you very much for writing again. I think its extraordinarily nice
of you to write to me, and Vita is quite wrong if she thinks or fears that
anything you've said has annoyed me. It didn't in the least. And I hope I
didn't annoy you by what I said. Its very difficult, when one writes letters in
a hurry, as I always do, not to make them sound abrupt. I only want to
say how much I like your honesty.
     I dont think its much good discussing Bloomsbury, because if I couldn't
make you see what I think it means in my book, I certainly can't in a
letter. So I'll only say that I dont think your quotation from one of Roger's
letters represents what he thought—for there are other quotations that give
quite a different view. Nor do I think it represents a point of view common
to all his friends. But aren't you taking what you call 'Bloomsbury' much
too seriously? I dont think that those people whom I suppose you to mean
had the very great gifts that are needed to alter society. What puzzles me is
that the people who had infinitely greater gifts than any of us had—I
mean Keats, Shelley, Wordsworth, Coleridge and so on—were unable to
influence society. They didn't have anything like the influence they should
have had upon 19th century politics. And so we drifted into imperialism
and all the other horrors that led to 1914. Would they have had more
influence if they had taken an active part in politics? Or would they only
have written worse poetry?
     I entirely agree with you when you say "You must educate your public.
Taste and appreciation can never improve until attitudes of mind are
changed." I felt that very much the other day when I lectured the W.E.A.
on poetry at Brighton. It seemed to me useless to tell people who left school
at 14 and were earning their livings in shops and factories that they ought
to enjoy Shakespeare. But how can we, if we remain artists, give them that
education, or change their conditions?
     I dont know whether I'm right in thinking from what you say in your
letter—"There is no doubt that I shall be more useful in Venice than in
Hyde Park"—that you feel it can be done. Does that mean that you
feel that you see something in pictures that Roger didn't, and that by

making people see this you can influence them in time to change their attitude without changing their education and conditions by political methods?

I hope you will be able to. It would solve many problems. Anyhow I think you've made a good beginning if you hate people who sit on the floor and despise humanity. So if my life of Roger helped to teach you that, it wasn't altogether wasted.

Here a young man from the War office interrupts; about putting up a pill box in our field. Also there is an air raid on. So excuse this very inadequate letter. Last Sunday we had five raiders almost crashing into the dining room. Then they machine gunned the next village, and apparently went on to Sissinghurst.

Vita says you've had an awful time at Chatham.

Yours ever
Virginia Woolf

Vanessa Nicolson

3635: To Dora Sanger[1]

Monk's House, Rodmell,
Lewes, Sussex

24th Aug [1940]

It was very nice of you to write about my life of Roger. I'm delighted that it interested you. I daresay I stressed the Quaker influence too much, but it certainly played a very large part in R's letters. The difficulty was that letters give a partial view; and for so much of his life I had only letters, and the family, who kept letters, predominated.

We so often think of you and Charlie. We are all congregated here, with many air raids.

V. W.

Daphne Sanger

3636: To Angelica Bell

Monk's House, Rodmell
[Sussex]

Tuesday [27 August 1940]

Darling Pix,

This letter shows you the esteem in which you are held in Rodmell. I leave it to you to arrange with the Rehearsers.[2] Then you will take a meal

1. The widow of C. P. Sanger (1871-1930), the barrister and editor of the standard work on wills. Virginia had known the Sangers through her brother Thoby (d. 1906).
2. Angelica Garnett now (1980) believes that this was a production of *A Midsummer Night's Dream*, planned by the Women's Institute of Rodmell, which she directed.

here, and examine your naked boys—the embroidery I mean. I've picked out private parts bright red. But its a bit of a muddle.

This is to say may we come over and see you and Brock [David Garnett] on Monday next—I think about 3. Then we could have a gossip. The witches are fairly on the ramp. Louie has adopted a 3 day old lamb. I'm now off to a fire [air raid] meeting.

Let me have a card.

V.

Texas

3637: To Ruth Fry   *Monk's House, Rodmell,*
                                     Sussex

28 Aug 1940

Dear Ruth[1]—yes of course we agreed that surnames were an abomination between us—

Thank you very much for your letter. I neednt tell you what a great relief and satisfaction it is to me that you should like my life of Roger. I know how I should have felt if someone were writing the life of my brother. And I was terribly afraid, as I wrote it, that you would find things that annoyed you, or would disagree with what I said. I did my best to let Roger tell his own life, but of course one cant simply do that. And it was a question, how far to intrude, and how far to suppress, oneself. I'm so glad you noticed the sentence I brought in to show his change toward your mother, and hers to him.[2] I felt it rounded off that long and sometimes very painful relationship. I know there should have been more dates, but so many events had to be telescoped in order to keep the book within bounds that dates often didn't seem to fit. Also there should have been a bibliography— I admit I shirked it, from laziness partly, partly that to be complete one would have had an almost endless chase through magazines and papers. I don't suppose he collected a tenth part of his writing.

When the nine children were born was a great puzzle even to Margery. I'm sorry I put you in the wrong house, and where was Roger born?[3]

It sold amazingly well till the first air raid on London, when the sales instantly stopped. Whether they'll recover I don't know. But I've had so many letters from his friends that I think it's reached them, and as you say, the reviews have been kinder much than I expected.

1. Ruth Fry (1876-1962) was Roger's youngest sister. She was a pacifist, and served as Secretary for the Friends War Victims Relief, 1914-18.
2. "The old restraint had gone and it was 'a real pleasure' to talk to her" (*Roger Fry*, p. 261).
3. At 6 The Grove, Highgate, which Virginia identifies in the opening sentence of her biography.

Once more, I'm so very glad that you liked it. And thank you for saying so.

I will send back the early picture of Highgate of Roger's, if I can find a safe way.

Please tell Lady Gibb[1] how glad I am she enjoyed the book.

Yrs Virginia Woolf

Thank you for sending Gerald Heard's article.[2] I've been in London so have not yet had time to read it.

Pamela Diamand

3638: To V. Sackville-West   *Monk's House, Rodmell,*
                               near Lewes, Sussex
Friday [30 August 1940]

I've just stopped talking to you. It seems so strange. Its perfectly peaceful here—theyre playing bowls—I'd just put flowers in your room. And there you sit with the bombs falling round you.

What can one say—except that I love you and I've got to live through this strange quiet evening thinking of you sitting there alone.

Dearest—let me have a line—let us meet next week. But one can scarcely bear it. Only we must.

Yr loving
V.

You have given me such happiness.
385 Lewes. Ring me up anytime.

Berg

3639: To Benedict Nicolson   *Monk's House, Rodmell,*
                               Lewes, Sussex
2nd Sept [1940]

Dear Ben,

You say 'next week'—I suppose thats now this week. No, if its this week, we shant be up at all. What I would suggest is, couldn't you possibly come here for a night? If so, ring up Lewes 385. We should very much enjoy seeing you. We could argue incessantly in between raids. And theres

---

1. Norah Gibb (who died later this year), wife of Sir Alexander Gibb (1872-1958), the civil engineer.
2. For Gerald Heard, see p. 366, note 2. This article has not been traced.

always a bed of sorts. If its the week of the 9th, then we may be up—I'm not sure; but would let you know.

In any case answer my letter at even greater length. I love getting your letters, and thinking out completely smashing replies. Only its easier to talk them, so we must meet.

Excuse this scrawl—to catch post.

I'm so happy you found the life of R. F interesting as well as infuriating. I was very anxious to know what you thought.

Yr ever
V. W.

Vanessa Nicolson

3640: To Mrs G. E. Easdale   *Monk's House, Rodmell,*
                                    Lewes, Sussex

3rd Sept 40

Dear Mrs Easdale,

I thought this year it would be impossible for you to remember the flowers—or if you did, you wouldn't be able to get them. And then the cardboard box came and there they were! So I shall have one blazing bunch all the winter. Thank you so much. I can only send you plums from our garden,—I dont suppose you want plums. We have a record crop. We live mostly down here; but go up to London—37 Mecklenburgh Sqre—every other week.

Yes, we are humming with Germans here—as we were playing bowls one came low down, and we took it for English till they started firing. For 2 days though we've been at peace.

Kent sounds much worse. But I agree—the country is better than London with raids or without. I saw the birth of Joan's baby in the paper. I'm so glad its over happily. Please congratulate her from us, only we hope she won't stop writing. And let us believe that some day we shall all meet—babies and all—in peace.

Thank you again for the flowers, and all your trouble.

Yrs sincerely
Virginia Woolf

University of London

3641: To Mrs R. C. Trevelyan   *Monk's House, Rodmell,*
                                      Lewes, Sussex

4th Sept 40

Dear Bessie,

It was delightful of you to write to me about my life of Roger. You have

425

found out exactly what I was trying to do when you compare it to a piece of music. Its odd, for I'm not regularly musical, but I always think of my books as music before I write them. And especially with the life of Roger,— there was such a mass of detail that the only way I could hold it together was by abstracting it into themes. I did try to state them in the first chapter, and then to bring in developments and variations, and then to make them all heard together and end by bringing back the first theme in the last chapter. Just as you say, I am extraordinarily pleased that you felt this. No one else has I think. And I dont wonder, for I was often crushed under the myriad details. It wasn't only the difficulty of making quotations fit—so many things had to be muted, or only hinted. And there is always a certain constraint, which one doesn't feel in fiction, a sense of other people looking over one's shoulder. I cant say how glad I am that you and Bob who both knew Roger so well think it a true portrait of him. Bob went all through his life even though, as so often happens, they met less often towards the end. I understand your being shy with him. I wasn't exactly shy, but I sometimes felt overpowered, and so uneasy. But nobody—none of my friends—made such a difference to my life as he did. And yet, writing about him, one had to keep that under.

Thank you so much for writing. I hope we may meet some day—we shall be a good deal in London this winter. But everything's difficult now. I'm so sorry about your eyes. Does it make a difference to your music?

With love from us both.

Yr affectionate
Virginia Woolf

Trinity College, Cambridge

3642: To David Cecil

Monk's House, Rodmell,
Lewes, Sussex

4th Sept [1940]

Dear David,

I liked very much getting a letter from my fellow biographer. I would have answered before, but was up in London—air raids: down here—more air raids. (London, by the way, is now 37 Mecklenburgh Square). When I'd finished my book, I thought, David's book is much better than mine, but then he didn't have such a difficult task. I doubt that it is possible to write a friend's life. In fact I came to the conclusion that it isn't, and only went on because I'd said I would. There's so much one can't say, and so much one mustn't say. Though the Frys were very good, I always felt them in the background. And then the switch over from quotation to narrative. And then the love affairs, and the quarrels with artists, and then the bare patches and the profusions—altogether its not a task I'd undertake again, but I'm immeasurably pleased if you got a vision of him, in spite of everything. I wish you had known him.

Its an age since we met. We've left Tavistock for Mecklenburgh, but live mostly down here. And you're in Shropshire. I hope you don't get German planes flying over your lawn, as we do. Not that they've done us any damage. And I hope you get time for Lord Melbourne, as well as the Oxford lectures.[1] I'm longing for a second volume of Melbourne.[2] Meanwhile I am deep in Coleridge. Have you ever tackled the life of Coleridge? I wish you would. I've just discovered the fact that Mrs Coleridge wore a wig—a short dry wig in the morning, like old grass. That explains a lot.

How is Rachel?[3] What's her baby like? Shall we ever meet in peace?—or in London?

I hope so. And thank you again for writing. Please, if you ever have time, write again. There's so much to talk about.

Love from us both.

Yrs ever V. W.

David Cecil

1. David Cecil was a Fellow of New College, Oxford.
2. Cecil's *The Young Melbourne* was published in 1939. His companion volume, *Lord M*, appeared in 1954.
3. His wife, the daughter of Desmond MacCarthy. Their first child, Jonathan Hugh, was born in February 1939.

Letters 3643-3674 (September–December 1940)

In September the fighter-battles over Rodmell were succeeded by bomber attacks on London, but the German planes were intercepted over Sussex and Virginia saw much of the intervening action. She seemed more exhilarated by it than frightened. When the banks of the River Ouse were breached by a bomb, she was entranced by the scenic effect. The bombers slowly gnawed at central London, which she quite often visited, and both her houses there were destroyed or rendered uninhabitable. Mecklenburgh Square was the first to go, in September, and then Tavistock Square in October, as well as Vanessa's and Duncan's studios in Fitzroy Street. The Woolfs removed their salvaged possessions to Monk's House and neighbouring cottages and barns, and Rodmell remained their only home till Virginia's death. The Hogarth Press was evacuated to Letchworth in Hertfordshire. Virginia was now writing journalism, and finished the draft of Pointz Hall. Her letters were almost exuberant, at times (especially when she wandered through battered London) inspired by a kind of patriotism. The invasion of Rodmell by the Anreps caused her more distress than the threatened invasion of Sussex by the Germans.

3643: To VIOLET DICKINSON   Monk's House, Rodmell,
                                             Lewes, Sussex

[8 September 1940]

My Violet,

(a raid is going on overhead, so dont expect much coherency—) You are an angel to toil through my efforts. This one was a damned effort. I had clouds of Quakers buzzing round me all the time I wrote. However, I was so devoted to him [Roger Fry] that I risked it. Did you ever meet him? I didnt get half his charm into the life—but you cant think what a job it was —Masses of love letters, bills, lectures, and so on, dumped on me—and I'm not a tidy woman by nature. Thank God its finished.

Leonard is out picking apples in the garden in spite of the planes. Do you get them?—oh there's the All Clear, which means I suppose they're off to London. I was going to say you ought to come and see our garden, which is the apple of Leonard's eye. As you can imagine, I never do a hands turn, but walk in the shade of the trees, and cant remember names. I've been wandering miles over the downs this afternoon, and must now read Katharine Furse's life of herself.[1]

I'm so old I could write a life of myself. But I remember too much. You, at Fritham [1902] laughing at our long skirts: and Theodore [Llewelyn] Davies hunting; and you—yes I remember all kinds of scenes with you—at Hyde Park Gate up in my room. One of these days I shall write about them. You were an angel to us,—d'you still wear that chain and the dolphin?—and why d'you think Nessa scorns you? I shall tell her tomorrow when she's coming over with her lovely daughter. Quentin works on a farm mercifully; and Clive sits up at night watching for Germans in a helmet. Leonard fights fires here. And so one day let us meet, and forgive this awful scrawl.

y. Sp[arroy].

Sussex

3644: To Ethel Smyth

Monk's House, Rodmell,
near Lewes, Sussex

11th Sept. [1940]

I've been meaning every day to write to you—that is I stop in the middle of something else and address a remark to you—but the moment never comes. And its not worth 2½ [stamp], I think, sending a thought: except that its quite worth 2½ getting a word from you. Yesterday we were up in London, and there was a crowd at Meck Sqre: a policeman stopped us: we got out—saw that the house just opposite ours across the road had been entirely crushed that night. A direct hit on top. It was nothing but a heap of bricks, smoking still. And we weren't allowed to go to 37, as a bomb was still in the square unexploded. Our house wasnt touched, but the windows are broken. So there was nothing for it but to come away. Everyone apparently in that house—one of those lovely houses at the side—had sheltered in the basement. All killed I suppose. We go up on Friday to arrange about moving the Press. and to bring back some of our valuables. that is if we're allowed. But everyone has been evacuated; the press cant work—And then we went and saw Holborn—my word—its like a nightmare. All heaps of glass, water running, a great gap at top of Chancery Lane; my typists office demolished.

I've just seen a plane shot down on the hill beside Lewes. We heard firing, ran out, and saw the plane swerve and fall, and then a burst of black smoke. Then the English plane circled and made off. There's the all clear.

1. Dame Katharine Furse, *Hearts and Pomegranates, Story of 45 Years, 1875-1920* (1940). She was Commandant-in-Chief of the Voluntary Aid Detachment (women's medical organisation) during World War I, and Director of the World Bureau of Girl Guides and Girl Scouts, 1928-38.

Thats why its so difficult to write a coherent letter. I try to write of a morning. Its odd to feel one's writing in a vacuum—no-one will read it. I feel the audience has gone. Still, so oddly is one made, I find I must spin my brain even in a vacuum.

But I want to know about you. Vita was coming but at the last moment she rang up. Bombs were dropping round Sissinghurst, and she had to stay, as she drives an ambulance. Rose Macaulay is doing the same in London. I admire that very much. Here we lead a disjointed jumping life. I had a niece staying here; another in a cottage. They collected friends in the airforce and so on. We had a fête: also a village play. The sirens sounded in the middle. All the mothers sat stolid. I also admired that very much. Oh I wanted to say: I've always admitted Maurice B[aring]. is a blind spot in me. I've no doubt you see whats there, and I dont. This refers to some remark of yours. The sale of Roger has been stopped completely by raids. Never mind: it had 3 weeks good run; and has landed me in endless letters. How people loved and hated him! Are you—doing what? Dear me: its true I should like to see you. You cohere like an orange globe, while the rest of the world scuds and streams.

V.

Post Script. Thursday [12 September]

I forgot to send this, so add a second sheet, by way of justifying my 2½ —though there's nothing to say.

Bomb in Meck Sqre still unexploded, everyone evacuated, but we go up tomorrow on the chance of being let in. For we must nail something over the windows. All our letters are left there and all work at the Press suspended. John Lehmann says we must evacuate the whole thing to the country. Yet the clerks seemed as tough as leather. And I've been writing about Coleridge,[1] and never noticed a siren, and I've been up on the hill picking blackberries for dinner, and lost a glove that was to have lasted a winter, and suddenly conceived the idea of a new book,[2] and really I think I can weather

1. Review of *Coleridge Fille: A Biography of Sara Coleridge*, by Earl Leslie Griggs (*New Statesman*, 26 October).
2. "Oh blackberrying, I conceived, or remoulded, an idea for a Common History Book—to read from one end of lit including biog: and range at will, consecutively" (AWD., 12 September 1940). For some time Virginia had been toying with the idea of a book on social history and its effect on literature, both British and possibly foreign. She worked on it intermittently until the end of her life, but left it unfinished. At first she called it *Reading at Random* or *Turning the Page*, and the first chapter was entitled *Anon* in her manuscript, and the second, *The Reader* (both *Berg*). The complicated history of this unfinished book, which took different shapes in her mind as she progressed, has been fully elucidated by Professor Brenda R. Silver in her '*Anon*' and '*The Reader*' (*Twentieth Century Literature*, Fall/Winter 1979).

—I mean weather cock—I mean brain spin—another ten years if Hitler doesn't drop a splinter into my machine. Churchill cheered me up.[1] Also this great gale thats blowing as it must have blown the other Armada. What touched and indeed raked what I call my heart in London was the grimy old woman at the lodging house at the back, all dirty after the raid, and preparing to sit out another. We, after all, have at least been to Italy and read Shakespeare. They havent: dear me, I'm turning democrat. And then, the passion of my life, that is the City of London—to see London all blasted, that too raked my heart. Have you that feeling for certain alleys and little courts, between Chancery Lane and the City? I walked to the Tower the other day by way of caressing my love of all that. We might be in the Strand, here at night, the raiders make such a noise of traffic—like buses and drays—in the sky. Now and then a bomb drops—but far away—Eastbourne I think. What about Woking? What does Mary [Ethel's maid] think? And Pan [sheepdog]? So you see, my thoughts curl round to you again, and indicate a letter. Werent we lucky to bring out our books when we did? I know I had something else, and very interesting to say: but cant remember, so must send this.

V.

Berg

3645: To William Plomer

Monk's House, Rodmell, Lewes, Sussex

15 Sept [1940]

Dear William,

It was just as well we put you off on Wednesday, wasn't it? It would have been an airy dinner—the windows are broken. We came up on Tuesday; the ruins were still smoking, a bomb timed to go off in an hour. But it didn't; and we went up again on Friday to get letters, settle the Press and so on, but the bomb was still unburst in the flower bed, so we had to retire once more. So we stay down here, for the present.

I wish you were out of London. The bombs are getting much too close to one's friends. What a sight Holborn was, my word! I dont much like driving in London during an air raid, but night must be much worse. Its odd, though, that one cant take it altogether seriously. Its like a very dreary game of hide and seek played by grown ups. Twice while playing bowls raiders have come over and been shot down in full view. One day they hedge-hopped over the tree at the gate. But its over so soon one hasn't

1. Churchill broadcast at 6 p.m. on 11 September, warning the country that the intensified bombardment of London might be a preliminary to a German invasion. He said: "It ranks with the days when the Spanish Armada was approaching the Channel and Drake was finishing his game of bowls."

time to think. Not at night though. They circle round like airy omnibuses: I wish they weren't going to you. We've been up and down most of the summer, and had a colony of Judith and her friends here all August. She remembers you—whats more reads and admires your poems. She's taken up with rather a dull young man from Tonbridge, but is off, as soon as she can get a passage, to America, where she has a scholarship.

If I'd known you were at Worthing I should have put out a feeler for a visit. Is there any chance (Hitler allowing) you would come for a week end? Till our windows are mended, we're fixed here. Do suggest one, if feasible. Its true we're very near the coast; but anyhow its a good deal better than London.[1]

I heard you had a job, but thought it was editing the Spectator—what is it?[2] It sounds dreary, unless its a comfort being useful. But I want Kilvert.[3] I take the unfashionable view that Kilvert—oh and Augustus Hare[4]—whose six volumes gave me acute pleasure—are more real than war. Why do people think whats unpleasant is therefore real? There are so many things to talk about: also I have some cheroots, so consider coming, and lets forget invasion. Please send a line to say if you're all safe.

Love from us both.

Yr
V.W.

Texas

3646: To Ethel Smyth

Monk's House, Rodmell,
near Lewes, Sussex

Sept. 20th [1940]

Your letter came this morning—the letter posted on 17th. I hastily continue my story. We went to London on Friday. Bomb still unexploded. Not allowed in. Off it went next day. Blew out all windows, all ceilings, and smashed all my china—just as we'd got the flat ready!—oh damn. Uninhabitable now apparently—Press has been moved to Letchworth[5]— What remains of it. Sale of Roger of course ruined.

1. Rodmell was only three miles from Newhaven, where the German 9th Army would have landed if 'Operation Sea Lion' had been carried out.
2. Plomer served in a clerical capacity in the Admiralty throughout the war.
3. See p. 377, note 1.
4. Augustus Hare (1834-1903), the biographer and writer of guide books, whose autobiography, *The Story of My Life*, was published in six volumes (1896-1900).
5. The Hogarth Press moved from 37 Mecklenburgh Square to Letchworth, Hertfordshire, where the staff occupied a few rooms in the premises of the Garden City Press, which had printed many of their books. It operated from Letchworth for the remainder of the war, under John Lehmann's supervision.

I try to let down a fire proof curtain and go on reading, writing, cooking. Mabel, afraid of invasion here, has left.[1] Its a mercy: for now I'm kept busy. We go up on Tuesday to see what can be done at the flat, and rescue what we can get into the car.

The other day we drove through an air raid. London like a dead city. We took shelter at Wimbledon in a gun emplacement with an East end family whose house had been bombed. There they were as cheerful as grigs with a rug a kettle and a spirit lamp: had been there for 3 nights: wind blowing through gun holes.

Oh dear! I'm worried to think of you with an incendiary next you. Here save at nights its more peaceful—All the talk of invasion. I'm off to lay in supplies—not that, with this gale blowing, it seems imminent. Theyve got guns in front of the garden and all down the river.

This is only a stop gap. I'll write again.

So do you. Yes, I'm sure the safety curtain—a heavy iron drop over ones own scene—is the only preservative. But I admit it dont always work. Please write

V.

Berg

3647: To Vanessa Bell   *Monks House [Rodmell, Sussex]*

Tuesday [24 September 1940]

Leonard's account of what was said on the telephone is of course quite different from yours. He certainly told me that you had asked him to find out the address and had arranged that he should ring you up later. So we cant understand why you should have been surprised.

What I dont understand is why there need have been such a fuss to find a place for them in Sussex.[2] Theyve got their own house at Rodwell,[3] and, if they didn't want to be in London could easily have gone there. I admit I find it very annoying to have them in the village, but its a great relief that its only for a short time. From what you said I thought they meant to stay indefinitely.

I'm sorry if you thought I was unnecessarily angry. I dont suppose you

1. Mabel, who had been maid-of-all-work in London and occasionally at Monk's House for five years, left the Woolfs for Roger Fry's sister Isabel, and only Louie Everest, who lived in Rodmell, remained to look after the house.
2. Vanessa had told Helen Anrep that there was a furnished cottage to let at Rodmell, and Helen had decided to rent it for herself and her two children, Igor and Anastasia. The Anreps arrived on 23 September, but remained no more than a week.
3. Rodwell House, Baylham, Suffolk, which had belonged to Roger Fry.

could possibly have prevented them coming. Once Helen knew about the cottage it was unavoidable.

Berg

3648: To Ethel Smyth   *Monks House [Rodmell,*
                                              Sussex]
25th Sept. 1940

The letter posted on the 22nd reached me on the 24th.

This is only to continue hastily the narrative. Up to Meck. Sq on Friday. Ceilings down, all windows in front broken; but although the mess is terrific—as if were moving in again—there's less serious damage than we expected. The worst for me is that much of my china and glass is smashed. And Lord—the bore of clearing up again! The Press has been moved to Letchworth. Extra cost to us £150: and we have Meck Sqre rent to pay and Tavistock too. Never mind—Sale of Roger I thought ended for good; but suddenly its started again. this week.

Thats my budget; and I admire your good heart for wishing to know. Oh and Mabel—she was my cook general. The delight of being without a maid in the house is such that I dont mind an hour's cooking—indeed its a sedative. I've been bottling honey. My present grumble is that friends whom I dislike [the Anreps] (unreasonably I admit) are refuging in the village. Why does this annoy me more than the war? Because its an ignoble fret— having them dropping in.

Well, I wish I could see you. A very nice long letter from Arthur Ponsonby about Roger. I'm telling him I live in her youth owing to your brilliant portrait.[1] D'you remember how she cut her nails? Thats what I call portrait painting. This naturally leads to the next vol. of your auto-biography. Please clear the schoolroom table and set to. London looked merry and hopeful, wearing her wounds like stars; why do I dramatise London perpetually? When I see a great smash like a crushed match box where an old house stood I wave my hand to London. What I'm finding odd and agreeable and unwonted is the admiration this war creates—for every sort of person: chars, shopkeepers, even much more remarkably, for politicians—Winston at least, and the tweed wearing sterling dull women here, with their grim good sense: organising First aid, putting out bombs for practise, and jumping out of windows to show us how. We burnt an

---

1. Ethel's description of Lady Ponsonby appeared in *As Time Went On* (1936). She was a lady-in-waiting to Queen Victoria, and Ethel's stormy friendship with her lasted nearly 30 years until Lady Ponsonby's death in 1916. Arthur Ponsonby (1871-1946), her son, was created Lord Ponsonby in 1930, and became leader of the Labour party opposition in the House of Lords.

incendiary bomb up on the down last night. It was a lovely tender autumn evening, and the white sputter of the bomb was to me, who never listened to the instructions, rather lovely. I'd almost lost faith in human beings, partly owing to my immersion in the dirty water of artists envies and vanities while I worked at Roger. Now hope revives again.

V.

Berg

3649: To Hugh Walpole   *Monk's House, Rodmell,*
                                         Lewes, Sussex

29 Sept 40

Dearest Hugh,

We drove up to Meck Sqre on Tuesday morning and found—well, what you saw. The bomb had fallen that night. I'm glad we weren't there. Then there were three more time bombs in the square. So for ten days we weren't allowed into the Square. Then the bombs went off—most of our ceilings fell, and the Press has had to be evacuated to X

I make this mark to show the point at which a bomb shook the window so violently that the pen jumped out of my hand. Theres an air raid going on—I've just been out into the garden to have a look. Theres a pop-pop pop up in the sky—then a crash somewhere over towards Newhaven. Now its quieted down though theres one hornet up in the clouds—and I continue: Press has been moved to Letchworth.

Meck: Sqre being uninhabitable, here we stay, but come up every week or so and see more of Bloomsbury destroyed. Monday Nessa's and Duncan's studios were burnt out—in [No. 8] Fitzroy Street. A frigidaire and a statue the only survivors.

I'm glad at anyrate you've left the flat where I had such a memorable tea.[1] D'you remember the picture falling, and the lurid light on the Park, and Rupert Hart Davis coming in? I saw they'd been very close at hand— the bombs I mean.

No, I've no fears for your chastity in the shelter,[2] but wish you were here at the moment; and put out a feeler for another letter, should you be inclined—should this letter reach you. Are you reading, writing? Yes, I hope so.

Love from us both

V. W.

Texas

1. Hugh Walpole had left 90 Piccadilly for the house of his servant and companion, Harold Cheevers, in Hampstead Garden Suburb.
2. Every night during the London Blitz, Walpole went to the garden-shelter with Harold's wife Ethel Cheevers, and the Cheevers's pekinese. (See Rupert Hart-Davis, *Hugh Walpole*, p. 431.)

3650: TO ANGELICA BELL
Monk's House, Rodmell,
Lewes, Sussex

1st Oct 1940

Dearest Pixy,

I think this is quarter day. . . . Here comes a pause. There's so much to say I'm like a bottle turned upside down. The fires—Mecklenburgh Square in ruins—the Anreps. My woolwork. How, where, which? Well, Nessa will have told you about the fires. Nessa and Duncan came to tea yesterday. Oh we had such a row about the Anreps! Think of having that spawn in the village. Cant post a letter without seeing a face like a codfish in embryo.[1] [. . . 15 words omitted . . .] Their minds too—how amorphous. Their manners non-existent—save when they hurl a club at that soft bear their mother. Enough.

You see how profoundly I'm in need of you. I think of you almost incessantly. I dream of you. I think Angelica—oh Angelica!—look up and see Ba's [Anastasia] great gargoyle gutter dripping. So you see, the Anreps have their uses, because they—no I wont finish that sentence; because it would flatter you: to be called a Mozart quintet played by angels on a spinet.

About my woolwork: are you sending it? We had Ben to stay [on 6 September], Nicolson, I mean 7 foot high; a very Guardsman, but a bit stiff in the top knot. What other news? Mostly village gossip. There's Mrs Chavasse, makes moccassins out of rabbits; Mrs Ebbs—"My passion, Mrs Woolf, is for the stage": and Miss Emery who gave me a loaf. Leonard then gives her a gallon of apples. Most afternoons I spend appling. D'you know they have all to be stood on their twigs or they rot? And we took the honey. We crushed it in a muslin bag and it dripped pure gold for 48 hours. then I decanted it. We have 30 bottles. Thats the sort of thing Brock [David Garnett] would like to get his snout into. I suppose you sit down to table with a congeries of moles. "What that?" says Brock, looking up. And a large fat grey form—now I must play bowls—shuffles in. A howling wind. A raider shot down at Caburn. A Private in the air force comes to play chess with Leonard. His name is Ken [Sheppard]. He is in love with a dairy maid. He is very beautiful, but proletarian. News! News! Please write. A great whirl of the witcherinas tonight.

V.

Texas

3651: TO V. SACKVILLE-WEST
Monk's House, Rodmell,
near Lewes, Sussex

4th Oct. [1940]

"Oh I'm glad"—those were the very words Leonard spoke when I

1. The Anrep children, Igor and Anastasia.

said Vita says she'll come. If you could hear what the Wolves usually say when people say theyre coming—.

So do. *Wednesday* we suggest: and the compact is you stay for Thursday luncheon.

Whats the matter with Ethel? Is it a mood, or anything serious? I cant make out. This morning's letter again refers to "an exquisite letter from Vita".

Air raids pretty constant. Two bombs as I ordered dinner, a mile away in the marsh.

Mecklenburgh Sq$^{re.}$ uninhabitable. Two houses destroyed. Ours has no glass or ceilings. Press moved to Letchworth—

But we'll keep our travellers tales till we meet

Yrs in haste as you see—and Lord
what a dirty sheet—

V.

Berg

3652: To J. R. Ackerley   *Monk's House [Rodmell, Sussex]*

4th Oct [1940]

Dear Joe,[1]

The Sitwell book has just come.[2] I'll have a look at it and see what I think its worth. I almost always like memoirs—on the other hand, the Sitwells, as a family, bore me. Leonard says he will do the other book,[3] if you will send it.

Travelling on our line isnt easy, but if you could ever come for a week-end, we should be delighted. Its comparatively quiet—though 2 bombs have just dropped in the marsh and we have fights of course. But they pass over, and in London they remain. I'm amazed at the courage of the Cockneys and wish you and William weren't among them.

So suggest any time you will.

Yours,
Virginia Woolf

Washington State University, Humanities Library

1. Joe Ackerley (1896-1967) was Literary Editor of *The Listener*, and a great friend of William Plomer.
2. Virginia reviewed *Two Generations*, edited by Osbert Sitwell, in *The Listener* on 31 October.
3. Leonard wrote nothing for *The Listener* until April 1941, when he reviewed a series of pamphlets called *The Democratic Order*, ed. Francis Williams.

3653: To Donald Brace   *Monk's House, Rodmell,*
                                          Lewes, Sussex
Typewritten
6th Oct 1940

Dear Mr Brace,

Mr Jack Morgan,[1] of J.P. Morgan and Co, has cabled to a friend of his in London, Lord Bicester,[2] asking him to request me to delete two sentences in my Life of Roger Fry. As he says that they give him and the Morgan family great pain, I have had to agree. Probably he has already applied to you. But I said I would write to you in confirmation. The first sentence is on page 141; beginning "I knew the answer beforehand." The second is on the middle of page 144 beginning "I always wondered."[3]

I told him that I thought the book was already in print, and that it would be impossible to make the corrections. Should there be a second edition, perhaps you will bear them in mind. It has already gone into a second edition over here, so that nothing can be done at present. Privately, I think the objection is unreasonable, but of course I did not like to refuse.

Owing to an air raid on Mecklenburgh Square we have had to move the Press to Letchworth. And as our new flat was damaged we are living entirely down here. I need not say that conditions are very unpleasant in England—but we are carrying on, and look forward one of these days to meeting you again.

With best wishes, and apologies for troubling you,

yours sincerely,
Virginia Woolf

Harcourt Brace Jovanovich

3654: To Ethel Smyth   *Monks House [Rodmell,*
                                         Sussex]
Sat. Oct 12th [1940]

Ethel dear, please tell me soberly precisely what you mean when you say you have diabetes. What does Dr Plesch say? I know you had some

1. John Pierpont Morgan (1867-1943), the son of J. Pierpont Morgan (1837-1913), the banker and art connoisseur, with whom Roger Fry had travelled in Italy in 1907.
2. 1st Lord Bicester (1867-1956), Chairman of Morgan, Grenfell & Co. Ltd., and many other businesses.
3. Both sentences occur in a later account by Roger Fry of his Italian journey with Morgan in 1907: "I knew the answer beforehand,—family heirlooms to be offered to Pierpont Morgan still sleeping upstairs in the arms of the elderly and well preserved Mrs Douglas" (*Roger Fry*, p. 141); "I always wondered that his mistresses in New York got such substantial subsidies as they did" (p. 144).

438

minor form of it. Has it become major? Well, I know there's insulin. I know people like Hugh Walpole flourish eternally when all riddled with it But I would like the exact facts. I've been gathering, partly from your handwriting, that you aren't as I last saw you—a Rose in June—the day I waved my hand at your valiant back. Lord how I admire you! Leonard showed me a tiny snapshot of you in some paper: and my heart—ah hah!— the organ you dont believe in—gave one of those pleasurable leaps when the blood fills it and a release from non-liking becomes a positive rapture. There she sat, with her little bow tie and her great forehead, my uncastrated cat, challenging the world, yet divinely compassionate of its (so to speak my) infirmities. Thats why I want facts about diabetes.

I cant for the like of me think what I can have said in that 10 minute note [Letter 3648] that deserved copying—I'm not outraged; I'm flattered.[1] Only I wish I knew what flying bird I brought down without knowing—I dont think I've ever taken more time than it takes to form a word in writing to you. A proof of our intercommunicativeness. Hasnt it been a queer collocation, the two people who have nothing alike, except—well, I cant go into that. I suppose I told you how I saw you years before I knew you?— coming bustling down the gangway at the Wigmore Hall [in November 1919], in tweeds and spats, a little cocks feather in your felt, and a general look of angry energy,[2] So that I said thats Ethel Smyth!—and felt, being then a mere chit, she belongs to the great achieved public world, where I'm a nonentity. You reminded me of a ptarmigan—those speckled birds with fetlocks.

Did I tell you, I forget, that Nessa's and Duncans studios have been bombed and burnt out?—about 100 canvases, and all the furniture and so on? Happily they'd both brought most valuables down here. But its odd, being destroyed. Mecklenburgh is now mended, as to glass; but I shant sleep there just yet, only go up and retrieve what's portable. I wish I didn't feel myself a coward. Most of my friends are as chirpy as crickets, working at the Treasury, sleeping in basements. When the bombs make our windows rattle I always jump. I dont like sitting of an evening and thinking the drone which is weaving its web above me is about to drop. It doesnt upon us—only on the convent at Newhaven, or some field. And I feel convinced we shall all survive. But thats because I want to . . . so many Surinam toads (thats Coleridge) breeding in my head.[3]

Vita was here for a night. I always fall into a warm slipper relation with her instantly. Its a satisfactory relationship. Sans Gwen its so simple. Gwen,

1. Ethel had written to Virginia: "Those letters of yours intoxicate me like a phrase of Mozart's" (7 October 1940, *Berg*).
2. See Virginia's contemporary description of this event in a letter to Lytton Strachey (Vol. II, Letter 1100).
3. In his *Letters* Coleridge refers to himself as a 'Surinam toad', creatures which carry their eggs on their backs.

she says is 'as a child' to her; the truth about Gwen is that she's a complete egotist. Now I dont mind egotism if there's an ego. If theres not, its boring.

Do I read you rightly when I apprehend that you're beginning again, where you left off, your memoirs? I hope so. Then I shall have another thread making continuity in our present blankness. Leonard wants me to help apple picking, so I must stop, and take my seat in the heart of a tree, with pale green globes hanging round me.

And what I want is facts about diabetes.

Yr
V.

Berg

3655: To V. Sackville-West   *Monks House, Rodmell*
                                    [Sussex]

15 Oct. [1940]

Lord what an embarrassing situation you created on Monday morning! The postwoman, that virginal and antique woman, brought a wooden box and said, "Please will you examine the goods?" So Leonard opened the box in her presence, and extracted—a po! And it wasn't a whole po—only the cheek of a po—as the poor woman said. But he swore, blushing like a rose, that it was quite undamaged. And she also blushed; and then we disinterred the whole po, all in bits—the handle, the bottom—Oh what a po it must have been! a double po—a Sackville po! And to think of your packing it and sending it and then that they should have broken it! There it is in the hall—the relics of the po—its heartbreaking. We shall never have one like it—what it would have meant say to Sibyl when she comes!—and then I rummaged further and found cuddled round the po masses and masses of the finest wool. How can you say it wants dyeing? Its a most harmonious mothy colour, and Louie[1] says you've sent enough for a jersey for me, and for socks for Leonard. Oh how can we ever thank you sufficiently— the two old Wolves dressed in real sheeps clothing—not ordinary sheep either—Jacobs sheep[1] which came in before the conqueror. Dear me, dear me, we were so exhilarated, what with the postwoman and the po we hardly settled into work all day.

Yes, you are an angel. And had you been criminal about—whatever it was—Doran,[2] all would be forgot and forgive—But you weren't criminal.

---

1. The brown and white breed of sheep at Sissinghurst.
2. Doubleday, Doran, the American publisher of Vita's *Country Notes in Wartime*. Vita had arranged its publication without consulting Leonard, who had published it in England.

Leonard aquits you of all intent: dont we always say, of all our authors Vita is the magnanimous Rose, the peach of perfection? dont we both like you (I put 'love' for my word) better every time we see you. And oh dear, the relics of the po in the hall make me laugh every time I cook my dinner, as I must. Its to be baked haddock.

V.

Berg

3656: To T. S. Eliot   *Monk's House, Rodmell,*
                                        Lewes, Sussex
Typewritten
17th Oct [1940]

My dear Tom,

I was greatly touched to receive your yellow book.[1] According to our compact, I say nothing of the printed matter.

I dont know where to begin—its so long since we met. And so much of London has been destroyed—I daresay youve seen Mecklenburgh, and gathered that we've had to move the Press; again, all our windows are out. So we only dip into London for a day.

I'd had it on the tip of my pen to ask you down, would it still be possible? A week end? The middle of a week? August and Sept. were so littered with fragments I couldn't fix any day. But at the moment, the trains are running; we're almost always alone. It would be a treat to see you. So consider if you could come.

Here I must skip all the questions I want to ask. Where are you? How are you? And so on. We go up tomorrow for the day to salvage what we can. Fabers[2] was all standing last time. Today we hear that Tavistock is gone.[3]

All I ask then is a card to say you will come; if you cant; then a letter please, with a complete account. But seeings better than writing.

And so with thanks from your very grateful but not very articulate old crone:

Virginia

Mrs T. S. Eliot

1. *East Coker* (1940).
2. In Russell Square, Bloomsbury. Eliot was a Director of Faber & Faber.
3. 52 Tavistock Square, where the Woolfs had lived from 1924 until moving to Mecklenburgh Square in 1939, was totally destroyed by a bomb. The Woolfs were still paying rent for it, but it was unoccupied and almost empty of furniture.

Monk's House, Rodmell,
Lewes, Sussex

Saturday [26 October 1940]

I cant tell you, my darling—this is the way Aunt [Mary] Fisher's letters
always began—no, My darling child. . . . I cant tell you what a delight it
was to get your and good Brock's [David Garnett] letters. What would
Aunt Mary have said to Brock? Well, she'd have forgiven Brock, but she'd
never never never have forgiven you. She was a chaste woman—13 children,
4 miscarriages. But why do I waste paper on Aunt Mary?

Yesterday we heard a whistle of bombs as we played bowls, and down
they plumped—4 in a row—in the field at the top. All the mothers in
Rodmell at once ran screaming: "The Bus! the Bus!" because the childrens
Bus was coming along the road. But God was good; nobody was hurt; and
I had the great delight of seeing the smoke and being within an inch of
Heaven.

This is a great score over Nessa.

Mummy says she's found you the most perfect house in the most perfect
place[1]—oh far better than Rodmell. So of course I'm wild to take it myself
—which indeed we must [sic] store our furniture somewhere, Meck. Sqre.
being a mere splinter of glass, the wind blowing in and out of my cup-
boards and the books all down. As for 52 Tavistock,—well, where I used
to dandle you on my knee, there's Gods sky: and nothing left but one
wicker chair and a piece of drugget.

Isnt life a whirligig? But do remember to send me some coloured papers,
all the same. Did I tell you about my rug? After an infinity of time, spent,
now writing, now reading, my true gift has at last proved to be rug making.
I make rugs of all colours: some say they never wear out. But thats no
reason why I shouldn't have your papers. Mummy is altogether flummoxed
—danderrydown flummoxed, as she calls it—about your design. Saying this
she combed her hair all up the wrong way. It was an awful spectacle. So
whats to be done? She says you've got it.

There is not very much news: but what there is of it is a mixture. Mabel's
friend, who used to take her to the dogs [races], is dead:[2] so she came back,
just as we were hoping we'd got the house to ourselves. But she's cheered
up amazingly. For one thing, the next door house was bombed: she is a
stormy petrel, only happy in a gale. Yet she looks like a Doyenne de
Comice pear. So I cant find one word to fit her. If you want a stormy petrel
who's a pear, you've only to say so.

Judith has arrived in America.[3] The Anreps are gone—I think to the

1. Claverham Farm, Berwick, about four miles from Charleston, where Angelica
   and David Garnett lived for about nine months. They married in 1942.
2. He was called 'Charles', and Virginia believed his surname to be 'Stanford'.
3. Judith Stephen was a post-graduate at Bryn Mawr.

Enfields.[1] If you know Mrs Enfield, and can distinguish her from Margery Strachey, you will echo what I say, which is, I'd be dead in a field, rather than stay with Enfield. You see when I write to you, I'm almost mistress of the other art of poetry. I daresay you're putting the pot on and wont want to spell out any more. Oh Lord, I've forgotten the fish. What shall we have for dinner? The old mutton once more? But it was never much of a joint in its heyday.

Its a tearing gale, and the Witcherinas are floating past in a roaring rhapsody of circumgyration. So I must wing my way round the Bowling Green. I've just been to see the [bomb] craters. If you look at the moon through a telescope, thats what they're like.

Do thank Brock for his most entirely sustaining and yet so light and yet so nourishing letter: and ask him to write another, only *one* kiss for him though: the rest for me.

Leslie Humphreys is here.

Texas

3658: To Ethel Smyth

Monk's House, Rodmell, near Lewes, Sussex

14th Nov 1940

If I had an orderly mind (as you have) I should divide this letter into A B C D (as you do) and then treat each subject separately. First, there's diabetes. Well, I'm thankful. So Plesch was more or less right: anyhow I dont care if its Plesch or its Smellie[2] so long as you're bounding like an air ball which has slipped out of the old womans grasp (I refer to a childish incident in Kensington Gardens, when this happened, and how I jumped for joy! She stood at the gate with a vast billowing bundle.) Then Hilda.[3] I'm sorry—not personally sorry, generally sorry. I didnt get on with her—she seemed so dried, so official; and I grieve to say my last encounter was a little tart on my side—She asked me to write some damned book for some damned series. It was to be patriotic, at the same time intellectual; also badly paid. And I thought her intolerably imperceptive of what I consider the irreconcilable differences. But publicly I admired: and I'm sorry she was run to death by the poisoned arrows of Dottys egotism. Did you mean, by

1. Ralph (1885-1973) and Doris Enfield (*née* Hussey). He was an agricultural economist, and she had published with the Hogarth Press a book called *L.E.L.*, *A Mystery of the Thirties* (1928).
2. Ethel had left her regular doctor, Dr Plesch, for Dr Smellie, a young Scottish doctor whom she liked for sticking to his name.
3. See p. 191, note 2. Hilda Matheson died on 30 October at the age of 52. In the last years of her life she lived in a farmhouse on Dorothy Wellesley's Sussex estate.

the way, that Dottys daughter said she had no connection with Dotty? In your letter Dotty and Mrs Matheson became slightly mixed. I see that Gwen has become Countess of something:[1] so may be she'll remove to St. Michaels Mount. I doubt that Vita ever said definitely she was bored. I think the relationship has spread and slackened, not been ended. Here I skip to "wearing her wounds like stars". You said I got that from HB. No. no. Its —I think Marvell, or one of the 17th Century poets. [*not traced*] Which I'm not sure; but its been walloping about in my head these 30 years.

Another bomb in Meck Sqre: did I tell you? All the books down again. Did I tell you we half think of moving the furniture here? We brought down a car load last week. Then, to my infinite delight, they bombed our river. Cascades of water roared over the marsh—All the gulls came and rode the waves at the end of the field. It was, and still is, an island sea, of such indescribable beauty, almost always changing, day and night, sun and rain, that I cant take my eyes off it. Yesterday, thinking to explore, I fell headlong into a six foot hole, and came home dripping like a spaniel, or water rugg (thats Shakespeare).[2] How odd to be swimming in a field! Mercifully I was wearing Leonards old brown trousers. Tomorrow I buy a pair of cords for myself. Its raining—raining . . . and I've been walking, walking. The road to the Bridge was 3 foot in water, and this meant a 2 mile round; but oh dear, how I love this savage medieval water moved, all floating tree trunks and flocks of birds and a man in an old punt, and myself so eliminated of human feature you might take me for a stake walking.

And tell me your opinion of Margot Oxford. For some reason she writes to me passionately daily. She sent for me in London, and told me the story of her sexual organs. Cold, as you can imagine. But do tell me, whats *your* version of her? You, whose eyes see so much further than mine. She says, will I write a long letter, explaining my beliefs! will I give her a book —she's now at the Savoy Hotel, sitting up at 3 am. being bombed; but bomb proof; and writing, writing—all in pencil. Tell me what it means.

Your quondam friend, Dr Gordon,[3] has written me about 10 pages of violent abuse of Roger Fry. Again I ask why? She never met him. She says she hates him; and that he's the spit and image of Russells Viper—a snake whose bite is small but deadly.

Now I must put on our dinner—To do this I must crash through a

1. The 2nd Lord St Levan died on 10 November, and was succeeded by his nephew Francis St Aubyn, Gwen's husband. He inherited St Michael's Mount in Cornwall.
2.   "Ay, in the catalogue ye go for men;
      As hounds and greyhounds, mongrels, spaniels, curs,
      Shoughs, water-rugs, and demi-wolves are clept
      All by the name of dogs."
                      Macbeth, III, i.
3. Violet Gordon-Woodhouse, the harpsichordist.

meeting of farm labourers which Leonard is holding in the hall. They are going to grow co-operative potatoes; each man his strip. Why am I so much shyer of the labourer than of the gentry? I am almost—what d'you call a voracious cheese mite which has gnawed its way into a vast Stilton and is intoxicated with eating—as I am with reading history, and writing fiction [*Pointz Hall*] and planning—oh such an amusing book on English literature.[1] Only room for exhortation: Write.

V

Berg

3659: To V. Sackville-West

Monk's House, Rodmell,
near Lewes, Sussex

15th Nov. [1940]

I have been trying, for the past ten days, to write to you, but something has always interrupted. Village life without Mabel to cook and fifteen people coming to hear Leonards lecture (on democracy): then buying bits of fish: I say all this chops up my day. But does not diminish my love, nor my gratitude. It is angelic of you to wish me to write another book. At the same time devilish. Havent I 20 books sizzling in my head at the moment? Then you tempt me with old Bess.[2] It is tempting of course. But I doubt if old Bess is my bird. I think she's neither one thing or the other. I mean Orlando was imagination: Roger fact. But Bess is after all, though much spangled with Elizabethan finery, an historic figure. I should have to grub. And I dont like shoddy history. And there's already a fat book about her.[3] I think I'll compromise, and make her a Common Reader. But all my books, including the DNB. are lying on the floor in London. I've handed on the other suggestion: Bates and Robinson.[4] For some reason I've a prejudice against Bates. Why, I dont know. Also: Why dont you do Bess? another bomb fell on Meck Sqre.

Years ago I went over Hardwick when old Lady Louisa Egerton[5] lived there. She had a face like a horse. She was very good to us. The Carnarvons

---

1. *Reading at Random* or *Turning the Page*. See p. 430, note 2.
2. Elizabeth Shrewsbury, known throughout history as 'Bess of Hardwick' (Derbyshire), after the great house she built there in 1590-4. The third daughter of an insignificant squire, she married four times and became the richest and most formidable woman in England, with one exception—the Queen.
3. *Bess of Hardwick* (1910), by Mrs Stepney Rawson.
4. Vita had suggested that John Lehmann should consider the work of Ralph Bates and (?) Robinson for *New Writing*. Lehmann did not publish Robinson, but Bates's story *The Launch* appeared in *New Writing* in January 1941.
5. The only daughter of the 7th Duke of Devonshire. She married in 1865 Admiral Francis Egerton, and died in 1907. In her widowhood she lived at Hardwick, then a property of the Dukes of Devonshire.

had lent us Teversal.[1] I was then emerging from madness. And she took us and showed us the house—I remember the windows. There was a motto, wasn't there, in stone, on the roof?[2] And two very plain Egerton daughters. I havent thought of them for years.

"Tell Virginia I am sending butter ..." Leonard gave me this tremendously exciting scrap out of your letter. Lord what a mint of things you've given me. Wool. Butter. Bess of Hardwick—to name the most recent additions.

About Hilda [Matheson]—I was sorry; not personally, for somehow I didnt adhere. She seemed made of the wrong substance. But that doesn't make me blind to her values—Ethel began her letter "*Vitas* death makes me very unhappy ..." What about Dotty? Ethel went on to say that Dottys daughter [Elizabeth] had quarrelled with her. She met her at the funeral. But I dont go by what old Ethel says.

Look. Vita ... You *must* come here instantly. Not to see me. To see the flood. A bomb burst the Banks. We are so lovely—all sea, right up to the gate. I've never seen anything more visionary lovely than Caburn upside down in the water. Flocks of gulls. Do come at once. Oh and a boat: and haystacks in the flood.

V.

Berg

3660: To Elizabeth Robins   *Monk's House, Rodmell,*
                                   Lewes, Sussex
17th Nov 1940

Dear Miss Robins,

I heard from Octavia [Wilberforce] the other day that you have reached America safely. Now I calculate that you must have had your three weeks in which to recover. So, am I being impertinent and intrusive if I write to ask—are you going on with your book?[3] I know from experience that either one is going on, or has good reasons for not going on. All the same I cant help putting to you the readers case: which is simply, please if you can give us another volume. Most books come to an end and one forgets

1. The Manor House, Teversal, Nottinghamshire, owned by the 4th Earl of Carnarvon, whose daughter Margaret married Virginia's half-brother George Duckworth. Virginia stayed there in September 1904, while she recovered from her illness following Leslie Stephen's death.
2. Not a motto, but the initials 'E.S.' (Elizabeth Shrewsbury) repeated six times in letters six-feet high on the parapets.
3. Elizabeth Robins wrote no book after the autobiographical *Both Sides of the Curtain* (1940), but the manuscript which she completed earlier, *Raymond and I*, was published posthumously in 1956.

them. But your book hasn't come to an end, and I haven't forgotten it. Thus you have put me into the position of a spider, dangling at the end of a thread, which it cant attach to anything, unless you will help it. I implore you to have pity on Virginia suspended on a thread. And I believe you've left lots of people in the same predicament. Well, I wont say any more except that I do beg of you to go on. And if this comes at the wrong moment, please forgive me.

This moment, here in my garden room, happens to be so lovely I can't keep my eyes on the paper. A bomb burst the river bank: and we are flooded all over the marsh—The sea comes almost to our gate. And the gardener has just called me to come and look at a swan. So you see the bombs so far have been kind to us. I suspect we seem, at a distance, far worse than we seem to ourselves. I hope to see Octavia some day. And end with our affectionate double regards—Leonard's and mine.

Yr
Virginia Woolf

Sussex

3661: To Dr Octavia Wilberforce   *Monk's House, Rodmell*
                                        [Sussex]

23rd Nov [1940]

Dear Octavia,

I had already written to Miss Robins—so I return the envelope and the cutting. Many thanks. I never thought to send by air mail. I must take your word for it that it wont enrage her.

I'm sorry the Americans wont take the book,[1] but they seem given over to patriotic orgies, according to a niece of mine [Judith Stephen] at Bryn Mawr.

We are bringing our London things down here, half ruined, I'm afraid by damp. I envy you your dry volumes—my poor old books are like tramps.

Yr
Virginia Woolf

Sussex

3662: To V. Sackville-West   *Monk's House [Rodmell,*
                                  Sussex]

29th Nov [1940]

I wish I were Queen Victoria: then I could thank you—From the depths of my Broken Widowed heart. Never never Never have we had such a

1. Harcourt, Brace had rejected Elizabeth Robins's *Both Sides of the Curtain.* See Letter 3542.

rapturous astounding glorious—no, I cant get the hang of the style. All I can say is that when we discovered the butter in the envelope box we had in the household—Louie that is—to look. Thats a whole pound of butter I said. Saying which I broke off a lump and ate it pure. Then in the glory of my heart I gave all our weeks ration—which is about the size of my thumb nail—to Louie—earned undying gratitude; then sat down and ate bread and butter. It would have been desecration to add jam.

You've forgotten what butter tastes like. So I'll tell you—its something between dew and honey. Lord, Vita!—your broken po, your wool, and then on top your butter!!! Please congratulate the cows from me, and the dairy maid, and I would like to suggest that the calf should be known in future (if its a man) as Leonard if a woman as Virginia.

Think of our lunch tomorrow: Bunny Garnett and Angelica are coming; in the middle of the table I shall put the whole pat. And I shall say: Eat as much as you like and I cant break off this rhapsody, for its a year since I saw a pound, to tell you anything else—I dont think anything else seems important.

Its true all our books are coming from the ruined house tomorrow: all battered and mildewed. Its true I've been made treasurer of the Women's Institute [Rodmell]: also I want to ask you about lantern slides of Persia; and will you come and talk: But this is mere trifling. Bombs fell near me: trifles; a plane shot down in the marsh: trifles: floods damned—no, nothing seems to make a wreath on the pedestal fitting your butter.

They've never sent me your book [*Country Notes in Wartime*] from the Press, damn them.

Here L breaks in: if I'm writing to you, will I add his deepest thanks for the butter

V.

Berg

3663: To Edward Sackville-West   *Monks House, Rodmell, Lewes [Sussex]*

Typewritten
Sunday 1st Dec. [1940]

My dear Eddy,

Forgive this typing; but my hands are so cold this bitter morning out in the garden room that I cant move a pen.

Derrick Leon was in a furniture shop in Wigmore Street. He wrote a very good novel, Livingstones,[1] about his life there; but later became a feeble copy of Proust and we couldn't go on publishing him. He's a Jew;

1. *Livingstones: A Novel of Contemporary Life* (1933). His next novel was *Wilderness* (1935), published by Heinemann's. In 1940 he published *Introduction to Proust*.

hardbitten; very competent. He was with Fortnum and Masons; then got tuberculosis; and now writes from some country cottage where he's recovering. I liked him; he was dark: inscrutable; but I never knew much more about him. My impression was that he'd got lost between two worlds; but might pull through.

I write with the usual air raid going on; distant droning; a bomb now and then. It is confusing as you say. Sometimes the country is so heavenly and reading and writing become so absorbing I'm very happy; then all at sea. Its like living on an island. Rodmell of course pulls us in to various societies; all very simple; I've not seen a clever person this six months, save the family over the way [at Charleston]. I daresay its good for one; but oh lord—how bare and barren in many ways.

Our new flat being now a heap of glass and plaster, we have no home in London. Tavistock is hanging in the air too—I see my drawing room panels[1] suspended over the rubble. And Nessa and Duncan are burnt out. So let us keep up this spiderlike conversation from time to time. Ben appeared the other day—an odd sample of the young man cut adrift, Vita too. But she's firmly anchored and as adorable as ever.

Excuse this scribble. Every twig is about half frost; Caburn hidden; and guns in the distance. Love from us both.

Yours V.W.

Berg

3664: To Ethel Smyth

Monks House, Rodmell
[Sussex]

Dec. 6th 1940

If you want to know, Ethel Smyth, Dame, Commander of the British Empire, why I've not written before, it is because I've had to empty the whole of 37 Meck Sqre into this cottage. Oh I cant go into the dreary details—how we went to London and found mushrooms sprouting on the carpets, pools standing on the chairs, and glass to the right left and then a ceiling fell. So we hired vans. Three days ago they arrived. A deluge. In the middle of unloading beds etc into the farm house where we've hired 3 rooms the farmer [Mr Botten] flew into a panic—said we must stop: said he wouldnt allow another handful to be added—suddenly remembered that his attics would catch fire if struck by a bomb; and so cast us out into the flood, and we had to bring half the impedimenta here. So I'm all black and blue with moving. And the house is packed like an emporium. And 4 tons of books came yesterday. And the Printing Press and all the type come tomorrow. This bores me so, I cant even write it. Boredom and distraction

---

1. Painted by Vanessa and Duncan in 1924.

and fights with matter, have been hag riding me this fortnight. And lectures in the hall; and 15 people to seat and warm. And the Womens Institute elects me Treasurer. And I have to collect 30 sixpences and pay Mrs Freeth 2/3 for hire of hall.

Now let us talk of something interesting. I was going to say why dont you write a Common Reader review of music? Now consider that. Write your loves and hates for Bach Wagner etc out in plain English. I have an ulterior motive. I want to investigate the influence of music on literature. But there's not a book on music that gives me a hint—Parry[1] all padding. What about Tovey?[2] Too metaphysical. Ethel is the [*last page missing*]

[*added on top of page:*]
Never never keep letters, Ethel. Theyre the devil when it comes to a move.

Berg

3665: To Dr Octavia Wilberforce   *Monk's House, Rodmell*
                                                    [Sussex]
17th Dec [1940]

Dear Octavia,

You know by this time how bad I am at answering letters: I ought to have thanked you before for sending Miss Robins' book.[3] I've put it carefully in the shelf, and shall begin when I'm quit of reading books for an article.[4] It was very good of you to think of it: and lend so valuable a copy.

Oh yes we will eat your cream gratefully and defy the flue—But we have loads of apples. Also Books. So lets make a Barter. And let us know beforehand when you're coming so that we mayn't be over the hill somewhere.

Your
Virginia Woolf
so cold she cant
hold a pen.

Sussex

1. Sir Hubert Parry (1848-1918), the composer and teacher. His *Art of Music* appeared in 1894.
2. Sir Donald Tovey (1875-1940), the composer, conductor, and author of *Essays in Musical Analysis* (1935-39).
3. Probably one of Elizabeth Robins's many novels, the best of which was *The Magnetic North* (1904).
4. *Ellen Terry* (*New Statesman*, 8 February 1941).

18th Dec. [1940]

Did you really mean me to take you at your word?

Well, I have. Last night, our 21st birthday celebration, after we'd eaten our chocolate cake, Mrs. Chavasse, the President,[1] rose and announced; "Ladies, I have the pleasure of informing you that Mrs. Harold Nicolson, equally well known as Vita Sackville West, has consented to lecture to us on Persia in February!!!"

Loud cheers. General enthusiasm. A vote of thanks was then given to Mrs. Woolf for having secured you.

Lord! dont go and say you wont! You cant think how they beamed and boomed over you. They've all heard you on the wireless. Miss Gardner our secretary has The Land by heart. The one passion they all share is for Persia. What about slides? I said you'd illustrate your travels. We will get a lantern if you want one.

Its the 3rd Tuesday in February.

meeting at 2.45.

You lunch here at 1. You sleep here. If you insist you go home after lunch on Wednesday.

But details can wait. Only tell me you'll come; and accept my—oh accumulated blessings.

You cant think how excited they were—never having been beyond Lewes in their lives. And you—whose voice they know; whose husband's voice they know—

All 37 Meck' Sqre has now been dumped here; and we're in the devil of a hobble and mess.

Yr V.

Berg

19th Dec [1940]

Dear Bob,

I've been so grateful to you the last few nights for giving me something that I enjoy reading.[2] I'm not enough of a scholar to know how close the translation is but I get the sense of being in a civilised world; and its so lovely, and so amusing: so lasting.

Of course once more your own dialogue makes the return to my old

1. Of the Women's Institute, Rodmell. Virginia was the Treasurer.
2. R. C. Trevelyan's *Translations from Horace, Etc, with Two Imaginary Conversations* (1940).

plea—that you should give us your prose side. Its not so magnificent as the poetic, I know. But I should like a note book of daily fragmentary comments: books, views, people, all as it comes.

This is a grudging way of thanking you: except that it means I want more.

Much love from us both,

Yr ever
Virginia Woolf

Sussex

3668: To ANGELICA BELL

Monk's House, Rodmell
[Sussex]

21st Dec [1940]

Dearest Pixie,

I sent off to you yesterday by post from Brighton (we had an ad.lib.) a small present—a coat to wit. A ticket is attached to it. If, as may well be, you want to change it, take the ticket and coat to the second floor of the Galeries Lafayette—the skirt, coat, blouse department—where a tall motherly lady has agreed to change it for you. I also enclose a modest cheque—part present, part—indeed the greater part—payment for the new Leda[1] at whom I'm working. A most ravishing lady.

The gaieties of Rodmell have been incessant.

Oh what about your lecture?[2] It was announced the other night at a 21st birthday assembly. And the population rose and cheered. Can you project your photographs on a lantern?

No time for more.

Virginia

We have a blue short haired kitten. He has just eaten my pen—hence the difficulty in writing.

Texas

3669: To ANGELICA BELL

Monk's House, Rodmell,
Sussex

Typewritten
Monday [23 December 1940]

Dearest Pix,

Your letter just come. I write in haste, with a trembling paw; so had better type. Did I say, you can change the coat, which I snatched in haste

1. The most recent of Angelica's designs for Virginia's embroidery.
2. To the Women's Institute on the subject of *How to Produce a Play*.

in the dark? If you take it to the Lafayette, there's a kind old woman who said you could choose any other more desirable object.

I suggest that you come to tea on Saturday next; stay the night; then we can make Mummy ask us all to Sunday lunch; any how, if not, take you over in the car.

Are your pictures adaptable to a lantern? The Institute said they would get a lantern if they were. Oh they were so agog when I told them; one of them acted in Carl Rosa [Opera Company]. However, no time for all this. I'm dashing to Lewes to meet Mummy.

Witcherina varissima but unkissed.

[*handwritten:*]

The Wolf and the Goat[1] are the joy of my mantlepiece. And old Lady Oxford sent me her legacy—worth £400—what d'you think it is?[2]— Come and see.

Texas

3670: To Ethel Smyth   *Monks House, Rodmell*
                                        [Sussex]
24th Dec. 1940.

I've only ten minutes before driving off across the hill to lunch with Rogers mistress, Helen Anrep.[3] I've been so badgered, that as you see, my hand trembles. Its partly that damned mess of books and things; I cant make a warm hollow for myself; my mind is churned and frothed; and to write one must be a clear vessel. Never mind; you dont care much; I mean I scribble to you as I scribble in my diary.

I'm awfully proud—thats not the right phrase—that you've started again on the autobiography, partly owing to me. I was thinking the other night that there's never been a womans autobiography. Nothing to compare with Rousseau. Chastity and modesty I suppose have been the reason. Now why shouldnt you be not only the first woman to write an opera, but equally the first to tell the truths about herself? Isnt the great artist the only person to tell the truth? I should like an analysis of your sex life. As Rousseau did his. More introspection. More intimacy. I leave it to you; for as you see I cant make my pen take my ply this cold morning. Margot [Oxford] has gone raving mad. She sent her car 120 miles yesterday here to bring me a bronze bust of Voltaire which she'd left me in her will. Why? I cant conceive. She was to have come herself. Can you explain this sudden rapture?

1. Hand-coloured 19th-century prints.
2. A statuette of Voltaire.
3. At Alciston Farmhouse, southeast of Charleston.

We're devilish poor. Lord, what a bill for rent and removal, and no money coming in, and the taxes! I shall have to write and write—till I die—just as we thought we'd saved enough to live, unwriting, till we died! But its a good thing—being buffeted, and not cosseted. How does it affect you? Are you ruined, I mean can you pay your bills out of income? Yes, I will come one day soon. Because I must exchange ideas; and I want to see you in your surroundings. But how?

This is a scribble, but write, and I will try to find a better mood soon.

Yr

V

Berg

3671: To Dr Octavia Wilberforce

[Monk's House, Rodmell, Sussex]

Christmas Eve [1940]

Your cow[1] must be a miracle. It has produced the best cream and the best milk that Leonard and Virginia Woolf have ever eaten.

Best wishes and thanks

Leonard Woolf   Virginia Woolf

Sussex

3672: To V. Sackville-West

Monks House [Rodmell, Sussex]

Boxing day [26 December 1940]

If my admiration for you could be increased, it would be by the fact that your divine butter arrived on Christmas morning. Anybody else, I that is, would have sent it any other day. As it was, Leonard and I, economising with a duck this year, had such an orgy of butter eating it was worth ten turkeys. Oh what a gift!

Oh Vita what a Cornucopia of Bounty you are!

A broken po.

A Jacobs fleece

Two pounds of fresh butter.

And I never give you a thing—I wonder why that is. Then I have to add about £2,000 from your books. let alone the meaning of 'em.

1. In the absence of Elizabeth Robins in America, Octavia Wilberforce continued to administer the Sussex farmhouse in Henfield, which had been converted into a rest home for professional women.

Have you got a life of Bess of Hardwick; a life of Lady Clifford;[1]—well, if you have, bring them, on loan, when you come. Another Bounty. Yes, of course we'll get the Lantern—and would you like me to ask Edith [*sic*] Jones[2] to lunch? That would save you going, which would be intolerable; and I'd slip out into the garden and leave you. Not that I want to—Lord no. I can talk 24 hours without stopping. I mean to you, not to her. Whats all this about Dotty? Ethel is catastrophic in the extreme. Oh I must tell you, Lady Oxford sent her chauffeur here with her legacy for me —a bronze bust of Voltaire. I think she loves me; please note.

V. and P.

Your book [*Country Notes in Wartime*] has sold 1862 copies. Very good.

Berg

3673: To Shena, Lady Simon   *Monk's House, Rodmell,*
Lewes [*Sussex*]

29th Dec 40

Dear Shena,

Leonard gave me a card the other day in which you made me responsible for one of your many generosities. I didn't deserve it.

But what I want so much to know is what's been happening to you—a large question.

I cant ask you to come to tea, because the flat is now half ruined by bombs; and all the furniture moved here, and we've no roof in London. You must come when you visit your brother in law.[3]

We're now villagers completely. And its a very odd life. If you come I'll ask the clergyman's wife to tea.

But what I should like, if you've time, is a line to say how you are.

Yr Virginia Woolf

Sussex

1. Lady Anne Clifford was the daughter of the Earl of Cumberland. She was married first to the Earl of Dorset, and secondly to the Earl of Pembroke. She died in 1676, leaving a diary, which Vita published with an introduction in 1924. A biography of her had been written in 1922 by George C. Williamson.
2. Enid Bagnold (Lady Jones). See p. 183, note 1.
3. Rear Admiral Tufton Beamish (1874-1951), Conservative Member of Parliament for Lewes, 1924-31 and 1936-45. In 1914 he married Margaret Simon, Shena's sister-in-law, and they lived at Chelwood Gate, near Haywards Heath, Sussex.

3674: To Dr Octavia Wilberforce *Monk's House, Rodmell*
[Sussex]
31st Dec [1940]

Dear Octavia,

I never heard a more absurd "business proposition" as you call it. A month's milk and cream in return for an unborn and as far as I can tell completely worthless book.[1] I've lost all power over words, cant do a thing with them. What we suggest is that if you would send your bounty say Monday and Friday to Lewes we would meet it. And return—well, apples? Thats about the only thing we can return. Of course, milk and cream are at the moment worth tons of apples. We know this, and can only put it on record that we realise it all—your generosity, and the trouble, and the really miraculous gift.

Your quotations, far from enraging, put me up a peg. Of course the Roger Fry was more or less an experiment in self-suppression, as E. R. [Elizabeth Robins] guessed. But I was afraid I'd somehow suppressed him too. It was a touch and go business—either too much colour or too little. But on the whole, I'd rather there were no biographer, than a mix up of the two. I suppose the really expert somehow combine both, rightly.

You cant write long enough letters to *this* author—but, having been book lugging, up at our hired room, I cant, as you see, make my hand cease to tremble. Now as a doctor, your hand is firm. So you can write. One of Roger's eccentricities was that he never analalysed character, but always art. I daresay the reason for his mastery.

Let me know about the bargain.

Yr V. W.

This sheet of paper came out of our bombed house—thats the dirt on it—bombs.

Sussex

1. In return for milk and cream, Dr Wilberforce had asked Virginia for a copy of her next book, which was *Between the Acts*.

Letters 3675-3701 (January–mid-March 1941)

Virginia had finished Pointz Hall (Between the Acts) *in November, and was now revising it at Monk's House. She also made some progress with her history of literature. She and Leonard made two day-expeditions to London, where she wandered sadly through the broken streets, and once they went by train to Cambridge, calling at Letchworth to see the Hogarth Press in its wartime premises. In Sussex life was quiet enough, though at night the enemy bombers still burbled their way overhead to London, and with the approach of spring a German invasion of the south coast was again expected. There were occasional visitors to Rodmell, among them Elizabeth Bowen and Octavia Wilberforce, and Vita, who spent a night there on* 17 *February. In late January Virginia went through "a trough of despair", but her letters remained cheerful, and she was making plans for April—Eliot was to visit Monk's House, and Virginia hoped to see Vita at Sissinghurst and Ethel Smyth at Woking.*

3675: To SIBYL COLEFAX

Monk's House, Rodmell, Lewes [Sussex]

4th Jan 1941

Dearest Sibyl,

Of course you've only to suggest any Friday. Not, if you'll take my advice, in January. Our hearts are warm, but oh the cold here! Driving snow; downs white; birds frozen; and my hand a mere claw. But in February? As I say, suggest it; but you know it's a bare barn, this house,—your blood's on your own head if you come. But I'll fry you an egg, and we can crouch over the fire. No Desmond; no Moore. The old Wolves huddle like rooks alone on their tree-top.

My only boast is that Margot [Oxford] has given me a statue.

Yrs Virginia

Michael Colefax

3676: To DR OCTAVIA WILBERFORCE

Monk's House, Rodmell, Sussex

Thursday [9 January 1941]

Dear Octavia,

Oh dear—now you've telephoned, and I was just about to write. We cant come to the concert, as Leonard lectures, and theres the Blackout and the chairs to see to.

I'm sorry. Think of eating Turkey! and I want to continue the argument—the very one-sided argument; books v. cream.[1] I dont see how you can brave it out. Nothing we both ever to the end write can outweigh your milk and cream at this bitter and barren moment. Besides, having some to spare, I gave Louie a jug; and so the Everest family bless your name, having porridge for breakfast. I'll keep the boxes. The cartons came unscathed.

Yesterday I had a long long letter from Rachel Dyce Sharp,[2] which I'll show you when you come. I think the woman's whirling raving mad—however.

This hand doesn't shake from book hugging, but from rage. Louie being gone to a funeral, I cooked lunch: and the rice floored me. Thats why I rage, and am now consulting a cookery book. So how am I to write *your* book?

My father's been done already. F. W. Maitland.[3]

But I'm too rice-infested to make any sense. So forgive; and I'm so sorry I forgot to answer before.

Yr V. W.

Sussex

3677: To Elaine Robson   *Monk's House, Rodmell,*
                                          Lewes, Sussex

10th Jan 1941

My dear Elaine [aged about 9],

The Blue Cat, whose name is Peat, has asked me to write you a letter as he has not yet learnt how. Well he has a fine story to tell you. When I—that is Virginia—came into the hall yesterday I saw Peat playing with my glove. Suddenly the glove began to whistle. Then I looked and saw the

1. See Letter 3674.
2. One of the proprietors of The Violet Nurseries in Henfield, Sussex, and the sister of Clifford Sharp, formerly Editor of the *New Statesman*. She wrote three or four letters to Virginia, one of which is summarised in a letter from Octavia Wilberforce to Elizabeth Robins (23 December 1940, *Sussex*). Miss Sharp had written to complain about a 'repulsive' passage in *Roger Fry*, in which Fry described the vicious beatings of his schoolmates by the masters. One boy was being caned, when suddenly he could no longer control his bowels and 'let fly' (*Roger Fry*, p. 33).
3. Frederick William Maitland (1850-1906), Professor of English Law at Cambridge, had known the Stephen family for many years, and married Virginia's cousin Florence Fisher. His *Life and Letters of Leslie Stephen* appeared in 1906.

fingers move. Then I looked again and saw it was a Bat. "Leonard! Leonard!" I shrieked. "The Cat has caught a bat!!" He thought it was a joke, so he didn't come. He was sawing up wood. Then I got a flower pot and put it over the Bat. But, when Leonard came, the bat was dead. So Peat ate him for his supper. Then we had a great flood, because a bomb burst the river Bank. And we saw all the moles swimming for dear life, only their paws are so short compared with their bodies they didn't get far. Then three great hares came and sat in the road. Now the flood is gone. All the marsh is frozen, and I can see three black spots which are really three red cows or hares.

Have you had any adventures? I wish you would write and tell me and I will tell Peat. He likes verse better than prose. He and Sally are curled up on the mat to keep each other warm. Only poor Sally is listening for Leonard to come. One of her ears is trembling. Leonard is sawing up wood. When I have written this letter I am going to cook a fish which I bought in Lewes. I went on my bicycle, and the bicycle ran down the hill like a toboggan. If it freezes again we shall skate on the lily pool. Have you skated yet? This is the end of the paper.

Peat made that mark—It is a cat's kiss. Leonard says he sends his kiss too X. That is it. Mine is this x. So I must use this bit of paper to say goodbye. Give our love to Mummy, Daddy, Philip and the baby.

Your affectionate
Virginia

Sussex (typescript copy)

3678: To Ethel Smyth

Monks House, Rodmell
[*Sussex*]

12th Jan 41

Well, well, how time passes. Did I ever thank you for your offer of a £10 note, which was to turn into a car, and the car was to take me to Woking—etc etc—No, my sudden financial anguish was only due to doing the years accounts with Leonard, Like my father, I can always conjure up bankruptcy. But unlike my father Leonard has no money complex. So we can rub along cutting a servant, cutting clothes; but otherwise not encroaching on capital yet. Oh yes, I can write: I mean I've a fizz of ideas. What I dread is bottling them to order. Didn't we start the Hogarth Press 25 years ago so as to be quit of editors and publishers? Its my nightmare, being in their clutches: but a nightmare, not a sane survey.

I'm interested that you cant write about masturbation. That I understand. What puzzles me is how this reticence co-habits with your ability to talk openly magnificently, freely about—say H.B. I couldn't do one or the other. But as so much of life is sexual—or so they say—it rather limits autobiography if this is blacked out. It must be, I suspect, for many generations, for women; for its like breaking the hymen—if thats the membrane's name—a painful operation, and I suppose connected with all sorts of subterranean instincts. I still shiver with shame at the memory of my half brother,[1] standing me on a ledge, aged about 6, and so exploring my private parts. Why should I have felt shame then?

But why should I be writing these sexual speculations now? Every other second I take my eyes off the page to look at the elms outside—burning orange against a deep blue. Then theres the little cross of the Church against the snow. Only the snow is going. Yesterday it was a livid purple. Lord! How quickly the sun sets! Only one red slope now is left on Caburn. But I must add the smoke convoluting out of Asheham Cement Works is a ruffled pink that absolutely defies description—you'll be glad to hear.

How odd it is being a countrywoman after all these years of being Cockney! For almost the first time in my life I've not a bed in London. D'you know what I'm doing tomorrow? Going up to London Bridge. Then I shall walk, all along the Thames, in and out where I used to haunt, so through the Temple, up the Strand and out into Oxford Street, where I shall buy maccaroni and lunch. No. You never shared my passion for that great city. Yet its what, in some odd corner of my dreaming mind, represents Chaucer, Shakespeare, Dickens. Its my only patriotism: save one vision, in Warwickshire one spring [May 1934] when we were driving back from Ireland and I saw a stallion being led, under the may and the beeches, along a grass ride; and I thought that is England.

Well, dearest Ethel, how damned generous you are, breaking, or ready to break, a golden lump off your hoard, all to buy a visit from me. I happen to be very humble just now. I cant believe in being anyone. So I say with amazement, yet Ethel wants to see me! We shall meet one of these days. By the way, youre coming to stay in the Spring: you will address the Womens Institute (as Vita is doing) then youll sleep here. Never mind Leonard. He is a good man: in his heart he respects my friends. But as for *my* staying with *you*, for some occult reason, he cries No no No. I think its a bad thing that we're so inseparable. But how, in this world of separation, dare one break it? I'm working really rather hard (for me)[2] but whats the good of what I write, I havent the glimpse of an idea. You'll say, its good for you. So it is, I've no doubt. Certainly I should swing like a frantic pendulum otherwise. And now I must 1. make soup. 2. make butter. Tell me how your book is going—for that's what I want.

V.

1. Gerald Duckworth (1870-1937). See Virginia's description of this encounter in *A Sketch of the Past* (*Moments of Being*, p. 69, 1976), which she had written between April 1939 and November 1940.
2. Virginia was revising *Between the Acts*.

If you want to know where I get my (ahem!) charm, read Herbert Fisher's autobiography. Marie Antoinette loved my ancestor: hence he was exiled; hence the Pattles, the barrel that burst, and finally Virginia.[1]

Berg

3679: To Philip Hugh-Jones   *Monks House, Rodmell,*
                                               Lewes [Sussex]
18th Jan 41

Dear Philip,

I am so glad that you enjoyed my life of Roger Fry. I wish you had known him—he was far the most 'exciting' person to meet I've ever known. He was always bubbling with new ideas and adventures, even when the last one had gone smash, like the Omega. I was glad to be able to rescue one of his blue Omega plates from the ruins of Mecklenburgh Square. We have had to move all our furniture down here, as after a landmine broke all the windows for a second time, our flat became uninhabitable. So we are now without a house in London and live entirely here; with our books and beds boarded out in various rooms in the village.

I'm glad you're in Edinburgh [to study medicine], and not London, which is a melancholy place now. Last week I walked through the ruins of the Temple. If you come to Sussex I hope you will visit us.

Please remember us both to your mother.[2]

                                               yrs Virginia Woolf
Philip Hugh-Jones

3680: To V. Sackville-West   *Monks House, Rodmell*
                                               [Sussex]
19th Jan [1941]

I must buy some shaded inks—lavenders, pinks violets—to shade my meaning. I see I gave you many wrong meanings, using only black ink. It

1. The autobiography of Virginia's cousin H. A. L. Fisher appeared posthumously in 1940 as *An Unfinished Autobiography*. Virginia's great great-grandfather was Antoine, Chevalier de L'Etang, a reputed lover of Marie Antoinette. One of his three daughters was Adeline (1793-1845), who married James Pattle. Pattle reputedly drank himself to death in India, and his body was brought home in a cask of spirits, which exploded during the voyage. Ethel had already told this story in *Impressions That Remained*. The legends about Pattle are discussed in Brian Hill's *Julia Margaret Cameron*, 1973.
2. See p. 71, note 1.

was a joke—our drifting apart. It was serious, wishing you'd write. It was not true that I disliked Hilda [Matheson]. I only felt—What? Something opaque, pulverising: my fault, as much as hers. And one pang of wild jealousy seized me, inopportunely, dining at Sibyls. No, no, I must buy my coloured inks. As for Irene;[1] yes: a certain discomfort; as if the past rose between us. I was sorry for one of her trophies—a nice young man she met at my house,[2] at once captivated then—I thought—dropped; whereupon he was killed in the war. But no: I must get my coloured inks. She never bedded, only waved flags from her castle tower: and it was a little exacerbating when my brother went off at a gallop. Thats all.

The slide[3] arrived safe. But Miss Gardner (who's had a story accepted by Horizon and is thus in the 7th Heaven[4]) says we must get a Lantern. The Epi-dia-scope (Greek for looking through and over, I think) wont take slides only photographs. But you haven't photographs, I suppose? Anyhow its easy to come by the Lantern. As for the Epi-dia-scope, I've run mad hunting one down in Lewes for Angelica's lecture on The Stage tomorrow.

What did you say when Violet T. asked you a leading question?[5] I still remember her, like a fox cub, all scent and seduction coming to 52: and abstracting The Common Reader. Now why did you love her? And did you love Hilda? We must go into all this. I rather think I've a new lover, a doctor, a Wilberforce, a cousin—ah! does that make you twitch! Am I still on the 3rd rung from the top? A sudden thaw: a spring day; and crocuses out in a pot.

Potto and V.

My blue envelope I bought from a bombed shop in Chancery Lane, cheap. Lord, what chaos in the Temple! All my lovely squares gone.

Look at Margots ravings[6]—and destroy.

Berg

1. Irene Noel (d. 1956), who married the politician Philip Baker (Noel-Baker) in 1915. Virginia had known her as a girl.
2. Tudor Castle, who worked in the Admiralty and died in the First War. See Volume I, Letter 512.
3. For Vita's lecture on Persia (18 February) for the Rodmell Women's Institute.
4. *The Land Girl*, by Diana Gardner, was published in *Horizon*, December 1940.
5. Violet Trefusis (1894-1972), the daughter of George and Alice Keppel, had a passionate love affair with Vita in 1919-20, and the two women eloped together to France from where their husbands retrieved them. Virginia had met Violet in November 1932. See Volume V, Letter 2660.
6. One of Lady Oxford's frequent and intimate letters to Virginia.

3681: To the Assistant Editor of Harper's Bazaar
Monk's House, Rodmell,
Lewes, Sussex

Typewritten (carbon copy)
23 January, 1941

Dear Sir,
Your letter of 21 January astonishes me. Three months ago *you* wrote to *me* saying that the American office had cabled to you "clamouring for" a story from me.[1] I was not prepared to submit a story unless commissioned and you then wrote to me on October 25th saying that "it would definitely be a commission from America" and "if you can let me have a story for them as soon as possible we would use it ourselves this side in the next issue to press." You acknowledged receipt of the story on November 4, nearly three months ago. Since that date I have heard nothing from you, my letters remained unanswered, and the story was not used in your next issue. You now write me a letter from which I gather that you propose, without apology, to repudiate your agreement

Yours faithfully
[*unsigned*]

Sussex

3682: To Dr Octavia Wilberforce
Monk's House
[*Rodmell, Sussex*]

Jan 25th [1941]

I never thanked you—dear me—for the receipts [recipes] which I have laid in my drawer. As for Riding Hood's basket, that is our bi-weekly miracle: really twice a week we have a festival at your expense, and Louie has porridge for breakfast.

This damp dismal day its like a sun in the fog. If I cant write, I can eat. As for writing, its a washout.

Should you be our way, look in: but this is only by way of thanks, in a rush and a hurry.

Yr
V. W.

Note the envelope, bombed stock from a lawyer's office bought cheap in Chancery Lane.

Sussex

1. The story (*The Legacy*) was first published in *The Haunted House and Other Short Stories* (1943).

463

3683: To Shena, Lady Simon   *Monk's House, Rodmell*
                                             [Sussex]

25th Jan [1941]

My dear Shena,

I was so glad to get your letter and write this by way of giving you an excuse—if you want one—to write again.

I had enough imagination to suppose that you'd be in the thick of it. And I rather envy you. It seems a little futile to boil with rage as I do about twice a week—in these marshes. This morning it was the soldiers saying women were turning them out of their jobs. The human race seems to repeat itself insufferably. I should like to know about rates—I've a personal interest now, fighting the Foundlings about our wrecked flat[1]—And Leonard says I'm to tell you how much he admired your pamphlet on Education. This is incoherent, but I'm trying to light a fire, this damp day, of green wood.

No, I dont see whats [to] be done about war. Its manliness; and manliness breeds womanliness—both so hateful. I tried to put this to our local labour party: but was scowled at as a prostitute. They said if women had as much money as men, they'd enjoy themselves: and then what about the children? So they have more children; more wars; and so on. This is not a contribution to the problem, only a groan.

I dont see why, if you can ever come south, you shouldnt stay here? only its unlikely I suppose, that you should come south. Consider us, if you dont mind a hard bed, a very small room, and dinner cooked by me. I wont ask Mrs Ebbs [rector's wife]—I've never asked her—I intend some day to ask her—that was how I came to think if you were here I would ask her. We live in the heart of the lower village world, to whom Leonard lectures on potatoes and politics. The gentry dont call.

I'm glad you got a glimpse of Roger Fry. If I could have shirked all the relations, I might have said more—But as it is—no, I dont think one can so disregard human feelings:—a reason not to write biographies,—yet if one waits the impression fades. Herbert Fisher [his *Autobiography*] rather nettled me. I dont like being exposed as a novelist and told my people[2] are my mother and father, when, being in a novel, they're not.

It was rather charming, though, his book, in the beginning, but then Lettice [Mrs Fisher] and the Cabinet between them flattened it out. That was true of him too;—

---

1. The Foundling Hospital (Thomas Coram Foundation) was the landlord of 37 Mecklenburgh Square.
2. Mr and Mrs Ramsay in *To the Lighthouse*.

But my fire must now be completely taken in hand: and you see, I've given you a very good excuse to write another letter.

Yr

Virginia Woolf

Sussex

3684: To Enid Bagnold   *Monk's House, Rodmell,*
                                          Lewes [*Sussex*]
26 Jan [1941]

Dear Enid,

Vita is coming here on the 18th. I wonder if you would come over to lunch on the 19th (a Wednesday) at one? It would be a great pleasure if you would. She says you have a phaeton and a hunter that jumps gates. We are down here, bombed out of London.

Vita is lecturing the Women's Institute, so I promised her I'd try and give her a treat next day.

Yrs

Virginia Woolf

Mrs J. L. Manning

3685: To Ethel Smyth   *Monks House, Rodmell*
                                          [*Sussex*]
Feb 1st 41

I've written you ever so many beautiful letters—cigarette letters—you know the kind, when one's devotion to Ethel rises like a silver smoke, too fine for words. These are the letters I write you, about 3 on a wet windy morning. Unlike Margot, I dont keep a pencil at my head and I forget where we left off—you were going into the snow in snow boots. You had seduced the wife of the woodcutter—and then? I have a far away lover, to match your translator—a doctor, a cousin, a Wilberforce, who lives at Brighton and has—by a miracle—heard of you. If I were in London, I'd ask you to meet. She has a herd of Jersey cows and sends me a pot of cream weekly. Oh theres Margot—I cant fathom her—I get now almost daily a letter written in bed at 3 am in the Savoy. Why at this last lap of time should she fabricate an entirely imaginary passion for me, who am utterly incongruous "You and Frances Horner"[1] she says this morning "are the only women I've ever loved". The rest of womenkind, as I can well imagine,

1. Lady Horner (*née* Graham, 1854-1940), whose daughter married Margot's stepson, Raymond, eldest son of Herbert Asquith, the Prime Minister.

465

seeing her clothes, she hates. Yet she assures me she never bedded with a lover. And why assure me of anything? Is it that at the end of life she must somehow still collect some mirror? and I, being unused, still reflect whats no longer there? I suppose her lovers, male, are now grizzly old Peers, with whom its no use flirting. Extend your lighthouse Beam over this dark spot and tell me what you see.

You were saying, werent you, you wanted to see Osberts Ankor?[1]— I heard from him tother day—after a lapse of years. He sent me his Aunt's diaries;[2] in which you occur. Did I tell you?—or was this silver smoke? I think you came into the Taits[3] drawing room, smoking. which shocked Florence Sitwell, who was, perhaps is, a perfect lady. I dont care for Osberts prose: the rhododendrons grow to such a height in it. But it was an amusing book. Also I read with gratitude, Mrs Dugdale[4]—what did she call it? some memoirs, but very light, shapely, and composed. How well people almost always write about themselves!

Did I tell you I'm reading the whole of English literature through? By the time I've reached Shakespeare the bombs will be falling. So I've arranged a very nice last scene: reading Shakespeare, having forgotten my gas mask, I shall fade far away, and quite forget. . . . They brought down a raider the other side of Lewes yesterday. I was cycling in to get our butter, but only heard a drone in the clouds. Thank God, as you would say, one's fathers left one a taste for reading! Instead of thinking, by May we shall be— whatever it may be: I think, only 3 months to read Ben Jonson, Milton, Donne, and all the rest! Today however, to make me quicken my pace, I saw a yellow woodpecker bright green against ruby red willows. Lord! how I started, and then saw coming across the marsh, Leonard, looking like a Saxon Earl, because his old coat was torn and the lining flapped round his gum boots.

I did walk through London the other day—Oh but I told you about the Temple, didnt I, all rubble and white dust?—and how, to put heart into me, I ate Turkey at Buszards [Oxford Street]? I have so seldom gloried in food, all alone. But there must be an end to this drivel, because I must earn

1. The group of ruined Buddhist temples in the jungles of Cambodia which Osbert Sitwell had visited in 1934. In 1939 he published a description of his trip in *Escape With Me*.
2. *Two Generations: Reminiscences of Georgiana C. Sitwell and Journal of Florence A. Sitwell*, ed. Osbert Sitwell, 1940.
3. Archibald Campbell Tait, the Archbishop of Canterbury, 1868–82. His daughter Edith married Randall Davidson, who also became Archbishop of Canterbury. Davidson's brother Harry married Ethel's eldest sister Alice.
4. Blanche Dugdale (*née* Balfour), the niece of Arthur Balfour, whose biography she published in 1936. Her memoirs were called *Family Homespun* (1940).

10 guineas reading a vast fat book about Mrs Thrale.[1] I'm in the 16th Century, and its a wrench to jerk to the 18th.

I read and read like a donkey going round and round a well; pray to God, some idea will flash. I leave it to nature. I can no longer control my brain. I am in touch with Enid Jones, who is coming to meet Vita; who is coming to lecture the Institute; and so shall I hope send a message to Maurice Baring.[2]

Now, Ethel dear, you will perhaps very kindly write to me. You see what a long letter this is: also dated. Not a very coherent letter; but Leonards sawing logs under the window; and the marsh is all emerald green again, and the elms barred with rosy clouds, and pale pure blue behind that funny little extinguisher—the Church. For the past 3 weeks I've lived like a moth in a towel. Did I tell you I can now make lovely, rich, savoury vegetable soup? Tonight we shall have maccaroni au gratin and my lovers [Wilberforce] cream. But now, in Gods name, I must open this damned industrious American [Clifford], who's spent 20 years shadowing Mrs Thrale. I would like to ask, quite simply, do you still love me? Remember how I waved that day in Meck Sqre. Do love me.

V.

Berg

3686: TO DESMOND MACCARTHY   *Monk's House, Rodmell,*
                                                          Lewes [Sussex]
Typewritten
2nd Feb [1941]
                    Re article in Sunday Times[3]

No, no, no, my dear Desmond—I really must protest. *I* never sat on top of a tower! Compare my wretched little £150 education with yours, with Lytton's, with Leonard's. Did Eton and Cambridge make no difference to you? Could the Hawk have been so affable and so hawklike without it?[4] Would Lytton have written just as well if he'd spent his youth, as I did mine, mooning among books in a library? I assure you, my tower was a mere toadstool, about six inches high. And when you say "She herself as a writer owes everything to having seen the world from a tower which did

1. Review of *Hester Lynch Piozzi*, by James L. Clifford (*New Statesman*, 8 March 1941). It was the last review that Virginia wrote, and she wrote eight drafts of it, which Leonard sent to Professor Clifford after her death.
2. Both Enid Bagnold (Lady Jones) and Maurice Baring lived in Rottingdean, Sussex.
3. In the issue of 2 February Desmond MacCarthy reviewed *The Leaning Tower*.
4. Desmond MacCarthy had used the pseudonym 'Affable Hawk' when he reviewed regularly for the *New Statesman*.

not lean"[1] you make me gnash my teeth. If you knew my inadequacy; what shifts and squeaks I'm put to every time I dip my pen! Of course I'm not on the ground with the WEA but I'm about four thousand five hundred and fifty pounds nearer them than you are. So I'm right to say 'we' when I talk to them; just as I'm right to say 'they' when I look up, as I do with constant envy and admiration, at you.

This is the brief residue of a three hours argument with Leonard. So I thought I'd pop my conclusion in an envelope and send it you.

No chance I suppose of another week end? How nice the last one was— And are you at Ham [Wiltshire]? If so, give Molly my love.

The cold has reduced my hand to such a frozen claw that I type; but the pleasure with which I read you remains warm.

Yr Virginia

Mrs Michael MacCarthy

3687: To Enid Bagnold

Monk's House, Rodmell, Lewes [Sussex]

Typewritten
Sunday [2 February 1941]

Dear Enid,

What a muddle! Vita said how much she'd like to meet you. I said, Then I'll ask her over ... Vita said, Perfect. Not a sign that she'd invited herself to you.

Perhaps we'd better leave it as it is—if you'll be so angelic as to come here. I know its asking a lot. And its not true that I hate leaving my house— not at all. But this we can discuss when you come. So we expect you at One on the 19th.[2]

If you should ever see Maurice Baring, could you convey my respectful affection?

Why are you North End House in the Telephone; and Elms on your paper?[3]

Yr
Virginia Woolf

Enid Bagnold

1. The sentence continued, ". . . and I think that, except as a sign of sympathy, she ought not to have used the pronoun 'we' in addressing an audience of working men".
2. Vita came to Monk's House for the night of the 17th, and on the 18th, before Vita gave her lecture to the Women's Institute, Enid Bagnold lunched with her and Virginia.
3. Both houses, facing each other across the Rottingdean green, belonged to the Jones. Kipling had stayed with his uncle Edward Burne-Jones at North End House, and lived at The Elms, 1897-1902.

3688: To the Editor of Harper's Bazaar

Monk's House, Rodmell,
Lewes, Sussex

Typewritten (carbon copy)
3 February, 1941

Dear Sir,

I have to thank you for your letter of 31 January, but there has been no muddle or misunderstanding on my side.[1] I have had no cable, letter, or any other communication either from Mr Davis or Miss McFadden. I had a letter from your office asking me for a story, saying that the American office had cabled to you. As I was engaged on a book at the time. I was not anxious to do it immediately and I replied that I had nothing by me, but had some stories roughly sketched out in my London house and would get them and look at them when I was next in town. I also enquired whether this was a commission, as I was not prepared to write a story except it was commissioned. I then received letters from your office pressing me to get the stories from my London house so that you could send one on the Clipper [air mail] to the U.S.A. as that was the repeated cabled request from your American office and informing me that "it would definitely be a commission from America". (See your letters of October 14, 20, and 25). I do not see that there is any "muddle" or "misunderstanding" about this, but a perfectly plain, legal contract. At some inconvenience to myself, I went up to town, got the rough sketches, wrote a story from one of them, and sent it to your office. I was told also that the story would be used here by you. The story was acknowledged, but after that I heard nothing from you and my letter remained unanswered. You now inform me that "they do not want" the story, but "are tremendously keen" about something else. I presume that payment will be made for the story commissioned by you— which will bring in foreign exchange as effectively as if it had been printed— and after that I will consider any suggestion which Miss McFadden cares to put before me.

Yours faithfully
[*unsigned*]

Sussex

3689: To V. Sackville-West

Monks House [Rodmell,
Sussex]

4th Feb. [1941]

Oh dearest Vita, what an overflowing Cornucopia you are! How you pet pamper and spoil me! Nothing could have come more pat than your pat. I'd shaken a bottle of milk for an hour; at last a yellow lump appeared: I put

1. See Letter 3681.

it on the kitchen table. The cat ate it—So when the post came, it was like the voice of God in answer to our prayers. What did Staples [Nicolsons' cook] say when she found it gone? Yes, I'm a butter maker now, and it takes the devil of a time.

Also: what am I wearing at this moment? Jacobs Ram. Louie made me a thick warm jersey. Its saved my life I live in it. And its a lovely colour— The whole county envies me. Dear me, how you rain blessings—Enid, by the way, writes (perhaps slightly aggrieved) that you said you'd lunch with *her*. So will I come too? I've said no. She must come here; and she will. Yes, we'll get the Lanthorn [for Vita's lecture].

I'm going to London tomorrow to walk among the ruins. Did I tell you all my books are to bits?—so, if you have Lady Ann Clifford[1] or any other Elizabethan biographer—dear me—I'm asking another favour; but could you bring them?

Its the very devil writing when every book lies at the bottom of a vast hole up at the blacksmiths

Many are utterly ruined.

So goodby till 18th to which I look forward as a drowning sailor to a Spice Island.

V.

Who is the Countess of Gall

Berg

3690: To Ethel Smyth   *Monks House* [*Rodmell, Sussex*]

Saturday [8 February 1941]

Dearest Ethel—of course I minded your distemper with me, but of course I put it down to misery. And now your card makes all safe and sound again:[2] I only scrawl this by way of a hug, which indeed I'd like to give you, loving your warm heart—Leonard says, he has not read Curry:[3] he says he doesnt believe in Federal Union *now*. He says he's given all his views on that in his 2/6 book. War for Peace.[4] If you'd like to read it—I think its very masterly—I'll send it.

1. See p. 455, note 1.
2. Ethel to Virginia (5 February 1941): "Pay no attention to my grumble of yesterday. After all, you have given, and give me the greatest joy of my latter end. As it said in that wonderful American poem: 'I am content,' said the soldier. Yes, by God I *am*. Bless you, my dear" (*Berg*).
3. William Burnlee Curry, *The Case for Federal Union* (1939), in which he argued that the creation of an international government, based on the federal model of the United States, would ensure world peace.
4. *The War for Peace* was published by Routledge in 1940.

Lord! What a horror about the insects WC on Pans nose! Enough to make anyone tart even with a woman who loves you with every fibre of what is in fact a damned good heart. I was out of spirits I admit all day after your letter. And what d'you mean, I ask, by your "you might do a tiny bit of direct work for your living . . ." Ought I, d'you mean, not to write articles? I agree. The Thrale¹ is nonsense, too, as I have to press it all into 6 pages—damn these editors!

Off to Letchworth and Cambridge next week to see the Press.² Oh Lord, what an effort moving in this weather and these conditions. Our line was blown up on Wednesday and it took 3 hours to get back from London

Yr inarticulate but adoring

V.

Berg

3691: To Mary Hutchinson
Monks House, Rodmell, Lewes [Sussex]

Typewritten
10th Feb. [1941]

Mary! Weasel! I've been trying to write this letter in hand writing, but my hand is like the cramped claw of an aged fowl: so I turn to the type. Please forgive. An odious habit.

No, I dont think I *can* write about The English and French.³ I've sat staring at it, but its too vast, too oleaginous. Nothing whatever happens. You see one has to approach ones subject with a little thrill—as if you were opposite and I suddenly gave you a rose. So I've told your old Bugger that I wont do that; but if they allow an English subject, a writer, then I'll do my best. If one could amuse the French—poor people, I would. Salute the man in your basement⁴ from me. I read his story in the paper. And to think of you on a battleship!⁵

As you say, wheres one to begin? Yes, Leonard has got a purple

1. See p. 467, note 1.
2. See p. 432, note 5.
3. For the magazine *France Libre*, edited by André LaBarthe and Baroness (which Virginia misread as 'Bugger' in Mary's letter) Moura Budberg, the Russian-born lover of Maxim Gorky and later of H. G. Wells. The Baroness invited Virginia to write an article comparing French and English women writers.
4. A young Frenchman who had escaped to England in a glider which he had assembled himself, collecting each part and keeping it hidden until a gale arose strong enough to blow him across the Channel.
5. Mary had been visiting her son Jeremy, who was serving in the Royal Navy.

hyacinth. And the flood has gone. Then the snow came, and I made green holes in the grass every time I came out here to my Lodge. Now the snow has gone. Life is rapid but eventless. We take tea at Charleston: Clive is digging a trench; Nessa feeding fowls; Duncan painting Christ; Quentin driving a tractor—all as it was in 1917. Tomorrow we go for a jaunt, to Cambridge, taking the Press at Letchworth in our way. And we shall dine with my dear Dadie [Rylands]; and shall I give him your love? Then Elizabeth Bowen comes; then Vita, to address the Womens Institute on Persia; then—why not Mary? But one cant lift a fringe of the future. Thats whats so odd—the blank space in front. Last time I heard from Tom [Eliot], he was domesticating with Hope Mirrlees:[1] spiritually, of course. But save for a gloomy stone dumb visit from Oliver Strachey, I've hardly seen a human being out of the roaring whirlpool of village life. Nessa rings up to say that Helen Anrep is being driven out of Sussex by soldiers. What else? Oh I read a great many books, and cook vegetable soup for dinner. Dear me, can you account for the Sitwells?[2] Maliciously I'm amused; but professionally—I must not say what, for fear I shall be hauled into the Law Courts. Margot pelts me with letters written at dawn in pencil. But somehow I feel she's insatiably, madly, greedy; so I'm not much flattered. I told you how she sent a bust of Voltaire all the way by car?

Thats all the news I can send at the moment, which is a lovely blue and white spring moment; and the snowdrops are out; and the crocuses showing. This is not to describe spring; but to bribe a weasel south. I dreamt all one night about Barbara.[3] And Victor had grown a mere spindle of a man. I must now cycle into Lewes to get our butter. All the time the Prime Minister was speaking I was shaking a bottle; just as he reached the peroration the butter came! Is this a symbol?

Give both our love: to Jack [Mary's husband]; to Barbara; to Jeremy [her son]; to Jeremys wife;[4] and taking out your little mirror, imagine that I am just about to print a kiss on your nose.

Virginia

Texas

1. The writer (1887-1978), whose *Paris: a Poem* (1920) was one of the Hogarth Press's earliest publications.
2. Edith, Osbert and Sacheverell Sitwell were suing Hamilton Fyfe and the left-wing paper *Reynolds News* for publishing this comment: "[Their] energy and self-assurance pushed them into a position which their merits could not have won.... Now oblivion has claimed them, and they are remembered with a kindly, if slightly cynical, smile." The Sitwells won their case; each was awarded £350. See *Facades* (John Pearson, 1978), pp. 338 and 344.
3. Mary's daughter, who had married Victor Rothschild in 1933.
4. In 1940 Jeremy Hutchinson married the actress Peggy Ashcroft.

3692: To Philippa Strachey   Monk's House, Rodmell
                                                    [Sussex]
17th Feb [1941]

Dear Pippa,
    I found your letter here, and am very grateful. It was angelic of you to
go into the matter. Alas, Leonard has plumped in favour of it—so I've
accepted—I neednt say how reluctantly.¹ But I suppose it dont much
matter. I can always resign in a huff at a word from you.
    What a bore it was that you weren't at Cambridge! We had a long
gossip with Pernel,² and felt as if we'd had a hot bath—it was so clean
warm and civilised. But we couldnt stay this time. Next time we must see
you, which would rejuvenate us. I suppose you cant come south?—no—
How d-d this war is!

                                                    Yr Virginia
Strachey Trust

3693: To George Rylands   Monk's House, Rodmell
                                                    [Sussex]
19th Feb [1941]

Dearest Dadie,
    I had meant to thank you before for the extraordinarily happy evening
you gave us. It was only that coming back here to find Elizabeth [Bowen],³
Vita and Lady Jones I couldn't seize a pen. It remains like an oasis, last
Wednesday, not a mirage—in the desert.
    I've ordered the books you bade me, and thank you for everything and
we both send our love.

                                                    Yr
                                                    Virginia
George Rylands

1. A committee concerned with the London-National Society for Women's
Service, of which Philippa Strachey was Secretary.
2. Pernel Strachey, Philippa's sister, who was Principal of Newnham College,
Cambridge, 1923-41.
3. Elizabeth Bowen spoke of this visit on 15 February (*Recollections of Virginia
Woolf*. Ed. Joan Russell Noble, 1972): "The last day I saw her I was staying at
Rodmell and I remember her kneeling back on the floor—we were tacking
away, mending a torn Spanish curtain in the house—and she sat back on her
heels and put her head back in a patch of sun, early spring sun. Then she laughed
in this consuming, choking, delightful, hooting way. And *that* is what has
remained with me."

3694: To Dr Octavia Wilberforce   *Monk's House*
                                    [Rodmell, Sussex]
[23 February 1941]

Dear Octavia,

You've reduced me not to silence quite, but to a kind of splutter—I mean, the cream: the cheese: the milk. I dont see how to begin: and twice a week the debt mounts. And you dont come here so that I could speak by word of mouth. Dear, dear—I'm dumb. But can just say we had a magnificent feast of cheese last night: not had one since September: and seldom any so suave and sweet and yet sour. No I didn't add sugar. For there was a natural sweetsour in it that was best unmixed.

We too have been turmoiled, not, I expect, for any such good purpose as you. Only going to Cambridge, to Letchworth, and somehow having a run of visitors in the house.

Should you be able to come over, please suggest it. And—have I the face to add—does your cook find any Seville oranges in the Brighton shops? None here. I daresay none anywhere.

But I only want to suggest a visit some time.

                                    Yr
                                    V.W.
Sussex

3695: To Ethel Smyth   *Monks House [Rodmell,*
                        Sussex]
1st March [1941]

Do you know, I have written you three separate letters, and torn each of them up? This is a fact. Partly, they were d—d dull: partly something always interrupted. Ever since we came back from Cambridge—30 hours in train journeys: £6 on hotel bills, all for Leonard to spend two hours at Letchworth—I've been in a fret. People kept turning up. Oh yes—there was Vita, and Enid Jones to lunch. You know, if one's only got a half daily maid its difficult, getting food together: and the wine had run out; and the duck was all strings and blue sinews. However Enid was as dapper as a dab chick. A brick I think would be the proper word—something a bit gritty and granular; but hard to the foot. Of course she—an old love I fancy—wanted to be alone with Vita; and there I was; and it was pelting wet, the cat had scratched a hole in the chair cover, and a visiting dog had lifted his leg against the table—In short there was an atmosphere of the sordid and squalid. I gave her your message, and she kindled, and said I was to tell you—it was when I got to this point in the other letters that I stopped: it bores me so repeating messages; she said Maurice [Baring] is much better on his Scotch island and she thinks that half his troubles are caused by the

474

Rheumatic air of Rottingdean. Now I have told you that; and added her love, and admiration: but I remember once sending you my love, and you snubbed me.

Then you sent me that 6d book [Curry's]: which I've not read, nor Leonard either. I am at the moment trying, without the least success, to write an article or two for a new Common Reader. I am stuck in Elizabethan plays. I cant move back or forwards. I've read too much, but not enough. Thats why I cant break into politics. Do you ever get glued, on a fly paper, as I do, when I'm trying to make myself master of something? I always trust that on the next page I shall free my legs. I have a mystic belief that if one goes on persistently the match box flame will spurt. But oh dear me, it hasnt.

If you want to picture me at the moment then you must strew the floor with mouldy dramatists; and how am I to picture you? Do you feel, as I do, when my head's not on this impossible grindstone, that this is the worst stage of the war? I do. I was saying to Leonard, we have no future. He says thats what gives him hope. He says the necessity of some catastrophe pricks him up. What I feel is the suspense when nothing actually happens. But I'm cross and irritable from the friction of village life. Isn't it foolish? But no sooner have I bound myself to my book, and brewed that very rare detachment, than some old lady taps at the door. How is she to grow potatoes or tomatoes? If that were all, I wouldnt mind. But she spends an hour, prodding her stick into the lawn, one thing following another. My theory as to that is that we have to pay the price of detachment by being tethered down. Do doctors widows come to your lawn, just as you're writing—and then what d'you do?

I cant deal with Margot [Oxford]. Every other day she writes to me. I cant answer. I gather she cruises about the Savoy cadging dinners. When they fail, she writes to me. I'm amused that she said the very same thing to Lady Balfour. Thats what I feel—her words are used already, so they dont fit. Two things I have now got to do: one, to find a flat in Brighton for Roger Fry's mistress [Helen Anrep]: the other to buy 2 tons of hay for Octavia Wilberforce's cows. She says theyre so thin you could put a safety pin through them. You see, I'm no good at practical affairs: I'm fished out of my element and lie gasping on the ground. Thats why, I suppose, I cant write to you. But if you wrote to me I should recover the tone of your voice at least. Do tell me, what are you doing? Pan's lice. Mary [maid]: anything. Excuse this drivel.

V.

Berg

4th March [1941]

Oh dearest Creature—now you've topped the whole hill of your bene-
factions with a firelighter. Po: butter: wool: books: firelighter on top.
There you must stop. You cant add anything to fire. You see the poetic
fitness of ending there. What a magnificent conception of life you have—O
damn the law. Leonard says we cant use your petrol. Another gift. But it
appears there's a Bus. Couldnt we arrange that?[1] I suppose your orchard is
beginning to dapple as it did the day I came there. One of the sights I shall
see on my death bed.

I suppose you havent any Hay to sell? Octavia Wilberforces cows at
Henfield, which give us butter, are starving. So I said I'd ask.

Silence means no.

I've been ranging the country this afternoon, asking for hay. Not a blade
to be had.

No, I've not read Enids play [*Lottie Dundas*]. Would she lend it me?
Is it a masterpiece? or merely a moneymaker? The Anrep flat fell through,
damn it.

Oh to think I shall never sit in the cold again. Aint this a pretty pattern
for a letter?[2]

Berg

3697: To Dr Octavia Wilberforce   *Monk's House*
                                                          [*Rodmell, Sussex*]
Typewritten
Tuesday [4 March 1941]

Dear Octavia,

Excuse this typing; which is my method of trying to be exact and
practical. Its about the flat. I find that Helen Anrep wants two bed rooms; if
possible three; kitchen and bath room; and sitting room. She cant afford
more than £50. I imagine this puts it out of the question. Should you hear
of anything, then tell me; but on no account trouble. Also, as far as I can
make out, the old part of Brighton is what she likes. Whether this is dearer,
or cheaper, I dont know. There! That sounds very pat.

And now of course typing dont suit any other kind of letter. So I wont

1. Vita offered to take Leonard and Virginia to Ellen Terry's house at Smallhythe,
   six miles from Sissinghurst, near Tenterden, Kent, where Ellen Terry's daughter,
   Edith Craig, lived with Christopher St John.
2. Virginia had written around the edges of the paper.

begin on the question of my living portrait. All I say is, I see that no one can be asked to sit. Why should they? Wouldnt it be a kind of torture? It was only a wild flitting dream. I will try to write to Miss Robins. No, no, no, I cannot write on a typewriter; and so must give over and say once more, what a damned generous woman you are. Have you any use for bottled gooseberries? Many pots here if you would take them.

[*handwritten:*]
All the same, I add in handwriting I think you're very paintable, as the painters say. Now I wonder why? Something that composes well—Perhaps reticence and power combined: and then theres the garden at Lavington.[1]

Sussex

3698: To T. S. Eliot   *Monk's House, Rodmell,*
                                          Lewes [*Sussex*]
Typewritten
8th March [1941]

My dear Tom,
    "With Mr Eliot's compliments"—how can I answer that very brief communication? Only I suppose by returning Mrs Woolf's comps. As you know, profound inhibitions prevent me from saying anything about the poem.[2] Happily, they dont prevent me from thanking you very profoundly for remembering Mrs Woolf.
    I have had it on the tip of my typewriter these many weeks to suggest that time is passing; and it would be a great pleasure to fix a point and see you. I suggest 5th of April week end. I do so very tentatively, because I know—havent we just been to Cambridge and back—the horror of trains. But our line is still better than some. Then there's the lack of civility here. Its a dripping day; the water has come through the kitchen ceiling.
    All the same, if you would venture, there's nothing we should like better. Or the middle of the week, if thats more to your liking.
    So much water has flowed under the bridge that I feel at sea; and so conclude.
                                          Yr aff
                                          Virginia
Mrs T. S. Eliot

1. Lavington House, East Lavington, near Chichester, Sussex, the family seat of the Wilberforces, where Octavia was born.
2. *The Dry Salvages*, published in *New English Weekly* (27 February 1941).

Monks House [Rodmell,
                                              Sussex]

10th March [1941]

Yes, yes yes, of course I agree with you. This refers to Mr. Currys book,[1] which I've just read. But then of course I'm not a politician, and so take one leap to the desirable lands. L's view would be, I think, that ones got to plod along the road, indeed to make it, before one gets there. But Lord! what a relief to have a vision! and I'm glad you're beating up an audience in Woking:

What I really write to say though is—how damnable these separations are! Letters, no letters; then letters again. Shall I come down for a night? I could now, on a Wednesday—in April—go back early Thursday.

But I daresay you cant manage. Anyhow youre off to Winnie.[2] But when youre back lets try to bridge this solitude. I would bring my rations. I'm in the dither of trying to contrive spring cleaning. Oh our carpets—I spent 2 hours carpet beating, and still the flakes of our bombed ceiling flock, and drown the books just dusted. I'd no notion, having always a servant, of the horror of dirt—

No: politics at the moment seem more pressing than autobiography. We have the drone of raiders every night, and the village is now fire spotting—chiefly incendiaries away over the hill.

So no more, for I'm off to Lewes about beating carpets, and only write this because, having done curry, I thought, belatedly, to wave a hand of thanks.

V.

Berg

Monk's House, Rodmell,
                                               Lewes [Sussex]

March 13th [1941]

Dear Miss Robins,

I was very sorry to hear from Octavia [Wilberforce] that you had had an accident. Selfishly, I'm afraid it may interfere with the book that I'm looking forward to.[3] But I remember a saying of Henry James—all experiences are of use to a writer. I think he was talking about a nervous breakdown. So may it be worth a broken bone.

I now go on to say that I've been cycling into Lewes—not a very interesting remark, save that it connects with Octavia. Has she told you,

1. See p. 470, note 3.
2. Winnaretta, Princesse de Polignac. See p. 42, note 2.
3. See p. 446, note 3.

I wonder—no, I dont suppose she has—of her amazing bi-weekly bounty —cream, milk, sometimes a cheese? Thats what I've been fetching. You cant think how it brightens our weekly bill of fare. Also, to fetch her empty basket, she sometimes comes over, and this has been, is, and will be, I hope, a great treat. Is it our drop of blood in common? Anyhow we sit over the fire, as if we'd known each other in the woods at Lavington. Its odd how our lives have run just not meeting but through the same country. Thats the sort of woman I most admire—the reticence, the quiet, the power —Here I can imagine her look of enquiry—why? Well its difficult to say why. Its the variety and the calm partly. As you can imagine, she's healing the sick by day, and controlling the fires by night.

At this moment theres a flood of yellow flowers in the garden—And the view from my window is like a block of flawed emerald, half green, half blue. And what I wonder are you doing at this moment?

Its amazingly peaceful here, you can almost hear the grass grow; and the rooks are building; you wouldnt think that at 7.30 the planes will be over. Two nights ago they dropped incendiaries, in a row, like street lamps, all along the downs. Two hay stacks caught and made a lovely illumination—but no flesh was hurt. Indeed, every bomb they drop only casts up a crater so far. Its difficult, I find, to write. No audience. No private stimulus, only this outer roar. And in these circumstances, Octavia is very refreshing. Leonard asks me to add his respects to my love, and we both often think of you and the book.

Yrs

V.W.

Sussex

3701: To Ruth Fry

Monks House, Rodmell,
Lewes [Sussex]

16th March [1941]

Dear Ruth,

Yes, I was very pleased with the reviews of Roger—especially the ones that abused him, for it shows how much bite he still has. But the one I liked best was J. T. Sheppards in the Cambridge Review, for that said that Roger Fry was there and not V.W., which was what I wanted.

You've been so good, taking an interest in it, I mean considering me, the author—thank you so much. It still goes on selling; but owing to an idiotic blunder, the Press gave me no time to correct misprints and mistakes. I must apologise; and will put them in, should there be another edition.

We are being a good deal bombed at the moment. Rows of incendiaries fell on the farm two nights ago and burnt haystacks, but so far no one has been hurt.

479

I suppose Thorpeness [Suffolk] is about as much of a target as we are.
Hoping we shall both escape, and meet some day.

Your affectionate,
Virginia Woolf

Pamela Diamand

Letters 3702-3710 *(March 18-28, 1941)*

On 14 March Virginia and Leonard had met John Lehmann in London, and asked him to read the typescript of her new novel, Between the Acts. *He was delighted by it, but Virginia decided that it needed extensive revision before publication. For some time she had been feeling acutely depressed, and began to hear voices. On 18 March she may have attempted to drown herself. Leonard, alarmed by her mental condition, consulted Octavia Wilberforce, and took Virginia to see her in Brighton. On the next day, Friday 28 March, Virginia wrote the third of her suicide letters, and at about 11.30 a.m. walked the half-mile to the River Ouse, filled her pockets with stones, and threw herself into the water.*

3702: TO LEONARD WOOLF   [*Monk's House, Rodmell,*
                                                                  Sussex]
Tuesday [18? March 1941]

Dearest,[1]

I feel certain that I am going mad again: I feel we cant go through another of those terrible times. And I shant recover this time. I begin to hear voices, and cant concentrate. So I am doing what seems the best thing to do. You have given me the greatest possible happiness. You have been in every way all that anyone could be. I dont think two people could have been happier till this terrible disease came. I cant fight it any longer, I know that I am spoiling your life, that without me you could work. And you will I know. You see I cant even write this properly. I cant read. What I want to say is that I owe all the happiness of my life to you. You have been entirely patient with me and incredibly good. I want to say that—everybody knows it. If anybody could have saved me it would have been you. Everything has gone from me but the certainty of your goodness. I cant go on spoiling your life any longer.

I dont think two people could have been happier than we have been.

                                                                  V.

British Library

1. On 11 May 1941 Leonard noted at the foot of this letter: "This is the letter left for me on the table in the sitting room which I found at 1 on March 28." For a discussion of the dating of this letter, and of the other suicide-notes, see Appendix A. A facsimile of the letter is published opposite p. 184 of *A Marriage of True Minds* (Spater and Parsons, 1977).

Monk's House, Rodmell,
                                              Lewes [Sussex]
Typewritten
20th March [1941]

Dear John,
   I've just read my so called novel [*Between the Acts*] over; and I really
dont think it does. Its much too slight and sketchy. Leonard doesnt agree.
So we've decided to ask you if you'd mind reading it and give your casting
vote? Meanwhile dont take any steps.
   I'm sorry to trouble you, but I feel fairly certain it would be a mistake
from all points of view to publish it. [*handwritten:*] But as we both differ
about this, your opinion would be a great help.
                                              Yours
                                                Virginia

I hope youre sending the manuscripts—I should like to do them.[1]

British Library

3704: To Lady Cecil   *Monk's House, Rodmell,*
                                              Lewes [Sussex]
21st March [1941]

My dear Nelly,
   To begin with business—Leonard's review[2] came out in the N.S. on
the 15th February.
   I'm glad that business has caused you to break ten years of silence.
When petrol is scarce, one must have recourse to ink—I wish we could
come over [to Gale, Chelwood Gate]—but the car only gets as far as Lewes
once a week.
   I'm so sorry that Lord Robert never sent me his book. I should have
liked to read it in my own copy. I read it in Leonard's, and wished for more.
There wasnt, even for me, a non-politician, a word too much about the
League, but I wished for more about Grove End Road [London] and the
room looking onto the garden, and you. Is this vulgar? I suppose so. I'm
greatly flattered that his old opinion of me—a wrinkled hag—has another

1. John Lehmann described in his book his meeting with the Woolfs in London on
   14 March: "Before we left, [Virginia] suddenly said she had nothing to do now,
   and could I send her some reading. I told her I would gladly pick out some
   manuscripts from the latest batch that had arrived for *Folios of New Writing*, if
   she really meant it. She eagerly agreed" (Lehmann, *Thrown to the Woolfs*, p. 100).
2. Of Lord (Robert) Cecil's autobiography, *A Great Experiment* (1941). He was
   British representative on many League of Nations and disarmament conferences.

side to its face.[1] Often when I turn over my old scrap book at night I pause at the Gale page.

I'm glad you liked Leonard's book [*The War for Peace*], and gave it to a sceptic. It seemed to me the only kind of thing worth writing now. Do you find you can read the novelists? I cant. Still, I agree that this war's better than last, and ever so much better than the last 5 years of peace. We've been bombed out of London and live entirely here now. Leonard lectures the village on politics. We see Vanessa occasionally—most nights the raiders go over. Last week the haystacks blazed and incendiaries lit up the downs. I cant help wishing the invasion would come. Its this standing about in a dentist's waiting room that I hate.

Are you at last obediently writing your Memoirs? That would complete Lord Roberts. Leonard sends his duty and I my love.

Yrs
Virginia Woolf

Marquess of Salisbury (Cecil Papers)

3705: To Lady Tweedsmuir   *Monk's House, Rodmell,*
                                  Lewes [Sussex]

[21? March 1941]

Dear Susie,[2]

How very nice of you to write! I hadnt liked to write to you, but I did want to hear about you. I know how difficult it must be, making a fresh start.[3] But you have a great deal more than most of us to look forward to. Elizabeth [Bowen] told me too of all your war activities. I expect that is a help too. I wanted also to write to you when your mother died. The memory of her goes back so far in my life—I remember 'dining out' for the first time in your house, after your father's death—and I remember him too coming to see us, and admiring him, as a child.[4] Isn't one of your sons like him? I saw a photograph, and thought so.

We have been completely bombed out of London, and lead a rather vegetable existence here, surrounded by the melancholy relics of our half destroyed furniture. All this afternoon I've been trying to arrange some of my father's old books.

1. Lord Cecil did not mention Virginia in his book. For 'wrinkled hag' see last paragraph of Letter 3404.
2. On 3 April 1941 Leonard sent this letter to Lady Tweedsmuir, saying, "I think you may like to have this letter, which was almost the last which Virginia wrote, but which she did not post."
3. Lord Tweedsmuir (John Buchan) had died in Canada on 11 February 1940.
4. Lady Tweedsmuir's father, Norman Grosvenor, son of the 1st Baron Ebury, died in 1898 when Virginia was 16. His wife Caroline (*née* Stuart-Wortley) died in 1940. She had been a novelist, a painter and a feminist.

Only now and then do I come to London at present. May I let you know a date later in case we could meet? I'm always rather rushed—thats the worst of it, as we've nowhere to stay in town.

Yes, I think thats a very good idea—writing letters from the country to America. I cant say that we're very peaceful here. Last week there were 50 incendiaries on the farm, and the stacks were burnt. Most days we have a raid—in fact the siren has just gone for the second time today. No one pays it any attention—I wonder if [Elsfield Manor] Oxford is more peaceful? Yes, do write about it. Wasnt Elizabeth's book[1] good? And thank you for writing to me—I was glad to hear of you after all this time.

Yr affate
Virginia

Lady Tweedsmuir

3706: To V. Sackville-West

[*Monk's House, Rodmell, Sussex*]

Saturday [22 March 1941]

Look at this letter [*lost*], sent to the New Statesman, addressed to 'Miss Virginia Woolf'.—What a queer thought transference! No, I'm not you. No, I dont keep budgerigars.

Louie's survive: and she feeds them on scraps—I suppose they're lower class, humble, birds. If we come over [to Sissinghurst], may I bring her a pair if any survive?[2] Do they die all in an instant? When shall we come? Lord knows—

Berg

3707: To John Lehmann

Monk's House, Rodmell, [*Sussex*]

Typewritten
Sunday [23 March 1941]

Dear John,
I have gone through these MSS[3] as far as I can. But my head is very stupid at the moment.

The only ones that are I think worth considering are: Mr Robinson's

1. Probably *The Death of the Heart*, by Elizabeth Bowen, 1938.
2. Many of Vita's budgerigars had died, owing to shortage of bird seed.
3. See p. 482, note 1.

poems; and Mr Urquart's story.[1] Both have distinct merit, I think; though both are border line cases.

Yours ever
[*unsigned*]

Texas

3708: To Vanessa Bell

[*Monk's House, Rodmell, Sussex*]

Sunday [23? March 1941]

Dearest,

You cant think how I loved your letter.[2] But I feel that I have gone too far this time to come back again. I am certain now that I am going mad again. It is just as it was the first time, I am always hearing voices, and I know I shant get over it now.

All I want to say is that Leonard has been so astonishingly good, every day, always; I cant imagine that anyone could have done more for me than he has. We have been perfectly happy until the last few weeks, when this horror began. Will you assure him of this? I feel he has so much to do that he will go on, better without me, and you will help him.

I can hardly think clearly any more. If I could I would tell you what you and the children have meant to me. I think you know.

I have fought against it, but I cant any longer.

Virginia

British Library

1. Lehmann rejected Robinson's poems. Fred Urquhart's story was *To-morrow Will Be Beautiful* (*New Writing*, No. 8, 1941).
2. On 20 March Vanessa wrote to Virginia: "You *must* be sensible. Which means you must accept the fact that Leonard and I can judge better than you can. Its true I havent seen very much of you lately, but I have often thought you looked very tired and I'm sure that if you let yourself collapse and do nothing you would feel tired, and be only too glad to rest a little. You're in the state when one never admits whats the matter—but you must not go and get ill just now. What shall we do when we're invaded if you are a helpless invalid—what should I have done all these last 3 years if you hadnt been able to keep me alive and cheerful. You dont know how much I depend on you. . . . Both Leonard and I have always had reputations for sense and honesty so you must believe us. . . . I shall ring up sometime and find out what is happening" (*Sussex*, papers of Leonard Woolf).

3709: To John Lehmann   *Monk's House, Rodmell,*
                                         Lewes [*Sussex*]
Typewritten
[27? March 1941]

Dear John,[1]

I'd decided, before your letter came,[2] that I cant publish that novel as it stands—its too silly and trivial.

What I will do is to revise it, and see if I can pull it together and so publish it in the autumn. If published as it is, it would certainly mean a financial loss; which we dont want. I am sure I am right about this.

I neednt say how sorry I am to have troubled you. The fact is it was written in the intervals of doing Roger with my brain half asleep. And I didnt realise how bad it was till I read it over.

Please forgive me, and believe I'm only doing what is best.

I'm sending back the MSS [for *Folios of New Writing*] with my notes.

Again, I apologise profoundly.

                                         Yours,
                                         Virginia Woolf
British Library

3710: To Leonard Woolf   [*Monk's House, Rodmell,*
                                         Sussex]
[28 March 1941]

Dearest,[3]

I want to tell you that you have given me complete happiness. No one could have done more than you have done. Please believe that.

1. The date when Virginia wrote this letter is not quite certain, but it was posted by Leonard late on 27 March with a covering note telling Lehmann "that Virginia was on the verge of a complete nervous breakdown" (*Thrown to the Woolfs*, p. 101). It reached him on Saturday 29 March, after Virginia was dead.

2. The sequence of events was as follows. On 14 March, when Virginia, Leonard and Lehmann met in London, it was agreed that Lehmann should read the typescript of *Between the Acts*. He assumed from their conversation that there was no doubt that it would be published shortly, and caused the book to be announced in the Spring-books issue of the *New Statesman*. Later he received Virginia's letter of 20 March (No. 3703), and wrote to her apologising for his action. Then he read the book, and praised it enthusiastically in another letter. Virginia's reply is the letter above.

3. On 11 May 1941 Leonard wrote on the reverse of this letter: "This letter was not the one left for me by V. I found it later in the writing block on which she was writing when I went out to see her in the Lodge about 11 on the morning of March 28. She came into the house with me, leaving the writing block in the Lodge. She must, I think, have written the letters which she left for me and Vanessa in the house immediately afterwards."

486

But I know that I shall never get over this: and I am wasting your life. It is this madness. Nothing anyone says can persuade me. You can work, and you will be much better without me. You see I cant write this even, which shows I am right. All I want to say is that until this disease came on we were perfectly happy. It was all due to you. No one could have been so good as you have been, from the very first day till now. Everyone knows that.

V.

You will find Roger's letters to the Maurons in the writing table drawer in the Lodge. Will you destroy all my papers.

British Library

Virginia's body was found by some children, a short way down-stream, on 18 *April, and an inquest was held next day at Newhaven. The verdict was 'Suicide while the balance of her mind was disturbed'. Her body was cremated at Brighton on* 21 *April, with only Leonard present, and her ashes were buried under a great elm-tree just outside the garden at Monk's House, with the last words of* The Waves *as her epitaph, "Against you I will fling myself, unvanquished and unyielding, O Death!"*

Dearest,

I want to tell you that you have
given me complete happiness. No one
could have done more than you have done.
Please believe that.

But I know that I shall never get over
this: & I am wasting your life. It is this madness.
Nothing anyone says can persuade me.
You can work. & you will be much
better without me. You see I can't
write this even, which shows I am right.
All I want to say is that until this
disease came on we were perfectly
happy. It was all due to you.
No one could have been so good as
you have been. from the very
first day 'till now: everyone knows that

V.

You will find them, I think, in the drawer in the —
room. I have put them in the drawer. & will
you destroy all my papers.

Appendix A

THE DATING OF VIRGINIA WOOLF'S
LAST LETTERS

HITHERTO it has been generally assumed that Virginia Woolf wrote all three of her suicide letters on the very day (Friday 28 March 1941) when she took her life. Leonard Woolf himself said so in a note which he added to her last letter shortly after her death (see p. 486, note 3), and again in his autobiography *The Journey Not the Arrival Matters*, p. 93. Quentin Bell took the same view in his biography of Virginia (II, p. 226). The purpose of this Appendix is to argue for an alternative chronology, that her suicide was premeditated by ten days, and that the three letters were written on the 18th, 23rd and 28th March respectively. The letter which Quentin Bell considers to be the last of the three, we deduce to be the first. In this volume the letters have been placed in accordance with this assumption.

Both Leonard Woolf and Quentin Bell either overlooked the dates 'Sunday' and 'Tuesday' written at the head of two of the letters, or believed that Virginia was so distraught that she misdated them. Neither of them appears to have regarded it as strange that Virginia, if their chronology is correct, should have written to Leonard two very similar letters within the same half-hour, but given her distress, this is of course possible.

However, it is unlikely that Virginia misdated the letters so erratically. She occasionally made errors in the number part of her letters (writing Wednesday 27th when it was the 26th), but seldom mistook the day of the week, certainly not by several days. Although she was obviously under great stress when she wrote the three letters, her handwriting (see the facsimile reproduction of the last of them opposite), and her method of expressing herself, were not abnormal, although in two of them she wrote, "You see I cannot write this properly". It is possible that she made the error which Leonard Woolf and Quentin Bell imply, but it seems to us that the more likely explanation is that when she wrote 'Sunday' and 'Tuesday', she wrote the letters on those actual days, and there is other evidence to support this view.

But which Sunday? Which Tuesday? And when was the undated letter (3710) written? The last question is the easiest. Leonard says that he found it on the writing-pad in Virginia's garden-hut ('lodge') soon after he found the other two letters in the house. He implies in his near-contemporary note and in his autobiography that he saw her writing it in her hut at about

11 a.m. on the day of her suicide, 28 March. It has the ring of a final testament ("Will you destroy all my papers"). It was almost certainly the last time she used her pen.

We have dated the 'Sunday' letter to Vanessa (3708) to 23 March mainly because of its first sentence, "You cant think how I loved your letter". We know that Vanessa wrote to Virginia on Thursday 20 March the letter (quoted in part on p. 485, note 2) which survives among Leonard's papers in Sussex University, and this is probably Virginia's reply to it. If she had written it on the previous Sunday (16 March), there would have been no Vanessa letter to answer, and we would have to suppose that she first confided her suicidal intention to Vanessa alone, without telling Leonard, which is improbable. By the next Sunday (30 March) Virginia was dead.

The 'Tuesday' letter to Leonard (3702) is editorially dated 18 March, in preference to 25 March, for two reasons. First because, as has been said above, Virginia would have been more likely to tell Leonard that she intended to die before she told Vanessa. Secondly, because it fits the incident which Leonard describes in *The Journey Not the Arrival Matters*, pp. 90-1:

> "There is a note in my diary on March 18 that she was not well and in the next week I became more and more alarmed. I am not sure whether early in that week [the 18th itself?] she did not unsuccessfully try to commit suicide. She went for a walk in the water-meadows in pouring rain and I went, as I often did, to meet her. She came back across the meadows soaking wet, looking ill and shaken. She said that she had slipped and fallen into one of the dykes. At the time I did not definitely suspect anything, though I had an automatic feeling of desperate uneasiness."

The physical characteristics of the three original letters now in the British Library give us a little help. Two of them ('Sunday' to Vanessa, and the undated letter to Leonard) are written on paper 8 in. × 10 in. torn from the same pad. The 'Tuesday' letter to Leonard is written on slightly smaller paper, 6½ in. × 8 in., which increases the likelihood that it was written on a separate occasion. The ink and penmanship of all three is identical, although on the undated letter the ink starts paler, as if it was running dry and had to be replenished halfway through. The 'Sunday' and 'Tuesday' letters were folded and put in blue envelopes, addressed to Vanessa and Leonard respectively. These were the two letters found in the house. The undated letter was left unfolded and unenclosed in the garden-hut.

Virginia's contemporary letters to other people (John Lehmann, Vita, Lady Tweedsmuir and Lady Cecil) naturally make no mention of her intended suicide, and are fairly normal in tone. In her diary, of which the last entry is dated 24 March, there is no hint of suicide, and its mood is not markedly eccentric or sombre, given that she had just passed through a second winter of war. The only obvious sign of distress in any of the letters, apart from the suicide notes, is contained in her instructions to John Lehmann to postpone the publication of *Between the Acts*, which she imagined to be "too slight and sketchy" (3703) and "too silly and trivial" (3709), and a single sentence to Lehmann, "My head is very stupid at the moment", which she wrote on 23 March, the suggested date of her suicide letter to Vanessa.

The reasons why Virginia Woolf killed herself are discussed in the Introduction to this volume. Here we are concerned only with dating the stages by which she reached her decision. Our conclusion is that on Tuesday 18 March she attempted suicide and wrote Leonard a note to explain her motive. Her attempt failed. Five days later she confirmed her intention by writing to Vanessa, but did not post the letter or leave it and the earlier one to Leonard where they could be found. Five further days elapsed before she wrote her second letter to Leonard, leaving it where she had written it, in her garden-hut, and took her two earlier letters into the house before setting out for the river.

This reconstruction of events relies mainly on her superscriptions 'Tuesday' and 'Sunday', but it is supported by other clues. Leonard's alternative assumption, shared by Quentin Bell, that the three letters were all written on the day of her suicide, cannot be conclusively disproved.

Appendix B

THESE letters are arranged in chronological order. The letter 'a' has been added in each case to the number of the letter which immediately precedes it in the volumes already published.

75a: To Violet Dickinson   [22 *Hyde Park Gate, S.W.*]
[early April 1903]
[*missing last page of letter 75*]

otherwise empty? She [Vanessa] and Adrian are going to share the studio and halve her bedroom, as otherwise we're one room short—and this enormous sort of Rufus [red] coloured wardrobe taking up the whole of one side. All her clothes can be pegged—but Gerald [Duckworth] when we suggested selling said "Oh my dear—the associations" it has a family pedigree—and George [Duckworth] thinking it ought to make part of our marriage trousseau—only the husband isn't ready.

I know you are going to spend the day with the dead and dying—and then a week with someone whose religion doesn't carry her through, which must be the worst kind of state to be in. Sparroy is rather garrulous tonight, but blesses you and embraces, and you might write her a letter too.

Yr Sp:

Mrs Ina Wolf

339a: To Vanessa Stephen   [46 *Gordon Square, Bloomsbury*]
[6 February 1907]

Address of Congratulation
to our
Mistress
on her
Approaching Marriage[1]

1. Vanessa and Clive were married on the next day.

Dear Mistress,

We the undersigned three Apes and a Wombat[1] wish to make known to you our great grief and joy at the news that you intend to marry. We hear that you have found a new Red Ape [Clive Bell] of a kind not known before who is better than all other apes because he can both talk and marry you: from which we are debarred.

We have examined his fur and find it of fine quality, red and golden at the tips, with an undergrowth of soft down, excellent for winter. We find him clean, merry, and sagacious, a wasteful eater and fond of fossils. His teeth are sharp, and we advise that you keep him on Bones. His disposition is Affectionate.

We therefore commend your marriage, and testify that you will make an excellent Mistress for any Ape or Wombat whatsoever. You are very understanding of Apes, loving and wholesome, vigilant after fleas, and scourging of all Misdoing.

We have been your humble Beasts since we first left our Isles, which is before we can remember, and during that time we have wooed you and sung many songs of winter and summer and autumn in the hope that thus enchanted you would condescend one day to marry us. But as we no longer expect this honour we entreat that you keep us still for your lovers, should you have need of such, and in that capacity we promise to abide well content always adoring you now as before.

With Humble Obeisance to our Mistress

We sign ourselves,

Her devoted Beasts

Billy

Bartholomew

Mungo

and

WOMBAT

The Sixth of February,
nineteen hundred and seven.
Year of our Lord.

Texas

---

1. Although this letter carried four signatures, it was in fact written and signed by Virginia alone, who called herself collectively 'the apes'. 'Wombat' may have been a name for her dog Garth.

977a: To Mary Hutchinson   *Hogarth House, Paradise Road,*
                             Richmond
8th Oct. [1918]

Dear Mary,

   We were very sorry you didn't come—not that Asheham is a good
house for colds. However, I was partly right in my guess. What I should
suggest is that you should send me the story as it is[1]—you can't possibly
tell anything about it. Please do. The Press is champing for work, and this
modesty is, I'm sure, a nun's veil to your writings—they mustn't for ever
keep their chastity unexposed. I am writing to Eliot; and I believe we've
got a poem by Murry, and Carrington's woodcuts and a story of mine.[2]

   Do come and see me. [Mark] Gertler said you were for ever in the
country, having taken some great actors house,[3] but we shall be here till
Christmas, so please ring up or write and suggest a time if you're in London.

                                             Yours
                                             Virginia Woolf
Texas[4]

990a: To Duncan Grant   *Hogarth House, Paradise Road,*
                            Richmond, Surrey
Friday [29 November 1918]

My dear Duncan,

   Is it possible that you have finished reading Tarr [Wyndham Lewis's
novel, 1918] by this time, and would lend it to me? I was so rash as to say
to Eliot the other night that Wyndham Lewis and Ezra Pound were the
biggest humbugs unhung, and then had to own that this was mere inspira-
tion on my part, as I have never read a word of either of them. So if you
could lend it to me, I should be very grateful.

   I cant think of any gossip to send you, as I have lavished myself in page
after page of unrequited garrulity to Nessa. O but there is one item, so to
speak, of immense possibility. I told Nessa that Roger sent my letter to

1. The Hogarth Press published nothing by Mary Hutchinson until *Fugitive Pieces*
   (1927).
2. In May 1919 the Hogarth Press published T. S. Eliot's *Poems*, J. Middleton
   Murry's *The Critic in Judgment*, and Virginia's *Kew Gardens*, but no collection
   of woodcuts by Carrington.
3. Glottenham, near Robertsbridge, Sussex. It belonged to Beerbohm Tree, the
   actor-manager.
4. These letters to Mary Hutchinson are now in the Humanities Research Center,
   The University of Texas, at Austin, Texas. They are subject to a non-publication
   restriction which has been waived by Lord Hutchinson (Mary's son) so that they
   can be included in this edition.

Marie Beerbohm [the actress] and the other way round. Yesterday I was rung up by Roger in a state of some agitation. First he assured me that no harm whatever had been done; and then he said "I had written to ask you to meet someone, who has a most interesting story to tell you." Here he paused. "It's a story about your father and mother. They made a mistake you know." "What sort of mistake?", I asked. "O a mistake with very remarkable consequences—" "Am I Mr Lowell's[1] daughter?", I cried. "No, no, its not that you're illegitimate—its something that you'll enjoy immensely—but I'm not going to tell you what until I see you." Now whatever it is he has clearly told Marie Beerbohm, in the letter that went wrong; but what can it be? Perhaps Nessa is the offspring of George [Duckworth] or Adrian of Walter Headlam.[2] Anyway Marie Beerbohm will have told the whole of London, so theres no use in trying to conceal the Duckworth blood, and she'd better make a clean breast of it, tell Nessa, and we'll none of us think a penny the worse of her. Hell, I'm glad it isn't me.

Ottoline continues her machinations apparently. The other day Desmond and Leonard went to tea with Katherine [Mansfield] and [Middleton] Murry. There they found Ott. She had arrived unexpectedly, saying that Desmond had asked her to meet him there—as far as we can make out a complete lie—for the purpose I suppose of keeping an eye on us. Please remind Bunny that his name rhymes with Honey, and if one says Garnett one thinks of Harnett.[3]

Yrs
V.W.

Estate of Duncan Grant

1046a: To Mary Hutchinson   *Hogarth House, Paradise Road,*
                              Richmond, Surrey

Friday [16 May 1919]

Dear Mary,
    Thank you for the cheque [for subscription to the Hogarth Press]. If you should ever want more than one copy of anything, it would be quite easy to send it after they come out. If you ever thought of people who might like to subscribe, I should be very grateful for names; I am making great efforts to get a tolerable circle, who can be counted on, but its very difficult.

1. James Russell Lowell (1819-91), the American poet and critic, was a friend of Leslie Stephen and 'Godfather' of Virginia.
2. The classical scholar (1866-1908) and Fellow of King's College, Cambridge, with whom Virginia had a flirtation in 1907.
3. Perhaps a pun on 'hornet'. David Garnett was keeping bees at Charleston.

I am sending back the Little Review.[1] When I came to read it, I found one month left out. I hope you forgot to send it; I've looked everywhere and don't seem to have it. But if it *was* sent, I will get another out of Miss Weaver.

I am sending an old scrap book of reviews—the first I ever wrote, and some later ones mixed up. I haven't read them through lately, but I dont think they can make very amusing reading seeing that they were written with the sweat of my brow, and generally in complete ignorance. But you won't believe that I'm really modest. Could you promise to send them back, anyhow, whether read or unread, in a week if possible? I want to go through all my reviews, and see if I couldn't run them together somehow in a general disquisition about literature:[2] and I thought of starting next week. If you would send any criticisms or suggestions this is the very moment they would come in useful. I take a beating, I may add, like a well-trained spaniel.

Yours Virginia Woolf

By the way, there are other occupations for hot days besides reading old reviews—ahem!

Texas

1053a: To Logan Pearsall Smith

Asheham House, Rodmell,
Lewes [Sussex]

May 30th [1919]

Dear Mr Pearsall Smith,

Many thanks for taking so much trouble on our behalf. Things have been going much better this last week. Mr Bain [bookseller] has taken some copies, and we've got several new subscribers. I shall write for the Italian end papers, which I have always wanted to get. The Omega is very good, I think, but at the same time expensive of course, and very difficult to handle.[3]

I'm sure that you're not an infallible judge of your own writing; so

1. The journal of experimental poetry and prose edited from 1917-19 by Ezra Pound. In 1919 it was serialising Joyce's *Ulysses*, which Virginia read for *Modern Novels* (*TLS*, 10 April 1919), reprinted in *The Common Reader* as *Modern Fiction*. In April 1918 Harriet Weaver, Editor of the *Egoist*, offered *Ulysses* to the Hogarth Press, but it was beyond their powers to publish it.
2. Virginia did not pursue this idea, but she revived it in another form with her *Common Reader* (1925).
3. A second edition of *Kew Gardens* was printed in June 1919 by Richard Madley, the printer for Roger Fry's Omega Workshop books.

please let us see the stories[1]—or have you nothing else? The only test, I believe, is the test of one's own pleasure in writing, which vanishes, but does not in vanishing affect the writing itself.

Having taken so much trouble, I am now going to ask you to take more—at least to tell me the name of the American publisher[2] who might be ready to look at my novel. I should be very grateful, as I am now negotiating with Gerald Duckworth.

We hope you will come and see us again. We come back to Richmond next week.

Yours very sincerely
Virginia Woolf

Library of Congress

1148a: To Hope Mirrlees   [*Hogarth House, Richmond*]

[end October 1920]

Dear Hope,

Please excuse this notepaper, and do not expect sense or wit from a poor wretch on the outskirts of a Bridge party—Adrian, Karin [Stephen] and Leonard are playing. I was very glad to hear from you, and would like still better to see you. Why don't you come and stay with us for a weekend? Then we can discuss Miss Rose Macaulay, Miss [Edith] Sitwell, Faith Henderson,[3] and Virginia Woolf. Poor dear Rose, judging from her works, is a Eunuch—thats what I dislike about Potterism.[4] She has no parts. And surely she must be the daughter of a don? Faith I dislike; Miss Sitwell I haven't read, but I would if you would lend her to me.[5] Are you writing? I ask as a publisher. We have a partner [Ralph Partridge], and now take it very seriously. Do send us something: verse or prose[6] —

I'm glad you liked my story.[7] It was written too quick, but I thought it had some points as a way of telling a story: later perhaps one might improve. But God knows how one is ever going to live long enough to write *any*thing.

1. In 1920 the Hogarth Press published Logan Pearsall Smith's *Stories From the Old Testament*.
2. Macmillan's, New York. Virginia's second novel (*Night and Day*, 1919), which in England was published by her half-brother Gerald Duckworth, was published in America, not by Macmillan's, but by Doran.
3. Faith Henderson (b. 1889), the sister of Nicholas Bagenal and wife of Hubert, the future Editor of the *Nation & Athenaeum*.
4. Rose Macaulay's satirical novel (1920).
5. In 1920 Edith Sitwell published a volume of poetry called *The Wooden Pegasus*.
6. After *Paris: A Poem* (May 1920), the Hogarth Press published nothing by Hope Mirrlees.
7. *Solid Objects* (*Athenaeum*, 22 October 1920).

Do suggest a visit—bearing in mind that it will be uncomfortable, and slovenly, and we are steeped in printers ink—still I will ask someone to meet you—Karin sends her love, and must now go home to continue her dissection of a human buttock [1] —

Yours
V.W.

Mrs T. S. Eliot

1208a: TO VANESSA BELL   [46 *Gordon Square, W.C.*1]

[1921?]

I looked in to consult you about the servants.[2] Angelica is perfectly well and had a very good night. But this morning my Nelly [Boxall] gave me notice on the ground that we had too many people yesterday. I feel pretty certain that the real reason is that she and your Nelly [Brittain] have arranged that she is to offer to come to you. Lottie [Hope] has *not* given notice and seems very depressed. This may be entirely guesswork on my part, and Nelly may only be in one of her usual states. But she was very odd in her manner, evidently trying to rake up reasons for going, and I know that she and your Nelly have been having great confabs.[3] I should very much like to know what you mean to do about it—of course I feel rather desperate, as anyhow there will be ructions between her and Lottie—O God what a nuisance it all is! I expect you'll get a letter from N. tomorrow morning. Would you ring me up as early as you can; I dont want her to think that I'm completely hood winked. But of course she'll change her mind a dozen times. I merely said that she had much better go if she thought the place too hard.

Lottie told me that they had so many easy days that one hard day didn't matter—from which I gather Nelly must have gone off on a line of her own.

V.

Berg

1236a: TO LADY CECIL   *Monk's House, Rodmell,*
                              Lewes [*Sussex*]

April 9th [1922]

My dear Nelly,
    I ought to have written before. Your letter arrived in the midst of a

1. Both Karin and Adrian Stephen were studying medicine.
2. Virginia hurriedly wrote this note in Vanessa's rooms in Gordon Square.
3. For a group photograph of Lottie Hope, Nelly Boxall, and Nelly Brittain, and Angelica (aged about 3½), see Volume II, opposite p. 484.

domestic crisis—a maid [Lottie Hope] having an operation—on top of which we moved down here.

It would give us great pleasure if we might come over [to Gale, Chelwood Gate, Sussex] and spend a day with you—We shall be here till the 27th, and though Leonard is digging potatoes and can't be got at, I feel sure that the trains work out conveniently from Lewes to East Grinstead.

L. is in the middle of Lady Gwendolen's second volume.[1] Did I tell you how enthusiastic Lytton Strachey was: But he refuses to believe (and so do I, for the credit of our trade) that Lady G. hasn't been trained to pen and ink secretly for years.

As for poor Elizabeth,[2] it is your duty to tell her the truth. I hear nothing but groans from those who have drunk her champagne, and now have to give thanks for presentation copies suitably enscribed.

Your affate
Virginia Woolf

I think all days between 20th and 27th are the same to us, if you would choose the best for you.

Marquess of Salisbury (Cecil Papers)

1245a: To Roger Fry   52 *Tavistock Square, W.C.*1

Monday [15 May 1922]

My dear Roger,

I'm sending back one of the tickets [to Roger's lecture], as I'm sure there are people who want it. Elly [Dr Elinor Rendel] says I must keep out of hot rooms at present—its only I've upset the rhythm of my heart—whatever that means—nothing of any importance, but its such a bore getting faint in public, that I'm submitting.

I suppose you wouldn't be a kind man and let me read your lectures in MS if you have an MS. I dont like missing your words—you know I have a misguided respect for them.

L. cant go to the lecture tomorrow, but someone else wants to—so may we keep the ticket, and L. will go next time.

yr Virginia

Sussex

1. *Life of Robert, Marquess of Salisbury, Volumes I & II* (1921), by Lady Gwendolen Cecil, his daughter.
2. Elizabeth Bibesco, the novelist. She was the daughter of the Prime Minister, Herbert Asquith, and married in 1919 Prince Antoine Bibesco, the Roumanian diplomat, playwright, and editor of the letters of Marcel Proust.

1291a: To Duncan Grant   *Monk's House, Rodmell*
                                          [Sussex]
[26 September 1922]

My dear Duncan,
    There is a sale at Cobbe Place, Beddingham tomorrow, Wednesday,
which I shall attend. I shall get there about 2.30. Perhaps you would join me.
It isn't the farm which I spoke of. That sale is not till Wednesday, 4th.
However, I daresay Sir Alfred Bosanquet[1] had some fine works, and I
want to rummage in Cobbe Place—it is the house behind the wall you pass
on the road to Asheham.
    I am involved in awful crises owing to Tom's visit, and the crass idiocy
of Ottoline. But it is a long story.[2]
    You might of course come to lunch and we could then go on after-
wards.

                                                              V.W.
Anyhow you might come one day.

Estate of Duncan Grant

1300a: To Mary Hutchinson   *Hogarth House, Paradise Road,*
                             Richmond, Surrey
Thursday [12 October 1922]

Dear Mary,
    A misunderstanding!
    I thought the message from you was that you would go and see Mrs
Eliot and discover their views [on the Eliot Fund], which would be imparted
to me on Thursday. Therefore I said don't do this; as I've seen Tom.
However Leonard says I misunderstood him, and I'm glad to think that
my invitation was independent of this infernal business which is losing me
all my friends, my hair, my time, my temper. Nor will poor Tom benefit
by a penny, that I can see.
    We are now in the whirl of getting the books out, and it is rather difficult
to make engagements. So I'll try to come to tea next Thursday; but you
must not keep the day, and I will send a card to say whether I can. Horrors
of various kinds develop at a moments notice, and one has to sit down and
write reams of envelopes or dash off to the city. The last crisis is that our

1. Sir Albert Bosanquet (1837-1923). He was a barrister, and Chairman of the East
   Sussex Quarter Sessions, 1912-21. Cobbe Place, a mile across the river from
   Rodmell, was bought in 1967 by Quentin and Olivier Bell.
2. Virginia, Ottoline Morrell and Richard Aldington were attempting to raise a
   fund for T. S. Eliot, to enable him to leave his job at Lloyd's Bank and concentrate
   on his writing.

edition of Andreev[1] is kept in bond at Hull until we have fought the act of 1887 which requires all books printed in Germany to say so, on the flyleaf in letters not less than one inch high.

Well, you can't say that the handwriting of this does me credit.

Yours
V.W.

Texas

1303a: To Logan Pearsall Smith
Hogarth House, Paradise Road, Richmond, Surrey

26th Oct. 1922

Dear Mr Pearsall Smith,

It is very good of you to like *Jacob's Room*, and I am much pleased that you should. I don't think it is quite a success, but I hope (perhaps vainly) that the next one will be. The effort of breaking with complete representation sends one flying into the air. Next time I shall stick like a leech to my hero, or heroine. But please excuse this egotism.

We shall be delighted to see you with Mr Whitall[2] on Saturday about 4.30. I had meant and wished to ask him before, but Leonard has been very busy, and I have been dribbling along with the relics of influenza.

Yours very sincerely
Virginia Woolf

Library of Congress

1352a: To Mary Hutchinson   *Hogarth [House, Richmond]*

[26 January 1923]

Dear Mary,

I hear from Aldington that we *must* make a special effort to get fresh subscribers: it is most important: there are real reasons which I cannot, at present, divulge.[3] Would you undertake to write to your friend Schiff[4]

1. *The Dark*, by Leonid Andreev, was published by the Hogarth Press in January 1923.
2. James Whitall, Logan Pearsall Smith's American cousin, had offered in August to take over the financial management of the Hogarth Press, but Leonard refused him.
3. T. S. Eliot had almost decided to leave his job in Lloyd's Bank, and needed an alternative income.
4. Sydney Schiff, the novelist, who wrote under the name of Stephen Hudson.

and beg him to send out more circulars? Aldington attaches importance to this; I don't know Schiff. I will put the screw on Harry Norton.[1]

Oh what a curse of scorpions it all is! Tom has taken the £50.

As I say, there are real and pressing reasons.

So forgive
V.W.

Texas

1377a: To Olive Temple   *Yegen [Spain]*

5th April [1923]

Dear Mrs Temple,[2]

We feel that we did not thank you at all sufficiently for the great kindness you showed us. We enjoyed every minute of our time with you, and came on here much refreshed.

Happily we had a lovely day for our ride yesterday, as it was a long one. We did not reach Yegen till 9 in pitch darkness. But this won't mean much to a traveller like you.

We very much hope you will give us a chance of seeing you in England. My husband wants me to say how much he enjoyed his talk with Mr Temple, and hopes he will be able to go on with them later.

Please remember us both to him.

Yours very sincerely
Virginia Woolf

Mrs Harold G. Reise

1380a: To Mary Hutchinson   *Alicante [Spain]*

perhaps Wednesday 18th April [1923]

Dear Mary,

I was much touched to get your letter, and if there had been white cliffs should have looked at them tenderly—but there was only Aldous Huxley's head.[3] It is all a very very long time ago. We have climbed so high, and talked such a lot. I have become a confirmed continentalist, and

1. H. T. J. Norton (1886-1937), the mathematician and Fellow of Trinity College, Cambridge.
2. Olive Temple (*née* Macleod), the wife of Charles Lindsay Temple (1871-1929), former Governor of Northern Nigeria. Leonard and Virginia stayed with them in Granada before going on to visit Gerald Brenan at Yegen in the Sierra Nevada.
3. Mary had affectionately asked her to think of her as Virginia left the English coast on her way to Spain. Aldous Huxley was on the same cross-Channel steamer.

can't think why we submit to a mitigated version of life at Hammersmith and Richmond. Here it is always fine, always indolent; one drinks coffee, listens to the Band, ships come in, old men spit; last night I did not sleep till 4, because of bugs. At 4 Leonard extricated a camel shaped lump of purple tissue from the hairs of my blanket. It burst with an odious smell into thick blood. So do not expect much continuity, cogency, or clarity from me. I am sitting in a Spanish gentleman's Club, to which travellers are admitted. There is only one old gentleman and his spittoon in the midst of a vast yellow chamber, set tight round the walls with wicker chairs, and in the midst breadths of white marble and vistas of billiard tables and courtyards and arum lilies beyond.

We are waiting for a ship to take us to Barcelona, but owing to the feast of the conception of the Virgin the ship remains at Carthagena, and so we grill here, watching the ships, listening to the band as I say. But we have been among the eternal snows [at Yegen], on mule back, and crouched over olive wood fires with deformed Catalans at midnight. Also at Granada with the Temples—highly aristocratic elderly people, expecting Mrs [Margot] Asquith the day after. In short, I cannot even begin to chatter. I should overpower the whole of River House [Hutchinsons' house, Hammersmith]. My voice would begin with the boiled egg and continue with the heavenly mushrooms and grilled chops at lunch. The 8ts would row past and row back and still I should be talking.

Gerald [Brenan] is a very sympathetic, but slightly blurred character, who owing to solitude and multitudes of books has some phantasmagoric resemblance to Shelley. Otherwise he is intelligent, and as we share certain views upon English prose, our tongues wag—mine like a vipers, his like a trusty farmyard dogs. He has a slight impediment in his speech. I like young men who have not had the dew frozen hard at Cambridge. In short, he admires a sentence or two in one of my books. Hush! Hush! Mary is looking for the ruler—ebony black—with which she snubs my perspiring snout.

I hope for a week in Paris. Leonard, of course, has to rush back in order to issue Maynards paper[1]—to which Mary Hutchinson is going to contribute some serious and well informed articles upon *Dress*. This, which I mean simply and affectionately, you take like a nervous mare with your ears laid back and one long white tooth showing. Ah, how hard it is to establish communication with any human being! I must stop. But, observe, I have said nothing about olives, oranges, lemons, palms; or the Eliots. I am reading Proust, I am reading Rimbaud. I am longing to write.

yrs V.W.

Texas

1. Leonard had just been appointed Literary Editor of the *Nation & Athenaeum*, of which Maynard Keynes had recently taken control.

Wednesday 9th? Jan [1924]

My dear Mary,

I would have written before—I'm not simply waiting like a spaniel begging for hot buttered toast, for my present—I've been whelmed though in domestic revolutions and scarcely in my five wits. Just this moment I've bought number 52 Tavistock Sqre.—at least, please God to see the lease through. And entirely changed my way of life. But come to our house warming next month, and you shall hear it all.

I met someone—Francis Birrell[1]—who said he'd been dining with you, which means I hope that influenza is gone. Still, aren't I entirely engrossed in my new house? Cant you see through all my pretences of friendship? Our house has a billiard room, two solicitors, a roof garden (but the damp comes through) a W.C. without proper access to the air, and one wall that aint plumb. But then, the rates—the rent—the basement—The library's going to be in the kitchen: Dadie and Joad[2] in the scullery: the press in the old gent's billiard room: L and I right on top, with an unexampled view behind of the Lights of London: in front nothing but greenery and young things playing tennis. Here my dear Mary, we will sit and watch the sun rise: we will give great parties, which will range the cellars, and tap at the deed boxes, and waltz between the presses, and sit out on top of the skylight. (Where is it that they eat quails on top of a skylight?) Yes, the third act of my drama shall be at 52 Tavistock Square: a little fantastic, I daresay, but you must admit, incredibly glorious.

Oh God, says Mary, is there nothing interesting in this letter? No gossip, no news, nothing even about a book? Well you see Saxon, with four lunatics and a toothless mother, is coming to Hogarth:[3] I'm waiting him this minute. My walls will echo with piping Tom's cry, and the shouts of Miss Churchill, who except for shouting is harmless, they say. Then did I tell you, how Nelly [Boxall] and Lottie [Hope] are going—so that I may have a divine ghostly cook who glides in and out, never sleeps, or eats butchers meat, but lays the table and disappears, and I need never, never never stop writing or talking, which ever it happens to be?

No, says Mary; and I dont want to hear any more. If Virginia's going on like this about her house, as well as—I mean if we've got to admire 52 Tavistock Square and the WC and the basement, as well as the dress, the genius, the face, the charm, the shoes, the stockings, the wit, the letters, the

1. Francis Birrell (1889-1935), the son of Augustine Birrell the Liberal statesman, and David Garnett's partner in a Bloomsbury bookshop.
2. George Rylands and Marjorie Joad, both employees of the Hogarth Press.
3. Saxon Sydney-Turner and his mother, who cared for mental patients in her home, had acquired the lease of Hogarth House.

character, the temper, the manners, the shoe laces, the finger nails, the way she comes in, and the way she goes out—then, my dear Mr Bell, says Mary, I say your sister in law's high at the price.

Not a bit yet, says the gallant Clive; But here I must stop.

Rather a nice letter Mary? Eh?

yrs VW

Texas

1442a: To Mary Hutchinson   [*Hogarth House, Richmond*]

[15 February 1924]

Mary!!!!!

The usual shortage of letter paper makes it necessary to use this professional sheet. Don't you smell me? I am like a civet. Leonard detests me. I think myself too, too, too lovely. Yes: you've entirely altered my life, and given a new channel for vanity to flow in. As you may have guessed, that inexplicable and most detestable prudery which for 10 years led me to make sanitary towels out of Kapok down rather than buy them, has always prevented me from saying to a powdered shop girl 'I too am a woman. . . . I want powder too.' Now you have removed an inhibition, ruined a home, intoxicated a heart, and made me for life your slave, suppliant, servant, debtor. No: I can say no more.

Tom's [Eliot] dining tomorrow; and I shall be very curious to observe whether rouge on the lips, quickens his marmoreal heart.

And yours, Madam? Have you one?

We ladies who powder—you see you've admitted me to the great company of *real* women—the desire of my heart.

VW

Texas

1472a: To Mary Hutchinson   52 *Tavistock Square, W.C.*1

23rd May 1924

My dear Mary,

I have been asked by the Hogarth Press to lay before you a proposal which we hope you will consider—that you should write us a book upon dress.[1] What we have in mind is a book with a practical bearing—it might be for those who have little to spend—but treated in a whimsical and imaginative way, with diversions in your own method, and perhaps black

1. Mary rejected this idea.

and white drawings. We feel sure you would write something enchanting. We should like to produce it for next Christmas.

Do consider this and let us know. Or suggest any better idea that occurs to you. We much want to have you on our list.

Ever yours
Virginia Woolf

Texas

1507a: TO THEODORA BOSANQUET   52 *Tavistock Sqre, W.C.*1
[7 November 1924]

Dear Miss Bosanquet,[1]

I think your essay is a great success, and I'm glad you did not keep it to tinker at, for I think you have suggested everything, and further work might well have spoilt it. As it is, you have got an immense deal into it, and made it come together perfectly as a whole. It interested me from first to last. One can never tell about the public, but I am sure it ought to have a success with anyone who cared for Henry James and his work, and I think we are very lucky to get it.

Yours sincerely
Virginia Woolf

Houghton Library, Harvard University

1538a: TO MARY HUTCHINSON   52 *Tavistock Square, W.C.*1
[16? February 1925]

My dear Mary,

Really really, weasels oughtn't to walk the streets full of flowers—they are sinister underground creatures: never have I seen my room so gay and weaselish. A thousand thanks: and I'm already better, and feel rather Tomish.

All my arguments have been entirely disregarded. Aldington has set his heart on making a journalist of Tom,[2] and as far as I can make out, they are now trying to get support for the Criterion and start him on that and any other odds and ends they can come by.

It is not accomplished yet: and knowing Tom, perhaps never will be.

1. Theodora Bosanquet was Henry James's secretary in the last years of his life. She wrote an account of him in *Henry James at Work*, published by the Hogarth Press in November 1924.
2. Eliot remained at Lloyd's Bank until the autumn of 1925, when he resigned to devote himself to writing and editing the new journal *Criterion*.

But my cottage is called a mere palliative, and I a miserable chicken hearted woman for suggesting it. Don't I know that Tom lives in a *basement*, that his position is degrading, insecure, ruinous to his health, destructive of his writing. Fashion notes for [Dorothy] Todd [Editor, *Vogue*] are far preferable: so why ask my advice at all?

But come on Monday, 4.45. I dont think, alas, there is any use in our discussing Tom: we shall only have to help him to articles; so will not dine; but my dinner is coming off soon.

VW

All about Tom is needless to say confidential. I'll show you the letters.

Texas

1559a: To Lady Cecil

Monk's House, Rodmell
[Sussex]

[May 1925]

My dear Nelly,

It is very nice of you—and very surprising—to go on reading your old friends works. I never expected you to. So far, the old gentlemen have said nothing, though I daily expect one of them to discover Evelyn[1] and give me a scolding.

But you would be nicer still if you told me when you are in London, and asked me to come and see you. Now you retire to Gale, and I'm at Tavistock Square till August, so what chance is there of discussing the Brontës and a million other subjects? You always had a strong strain of perversity in you from your earliest days: Lambton blood, I suppose.[2]

My house, you will be amused to hear, has been a mere ante room to the House of Lords the past fortnight. Leonard has been caballing about Kenya day and night, and I have several times been shut out of his study while the great discoursed. He is very sceptical, I regret to say, of the government promises. Does Lord Balfour carry conviction to your mind?[3] One of our authors is a fiery and intractable Scotchman called Norman Leys, whose

1. *Rambling Round Evelyn*, an essay about the diaries of John Evelyn (1620-1706), published in *The Common Reader*.
2. Nelly Cecil was born Eleanor Lambton, daughter of the 2nd Earl of Durham. Her husband Robert was created Viscount Cecil in December 1923.
3. Arthur Balfour (1848-1930), previously Prime Minister, was now Lord President of the Council in Baldwin's government, and took a leading part in the discussion of Imperial affairs. There was no immediate crisis in Kenya, but a continuing debate about the rival claims of the white settlers and the native Africans to the Kenyan Highlands.

book on Kenya we published [in November 1924]. He is a perfect Saint and martyr, but not altogether easy company in the house.

We shall be here (we're down for Sunday and it is pouring of course) all August and September. Surely a Viscountess has a motor car, and being a lady of the kindest heart, comes to visit her humble friends? We have wild schemes of building here; but I don't believe you much mind a very scratch bed and scratcher dinner.

So propose a day, and then we will sit in my garden hut, and you shall tell me the whole story of your life, (as if you would dream of such a horror!) and anyhow we can always talk about—all sorts of things. Why have you never written anything for the Hogarth Press?

Your affate
V. W.

Marquess of Salisbury (Cecil Papers)

1581a: To Mary Hutchinson   *Monks House, Rodmell*
                              [Sussex]
Monday [14 September 1925]

My dear Mary,

These postcards are all very well, but why not write me a letter?

I am leading a diminished, impoverished, suffocated life, bed in the morning, garden, or fire in the afternoon: and in these circumstances watch for the post. Please write—anything, so be that it takes me half an hour to get through.

Tom's character is sadly aspersed.[1] I must leave Clive to give you the details, which he will, I know, with pleasure.

I still stick to the rags and tatters that remain (of Tom's character) with the tenacity of a leech, but get little help from Leonard. But suppose a little boy was beaten every day, and had his fingers shut in doors, and dead rats tied to his tail coat—that is Tom's predicament I maintain—he might fail in that manly and straightforward conduct which we all admire.

I am afloat in 12 volumes of ancient and incredibly vapid 18th Century autobiographies: nobody could survive in that flood but me: and now, in the 6th vol. of Mrs Bellamy's apology,[2] the print is sticking to the page opposite. Never mind. But what about Mary's book? Eh?

Will you do a kind act for me, if you have the chance? Viola Tree

1. The Woolfs had offered to reprint *The Waste Land*, but Eliot gave it to Faber & Gwyer, whom Eliot had recently joined, although the contract with the Hogarth Press was never cancelled.
2. George Anne Bellamy (1727-1788), the notorious English actress, whose *Apology* (1785) was published in six volumes.

suddenly offered to come here on a bicycle with her manuscript.[1] L said I was ill and asked her to send it. She has not answered a word, and we fear she may be huffed. Would you assure her that it is literally true—I haven't seen a soul, and am still incapable of entertaining; but we would read it instantly, if she sent it by post. She is such a merry go round however, that I daresay the whole thing ran off her back in a vapour.

Tell Jack [St John Hutchinson] I long to discuss the affaire Eliot with him. Good Weasel, get your pen and ink.

yrs V.W.

Texas

1612a: To Lady Ottoline Morell

[52 *Tavistock Square, W.C.*1]

[January 1926]

Dearest Ottoline,

It is wonderful of you to keep up still such an interest in the doings of your troupe—for I always think of myself as performing in the ring for you in your exalted box. Why aren't you still seated in Bedford Square, in the place of the autocratic Margot [Oxford]?

I'm so sorry you've been ill, and are you really cured? It sounds horribly drastic, retiring to Wales to be made well.[2]

It was all my own fault, getting ill this autumn—so I am told. One's friends are very candid, aren't they? I'm told to give up all pleasure and do nothing but work. So please don't come to London just yet, and dont give any parties—or don't let people tell me of them.

I met Siegfried Sassoon[3] at a concert the other night, and he stirred me to great excitement by saying that you are writing your memoirs and I hope to goodness this is true. Please do it. I think it is one of the things you owe the world. Then let me have them, and publish them, and write a character of you, to supplement the works of Lawrence, Sitwell, and Aldous and Cannan[4]—what a tribe, to be sure! Write everything as fast as you can, as it comes into your head, and it will be a masterpiece. Pick us all to pieces. Throw us to the dogs. It is high time you came off your heights and did a little dusting in a high-minded manner.

1. Of *Castles in the Air: The Story of My Singing Days*, which the Hogarth Press published in April 1926. Viola Tree (1884-1938) was the daughter of the actor-manager Sir Herbert Beerbohm Tree.
2. Ottoline was undergoing a cure at Ruthin Castle, North Wales.
3. The poet and novelist (1886-1967), author of *Twelve Sonnets* (1911), *Memoirs of a Fox-Hunting Man* (1928) etc.
4. D. H. Lawrence had caricatured Ottoline in *Women in Love* (1920) and Aldous Huxley in *Crome Yellow* (1921). Neither the Sitwells nor Gilbert Cannan (1884-1955) are known to have done the same.

Will you thank Julian [Morrell] for a very charming Xmas card? I was greatly touched, and hope she'll come and see us, if she ever condescends to London.

Only write your memoirs.

Yr. V.W.

Texas

1647a: To Tom Driberg   *Monks House, Rodmell,*
                                          Lewes, Sussex
June 13th [1926]

Dear Mr Driberg[1]

It was very good of you to tell us about Miss Steins lecture. We had meant to suggest to her that she should write something of the kind for the Hogarth Press, but had not the chance of talking to her at Edith Sitwell's party.[2] We have now written and asked her to let us see her paper. It sounds most interesting; and I hope very much that we shall be able to bring it out in our series.[3]

Many thanks for writing to me.

Yours sincerely
Virginia Woolf

I will ask her to include the poems if possible.

Drew Ponder Greene

1652a: To Lady Ottoline Morrell
                                          52 Tavistock Square, W.C.1
[early July 1926?]

Dearest Ottoline,

I have been meaning to write, but I wrote you such a charming and flattering (but sincere) letter in the train coming home,—I mean I made it up—that I find it difficult to write a real letter. It was all about being grateful to you and Philip for having taken so much pains these 20 years to give me pleasure. I became sentimental at the thought of Bedford Sqre, and Peppard.[4] This is all very awful, I said to myself, as the train reached Paddington.

1. Tom Driberg (1905-76) was then an undergraduate at Oxford. Later he had a distinguished career in journalism and politics.
2. On 1 June 1926. See Letter 1644, Volume III.
3. Gertrude Stein's *Composition as Explanation* was published as one of the Hogarth Essays in November 1926.
4. The Morrells lived at 44 Bedford Square, Bloomsbury, in 1907-15, during which time they had a country cottage, Peppard, near Henley-on-Thames. They moved to Garsington Manor, Oxford, in 1915.

One never does write these charming letters, partly, I suppose, because one is afraid of getting one's feelings wrong in writing. All you can know, therefore, is that I was very happy at Garsington, and very sentimental about you, Garsington and Philip in the train.

I entirely disagree with Desmond [MacCarthy]. The memoirs[1] seem to me to improve (Leonard sent them off in a fright, or I would have marked passages.) I think you become more definite and exact as you go on. Beware of kindness. Imagine you are writing of people long dead, or unable to read. If you muffle up your feelings, you wont give real pleasure;—but I'm only anxious that we shall all figure truthfully for the sake of literature. Also, do not be too shrinking about yourself. A little outspoken vanity would be refreshing. Then I liked your reflections upon life—I would dash them down, if I were you, pall mall. You always, it seems to me, fall on your feet. I go on saying enviously What a subject! What a book! It is splendid —beginning with the empty rooms; then Italy; then Bedford Square. I assure you, you have no need to be nervous: no: be bold and lavish, and say whatever comes into your head. And please let me see the next lot soon.

Your afft
VW.

Texas

1676a: To Virgil Barker: 52 *Tavistock Square, W.C.*1

Typewritten
27th September, 1926

Dear Mr Barker,[2]

I am so much annoyed to find that the article I sent you, Some Thought on the Cinema, has been printed in the New republic. It appeared some time in August,[3] when I was in the country, or I would have written to you before.

The New republic has an arrangement with the Nation by which it can take certain articles which are sent to it in proof. The Secretary at the Nation is convinced that no proof was sent, and I can only suppose that some one in the New republic took the article in ignorance. We have written to complain. I can only offer you my sincere apologies and hope that as the publication was so much later than yours that no harm was done to The Arts.[4]

You were so good as to ask me to send you the articles of a more

1. Ottoline was writing her memoirs, based on her diaries and correspondence, but they were not published until after her death, when they were edited by Robert Gathorne-Hardy in two volumes (1963 and 1974).
2. Editor of *Arts* (New York).
3. *The Movies and Reality* (*New Republic*, N.Y., 4 August 1926).
4. Where the article appeared as *Cinema* in June 1926.

literary nature from time to time. I wonder whether an article on the diaries of Benjamin Haydon, the historical painter, would interest you? A reprint is appearing here in a few weeks. They are of great literary and artistic interest, as you are probably aware. As I should not publish the article in England, I ought to mention that my fee would be £20.[1]

I should be much obliged if you would let me know at the earliest opportunity whether you would like to have the article. It would run to about 1,500 words. I could let you have it by the middle of October.

Yours sincerely
Virginia Woolf
(Mrs Woolf)

Archives of American Art, Smithsonian Institution

1676b: To Mary Hutchinson   *Monks House, Rodmell*
                                                   [Sussex]
Friday Oct. 1st [1926]

My dear Flinders,

That devil Vita, having put us off twice and finally not come has made it too late to suggest your coming before we go. What a bore! But I dont suppose you would have. Please come next year though.

Now about your manuscript [*Fugitive Pieces*]. Is it done? I can see you flinch. But its no good prevaricating and titivating. Heave it into the post at Angus's [Davidson] head this very night after dinner. What about George Moore?[2] Do get him. Perhaps you're still away. We go on sitting in the sun; like old crones over the fire, gossiping endlessly but come back on Tuesday. Rather a bore, in some ways, to put on the shackles of life: but also rather exciting. What about [Dorothy] Todd? What about—everybody?

I say, will you buy me a hat one of these days? I can't lunch with Sybil [Colefax] in black felt which has been [in] the river again. Would you? (buy, not lunch—Oh no! not in black felt). I can't imagine where hats are sold: now you know this and its part of your incessant fascination. I think its in an alley, paved, with bottle glass windows. An old woman, who knew your grandmother—no, I've got it all wrong.

Leonard is buying dung off Mrs Bolton outside my lodge door. I am soaking in the embers of the sunset, with one finger broken, but a heart that is perfectly sound.

1. Virginia published a review of *The Autobiography and Memoirs of Benjamin Robert Haydon* in the *Nation* (18th December 1926), and it was reprinted in the *New Republic* (29 December 1926).
2. Virginia had met the novelist George Moore in March 1926 at Mary's London house.

Now, Mary, to your writing; and lets have no more airs and graces. There's Peter out on Thursday:[1] every day I expect a stiletto in the ribs at the hand of Topsy [Lucas], who, I'm told, is furious that we dont recognise the divine genius of that stiff little prig (but adorable man I quite agree) her husband. Tell me whats the news.

yrs VW

Texas

1707a: To Donald Brace   52 *Tavistock Square, W.C.*1

Typewritten
9th January 1927

Dear Mr Brace,

I enclose the agreements. We have inserted another clause which I hope you will agree to. If you do perhaps you would add it to the second copy and return it to me. Except for this one change, everything is agreed to by me.

I have had a letter from Mrs Van Doren,[2] and hope that we may be able to arrange a visit to America in the Spring, but have not yet had time to hear from her. In that case, we shall much look forward to seeing you.

Faithfully yours,
Virginia Woolf

I am afraid that the MS of my novel [*To the Lighthouse*] that I sent you was in an extremely rough state. Large parts have been rewritten since.

Harcourt Brace Jovanovich

1761a: To Leonard Woolf   [*Monk's House, Rodmell,*
                                   Sussex]

Monday [23 May 1927]

Very good night. Feeling very well. Pinka has been an angel—slept in her box in the bathroom. She was very restless after you went and rushed to the gate, and then to your room with her nose to the ground. In fact the whole evening she was watching for you. When I was in the garden, the Wellers arrived on a motor bicycle to call on Nelly [Boxall]. Percy [Bartholomew, gardener] told them she was gone. I suppose it was the Wellers—a young woman, he said.

1. F. L. Lucas, *The River Flows* (October 1926).
2. Irita Van Doren, Editor of the *Weekly Book Supplement* of the *New York Herald Tribune*.

I heard from Vita this morning that she may possibly come this evening and spend the night—but has to be at Long Barn for lunch tomorrow. Possibly I might get her to motor me to East Grinstead. Anyhow don't meet me at Victoria. But I think its very unlikely that she will come. As I sat in the garden this morning I heard a noise like an aeroplane just over my head, looked up, and saw a swarm of bees. I was rather afraid that they would settle on me and sting me to death, or infest me permanently, but they went over the terrace at a great rate—a terrific swarm of them—Then I saw a Cinnabar Moth. The tits are sat on by the mother all day. I'm now taking Pinka to the river. Its a perfect day. If you were here, I should be tempted to stay—as it is, I shall be back for tea. All letters came by first post. I am asked by Watts [literary agent] to write 3,000 words of recollections of my father for the Rationalist Annual—is this the Lighthouse?

Don't you think it might be a good thing to advertise the Marionette[1] in the programme of the Marionettes at the Scala?

I wonder what happened with Riding.[2]

Tell Nelly I've bought a pound of butter at Bottens [local farmers], and will bring most of it back—also 1 shillings worth of cream, so I'm living in luxury. Pinka sends 3,000 kisses. Marmots 20,000. Mandril[3] 2 million.

Sussex

1781a: To Lady Ottoline Morrell

52 *Tavistock Sqre.*, *W.C.*1

[July 1927]

Dearest Ottoline

It was very nice of you to write. As usual, you made my head swim with beauty,—I walk about London making up phrases about you. Isn't it a pleasure to you that you have this effect on people? I'm not going to write it down though, only to continue to be a humble and dumb faithful servant.

I should like to describe your dress; and then the pictures, and the colours.

But also, besides this, I liked just sitting and chattering.

1. *The Marionette*, a novel by Edwin Muir, was published by the Hogarth Press in 1927, and Virginia was suggesting that it be advertised in the programme of the Italian Marionettes, then showing at the Scala Theatre, London.
2. Laura Riding, the poet, whose *Voltaire* the Hogarth Press published in November.
3. 'Mandril' and 'Marmots' were the two names which Virginia gave to herself when writing to Leonard.

Thank you so much for letting me come.[1]

Your
Virginia

If Philip does beard Sybil Colefax tomorrow, do ask him to bring me Turner's Aesthetes,[2] to read on the journey,[3] I will send it back.

Texas

1795a: TO JACQUES-ÉMILE BLANCHE   [*Monk's House, Rodmell, Sussex*]

3rd August 1927

Dear M. Blanche,[4]

It was most good of you to send me your books.[5] I had plenty of room for them and dipped into them even crossing the Channel. Now I am settling down to read [George Frederick] Watts, and shall get your novel [*Aymeris*] from London. It was a great pleasure to find my name written in each.

We are delighted—that is my husband, our partner and myself—are delighted that you will consider writing something for the Hogarth Press.[6] Of all your suggestions, we think the Glamour of London the most attractive. I think that a book in which you gave your memories of people and of the place itself some years ago would have the greatest interest for English readers. There might be illustrations, and there would be no difficulty in getting it translated.

May we hope then that you will start on this when the work you told me about is finished? I will write and remind you later.

I will send you an untouched photograph of myself[7] directly I have one —in a week or so.

1. To 10 Gower Street, Bloomsbury, where Ottoline had just moved from Garsington.
2. W. J. R. Turner's novel *The Aesthetes* (1927), which cruelly portrayed Ottoline as Lady Virginia Caraway. Two of the other characters are Esmond Darthy (Desmond MacCarthy) and Dytton (Lytton Strachey).
3. To stay with Ethel Sands and Nan Hudson in Normandy.
4. Jacques-Émile Blanche (1861-1942), the French portrait painter and writer, who had a house near Ethel Sands' in Normandy, where Virginia had recently met him.
5. *Les Cahiers d'un Artiste* (1914-19).
6. Blanche never published anything with the Hogarth Press.
7. For his article *Entretien avec Virginia Woolf*, published in *Nouvelles Littéraires* (13 August 1927).

Please remember me to Madame Blanche and believe me, with many thanks for the books,

Yours sincerely,
Virginia Woolf

P.S. I have just read the Berthe Morisot and the Frederick Watts [in *Cahiers*] with great enjoyment

Mrs G. Casadavan

1799a: To Jacques-Émile Blanche [*Monk's House, Rodmell, Sussex*]

20th August 1927

Dear M. Blanche,

I have been away for a few days and come back to find the Nouvelles Litteraires waiting for me with your most generous and charming article in it. Had I known what notes you were taking the other day at Auppegard I should have done my best to say something more intelligent. But indeed you have seen so much more than there was to see, and have said it so much more brilliantly than I could have done had I tried that I am glad to leave well alone. It would not be easy for me to tell you what pleasure your appreciation of my work gives me. I should have thought there was so much that was barbarous and offensive to a French ear—for which, as I told you, I have the highest respect—in what I do that I am surprised as well as gratified. However, as I read your article, I feel that I owe much, in every way, to your own imagination, which has the advantage not only of being French, but of being a painter's. I have boasted so much of this article that C. Bell implores me to give him a copy. This I will not do as I have only one, but should you have any to spare, it would be most kind if you would send him one to Charleston.

I can't help feeling a little guilty that you should have spent your time translating words of mine. They read much better to me in French than in English, and again I feel deeply grateful to you for trying to convey my words to French readers.[1] That you should have taken so much trouble on my behalf seems to me most remarkable. I am still waiting for my bookseiler to send me a copy of your novel. Meanwhile I think with great interest of the book on London which we hope to have from you.

Believe me, with many thanks,

Yours sincerely,
Virginia Woolf

1. In his article Blanche included his translation of the first few pages of *To the Lighthouse*, and the same issue of *Nouvelles Littéraires* contained his translation of *Kew Gardens*.

P.S. I hope to send you a photograph in a few days if you still want one. I did not mean to paint an exact portrait of my father in Mr Ramsay. A book makes everything into itself, and the portrait became changed to fit it as I wrote. But this is of no great importance. My mother died when I was 13 so that the memory of her in Mrs Ramsay is also very distant.

Mrs G. Casadavan

1807a: TO JACQUES-ÉMILE BLANCHE [*Monk's House, Rodmell, Sussex*]

Typewritten
[5 September ? 1927]

Dear Monsieur,

I must again thank you—but this time I will typewrite so that you may not be bothered by my handwriting—for your kindness. Stock has already written to the Hogarth Press about translating Mrs Dalloway. A lady has been translating it for some time, so I have referred them to her. If it should appear as a book I shall owe you many thanks.[1]

At last, after much delay my bookseller has discovered that your novel is not written in English. He had been looking for it among English publishers' lists. He has now started afresh and I wait in hope. You can judge by this what a barbarous people we are, and how much I rejoice that my great grandmother was a Frenchwoman.

I have seen Mr Warren;[2] but that is all. He was surrounded by young men of great beauty carrying violins. I have peeped in through his windows and seen what [I] take to be Greek statues. Roger Fry has been to tea: but I gather that the female sex is not his favourite.

I hope you are within sight of beginning your book for us. We shall easily find you a translator.

Yours sincerely,
Virginia Woolf

Mrs G. Casadavan

1812a: TO JACQUES-ÉMILE BLANCHE [*Monk's House, Rodmell, Sussex*]

[17 September 1927]

Dear M. Blanche,

I cannot wait any longer to thank you for sending me a copy of Aymeris.

1. In 1929 Stock published a French translation of *Mrs Dalloway* by S. David.
2. Edward Perry Warren (1860-1928), the American expert on classical art, who lived at Lewes House, Sussex.

I have been waiting to be able to sit down quietly and enjoy it. But I see no chance of this as yet. I have sold my soul to an American paper and have to spend the next three weeks doing nothing but read American books in order to write foolish articles.[1] Meanwhile your book lies on my table and I don't dare dig in it. I look at the pictures which are enough to lure me on. It was very good indeed of you to give it to me. I own that I shall try to make it yield a picture of you—such is my bad habit in reading novels. I shall make up a story of your life and character which I have no doubt will be purely imaginary. But it will give me I know the greatest pleasure. But I must now turn to an American professor called Peck who in spite of his name has written two vast volumes upon Shelley. How much I should prefer one book about Monsieur Blanche!

Believe me.

Yours sincerely,
Virginia Woolf

Mrs G. Casadavan

1826a: To Donald Brace   52 *Tavistock Square, W.C.*1

Typewritten
30th Oct 1927

Dear Mr Brace,

You asked me to send you particulars of the little book I am writing.

So far as I can tell at present it will be called Orlando, a Biography, and will be modelled to some extent upon the history of a real English family.

Orlando, the hero, will live from the days of Elizabeth to the present time, and will become a woman half way through. It will be completely fantastic, and written very simply, rather in the manner of different writers, like Defoe and Lord Macaulay. I hope to have eight illustrations taken from real portraits of contemporary people. There will be a preface, notes and appendix, and it will imitate in get up and arrangement the usual biography. It will run to about 40,000 words I suppose. Of course I may find that I cannot do it, and have to give it up, or it may be impossible to get it done for this spring. But I will send you a typed copy of the first chapter (about 10,000 words) by the beginning of December, and one photograph.

With best wishes
yours sincerely
Virginia Woolf

1. Reviews of Ernest Hemingway's *Men Without Women* (*New York Herald Tribune*, 9 October 1927); and *Shelley: His Life and Work*, by Walter Edwin Peck (*Herald Tribune*, 23 October 1927).

If there are any other facts you would like please let me know.

Harcourt Brace Jovanovich

1840a: To Jacques-Émile Blanche
[52 *Tavistock Square, W.C.*1]
5th Dec. 1927

Dear M. Blanche,

I have been waiting to write to you until I could be sure I had found a translator. I had my hands on the very man, but he is now going to Siam. I am sure it would be safer if you could recommend somebody. My knowledge of French is not good enough to check a translation. If you would make any suggestion I would carry it out. Between us I am sure we can get the book well done; but my own experience of translations is so disastrous that I don't want to run risks with your book.[1] We are very glad it is getting into shape. I much look forward to reading it. I am glad that Tavistock Square was in a respectable mood. This is no longer. We are surrounded by unfortunate ladies, who use the summer houses in the garden for purposes of their own.

Yours sincerely,
Virginia Woolf

Mrs G. Casadavan

1843a: To Vanessa Bell   [52 *Tavistock Square, W.C.*1]
[early January 1928]

Dearest,

Could you have the angelic goodness to bring up a shiny black waterproof, which I must have left somewhere—not, I think, in my bedroom, or I should have seen it.[2] God knows where I took it off. But the floods are so great here, I badly want it.

I am leading a strict hygienic life—not out once, only decorous visits—as from Tom for example, whose pomp was such, and inuendoes about Vivien's [Mrs Eliot] sanity, that we both guffawed behind our hands. Then Tommie [Stephen Tomlin]—a much more lively sprite yesterday: in despair over Maynard's party. I hear you're drawn in—what weakness you do show to be sure! Roger rang up to say his affairs were in a crucial state and

1. *Mes Modèles* (1928) were literary portraits of Maurice Barrès, André Gide, Marcel Proust, George Moore, Thomas Hardy and Henry James—all of whom had sat to him for their portraits.
2. Virginia and Leonard spent the nights of 24-26 December 1927 at Charleston.

moving rapidly, which he wanted us to come and discuss, but we couldnt. What is up now, I wonder?

When shall you be back?

And do you love me?

And 1, million thanks for our happy luxurious lascivious Christmas. I've never enjoyed myself so much.

Remember the mackintosh

VW

Berg

1876a: To St John Hutchinson   *Fontcreuse, Cassis,*
                                                              France
3rd April 1928

My dear Jack,

We have been motoring across France for the last six days and I found your letter waiting for me here. It was very nice of you to write, and to be pleased at my prize.[1] I feel slightly ridiculous, but also rather pleased, I must admit.

This is a very lovely house, and we are in Vanessa's vineyard; Endless pictures are being painted. Nan Hudson is on her way up to lunch. It is very hot in the sun, very cold in the shade. I think motoring through France is the greatest pleasure in life—only one eats too much.

Love to Mary and many thanks for your letter. Come and see us soon, and will you please turn over in your mind a possible pamphlet for the Hogarth Press?[2] Surely the law needs showing up? But any point of view that occurs to you will be to our liking.

Yours ever
Virginia Woolf

Texas

1908a: To Rosamond Lehmann   *Monks House, Rodmell*
                                                                [Sussex]
July 2nd [1928]

Dear Rosamund,

I'm so sorry that you've been ill—I was just about to write and ask you to come and dine, but Leonard says you are staying down in the country. What a bore being ill is, except that—well, there are a great many consolations I know, but I cant remember them at this moment—except that its

1. Virginia had been awarded the *Femina Vie Heureuse* prize for *To the Lighthouse*.
2. St John Hutchinson never wrote for the Hogarth Press.

rather nice lying in a garden—feeling enormously wise, which I dont do when I'm taking an active part in life. In ten minutes or so we are driving back to London, and I dont expect to feel wise when I'm talking to, shall we say, Sibyl Colefax or Rebecca West—who's a very nice woman, though. I met her the other day at a party that Nessa and Duncan gave,[1] and was amused to find how awed one still is by celebrities, and then they turn out to be much like other people. She is rather fierce, and I expect has some bone she gnaws in secret, perhaps about having a child by Wells. But I couldn't ask her. Perhaps you know her.

Are you able to go on with your book?[2] I hope so. I like walking about in your mind, and telling myself this is what is going to happen next, and so on. No doubt I'm all wrong. Are you writing about the same people, or have you come out in an entirely new world, from which you see all the old world, minute, miles and miles away? These questions are only questions—no answer needed, unless one day you feel inclined to write.

Now I must throw my nightgown into a bag. I've just picked all the sweet peas, and our dining room table looks like the whole of Covent Garden at dawn. I hope we shall see you in the autumn.

Yrs Virginia Woolf

Oh how do you spell your name? [Mrs Wogan Philipps]

King's

1908b: To V. Sackville-West   52. [*Tavistock Square, W.C.*1]

Friday [6 July 1928]

This is your property. Many thanks. Came home [from Long Barn] like a costers barrow flowerladen. Old Miss Pritchard[3] insisted on carrying my bag up. Rooms entirely garlanded. Some flowers for Pinkers [spaniel] wedding wreath tomorrow.

I find a letter from my French translator,[4] 4 pages long, asking me to interpret, to annotate to explain every other sentence: as for instance.

red hot pokers—are these iron spikes painted red?

Lady Margaret Duckworth rings me up to ask me to lunch to meet Herbert Fisher; will I come and sit with Sir George who has lumbago.

A letter from America to say will we go there for 3 months if paid £800 and give 10 lectures and write 12 articles.[5] and so on.

1. Virginia met Rebecca West at a party in May of this year, but it was given by Dorothy Todd. She had a son, Anthony West, by H. G. Wells.
2. Rosamond Lehmann's second novel, *A Note in Music* (1930).
3. The sister of one of the solicitors who leased part of 52 Tavistock Square.
4. M. Lanoire, translator of *To the Lighthouse*.
5. This invitation, like all Virginia's other invitations to visit America, was declined.

Long Barn seems Paradise—Oh dear oh dear—if I had you and the country!

Berg

1911a: To Alice Ritchie   *Monks House, Rodmell,*
                                       Lewes [Sussex]
Aug 3rd. [1928]

Dear Miss Ritchie,[1]

It was a great pleasure and surprise to me to get your letter. I was rather alarmed to hear that you were reading Orlando, for you are the first person besides my husband to read it. I wrote it (for me) so quickly and in such a random frame of mind that I couldn't feel sure when I read it over that it would convey much to anybody else. I was so bored by writing criticism that I dashed it off, by way of a joke, and then it got, as I thought probably too long, and some parts too serious and others too extravagant. But I couldn't begin re-writing, as no doubt I ought. Any how, I am very pleased that you like it, and it was very good of you to bother to write and say so. But I must give you a copy when it is published. I altered the proofs a little at the end, and tried to do away with one very awkward break. But I daresay I made it worse.

We've just had another novel about Geneva[2] sent in by a man called Benson who lives there. It is amazingly on the same lines, in setting and even in atmosphere, as yours: and very interesting. I wonder if you knew him?

I hope that you've had time to write some more fiction, now that you are rid of the press for a time. The praises of the Peacemakers reach me from all sorts of unexpected quarters.

Would you, by the way, say nothing about Orlando until it's published —I mean of its story or the characters, so that the surprise, such as it is, may be fresh.

                                 Yours sincerely
                                 Virginia Woolf

Mrs Ian Parsons

1. Alice Ritchie published two novels with the Hogarth Press, *The Peacemakers* (May 1928) and *Occupied Territory* (1930), and also travelled books for them. She was the sister of Mrs Ian ('Trekkie') Parsons.
2. *Dawn on Mont Blanc* by Wilfrid Benson. Hogarth Press, February 1930.

1937a: To V. Sackville-West   [52 *Tavistock Square, W.C.*1]
Telegram
[12 October 1928]

Your biographer is infinitely relieved and happy.[1]

Kate Stout

1942a: To Roger Fry   52 *Tavistock Square* [*W.C.*1]
Tuesday 16th Oct. [1928]

My dear Roger,
    What an idiotic thing I have done!—in my delight at getting a letter
from you, I must have thrown it up into the air, and then it fell into a waste
paper basket, I suppose—anyhow it's gone. So what your address is
[travelling in France], I don't know; and must ring up [48] Bernard Street
and ask Highland Mary [maid]. But before this happened, Mrs Cartwright[2]
had been informed. You sound very happy and sensible: I am happy, but
not sensible. Why does one lead the life one does?[3] I have been lunching
with Sibyl [Colefax] to meet Noel Coward; and I enjoyed it, but then I
have no time to read Paradise Lost; and if I lunch with Sibyl, I must give
her tea; and then, Roger, who should come here too, goes off to Weston
Super Mare on the pretext that he has to bury a brother.[4] So it goes on.
Tomorrow we are dining with the Hutchinsons—and here I interpolate
that there's a good deal to be said for Mary [Hutchinson] in my view—
anyhow she doesn't cock a doodle about the place as Clive does—and going
to the Eliots to discuss Tom's new poems; but not only that—to drink
cocktails and play jazz into the bargain, Tom thinking one can't do anything
simple. He thinks this makes the occasion modern, chic. He will, no doubt,
be sick in the back room; we shall all feel ashamed of our species. He has
written some new poems, religious, I'm afraid, and is in doubt about his
soul as a writer. So you see how my time is spent, leaving out all the washing
and buying shoes, and ordering a new dustbin, because Mrs Cartwright
says she gets a sore throat from our potato peeling.
    Noel Coward was rather interesting. He says the English theatre is so
degraded that he will not produce any serious work here in future. He says

1. This was Virginia's reply to Vita's telegram saying that she had just finished
   reading *Orlando* and was delighted by it.
2. The Manager of the Hogarth Press, 1925-30.
3. Roger Fry replied on 3 November 1928 (*Letters of Roger Fry*, ed. Denys Sutton,
   1972): "It's really a curse that we have become so notorious and that means so
   recherché by all the people whose intellectual life consists in pure snobbism."
4. Portsmouth Fry, who contracted an illness in youth and became a lifelong invalid.

the middle classes make his life a burden. Old women in Gloucester write and abuse him for immorality. Lord Cromer[1] can force him to leave out any sentence, or ban the whole play. He says they are infinitely more civilised in America and Berlin. So he is off to produce his plays in New York. There he makes £1000 a week, and he can say what he likes. Leonard, Morgan [Forster] and I have all got to appear in Court in defence of Miss Radcliffe Hall's Sapphistic novel [*The Well of Loneliness*, 1928]—which is so pure, so sweet, so sentimental, that none of us can read it—But you will be surprised to hear that the railwaymen who were ordered by the Customs to remove 500 copies of the book from the ship at Dover (it is being published in France) were so indignant at the injustice of the Law that they sent Radcliffe Hall a letter of sympathy! You must admit that the English are odd.

I am sending you my new book [*Orlando*] (this reads very professional) chiefly because I took the liberty of mentioning you in the preface. It is a joke, and therefore of course is being taken as a serious historical study, or allegory.

When are you coming back? Soon, I hope, for I want to talk to you more than I can say.

I must stop now and go and see that the drawing room is tidy (so to speak) as we're having a party—So that is the way we live.

Love to the woman A. [Anrep]. I thought her reference to the Queen in bad taste; but love all the same.

Ys Virginia

PS. I have left this letter so long that I am ashamed to send it. But Nessa has never given me your address. Oct. 22nd.

Pamela Diamand

1972a: To CLIVE BELL   [52 *Tavistock Square, W.C.*1]

Boxing Day [1928]

Dearest Clive,

Leonard's knowledge of Champagne being elementary rusty and meagre, I'm sure I underpaid you. I read in a list the other night that Champagne costs never less than 20/- so I enclose 10/- more.

Now all the haggling and cheque writing would be unnecessary if you had been *open*. Thats what our grandparents would have called it—I regret

1. The 2nd Earl of Cromer (1877-1953), who had become Lord Chamberlain in 1922. In addition to his other functions, he was Censor of plays.

that at this season, of all seasons, with our Saviour in the manger, you should have been guilty of deceit.

The world has come to an end—expired quite quietly, and no one much minded. No letters, telephones, bulletins: the King may be dead:[1] but I confess we have had Gerald Brenan, Roger [Fry] and Margery [Strachey] here till the other minute, and my head spins.

I am writing to your wife from Rodmell.

May we meet soon.
V

Quentin Bell

1985a: To Mary Hutchinson   [*Berlin*]

Postcard
[24 January 1929]

We have just been seeing Sans Souci[2] in a snow storm. It is incredibly ugly—Berlin I mean—very cold; but extremely gay. I dined on the top of the Eiffel tower [*Funkturm*] last night with Vita, who sends her love.

Texas

2008a: To Jacques-Émile Blanche
                    [*52 Tavistock Square, W.C.1*]
March 8th, 1929

Dear M. Blanche,

A friend of mine has just sent me a copy of your article on Orlando.[3] It is more than good of you to have written it. I think this is the only, or among the three only intelligent reviews I have had, and bears out my theory that the French carry a much sharper pen in their hands than we do. What most pleases me is the fact, what I think I discover in the midst of all your kindness, that you do not like the new book as well as you did the old. I myself think The Lighthouse much better—indeed Orlando was a joke, as you guess, dashed off as a relief from writing too many critical articles—but I am delighted if it gave you an evening's fun. I do not want

1. King George V had been seriously ill since 21 November, but he recovered and lived until January 1936.
2. Frederick the Great's palace at Potsdam.
3. *Un nouveau roman de V. Woolf* (*Nouvelles Littéraires*, 16 February 1929).

to bother you about your promise, extorted at Auppegard, that you would some day send us a book; but on my part I have not forgotten it.

With many thanks.

Yours sincerely,
Virginia Woolf

Mrs G. Casadavan

2026a: To Mary Hutchinson

Monks House, Rodmell
[Sussex]

Monday [6 May 1929]

Well, Weazel, I was very sorry not to see you at the lecture[1] but the truth was I had to take my niece [Judith Stephen] to the Coliseum, and by the time we had seen the last juggler and lady in yellow satin my head spun. Weazels would have seemed snakes.

But when shall I see you? Life seems nothing but a cascade. Shall you come to tea with me one day? But I suppose you are flitting in the dusk from one arc lamp to another. My vision of you is almost entirely unreal. You come out at night; you drop orchids in the mud, and have them washed in warm water with cotton wool.

I am running on because Leonard is in the W.C. and I am left in charge of Pinka, who is on heat and therefore all agog for life. We are down here to see about making a new room[2]—this we have been seeing about for 3 months now, and not a stone is laid. But when the stones are laid you will have to brave the eternal sea mist and south west gale and come here. I should provide you with the works of Ronald Firbank[3] which I am reading with some unstinted pleasure and we would walk on the terrace and see the lights of Lewes twinkle like the necklace which you are just letting curl in a circlet on your dressing table.

Clive is in Cassis, to me rather dreary and like coffee cups after a party; but he won't go to Saigon apparently. He means to live in Paris for a year. Dear, dear, how depressing is all this, this yellowing and falling of one's friends. He seems to me still redeemable, but how?

Here is Leonard. I must go to my lodge and write a page of the dullest book in creation [*A Room of One's Own*]. And then we drive up to London: and then—and then—what will happen then?

1. At 37 Gordon Square, where Charles Mauron lectured on Mallarmé.
2. The Woolfs were planning two rooms, a bedroom for Virginia, opening onto the garden, and a sitting-room above it.
3. The novelist (1886-1926), whose highly stylised works included *Valmouth* (1919) and *Sorrow in Sunlight* (1925).

I like Weasels to kiss: but as they kiss to bite: and then to kiss. I like
alternations and variety.

V

And Tom—Have you heard the latest?[1]

Texas

2036a: To Mary Hutchinson   *Fontcreuse, Cassis*
                                             [*France*]

8th June 1929

Dearest Weasel,
    The Isle of Wight seems a long way away, and I cant help feeling that
it is too hot to be in Parliament—at the same time I'm very sorry that
Jack did not win[2]—an impossible event, I suppose. I daresay it was the fact
of having married a weasel that did it. But what an infernal bore—all those
meetings and speeches for nothing. Do they give him a safe seat now? Is
any seat safe now? Will he turn Labour? Anyhow, please give him Leonard's
and my love.
    We left the day after the Election, and dined with Roger and Helen and
Quentin and Clive in Paris—all much as usual, except that Roger is once
more infested with doctors and treatments, and Helen's mother is dead and
Clive depressed me—but he's going to live in Paris for ever. And I cant
say why I was depressed, unless you'll come and see me.
    But how will that ever be? Does London exist? Here all is heat and vine-
yards; people swim about naked in the air. One prays that a ladies legs may
be shapely. The human figure has regained the place which, as you may
know, it had in Greece. Shapely or not—and alas, often it is a mere barrel
of flesh, in which bones are lost like needles and perhaps dont exist,—everyone is shameless—the effect of the wine and the heat. I like the atmosphere
so much that I think of buying a house in a wood this afternoon.
    Nessa and Duncan live a kind of bubbling seraphic life, with Angelica
and Judith[3] sporting like dolphins, naked too. They are infinitely happy,
busy, full of small errands and businesses; giving lifts to old ladies, entertaining the Colonel [Teed], (whose mistress [Jean Campbell] has gone off
to induce a miscarriage, her 6th, in Geneva); and today there is a grand
swimming race, and a picnic, and presents, bought in Cassis, for everybody.
It is certain that Mrs Curry will lose; for among other curiosities, we have
all sorts of cups without saucers, broken teapots, by which I mean—but

1. Simply that Vivien Eliot's legs were swollen.
2. St John Hutchinson had contested the Isle of Wight constituency as a Liberal in
   the General Election on 30 May. He did not stand for Parliament again.
3. The 10-year-old daughter of Nicholas and Barbara Bagenal.

dont ask me in this heat to be exact—that there is not a single whole couple in Cassis. They are all odds and ends. Some breed cocker spaniels, all paint.

But this will be boring you horribly. You will be dining at Boulestin's [restaurant] tonight, with a lady. And you will be wearing a tight back dress with many flounces and a white camellia. We, on the contrary, dine out on the terrace; and I'm not allowed to say 'theres a shooting star' because by the time they look, its shot. Suddenly it becomes very cold and we go and sit in the studio. Then Leonard and I stumble to bed, through the vines, to the croak of frogs. A pleasant life—yes: but I should like a little gossip with Weasel; and shall be back in 10 days. Leonard sends his love—

Virginia

Texas

2220a: To Janet Vaughan   *Monks House, Rodmell*
                                               [Sussex]
17th Aug. [1930]

My dear Janet,[1]

I hastily send this off, on seeing in the Daily Telegraph about Mr Gourlay.[2] But I dont know if you are in England. Anyhow, we want to aim our love and congratulations at your head—both of us—old married people as we are. I can assure you, no state in the world is half so pleasant. I hope Mr Gourlay was the young man who once charmed me behind a counter. And I hope you'll come and see us. And that you're back from Chicago.

Anyhow, incoherent and harried as I am, I send, dear Janet, what is really a token of deep affection, remembering Madge, and feeling dumbly and curiously some feeling of maternal affection (though I've no right) in her place for you.

yr V.W.

Sussex

2339a: To Ethel Smyth [52 *Tavistock Square*,] *London.* [*W.C.*1]
[23 March 1931]

Nessa has rung up to say the party is fixed for Thursday next at 9—a cold dinner, I imagine. and a few people of her inviting.

1. Janet Vaughan (b. 1899) was the daughter of Virginia's old friend Margaret ('Madge') Vaughan (*née* Symonds) and William Wyamar Vaughan, Virginia's cousin, the Headmaster successively of Giggleswick, Wellington and Rugby. She became a distinguished physician and Principal of Somerville College, Oxford, 1945-67.
2. David Gourlay, Director of Wayfarers Travel Agency, Bloomsbury. Janet was engaged to him.

I've just read your letter hastily—about HB's [Henry Brewster] writing
—As I say my remarks applied to his letters; I should never say that his
books were badly written because they're not literary—in fact, for me,
like most Americans, he is much too literary in one sense—too finished,
suave, polished and controlled; uses his brains and not his body; and if I
call him not a born writer, its because he writes too well—takes no risks—
doesn't plunge and stumble and jump at boughs beyond his grasp, as I,
to be modest, have done in my day; and you. It trickles off me—his beauty
—instead of raising the nerves in my spine—But this is the way with all
Americans—they cant throw things about as we do. cant take liberties:
are so d—d refined for example Henry James. Enough: I'm rushed; and
incoherent.

Berg

2489a: To Jacques-Émile Blanche
[52 *Tavistock Square, W.C.*1]
22 Dec. 1931

Dear M. Blanche,
     I am delighted to hear from you again, and particularly glad that you
liked The Waves. I am sending you a few reviews—but Desmond McCarthy
though he says he is writing about The Waves has not yet finished, and I
doubt that he will publish anything before March, if then. Our English
reviewers have been for the most part kind, but seldom intelligent. Thus I
shall look forward with special interest to what you have to say and I hope
you will let me know where I can read you. It is very good indeed of you to
interest yourself once more in my books. I always feel that I owe a great
deal of the interest that the French take in my work to you. A professor
Delattre has actually written a book on me![1]
     I am afraid the French show,[2] from what I hear, is not going to turn
well. Everybody is tired, angry, spiteful, and if we don't abuse the Americans
we abuse the French. Here, privately, we are very anxious about Lytton
Strachey who is desperately ill; and what with one thing and another
London is not a cheerful city. We are also covered in yellow fog—in the
midst of which your letter is a cheerful omen for me, for which I thank you.
     Believe me, dear M. Blanche,
                                             Yours very sincerely,
                                             Virginia Woolf

Mrs G. Casadavan

1. Floris Delattre, *Le Roman psychologique de V. Woolf* (1932).
2. The exhibition of French art, at the Royal Academy, mainly of 19th-century
paintings. It opened on 1 January 1932 and ran for 2½ months.

2899a: To John Carter   52 *Tavistock Square, W.C.1*

3rd June 1934

Dear Mr Carter,

Many thanks for your letter. I am delighted to hear that your book is coming out,[1] and shall read it with the greatest interest. I was much amused by the efforts of Mr Wise to anticipate judgment in the T.L.S., but they did not seem to me to carry conviction.

I gather from letters that I have had from America that your revelations are awaited there with the greatest excitement in Browning circles, and I hope the book will have a great success.

Yours sincerely,
Virginia Woolf

I must apologise for making a guess at your initial, but being in bed with influenza I have lost your letter and the prospectus.

Texas

2939a: To Stephen Spender   52 *Tavistock Square, W.C.1.*

21st Oct [1934]

Dear Stephen,

I've just read your article on Wyndham Lewis's book in the Spectator.[2] It was very nice of you to defend me. I haven't read him and I shant. For the past 20 years he's been abusing what he calls Bloomsbury; so I feel I know all about it and dont care a broken tea cup. But if I did, I should be more than placated by your generosity.

I dont know if you're still in Vienna, and I've lost your address, so I must send this round by the Spectator.

How has your long poem [*Vienna*, 1935] got on? I want very much to

1. In 1934 John Carter and G. Pollard published *An Enquiry into the Nature of Certain 19th Century Pamphlets*. By testing paper, type design, and handwriting where possible, Carter and Pollard exposed 54 'first editions' as forgeries, including an edition of Elizabeth Barrett Browning's *Sonnets From the Portuguese*, dated 1847. Thomas James Wise (1859-1937) was the book collector and bibliographer who had accepted these pamphlets as genuine, and in the *TLS* for 24 May 1934, he attempted to defend the dating of the Browning *Sonnets*.

2. *Men Without Art* by Wyndham Lewis, reviewed by Spender in the *Spectator* on 19 October 1934. Lewis had complained that he had been "suffocated" by Virginia. Spender replied: "Why should Mrs Woolf seem to suffocate Mr Lewis? And if he seems suffocated by Mrs Woolf, why should he object to her being suffocated by Messrs Bennett, Wells and Galsworthy? He ought to be pleased."

read it. We are back here: Rosamond is coming to dinner: Ottoline is giving a tea party.

I hope you'll come when you are back, and let us go on with the argument we started that day with Hugh [Walpole] and William [Plomer]— and then I'll tell you the story of Wyndham and the Omega—(only its sordid and morbid and not at all to the credit of human nature.)[1]

Yours
Virginia Woolf

Texas

3007a: To Marcel Boulestin   52 *Tavistock Square, W.C.*1

April 8th [1935]

Dear M. Boulestin,[2]

I have been away for the weekend or I would have written. It is extremely kind of you to ask us to lunch; and I am very sorry that my husband is engaged both tomorrow and Wednesday, but lunch is a difficult time for him. Yes, my cook [Mabel] has thoroughly enjoyed your lessons, and I have just been reaping the benefits. I wish that I could offer you anything as satisfactory as your sole with mushroom sauce, but can only sign myself with gratitude

Yours sincerely
Virginia Woolf

Michele Tempesta

3064a: To Lady Cecil   *Monks House, Rodmell, Lewes, Sussex*

Saturday [28 September 1935]

I was just saying to myself, why do I never see Nelly? She was coming to see me, and she never did—this was what I was saying on the downs the day before yesterday, and then there's the second post, with your letter.

Yes, the Captain[3] was mine—at least, being horribly bored by Abyssinia [Italian invasion] I took down the first book I saw that looked unlike the

---

1. In 1913 Wyndham Lewis quarrelled with Roger Fry over a commission to decorate a room in the *Daily Mail's* Ideal Home Exhibition, and with three other painters he broke off relations with Fry and his Omega Workshops.
2. Proprietor of the famous subterranean restaurant in Covent Garden.
3. *The Captain's Death Bed* (*TLS*, 26 September 1935), an essay about the novelist Captain Frederick Marryat (1792-1848).

state of things in the Times, and I rather liked the story of the roses and the looking glasses.

By the way, what a pity Lord Robert—I always think of him in this immature state[1]—didn't write criticism, instead of ruling the world. But all I want to say is, we shall be back in October: so please do ring up—Anyhow come. No room for more.

V.W.

Marquess of Salisbury (Cecil Papers)

TO LEONARD WOOLF   [*Monk's House, Rodmell,*
                                              Sussex]
[n.d.]

Dearest M.

A perfect night—slept from 11.30 to 7.30 without waking. Very fine morning—good breakfast, no headache—am just going to begin writing.

Love from all animals. Could you possibly get me 2 packets of cigarettes? Shall come back tomorrow for certain.

M
D & D
Grizzly

Sussex

1. Lord Robert Cecil was created Viscount Cecil of Chelwood in 1923.

Index

Index

The numbers are page-numbers, except in the 'Letters to' section at the end of individual entries, where the letter-numbers are given in italics. Letters numbered with the suffix 'a' are in Appendix B, pp. 492-532.

Abbreviations: V. stands for Virginia Woolf; L. for Leonard Woolf; Vita for V. Sackville-West; ES. for Ethel Smyth.

Bagenal, Barbera, 147 & *n*, 191
Bagenal, Judith, 527 & *n*
Bagenal, Nicholas, 113, 147*n*
Bagnold, Enid (Lady Jones), 183 & *n*, 297
& *n*, 455, 465, 468 & *n*, 474, 476
Letters to: Nos. *3684, 3687*
Bailey, John Cann, 90 & *n*
Balfour, A. J., 76*n*, 507 & *n*
Balfour, Lady (Elizabeth), 8 & *n*, 56*n*,
267 & *n*, 401, 475
Baring, Maurice: ES.'s friend, 51 & *n*;
V.'s low opinion of his books, 62,
66, 68, 93; his religion, 67 & *n*; V.
likes him, 70; on *The Years*, 118;
ES.'s biography of, 142, 190, 211,
219; and Dr Alexander, 118 & *n*, 177,
183; V.'s 'blind spot', 430; his health,
474-5
Barker, Virgil, 511 & *n*
Letter to: No. *1676a*
Barnes, Djuna, 95*n*, 96
Barnes, George, 83 & *n*, 84, 219 & *n*
Barrie, J. M., 169*n*
Bartholomew, Percy, 54, 164, 399
Basque Refugees, 139 & *n*
Bates, Sir Percy, 38*n*
Bates, Ralph, 445 & *n*
Bath, Marquess of, 237*n*
Bayeux, France, 340
Baynes, Keith, 142 & *n*
BBC: V. broadcasts for, 108 & *n*, 110, 125,
126
Beale, Oswald, 279
Beamish, Admiral Tufton, 455*n*
Beaton, Cecil, 126 & *n*
Bedford, Duke of, 72 &*n*; Duchess of,
300 & *n*
Beecham, Miss H. H.
Letter to: No. *3123*
Beefsteak Club, 285 & *n*
Beerbohm, Marie, 495
Beerbohm, Max, 18 & *n*, 295, 299, 333
Beeton, Isabella, 58 & *n*
Bell, Angelica (Mrs David Garnett): V.
imagines in old age, 20; clothes, 33;
V.'s allowance to, 69, 218, 269, 361,
377; acting, 85, 118; V.'s youth more
interesting?, 94; after Julian's death,
148; quick wits, 158; tact, 161; at
Sissinghurst, 168 & *n*; 'exquisite
Jerboa', 173; in Paris, 178; acting
with St Denis, 178*n*; praised by
Colefax, 194; dancing, 227; acts in

Gammer, 263 & *n*; at Cassis, 291,
527; her postcards, 300; gives up
stage for painting, 304; Spanish
relief-work, 319 & *n*, 320; Village
Players, 322-3, 324; 'pearl pink
cloud', 368; with David Garnett,
405 & *n*, 423, 436, 442; V.'s 'rights',
405 & *n*; directs Rodmell play, 422
& *n*; at Monk's, 448; designs for V.'s
embroidery, 423, 452 & *n*; lectures,
452, 462; marries David Garnett, 442*n*
Letters to: Nos. *3317, 3339, 3429,
3439, 3475, 3500, 3504, 3532,
3555, 3559, 3577, 3616, 3636,
3650, 3657, 3668-9*
Bell, Clive: 'a flibbertigibbet', 20; 'plagiarised' Roger Fry, 20; not member of
Apostles, 20 & *n*; 'affable', 32; after
Julian's death, 151; and Janice Loeb,
153, 173, 176, 284-5; getting bald,
168; book on Julian, 245; *Warmongers*, 293 & *n*; Loeb tiring of him,
302; restive at Memoir Club, 337; on
Roger Fry, 410-11; war-work, 429;
on his wedding-eve, 492-3; 'redeemable', 526; in Paris, 527; *mentioned*, 59,
206, 208, 209, 214, 331, 368, 472, 516
Letters to: Nos. *3135, 3221, 3225,
3410, 3624; 1972a*
Bell, Colonel Cory, 291
Bell, Graham, 346 & *n*
Bell, Julian: memoir of Roger Fry, 8 & *n*,
18, 33, 176, 372; in China, 8*n*, 21, 32;
Work for the Winter, 19 & *n*;
Mallarmé, 84 & *n*; post-China plans,
85 & *n*; returns from China, 113*n*;
proposes to go to Spain, 116 & *n*,
123, 131; killed in Spain, 146 & *n*,
148*n*, 161 & *n*; 'grandeur in his
death', 150; but 'a complete waste',
162; his motives, xiv-xv, 151;
memorial volume proposed, 155 & *n*;
Letter to E. M. Forster, 166 & *n*, 167;
Letter to C. Day Lewis, 176 & *n*;
Keynes's obituary of, 192 & *n*;
Mauron's memoir of, 206; Su-Hua
Ling (Mrs Chen), 221*n*, 223; irrational desire to fight, 235; biography of?, 245; *Julian Bell* published,
275 & *n*, 292, 300; Vita thinks about,
357 & *n*; 'always changing', 372; V.
always thinks about, 381-2, 385
Letters to: Nos. *3101, 3111, 3126, 3189*

Letters to: Nos. *3096, 3108, 3127, 3217, 3321, 3359, 3455, 3483, 3493-4, 3511*

Boxall, Nellie, 498 & *n*

Brace, Donald (Harcourt, Brace): *The Years*, 179; *To the Lighthouse*, 180 & *n*, 513; *Three Guineas*, 268; V. recommends Robins to, 349-50; *Roger Fry*, 383; J. P. Morgan in *Fry*, 438 & *n*; V. explains *Orlando* to, 518
Letters to: Nos. *3320, 3347, 3436, 3542, 3586, 3653; 1707a, 1826a*

Braithwaite, Richard and Margaret, 19 & *n*, 20

Brenan, Gerald, 502*n*, 503, 525

Brewster, Henry, 38 & *n*, 39, 112*n*, 389, 404, 406, 529

Brighton, Sussex, 167, 394-5, 452, 487

Brittain, Nelly, 498 & *n*

Brittain, Vera, 378 & *n*, 379, 380
Letter to: No. *3578*

Brittany, V. and L. visit, 333, 336-41

Brontë, Charlotte, 259

Brontë, Emily, 329 & *n*

Brooke, Rupert: his letters, 31 & *n*, 32, 68; and Margaret Keynes, 139; and Ka Arnold-Forster, 363 & *n*

Brown, Isabel, 139

Browning, Elizabeth Barrett, 131*n*

Brunete, Spain, 148*n*

Bryant, Sir Arthur, 31 & *n*

Budberg, Baroness Moura, 471 & *n*

Budock Vean, Cornwall, 39-40

Bussy, Dorothy and Simon, 58*n*, 71, 100, 143*n*, 338 & *n*, 367 & *n*, 368-9*n*
Letters to: Nos. *3171, 3207, 3564*

Bussy, Jane ('Janie'), 58 & *n*, 101, 163
Letter to: No. *3157*

Butler, Samuel, 238 & *n*

Butts, Anthony, 138 & *n*, 172

Butts, Mary, 138 & *n*, 168, 172 & *n*

Byron, Lord, 305 & *n*

Caburn, Mount (Lewes), 155, 315, 460

Caen, Normandy, 341

Caerhays, Cornwall, 40 & *n*

Callimachi, Princess Anne-Marie, 231*n*

Cambridge University: The Apostles, 9 & *n*, 20 & *n*; V. plans visit to, 10; cancelled, 15; women's colleges, 132 & *n*, 133 & *n*, 372; in Munich crisis, 280; in wartime, 402; V. visits, 472, 473-4

Campbell, Jean (Cassis), 194 & *n*, 291*n*, 527

Canada, 234 & *n*

Cannan, Gilbert, 509 & *n*

Canterbury, 8

Carnac, Brittany, 336 & *n*, 341

Carroll, Lewis, 362 & *n*

Carter, John, 530 & *n*
Letter to: No. *2899a*

Carter, R. C., 397 & *n*

Cartwright, Mrs (Hogarth Press), 523 & *n*

Case, Emphie, 93*n*, 114, 118, 131, 145
Letter to: No. *3253*

Case, Janet: illness, 93 & *n*; memories of youth, 94; taught Diana Cooper, 135 & *n*; V. and L. visit, 114 & *n*, 117, 118; dying, 124; operation, 132, 134; dies, 145*n*, 184; V.'s obituary of, 145*n*
Letters to: Nos. *3203, 3228, 3233, 3251, 3257, 3264, 3269*

Cassis, France, 294, 520, 527-8

Castle, Tudor, 462*n*

Cavendish, Lady F., 267 & *n*

Cecil, Algernon, 198 & *n*

Cecil, Lord David: *The Young Melbourne*, 19 & *n*, 315, 427; Jane Austen lecture, 22 & *n*; 'young, happy', 122; on *Roger Fry*, 426
Letters to: Nos. *3113, 3642*

Cecil, Guendolen, 198 & *n*

Cecil, Lady Gwendolen, 499 & *n*

Cecil, Lady ('Nellie'), 43 & *n*, 122, 242, 482, 507, 531
Letters to: Nos. *3239, 3404, 3704; 1236a, 1559a, 3064a*

Cecil, Rachel (Lady David), 19 & *n*, 122, 427 & *n*

Cecil, Viscount (Robert), 85 & *n*, 87, 122, 482*n*, 532

Chabrun, Jacques, 173 & *n*, 177, 182

Chamberlain, Joseph and Mary, 103 & *n*

Chamberlain, Neville, 273-4*n*, 278-80*n*, 353

Chapman, R. W., 87 & *n*
Letter to: No. *3191*

Charles Edward, Prince, 245 & *n*

Charleston, Firle, Sussex: play at, 69; family dinner, 100; in wartime, 368

Charterhouse (London), 220 & *n*

Chateaubriand, Vicomte, 203, 210, 333

Chaucer, Geoffrey, 304, 314, 322

Chavasse, Mrs (Rodmell), 395, 436, 451

Dickinson, Oswald ('Ozzy'), 51, 156 & *n*
Dickinson, Violet: Memoir of Stephen family, 28 & *n*, 43, 158; returns V.'s own letters, 87, 89 & *n*, 90, 94; at Fritham, 118 & *n*, 429; breaks leg, 156-7; her height, 158; book given to V. in 1905, 184; cared for V. in 1904, 237; on *Roger Fry*, 428
    Letters to: Nos. *3120, 3138, 3178, 3192, 3195, 3197, 3231, 3235, 3242, 3293, 3324, 3398, 3643; 75a*
Disraeli, Benjamin (Lord Beaconsfield), 216
Dordogne, France, 128-30, 135, 140
Douarnenez, France, 360 & *n*
Douglas, Charles, 321
    Letter to: No. *3496*
Douie, Vera, 145*n*, 232
Drake, Mr and Mrs Bernard, 364 & *n*
Dreadnought hoax (1910), 17 & *n*; V.'s lecture on, 407 & *n*
Driberg, Tom, 510 & *n*
    Letter to: No. *1647a*
Droitwich, 70 & *n*
Dryburgh Abbey, Scotland, 247 & *n*
Duckworth, Sir George, 28 & *n*, 56, 70, 71 & *n*, 90, 103 & *n*, 236, 492
Duckworth, Gerald, 23 & *n*, 28 & *n*; sexual advances to V. in childhood, 460 & *n*; 492, 497 & *n*
Duckworth, Lady Margaret, 14 & *n*, 446*n*, 521
    Letter to: No. *3106*
Duckworth, Stella, 372 & *n*
Dufferin and Ava, Marquess of, 414 & *n*
Dugdale, Blanche, 76 & *n*, 466 & *n*
Dunkirk, evacuation from, 400 & *n*
Dunvegan Castle, Skye, 244 & *n*

Easdale, Mrs G. E., 24 & *n*, 25 & *n*, 365, 425
    Letters to: Nos. *3117, 3258, 3561, 3640*
Easdale, Joan (Mrs Rendel), 24*n*, 135 & *n*, 136, 292, 299, 365 & *n*, 425
Eastwood, Mrs Hugh de C. (Elinor Smyth), 47 & *n*, 51
Ebbs, Mrs (Rodmell), 157, 231, 280, 391, 418, 436, 464
Eden, Sir Timothy, 118*n*
Edward VIII (Duke of Windsor): 'a bounder', 10-11; abdication of, 91

& *n*, 95*n*; Archbishop on, 107 & *n*, *Nahlin* cruise, 134 & *n*; married, 194*n*; Colefax's inside story of, 194, 197
Egerton, Lady Louisa, 445 & *n*
Eliot, T. S. ('Tom'): championed by Edith Sitwell, 10*n*; V. on his *Collected Poems*, 29, 33, 73; V. 'could have loved', 59; attacked by F. L. Lucas, 85 & *n*; in green muffler, 99; praises Ottoline Morrell, 127; stays with Bruce Richmond, 144 & *n*, 230*n*; proposes publish Julian Bell's essays, 154-5*n*; on God, 171; at Monk's House, 173, 178, 194; on *Julian Bell*, 176; unpublished doggerel, 188*n*; 'Old Possum', 188*n*, 213; 'antique respectability' of, 198; *Family Reunion*, 198, 322 & *n*; at Monk's again, 367; lecture in Italy cancelled, 398 & *n*, 400; *East Coker*, 398 & *n*, 441; V. represents at Ottoline's funeral, 231; in fancy-dress as Crippen, 313 & *n*; with Hope Mirrlees, 472; *The Dry Salvages*, 477 & *n*; V. invites to Monk's again, 477; V. on Pound, 494; Eliot Fund (1922-5), 500 & *n*, 501-2, 506-7; *Criterion*, 506 & *n*; conduct not quite straight, 508; *The Waste Land* (reprint), 508 & *n*; Vivien Eliot, 519, 527*n*; smart tastes, 523
    Letters to: Nos. *3122, 3271, 3277, 3289, 3331, 3336, 3364, 3389, 3497, 3608, 3656, 3698*
Ellis, Havelock, 386 & *n*
Elton, Charles, 321 & *n*
Emery, Miss (Rodmell), 50, 164, 436
Enfield, Ralph and Doris, 443 & *n*
Erasmus, 362, 368
Ervine, St John, 7, 10 & *n*
Eugénie, Empress, 154*n*
Euston Road School of Painting, 194 & *n*, 204-5, 208, 300, 346*n*
Evelyn, John, 507 & *n*
Everest, Louie, 54 & *n*, 107, 152, 353, 410, 433*n*, 448, 484

Faber, Geoffrey, 409*n*
Fabian Society, 303 & *n*, 401
Falmouth, Cornwall, 39-41
Farrell, Sophie, 308 & *n*
Fawcett (Marsham St.) Library, 145 & *n*, 231, 232, 234, 236, 239

Humphreys, Leslie, 353 & *n*, 361, 405, 411, 443

Hunt, Holman, 70 & *n*

Hutchinson, Barbara, 131*n*, 472

Hutchinson, Jeremy, 413, 471*n*, 472*n*, 494*n*

Hutchinson, Mary: and Vita, 101; V. dines with, 134; dines with V., 375; V. encourages her to write, 494, 503, 505-6; V. sends her earliest articles to, 396; Eliot Fund, 500, 501-2, 506-7; River House, 503; gives V. powder, 505; V. on Eliot's character, 508; *Fugitive Pieces*, 512 & *n*; V.'s tribute to, 523; V.'s vision of, 526, 528

Letters to: Nos. *3691*; *977a*, *1046a*, *1300a*, *1352a*, *1380a*, *1438a*, *1442a*, *1472a*, *1538a*, *1581a*, *1676b*, *1985a*, *2026a*, *2036a*

Hutchinson, St John ('Jack'), 291 & *n*, 295, 375, 405, 527 & *n*

Letter to: No. *1876a*

Huxley, Aldous: palmistry, 3*n*, 5; *Eyeless in Gaza*, 7; in Buenos Aires, 13; peace propaganda, 83; *Brave New World*, 361; in 1923, 502 & *n*

Huxley, Julian, 144*n*, 181

Huxley, Maria, 3 & *n*

Ibsen, Henrik, 10 & *n*, 20, 22-3, 24, 74 & *n*, 349-50

Intellectual Liberty Committee, 99 & *n*

Invasion of Britain, threat of, 431*n*, 432*n*, 433, 483

Ireland: Nationalists murder an Admiral, 24 & *n*; V.'s visit to in 1934, 45; 'rebels' in London, 312 & *n*

Irving, Sir Henry, 350 & *n*

Isham, Virginia, 323 & *n*

Isherwood, Christopher: proposed partner in Hogarth Press, 200*n*; in China with Auden, 259 & *n*; 'nimble, inscrutable', 299; V. sees his play, 317*n*, 318; goes to America, 328

Italy: in Munich crisis, 279; V.'s love of Rome, 321, 387; invades Albania, 326*n*, 327

James, Henry, 478, 506 & *n*, 529

Janin, René, 172 & *n*

Jekyll, Gertrude, 157 & *n*

Joan of Arc, 49-50

John, Augustus, 417

John, Katherine, 84 & *n*, 154 & *n*, 346*n*

Johnson, Dr Samuel, 190, 245 & *n*

Jones, Alice, 33, 71*n*

Joyce, James, 496*n*

Juliana, Queen of the Netherlands, 210 & *n*

Kauffer, Ann McKnight, 313 & *n*

Letter to: No. *3484*

Kenney, Susan, xvii

Kent, Duke of, 194 & *n*

Kernahan, Coulson, 299 & *n*

Keswick, 298 & *n*

Kew Gardens, 220

Keynes, Lydia (Lopokova): acts Ibsen, 10 & *n*, 20, 22-3; asks L.'s advice, 34; on Keynes's illness, 176, 179; at Monk's House, 196-7; in Munich crisis, 280; and Janice Loeb, 284-5

Letter to: No. *3256*

Keynes, Margaret, 138 & *n*

Letter to: No. *3263*

Keynes, John Maynard: his *General Theory*, 10 & *n*; V. spends Christmas with, 96, 100; seriously ill, 129 & *n*, 131; *Essays in Biography*, 129 & *n*; recuperates, 133, 134, 139, 173, 179; on Julian Bell, 149, 192 & *n*, on Macaulay, 193; Christmas at Monk's House, 194, 196-7; Lewes theatre, 197; in Munich crisis, 280 & *n*, 285; 'a great man', 287; Cambridge, 287 & *n*; Dr Plesch, 327 & *n*, 376; his political influence, 420

Letters to: Nos. *3249*, *3252*, *3282*, *3314*, *3338*

Kidd, Ronald, 234

Kilham Roberts, Denys, 188 & *n*

Letter to: No. *3330*

Kilvert, Francis, 266 & *n*, 377 & *n*, 432

Kipling, Rudyard, 13 & *n*, 468*n*

Kirkby Lonsdale, Cumberland, 250 & *n*

Koteliansky, S. S., 146 & *n*

Letters to: Nos. *3274*, *3278*

Lamb, Charles, 259

Landowska, Wanda, 217 & *n*

Lane, Allen, 188*n*

Lane, Sir Hugh, 120 & *n*

Lang, Archbishop Cosmo Gordon, 107 & *n*

Lange, Miss (Hogarth Press), 105, 106, 241*n*

Larter, Mrs (Rodmell,) 281

Mabel (Woolfs' cook), *see* Haskins, Mabel

McAfee, Helen (*Yale Review*), 189 & *n*, 306, 316
Letters to: Nos. *3333, 3472, 3488*

MacCarthy, Desmond: illness, 19; long talk with V., 111; lectures on Leslie Stephen, 125 & *n*, 130; Memoir Club, 337; at Monk's, 400; reviews *Roger Fry*, 410 & *n*; and Ottoline Morrell, 495, 511
Letters to: Nos. *3623, 3686*

MacCarthy, Molly (Mrs Desmond): Memoir Club, 82, 337; gall-stones, 206, 208; V.'s admiration for, 337
Letters to: Nos. *3187, 3353, 3357, 3520*

Macaulay ,Rose, 16 & *n*, 21 & *n*, 193, 402, 430, 497

Macaulay, Thomas Babington, 45, 48, 54

Macdonald, Flora, 245 & *n*

MacDonald, Ramsay, 383*n*

McDougall, Angus, 126

McKechnie, Nurse, 51 & *n*, 57

MacKenna, Stephen, 96 & *n*

Macmillan (N.Y. publishers), 497 & *n*

MacNeice, Louis, 171*n*, 381*n*

McNeil, Daisy, 266 & *n*, 368

McTaggart, John, 6 & *n*

Madge, Charles, 34*n*, 172*n*, 351 & *n*

Mair, John, 370 & *n*

Maitland, F. W., 458 & *n*

Mallarmé, Stéphane, 84 & *n*

Mallory, George, 363 & *n*

Manchester, 115 & *n*, 303

Mandeville, Bernard de, 226

Mansfield, Katherine, 495

Marryat, Capt. F., 531 & *n*

Marsh, Edward, 31 & *n*

Martin, Amelia (Sackville-West), 191 & *n*

Martin, Kingsley: in Rhineland crisis, 19 & *n*; 'the Bore', 55; in Munich crisis, 274, 275-6, 280; defeatism, 292; in wartime, 366, 402
Letter to: No. *3310*

Mary Ward Settlement, 275 & *n*

Mass Observation, 172*n*

Matheson, Hilda: 191 & *n*, 388*n*; dies, 443 & *n*; V.'s view of, 446, 462

Matisse, Henri, 143 & *n*, 145 & *n*

Maugham, Somerset, 112*n*, 203 & *n*, V. meets, 299

Mauron, Charles: letters from Roger Fry, 7 & *n*, 9, 33, 85, 487; Mallarmé, 84

& *n*; on Julian Bell's future, 85; at Charleston, 160 & *n*; memoir of Julian Bell, 176 & *n*, 206; at St Rémy, 274*n*, 285 & *n*; lectures, 526 & *n*

Mauron, Marie, 163, 274*n*, 285

Maxse, J. H., 198 & *n*

Maxse, Leo, 198 & *n*

Mayor, Beatrice, 364 & *n*

Mecklenburgh Square, No. 37: Woolfs take lease of, 332*n*, 338; move to, 344ff; description of, 350; settling in, 353, 357; first occupy, 363, 391; badly damaged by bombs, 429-31, 432, 434; damaged again, 441, 442, 461; books etc. moved to Monk's House, 449, 451, 470

Melrose, Scotland, 247

Memoir Club, xiii, 82 & *n*, 287 & *n*, 337

Michelet, Jules, 312 & *n*

Mirrlees, Hope, 472 & *n*, 497-8
Letter to: No. *1148a*

Mitchison, Naomi, 114 & *n*
Letter to: No. *3227*

Mitz, Mitzi (L.'s marmoset), 75, 124, 130; dies, 307

Mockford, Mrs (Rodmell), 12

Moir, Miss (*Forum*), 276-7

Molière, Jean-Baptiste, 110 & *n*, 160*n*

Monk's House, Rodmell: political meetings in, 107, 270, 353, 391; V.'s sittingroom, 107; kitchen improvements, 132; embroidery and mirror, 198 & *n*, 266; new library for L., 251 & *n*, 286; balcony, 262*n*; hospitality of, 270; V.'s happiness in, 286; at start of war, 359; electric stove, 383, embroidery, 423, 452; London books etc. moved to, 449, 451, 470; new rooms, 526 & *n*
Garden at: zinnias, 58; poplars, 75; tortoises, 134; topiary, 140; the vine, 153; pond, 166-7, statues, 184; dew-pond, 348; rock-garden, 388; apples and bees, 436; V. never works in, 428; V.'s garden-hut (lodge), 73, 153, 228, 447, 472, 486*n*
See also under Rodmell

Montaigne, Michel de, 125 & *n*, 216

Moore, George, 512 & *n*

Moore, G. E., 37 & *n*, 287*n*, 398 & *n*, 400

Morgan, Charles, 77 & *n*

Morgan, J. Pierpont, 438 & *n*

Morley College, 419 & *n*

Morley, John, 383 & *n*

Morrell, Julian, 510

Morrell, Lady Ottoline: her Memoirs, 45 & *n*, 509, 511; on Abdication day, 91*n*, 95; illness, 140 & *n*; Duke of Portland, 203 & *n*; V.'s affection for, 212; dies, 223 & *n*, 225; V.'s obituary of, 223*n*, 225; funeral, 226 & *n*, 227; V. fond of her, 227; her salon, 282; memorial to, 340; epitaph, 345; keeping her eye on Bloomsbury, 495; satirised by Lawrence and Huxley, 509 & *n*; and by W. J. Turner, 515*n*; V. at Garsington, 510-11

Letters to: Nos. *3094, 3105, 3141, 3150, 3179, 3198-9, 3204, 3247, 3265, 3349, 3368; 1612a, 1652a, 1781a*

Morrell, Philip, 71*n*, 127 & *n*, 211 & *n*, 214, 223, 227, 228, 305, 340, 405 & *n*

Letters to: Nos. *3280, 3362*

Morris, William, 408 & *n*

Mortimer, Raymond, 47 & *n*, 274, 356 & *n*

Letter to: No. *3550*

Muir, Edwin, 514 & *n*

Munich crisis (1938), 273-81

Murry, Middleton, 33 & *n*, 136*n*, 495

Mussolini, Benito, 279, 326*n*

Nash, Rosalind, 149

National Gallery, 276

Nef, Elinor Castle and John Ulric, 142 & *n*, 143, 144, 145

Letters to: Nos. *3267-8*

Ness, Loch (monster), 244

Nevill, Lady Dorothy, 320 & *n*

Nevinson, H. W., 58

Newcome, Colonel, 220 & *n*, 221

Newhaven, Sussex, 432*n*, 439

Newman, Lyn and Max, 19 & *n*

New Statesman, V.'s letter to: No. *3566*

New Writing, 34 & *n*, 200*n*, 252, 364*n*, 374, 408*n*, 445 & *n*, 482*n*

Nicholls, Mrs (Hogarth Press), 241 & *n*, 244, 276, 284, 297, 357, 408

Nichols, John Bowyer, 75 & *n*, 76

Nichols, Robert, 75 & *n*, 76

Nicolson, Benedict (Ben): 'indolent, muffed', 165 & *n*; dines with V., 232, 253; helps V. with *Roger Fry*, 264-5*n*, 329 & *n*, 330, 342*n*; job with royal pictures, 329 & *n*; in Army, 398 & *n*; criticises *Roger Fry*, and V.'s re-

joinders, 413-14, 419-22; stays at Monk's House, 436, 449

Letters to: Nos. *3416, 3431, 3509, 3527, 3534, 3607, 3627, 3633-4, 3639*

Nicolson, Harold: invites V. to meet Lindbergh, 18 & *n*; fund for Colefax, 98 & *n*; with V. at Sissinghurst, 171; broadcasts, 267 & *n*; in Munich crisis, 274*n*, 278; his diaries, 279 & *n*; sailing ketch, 307*n*; foresees war, 346

Nicolson, Nigel, 165 & *n*

Night and Day (magazine), 197 & *n*

Noel-Baker, Philip and Irene, 277 & *n*, 462 & *n*

Nohant, Château de (George Sand), 130 & *n*, 131, 141

Northease, Sussex, 293

Norton, H. T. J., 128*n*, 502 & *n*

Noyes, Alfred, 321 & *n*

Oban, Scotland, 248-9

Ocampo, Victoria: invites V. to Argentina, 13, 35 & *n*; lectures on V., 166 & *n*; her butterflies, 167, 284 & *n*; in London during Munich crisis, 273, 277, 283; meets Vita, 309-10*n*; V.'s description of, 310; travelling, 334; V. complains of photography incident, 342-3*n*, 351

Letters to: Nos. *3228, 3304, 3445, 3450, 3453, 3477, 3516, 3528*

O'Faolain, Sean, 313 & *n*, 391 & *n*

Olivier, Brynhild (Popham), 97 & *n*

Olivier, Edith, 230 & *n*

Olivier, Noel (Richards), 31, 97 & *n*, 274

'Omega', 419, 461, 496, 531 & *n*

O'Neill, Eugene, 381 & *n*

Order of Merit, 195 & *n*, 308 & *n*

Origo, Iris, 6 & *n*, 8, 11

Orlando: paperback, 40-41*n*; Spanish translation, 167 & *n*; 'imagination', 445; V. describes it to Donald Brace, 518; started as a joke, 522; telegram to Vita, 523; not an allegory, 524; 'an evening's fun', 525

Ouida (Louise de la Ramée), 302 & *n*

Ouse, River (Sussex): floods, 2; bridge over, 158*n*; V. walks along, 173; 'as big as a large snake', 328; V. loves it, 352; military defences of, 409, 433; banks breached by bombs, 444, 446, 459; V. drowns in, 481

3530, 3533, 3565, 3603, 3660, 3700

Robson, Elaine, 174 & *n*, 316, 339, 458-9
 Letters to: Nos. *3313, 3487, 3523, 3677*
Robson, William, 131 & *n*, 150
 Letter to: No. *3284*
Rocamadour, France, 128-9
Rochester, Kent, 317 & *n*
Rodmell, Sussex: floods, 2; bungalows, 184; foot-and-mouth disease, 193, 196; L. as school-manager, 227, 233; in Munich crisis, 277, 280; at start of war, 357, 391; village play, 391 & *n*, 400, 418, 422*n*, 430; air-raids, 402, 406, 422, 429-30, 439, 442; fire-drill etc., 405 & *n*, 408; anti-invasion defences, 433; river-bank breached, 444, 446, 459; Women's Institute, 448, 451, 452 & *n*; village interrupts V.'s work, 475. *See also* under Monk's House; Ouse, River
Roger Fry: A Biography: V.'s feeling for him, 426; his art-criticism, 3; Mauron and Dickinson letters, 7, 9; Julian Bell memoir, 8 & *n*, 18, 33, 176, 372; V.'s progress with, 9, 44; and Clive Bell, 20; Mallarmé's poems, 84 & *n*; 'horrors of book-making', 104; V. resumes, 110 & *n*, 135-6; boxes of letters, 169; Helen Fry, 186, 264 & *n*, 268; V. resumes book again, 226; Rothenstein's letters, 254 & *n*; Trevelyan memories, 255*n*, 258, 264; this 'barren nightmare', 262; his art-history, 264-5, 285, 415; difficulties of biography, 267, 271, 285; Post-Impressionist show, 279 & *n*; V. reaches 1911, 285; problem of Vanessa's affair with Fry, 285 & *n*; Hampton Court, 294 & *n*; 'a huge glow', 305; and Mark Gertler, 324; 'toiling, revising', 326; Ben Nicolson helps, 330 & *n*, 342; slow progress, 347; 'working like a nigger', 362; rewriting, 374, 376; 'cabinet-making', 381; finished, 383; Vanessa's and L.'s opinions of, 385 & *n*; Fry's family approve, 386, 389; proofs, 397, 399; Shaw gives V. a Fry picture, 402
 Published, 406*n*; reviews, 410 & *n*, 411 & *n*; Clive Bell and Trevelyan on, 411-12; V.'s defence of Fry

to Ben Nicolson, 413-14, 419-22; difficult to write, 411, 416, 426; his influence on painters, 417; V.'s biographical method, 417, 426; sales, 418, 430; Quaker element in, 422; no bibliography, 423; 'libel' on J. P. Morgan, 438 & *n*; violent abuse of, 444, 458 & *n*; 'experiment in self-suppression', 456, 479; Fry's capacity to excite, 461; misprints, 479
 Letters to Fry (in App. B.): Nos. *1245a, 1942a*
Roman Wall, *see* Hadrian's Wall
Rome: V.'s love for, 321, 387
Roosevelt, Franklin D., 327 & *n*
Rose, Philip, 293
Rosinsky, Herbert, 277 & *n*
Rothenstein, Michael, 302 & *n*
Rothenstein, Sir William, 254 & *n*, 287, 290 & *n*, 346, 368, 416
 Letters to: Nos. *3417-18, 3458, 3619, 3630*
Rothschild, Victor (Lord), 131 & *n*, 472
Rousseau, J-J., 453
Russell, Bertrand and Patricia: *Amberley Papers*, 65 & *n*, 69 & *n*, 72-3, 77; *Which Way to Peace?*, 83
Ruthin Castle, Wales, 131 & *n*, 173, 179, 509*n*
Rutland, Duke of, 135 & *n*
Rylands, George ('Dadie'), 10 & *n*, 84, 125*n*, 217 & *n*, 318 & *n*, 472-3
 Letters to: Nos. *3243, 3370, 3491, 3529, 3693*

Sackville, Lady (Vita's mother): dies, 12 & *n*; V.'s opinion of, 175, 185
Sackville, Thomas (Earl of Dorset), 329 & *n*, 351
Sackville West, Edward ('Eddy'): book on de Quincey, 33*n*; quarrel with V. made up, 46 & *n*; unhappiness, 350-1*n*; diary of, 366 & *n*; at Monk's, 374, 376
 Letters to: Nos. *3218, 3562, 3663*
Sackville-West, V. (Vita, Mrs Harold Nicolson): summary of later relations with V., xii-xiii; and Gwen St Aubyn, 2, 4, 440; not in disgrace with V., 11; her mother dies, 12; 'always affectionate', 42; V.'s opinion of *Saint Joan*, 49-50, 56, 57, 88; in Sahara, 121 & *n*; V. at Sissinghurst (*q.v.*); 'affair with

Letters to: Nos. *3092, 3175, 3230, 3238, 3240, 3573, 3587; 2939a*
Spira, Mela, 311 & *n*, 319
Sprott, W. J. H. ('Sebastian'), 414 & *n*, 416
Letter to: No. *3629*
Stanford, Charles, 442 & *n*
Staples, Mrs (Vita's cook), 125 & *n*, 470
Stein, Gertrude, 230, 510 & *n*
Stephen, Adrian, 17*n*, 84, 99, 100, 168, 313*n*, 371, 372
Stephen, Ann (Llewelyn Davies): at Cambridge, 9 & *n*, 10, 15-16, 84, 139-40; engaged, 143, 169, 179, 227; married, 251*n*; at Monk's House, 284, 293, 305; her letters, 373; in Dublin, 391, 400
Stephen, Barbara (Nightingale), 204 & *n*
Stephen, Dorothea, 204 & *n*
Stephen, Sir Harry, 23*n*, 204 & *n*, 209
Stephen, James, 23*n*, 204 & *n*, 209
Stephen, Judith: Russell praises, 84; going to Cambridge, 172; at Monk's House, 178; new house, 204 & *n*; at Cambridge, 400, 402; and Leslie Humphreys, 411, 432; in America, 442 & *n*, 447; in childhood, 526
Letters to: Nos. *3546, 3570, 3610*
Stephen, Julia (V.'s mother), 32
Stephen, Karin, 84, 372, 498,& *n*
Stephen, Leslie (V.'s father): house at Lyme, 25*n*; headaches, 32; when dying, 51; *Study of English Literature*, 86 & *n*; MacCarthy lectures on, 125 & *n*, 130; walking, 157-8; 18th century literature, 172 & *n*; his library, 234; scholars' interest in, 333; V. eavesdrops on, 334-5; his manuscripts sold, 365 & *n*, 371; and O. W. Holmes, 402; biography of, 458 & *n*; V. teased by Fry on her paternity, 495; in *Lighthouse*, 517
Stephen, Thoby (V.'s brother), 33, 38, 148*n*, 372
Stern, G. B., 126 & *n*
Storrs, Sir Ronald, 89 & *n*, 183
Strachan, Miss (Hogarth Press), 300
Strachey, Christopher, 9 & *n*
Strachey, James, 100 & *n*, 330
Strachey, Lytton: book by David Cecil about?, 19 & *n*, 22; in Devon (1911), 37 & *n*; book by V. about?, 44 & *n*; influence on Vita, 50; attacked by critics, 65; his letters malicious, 100 & *n*; friendship with V., 289 & *n*; Horace Walpole, 330-1; he and V. in their youth, 372; his influence, 420
Strachey, Marjorie, 253 & *n*, 315, 525
Strachey, Oliver, 472
Strachey, Pernel, 15 & *n*, 145, 239, 473
Letter to: No. *3107*
Strachey, Philippa ('Pippa'), 104 & *n*, 145 & *n*, 374
Letters to: Nos. *3215, 3273, 3572, 3692*
Strachey, Ray, 74*n*
Strathmore, Lady, 247*n*, 249
Sutcliffe, Mr, 370
Letter to: No. *3567*
Swift, E. T., 314 & *n*
Sydney-Turner, Saxon, 133, 138*n*, 147*n*, 372, 504 & *n*
Letters to: Nos. *3255, 3279, 3295, 3399*

Tait, Archbishop A. C., 466 & *n*
Tate Gallery, 293
Tavistock Square, No. 52: Woolfs purchase lease, 504; think of leaving, 298, 332 & *n*; neighbouring houses demolished, 326, 329; Woolfs leave, 344ff; destroyed by bomb, 441 & *n*, 442, 449; a disreputable area, 519
Taylor, Jeremy, 332 & *n*
Teed, Colonel (Cassis), 194 & *n*, 291 & *n*, 300, 527
Temple, Olive and Charles, 502 & *n*
Letter to: No. *1377a*
Tennant, Stephen, 57 & *n*, 296, 419
Terry, Ellen, 232*n*, 476*n*
Thomas, Dylan, 10*n*
Thomsett, Mr and Annie (Rodmell), 270 & *n*
Thompson, John H., 92 & *n*
Letter to: No. *3201*
Thrale, Hester (Mrs Piozzi), 467 & *n*
Three Guineas: and Julian Bell's death, xv; V.'s first ideas for, 44 &*n*, 60; starts writing, 85 & *n*; women at Cambridge, 132 & *n*, 133 & *n*, 372; 'my war pamphlet', 159; finishing, 173; jacket, 206; notes at end of, 217 & *n*, 235, 251; 'my worst book', 218 & *n*; 'Outsiders', 229 & *n*, 236-7, 239, 303; published, 231; 'repeats theme' of *The Years*, 231; comments